Frommer's®

1st Edition

Northern New England

by Wayne Curtis

WHITE MT.   HWY 302
NOTCH LAND INN

Macmillan • USA

ABOUT THE AUTHOR

Wayne Curtis is the author of *Maine: Off the Beaten Path* (Globe Pequot) and numerous travel articles in newspapers and magazines, including the *New York Times, National Geographic Traveler,* and *Outside.* He lives in Portland, Maine, where he endeavors to support local microbreweries and minor-league baseball.

MACMILLAN TRAVEL

A Simon & Schuster Macmillan Company
1633 Broadway
New York, NY 10019

Find us online at **http://www.mgr.com/travel**
or on America Online at Keyword: **Frommer's.**

ISBN 0-02-861141-1
ISSN 1090-5502

Editors: Lisa Renaud, Ian Wilker
Production Editor: Zackary Martin
Design by Michele Laseau
Map Editor: Douglas Stallings
Digital Cartography by Ortelius Design
Maps copyright © by Simon & Schuster, Inc.

SPECIAL SALES

Bulk purchases (10+ copies) of Frommer's and selected Macmillan travel guides are available to corporations, organizations, mail-order catalogs, institutions, and charities at special discounts, and can be customized to suit individual needs. For more information write to: Special Sales, Macmillan General Reference, 1633 Broadway, New York, NY 10019.

Manufactured in the United States of America

Contents

List of Maps

AN INVITATION TO THE READER

In researching this book, I discovered many wonderful places—inns, restorts, restaurants, shops, and more. I'm sure you'll find others. Please tell us about them, so we can share the information with your fellow travelers in upcoming editions. If you were disappointed with a recommendation, we'd love to know that, too. Please write to:

Wayne Curtis
Frommer's Northern New England, 1st Edition
Macmillan Travel
1633 Broadway
New York, NY 10019

AN ADDITIONAL NOTE

Please be advised that travel information is subject to change at any time—and this is especially true of prices. We therefore suggest that you write or call ahead for confirmation when making your travel plans. The author, editors, and publisher cannot be held responsible for the experiences of readers while traveling. Your safety is important to us, however, so we encourage you to stay alert and be aware of your surroundings. Keep a close eye on cameras, purses, and wallets, all favorite targets of thieves and pickpockets.

WHAT THE SYMBOLS MEAN

✪ **Frommer's Favorites**

Hotels, restaurants, attractions, and entertainment you should not miss.

⑤ **Super-Special Values**

Hotels and restaurants that offer great value for your money.

The following abbreviations are used for credit cards:

AE	American Express	EU	Eurocard
CB	Carte Blanche	JCB	Japan Credit Bank
DC	Diners Club	MC	MasterCard
DISC	Discover	V	Visa
ER	enRoute		

The Best of Northern New England

One of the greatest challenges of traveling in Northern New England is choosing from an abundance of superb restaurants, accommodations, and attractions. Where to start? Here's an entirely biased list of my favorite destinations, the places I always return to time and time again. Over years of traveling through the region, I've discovered that these are the places worth more than just a quick stop when I'm in the area. They're all worth a major detour.

1 The Seven Wonders of Northern New England

- **The Appalachian Trail:** The 2,100-mile Appalachian Trail runs from Georgia to Maine, stitching together some of the most spectacular scenery in northern New England. The trail enters the region in southwest Vermont, and winds through the lovely southern Green Mountains before angling toward the White Mountains of New Hampshire. From here, it makes its way through remote Maine lakes and hills before finishing up on the summit of Mt. Katahdin.

- **Lake Champlain** (Vermont): "New England's West Coast" is lapped by the gentle waves of Lake Champlain, that vast, shimmering sheet of water between Vermont and New York. To the west are the stern Adirondacks, to the east are the distant, rolling ridges of the Green Mountains. Sign up for a lake cruise, or just hop the ferry from Burlington for a cheap excursion across the lake and back. See chapter 5.

- **The Connecticut River** (Vermont and New Hampshire): The broad, lazy Connecticut River forms the border between New Hampshire and Vermont, and it's a joy to follow. You'll find wonderful vistas, peaceful villages, and evidence of the region's rich history, when the river was the superhighway of northern New England. See chapters 5 and 6.

- **Franconia Notch** (New Hampshire): It's spectacular to drive through this rocky gorge, which cuts through the craggiest part of the White Mountains, but it's even more wondrous if you stop and explore on foot or bike. Hike the flanking ridges, bike the pathway along the valley floor, or just lounge in the sun at the edge of Echo Lake. New Hampshire's famous Old Man of the Mountains lives here. See chapter 6.

- **Tuckerman Ravine** (New Hampshire): This glacial cirque high on the flanks of Mount Washington (New England's highest peak) seems part medieval, part Alps, and entirely otherworldly. Snows are blown across the upper lip throughout the winter, accumulating to depths of 70 feet or more. Skiers trek here from throughout the country in spring to challenge this sheer face, and hikers will find snow in this vast and shady bowl well into summer. See chapter 6.
- **Acadia National Park** (Maine): New England's only national park happens to be one of the nation's most popular. And it's no wonder. The fractured, rocky coastline is pounded by surf and surrounded by silent boreal forests; open summits of low mountains afford spectacular coastal views. See chapter 7.
- **Mount Katahdin** (Maine): Rising abruptly from a thick blanket of the North Woods forest, the nearly mile-high Mount Katahdin has an ineffable spiritual quality to it. It's the centerpiece of equally inspiring Baxter State Park, one of the last, best wildernesses of the eastern states. See chapter 7.

2 The Best Small Towns

- **Grafton** (Vermont): Just a few decades ago Grafton was a down-at-the-heels mountain town slowly being reclaimed by termites and the elements. A wealthy family took it on as a pet project, and has lovingly restored the village to its former self—even burying the electric lines to reclaim the landscape. It doesn't feel like a living history museum; it just feels right. See chapter 5.
- **Woodstock** (Vermont): Woodstock has a stunning village green, a whole range of 19th-century homes, woodland walks leading just out of town, and a settled, old-money air. This is a good place to explore by foot or bike, or to just sit on a porch and watch summer unfold. See chapter 5.
- **Montpelier** (Vermont): This is the way all state capitals should be: slow-paced, small enough so you can walk everywhere, and full of shops that still sell nails and strapping tape to real people. Montpelier also shows a more sophisticated edge, with its Culinary Institute, a theater showing art-house films, and several fine book shops. But at heart it's a small town, where you just might run into the governor buying a wrench at the corner store. See chapter 5.
- **Exeter** (New Hampshire): Exeter boasts a small museum covering life in revolutionary times, but the whole town is a living monument to a bygone era. The brick commercial downtown is trim and bustling; the prestigious Exeter Academy prep school recalls the era of Holden Caulfield of *Catcher in the Rye.* See chapter 6.
- **Fitzwilliam** (New Hampshire): With its sleepy, lost-in-time feel, Fitzwilliam seems caught in a time warp from the 1830s. You half expect to see a horse-drawn carriage circling around the idyllic green, which is ringed with some of the most charming architecture in the region. This is a great destination for explorers—few urban refugees have yet discovered the place, and it still has a beguiling, raw-around-the-edges feel. See chapter 6.
- **Castine** (Maine): Soaring elm trees, a peaceful harborside setting, plenty of grand historic homes, and a selection of good inns make this a great spot to soak up some of Maine's coastal ambience off the beaten path. See chapter 7.

3 The Best Places to See Fall Foliage

- **I-91** (Vermont): An interstate? Don't scoff (the traffic can be terrible on state roads). If you like your foliage viewing wholesale, cruise I-91 from White River Junction to Newport. You'll be overwhelmed with gorgeous terrain, from the gentle Connecticut River Valley to the sloping hills of the Northeast Kingdom. See chapter 5.

- **Route 100** (Vermont): Route 100 winds the length of the Vermont from Readsboro to Newport. It's the major north-south route through the center of the Green Mountains, and it's surprisingly undeveloped along most of its length. You won't exactly have it to yourself along the southern stretches on autumn weekends, but as you head further north you'll leave the crowds behind. See chapter 5.
- **Aboard the M/V *Mount Washington*** (New Hampshire): One of the more majestic views of the White Mountains is from Lake Winnipesaukee to the south. The vista is especially appealing as seen from the deck of the *Mount Washington,* an uncommonly handsome 230-foot-long vessel that offers a variety of tours through mid-October, when the lake is trimmed with a fringe of fall color along the shoreline. See chapter 6.
- **Crawford Notch** (New Hampshire): Route 302 passes through this scenic valley, where you can see the brilliant red maples and yellow birches high on the hillsides. Mount Washington stands guard in the background, and in fall is likely to be dusted with an early snow. See chapter 6.
- **The Blueberry Barrens of Downeast Maine:** Maine's wild blueberry barrens are ablaze with a brilliant cranberry-red hue in the fall. Wander the dirt roads northeast of Cherryfield through the upland barrens, or just drive on Route 1 between Harrington and Machias past the experimental farm atop aptly named Blueberry Hill. See chapter 7.

4 The Best Ways to View Coastal Scenery

- **Biking Route 1A from Hampton Beach to Portsmouth** (New Hampshire): You'll get a taste of all sorts of coastal scenery pedaling along New Hampshire's miniscule coastline. You'll begin with sandy beaches, then pass rocky headlands and handsome mansions before coasting into the region's most scenic seaside city. See chapter 6.
- **Sea Kayak Merchant's Row:** The islands between Stonington and Isle au Haut, rimmed with pink granite and capped with the stark spires of spruce trees, are simply spectacular. Exploring by sea kayak will get you to islands inaccessible by motor boat. Outfitters offer overnight camping trips on the islands. See "Enjoying the Great Outdoors" in chapter 7.
- **Hike Monhegan Island:** The village of Monhegan is clustered around the harbor, but the rest of this 700-acre island is all picturesque wildlands, with miles of trails crossing open meadows and winding along rocky bluffs. See chapter 7.
- **Drive the Park Loop Road at Acadia National Park:** This is the region's premier ocean drive. You'll start high along a ridge with views of Frenchman Bay and the Porcupine Islands, then dip down along the rocky shores to watch the surf crash against the dark rocks. Plan to do this 20-mile loop at least twice to get the most out of it. See chapter 7.

5 The Best Active Vacations

- **Biking Inn to Inn** (Vermont): Throughout the state, serpentine roads wind through the verdant hills and along tumbling streams. Several organizations will ferry your baggage from inn to inn; you provide the pedal power to get yourself from one point to the next. See "Enjoying the Great Outdoors" in chapter 5.

- **Skiing in Vermont:** Vermont has nearly two dozen ski areas, offering everything from the cozy friendliness of Bolton Valley to the high-impact skiing of towering Killington. Vermont has long been New England's ski capital, and they've learned how to do it right. See chapter 5.
- **Hiking the White Mountains** (New Hampshire): These rugged peaks draw hikers from all over the globe, attracted by the history, the beautiful vistas, and the exceptional landscapes along the craggy ridgelines. You can make day-hike forays and retreat to the comfort of an inn at night, or stay in the hills at the Appalachian Mountain Club's historic high huts. See chapter 6.
- **Canoeing** (Maine): Maine has thousands of miles of flowing rivers and streams, and hundreds of miles of shorelines along remote ponds and lakes. Bring your tent, sleeping bag, and cooking gear, and come prepared to spend a night under the stars listening to the sounds of the loons. See chapter 7.
- **Mountainbiking at Acadia:** John D. Rockefeller, Jr., built the carriage roads of Mount Desert Island so the gentry could enjoy rambles in the woods with their horses, away from pesky cars. Today, this extensive network makes for some of the most enjoyable, aesthetically pleasing mountain biking anywhere. See chapter 7.

6 The Best Skiing

- **Killington** (Vermont): The mountain's big and can be impersonal, but at 3,150 feet it has the highest vertical drop of any New England ski area. You can ski all day and still find new terrain. At night, you've got a mall's worth of restaurants to choose from. See chapter 5.
- **Mad River Glen** (Vermont): This notably feisty ski area hasn't given in to passing whims—like high-speed chairlifts and snowmaking—and maintains a stubborn pride in its challenging slopes and no-frills skiing. Longtime owner Betsy Pratt sold the mountain in 1995, and the cooperative of skiers who bought it seems determined to maintain its cranky charm. See chapter 5.
- **Wildcat Mountain** (New Hampshire): Set amid the White Mountain National Forest, Wildcat is a wonderful, remote ski area with a good range of slopes and the best mountain views of any ski area in New England. See chapter 6.
- **Sugarloaf** (Maine): New England's second biggest ski mountain has a friendly, bustling resort at its base and some superb skiing on its upper flanks. This is the place to be after a heavy snowstorm, when the snowfields offer the only lift-served above-treeline skiing in the east. See chapter 7.
- **Sunday River** (Maine): Sunday River just seems to keep on growing. As it expands its way along this ridge of challenging peaks, it continues to impress die-hard skiers with creative trail planning, tough steeps, and the best snowmaking in the east. See chapter 7.

7 The Best Destinations for Families

- **Montshire Museum** (Norwich, Vermont): This new children's museum, in a soaring, modern space on the Vermont–New Hampshire border, has wonderful interactive exhibits inside and nature trails winding along the Connecticut River. See chapter 5.
- **Weirs Beach** (New Hampshire): This is the trip your kids would plan if you didn't get in the way. Weirs Beach on Lake Winnipesaukee offers passive amusements like

train and boat rides that appeal to younger kids, and plenty of active adventures for young teens—like go-kart racing, waterslides, and video arcades. Their parents can recuperate while lounging on the lakeside beach. See chapter 6.

- **Cog Railroad** (Crawford Notch, New Hampshire): It's fun! It's terrifying! It's a great glimpse into history. Kids love this ratchety climb to the top of New England's highest peak aboard trains that were specially designed to scale the mountain in 1869. As a technological marvel, the railroad attracted tourists by the thousands a century ago. They still come to marvel at its sheer audacity. See chapter 6.
- **Waterville Valley** (New Hampshire): Waterville Valley knows what kids and teens are looking for, and it's not a quiet night in front of a crackling fire. It's snowboarding, and this mid-sized ski area has gone the extra distance to appeal to snowboarders with separate activities and even a separate mountain for the snowboard crowd. See chapter 6.
- **Monhegan Island** (Maine): Kids from 8 to 12 years old especially enjoy overnight excursions to Monhegan Island. The mail boat from Port Clyde is rustic and intriguing, the hotels are an adventure, and the woods are filled with magical fairy houses. See chapter 7.

8 The Best Places to Rediscover America's Past

- **Plymouth** (Vermont): President Calvin Coolidge was born in this high upland valley, and the state has done a superb job preserving his hometown village. You'll get a good sense of the president's roots, but also gain a greater understanding of how a New England village works. Don't miss the cheese shop still owned by the President's son. See chapter 5.
- **Shelburne Museum** (Shelburne, Vermont): Think of this sprawling museum as New England's attic. Located on 45 acres on the shores of Lake Champlain, the Shelburne Museum not only features the usual exhibits of quilts and early glass, but whole buildings preserved like specimens in formaldehyde. Look for the lighthouse, the railroad station, and the stagecoach inn. This is one of northern New England's "don't miss" destinations. See chapter 5.
- **Portsmouth** (New Hampshire): Portsmouth is a salty coastal city that just happens to boast some of the most impressive historic homes in New England. Start at Strawbery Banke, a historic 10-acre compound of 42 historic buildings. Then visit the many other grand homes in nearby neighborhoods, like the house John Paul Jones occupied while building his warship during the Revolution. See chapter 6.
- **Manchester** (New Hampshire): New England's history isn't all farming and shipbuilding. A driving tour of downtown Manchester, with its hulking and impressive 19th-century factories of brick lining the Merrimack River, will show another side of New England's storied past. See chapter 6.
- **Sabbathday Shaker Community** (New Gloucester, Maine): This is the last of the active Shaker communities in the nation—the only Shaker community that voted to accept new converts rather than to die out. The 1,900-acre farm, about 45 minutes outside of Portland, has a number of exceptional buildings, including some dating back to the 18th century. Visitors come to view examples of historic Shaker craftsmanship, and buy locally grown Shaker herbs to bring home. See chapter 7.

9   The Best Destinations for Literary Enthusiasts

- **Naulakha** (Brattleboro, Vermont): During his sojourn in Vermont, British writer Rudyard Kipling gained a reputation as being something of a strange bird. But his neighbors' whispers didn't stop him from writing *The Jungle Book* or *Captains Courageous* while living in Naulakha, a house he built outside of Brattleboro. Today, you can rent the home by the week and follow Kipling's footsteps through the countryside during your stay. See chapter 5.
- **Robert Frost Farm** (Sugar Hill, New Hampshire): Two of the most famous New England poems—"The Road Not Taken" and "Stopping by Woods on a Snowy Evening"—were composed by Robert Frost at this farm just outside of Franconia. Explore the woods and read the verses posted along the pathways, and tour the farmhouse where Frost lived with his family earlier this century. See chapter 6.
- **West Branch of the Penobscot River** (Maine): Henry David Thoreau ventured down this river by canoe in the mid-19th century, and found the woods all "moosey and mossy." They're still that way along the river today. A four-day canoe trip along part of his route includes a stop at tiny Chesuncook Village, where you can find the grave of Thoreau's host in a quiet, wooded cemetery. See chapter 7.

10   The Most Intriguing Historic Homes

- **Hildene** (Manchester, Vermont): This lavish summer home, built by Abraham and Mary Todd Lincoln's son Robert, offers a glimpse of how the other half lived late in America's gilded age. A prosperous businessman, the younger Lincoln built this summer retreat complete with a 1,000-pipe organ and extensive formal gardens. See chapter 5.
- **Drisco House** (Portsmouth, New Hampshire): The Drisco House is the most fascinating of the many structures at Strawbery Banke, the region's premier historic attraction. Half of this house was restored to its 1790s grandeur, and half left pretty much as it appeared in the 1950s. You'll learn plenty about how a house adapts to the technology and culture of the era. See chapter 6.
- **Canterbury Shaker Village** (Canterbury, New Hampshire): This historic village outside of Concord nicely captures the Shaker way of life, which stressed simplicity and industry. See the massive laundry room, or enjoy a Shaker-inspired meal at the elegant restaurant, followed by an evening candlelight tour of the village at its most peaceful. See chapter 6.
- **Saint-Gaudens National Historic Site** (Cornish, New Hampshire): Sculptor Augustus Saint-Gaudens has been overshadowed somewhat by his contemporary, Daniel Chester French, but his works were extraordinary and prolific. You'll learn all about the man and the artistic culture of the late 19th and early 20th century during tours of his studio and house, located in the peaceful Connecticut River Valley of southwest New Hampshire. See chapter 6.
- **Victoria Mansion** (Portland, Maine): Donald Trump had nothing on the Victorians when it came to material excess. You'll see Victorian decorative arts at their zenith in this elaborate Italianate mansion built during the Civil War years by a prosperous hotelier. It's open to the public for tours throughout the summer. See chapter 7.
- **Parson Fisher House** (Blue Hill, Maine): Parson Jonathan Fisher, who served as minister to the quiet town of Blue Hill in the late 18th century, was a man of extraordinary talents. A true renaissance man, he did everything from designing

his own house to building his own clocks to preaching sermons in five languages (including Aramaic). As if that wasn't enough, his primitive landscapes are widely regarded as among the best to emerge from the region. See chapter 7.

11 The Best Resorts

- **Woodstock Inn & Resort** (Woodstock, Vermont; ☎ **802/457-1100** or 800/448-7900): The 140-room inn was built in the 1960s with a strong colonial revival accent. Located right on the green in picturesque Woodstock, the inn offers easy access to the village, along with plenty of other activities, including golf on a course designed by Robert Trent Jones, indoor and outdoor pools, hiking, and skiing (both downhill and cross-country) in winter. See chapter 5.
- **White Mountain Hotel and Resort** (North Conway, New Hampshire; ☎ **802/457-1100** o̶ This tasteful, upscale resort opened just a few years ago, but it's imbued with old-fashioned comfort and charm. Located a few miles from the tacky bustle of North Conway, the White Mountain Resort offers golf, swimming, and hiking right at its front door. See chapter 6.
- **Mount Washington Hotel** (Bretton Woods, New Hampshire; ☎ **603/278-1000** or 800/258-0330): The last of the grand Edwardian resorts, the Mount Washington has come back from the brink of bankruptcy with its famed flair intact. This is the place to play golf, climb Mount Washington, or just sit on the broad porch and feel important. See chapter 6.
- **Balsams Grand Resort Hotel** (Dixville Notch, New Hampshire; ☎ **603/255-3400**, or 800/255-0600, 800/255-0800 in NH): It's like having your own castle on your own private estate. Set on 15,000 acres in far northern New Hampshire, The Balsams has been offering superb hospitality and gracious comfort since 1866. It has two golf courses, miles of hiking trails, and, in winter, its own downhill and cross-country ski areas. See chapter 6.
- **The Quisisana** (Center Lovell, Maine; ☎ **207/925-3500,** or 914/833-0293 in winter): It's a rustic Maine vacation with a musical twist. The waiters, chambermaids, and other staff are recruited from conservatories around the nation, and they perform everything from light opera to chamber music for guests at this pine-filled lakeside resort. Between performances there's ample opportunity for canoeing and hiking. See chapter 7.
- **The Colony** (Kennebunkport, Maine; ☎ **207/967-3331** or 800/552-2363): This rambling, gleaming white resort dates back to 1914, and has been nicely upgraded over the years without losing any of the charm. You can play shuffleboard, putt on the green, or lounge in the ocean-view pool. More vigorous souls cross the street to brave the cold Atlantic waters. See chapter 7.

12 The Best Country Inns

- **The Old Tavern at Grafton** (Grafton, Vermont; ☎ **802/843-2231** or 800/843-1801): This elegant village inn sits amid one of the most charming historic villages of northern New England. Modernized and thoroughly made over, the Old Tavern offers contemporary elegance with plenty of historic flair. See chapter 5.
- **Windham Hill Inn** (West Townshend, Vermont; ☎ **802/874-4080** or 800/944-4080): New innkeepers made over this historic inn in 1995, adding welcome amenities like air-conditioning while still preserving the antique charm of this 1823 farm house. It's at the end of a remote dirt road in a high upland valley, and guests are welcome to explore 160 private acres on a network of walking trails. See chapter 5.

- **Kedron Valley Inn** (South Woodstock, Vermont; ☎ **802/457-1473** or 800/
836-1193): Set at a quiet country crossroads just south of Woodstock, the Kedron
Valley Inn offers genuine comfort—this is no stuffy museum-quality setting.
Guests enjoy exquisite bedrooms, a private pond with two sand beaches, and a creative dining room that wins raves from discriminating diners. See chapter 5.
- **Twin Farms** (Woodstock, Vermont; ☎ **802/234-9999** or 800/894-6327): Just
north of Woodstock is the most elegant inn in New England. The price will
appall many of you (rooms start at $700 for two, including all meals and liquor),
but you'll certainly be pampered here. Novelist Sinclair Lewis once lived on this
300-acre farm, and today it's a aesthetic retreat that offers serenity and exceptional
food. See chapter 5.
- **The Inn at Thorn Hill** (Jackson, New Hampshire; ☎ **603/383-4242**): Designed
by famed architect Stanford White in 1895, this handsome inn is maintained in
a style that would make the master proud. It's decorated in a Victorian motif, with
comfortable guest rooms, lovely common areas, and a well-regarded dining
room—all within easy walking (or skiing) distance of the town of Jackson. See
chapter 6.
- **The White Barn Inn** (Kennebunkport, Maine; ☎ **207/967-2321**): Much of the
White Barn staff hails from Europe, and guests are treated with a continental
graciousness. The rooms are a delight, and the meals (served in the barn) are
among the best in Maine. See chapter 7.

13 The Best B&Bs

- **1811 House** (Manchester Village, Vermont; ☎ **802/362-1811** or 800/
432-1811): The 1811 House is one of the best historic inns around. If you want
your room decor to match the architectural style, you'll be content here. Everything is steeped in austere early American elegance—there's none of that kitschy
look that often afflicts places less adept at recreating a historical sensibility. See
chapter 5.
- **Inn at Round Barn Farm** (Waitsfield, Vermont; ☎ **802/496-2276**): The beautiful lap pool hidden beneath the monumental former barn is only one of the secrets concealed by this charming inn. The rooms are romantic, the surrounding
hillsides are the very picture of pastoral Vermont, and small touches everywhere
make guests feel very welcome. See chapter 5.
- **Adair** (Bethlehem, New Hampshire; ☎ **603/444-2600** or 800/441-2606): This
is one of the newer mansions in the White Mountains (it dates from 1927), but
innkeepers Patricia and Hardy Banfield have done a stellar job of infusing this
Georgian Revival with a time-honored elegance. Guests can relax here in profound
peace even though they're within easy exploring distance of White Mountain attractions. See chapter 6.
- **Pomegranate Inn** (Portland, Maine; ☎ **207/772-1006** or 800/356-0408):
Whimsy and history collide to good effect at this fine B&B in one of Portland's
most stately neighborhoods. The Italianate mansion is stern on the outside,
but inside it's alive with creative wall paintings and one-of-a-kind antiques. See
chapter 7.
- **Balance Rock Inn** (Bar Harbor, Maine; ☎ **207/288-2610** or 800/753-0494):
Hands down, the best coastal view in Maine can be had from the front patio of
the Inn at Balance Rock, which lies right on the water in Bar Harbor. You could
spend the whole day without wandering far from the patio—splashing in the pool,
lounging on the broad lawn, and sipping cocktails in the evening as dusk settles
over Frenchman Bay. See chapter 7.

- **John Peters Inn** (Blue Hill, Maine; ☎ 207/374-2116): Simple yet sophisticated refinement is the order of the day at this wonderful 1810 inn, located on 25 shorefront acres in Blue Hill. The rooms are comfortable, with a pleasantly historical feel, and you feel like you're the master of your own estate as you walk the common rooms and the grounds. See chapter 7.

14 The Best Moderately Priced Accommodations

- **Mad River Barn** (Waitsfield, Vermont; ☎ 802/496-3310 or 800/631-0466): It takes a few minutes to adapt to the Spartan rooms and no-frills accommodations here. But you'll soon discover that the real action takes place in the living room and dining room, where skiers relax and chat after a day on the slopes, and share heaping helpings at mealtime. Rooms with breakfast are $65 for two in summer, and $95 in winter. See chapter 5.
- **Inn of Exeter** (Exeter, New Hampshire; ☎ 603/772-5901 or 800/782-8444): The dark, richly appointed lobby feels like a private gentleman's club. The location, adjacent to one of the most exclusive prep schools in the nation, only enhances the clubby mood. Rooms are a good value at $75 to $100 for two. See chapter 6.
- **Red Hill Inn** (Center Harbor, New Hampshire; ☎ 603/279-7001 or 800/573-3445): Situated in the lush hills between Lake Winnipesaukee and the White Mountains, the Red Hill Inn has a faded Victorian grandeur that's been nicely updated without destroying the mood. It's hard to pry yourself away from the fireplace in the common room, but try to stir yourself, if only to explore the forest and fields around the inn. See chapter 6.
- **Philbrook Farm Inn** (Shelburne, New Hampshire; ☎ 603/466-3831): Go here if you're looking for a complete getaway. The inn has been taking in travelers since the 1850s, and they know how to do it right. The farmhouse sits on 1,000 acres between the Mahoosuc Mountains and the Androscoggin River, and guests can hike with vigor or relax in leisure with equal aplomb. Rooms for two are $130 or under, and that includes both breakfast and dinner. Ask about discounts for longer stays. See chapter 6.
- **Maine Stay Inn** (Camden, Maine; ☎ 207/236-9636 or 800-950-2117): It's by no means a budget inn (rooms run $80 to $130 for two), but you get a lot of hospitality for the money, and the accommodations are as nice as others I've seen for twice the price. The inn is within walking distance of both downtown Camden and the Camden Hills. See chapter 7.

15 The Best Alternative Accommodations

- **Camping in the Green Mountains** (Vermont): Whether your preferred mode of travel is by foot, car, canoe, or bike, you'll find plenty of good campsites in the verdant hills of Vermont. The state parks are well regarded, with many dating from from the Civilian Conservation Corps days. The national forest, aided by the Green Mountain Club, maintains dozens of backcountry sites and lean-tos offering secluded getaways far from the noise of everyday life. See chapter 5.
- **Appalachian Mountain Club Huts** (New Hampshire): For more than a century, the AMC has been putting up weary hikers at its huts high in the White Mountains. Today, the club still manages eight of them (each about a day's hike apart), serving up filling, family-style meals and offering sturdy bunks stacked three high in rustic bunk rooms. See chapter 6.

- **Little Lyford Pond Camps** (outside Greenville, Maine; ☎ via radio phone **207/ 695-2821**): It's accessible only by ski, snowmobile, or skiplane in winter, but that's the charm of this remote mountain lodge. (You can drive here in summer.) There's good hiking, canoeing, fishing, and skiing right out the front door of the century-old cabins, each of which comes complete with woodstove, gas lamps, and a private outhouse in back. See chapter 7.
- **Maine Island Trail Islands:** About 70 remote islands along the Maine Coast are open to camping, and from these remote, salty wildernesses you'll see some of the best sunsets imaginable. See "Sea Kayaking" in the "Enjoying the Great Outdoors" section of chapter 7.
- **Windjammers** (Maine): Maine has the East Coast's largest fleet of windjammers, offering travelers summertime adventure on the high seas. Most are berthed in the region between Bath and Belfast. You can explore offshore islands and inland estuaries, and learn how sailors once made the best of the wind. Accommodations in private cabins are typically spartan, but you'll spend most of your time on the deck luxuriating in the stunning views anyway. See chapter 7.

16 The Best Restaurants

- **Hemingway's** (Killington, Vermont; ☎ **802/422-3886**): Killington seems an unlikely place for a serious culinary adventure, yet Hemingway's will meet the loftiest expectations. The menu changes frequently to ensure that only the freshest ingredients are used. If it's available, be sure to order the wild mushroom and truffle soup. See chapter 5.
- **Inn at Sawmill Farm** (West Dover, Vermont; ☎ **802/464-8131**): Men are required (not requested) to wear jackets while dining in this elegant restaurant, housed in a former barn. The chef gets high marks for his presentation of dishes such as pan-seared salmon in saffron sauce, and oenophiles rave about the 36,000-bottle wine cellar. See chapter 5.
- **The Daniel Webster Room** (Hanover, New Hampshire; ☎ **603/643-4300**): Classic continental fare and more is cooked to perfection and expertly served in the elegant neoclassical dining room at the Hanover Inn, at the edge of the Dartmouth College campus. Try the filet mignon with foie gras. See chapter 6.
- **Street & Co.** (Portland, Maine; ☎ **207/775-0887**): Seafood is the big catch at this intimate Portland bistro, tucked down a narrow alley just a block from the waterfront. Low beams, dim lighting, and drying herbs hanging from the joists overhead set the mood. Diners are seated at copper-topped tables, designed to allow the waiters to deliver the steaming skillets of perfectly prepared seafood right from the stove. See chapter 7.
- **Porcupine Grill** (Bar Harbor, Maine; ☎ **207/288-3884**): The extravagantly crafted bar is the first thing you'll notice as you enter Bar Harbor's Porcupine Grill. But it's the food you'll remember when you leave. Everything is delicately prepared—even dishes with ginger or sun-dried tomato, ingredients that tend to overwhelm when they're used by less talented chefs. See chapter 7.
- **White Barn Inn** (Kennebunkport, Maine; ☎ **207/967-2321**): The setting, in an ancient, rustic barn, is magical. The tables are draped with floor-length tablecloths, and the chairs feature imported Italian upholstery. The food is to die for. Enjoy entrees such as grilled duckling breast with ginger and sundried cherry sauce, or a roast rack of lamb with pecans and homemade barbecue sauce. See chapter 7.

17 The Best Local Dining Experiences

- **Blue Benn Diner** (Bennington, Vermont; ☎ **802/442-5140**): This Bennington favorite, housed in a classic 1945 Silk City diner, has a barrel ceiling, acres of stainless steel, and a vast menu. Make sure you don't overlook specials scrawled on paper and taped all over the walls. And leave room for a slice of delicious pie, like blackberry, pumpkin, or chocolate cream. See chapter 5.
- **Curtis Bar-B-Q** (Putney, Vermont; ☎ **802/387-5474**): Located on a scruffy lot in Putney, Curtis Bar-B-Q serves up the most righteous, down-to-earth slabs of pork and beef in New England. Don't look for atmosphere. There isn't any—unless you count the signs decreeing that "All dogs must be leashed" as decor. Just order your meat from the blue school bus, and take it to an empty picnic table to enjoy. See chapter 5.
- **Daily Planet** (Burlington, Vermont; ☎ **802/862-9647**): Burlington's hip Daily Planet is a college bar that does a remarkable thing: It serves up great food at a good price. Noisy, yes, but informal, fun, and vibrant. See chapter 5.
- **Lou's** (Hanover, New Hampshire; ☎ **603/643-3321**): Huge crowds flock to Lou's, just down the block from the Dartmouth campus in Hanover, for breakfast on weekends. Fortunately, breakfast is served all day here, and the sandwiches, served on fresh-baked bread, are huge and delicious. See chapter 6.
- **Beal's Lobster Pier** (Southwest Harbor, Maine; ☎ **207/244-7178**): This Southwest Harbor institution is a superb spot to practice one of the great rituals of summer: eating a freshly boiled lobster while sipping on a Maine beer. It's nothing fancy (no lobster pound should be); the good view of the harbor and the relaxed atmosphere come at no additional charge. See chapter 7.

18 The Best Destinations for Serious Shoppers

- **Manchester** (Vermont): The dozens of outlet stores clustered in this handsome village include the usual high-fashion suspects, along with some notable individual shops. Head to Orvis, the maker of noted fly-fishing equipment, for a selection of outdoor gear and clothing. See chapter 5.
- **Portsmouth** (New Hampshire): Downtown Portsmouth offers a grab-bag of small, manageable, eclectic shops, ranging from funky shoe stores to high-quality art galleries. The downtown district may be small enough to browse leisurely on foot, but it packs in a broad assortment of stuff for sale that will appeal to most any taste. See chapter 6.
- **North Conway** (New Hampshire): Combine outdoor adventure with serious shopping along the 3-mile stretch of discount outlet stores that makes up most of North Conway. Look for Anne Klein, American Tourister, Izod, Dansk, Donna Karan, Levi's, Polo/Ralph Lauren, Reebok/Rockport, J. Crew, and Eddie Bauer in town, along with dozens of others. See chapter 6.
- **Route 1** (Kittery to Kennebunk, Maine): Antique hounds delight in this stretch of less-than-scenic Route 1. Antique mini-malls and high-class junk shops alike are scattered along the route, though there's no central antique zone. Among the best shops is Jorgensen's Antiques on Route 1 in Wells, which has a good selection of American and European furniture in two large buildings. See chapter 7.
- **Freeport** (Maine): L.L. Bean is the big name in this thriving town of outlets, but you'll also find Nike, Patagonia, J. Crew, Dansk, Brooks Brothers, and about 100 others. This is the most aesthetically pleasing of the several outlet centers in northern New England. See chapter 7.

2

Getting to Know Northern New England

lived on an island off the Maine Coast near Portland for four years, at the end of a mile-long dirt road. I had one other neighbor, whose house was a stone's throw across the road from me. For the first few months, our only contact was an occasional nod or wave, or a few cordial words exchanged if we ran into one another at the island store.

I didn't realize it at the time, but she was testing me. After six months she became a bit chattier, and eventually confessed that her biggest nightmare was having a neighbor who would come bursting through the door each day with a sing-song "Good Morning!" while bearing a basket of freshly baked blueberry muffins. I had kept my distance, proving I could be a good neighbor. We ended up as lasting friends.

Respecting privacy goes a long way in northern New England. It always has. And getting to know the region requires equal amounts of patience and persistence. Northern New England doesn't wear its attractions on its sleeve, waving them around for everyone to notice. It keeps its best secrets hidden in valleys and on the side streets of small villages. Your most memorable experience might be cracking open a boiled lobster at a lobster pound marked only with a scrawled paper sign, or enjoying a million-dollar afternoon view from a low-rent hill in Vermont's Green Mountains. There's no Disneyland or Space Needle or Grand Canyon here. Northern New England is the sum of dozens of smaller pleasures.

Which isn't to say that northern New England lacks attractions. It has the Green Mountains of Vermont, the White Mountains of New Hampshire, and Acadia National Park on the Maine Coast. It has wonderful, lost-in-time towns like Woodstock, Vermont, and Hancock, New Hampshire. But thinking of your explorations as a "connect-the-dots" endeavor linking the "major sights" with long drives is a sure-fire recipe for disappointment. It's better to plan a slow itinerary that allows you to enjoy the stretches between destinations, to explore the little villages and quiet byways.

What you'll find is an inviting blend of history, both human and natural. Northern New England wasn't a hub of colonial civilization, like Massachusetts or Virginia. But this region of rounded hills and fertile river valleys did attract early settlers, and thriving farms and villages dotted the countryside. In this century, northern New England labored under an extended economic malaise, which incidentally helped preserve many of the old villages. Farm fields that would have sprouted neighborhoods of suburban tract homes in a robust economy remained farm fields, and many villages are still dominated by churches and white clapboard homes that remain a far remove from the nearest mall.

And you'll find plenty of opportunities for rugged adventure. Some writers insist that northern New England's character is still informed by a grim Calvinist doctrine, which decrees that nothing will change one's fate and that hard work is a moral virtue. (New Englanders' dull acceptance that the Red Sox will never be victorious is often trotted out as evidence of the region's enduring Calvinism.) And sure enough, there are vigorous strains of Calvinism in outdoor recreation as practiced in New England. Here's how the locals entertain themselves: Hiking the severe, demanding paths of the White Mountains; swimming in the near-Arctic waters of Maine; and patiently waiting for fish to strike a fly while slowly being consumed by black flies along a northern Vermont river. In other words, don't expect posh resorts on sandy beaches where personal valets bringing you fresh towels and Evian.

That's not to say a trip here means lumpy mattresses and inedible food. On the contrary, in the past two decades luxurious country inns and restaurants serving food to rival the best of Boston have become part of the landscape. Enjoy these places. But to get the most out of your trip, be sure to leave enough time to put your heels up on a porch rail, or to wander out of town on an abandoned county road.

"There's nothing to do here," an inn manager in Vermont once explained to me. "Our product is indolence." And that's an increasingly rare commodity these days. Take the time to savor it.

1 The Regions in Brief

The Green Mountains   Extending the length of Vermont from Massachusetts to Canada, this undulating chain of forested hills and low mountains offers good hiking, scenic backroad drives, and superb bicycling. Much of the chain is part of the Green Mountain National Forest, which encompasses hiking trails, campgrounds, and wilderness areas. The best views can be had from atop the peaks in the northern half of the state. The most scenic drives are in the southern part of the state.

The Northeast Kingdom   Vermont's three northeastern counties form the Northeast Kingdom, the most remote and rural part of the state. While tourist amenities are few, the sense of exploring the rural far north is large.

The Lakes Region   Lake Winnipesaukee is the heart of the New Hampshire's Lakes Region, but many smaller lakes and ponds dot the landscape and offer quiet escapes.

The White Mountains   Starting in the mid-19th century, New Hampshire's White Mountains have attracted travelers seeking to experience the grandeur of the craggy, windswept peaks and explore the forests dotted with glacial erratics and clear, rushing streams. The region's best backcountry hiking and camping is found here.

Coastal Maine   Maine's rocky coast is the stuff of legend, art, and poetry. The term Downeast was born here—a reflection that ships sailing east had an easier go of it with currents and winds in their favor. South of Portland you'll find beaches broken by the occasional rocky headland. Northeast of Portland, the landscape becomes far rougher, with fractured rock battered by the sea and the beaches few and far between. The most popular (and crowded) destinations are around Ogunquit, Boothbay Harbor, Camden, and Mount Desert Island.

Acadia National Park   New England's only national park, Acadia attracts thousands of tourists who come to just sit on rocks and watch the surf. You can also hike

Northern New England

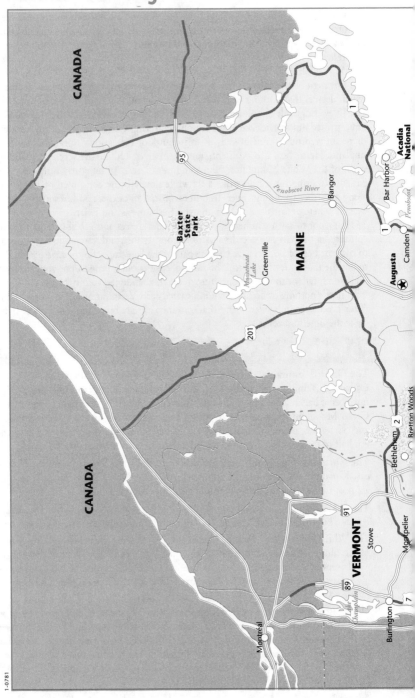

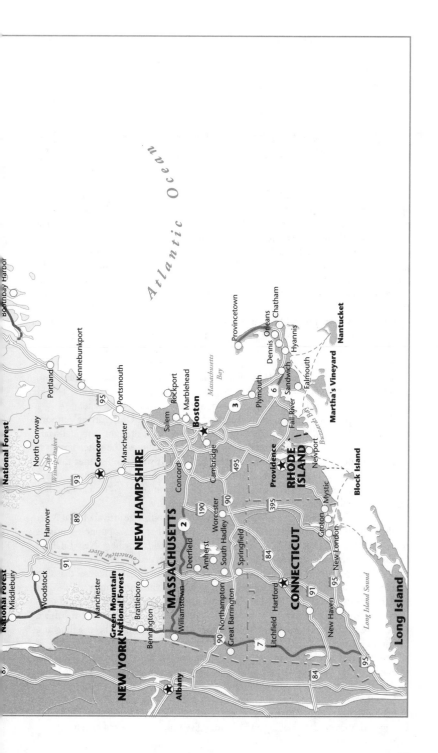

15

to the low, bald summits, and mountain bike on the elaborate network of forested carriage roads.

Maine's North Woods Consisting of millions of acres of uninhabited terrain, the North Woods is almost entirely owned by timber companies who harvest trees to feed their mills. Within this vast tree plantation are pockets of undisturbed wildlands that recall the era when Thoreau paddled and portaged his way north.

2 Northern New England Today

The most pressing issue facing the region today might be summarized in one word: Wal-Mart.

New England has always taken a quiet pride in its low-key, practical way of approaching life. "Use it up, wear it out, make do, or do without" is a well-worn phrase that aptly sums up the attitude of many in northern New England, an area still blessed with little crime and a vigorous work ethic.

Town meetings are still the form of government in many communities. Residents gather in a public place in town, usually in the grim season of February or March, and vote on the important issues of the day, like funding for their schools, road improvements, and even symbolic gestures, such as declaring their town a nuclear-free zone.

Where do the traditional town meeting, and the verities of thrift and parsimony, fit into an economic universe that includes Wal-Mart? Since Wal-Mart first appeared on the scene in these three states, there's been hearty debate over the matter. The *Maine Times,* a statewide alternative paper, took up the fight a few years ago when Wal-Marts first started appearing in Maine, claiming that the superstores would leave already troubled Main Streets in dire straits, and undermine values that Mainers held dear. "Stop Wal-Mart" bumper stickers started sprouting around the state.

Vermont has proven even more prickly about Wal-Marts. A University of Vermont survey in 1995 found that 62 percent of Vermont residents thought that Wal-Mart and other major chains should be discouraged from coming to the state. That was up from 50 percent in 1994 and 45 percent in 1993. It was also just after the first Wal-Mart came to Vermont—in a downtown Bennington location—and a second Wal-Mart was announced for the suburbs of Burlington. At press time, Wal-Mart had just cancelled plans for another store in St. Johnsbury.

Of course, Wal-Mart isn't just a superstore. It's a symbol. The arrival of Wal-Mart in New England marks a sea change, and it's a change that vocal opponents insist is not for the better. They say Wal-Mart heralds those trends northern New England has managed to avoid for some time— suburban sprawl, decaying downtown store-fronts, dependence on a low-wage job economy, and the arrival of businesses that ship their profits out of state rather than keeping them in the community. Wal-Mart strikes some as a harbinger of other problems to come, like crime, traffic, and con-gestion. (To be fair, others see Wal-Mart's arrival in happier, simpler terms: It's a place to get a better price on merchandise that local retailers have been selling at a premium for years.)

Behind the Wal-Mart debate is a central question that the region is just beginning to grapple with: What is the role of development in northern New England? If not Wal-Mart, what are the economic alternatives?

Development is a hot but not inflammatory issue—this isn't like the property rights movement in the West, where people are manning the barricades and taking hostages for the cause. (New England just isn't given to those kinds of extremes.) Few seem to think that development should be allowed at all costs. And few seem to think that the land should be preserved at all costs.

Without development, the offspring of longtime New England families will have no jobs, and Northern New England will be fated to spend its days as a sort of quaint theme park. But if development continues unabated, many of the characteristics that make this region unique—and attract tourist dollars—will vanish. Will Vermont be able to sustain its $2 billion tourism industry if the countryside is blanketed with strip malls and fast-food joints? That's not likely. The question is how to balance the conservation ethic with room for growth. And it's not a question that's likely to be resolved in the near future.

The debate over development takes unique forms in each part of the region. In Maine's North Woods, the vast, unbroken tracts of timberland have been discovered by second-home developers, who have bought prime waterfront property to build vacation homes. Environmentalists say that this fragmentation of the North Woods will forever destroy a valuable natural asset; one environmental group has proposed creating a new national park to preserve what's left. Landowners maintain that it's their land, and they have a right to do with it what they see fit. The road to an amicable settlement promises to be bumpy and long.

Northern New England's five-year economic boom in the late 1980s, which fueled much of the debate over development, slowed considerably in the 1990s, making the issue less urgent but no less critical.

Commentators point out that other social changes on the horizon could raise new conflicts. The rise of the information culture will make it increasingly likely that telecommuters and info-entreprenuers will settle in remote and pristine villages, running their businesses via modem and satellite. How will these affluent migrants adapt to clear-cutting in the countryside or increasing numbers of tour buses cruising their village greens?

Change isn't likely to come rapidly to New England. It rarely does. But there's a lot to sort out, and friction will likely increase, one Wal-Mart store at a time.

3 History 101

New England refuses to be divorced from its past. While cars, shopping malls, and condos have had their culture-shaping impact here as they have elsewhere in the U.S., these new inventions have yet to overwhelm the region's profound sense of history. That's especially true in northern New England. Travelers in Maine, New Hampshire, and Vermont will find clues to the region's rich past everywhere they turn, from stone walls running through now-dense woods, to spectacular Federal-style homes standing alone in the countryside. Like the earlier glaciers, powerful economic trends moved across the region, then retreated, often leaving ample evidence of their presence in their wake.

Here's a quick look at some historical episodes and trends that shaped these northern states.

INDIGENOUS CULTURE   Native Americans have inhabited northern New England since about 7,000 B.C. While New York's Iroquois Indians had a presence in Vermont, northern New England was inhabited mostly by Algonquin Indians known as Abnakis ("people of the dawn"), who lived a nomadic life, moving with the seasons and traveling to areas where food was abundant. After the arrival of the Europeans, French Catholic missionaries succeeded in converting many of the Native Americans, and most tribes sided with the French in the French and Indian

A Literary Legacy

The figure that dominates any discussion of northern New England's literary tradition must surely be Robert Frost (1874–1963). This exceptionally gifted poet, who some believe was the greatest of this century, was born in California but lived his life in Massachusetts, New Hampshire, and Vermont. In the New England landscape and community he found a lasting grace and rich metaphors for life. ("Two roads diverged in a wood, and I—/ I took the one less traveled by, / And that has made all the difference.")

Other writers from the region have also made their mark. Poet Henry Wadsworth Longfellow (1807–82) was born in Portland, lived much of his life in Boston, and was widely famed for his narrative poems. Sarah Orne Jewett of Maine has gained a following among serious scholars in recent years for her gentle stories of early life along the coast. Dorothy Canfield Fisher and Kenneth Roberts have done much to educate their readers about the history of Vermont and Maine, respectively. Edna St. Vincent Millay and Edwin Arlington Robinson both hailed from Maine. And May Sarton, who died in 1995, was highly respected for her journals as well as her fiction.

Northern New England's influence is more subtle than the output of its authors. Travels through the region greatly influenced the work of Henry David Thoreau and Nathaniel Hawthorne. Artemus Ward, a comic performer who hailed from Waterford, Maine, was a national sensation as a comic backwoods philosopher in the mid-19th century, and humorist Mark Twain widely credited Ward as an inspiration for his own style of humor.

Contemporary writers seem to be attracted to northern New England not so much for its community of writers, but for the privacy the region affords. In Vermont, this includes novelist Howard Frank Mosher, whose works invest the Northeast Kingdom with mystical qualities. New Hampshire seems to have attracted more than its share of popular writers, including poet Donald Hall, essayist Noel Perrin, travel writer Bill Bryson, naturalist Sy Montgomery, and noted crank P.J. O'Rourke.

Wars in the 18th century. Afterward, the Indians fared poorly at the hands of the British and never regained their stature in the region. Today, Indians are found in greatest concentration at several major reservations in Maine, including Indian Island in the Penobscot River, and two near the Canadian border in Washington County. Other than that, the few clues left behind by Indian cultures have been pretty much obliterated by later settlers.

SETTLEMENT, FARMING & TRADE   Settlement of the region began in earnest in the late 17th and early 18th centuries as colonists from Massachusetts pushed northward and arriving Europeans settled along the south coast. The first areas to be settled were lands near protected harbors on the coast (such as Portsmouth, N.H.) and along navigable waterways (like Brattleboro, Vt.).

During the 18th and early 19th century, the region followed two tracks. Residents of inland communities survived by clearing the land for farming and trading in furs. Vermont in particular has always been an agrarian state, and remains prominent in dairy products to this day. (It's no coincidence that Ben & Jerry's ice cream is manufactured there.)

Meanwhile, along the coast, the region prospered as boat yards were built in Maine's coves, and ship captains made tidy fortunes trading lumber for sugar and

Maine is also summer home to a number of notable authors, including Anne Beattie, James Michener, and Christopher Buckley. Maine is also the year-round home of Stephen King, who is considered not so much a novelist as Maine's Leading Industry.

And below are a few of my favorite books about this area, or written by regional authors.

In the Memory House by **Howard Mansfield.** This finely written book by a New Hampshire author provides a penetrating look at New England's sometimes estranged relationship with its own past. First published in 1993 and available in paperback.

Inventing New England by **Dona Brown.** A University of Vermont professor tells the epic tale of the rise of 19th-century tourism in New England in this uncommonly well-written 1995 study.

Lobster Gangs of Maine by **James M. Acheson.** An exhaustively researched 1988 study that answers every question you'll have about the lobsterman's life, and then some.

Northern Borders by **Howard Frank Mosher.** This magical novel, published in 1994, is ostensibly about a young boy living with his taciturn grandparents in northern Vermont. But the book's central character is really Vermont's Northeast Kingdom.

One Man's Meat by **E. B. White.** White was a sometime resident of a saltwater farm on the Maine Coast and frequent contributor to the *New Yorker*. His essays, composed in the late 1930s and early 1940s, are only incidentally about Maine, but you get a superb sense of place by observing the shadows. Still in print in paperback.

Vermont Traditions by **Dorothy Canfield Fisher.** Written in that somewhat overwrought style popular in the 1950s, this still remains the best survey of the Vermont character.

rum in the Caribbean. Even ice became a valued commodity, with Maine shipping tons of ice in insulated ships around the world—to the Caribbean, Brazil, and even India. More adventurous traders made the hazardous voyage to the Orient, bringing back lacquered furniture and Chinese paintings, which still turn up in country auctions to this day.

The pushing of the railroad into northern New England in the mid-19th century was another boon. The train opened up much of the interior and led to towns springing up overnight, such as White River Junction, Vt. The rail lines allowed the local resources—such as the fine marbles and granites from Vermont—to be easily shipped to markets to the south.

INDUSTRY   New England's industrial revolution took root around the time of the embargo act of 1807. Barred from importing English fabrics, Americans had to build their own textile mills to obtain cloth. Other common household products were soon also manufactured here, especially shoes, which became an industrial mainstay for decades. Towns like Lewiston and Biddeford, Maine, and Manchester, New Hampshire, became centers of industrial production. The spread of rail encouraged the growth of industry, as products could be shipped more easily to lucrative markets. There was another effect: In the mid-19th century, the composition of the local population began to change as French-Canadians immigrated to work in the factories. Today there's still a strong French-Canadian influence in Manchester, Biddeford, and Lewiston, a legacy of manufacturing days.

As with farming before it, manufacturing headed south, drawn by cheaper labor and closer access to raw materials like cotton and leather. Northern New England's industry began to die off slowly. Today paper manufacturing and electronics account for much manufacturing, but far more residents are employed by service providers and government than by manufacturers.

TOURISM In the mid and late-19th century, northern New Englanders discovered a new cash crop: the tourist. All along the eastern seaboard it became fashionable for the gentry and eventually the working class to set out for excursions to the mountains and the shore. The White Mountains of New Hampshire were among the first regions to benefit from this boom. By the mid-19th century, farmhouses were being converted to inns to accommodate those seeking inspiration in the clear mountain air. By later in the century, tourists were venturing throughout the region in search of the picturesque and sublime. "Summer" became a verb.

The 19th-century tourism wave crested in the 1890s in Bar Harbor, Maine, which was flooded by affluent visitors who spent time in their extravagant "cottages," and by the less prosperous, who occupied boarding homes and the lesser hotels. Several grand resort hotels from tourism's golden era still flourish in each of the three states.

SLUMBER While the railways allowed northern New England to thrive in the mid-19th century, the train played an equally central role in undermining its prosperity. The driving of the Golden Spike in 1869 in Utah, linking America's Atlantic and Pacific coasts by rail, was heard loud and clear in New England, and it had a discordant ring. Transcontinental rail meant farmers and manufacturers could easily ship goods from the fertile Great Plains and California to faraway markets, making it even harder for New England's hardscrabble farmers to survive. Likewise, the coastal shipping trade, already in difficult straits, was dealt a fatal blow by this new transportation network. And the familiar tourists found they could venture easily to the Rockies and other stirring western sites.

Beginning in the late 19th century and accelerating through much of the early 20th, New England lapsed into an extended economic slumber. As early as the 1870s, families commonly walked away from their farmhouses (there was no market for resale), and set off for regions with more promising opportunities. The abandoned, decaying farmhouse became almost an icon for New England, and open farmland that overspread much of northern New England was reclaimed by forest. With the the rise of the automobile, the grand resorts further succumbed, and many closed their doors as inexpensive motels siphoned off their business.

During the Great Depression, historian Bernard DeVoto toured New England. Of the depressed milltown of Fall River, Mass., he wrote, "To spend a day in Fall River is to realize how limited were the imaginations of the poets who have described hell."

BOOM Toward the end of the current century, much of northern New England has ridden an unexpected wave of prosperity, peaking in the late 1980s. During that decade, a massive real estate boom shook the region, driving land prices sky high as prosperous buyers from Boston and beyond acquired vacation homes or retired to the more alluring areas, like the Maine Coast and regions near ski mountains in Vermont. The rise of the information culture has also been a modest boon, allowing info-entreprenuers to settle in small villages and even on remote islands, yet still remain plugged in to the electronic info-structure. Tourism seems also to be rebounding as well as urbanites of the Eastern seaboard opt for shorter, more frequent vacations closer to home.

But the boom didn't last for long—real estate prices inevitably subsided, and the manic drive to develop lapsed. Business that depended on the boom went under, and a low-grade, lingering recession returned. And many communities never benefited from the boom at all; they're still waiting to rebound from economic malaise of earlier in this century. Especially hard hit have been places like northeastern Vermont and far down-east Maine, where residents still depend on dwindling local resources— timber, fisheries, and farmland—to eke out a living. For them, prosperity remains elusive.

4 The Natural Landscape

The natural history of northern New England is, quite literally, carved in stone.

The craggy White Mountains of New Hampshire, the famed rocky Maine coast, and the stony riverbeds that wind their way through pastoral Vermont are all evidence of the region's bedrock heritage. Visitors passing through much of northern New England will come away with impressions of brooding gray rock standing in only slightly contrast to the dark spruce and fir nearby. Even in those softer-edged parts of the region—where green farmland and leafy hills predominate—the muscular, undulating ridges suggest that you wouldn't dig too deep before hitting solid rock.

Complex geological events millions of years ago far beneath the earth's crust shaped much of New England's terrain. But it was the massive and powerful glaciers that left the most easily identifiable fingerprints on the landscape. All three states were overspread with thick glaciers during several epochs, with the first glaciers forming as long as one million years ago. The last of the mile-thick glaciers melted away and retreated from northern New England relatively recently—only some 12,000 to 13,000 years ago.

Glaciers had an outsized hand in shaping the landscape. The sheer force and pressure of these massive ice sheets literally moved mountains and reconfigured valleys. As you travel, notice that many mountains are gently sloping on one side (often the north), but are fractured and craggy on the other. This resulted from glaciers grinding down the near side of the mountains as they moved through an area, then cracking and "plucking" mountainsides as they came over the crest. This is most plainly seen on "the Porcupines," a group of islands off Bar Harbor near Acadia National Park in Maine. The force of glacier movement also created dramatic, rocky bowls, called cirques, high in the mountains—spectacular Tuckerman Ravine on Mount Washington is the most stunning example of this. Also notice the shape of the mountain valleys as you travel. Few are "V"-shaped and steep-sided, as you might find in the West; they're more often "U"-shaped, gouged out by slow-moving rivers of ice.

The glaciers took a sledgehammer to New England's landscape, but here and there they also employed a more delicate touch. The northern woods are littered with "glacial erratics," boulders that were wrested from mountains (sometimes far away) and deposited by the melting ice in incongruous, sometimes precarious spots. Geological gumshoes will find plenty more evidence of the glaciers as they travel, with many landforms tagged with names seemingly from The Hobbit—kettles, eskers, drumlins, and kames. It's out of the scope if this introduction to detail the glacial landscape, but other good resources exist, including the excellent introduction, Glaciers & Granite: A Guide to Maine's Landscape and Geology by David L. Kendall (Down East Books). Greenfield State Park in southern New Hampshire boasts a variety of glacial landforms, and is well worth visiting if you're curious about New England's glacial past. Atop northern New England's bedrock foundation is a relatively thin veneer of mixed forest, which home a range of wildlife well adapted to the northern climate and terrain.

You'll discover two basic types of forest in the region. In southern Vermont and New Hampshire, and in southwest Maine along the coast to near Acadia National Park, the land is blanketed with a leafy forest dominated by northern hardwoods, such as maple and beech, mixed with gracious white pines and hemlocks. This is the classic New England forest that, in autumn, attracts throngs to see the brilliant displays of fall foliage. In the northern reaches of the region, the forest is more stern and severe, dominated by the sharp, humorless spires of spruce and fir, the mood lightened here and there by thickets of birch. This is the forest explored by Thoreau in the mid-19th century, and one now prized by timber companies for its softwoods, which provide the raw material for paper mills and lumber.

While traveling in the mountains, notice the changes in the forest landscape as you you rise in elevation. This is especially notable in the White Mountains. You might hike through a leafy hardwood forest at the beginning of an ascent, then pass through spruce and fir forest before coming onto an Arctic landscape. As early as 1839, Thoreau determined that every 400 foot gain in elevation was equivalent to traveling 70 miles north. The scientist C.H. Hitchcock concurred, noting that the summit of Mount Washington corresponded with Labrador and Greenland. "It is an arctic island in the temperate zone," he wrote. The Maine Coast shares some similarities. The cool summer temperatures (resulting in part from Arctic ocean currents that sweep along the shores) create an ecosystem that you'd expect to find at a far more northerly latitude.

A rule of thumb in biology is that diversity diminishes as you head further north, but abundance increases. That's true here with wildlife. The critters who live here exist in great numbers. Watch for Eastern coyotes, fox, wild turkeys, and beavers. Deer aren't as common as in the Mid-Atlantic states (although they're abundant enough to cause gardeners headaches on Maine's islands), but you may see moose and black bear at the edge of the denser forests. (Good places for moose-spotting are northernmost New Hampshire, and in Maine's Rangeley and Moosehead lakes region.) Along the coast, keep an eye peeled for herons, ospreys, and bald eagles; in the higher mountains, listen for the melancholy "quork-quork-quork" of the ravens. On the lakes, look for the beautiful, black-headed loons, and listen for their raucous whooping in the evening.

And the hand of man has influenced the look of the land. With the decline of agriculture early in this century, the forest reasserted itself, reclaiming fields and farmhouses. Today, it's not uncommon to come across stone walls in the midst of dense woods (built by farmers clearing rocks from their fields), or to stumble across the old cellar holes of farmhouses that once dotted remote valleys and high hillsides.

One final note: It would be disingenuous to write of the regional landscape without mentioning insects. You will experience them if you come here for camping, canoeing, or hiking, especially in early summer. Of particular note are mosquitos and black flies. Mosquitos will be familiar to most visitors. The black fly may not.

You will hear locals often speak of dreaded black flies, and you may see them commemorated on T-shirts. (One popular slogan puts it accurately: "Black flies don't just bite, they suck.") Black flies are far smaller and nastier than common house flies, and many visitors confuse them with gnats. Black flies like to buzz jerkily around your eyes and nose, occasionally making kamikaze dives. But they'll rarely land and bite on your open skin; while some are distracting you with nostril sorties, others will stealthily slip into cuffs and collars, tap you for a small donation of blood, then fly off and leave an itchy welt. Needless to say, this is most irritating.

A simple if slightly dorky defense is to button your cuffs and top shirt button, and tuck your cuffs into your socks. Most insect repellents also work decently against black flies—slather it on your wrists, ankles, and neck. But there's only one fool-proof solution: Explore the woods in late summer or fall, after the insect population has greatly diminished.

5 A Taste of New England

The quintessential New England meal is the clambake. If you're adventurous, here's how it's done: Start by digging a deep pit at the beach. Build a roaring fire of driftwood and throw in some beach stones to absorb the heat. Cover the hot ashes and stone with a layer of seaweed, then throw in live lobsters. Add more seaweed, then corn on the cob, then another layer of seaweed followed by clams and a final topping of seaweed. Let sit. When the clams have opened, dig everything up and serve with lots of fresh butter. (A less gritty, easier version can be made in a large stockpot on your stove. Or easier still, let someone else do the work. Ask around in your travels—some restaurants and inns feature clambakes during the summer.)

All along the coast you'll be tempted by seafood in its various forms. Live lobster can be had off the boat at lobster shacks all along the Maine coast. The setting is usually rustic—maybe a couple of picnic tables and a shed where huge vats of water are kept at a low boil. A lobster dinner might include corn on the cob or some seafood chowder, and it isn't likely to cost more than $10 per person. Just ask if your lobster includes melted butter (not margarine, which does little to enhance the lobster's flavor).

And then there are the ubiquitous fried fish joints, where you can get everything from cod to clams deep fried with a breaded crust and served with a wedge of lemon or tartar sauce. Tasty, but not very wholesome if you're watching your waistline. (A friend of mine once likened eating a bucket of fried claims to consuming a container of spackle followed by a shot of Mazola.) The more upscale seafood restaurants offer fresh fish cooked over a grill, or gently sauteed.

Inland, be sure to sample the local products. This includes delectable maple syrup, of course, which is sold at farmhouses and farmstands throughout the region. (Look for the homemade signs tacked to a tree at the end of a driveway.) Check the label for Grade A syrup certification; it's lighter and sweeter than the heavier, more tart Grade B. Cheese is a Vermont specialty, especially the strong cheddar produced in cheesehouses throughout the state. Look also for Vermont's famed apple cider, and Maine's wild blueberries.

Later in the summer, small farmers across the region set up stands at the end of their driveways offering fresh produce straight from the garden. Don't pass these by. You can usually find fresh berries, delicious fruits, and sometimes home-cooked breads that make excellent snacks on the road. These stands are rarely tended; just leave your money in the coffee can.

Restauranteurs haven't overlooked New England's bounty. Many fine restaurants throughout the region serve up delicious meals consisting of local ingredients—some places even tend their own gardens for fresh greens and herbs. Some of the best restaurants are set well outside of the cities, borrowing from the French tradition of classic country inns serving superior food in pastoral settings. Talented chefs have taken basic ingredients that would have been familiar to the Pilgrims and adapted them to more adventurous palates. I'm thinking of some of the fine meals I've enjoyed while researching this guide, such as curried pumpkin soup, venison medallions with shiitake mushrooms, and wild boar with juniper berries.

But you don't have to have a hefty budget to enjoy the local foods. A number of regional classics fall under the "roadfood" category. Here's an abbreviated field guide:

Beans   Boston is forever linked with baked beans (hence the nickname "Beantown"), but the sweet, earthy beans remain popular throughout the region. Saturday night supper traditionally consists of baked beans and brown bread, and some diners still offer up beans with breakfast. (Try it!) B&M Baked Beans are canned in a old-fashioned plant overlooking the bay in Portland, but for more local flavor, watch for community bean suppers, frequently held on weekends.

Moxie   Early in this century, Moxie outsold Coca-Cola. Part of its allure was the fanciful story behind its 1885 creation: A traveler named Lieutenant Moxie was reputed to have observed South American Indians consuming the sap of a native plant, which gave them extraordinary strength. The drink was "re-created" by Maine native Dr. Augustin Thompson, who marketed it nationwide. It's still a popular drink in New England (it's now actually manufactured by Coca-Cola), although some folks liken the taste to a combination of medicine and topsoil.

Muffins   These have long been a New England institution. A blueberry muffin is the classic choice, but a wide variety of fresh-baked muffins is available at bakeries, restaurants, and even convenience stores throughout the region. At some traditional places, blueberry muffins are even served with dinner.

Lobster Rolls   Lobster rolls consist of lobster meat plucked from the shell, mixed with just enough mayonnaise to hold it all together, then served on a hot-dog roll. I'll admit to being a heretic when it comes to lobster rolls—I've never really liked them all that much (a boiled lobster served with butter seems a much better use of the crustacean), but others rave about them. They're available at roadside stands and restaurants throughout Maine—even most McDonald's in Maine offer a seasonal lobster roll that aficionados say is pretty good.

Pies   New Englanders are serious about their pies, and it remains a popular desert throughout the region. Apple, blueberry, pumpkin, and mincemeat are the traditional favorites, but you can usually find a good selection of cream pies as well.

Red Dogs   These garish red hot dogs are a perennial favorite among kids, and a lot of older New Englanders. While there's no real difference in taste or content than the regular dogs, there's something unique—and somehow tastier—about eating a hot dog the color of a maraschino cherry.

Finally, I should mention beer. New England has more microbreweries than any other region outside of the Pacific Northwest—Maine alone had 22 at last count. Many small towns are even getting their own brewpubs, leaving some to wonder if a shake-out is overdue. In general, Vermont's brews tend to be a bit lighter, and include a number of excellent lagers; those brewed Maine and New Hampshire tend to be the more robust brown and red ales, stouts, and porters.

Among the best brewpubs are the Portsmouth Brewery, Stonecoast Brewery (Portland), Federal Jack's Brew Pub (Kennebunkport), Vermont Pub & Brewery (Burlington), and the Windham Brewery at the Latchis Grille (Brattleboro). If you're buying beer for the road, I'd recommend the excellent Smuttynose Brown Dog Ale, Geary's Hampshire Ale, or the Carrabassett India Pale Ale, although there are dozens of other tasty choices.

6 New England Style

When folks talk of northern New England "style," it usually conjures up a mental picture of church steeples and white clapboard. But New England style transcends those simple objects. Spend enough time here, and you'll realize New England style is defined by its scale, which is at once very grand and very human.

The scale is found in how the creations of people—whether public institutions, humble homes, or vessels on the water—relate to the landscape. You'll see it in the way a slender church spire rises from a wooded valley floor, or a silo from a hilltop farm. You'll find it in the way handsome homes cluster around a village green, or a low block of rowhouses curves toward the waterfront in a coastal city. You'll see it in the size of a lobster boat bobbing in a rocky cove, in the dimensions of a perfect Federal house, and in the graceful surviving elm trees planted at the edge of a lane.

The building blocks of New England style, of course, are its early homes. You can often trace the evolution of a town by its architecture, as styles evolve from simple boxlike homes to elaborate Victorian mansions. This primer should aid with basic identifications:

Colonial (1600–1700)   The New England house of the 17th century was a simple, boxy affair, often covered in shingles or rough clapboards. Don't look for ornamentation; these homes were designed for basic shelter from the elements, and are often marked by prominent stone chimneys. Architecture of this style is rather rare in northern New England, which was generally settled quite a bit later than Massachusetts. A good example is the Sherburne House (ca. 1695), at Strawbery Banke in Portsmouth, N.H.

Georgian (1700–1800)   Ornamentation comes into play in the Georgian style, which draws heavily on classical symmetry. Georgian buildings were in vogue in England at the time, and were embraced by the affluent colonists. Look for Palladian windows, formal pilasters, and elaborate projecting pediments over the main doorway. Some homes like Portsmouth's impressive Wentworth-Gardner House were made of wood but designed to look like masonry. Portsmouth is the best destination for viewing Georgian homes.

Federal (1780–1820)   Federal homes may best represent the New England ideal. Spacious yet somehow austere, Federal homes are often rectangular or square, with low pitched roofs and little ornament on the front (although carved swags or other embellishments might be seen near the roof line). Look for fan windows and chimneys bracketing the building. Excellent Federal-style homes are found throughout the region, many of them dating from the period of exceptional prosperity here prior to the Embargo of 1807. Kennebunkport, Maine, is rich with Federal homes set in tranquil neighborhoods.

Greek Revival (1820–1860)   The easiest-to-identify Greek Revival homes feature a bold projecting portico with massive columns, like a part of the Parthenon grafted onto an existing home. The less dramatic homes may have subtle pilasters, or simply be oriented such that the gable faces the street, lending the impression that it has a triangular pediment. Greek Revival didn't catch on in New England quite the way it did elsewhere in the country, but some fine examples exist, notably in Newfane, Vt., which is virtually a museum of Greek Revival architecture.

Victorian (1860–1900)   This is a catch-all term for the jumble of late 19th-century architectural styles that emphasized complexity and opulence. The best known Victorian style is the tall and narrow house with mansard roof and prickly looking roof cresting. A wonderful example of this is the author Stephen King's spooky house in Bangor, Maine. But the style also includes squarish Italianate homes with wide eaves; one of the best examples in the country is the huge brownstone Victoria Mansion in Portland.

Stretching the definition a bit, Victorian can also include the Richardsonian Romanesque style, which was popular for railroad stations and public buildings. A superb Richardsonian building is the red sandstone Fairbanks Museum in St. Johnsbury, Vt., built in 1889.

Shingle Style (1880–1900)   This uniquely New England style arose in late 19th century, and quickly became the preferred look for vacation homes among the very affluent. These homes marked by a profusion of gables, roofs, and porches, and were typically covered with shingles from roofline to foundation. Shingle-style homes project a sense of leisure and wealth. A number of the great "cottages" of Bar Harbor, Maine, were constructed in this fashion.

Modern (1900–present)   Quite frankly, the three states have produced little in the way of notable modern architecture. This is even true in commercial architecture, a field in which much of the nation saw tremendous creativity in this century. But remember that New England peaked economically in the late 19th century. The subsequent lull did much to preserve the older architecture that lends the region its character, but little to produce modern buildings worthy of note. In the 1980s a number of huge, ostentatious vacation homes sprouted during the boom, especially high on mountains near resorts and on rocky coastal promontories. My feeling is that architectural historians are likely to judge most of these homes quite harshly.

Among idiosyncratic architectural styles to watch for is the "classic" New England farmhouse. These are huge and rambling, with the old barn connected to the main house with one or two intermediary buildings. This set-up allowed the farmer to perform his barn chores in winter without having to brave the frigid winds. This style—locally called "big house, little house, back house, barn"—not only describes a building style, but even became part of a well-known jump-rope rhyme. These farmhouses are relatively common throughout the region.

Where do you go to discover the New England style? Northern New England is unusually blessed with perfect and near-perfect villages. Architecture buffs should head to Orford, N.H.; Castine and Kennebunkport, Maine; or Woodstock, Vt. Aficionados of village greens will like Newfane, Vt., Whitefield, N.H.; and Bethel, Maine. If it's that ineffable small-town feel you're looking for, set your sights on Grafton or Dorset, Vt.; Waterford, Me.; or Fitzwilliam, N.H.

New England is best appreciated when you're out of your car. Driving through a wonderful village, circling the green twice before heading onward, seems somehow unclean, like showing up at a wedding in sweaty gym clothes. You really need to get out and stretch your legs, if just for a few minutes, to really appreciate the human scale of many of these towns. Take the time to walk the tree-lined streets, or wander into a venerable church. These minor adventures often seem comforting and serene, like coming home after a long journey.

Planning a Trip to Northern New England

3

This chapter is designed to provide most of the nuts-and-bolts travel information you'll need before setting off for northern New England. Browse through this section before you hit the road to ensure you've touched all the bases.

1 Visitor Information & Money

VISITOR INFORMATION   It often seems that northern New England's leading cash crop is the brochure. Shops, hotels, and restaurants frequently feature prominently placed racks of colorful pamphlets touting local sights and accommodations. These mini-centers can be helpful in turning up unexpected places, but for a more comprehensive overview you should head for the state information centers or the local chambers of commerce. Chamber addresses and phone numbers are provided for each region in the chapters that follow. If you're a highly organized traveler, you'll call in advance and ask for information to be mailed to you. If you're like the rest of us, you'll swing by when you reach town and hope the office is still open.

All three states are pleased to send out general visitor information packets and maps to travelers who call or write ahead. Here's the contact information: **Maine Publicity Bureau,** P.O. Box 2300, Hallowell, ME 04347 (☎ **207/623-0360** or 800/533-9595 outside Maine); **New Hampshire Office of Travel and Tourism,** P.O. Box 1856, Concord, NH 03302 (☎ **603/271-2343** or 800/258-3608 for seasonal information); **Vermont Travel and Tourism,** 134 State St., Montpelier, VT 05602 (☎ **802/828-3237** or 800/837-6668 for general information, or 800/833-9756 to receive information by fax).

If you're connected to the Internet, there's a rapidly growing horde of information available on the World Wide Web. Many inns and restaurants are putting up their own sites, and entrepreneurs offer packaged tourism information. Many of these sites are the equivalent of electronic brochures, offering much the same information you'd find at information racks around the state. Be sure to distinguish which are paid advertising, and which are the opinions of travelers or residents. (Some cagey advertisers try to make it sound as if they're offering independent advice.)

My favorite sites are those run by cranky folks offering honest and sometimes jaundiced views of various destinations. Find these by using a search engine like Alta Vista (http:www.altavista.digital.com).

Type in string of terms outlining your interest (e.g., "New Hampshire white mountains hiking"). You'll get a huge haul of sites, most of which you'll throw back but some of which will be helpful or amusing or both.

Other good places to begin an Internet search are the official information pages maintained by each state. The Web addresses are: Maine: http://www.state.me.us/, New Hampshire: http://www.cit.state.vt.us/, Vermont: http://www.cit.state.vt.us/.

MONEY   Here's a scene I've seen repeated a number of times. A young couple, most likely just out of college, stand at a tourist information center looking rather despondent. "Isn't there anything cheaper?" one asks. "No, that's a good price," responds the person at the desk. "You won't find anything better."

Budget travelers accustomed to turning up basic motels for $25 or $30 in other parts of the country are in for a bit of a shock in northern New England, at least during peak travel seasons. In mid-summer there's simply no such thing as a cheap motel in the most popular areas, like Winnipesaukee, southwest Vermont, Camden, or Bar Harbor. Motels where you might expect to pay $40 per night might well command $90 on a Saturday in August. (To be fair, many of the innkeepers in these northern latitudes must make all their profit in what amounts to a two- or three-month season.)

What are the alternatives?

• **Travel in the off-season.** Inexpensive rooms are often available in April or May. If that's a little too bleak, consider traveling between Memorial Day and July 4th, when you can often get discounts or good deals on packages as innkeepers get ready for the crowds of high summer. The best "off-season" period to my mind is September. The weather is good, and many inns and hotels cut their prices for two or three weeks between the summer and foliage periods.

• **"Commute" from lower-prices areas.** If you're willing to drive a half-hour to an hour to reach prime destinations, you can often find cheaper lodging in less glamorous settings.

• **Camp.** All three states offer great camping opportunities at both public and private campgrounds, with prices ranging from $8 to $25 per night. Because the region is relatively undeveloped, you can often find camping within a short drive of even major cities.

Traveler's checks are commonly accepted everywhere, although some smaller shops may balk at cashing $100 checks. Cash machines (ATMs) are easy to find in the more populated areas and regions that cater to tourists. But don't count on finding machines in the smaller villages in the more remote parts of the region. Stock up on greenbacks when you can. To locate the nearest machine in the **Plus** network, call **800/843-7587.** For the **Cirrus** network, call **800/424-7787.**

2 When to Go

THE SEASONS

The well-worn joke about the climate in northern New England is that it has just two seasons: winter and August. There's a kernel of truth to that, but it's mostly a canard to keep outsiders from moving here, repeated the same way the Pacific Northwest "celebrates" its 11-month "rain festival."

In fact, the ever-shifting seasons are one of those elements that make New England so distinctive. With one exception, the seasons are long and well-defined in Northern New England.

SUMMER   The peak summer season runs from July 4th to Labor Day. Vast crowds surge into northern New England during these two holiday weekends, and the level of activity remains high throughout July and August. This should be no surprise: Summers are exquisite here. The forests are verdant and lush, the sky can be an almost lurid blue and the cumulus clouds brilliantly white. In the mountains, warm (rarely hot) days are the rule, followed by cool nights. Along the coast, ocean breezes keep the temperatures down, and often produce vichyssoise fogs that linger for days. (In Portland, it tops 90 degrees only four or five days a year on average.)

The weather is determined by the winds. Southwest winds bring haze, heat, and humidity. The northwest winds bring cool weather and knife-sharp vistas. These systems tend to alternate during the summer, with the heat arriving stealthily and slowly, then getting exiled by stiff, cool winds rising from the north a few days later. (The change from hot to cool will sometimes occur in a matter of minutes.) Rain is rarely far away—some days it's an afternoon thunderstorm, sometimes it's a steady drizzle that brings a four-day soaking. On average, about one day in three will bring some rain. Travelers should come prepared for it.

For most of the region, mid-summer is the prime season. Expect to pay premium prices at hotels and restaurants. The exception is around the empty ski resorts, where you can often find bargains. Also be aware that early summer brings out the black flies and the mosquitos in great multitude, a state of affairs that has spoiled many north country camping trips. Outdoorspeople are best off waiting until after July 4 if they want to avoid fate as human pincushions.

AUTUMN   Don't be surprised to smell the tang of fall approaching as early as mid-August, a time when you'll also notice a few leaves turned blaze-orange in otherwise verdant maples at the edges of wetlands. Fall comes early to northern New England, puts its feet up on the couch, and stays for some time. The foliage season begins in earnest in the northern part of the region by the third week in September; in the south, it reaches its peak by the middle of October.

Fall in New England is one of the great natural spectacles of the United States. With its rolling hills tarted up in brilliant reds and stunning oranges, fall is garish in a way that seems determined to embarrass understated New England. Along winding country roads you'll find heaps of pumpkins for sale under fiery red sugar maples, and crisp apples available by the bushel. Take the time to scout out the farmstands, where you'll be amazed at the fertility of this otherwise flinty land.

Keep in mind this is the most popular time of year to travel—bus tours flock to New England in early October like so many migrating geese. As a result, hotels are invariably booked solid. Local radio stations at times put out calls for residents to open their doors to stranded travelers who otherwise would have to sleep in their cars. Reservations are essential. And expect to pay a foliage surcharge of $10 or $20 per room at many inns.

All three states maintain recorded foliage hot lines to let you know when the leaves are at their peak: call **Maine** (☎ **800/533-9595** or 207/623-0363), **New Hampshire** (☎ **800/258-3608**), or **Vermont** (☎ **802/828-3239**).

WINTER   New England winters are like wine—some years are good, some are lousy. During a good season (like the winter of 1995–96), plenty of light, fluffy snow blankets the deep woods and fills the ski slopes. A good New England winter offers a profound peace and tranquility. The muffling qualities of fresh snow can bring a thunderous silence to the region, and the hiss and pop of a wood fire at a country inn can sound like an overwrought symphony. During these winters, exploring the forest on snowshoes or cross-country skis is an experience that borders on the magical.

During the other winters, the lousy ones, the weather brings a nasty melange of rain and sleet. It's bone-numbing cold, and bleak, bleak, bleak. Look into the eyes of the residents on the street during this time. They are all thinking of the Caribbean.

The higher you go in the mountains, and the further north you head, the better your odds of finding snow and avoiding rain. Winter coastal vacations can be spectacular (nothing beats cross-country skiing at the edge of the pounding surf), but it's a high-risk venture that could well yield rain rather than snow.

Ski areas naturally are crowded during the winter months. They're especially so during school vacations, when most ski resorts take the rather mercenary tactic of jacking up rates.

SPRING   Spring lasts only a weekend or so, often around mid-May, but sometimes as late as June. One day the ground is muddy, the trees barren, and gritty snow is still collected in shady hollows. The next day, it's in the 80s, trees are blooming, and kids are swimming in the lakes. Travelers must be very crafty and alert if they want to experience spring in northern New England. This is also known as mud season, and it's a time many innkeepers and restauranteurs close up for a few weeks for repairs or to venture someplace warm.

Burlington, Vermont's Average Temperatures

	Jan	Feb	Mar	Apr	May	Jun	July	Aug	Sep	Oct	Nov	Dec
Avg. High	25	27	38	53	66	76	80	78	69	57	44	30
Avg. Low	8	9	21	33	44	54	59	57	49	39	30	15

Portland, Maine's Average Temperatures

	Jan	Feb	Mar	Apr	May	Jun	July	Aug	Sep	Oct	Nov	Dec
Avg. High	31	32	40	50	61	72	76	74	68	58	45	34
Avg. Low	16	16	27	36	47	54	61	59	52	43	32	22

NORTHERN NEW ENGLAND CALENDAR OF EVENTS

January

☒ **New Year's & First Night Celebrations,** regionwide. Portland, Portsmouth, and Burlington, among others, all celebrate the coming of the New Year with plenty of activities for families and friends at venues spread across each city. Greet January with fireworks at midnight. Check with local chambers of commerce for details.

February

- **Dartmouth Winter Carnival,** Hanover, N.H. Huge and elaborate ice sculptures grace the Green during this festive celebration of winter, which includes numerous sporting events and other winter-related activities. Call **603/646-1110** for information. Mid-month.

- **Mt. Washington Valley Chocolate Festival,** North Conway, N.H. Earn your chocolate by cross-country skiing from inn to inn, picking up sweets at each stop. Look for other events sure to please the chocoholic in and around town. Call **800/367-3364.** Late February.

- **Stowe Derby,** Stowe, Vt. The oldest downhill/cross-country ski race in the nation pits racers who scramble from the wintry summit of Mt. Mansfield into the village on the Stowe Rec path. Call **802/253-3423** for details. Late February.

March

- **Super Winterfest,** Ludlow, Vt. A weeklong festival throughout the town featuring skiing, ice fishing, snow hockey, fireworks, and a parade. Call **802/228-1229.** Early March.
- **Maine Boatbuilders Show,** Portland, Me. More than 200 exhibitors and 9,000 boat aficionados gather as winter fades to make plans for the coming summer. A great place to meet boatbuilders and get ideas for your dream craft. Late March.

April

- **Sugarbush Spring Fling,** Waitsfield, Vt. Ski-related events herald the coming of spring and the best season for skiing. Special events for kids. Call **802/583-2381.**

May

- **Annual Basketry Festival,** Stowe, Vt. A weeklong event with displays and workshops by talented weavers. Mid-May.
- **Lilac Sunday,** Shelburne, Vt. See the famed lilacs (more than 400 bushes) at the renowned Shelburne Museum when they're at their most beautiful. Call **802/985-3346** for details. Mid- to late May.
- **Mayfest,** Bennington, Vt. Main Street is blocked off to cars and filled with food vendors and craftsman at this late spring/early summer community event. Call **802/442-5758.** Late May.
- **Open Studio Weekend,** throughout Vt. Artists throughout the state open their doors to the public, offering a first-hand glimpse at how it's all done. Call **802/223-3380.** Late May.

June

- **Old Port Festival,** Portland, Me. A day-long block party in the heart of Portland's historic district with live music, food vendors, and activities for kids. Call **207/772-2249** for information. Early June.
- **Market Square Weekend,** Portsmouth, N.H. This lively street fair attracts hordes from throughout southern New Hampshire and Maine into downtown Portsmouth to dance, listen to music, sample food, and enjoy summer's arrival. Call **603/436-2848.** Early June.
- **Lake Champlain Balloon and Craft Festival,** Essex Junction. New England's largest balloon festival draws thousands of spectators to see these graceful craft float above the quiet landscape. Call **802/899-2993.**
- **Motorcycle Week,** Loudon & Weirs Beach, N.H. Tens of thousands of bikers descend on the Lake Winnipesaukee region early each summer to compare their machines and cruise the strip at Weirs Beach. The Gunstock Hill Climb and the Loudon Classic race are the centerpieces of the week's activities. Call **603/783-4931.** Mid-June.
- **Great Kennebec Whatever Week,** Augusta, Me. A community celebration to mark the cleaning up of the Kennebec River, culminating in a wacky race involving all manner of watercraft, some more seaworthy than others. Call **207/623-4559** for details. Late June.

July

- ✪ **Independence Day,** regionwide. Communities throughout all three states celebrate July 4th with parades, cookouts, road races, and fireworks. The bigger the town, the bigger the fireworks. Contact local chambers of commerce for details.

- **Moxie Festival,** Lisbon Falls, Me. A quirky community festival celebrating a soft drink that once outsold Coca-Cola. Call **207/783-2249.** Early July.
- **Street Festival,** Hanover, N.H. This one-day bazaar attracts more than 100 vendors to sell their wares in this picturesque town. There's also live entertainment. Call **603/643-3115** for information. Mid-month.
- **Vermont Quilt Festival,** Northfield, Vt. Displays are only part of the allure of New England's largest quilt festival. You can also attend classes, and have your heirlooms appraised. Call **802/485-7092.** Mid-July.
- **Revolutionary War Days,** Exeter, N.H. Learn all you need to know about the War of Independence during this historic community festival, which features a Revolutionary War encampment and dozens of reenactors. Call **603/772-2622.** Mid-July.
- **Marlboro Music Festival,** Marlboro, Vt. This is a popular six-week series of classical concerts featuring talented student musicians performing in the peaceful hills outside of Brattleboro. Call **802/254-2394** for information. Weekends from July through mid-August.

August

- **Maine Lobster Festival,** Rockland, Me. Fill up on the local harvest at this event marking the importance and delectability of Maine's favorite crustacean. Enjoy a boiled lobster or two, and take in the ample entertainment during this informal waterfront gala. Call **207/596-0376** or 800/562-2529. Early August.
- **Maine Festival,** Brunswick, Me. A three-day festival showcasing Maine-made crafts, music, foods, and performers. Boisterous, fun, and filling. Call **207/ 772-9012.** Early August.
- **Southern Vermont Crafts Fair,** Manchester. More than 200 artisans show off their fine work at this popular festival, which also features creative food and good music. Early August.
- **Annual Star Party,** St. Johnsbury, Vt. The historic Fairbanks Museum and Planetarium hosts special events and shows, including night viewing sessions, during the lovely Perseid Meteor Shower. Call **802/748-2372.** Mid-August.
- **Blueberry Festival,** Machias, Me. A festival marking the harvest of the region's wild blueberries. Eat to your heart's content. Call **207/794-3543.** Mid-month.
- **Blue Hill Fair,** Blue Hill, Me. A classic country fair just outside one of Maine's most elegant villages. Call **207/374-9976.** Late August.

September

- **Vermont State Fair,** Rutland, Vt. All of Vermont seems to show up for this grand event, with a midway, live music, and plenty of agricultural exhibits. Call **802/ 775-5200** for details. Early September.
- **Windjammer Weekend,** Camden, Me. Come visit Maine's impressive fleet of old-time sailing ships, which host open houses throughout the weekend at this scenic harbor. Call **207/236-4404.** Early September.
- **Blessing of the RVs,** Colebrook, N.H. Recreational vehicle owners gather at the outdoor Shrine of Our Lady of Grace each year to fraternize and have their land craft blessed by a priest. Call **603/752-3142.** Late September.
- ✪ **Common Ground Fair,** Windsor, Me. An old-time state fair with a twist: the emphasis is on organic foods, recycling, and wholesome living. Call **207/ 623-5515.** Late September.

October

- **Northeast Kingdom Fall Foliage Festival,** Northeast Vermont. A cornucopia of events staged in towns and villages throughout Vermont's northeast corner heralds the arrival of the fall foliage season. Be the first to see colors at their peak. Call **802/748-3678** for information. Early October.

○ **Fryeburg Fair,** Fryeburg, Me. Cotton candy, tractor pulls, live music, and huge vegetables and barnyard animals at Maine's largest agricultural fair. There's also harness racing in the evening. Call **207/985-3278.** A week in early October.

• **Harvest Day,** Canterbury, N.H. A celebration of the harvest season, Shaker-style. Lots of autumnal exhibits and children's games. Call **603/783-9511.** Mid-month.

November

• **Victorian Holiday,** Portland. From late November until Christmas Portland decorates its Old Port in a Victorian Christmas theme. Enjoy the window displays, take a free hay ride, listen to costumed carolers sing. Call **207/772-6828** for details.

December

• **Christmas Prelude,** Kennebunkport, Me. This scenic coastal village greets Santa's arrival in a lobster boat, and marks the coming of Christmas with street shows, pancake breakfasts, and tours of the towns' inns. Call **207/967-3286.** Early December.

○ **Candlelight Stroll,** Portsmouth, N.H. Historic Strawbery Banke gets in a Christmas way with old-time decorations and more than 1,000 candles lighting the 10-acre grounds. Call **603/433-1100** for information. First two weekends of December.

• **Woodstock Wassail Celebration,** Woodstock, Vt. Enjoy classic English grog, along with parades and dances, at this annual event. Call **802/457-3555.** Early December.

3 The Active Vacation Planner

Northern New England is a superb destination for those who don't consider it a vacation unless they find some outdoor adventure. Hiking, canoeing, and skiing are among the most popular activities, but there's also rock-climbing, sea kayaking, mountain biking, road biking, sailing, winter mountaineering, and snowmobiling. In general, the further north you go in the region, the more remote and wild the terrain becomes.

One terrific resource is another Frommer's publication, *Outside Magazine's Adventure Guide to New England.* It covers all kinds of outings for travelers of every ability level.

For pointers on where to head, see the "Enjoying the Great Outdoors" section at the beginning of each state chapter. More detailed information on local services is included in each regional section.

GENERAL ADVICE   To get into the woods or the mountains, the basic advice is simple: Head for the green. Look for those green-shaded areas on the map where you'll find the highest concentration of public lands. These include the Green Mountain National Forest in Vermont, the White Mountain National Forest in New Hampshire, and Baxter State Park and Acadia National Park in Maine. Adventure travel outfitters and suppliers can often be found in towns at the perimeter of these areas.

Some added advice: To find real adventure, plan to stay put. I've seen too many travelers get frustrated by trying to bite off too much—planning some biking in Vermont, some hiking in the White Mountains, then maybe a little kayaking off Acadia in Maine, all in one week. That's only a good formula for developing a close, personal relationship with your car. I'd advise adventurers to pick just one area, then settle in for a few days or a week, spending the long summer days exploring locally by foot, canoe, or kayak. This will give you the time to enjoy an extra hour lounging at a remote backcountry lake, or to spend an extra day camped in the backcountry. You'll also learn a lot more about the area. Few travelers ever regret planning to do too little on their vacations. A lot of travelers regret attempting to do too much.

FINDING YOUR WAY   Travelers used to hire guides to ensure they could find their way out of the woods. With development encroaching on many once-pristine areas, it's now helpful to have guides to find your way into the woods and away from civilization and its long reach. Clearcuts, second-home developments, and trails teeming with weekend hikers are all obstacles to be avoided. And local knowledge is the best way to find the most alluring, least congested spots.

Travelers have three choices: Hire a guide; sign up for a guided trip; or dig up the essential information yourself.

Guides of all kinds may be hired throughout the region, from grizzled old fishing hands who know local rivers like their own homes to young canoe guides attracted to the field because of their interest in the environment. Among the most experienced, well-liked guides in the region are Alexandra and Garrett Conover of Maine's **North Woods Ways,** R.R. #2, Box 159A, Guilford, ME 04443 (☎ **207/997-3723**). The couple offers canoe trips on northern Maine rivers (and beyond), and are well versed in North Woods lore. Elsewhere, check with the chambers of commerce for suggestions on local guides.

Guide-led adventure tours are increasingly common throughout the region, with trips ranging from afternoon llama treks to week-long sea-kayak expeditions. Among the most respected outfits for inland exploration are **New England Hiking Holidays,** P.O. Box 1648, North Conway, NH 03860 (☎ **800/869-0949**), and **Vermont Bicycle Touring,** P.O. Box 711, Bristol, VT 05442 (☎ **802/453-4811**). To view Maine from a low perch on the water, try an island camping adventure traveling by sea kayak with **Maine Island Kayak Co.,** 70 Luther St., Peaks Island, ME 04108 (☎ **207/766-2373**).

Guidebooks to the region's backcountry are plentiful and diverse. **L.L. Bean** in Freeport, Maine, and the **Green Mountain Club** headquarters in Waterbury, Vermont, both have an excellent selection of guidebooks for sale, as do many local bookshops throughout the region. Catalogs of local guidebooks are also available by mail. Contact the **Appalachian Mountain Club,** 5 Joy St., Boston, MA 02108 (☎ **617/523-0636**) or **Backcountry Publications,** P.O. Box 175, Woodstock, VT 05091 (☎ **800/245-4151**).

Local outdoor clubs are also a good source of information, and some offer trips open to nonmembers. The most established of the bunch is the Appalachian Mountain Club (see address above), whose chapters run group trips almost every weekend throughout the region, but especially in northern New Hampshire. Other groups include the **Green Mountain Club,** RR#1, Box 650, Route 100, Waterbury Center, VT 05677 (☎ **802/244-7037**) and the **Maine Outdoor Adventure Club** (☎ **207/828-0918** for a recorded hotline in Portland).

Another obvious but often overlooked source of information are shops that cater to active travelers. Cross-country ski shops, bike dealers, fishing suppliers, and camping shops are all potentially rich resources about the best local destinations. Clerks, managers, and other customers might be able to point you to the best trails and rivers. Come in early or late, wait until a lull, make a small purchase, befriend a staffer, and methodically mine their local expertise.

LEARNING & SPECIAL-INTEREST VACATIONS   A rewarding way to spend a vacation is to learn a new outdoor skill or add to your knowledge while on holiday. There are plenty of options in northern New England, ranging from formal week-long classes to one-day workshops.

Among the better choices:

- **Learn to fly-fish** on New England's fabled rivers. Among the region's most respected schools are those offered by Orvis (☎ **800/548-9548**) in Manchester, Vt., and L.L. Bean (☎ **800/341-4341**) in Freeport, Maine. (L.L. Bean also offers a number of shorter workshops on various outdoor skills through its Outdoor Discovery Program; call **207/865-3111**).
- **Learn about birds and coastal ecosystems** in Maine. Budding and experienced naturalists can expand their understanding of marine wildlife while residing on 333-acre Hog Island in Maine's wild and scenic Muscongus Bay. Famed birder Roger Tory Peterson taught birding classes here in the past, and the program has a stellar reputation. Contact the **National Audubon Ecology Camp,** 613 Riversville Rd., Greenwich, CT 06831 (☎ **203/869-2017**).
- **Sharpen your outdoor skills.** The **Appalachian Mountain Club,** 5 Joy St., Boston, MA 02108 (☎ **617/523-0636**), has a full roster of outdoor adventure classes, many of which are taught at the club's Pinkham Notch Camp at the base of Mount Washington in the heart of the White Mountains. You can learn outdoor photography, wild mushroom identification, or backcountry orienteering, for starters. In winter, ice climbing and telemark skiing lessons are held on the slopes of the rugged White Mountains. Classes often include accommodations, and most are reasonably priced. Call or write for a course catalog.

4 Choosing a Small Inn or B&B

"The more we travel," said the couple next to me one morning at a New Hampshire inn, "the more we realize why we go back to our old favorites time and again." The reason for their comment? They were forced to change rooms at 2am when rain started dripping through the ceiling.

Northern New England's inns and B&Bs offer an alternative to the homogenized, cookie-cutter hotel rooms that seem to line U.S. highways coast-to-coast. In Maine, New Hampshire, and Vermont, you can stay in inns that are two centuries old and rich in historical associations. You can sleep in quirky rooms furnished with stunning antiques and filled with intriguing geegaws that the innkeepers trust you won't walk off with. (Chain hotels even bolt their horrid artwork to the walls.)

Of course, as that unfortunate couple learned, there are reasons why some people prefer cookie-cutter rooms. Predictability isn't always a bad thing. In a chain hotel, you can be reasonable certain water won't come dripping in through your ceiling at night. Likewise, you can bet that beds will be firm, that the sink will be relatively new and lacking in interesting sepia-toned stains, that you'll have a TV and telephone and a lot of counter space next to the bathroom sink.

But the only true way to develop a list of "old favorites" is to take some chances, for which you anticipate unexpected adventures. With some luck, you'll stumble into Ralph Waldo Emerson's idea of simple contentment: "Hospitality consists in a little fire, a little food, and an immense quiet," he wrote in his journal.

Selecting an inn to start your quest can be a bit overwhelming, what with hundreds of inns and B&Bs now operating across the region, up from just a few dozen a couple of decades ago.

Indeed, the distinction between B&Bs and inns is increasingly blurred. Generally speaking, B&Bs serve just breakfast, and inns serve breakfast, dinner, and often lunch. But these differences don't always translate into the higher level of service or more graciousness on the part of the hosts at the inns. B&Bs can be more elegant and well-appointed than many inns, dinner be damned. Indeed, the places listed in the "Best B&Bs" section in the prior chapter all have the air of gracious inns that just happened to have overlooked serving dinner.

Because small inns reflect the personalities of their owners, you may find yourself uncomfortable even if the service is impeccable and the cleanliness unimpeachable. One place might be too "foofy," as one of my friends refers to certain inns, with ruffles everywhere, busy wallpaper, and sachets that bring to mind a tragic perfume factory explosion. Maybe the innkeepers are too gregarious, or consider innkeeping a form of therapy. Another friend of mine refuses to stay any place where he thinks the innkeepers want to be his friend. So he strikes off any place with fewer than four guest rooms, believing that the owners are in it mostly for the company. (Sometimes that's right, but mostly not.)

There are a few simple steps you can take to reduce the risk of wretched evenings far from home:

- **Ask your friends.** Word of mouth is the most reliable way to go, especially if you have close friends who've traveled in the region and who know your tastes and preferences.
- **Call for the brochure.** A phone call will not only bring you a brochure, which often provides clues as to the innkeeper's sense of style, but also you'll get a chance to chat briefly with the staff (or quite possibly with the owner), and gauge their friendliness and professionalism. A dog barking in the background might be a good sign, or a bad one. It all depends on your interpretation.
- **Stop by unannounced.** Don't hesitate to walk right in a place that catches your eye. Some of the best finds turn up this way. One thing I've learned after visiting more than 300 or so establishments in researching this and other books is that I still can't reliably gauge from the outside what a place will be like on the inside. It's invariably a surprise, sometimes for the better, and sometimes not. An unannounced visit is also a good way to measure the hospitality of the host. Was the greeting a bit chilly? Or pleasant and warm?
- **Ask to see your room** before you sign on the dotted line. Inn rooms are almost always idiosyncratic, and often vary widely. The more lavish mansions had quarters for the servants, and no enterprising innkeeper lets these rooms go unused. Visions of upstairs grandeur can be easily deflated by downstairs reality. Most innkeepers are happy to let you look around, but be aware that nicer rooms typically fetch a higher price.

5 Tips for Travelers with Special Needs

FOR TRAVELERS WITH DISABILITIES Prodded by the Americans with Disabilities Act, a growing number of inns and hotels are retrofitting some of their rooms for people with special needs. Most innkeepers are quite proud of their improvements—when I arrive for a site visit, they're invariably quick to show me their new rooms with barrier-free entrances, wheelchair-accessible showers, and fire alarms equipped with strobe lights. Outdoor recreation areas, especially on state and federal lands, are also providing trails and facilities for those who've been effectively barred in the past.

Accessibility is improving regionwide, but improvements are far from universal. When in doubt, call ahead to ensure that you'll be accommodated.

Wilderness Inquiry, Fifth Street SE, Box 84, Minneapolis, MN 55414 (☎ **800/ 728-0719** or 612/379-3858), offers adventure travel packages for disabled travelers nationwide, including a canoe trip on the Moose River in Maine.

FOR SENIORS   New England is well-suited for older travelers, with a wide array of activities for seniors and discounts often available. It's wise to request a discount at hotels or motels when booking the room, not when you arrive. An identification card from the **American Association of Retired Persons (AARP),** 601 E St., NW, Washington DC 20049 (☎ **202/434-2277**), can be invaluable in obtaining discounts.

Excellent programs for seniors are offered by Elderhostel, which is based in Boston. These educational programs for people over 55 years old are reasonably priced, and include lodging and meals. Participants can study everything from the art of downhill skiing to the art of autobiography. The locations where these classes are held are often intriguing and dramatic. For more information, contact **Elder- hostel,** 75 Federal St., Boston, MA 02110 (☎ **617/426-7788**).

FOR FAMILIES   Few families don't find a raft of things to do with kids in north- ern New England. The natural world seems to hold tremendous wonder for the younger set—an afternoon exploring the mossy banks and rocky streambeds is an adventure. Older kids like the challenge of climbing a high mountain peak or learning to paddle a canoe in a straight line. As for teenagers, well, there are the video arcades of Weirs Beach, New Hampshire, and Old Orchard Beach, Maine.

Be sure to ask about family discounts when visiting attractions. Many places offer a flat family rate that is less expensive than paying for each ticket individually. Some parks and beaches charge by the car rather than the head.

Be aware that many inns cater to couples, and kids aren't exactly welcomed with open arms. Many inns don't allow kids, or strongly prefer only children over a cer- tain age. Innkeepers will let you know when you make your reservation, but you should mention that you're traveling with kids. Anyway, it's often wise to mention that you're a family when booking a room; often you'll get accommodations nearer the game room or the pool, making everyone's life a bit easier.

Recommended destinations for families include Weirs Beach and Hampton Beach in New Hampshire, and York Beach and Acadia National Park, Maine. North Conway, N.H. also makes a good base for exploring with kids. The town has lots of motels with pools, and there are nearby train rides, aquaboggans, streams suitable for splashing around, easy hikes, and the distraction known as Story Land.

Several specialized guides offer more detailed information for families on the go. Try *Frommer's New England with Kids,* and *Best Hikes with Children in Vermont, New Hampshire & Maine* by Cynthia and Thomas Lewis.

FOR GAY & LESBIAN TRAVELERS   Northern New England isn't exactly a hotbed of gay culture, especially compared to Provincetown, on Cape Cod. But many gays and lesbians live and travel here and have found these three states accepting if not always welcoming. As elsewhere in the country, the larger cities are more accom- modating to an alternative lifestyle than the smaller towns.

Portland, Maine, has the most substantial gay population, attracting many refu- gees who've fled the crime and congestion of Boston and New York. Portland hosts a sizeable gay pride festival early each summer that includes a riotous parade and a dance on the city pier, among other events. Check with the local gay newspaper, **Community Pride Reporter,** for dates and details (☎ **207/879-1342**).

Portland's oldest gay club is **The Underground,** located at 3 Spring St. near the Old Port (☎ **207/773-3315**). Half of the place is a tidy, friendly bar and hangout; the other half is a disco with pulsing lights and loud, urban music. Other places to visit are **Blackstones,** 6 Pine St. (☎ **207/775-2885**), which has a low-key neighborhood bar feel to it, and **Sisters,** 45 Danforth (☎ **207/774-1505**), which draws many of the city's lesbians.

In Manchester, N.H., try **The Frontrunner** at 22 Fir St. It's open to members and their guests only, but you may be able to wangle your way in or sign up as a new member.

In Burlington, Vt., **135 Pearl,** 135 Pearl St. (☎ **802/863-2343**), is the place to go for dancing and live music.

As for resorts areas, Ogunquit on the southern Maine coast is a hugely popular destination among gay travelers and features a lively beach and bar scene in the summer. In the winter, it's decidedly more mellow. Try **The Club** (☎ **207/646-6655**) at 13 Main St. during the summer rush.

For a more detailed directory of gay-oriented enterprises in New England, track down a copy of **The Pink Pages,** published by KP Media (66 Charles St., #283, Boston, MA 02114; e-mail kpmedia@aol.com).

More adventurous souls should consider linking up with the **Chiltern Mountain Club,** P.O. Box 407, Boston, MA 02117 (☎ **617/859-2843**). This is an outdoor adventure club for gays and lesbians; about two-thirds of its 1,200 members are men. The club organizes trips to northern New England throughout the year, and its members can help with advice. The club also maintains a Web site at http://www.chiltern.org/chiltern/.

6 Getting There

BY CAR   Getting to northern New England by car doesn't require much in the way of special knowledge. Coming from the south, there are two main interstate highway corridors. I-91 heads more or less due north from Hartford, Ct., along the Vermont–New Hampshire border, then through northern Vermont to the Canadian border. The other major interstate corridor skirts Boston. Follow I-93 from north from Boston if your destination is the White Mountains; for Maine, take I-95, which parallels the southern Maine Coast before veering inland.

If scenery is your priority, the most picturesque way to enter northern New England is from the west. Drive through New York's Adirondack Mountains to Port Kent, N.Y., on Lake Champlain, then catch the car ferry across the lake to Burlington.

BY PLANE   Major commercial carriers serve Burlington, Vt.; Manchester, N.H.; and Portland and Bangor, Me. Airlines most commonly fly to these airports from New York or Boston, although direct connections from other cities, such as Chicago and Philadelphia, are also available. Many of the scheduled flights to northern New England from Boston are aboard smaller prop planes; ask the airline or your travel agent if this is an issue for you.

Several smaller airports in the region are served by feeder airlines and charter companies, including Rutland, Vt.; Rockport, Me.; and Bar Harbor, Me.

Many people who travel to northern New England find they pay less and have a wider choice of flight times by flying into Boston's Logan Airport, then renting a car there. Boston is about two hours by car from Portland, less than three hours from the White Mountains. If you're heading to the Bennington or Manchester area of Vermont, Albany, N.Y., is the closest major airport.

Airlines serving northern New England include **American** (☎ 800/433-7300), **Colgan** (☎ 800/272-5488), **Continental** (☎ **800/525-0280**), **Delta** (☎ 800/221-1212), **Northwest** (☎ 800/225-2525), and **USAir** (☎ 800/247-8786).

BY BUS   Express bus service is well run if a bit spotty in northern New England. You'll be able to reach the major cities and tourist destinations by bus, but few of the smaller towns or villages. Tickets are quite reasonable—about $12 one-way from Boston to Portland, or $45 from Boston to Burlington—and taking the bus requires no advance planning.

Two major bus lines serve northern New England. **Vermont Transit Lines** (☎ **800/451-3292** or 800/642-3133) is affiliated with Greyhound and serves all three states with frequent departures from Boston. **Concord Trailways** (☎ **800/639-3317**) serves New Hampshire and Maine, including some smaller towns in the Lake Winnipesaukee and White Mountains area. Concord Trailways buses are a bit more luxurious (and a few dollars more expensive) than Vermont Transit, and often entertains travelers with videos and music (piped through headphones) en route.

BY TRAIN   Train service is unfortunately very limited in northern New England. The Vermonter departs Washington, D.C., with stops in Baltimore, Philadelphia, and New York before following the Connecticut River northward. Stops in Vermont include Brattleboro, Bellows Falls, Claremont (N.H.), White River Junction, Montpelier, Waterbury, Burlington/Essex Junction, and St. Albans. A bus connection takes passengers on to Montréal. For schedule information or reservations, contact **Amtrak** at ☎ **800/872-7245.** Amtrak also maintains a Web site at http://www.amtrak.com/.

Rail service from Boston to Portland also serving seacoast New Hampshire, was slated to begin in 1994, but wrangling over track upgrades and other issues has severely delayed the process. At press time, it looked reasonably hopeful for service to resume in early or mid-1997. Contact Amtrak for more information.

7 Getting Around

One of my most fervent wishes is that someday I'll be able to travel around northern New England without my car, as my ancestors did. I'd like a reversion to historic times, when travelers could venture to the White Mountains or Maine's Mt. Desert Island or Vermont's Lake Champlain via luxurious rail car or steamship. Early in this century, visitors could even link one trolley line with the next to travel great distances between seaboard cities and inland towns.

Alas, the rise of car culture doomed New England's once-extraordinary mass transit system (visit the Trolley Museum in Kennebunkport, Maine, for a glimpse of this golden era), and today you pretty much need a car to do any serious exploring in the area. Yes, you can explore by canoe, bike, foot, or sea kayak—all of which beats staring dully through a bug-streaked windshield during a 10-hour touring day. But getting to areas where biking is best, or from one end of the river to the other, or to remote trailheads will likely require that car. There are some other options (see the sidebar for suggestions), or you can sign up for a guided bike tour or other adventure trip. But for the most part attempting to sightsee without the convenience of a car will mostly yield frustration and be a considerable waste of time.

BY CAR   The four major airports in Northern New England (see "Getting There," above) all host national car rental chains. Some handy phone numbers are **Avis** (☎ 800/331-1212), **Budget** (☎ 800/527-0700), **Enterprise** (☎ 800/325-8007), **Hertz** (☎ 800/654-3131), **National** (☎ 800/227-7368), **Rent-A-Wreck** (☎ 800/535-1391), and **Thrifty** (☎ 800/367-2277). You might also find independent car rental firms in the bigger towns, sometimes at better rates than those offered by the chains.

The most famous New England joke ends with the punchline "You can't get there from here." But you may conclude it's no joke as you try navigate through the area. Travel can be convoluted and often confusing; it's handy to have someone adept at map reading in the car with you if you veer off the main routes for some country-road exploring. North-south travel is fairly straightforward, thanks to the four major interstates in the region. Traveling east to west (or vice versa) across the region is a more vexing proposition, and will likely involve stitching together a route of several state or county roads. Don't fight it; just relax and understand this is part of the New England experience.

On the other hand, New England is of a size that touring by car can be done quite comfortably, at least in New Hampshire and Vermont. You can drive from Portland to Burlington quite easily in a day across the heart of the region. Maine is far larger than the other two states; when making travel plans, beware of two-sided maps that alter the scale from one side to the other. Remember when budgeting your time that Portland is closer to Manhattan than it is to Madawaska at the state's extreme northern tip.

Here are some representative distances between points:

Boston, Mass. to:
> Bar Harbor, Me. 281 miles
> Portland, Me. 107 miles
> North Conway, N.H. 138 miles
> Burlington, Vt. 214 miles

Portland, Me. to:
> Bar Harbor, Me. 174 miles
> Greenville, Me. 153 miles
> Rangeley, Me. 118 miles
> Manchester, N.H. 95 miles

Burlington, Vt. to:
> Brattleboro, Vt. 148 miles
> Killington, Vt. 92 miles
> Stowe, Vt. 37 miles
> Portland, Me. 232 miles

North Conway, N.H. to:
> Concord, N.H. 80 miles
> Bar Harbor, Me. 216 miles
> Portland, Me. 65 miles
> Burlington, Vt. 141 miles

Traffic is generally light compared to most urban and suburban areas along the east coast, but there are some exceptions. Traffic on the interstates leading from Boston can be sluggish on Friday afternoons and evenings in the summer. A handful of choke points, particularly on Route 1 along the Maine coast, can back up for miles as tourists seek to cross the two-lane bridges spanning tidal rivers. North Conway in New Hampshire is famed for its hellish traffic, especially during the foliage season. To avoid the worst of the tourist traffic, try to stay put on big summer holidays; if your schedule allows it, travel on weekdays rather than weekends; and hit the road early or late in the day to avoid the mid-day crunch.

If you're a connoisseur of back roads and off-the-beaten track exploring, DeLorme atlases are invaluable. These are produced for all three states, and offer an

Your Car: Leave Home Without It

Options exist for those who don't consider it a real vacation unless they put some distance between themselves and their cars. Here are a few suggestions:

- **Take a bus or fly into Portland,** Maine, where you can sign up for a guided sea kayak excursion. **Maine Island Kayak Co.** (☎ 207/766-2373) is just 20 minutes outside of the city by ferry on Peaks Island, and offers trips throughout the state all summer long. You can camp within the city limits on remote Jewell Island at the edge of Casco Bay, or head out for a few days along more remote parts of the coast.

- **Take Amtrak to Brattleboro,** Vt., and stay at the downtown Latchis Hotel, just a two-minute walk from the train station. From this base, you can explore this small town of brick architecture, fine restaurants, and quirky shops. Cross the river to hike Wantastiquet Mountain one afternoon. Another day, rent a canoe and explore the Connecticut River, or get a bike and head off into the hilly countryside.

- **Take a bus or fly into Bar Harbor,** Maine, then settle into one of the numerous inns or B&Bs downtown. Rent a mountain bike. By day, you can explore the elaborate network of carriage roads at Acadia National Park and cruise along picturesque Park Loop Road. By night, enjoy lobster and other fine meals at Bar Harbor's restaurants.

- **Fly to Bangor,** Maine, on a commercial flight. Hire a charter float plane to pick you up at the airport and deliver you to **Chesuncook Lake House** (☎ 207/745-5330) deep in the North Woods and far from any roads. Here, you can explore the lakeshore by foot, or rent a canoe to fish in some of the lake's remote coves.

- **Take the Concord Trailways bus to the Appalachian Mountain Club's Pinkham Notch Camp** (☎ 603/466-2725), high in the White Mountains. Spend a night here, then backpack for two days across the demanding, rugged mountains, staying at AMC's remote backcountry huts (all meals provided). At the end of your sojourn, catch the AMC shuttle back to Pinkham Notch, then the return bus back to Boston.

extraordinary level of detail, right down to logging roads and public boat launches on small ponds. **DeLorme's headquarters and map store** (☎ 207/865-4171) is in Freeport, Maine, but their products are available widely at book and convenience stores throughout the region.

If you're organized to a degree that sometimes alarms your family and close friends, I have an Internet Web site for you. MapQuest calculates distances and driving directions from thousands of points around the country. Although it seems a bit quirky for long-distance hauls, it's very good for shorter trips. Type in where you are and where you want to go, and the online software calculates the total distance and provides detailed driving instructions. Before departing you can plot your route and even print out a daily driving itinerary. The MapQuest site is at http://www.mapquest.com.

BY PLANE   Service between airports within the region is sketchy at best. You can find limited direct flights between some cities (such as Portland to Bangor), but for the most part you'll have to backtrack to Boston and fly out again to your final destination. Convenient it's not. And if you're the nervous type, remember to ask if you'll have to board a tiny puddle-jumper for your flight. See "Getting There" for airline phone numbers.

BY BUS   As mentioned above in the "Getting There" section, express bus service into the region is quite good. But beware of trying to travel within the region by bus. Quirky schedules and routes may send you well out of your way, and what may seem a simple trip could take hours. (A clerk at Vermont Transit explained to me that the 65-mile trip from Portland to North Conway was necessarily via Boston and would take approximately nine hours—about twice as long as traveling between these points by bicycle.) Traveling north-south between towns along a single bus route (e.g., Concord to North Conway, or Portland to Bangor) is feasible, bus east-west travel across northern New England is impractical.

BY TRAIN   Amtrak provides extremely limited rail travel within the region, and is mostly confined to a few stops in Vermont. See "Getting There," above. If everything goes according to plan, trains will also run from Boston to Portland in 1997, with stops in New Hampshire and along the southern Maine coast. Call **Amtrak** at ☎ **800/872-7245** for more information.

FAST FACTS: Northern New England

AAA   The Maine and Vermont AAA services are jointly managed from the club's headquarters in Portland, Me., but the national auto club has branch offices throughout northern New England to help members with trip planning, road service in the event of a breakdown, and discount tickets to events and attractions. Call 800/222-4357 for more information on membership.

American Express   American Express offers travel services, including check cashing and trip planning, through several affiliated agencies in the region. The office in Portland, Me., is located at 480 Congress St. (☎ 207/772-8450); in West Lebanon, N.H., at 24 Airport Rd. (☎ 603/298-5997), and in Barre, Vt., at 325 North Main St. (☎ 802/479-0541).

Business Hours   Most offices are open from 8 or 9am to 5 or 6pm. Shops usually open around 9:30 or 10am. Banks typically close at 3 or 4pm, but many have cash card machines available 24 hours. Post offices in larger cities may be open past 5pm, but it's best to call ahead before going out of your way. A few supermarkets are open 24 hours a day, but they're not terribly common in this part of the world. If you need quick provisions, look for one of brightly lit convenience stores (Christy's and Cumberland Farms are among the chains here), which are usually open until at least 10 or 11pm.

Emergencies   In the event of fire, crime, or medical emergency, dial 911.

Liquor Laws   The legal age to consume alcohol is 21, and all three states sell hard liquor through state-run stores. Beer and wine is available in grocery and convenience stores. Restaurants that don't have liquor licenses sometime allow patrons to bring their own adult beverages. Always ask first.

Maps   Maps of the region and individual states are commonly available at convenience stores and supermarkets for $2 or $3. All three states also offer free road maps at their official tourist information centers (you usually have to ask at the desk). For more detailed coverage of the region, consider purchasing Delorme Atlases, which are available for Maine, New Hampshire, and Vermont.

Newspapers/Magazines   Almost every small town seems to have a daily or weekly newspaper covering the events and happenings of the area. These are good sources of information for small-town events and specials at local restaurants—the day-to-day things that slip through the cracks at the tourist bureaus. The largest papers in each state are the Portland Press Herald (Maine), Manchester Union-Leader (New Hampshire), and the Burlington Free-Press (Vermont). Both Burlington and Portland have free alternative weeklies that are excellent sources of information on concerts and shows at local clubs.

Speed Limits   The speed limit on interstate highways in the region is generally 65 miles per hour, although this is reduced to 55 miles per hour near cities. State highways are a less formal network, and the speed limits (and the conditions of the roads) vary widely. Watch for speed limits to drop in one or two stages as you approach a settlement. *Be alert:* This is often where the local cop lurks.

Taxes   The sales tax in Vermont is 5%; in Maine it's 6%. In both states the rate increases to 7% for rooms and meals. There is no general sales tax in New Hampshire, but a "tourist" tax of 8% is levied on restaurant meals and hotel rooms.

Time   All three states are in the eastern time zone, as is the Canadian province of Québec to the north. The provinces of New Brunswick, Nova Scotia, and Prince Edward Island are in the Atlantic Time Zone, which is one hour earlier.

4 For Foreign Visitors

Most of the general information to ensure a pleasant trip will be found in the preceding introductory chapters. Some aspects of U.S. laws, customs, and culture that might be perplexing to visitors from Canada and overseas are covered in this chapter.

1 Preparing for Your Trip

ENTRY REQUIREMENTS

DOCUMENTS   Canadian citizens have it easiest when visiting the United States. Canadians need only present some form of identification at the border; a passport isn't necessary unless you plan to stay more than 90 days, although it may be helpful as identification for certain transactions, especially financial.

A number of countries are currently participating in the visa waiver pilot program, which allows travelers from these countries to enter the United States with just a valid passport and a visa waiver form. Check with your travel agency for the current rules and participating airlines and cruise lines. (The countries in this program in 1996 are Andorra, Austria, Belgium, Brunei, Denmark, Finland, France, Germany, Iceland, Ireland, Italy, Japan, Liechtenstein, Luxembourg, Monaco, Nether, New Zealand, Norway, San Marino, Spain, Sweden, Switzerland, and the United Kingdom.)

Other foreign visitors should apply for a U.S. visa at the embassy or consulate with jurisdiction over their permanent residence. You can apply for a visa in any country, but it's generally easier to get a visa in your own. Applicants must have a passport that's valid for at least six months beyond the dates they propose to visit, a passport-sized photo (1.5 inches square), and some indication that they have a residence outside the United States to which they plan to return. Applicants must also fill out a Form OF-156 (available free at all U.S. embassies and consulates). If you have a letter of invitation from a U.S. resident, that's sometimes helpful. Drug addicts and anarchists need not apply.

Bear in mind that the U.S. government assumes that everyone visiting the U.S. plans to immigrate here illegally. Some regard this as a little presumptive and cynical, but that's how the system works under U.S. law. Therefore, it's up to the traveler to convince U.S. authorities otherwise. The more evidence you assemble to that effect, the easier it will be to get a visa. Especially helpful is an indication of how your trip will be financed.

Once in the country, foreign visitors come under the jurisdiction of the Immigration and Naturalization Service (INS). If you'd like to change the length or the status of your visa (for instance, from nonimmigrant to immigrant) contact the nearest INS office. Look in the local phone book under "U.S. Government."

Be sure to carefully check the valid dates on your visa. If you overstay one or two days, it's probably no big deal. If it's more than that, you may be on the receiving end of an interrogation by customs officials on your way out of the country, and it may hinder efforts to get another visa the next time you apply for one.

MEDICAL REQUIREMENTS Unless you've recently been in an area suffering from an epidemic (such as yellow fever or cholera), no inoculations are needed to enter the United States.

Not all prescription drugs that are sold overseas are necessarily available in the United States. If you bring your own supplies of prescription drugs (and especially syringes), it's wise to carry a physician's prescription in case you need to convince customs officials that you're not a smuggler or drug addict.

CUSTOMS REQUIREMENTS Jet and ship passengers will be asked to fill out a customs form declaring what goods they're are bringing into the country. Visitors planning to spend at least 72 hours in the United States may bring 200 cigarettes, 3 pounds of smoking tobacco, or 100 cigars (but no Cuban cigars), and $100 worth of gifts without paying any duties. Anything over these amounts will be taxed. No food may be brought into the country (this includes canned goods); live plants are also prohibited. Up to US $10,000 in cash may be brought in or out of the country without any formal notification. If you are carrying more than that amount, you must notify customs officials when either entering or departing the country.

MONEY

The basic unit of U.S. currency is the dollar, which is about enough to buy a large cup of coffee. The dollar consists of 100 cents. Common coins include penny (1¢), nickel (5¢), dime (10¢), and quarter (25¢). You may come across a 50¢ or $1 coin, but these are relatively rare. Dollar bills and coins are accepted everywhere, but some smaller shops won't accept larger bills ($50 or $100) because they lack sufficient change or are fearful of counterfeit bills. It's best to travel with a plentiful supply of $10 and $20 bills.

Foreign-exchange bureaus, so common in many countries, are rare in the United States, and are virtually nonexistent in northern New England. Many banks will exchange foreign currency for dollars, but it's often a time-consuming and expensive process. It's best to plan ahead and obtain dollars or dollar-based traveler's checks in your own country before departure.

Canadian dollars are commonly accepted in Maine, New Hampshire, and Vermont (all of which border Canada), although it's generally easier to use Canadian currency the closer to the border you are. Most hotels and many restaurants will accept Canadian currency at a discount close to its current trading value. Some places will periodically accept Canadian currency at face value as a part of a promotion to attract Canadian tourists; look for signs and advertisements to this effect in your travels.

TRAVELER'S CHECKS Traveler's checks are considered as good as cash in most U.S. shops and banks. Widely recognized brands include American Express, Barclay's, and Thomas Cook. With other types of checks, you might meet with some resistance, particularly in smaller towns. Some small shops may not cash checks of $100 or more if they have insufficient change; it's best to cash these at hotels or banks. Most banks will cash traveler's checks without charge.

CREDIT CARDS   Credit cards are becoming an increasingly common form of payment throughout the United States for everything from expensive hotel rooms to inexpensive gifts. It's not impractical to travel the country with no cash, just a credit card in your back pocket. Among the most commonly accepted credit cards are American Express, Discover, MasterCard, and Visa. Because American Express charges a higher rate for processing its transactions, a number of hotels and restaurants will claim not to accept the card, but will if it's the only card you have.

It's highly recommended to have at least one credit card (fully paid up) when you travel in the United States. Credit cards are commonly accepted in lieu of deposits when renting a car or a hotel room, and are often allowed as a form of identification.

Many ATM (automatic teller machines) will debit your credit card and provide cash on the spot. Don't ever give your card to anyone as a deposit; they should record the information on it and return it to you. Also be careful with your credit card receipts, as the information on them may be used by the unscrupulous to make purchases.

INSURANCE

Foreign visitors who are not insured are strongly urged to take out a traveler's insurance policy to cover any emergencies that may arise during their stay here. The United States does not offer national medical coverage for its residents; medical services are paid for either in cash or, more commonly, by an individual's insurance company. Be aware that hospital and doctors' costs are extremely high in the United States, and even a minor medical emergency could result in a huge extra expense for those traveling without insurance.

Comprehensive policies available in your country may also cover other disasters, including bail (in the event you are arrested), automobile accidents, theft or loss of baggage, and emergency evacuation to your country in the event of a dire medical situation. Check with your local automobile association (if there is one) or insurance company for detailed information on travelers' insurance.

Packages such as "Europe Assistance Worldwide Services" in Europe are sold by automobile clubs and travel agencies at attractive rates. **Travel Assistance International (TAI)** (☎ **800/821-2828** or 202/347-2025) is the agent for Europ Assistance Worldwide Services, Inc., so holders of this company's policies can contact TAI for assistance while in the United States.

Canadians should check with their provincial health scheme offices or call **HealthCanada** (☎ **613/957-3025**) to find out the extent of their coverage and what documentation and receipts they must take home in case they are treated in the United States.

SAFETY

Maine, New Hampshire, and Vermont have some of the lowest crime rates in the country, and the odds of anything untoward happening during your visit here are very slight. But all travelers are advised to take the usual precautions against theft, robbery, and assault.

Avoid any unnecessary displays of wealth when in public. Don't bring out big wads of cash from your pocket, and save your best jewelry for private occasions. If you are approached by someone who demands money, jewelry, or anything else from you, do what most Americans do: Hand over what the mugger requests. Don't argue. Don't negotiate. Just do what they say. Then immediately contact the police (see "Emergencies," below).

The crime you're statistically most likely to encounter is theft of your automobile. Break-ins can occur any time of the day or night. Don't leave any items of value in plain view; that offers a target that's tempting for even the casual miscreant. At the least, store your valuables locked securely in your trunk. Better still, keep them with you at all times.

There are very few neighborhoods in northern New England where you're likely to feel threatened. (This isn't the case in the bigger cities to the south.) Still, late at night you should look for a well-lighted area to get gas or if you need to step out of your car for any reason. Also, it's not advisable to sleep in your car at night at highway rest areas, which can leave you vulnerable to robbers passing through the area.

Take the usual precautions against leaving cash or valuables in your hotel room when you're not present. Larger hotels have safe deposit boxes. Smaller inns and hotels will not, although it can't hurt to ask to leave small items in the house safe. A good number of small inns don't even have locks on guest rooms doors. Don't be alarmed; if anything this is a good sign, indicating that there have been no problems here in the past. If you're feeling at all nervous about this, lock your valuables in your car trunk.

One personal note: I've traveled for many years in northern New England, often leaving my inn room door unlocked, and can't report a single unpleasant experience.

2   Getting to Northern New England

There are few international flights into northern New England, so the odds are you'll arrive by way of Boston, New York, or Canada. And the odds are better still that you'll arrive by car. Bus and train service reaches parts of Maine, New Hampshire, and Vermont, but it tends to be quite spotty and relatively expensive, especially if two or more are traveling together (It's often much cheaper to rent a car than to pay for two tickets). Note also that these states are best seen by exploring the countryside, which is virtually inaccessible by mass transportation. If you're dead set against renting a car, look for suggested vacations using public transportation in the previous chapter.

Many international travelers come to northern New England via Boston's Logan Airport or the three New York City area airports. Boston offers the easiest access to northern New England: Portland, the White Mountains, and the southern Green Mountains are two to three hours away by car. Figure on at least five hours of driving time to most attractions if you're coming from New York airports. European visitors heading to Maine should inquire about flights to Bangor; while the city isn't a major European destination, a number of flights en route to the West Coast stop here to refuel and it's sometimes possible to disembark.

Dozens of airlines serve New York and Boston airports from overseas, although New York gets far more overseas traffic. Some helpful numbers to call in London include: **American Airlines** (☎ 0181/572-5555), **British Airways** (☎ 0345/222-111), **Continental** (☎ 4412/9377-6464), **Delta** (☎ 0800/414-767), **United** (☎ 0181/990-9900), and **Virgin Atlantic** (☎ 0293/747-747).

Canadian readers may want to check flight availability and fares on **Air Canada** (☎ **800/268-7240** in Canada) and **Canadian Airlines International** (☎ **800/426-7000** in Canada).

Those coming from Latin American, Asia, Australia, or New Zealand will probably arrive in New England through gateway cities like Miami, Los Angeles, or San Francisco, clearing customs there before connecting onward. In this case, it may be easiest to book a flight directly to northern New England. Airports with regularly scheduled flights in the region include Portland and Bangor, Maine; Manchester, N.H.; and Burlington, Vt. Albany, N.Y. is another option, especially if your destination is southern Vermont.

Bus service is available from Boston's Logan Airport to several cities in Northern New England. Limited train service is also offered. See "Getting Around" in the previous chapter.

FAST FACTS: For the Foreign Traveler

Abbreviations   On highway signs and in publications you'll often see the states of northern New England abbreviated. Maine is "Me.", New Hampshire is "N.H.", and Vermont is "Vt." All capital letters are used when addressing mail for the U.S. Postal Service.

Automobile Organizations   Becoming a member of an automobile club is handy for obtaining maps and route suggestions, and can be helpful should an emergency arise with your automobile. The nation's largest automobile club is the American Automobile Association (AAA), which has nearly 1,000 offices nationwide. AAA offers reciprocal arrangements with many overseas automobile clubs; if you're a member of an automobile club at home, find out whether your privileges extend to the United States. For more information on AAA, call 800/222-4357.

Business Hours   Businesses are typically open from 9am to 5pm Monday through Friday. Banks typically shut down at 3 or 4pm, although ATM machines operate 24 hours. Most restaurants and some shops stay open until 8 or 9pm. If you need something after hours, head to the nearest mall, which is typically open until 9pm or so.

Climate   See "When to Go" in chapter 3.

Currency   See "Money," earlier in this chapter.

Drinking Laws   You must be 21 years old to legally drink alcohol in most of the U.S.   No matter what your age, state laws in New England are notoriously harsh on those who drive drunk. Know your tolerance. If you plan to exceed your tolerance in an evening, allow enough time for the effects to wear off, or imbibe within walking distance of your hotel or inn.

Driving   A current overseas license is valid on U.S. roads. If your license is in a language other than English, it's recommended that you obtain an International Drivers Permit from the American Automobile Association affiliate or other automobile organization in your own country prior to departure (see "Automobile Organizations," above).

Electricity   Electrical incompatibility makes it tricky to use appliances manufactured for Europe in the United States. The current here is 110-120 volts, 60 cycles, compared to the 220-240 volts, 50 cycles used in much of Europe. If you're bringing an electric camera flash, portable computer, or other gadget that requires electricity, be sure to bring the appropriate converter and plug adapter.

Embassies/Consulates   Embassies are located in Washington, D.C. Call directory assistance (☎ 202/555-1212) and request the phone number. (Directory assistance calls are free from most pay phones.)

A handful of countries maintain consulates in Boston. Among English-speaking countries, these include **Australia,** 20 Park Plaza, Boston, MA 02116 (☎ 617/542-8655); **Canada,** 3 Copley Place, Suite 400, Boston, MA 02116 (☎ 617/262-3760); **Great Britain,** Federal Reserve Plaza, 600 Atlantic Ave. (25th floor), Boston, MA 02210 (☎ 617/248-9555); **Ireland,** 535 Boylston St., Boston, MA 02116 (☎ 617/267-9330); and **Israel,** 1020 Statler Office Building, 20 Park Plaza, Boston, MA 02116 (☎ 617/542-0041). For other countries, contact directory assistance (☎ 617/555-1212).

Emergencies   In the event of any type of emergency, simply dial "911" from any phone. You do not need a coin to make this call. A dispatcher will immediately send medics, the police, or the fire department to assist you. If "911" doesn't work, dial "0" and report your situation to the operator. If a hospital is near when a medical emergency arises, look for the "Emergency" entrance, where you will be quickly attended to.

Gasoline   Gasoline is widely available throughout the region, with the exception of the North Woods region of Maine, where you can travel many miles without seeing a filling station. Gas tends to be cheaper further to the south and in larger town and cities, where the competition is a bit stiffer; you're better off filling up before setting off into remote or rural areas. Gas is available in several different grades at each station; the higher the octane, the more expensive it is. Cars tend to run a bit smoother and more efficiently with higher grades of gasoline, but rental cars will take any grade.

Many of the filling stations in New England have both "self-serve" and "full-service" pumps; look for signs as you pull up. The full service pumps are slightly more expensive per gallon, but an attendant will pump your gas and check your oil (you might have to ask for this). The self-serve pumps often have simple directions posted on them. If you're at all confused, ask anyone who happens to be around for instructions.

Holidays   With some important exceptions, national holidays usually fall on Mondays to allow workers to enjoy a three-day holiday. The exceptions are New Year's Day (January 1), Independence Day (July 4), Veterans Day (November 11), Thanksgiving (last Thursday in November), and Christmas (December 25). Other holidays include Martin Luther King, Jr. Day (third Monday in January), President's Day (third Monday in February), Easter (first Sunday following a full moon occurring March 21 or later), Memorial Day (last Monday in May), Labor Day (first Monday in September), and Columbus Day (second Monday in October). In Maine and Massachusetts, Patriot's Day is celebrated on the third Monday in April. On these holidays, banks, government offices, and post offices are closed. Shops are sometimes open and sometimes not on holidays, but assume almost all will be closed on Thanksgiving and Christmas Day.

Languages   Some of the larger hotels may have multilingual employees, but don't count on it. Outside of the cities, English is the only language spoken. The exception is along the Canadian border and in some Maine locales (including Old Orchard Beach, Biddeford, Lewiston, and Van Buren), where French is commonly spoken or at least understood.

Legal Aid   If a foreign tourist accidentally breaks a law, it's most likely to be for exceeding the posted speed limit on a road (it's the law U.S. residents most frequently run afoul of). If you are pulled over by a policeman, don't attempt to pay the fine directly—that may be interpreted as a bribe, and you may find yourself in graver trouble. You'll be issued a summons with a court date and a fine listed on it; if you pay the fine by mail, you won't have to appear in court. If you are arrested for a more serious infraction, you'll be allowed one phone call from jail. It's advisable to contact your embassy or consulate.

Mail   Virtually every small town and village has a post office; ask anyone on the street where it is and you'll be directed there. Mail within the United States costs 32¢ for a one-ounce letter, and 23¢ for each additional ounce; postcards are 20¢. Overseas mail to Europe, Australia, New Zealand, Asia, and South America is 60¢ for a half ounce, 40¢ for a postcard. A half-ounce letter to Mexico is 35¢; a one-ounce letter to Canada is 40¢. If in doubt about weight or costs, ask the postal clerk. Mail may also be deposited at blue mailboxes with the inscription "U.S. MAIL" or "United States Postal Service" located on many streets.

If you need to receive mail during your travels, have your correspondents address it to your name, "c/o General Delivery" at the city you are visiting. Go in person to the main post office to collect it; you'll be asked for identification (a passport is ideal) before it's given to you.

Newspapers/Magazines   Foreign newspapers and magazines are commonly found in Boston and Cambridge to the south, but are harder to track down in northern New England. Your best bet is to go to Borders Bookstore (Portland and Bangor, Maine), or Barnes & Noble (Augusta, Maine; Salem, Nashua, and Manchester, N.H.; and South Burlington, Vt.) Both chains have large stores and offer a decent selection of the overseas press.

Taxes   Visitors to the United State are assessed a $10 customs tax upon entering the country, and a $6 tax on departure. The United States does not have a value-added tax (VAT). The tax you most commonly come across is a sales tax (usually 5–6%) added on to the price of goods and some services. New Hampshire does not have a sales tax on goods, but does levy an 8% tax on hotel rooms and meals at restaurants.

Telephone and Fax   Pay phones are not hard to find except in the more remote regions. Shops that have public phones inside usually display a blue sign featuring a bell inside a circle outside the store.

Telephone numbers beginning with "800" or "888" are toll-free. Press "1" before dialing a toll-free number.

Phone directories are divided between Yellow Pages (stores and services, listed by category) and the White Pages (names, listed alphabetically). Be aware that some White Pages are sometimes further split between commercial and residential listings. Phone books are sometimes found at pay phones; failing that, ask to see one at a friendly shop or restaurant. To find a specific local phone number, dial "411" (no coin needed) and an operator will take your request. The Yellow Pages section often features maps of the local area and other information of interest to travelers.

Local calls cost 10¢ or 25¢ (depending on the state) for a limited amount of time. You can use a quarter for a 10¢ phone call, but you won't receive change. How far you can call on a local call varies from place to place, and the boundaries will often seem arbitrary. If you're uncertain whether a call is long-distance or not, try it as a local call. If a recorded voice comes on telling you to deposit more money for the first three minutes, that means it's a long-distance call.

Long-distance calls at pay phones tend to be very expensive, and you'll need a lot of coins. There are other options. At some phones you can use your credit card. And prepaid phone cards are available at many convenience stores and other outlets, typically for $5 or $10. Follow the instructions on the card (you'll call a toll-free 800 number first, then punch in a code and the number you wish to call). Long-distance charges using the cards are usually about 30¢ per minute, and is less expensive and more convenient than feeding coins into a pay phone.

Be aware that many hotels (notably the more expensive chain hotels) tack on a surcharge for local and long-distance calls made from your room. Even toll-free "800" number calls can cost you $1 or more. Ask about these charges when you check in. If your hotel does adds a high surcharge and you plan to make a number of phone calls, you're better off using a pay phone.

To charge the phone call to the person receiving your call, dial "0" then the area code and the number you're calling. An operator (or computer) will come on the line and ask your name, and will then call the number to ask permission to reverse the charges. If the person you're calling accepts, the call will be put through.

If you need to send or receive a fax (facsimile), ask at your hotel, or look in the Yellow Pages under "Fax Transmission Service." Many copy shops will provide this service for you.

Time All of northern New England is in the Eastern Time Zone—the same as Boston, New York, and the rest of the eastern seaboard. All states shift to Daylight Savings Time in summer, setting clocks ahead one hour in the spring (the first Sunday in April), and back again in the fall (the last Sunday in October).

Tipping Tipping is commonly practiced in the United States to recognize good service. Be aware that in restaurants, servers are typically paid a bare minimum and depend on tips for their wage. Tipping isn't considered optional, unless the service is unspeakably deplorable. For decent to good service tip 15%; for outstanding service 20%. Other suggestions for tipping include: bartenders, 10%–15%; bellhops, $1 per bag; cab drivers, 10% of fare; chambermaids, $1 per day; checkroom attendants, $1 per garment; parking attendants, $1. No tipping is expected at gas stations or at fast-food or other self-service restaurants.

Toilets Public toilets (commonly called "rest rooms") are increasingly scarce in the United States, and where they do exist they're often not fit for use. Restaurants have rest rooms for their customers; some will let people off the street use them, but many have signs indicating "For Patrons Only." This is remedied by buying a pack of gum or a cup of coffee. Fast food restaurants (like McDonald's or Burger King) are a good bet for reasonably clean toilets when traveling on the highways.

5 Vermont

A pair of East Coast academics raised a ruckus recently with a proposal to turn much of the Great Plains into a national park, and let the buffalo roam free again.

With all due respect, if there's any state that should be turned wholesale into a national park, it's Vermont. This would preserve a classic American landscape of rolling hills punctuated with slender white church spires and covered bridges (Vermont has more than 100). It would preserve the perfectly scaled main streets in towns like Woodstock and Bennington and Middlebury and Montpelier. It would save the dairy farms that fan across the shoulders of verdant ridges. But most of all, it would preserve a way of life that, one day, America will wish it had retained.

Without feeling in the least like a theme park, Vermont captures a sense of America as it once was. Vermonters still share a strong sense of community, and they respect the ideals of thrift and parsimony. They still prize their small villages and towns, and they understand what makes them special. In his 1996 state of the state address, Gov. Howard Dean said that one of Vermont's special traits was in knowing "where our towns begin and end." That alone speaks volumes.

Of course, it's not likely that Vermont residents would greet a national park proposal with much enthusiasm or equanimity. Meddlesome outsiders and federal bureaucrats don't rank high on their list of folks to invite to Sunday supper. At any rate, such a preservation effort would ultimately be doomed to failure. Because Vermont's impeccable sense of place is tied to its autonomy and independence, any effort to control it from above would certainly cause it to perish.

Happily for travelers exploring the state, it's not hard to get a taste of Vermont's way of life. You'll find it in almost all of the small towns and villages. And they are small—the suburbs of suburbs of some East Coast cities are far larger. Let the numbers tell the story: Burlington, Vermont's largest city, has just 39,127 residents; Montpelier, the state capital, 8,247; Brattleboro, 8,612; Bennington, 9,532; Woodstock, 1,037; Newfane, 164. (All these figures are from the 1990 census.) The state's entire population is just 560,000—making it one of a handful of states with more senators than representatives in Congress.

Vermont

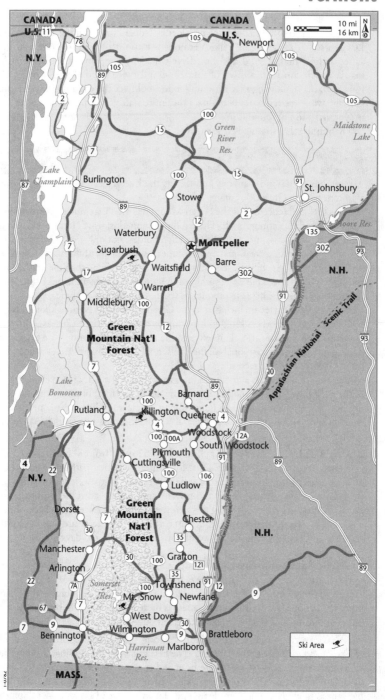

Of course, the numbers don't tell the whole story. You have to let the people do that. One of Vermont's better-known residents, Nobel Prize–winning author Sinclair Lewis, wrote 70 years ago: "I like Vermont because it is quiet, because you have a population that is solid and not driven mad by the American mania—that mania which considers a town of four thousand twice as good as a town of two thousand. . . . Following that reasoning, one would get the charming paradox that Chicago would be ten times better than the entire state of Vermont, but I have been in Chicago and not found it so."

Thankfully, that still holds true today.

1 Enjoying the Great Outdoors

Arizona has the Grand Canyon; Florida has the Everglades. And Vermont? Well, Vermont has the Green Mountains.

The chief difference is that the Green Mountains aren't so much a destination as part and parcel of Vermont itself. These rolling mountains, which form a north-south spine from the Massachusetts to the Canadian border, not only define Vermont, but also offer wonderful recreational opportunities, especially for those attracted to low-key adventures. These hills are less dramatic and more forgiving than the harsh White Mountains of northern New Hampshire, and more friendly than the spiky spruce and fir forests of Maine. These are mountains where you can feel at home.

About 500,000 acres are included in the Green Mountains National Forest, which offers some of the best hiking and mountain biking in the Northeast. But outdoorspeople needn't restrict themselves to the national forest land. State forests and parks contain some exceptional hiking trails, and even many privately owned lands are open to low-impact recreation.

This mix of wilderness and civilization gives Vermont much of its character. One of the great pleasures of exploring Vermont, whether by foot, bike, or canoe, is coming over a hill or around a bend and spying a graceful white steeple or a sturdy wooden silo, both of which are as integral to the landscape here as maple trees and rolling ridges.

BACKPACKING The Long Trail, running 262 miles from Massachusetts to the Canadian border, was the nation's first long-distance hiking path and remains one of the best. This high-elevation trail follows Vermont's gusty ridges and dips into shady cols, crossing federal, state, and private lands. Open-sided shelters are located about one day's hike apart, making this a convenient way to traverse the backcountry. The trail can be quite demanding in parts, and to hike the entire length requires stamina and experience. Shorter excursions of two or three days are, of course, entirely possible.

The best source of information about the Long Trail and other backcountry opportunities in Vermont is the **Green Mountain Club,** R.R. #1, Box 650, Route 100, Waterbury Center, VT 05677 (☎ **802/244-7037**), which publishes the Guidebook of the Long Trail. Club headquarters is located on Route 100 between Waterbury and Stowe, and is open weekdays until about 4:30 pm.

BIKING Vermont has but a handful of biking trails converted from abandoned rail-beds, and most are under 10 miles. The best known is the Burlington Bike Path, which runs along the downtown waterfront and continues for 9 miles along the shores of Lake Champlain. The Stowe Rec Path, which is not an old rail line, is also very pleasant as it winds through farmlands and along the edge of ski resort development.

Bike trails are secondary, however, since Vermont's backroads offer some of the most superb biking in the Northeast. Even Route 100 is spectacular along stretches; especially appealing is Route 100 north of Killington to Sugarbush. While sheer hills on some back roads can be excruciating for those who've spent too much time behind a desk, close scrutiny of a map should reveal routes that follow rivers and offer less gruelling pedaling.

Vermont also lends itself to superb mountain biking. Numerous county and town roads have been abandoned and offer superior backcountry cruising. Most Green Mountain National Forest trails are also open to mountain bikers (but not the Appalachian or Long trails). Mountain bikes are prohibited from state park and state forest hiking trails, but are allowed on the gravel roads through these lands. There's also a 10-mile pilot trail for mountain bikers in the Little River area of Mt. Mansfield State Forest that's worth checking out. Mt. Snow and Jay Peak ski areas, among others, will bring you and your bike to blustery ridges via lift or gondola, allowing you to work with rather than against gravity on your way down. The Craftsbury Center is your best bet if you're looking for backroad cruising through farmland rather than forest.

Organized inn-to-inn bike tours were invented in Vermont, and they remain a great way to see the countryside by day while relaxing in luxury at night. Tours are typically self-guided, with luggage transferred for you each day by vehicle. Try **Vermont Bicycle Touring** (☎ 802/453-4811), **Country Inns Along the Trail** (☎ 802/247-3300), **Bike Vermont** (☎ 800/257-2226), and **Cycle-Inn-Vermont** (☎ 802/228-8799).

CANOEING   Vermont offers exceptionally pleasant canoeing on a number of rivers and lakes. Lake Champlain offers protected canoeing on the east side of North Hero Island and Grand Isle; outside these waters, be aware that sudden winds can come up unexpectedly with disastrous results. Numerous small ponds within the Green Mountains lend themselves to a lazy afternoon's paddle.

Good paddling rivers include the Battenkill in southwest Vermont, the Lamoille near Jeffersonville, the Class II Winooski near Waterbury, and the Missisquoi from Highgate Center to Swanton Dam. The whole of the historic Connecticut River, while frequently interrupted by dams, offers uncommonly scenic paddling through rural farmlands. Especially beautiful is the seven-mile stretch between Moore and Comerford dams near Waterford. Rentals are easy to come by near Vermont's major waterways; just check the local Yellow Pages.

In the early 1990s the **Upper Valley Land Trust** (☎ **603/643-6626**) set up a network of primitive campsites along the Connecticut River, allowing canoeists to paddle and portage its length and camp along the riverbanks at night. Two of the campsites are accessible by car. Call for a brochure.

Vermont also offers a novel way to explore the state: canoeing inn-to-inn. These trips can usually be tailored for most ability levels, and offer leisurely touring at a pace that's perfect for Vermont. **Vermont Waterways** (☎ **800/492-8271**) offers weekend and five-day tours by canoe and sea kayak on the Connecticut River, Lake Champlain, the Lamoille, and Winooski rivers. Prices start at $380 per person for a weekend trip, which includes all meals and lodging at inns or B&Bs.

A helpful guide is Roioli Schweiker's *Canoe Camping Vermont & New Hampshire Rivers,* published by Countryman Press.

One final note: Those whose goal is to canoe long distances through wild lands will be better served in northern and eastern Maine.

FISHING Vermont attracts anglers from all over the eastern United States, who flock to its banks with spinners and flies. Both lake and river fishing can be excellent—if you know what you're doing. Vermont has 288 lakes of 20 acres or larger, hundreds of smaller bodies of water, and nearly countless miles of rivers and streams.

Novice fly fishermen would do well to stop by the sizeable **Orvis Catalog Store** (☎ **802/362-3750**) in Manchester to ask for some friendly advice, then perhaps try out some of the famed tackle on the store's small ponds. If time permits, sign up for one of the Orvis fly-fishing classes and have an expert critique your technique and offer some pointers.

Vermont's rivers and lakes are home to 14 major species of sportsfish, including landlocked salmon, four varieties of trout (rainbow, brown, brook, and lake), and large- and smallmouth bass. The 100-mile-long Lake Champlain attracts its share of enthusiasts angling for bass, landlocked salmon, and lake trout. In the south, the Battenkill is perhaps the most famed trout river (thanks in part to the proximity of Orvis), although veteran anglers contend that it's lost its luster. The Walloomsac and West rivers have also been rumored to give up a decent-sized trout or two. And don't overlook the Connecticut River, which the Fish and Wildlife Department calls "probably the best-kept fishing secret in the Northeast."

Fishing licenses are required and are available by mail from the state or in person at many sporting goods and general stores. License requirements and fees change from time to time, so it's best to write or call for a complete list: **Vermont Fish & Wildlife Dept.,** 103 South Main St., Waterbury, VT 05671 (☎ **802/241-3700**).

Two invaluable guides are *The Atlas of Vermont Trout Ponds,* and *Vermont Trout Streams,* both published by **Northern Cartographic,** 4050 Williston Rd., South Burlington, VT 05403 (☎ **802/860-2886**).

HIKING Vermont offers a spectacular range of hiking trails, from undemanding woodland strolls to lengthy treks along rugged, windswept ridges.

The two premier long-distance pathways in Vermont are the Appalachian and Long trails, which traverse some of the most dramatic terrain the state has to offer. Day hikes are easily carved out of these longer treks; see "Backpacking" above for information on the Green Mountain Club, which is the best source of advice on Vermont's trails.

The **Green Mountain National Forest** offers a total of 500 miles of hiking trails, from the Long Trail to pathways through lowland valleys. There is no single best area for hiking; just head to any of those big green areas on the state map and search out local information on trails. Any of the four Green Mountain offices will make a good stop for picking up maps and requesting hiking advice from rangers. The main office is in Rutland (☎ **802/747-6700**). District ranger offices are in Middlebury (☎ **802/388-6688**), Rochester (☎ **802/767-4261**), and Manchester (☎ **802/ 362-2307**).

In addition to the national forest, Vermont has in excess of 80 state forests and parks, many of which set the stage for superior hiking. Guides to hiking trails are essential to get the most out of a hiking vacation in Vermont. Recommended guides include the *Green Mountain Club's Day Hiker's Guide to Vermont,* and *50 Hikes in Vermont,* published by Countryman Press. Both are widely available in bookstores throughout the state.

SKIING Vermont has been eclipsed by upscale Western and Canadian ski resorts in the past few decades, but in many minds Vermont is still the capital of downhill skiing in the United States. The nation's first ski lift—a rope tow— was rigged up off a Buick engine in 1933 near Woodstock. The first lodge to accommodate skiers was built in Vermont at Sherburne Pass.

Sadly, the dismal economics of running a small ski area has taken its toll. The number of ski areas in the state has been steadily diminishing, from 81 in 1970 to 41 in 1987 to fewer than 20 today. But many of the remaining ski areas have vastly improved, putting money into high-speed lifts and state-of-the-art snowmaking.

Ski areas in Vermont vary widely, but each has its appeal. For those looking for the allure of big mountains, steep faces, and a lively ski scene, there's Killington, Stratton, and Stowe. Families and intermediates find their way to Mount Snow, Sugarbush, Pico, Okemo, Bolton Valley, and Smuggler's Notch. For old-fashioned New England ski mountain charm, there's Mad River Glen, Ascutney, Burke, and Jay Peak. Finally, those who prefer a small mountain with a smaller price tag make tracks for Middlebury Snow Bowl, Bromley, Maple Valley, and Suicide Six.

Vermont is also blessed with about 50 cross-country ski areas throughout the state. These range from modest mom-and-pop operations to elaborate destination resorts with snowmaking that extends the season and tides skiers over during snow droughts. The general advice is to head north, and head to higher elevations, where the best snow is usually found. Among the snowiest, best-run destinations are the Trapp Family Lodge in Stowe, the Craftsbury Nordic Center in the Northeast Kingdom, and Mountain Top near Killington. For a free brochure listing all the cross-country facilities, contact the **Vermont Dept. of Travel and Tourism** (☎ **800/837-6668**). The state also updates a recorded **cross-country ski report** every Thursday (☎ **802/ 828-3239**). A fax of the report is available by calling 800/833-9756.

Vermont also boasts one of the nation's premier long-distance cross-country ski trails, the 280-mile **Catamount Trail,** P.O. Box 1235, Burlington, VT 05402 (☎ **802/864-5794**), which parallels the Long Trail at a lower, more charitable elevation. Members who join the Catamount Trail Association receive a helpful newsletter and discounts at the touring centers along the route. The organization also offers guided tours on trail segments during winter weekends.

Inn-to-inn ski touring is catching on; contact the Trapp Family Lodge or the Craftsbury Center for information.

SNOWMOBILING   Vermont boasts a lengthy, well-developed network of snowmobile trails throughout the state. That's the good news. The bad news is that out-of-staters must pay their pound of flesh for the privilege of riding in Vermont. Nonresidents pay $22 to register their sled, and an additional $25 to join the Vermont Association of Snow Travelers (VAST). Snowmobilers must also join a local snowmobile club, with fees of $7 to $10. The fine for ignoring these rules is currently $117.50.

The best source of information on snowmobiling in Vermont is **VAST,** P.O. Box 839, Montpelier, VT 05601 (☎ **802/229-0005**), which produces a great newsletter and can help point you and your machine in the right direction.

Snowmobile rentals are hard to come by in Vermont, although guided tours are common. In southern Vermont, **High Country Snowmobile Tours,** located 8.5 miles west of Wilmington (☎ **802/464-2108** or 800/627-7533) offers tours between one hour and overnight. If you've never been on a snowmobile before but want to give it a whirl, rides around a 1.5-mile track are offered just south of Stowe at **Nichols Snowmobile Rentals** (☎ **802/253-7239**).

2 Southwestern Vermont

Southwestern Vermont is the turf of Ethan Allen, Robert Frost, Grandma Moses, and Norman Rockwell. As such, it may feel familiar to you even if you've never been here before. Over the decades, it's subtly become ingrained in America's cultural and geographic psyche.

The region is sandwiched between the Green Mountains to the east and the rolling hills of the Vermont–New York border to the west. The first town you're likely to hit is Bennington—a commercial center that offers up a selection of goods for locals and tourists alike. Northward toward Rutland the terrain is more intimate than intimidating, with towns clustered in gentle valleys along rivers and steams. Former 19th-century summer colonies and former lumber and marble towns exist side by side, with both offering pleasant accommodations, delightful food, and, in the case of Manchester Center, world-class shopping.

These outposts of sophisticated culture are within easy striking distance of the Green Mountains, allowing you to enjoy the outdoors by day and goose-down duvets by night. The region also attracts its share of weekend celebrities, as well as shoppers, gourmands, and those simply looking for a brief fantasy detour in the elegant inns and B&Bs.

Keep in mind when traveling here that two Route 7s exist. Running high along the foothills is the new Route 7, which offers limited access and higher speeds, resulting in a speedy trip up the valley toward Rutland. Meandering along the valley floor is Historic Route 7A, a more languorous route with plenty of diversions (antique shops, historic views) along the way. If you've got the time, take the slow road from Bennington to Manchester.

BENNINGTON

Bennington owes its fame (such as it is) to a handful of eponymous moments, places, and things. Like the Battle of Bennington, fought in 1777 during the American War of Independence. And Bennington College, a small but prestigious liberal arts school that's produced a bumper crop of well-regarded novelists in recent years. And Bennington pottery, which traces its ancestry back to the first factory here in 1793, is today prized by collectors for its superb quality.

Bennington is a pleasant, no-nonsense town with a handful of restaurants and stores still selling things that people actually need. The surrounding countryside, while defined by rolling hills, is afflicted with fewer abrupt inclines and slopes than many of Vermont's towns. The downtown is compact, low, and handsome, and boasts a fair number of architecturally striking buildings. In particular, don't miss the stern marble Federal building (formerly the post office) with its six fluted columns at 118 South St.

ESSENTIALS

GETTING THERE   Bennington is located at the intersection of Route 9 and Route 7. The nearest interstate access from the south is via at the New York Thruway at Albany, N.Y. From the east, I-91 is about 40 miles distant at Brattleboro.

VISITOR INFORMATION   The **Bennington Area Chamber of Commerce,** Veterans Memorial Dr., Bennington, VT 05201 (☎ **802/447-3311**), maintains an information office on Route 7 north near the veterans' complex. The office is open during business hours; after hours, you can pick up a map of Bennington and a list of attractions from the box outside the front door.

EXPLORING THE TOWN

Bennington's claim to history is the fabled Battle of Bennington, which took place August 16, 1777. While a relatively minor skirmish, it had major implications for the outcome of the war.

The British had devised a grand strategy to defeat the impudent colonies: divide the colonies from the Hudson River through Lake Champlain, then concentrate forces to defeat one half followed by the other. As part of the strategy, British General John Burgoyne was ordered to attack the settlement of Bennington and capture the military supplies that had been squirreled away there by the Continental militias in anticipation of hostilities. There, he came upon the colonial forces led by Gen. John Stark, a veteran of Bunker Hill. After a couple of days playing cat and mouse, Stark ordered the attack on the afternoon of August 16, proclaiming, "There are the redcoats, and they are ours, or this night Molly Stark sleeps a widow!" (Or so the story goes.)

The battle was over in less than two hours—the British and their Hessian mercenaries were defeated, with more than 200 enemy troops killed; the colonials lost but 30 men. This cleared the way for another vital colonial victory at the Battle of Saratoga, ended the British strategy of divide and conquer, and set the stage for a colonial victory in the War of Independence.

That battle is commemorated by northern New England's most imposing monument. You can't miss the **Bennington Battle Monument** if you're passing through the surrounding countryside. This 306-foot obelisk of blue limestone atop a low rise was dedicated in 1891. It resembles a shorter, paunchier Washington Monument. Note also that it's actually about six miles from the site of the actual battle; the monument actually marks the spot where the munitions were stored.

The monument's viewing platform, which is reached by elevator, is open 9am to 5pm daily from April through October. Admission is $1.

The monument is located on a leafy hill above the current town of Bennington. This area is called **Old Bennington,** and was the desired location for many of the town's better homes. Most are private, but they're impressive to see, set on oversized lots at a respectful distance from one another. Also in Old Bennington is the Old First Church. Built in 1805 with an open steeple, this church makes its way onto most lists of the most striking churches in New England. New England's favorite poet, Robert Frost, is buried in the church's cemetery.

Along the highway between Old Bennington and the current town center is the **Bennington Museum** (☎ **802/447-1571**). This intriguing collection traces its roots back to 1875; the museum has occupied the current stone-and-column building overlooking the valley since 1928. Nine galleries feature a wide range of exhibits, including furniture, glass, oil paintings, and pottery. Of special interest are the colorful, primitive landscapes by Grandma Moses (1860–1961), who lived much of her life nearby, and a glorious luxury car called the Wasp, 16 of which were crafted in Bennington between 1920 and 1925. The museum is open 9am to 5pm daily (until 7pm Friday through Monday in summer). Admission is $5 for adults, $4.50 for students and seniors, and $12 for a family with children under 18. Children under 12 enter free.

Bennington College was founded as an experimental women's college in the 1930s. It's since gone co-ed, and has garnered a national reputation as a leading liberal arts school (it also claimed the title of most expensive college in the United States for a time). Bennington has a reputation for teaching writing; W.H. Auden, Bernard Malmud, and John Gardner have all taught here. In the 1980s, Bennington produced

Southern Vermont

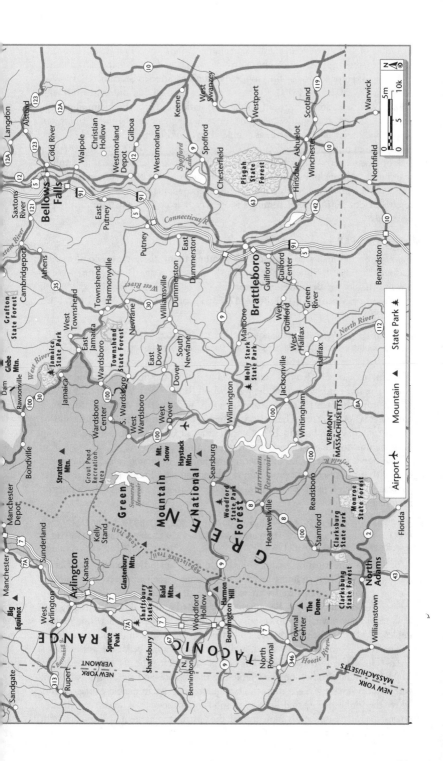

a number of prominent young authors, including Donna Tartt, Bret Easton Ellis, and Jill Eisenstadt. The pleasant campus north of town is well worth wandering about.

Finally, if you need to gas up, stop by **Hemmings Sunoco Station,** at 216 West Main St. (☎ **802/447-3572**). OK, so it doesn't look all that different from your average service station—but head inside. The station is owned by Hemmings Motor News, a successful, quirky magazine for car buffs. It's published in Bennington, distributed nationally, and serves as a bible of sorts for buyers and sellers of old cars. A tiny museum inside the station contains some splendid antique cars, and what for lack of a better term might be called automotive bric-a-brac. There's also automotive stuff for sale, including car books and Hemmings Motor News souvenirs. What's more, the station boasts another thing that was once standard at service stations coast to coast: clean restrooms. Hemming's is open daily from 7am to 10pm (until 9pm on Sunday).

WHERE TO STAY

Bennington has a slew of basic motels. Among them, three clean, comfortable, reasonably priced facilities are conveniently clustered along Route 9 just west of downtown. Try the **Bennington Motor Inn** (☎ **802/442-5479** or 800/359-9900), the **Paradise Motor Inn** (☎ **802/442-8351**), or **Mid-Town Motel** (☎ **802/ 447-0189**).

Four Chimneys. 21 West Rd., Bennington, VT 05201. ☎ **802/447-3500.** 11 rms. TV TEL. $85–$175 double including breakfast; $170–$250 including breakfast and dinner. AE, CB, DC, DISC, MC, V.

This striking Colonial Revival building will be among the first to catch your eye as your arrive in Bennington from the west. Set off Route 7 on a large, landscaped lot, it's an imposing white, three-story structure with, naturally, four prominent chimneys. (Local secret: The third chimney's a fake, added for the purposes of symmetry.) The inn, built in 1912, is at the edge of Old Bennington; the towering Bennington Monument looms above the backyard.

The carpeted guest rooms are inviting and homey, decorated in a casual country style with early American reproductions. About half have fireplaces; most also offer Jacuzzis. The inn is in the process of making over its rooms; ask for one that's recently been redone.

South Shire Inn. 124 Elm St., Bennington, VT 05201. ☎ **802/447-3839.** Fax 802/442-3547. 9 rms (1 with shower only). A/C TEL. Peak season $95–$150 double; off-season $80–$130 double. Rates include breakfast. AE, MC, V.

A locally prominent banking family hired architect William Bull to design and build this impressive Victorian home in 1880. It was an era when architects knew how to use big space and their patrons were willing to foot the bill. Today, guests can reap the benefits of that vision at Bennington's finest bed-and-breakfast, located a short walk from downtown. The downstairs is spacious and open, with detailing including leaded glass on the bookshelves, and intricate plasterwork in the dining room.

The guest rooms are richly hued, and most have canopy beds and working fireplaces (Duraflame-style logs only). The best of the bunch is the old master bedroom, which has a king-sized canopy bed, a tile-hearth fireplace, and a beautiful bathroom with hand-painted tile. Four more modern guest rooms are in the old carriage house, where the innkeepers spared little expense in the make-over. The carriage house's downstairs rooms are slightly more formal; the upstairs rooms are more intimate, with low eaves and skylights over the tubs.

WHERE TO DINE

Alldays & Onion. 519 Main St. ☎ **802/447-0043.** Reservations accepted for dinner, but not often needed. Sandwiches $2.25–$6.95; dinner $10.95–$14.95. AE, DC, DISC, MC, V. Mon–Tues 8am–6pm, Wed–Sat 8am–8pm.

First off, the name. For reasons that are not entirely clear, this eminently casual place is named after a turn-of-the-century British automobile manufacturer. Locals flock here to enjoy the wholesome, tasty sandwiches, the filling deli salads (like Cajun chicken and pasta salads), and tasty quiches and soups. More ambitious dinners are served later in the week, with entrees ranging from Southwest cowboy steak with skillet corn sauce to a more politically correct soba and stir-fried vegetables. The atmosphere is that of a small-town restaurant gussied up for a big night out—the fluorescent lights are bright, but the dark hues of the walls knock down the intensity a notch, and folk-rock background music mellows it further still. In summer, enjoy the airy screened-in patio.

☉ Blue Benn Diner. North St. (Route 7). ☎ **802/442-5140.** Breakfast $1.25–$5.95; sandwiches and entrees $1.95–$5.75; dinner $7.95. No credit cards. Mon–Tues 6am–5pm, Wed–Fri 6am–8pm, Sat 6am–4pm, Sun 7am–4pm. AMERICAN.

Diner aficionados make pilgrimages here to enjoy the ambience of this 1945 Silk City classic, with barrel ceiling and copious amounts of stainless steel. Blue stools line the laminate counter, on which you see plain evidence that more people are right-handed than left-handed by the wear marks. But even folks who don't give a fig for diners flock here for the tremendous value on food. The printed menu is vast, but don't overlook the specials scrawled on paper and taped all over the walls. Blue-plate dinner specials are $7.95, and include vegetables, rice, soup or salad, rolls, and Indian pudding for dessert. There's also a great selection of pies, like blackberry, pumpkin, and chocolate cream, that sell for $2.50 a slice (add 25¢ if you want it à la mode).

Four Chimneys. 21 West Rd. ☎ **802/447-3500.** Reservations recommended in summer. Main courses $13.75–$29.50. AE, CB, DC, DISC, MC, V. Tues–Sun 11:30am–2pm; daily 5–9pm. CONTINENTAL.

Chef Alex Koks trained in the Netherlands and serves up meals prepared with a continental flair at his well-regarded restaurant and inn. Located in an impressive manse in Old Bennington, the Four Chimneys specializes in meals prepared exactingly and served with panache. Diners might start with escargot with garlic sauce on puff pastry, or a unique mustard soup, then move on to duckling served with cherries, or a spicy sirloin steak served with red onion preserve. Guests can choose between two dining rooms depending on the season and their mood. In the warmer months, most migrate to the summery screened-in porch with its cane-seated chairs and brick floor. In winter, a more elegant interior room is spacious and formal without being unduly fancy.

ARLINGTON, MANCHESTER & DORSET

Vermont's rolling Green Mountains are rarely out of view in this cluster of hamlets. And in mid-summer the lush green hereabouts gives Ireland a good run for its money—verdant hues are found in the forests blanketing the hills, the valley meadows, and the mosses along the tumbling streams, making it obvious how these mountains earned their name.

These quintessential Vermont villages make ideal destinations for romantic getaways, aggressive antiquing, and serious outlet shopping. Each of the towns is worth visiting, and each has its own peculiar charm. Arlington has a quaint town center that borders on microscopic (U-turns are a popular pastime among travelers). To the north, Manchester and Manchester Center share a blurred town line, but maintain distinct characters. The more southerly Manchester has an old-world, old-money elegance with a campus-like town center centered around the columned Equinox Hotel. Just to the north, Manchester Center is a major mercantile center with dozens of outlets offering discounts on brand-name clothing, accessories, and housewares. A worthy detour off the beaten track is Dorset, an exquisitely preserved town of white clapboard architecture and marble sidewalks.

One caveat: With its proximity to the New York Thruway, just 40 miles east at Albany, the area attracts a disproportionate number of affluent weekenders from New York City—so the prices for inns and restaurants tend to be higher throughout the region. Those looking for a budget vacation will find better values to the north and east.

ESSENTIALS

GETTING THERE   Arlington, Manchester, and Manchester Center are located north of Bennington on Route 7A, which runs parallel to and west of the more modern, less interesting Route 7. Dorset is north of Manchester Center on Route 30, which intersects with Route 7A in Manchester Center.

VISITOR INFORMATION   The **Manchester and the Mountains Chamber of Commerce,** R.R. 2, Box 3451, Manchester Center, VT 05255 (☎ **802/362-2100**), maintains two information centers in Manchester Center in the summer. One is in a gray house two blocks north of the blinking light (open year-round). The other (open summer through foliage season only) is four blocks north of the blinking light in a white house on Adam Park Green. Hours are daily from 9am to 5pm (Sunday 9am to 2pm).

For information about outdoor recreation, the **Green Mountain National Forest** maintains a district ranger office (☎ **802/362-2307**) in Manchester on Routes 11 and 30 west of Route 7. It's open 8am to 4:30pm Monday through Friday.

EXPLORING THE AREA

Arlington has attracted more than its share of artists, writers, and celebrities over the years. The writer Dorothy Canfield Fisher and the painter Rockwell Kent lived here, and today a handful of celebrities, including producer Norman Lear, maintain summer homes nearby.

But Arlington owes its closest brush with fame to its association with painter and illustrator Norman Rockwell, who resided here from 1939 to 1953. Arlington residents were regularly featured in Rockwell covers for the Saturday Evening Post. If folks you bump into look familiar, that may be why.

Arlington maintains a small monument to its Rockwell legacy. Housed in a 19th-century Carpenter Gothic-style church in the middle of town, The **Norman Rockwell Exhibition** (☎ **802/375-6423**) features displays including many of those famous covers, along with photographs of the original models. Sometimes you'll find the models working as volunteers. Reproductions are available at the gift shop. Open 9am to 5pm daily in summer; open in the off-season 10am to 4pm weekdays and 10am to 5pm weekends. Admission is $1.

Between Arlington and Manchester you'll pass the entrance to **Skyline Drive** (☎ **802/362-1113**), a looping toll road that takes you to the summit of 3,835-foot Mount Equinox—which, incidentally, is the highest peak in Vermont not traversed by the Long Trail. The toll is $5 per car for the five-mile trip to the top, which affords open views of the Green Mountains to the east. Don't expect wilderness;

there's even a modest inn up top that's open May to October. The mountaintop is also accessible by hiking trail.

Manchester has long been one of Vermont's moneyed resorts, attracting prominent summer residents like Mary Todd Lincoln and Julia Boggs Dent, the wife of U.S. Grant. This town is well worth visiting just to wander its quiet streets, bordered with distinguished homes dating from the early Federal period. It feels a bit like you've entered a time warp here, and the cars driving past the green seem like anachronisms. Be sure to note the sidewalks made of irregular marble slabs. The town is said to have 17 miles of such sidewalks, made from the cast-offs of Vermont's marble quarries.

Seven miles north of Manchester on Route 30 is the village of Dorset. Fans of American architecture owe themselves a visit. While not nearly as grand as Manchester, this quiet town of white clapboard and black and green shutters has a quiet and appealing grace. The elliptical green is fronted by early homes that are modest by Manchester standards, but nonetheless are imbued with a subtle elegance. In fact, Dorset feels more like a Norman Rockwell painting than most Norman Rockwell paintings. The main action here is at Peletier's Store, which has been provisioning villagers for more than 175 years, although the product line is decidedly more upscale these days.

Museums & Historic Homes

✪ **Hildene.** Route 7A, Manchester. ☎ **802/362-1788.** $7 adults, $2 children 6–14. Tours daily from mid-May through Oct 9:30am–4pm. Special holiday tours Dec 27–29.

Robert Todd Lincoln was the only son of Abraham and Mary Todd Lincoln to survive to maturity. But he also achieved plenty on his own, earning millions as a prominent corporate attorney and serving as secretary of war and ambassador to Britain under three presidents. He also served as president of the Pullman Company (makers of deluxe train cars) from 1897 to 1911, stepping in after the death of company founder George Pullman.

What did one do with millions of dollars in an era when that was still something more than pocket change? Build lavish summer homes, for the most part. And Lincoln was no exception. He summered in this stately, 24-room Georgian Revival mansion between 1905 and 1926, and delighted in showing off its remarkable features, including a spectacular sweeping staircase and a 1908 Aeolian organ with its 1,000 pipes (you'll hear it played on the tour). And what summer home would be complete without formal gardens? Lincoln had gardens designed after the patterns in a stained glass window and planted on a gentle promontory with outstanding views of the flanking mountains.

A tour of the estate will give you a good sense of life here—descendents of Lincoln occupied the home until 1975, when they donated the property to the Church of Christ, Scientist, which later sold the property to the Friends of Hildene. Many of the furnishings are original, and a number of family mementos are on display.

Special Christmas candlelight tours are held at the end of December, and in winter 9 miles of cross-country skiing trails are maintained on the property, with the carriage house serving as a warming hut. Visitors pay a $7 skiing fee.

American Museum of Fly Fishing. Route 7A (a block north of the Equinox Hotel), Manchester. ☎ **802/362-3300.** Adults $3, children free. May–Oct daily 10am–4pm; Nov–Apr Mon–Fri 10am–4pm.

Warning: This is not the place to take diffident teenagers who complain that adults do boring things on vacation. It is, however, the place for serious anglers interested in the rich history and delicate art of fly fishing. The museum includes exhibits on the evolution of the fly-fishing reel, paintings and sculptures of fish and anglers, displays of creels, and dioramas depicting fishing at its best. You can see the fly-fishing tackle of some of the nation's more notable anglers, including Herbert Hoover, Andrew Carnegie, and Ernest Hemingway. And, naturally, there are extensive exhibits of beautifully tied flies, displayed in oak and glass cases.

SHOPPING

Manchester Center is one of several upscale factory outlet meccas in northern New England. Retailers include (take a deep breath) Pendleton, Bass Shoes, Timberland, Burberry's, Polly Flinders, Christian Dior, J. Crew, Seiko, Donna Karan, Coach, Van Heusen, Giorgio Armani, and Dansk. The shops conveniently cluster along a "T" intersection in the heart of Manchester Center. Most are readily accessible on foot, while others are a bit farther afield, requiring scuttling from one to the next by car.

If you need to take a break while shopping, head for **Bagelworks** (☎ **802/ 362-5082**) in Manchester Center on Routes 11 and 30, two doors down from McDonald's, (Chewy bagels, herby cream cheeses, and robust coffee are the order of the day.) There's limited seating indoors, but when the weather's nice you can take your snack to a small deck overlooking a stream, or head to the town park just up the block.

A couple of local shops are worth seeking out amid the high-fashion names. Orvis, which has crafted a worldwide reputation for manufacturing topflight fly-fishing equipment, is based in Manchester. The **Orvis Catalog Store** (☎ **802/362-3750**) is located between Manchester and Manchester Center, and offers rustic housewares, sturdy outdoor clothing, and, naturally, fly-fishing equipment. Two small ponds just outside the shop allow prospective customers to try before they buy.

Near the middle of Manchester Center at the intersection of Route 7A and Route 30 is the **Northshire Bookstore** (☎ **802/362-2200**), one of the best book shops in a state where reading is a popular pastime. In addition to great browsing, the store sponsors frequent readings by prominent authors.

SUMMER SPORTS

HIKING & BIKING   Superb hiking trails ranging from challenging to relaxing can be found in the hills a short drive from town. Get acquainted with what's where at the Green Mountain District Ranger Station (see "Visitor Information," above). Ask for the free brochure "Day Hikes on the Manchester Ranger District."

The Long Trail and Appalachian Trail (they overlap in southern Vermont) run just east of Manchester; one of the more popular day treks runs along these trails to Spruce Peak. Five miles east of Manchester Center on Routes 11 & 30 look for parking where the Long Trail/Appalachian Trail crosses the road. Strike out southward on foot over rocky terrain for 2.2 miles to the peak, looking for the blue-blazed side trail to the open summit with its breathtaking views of the Manchester Valley.

For more casual hiking, head to the oddly named Grout Pond Recreation Area, a 1,600-acre parcel formerly owned by the Boy Scouts. It's located east of Arlington on Forest Highway 6. The area offers 8.3 miles of easy hiking trails in the area around a tranquil 79-acre pond. Limited camping is available on the lake, with three sites accessible only by canoe.

A scenic drive northwest of Manchester Center you'll come to the Delaware and Hudson Rail-Trail, of which 20 miles have been built in two sections in Vermont. (Another 14 miles will eventually be developed across the state line in New York.) The southern section of the trail runs about 10 miles from West Pawlet to the state line at West Rupert, over trestles and past vestiges of former industry, such as the old Vermont Milk and Cream Co. Like most rail-trails, this is perfect for exploring by mountain bike. To reach the trailhead, drive north on Route 30 from Manchester Center to Route 315, then continue north on Route 153. In West Pawlet, park across from Duchie's General Store (a good place for refreshments), then set off on the trail southward from the old D&H freight depot across the street.

ON THE WATER   For a duck's-eye view of the rolling hills, stop by **Battenkill Canoe Ltd.** (☎ **802/362-2800** or 800/421-5268 from out of state) in Arlington. This friendly outfit offers daily canoe rentals on the scenic Battenkill and surrounding areas. Trips range from two hours to a whole day, and multiday inn-to-inn canoe packages are also available.

Aspiring anglers can sign up for fly-fishing classes taught by skilled instructors affiliated with **Orvis** (☎ **800/548-9548**), the noted fly-fishing supplier and manufacturer. The two-and-a-half-day classes include instruction in knot tying and casting; students practice catch-and-release fishing on the company pond and the Battenkill River. Classes are held from mid-April through Labor Day.

SKIING

Bromley. P.O. Box 1130, Manchester Center, VT 05255. ☎ **802/824-5522,** or 800/865-4786 for lodging. Vertical drop: 1,334 feet. Lifts: 6 chairlifts, 3 surface lifts. Skiable acreage: 175. Lift tickets: $39 weekends, $19 weekdays.

Bromley is a great place to learn to ski. Gentle and forgiving, the mountain also features long, looping intermediate runs that are tremendously popular with families. The slopes are mostly south-facing, which means some protection from the winter winds and the warmth of the sun. (Of course, it also means that the snow melts here first.) The base lodge scene is more mellow than at many resorts, and your experience here is likely to be very relaxing.

Stratton. Stratton Mountain, VT 05155. ☎ **802/297-2200,** or 800/843-6867 for lodging. Vertical drop: 2,003 feet. Lifts: 1 gondola, 9 chairlifts (including 1 six-person high-speed), 2 surface lifts. Skiable acreage: 478. Lift tickets: $48 weekends, $42 weekdays.

Stratton is striving to reinvent itself. Founded in the 1960s, it labored in its early days under the belief that Vermont ski areas had to have a Tyrolean flair. Hence, a Gothic clock tower, Swiss Chalet Nightmare architecture, and the overall feel of being Vail's younger, less affluent sibling. Stratton is working to leave the image of Alpine quaintness behind in a bid to attract a younger, edgier set. The jury is still out, but the resort appears to be heading in the right direction. The slopes are especially popular with snowboarders, a sport that was invented here when bartender Jake Burton slapped a big plank on his feet and aimed down the mountain. Expert skiers should seek out Upper Middlebrook, a fine, twisting run off the summit.

WHERE TO STAY & DINE

Gourmands who find the drive back to a hotel after a pleasant dinner an irksome interference with the evening's magic will be happy in the Manchester area. With one notable exception, the area's best restaurants happen to be located at local inns and hotels, so you can enjoy a meal, then idle by a fireplace before working your way slowly back to your room. Most the inns listed below also offer meals to the public, although several require reservations. It's always best to call first.

✪ **Arlington Inn.** Route 7A (P.O. Box 369), Arlington, VT 05250. ☎ **802/375-6532** or 800/ 443-9442. 18 rms (some with showers only, one with detached bath). A/C. Summer, Christmas, Thanksgiving, Presidents and Memorial Day weekends $80–$160 double; foliage season $90–$185 double; late fall through spring $70–$150 double. All rates include breakfast.

This stout, cream-colored Greek Revival home, built in 1848 for a railroad baron, seems better suited to the Virginia countryside. But it anchors the village well here, set back from the road on a lawn bordered with sturdy maples. Inside, the inn boasts a similarly courtly feel, with unique wooden ceilings adorning the first floor rooms, and a tavern that borrows its atmosphere from an English hunt club.

Innkeepers Deborah and Mark Gagnon, Boston refugees who acquired the inn in 1994, have taken strides to improve the inn's regal decor. Room rates vary widely, but even the least expensive rooms are well-appointed with period reproductions. The quietest rooms are in the detached carriage house, which many guests specifically request. The inn is no-smoking.

The Gagnons recently purchased the equally handsome 1830 Federal-style house next door, and have converted this into five more guest rooms, all of which have TV and telephone, and three of which have wood-burning fireplaces.

Dining/Entertainment: Dinners, served in the main dining room, include native produce and meats when available. Dinner choices change frequently, but might include an appetizer of duck, wild mushroom and sun-dried cranberry strudel, followed by a grilled veal chop served on a bed of artichokes, shallots, and fresh herbs. Entrees are priced from $18 to $24.

Barrows House. Rt. 30, Dorset, VT 05251. ☎ **802/867-4455** or 800/639-1620. Fax 802/867-0132. 28 rms (1 with shower only). A/C. $185–$245 double, including breakfast and dinner. B&B rates also available. Discounts available in midwinter and midweek. AE, CB, DC, DISC, MC, V.

Within easy strolling distance of the village of Dorset stands this compound of eight early American buildings, set on nicely landscaped grounds studded with birches, firs, and maples. The main house was built in 1784, and it's been an inn since the early 1900s. Some of the guest rooms have gas or wood fireplaces, and all share a small, country-style common area in the main inn. The inn offers limited rooms for smokers, and only some rooms have telephones.

Dining/Entertainment: Enjoy a before-dinner drink in the casual and cozy tavern with the trompe l'oeil bookshelves. The main dining area is a happy marriage of classical and contemporary. Sit in either the traditional country inn room, or the more modern greenhouse addition. The cuisine is contemporary New England, with entrees like Atlantic salmon with a sun-dried tomato pesto cream, or pan-roasted chicken breast with roasted peppers, shiitake mushrooms, and artichoke hearts. Entrees range from $9.95 to $18.75.

Dorset Inn. Church and Main sts., Dorset, VT 05251. ☎ **802/867-5500.** Fax 802/867-5542. 31 rms. $150–$195 double, $225–$295 suite. Rates include breakfast and dinner. AE, MC, V.

Set in the center of genteel Dorset, this former stagecoach stop was built in 1796 and claims to be the oldest continuously operating inn in Vermont. With 31 rooms, the Dorset Inn is fairly large by Vermont standards, but far more intimate than comparably sized places. The carpeted guest rooms, some of which are in a well-crafted addition built in the 1940s, are furnished in an upscale country style, with a mix of reproductions and antiques including canopy and sleigh beds. (All but two rooms have air conditioning, and only the two suites have televisions and telephones.) This is a no-smoking inn.

Dining/Entertainment: Guests mingle in the common rooms, which are vintage Vermont, with creaky wood floors, marble fireplace hearths, and hunt scenes adorning the walls. The tavern is wonderfully casual and pubby, panelled in dark wood with a stamped tin ceiling. The dining room is a bit more formal; many men ask if they should wear a jacket and tie to dinner, but the inn encourages informality. The luncheon menu doesn't vary much from the dinner menu, and includes basics like hamburgers and grilled Black Angus sirloin, along with vegetarian specialties like spinach canneloni stuffed with artichoke hearts and ricotta. Entrees at lunch are $6.50 to $9; dinners range from $8.50 to $18.50.

✪ **1811 House.** Route 7A, Manchester Village, VT 05254. ☎ **802/362-1811** or 800/432-1811. 14 rms, including three cottage rms. A/C. $160–$200 double. Rates include full breakfast. AE, DISC, MC, V.

This historic Manchester Village home, the first part of which was built in the mid-1770s, started taking in guests in 1811 (hence the name). And it often seems that not much has changed here in the intervening centuries. The warrenlike downstairs common rooms are rich with history—the pine floors are uneven, the doors out of true, and everything is painted in earthy, colonial tones. Even the exterior is painted a pheasant-brown color. The antique furniture recreates the feel of the house during the Federal period, and a delightful English-style pub lies off the entryway, complete with tankards hanging from the beams. For aficionados of early American culture, this is without question the place to be. This is a bed-and-breakfast; no evening meals are served.

The Equinox. Route 7A (P.O. Box 46), Manchester Village, VT 05245. ☎ **802/362-4700** or 800/362-4747. Fax 802/362-1595. 180 guest rms (8 with shower only). A/C TV TEL. $159–$289 double; $369–$549 suite. AE, DC, DISC, MC, V.

A blue-blood favorite, The Equinox dominates Manchester Village with its gleaming white clapboard and trim rows of columns. And make no mistake, its historic lineage notwithstanding (it was established in 1769), this is a full-blown resort with sports facilities, two dining rooms, and all the in-room amenities. As is fitting for its faux-Anglo charm, there's a even a British school of falconry affiliated with the inn that offers introductory classes at princely fees ($65 per person for a 45-minute introductory lesson).

Guest rooms, which were extensively renovated in 1991, are by and large decorated similarly in a country pine motif. The suites are a bit richer hued. Room prices vary widely based on size, but there's really not all that much difference between the largest and smallest rooms.

Next door is the grand Charles Orvis Inn, an 1812 home renovated by The Equinox in 1995. It offers nine elegantly appointed suites for $649 to $888 per night, including breakfast. Early reports suggest that this annex, while quite pleasant, is more than slightly overpriced.

Dining/Entertainment: Choose the dining room to fit your mood: There's the continental elegance of The Colonnade, where men are requested to wear jackets at dinner, or the more relaxed, clubby comfort of Marsh's Tavern.

Facilities: Golf course, indoor and outdoor pools, and a fitness room.

Inn at Ormsby Hill. Route 7A (near Hildene, south of Manchester Village), Manchester Center, VT 05255. ☎ **802/362-1163** or 800/670-2841. Fax 802/362-5176. 10 rms. A/C. $115–$205 double. Rates include full breakfast. Discounts midweek and off-season. AE, MC, V. Closed briefly in Apr.

Chris and Ted Sprague put themselves on the culinary and innkeeping map after opening the delightful Newcastle Inn in coastal Maine some years ago. Well, they're at it again. In September 1995 they sold the Newcastle, bought this historic inn, doubled the number of guest rooms, and polished the place to an lustrous splendor. The oldest part of the inn dates to 1764 (Ethan Allen was said to have hidden here), with a harmonious addition put on by Edward Isham, a prominent 19th-century Chicago attorney. His addition to the back of the house, designed to look like the interior of a steamship cutting upriver, now houses the dining room and offers guests wonderful morning views as they enjoy Chris's otherworldly breakfasts.

Guest rooms vary in size and style. Among the best are the Taft Room, with its vaulted wood ceiling, and the first-floor library, with many of Isham's books still lining the shelves. The newer rooms, in what used to be a dormitory when the inn housed a home for underprivileged boys, are somewhat smaller, but still tastefully done. All newer rooms feature whirlpools and gas fireplaces.

Dining/Entertainment: Chris offers guests a light supper upon arrival on Friday nights (at $15 per couple), and an optional four-course dinner Saturday night ($60 for two). Go with the dinner. You won't be disappointed.

The Reluctant Panther. West Rd. (P.O. Box 678), Manchester Village, VT 05254. ☎ **802/ 362-2568** or 800/822-2331. Fax 802/362-2586. 16 rms (some with showers only). A/C TV TEL. $165–$275 double, $210–$235 double during foliage season and Christmas week. Rates include breakfast and dinner. No children under 14. AE, MC, V.

The Reluctant Panther, located a short walk from the Equinox, is is easy to spot: It's painted a pale eggplant color and has faded yellow shutters, making it stand out in this staid village of white clapboard. It's run with couples in mind. This 1850s home is elegantly furnished throughout (as are guest rooms in an adjacent building, built in 1910), and features nice touches, including goose-down duvets and a split of wine in every room. Ten of the rooms have fireplaces, and one, the Mark Skinner suite, even features a wood-burning fireplace and a double Jacuzzi in the bathroom. Smoking is permitted in the lounge only.

Dining/Entertainment: As nice as the inn is, the Reluctant Panther is perhaps better known locally for its excellent dining. The first-floor dining room, decorated with floral prints, achieves the feat of being intimate without feeling crowded. (There's also a greenhouse with slate floor, which is very pleasant in summer.) The cuisine is European, prepared by Swiss-German chef Robert Bachofen, the former director of food and beverage at the Plaza Hotel in New York. The menu changes frequently, but expect entrees like grilled veal chops with ragout of shiitake and white mushrooms, or tuna steak with a minted cilantro-walnut salsa. Entree prices range from $18.95 to $24.95.

West Mountain Inn. River Road, Arlington, VT 05250. ☎ **802/375-6516.** Fax 802/ 375-6553. 18 rms (2 with shower only). Spring weekends, summer, and winter $152–$184 double; foliage season $172–$204 double; spring midweek $139 double. All rates include breakfast and dinner. AE, DISC, MC, V.

The West Mountain Inn is a handsome, rambling, white-clapboard building dating back a century-and-a-half. Sitting atop a steep, grassy bluff at the end of a dirt road one-half mile from the center of Arlington, it's a perfect place for travelers seeking sanctuary from the hectic modern age. The guest rooms, named after famous Vermonters, are nicely furnished with country and Victorian reproductions. The rooms vary widely in size and shape, but even the smallest has a surplus of charm and character. If the weather is uncharacteristically steamy, ask for one of the rooms on the top floor, which is air-conditioned. No smoking.

Dining/Entertainment: The inviting dining room is furnished in a hearty rather than cloying country style, with maple floors, pine walls, and green-and-white plaid tableclothes. Dinners include regional fare prepared and served with flair. Typical entrees are roasted quail with an orange-kiwi glaze, and steak au poive in a mushroom merlot demi. Dinner for nonguests is by reservation only, and is $30 fixed price.

WHERE TO DINE

✪ **Chantecleer.** Route 7A, 3¹/₂ miles north of Manchester Center. ☎ **802/362-1616.** Reservations recommended. Main courses $18.75–$27.50. Wed–Mon 6–9:30pm. Closed Mon in winter and for 2–3 weeks in Nov and Apr. CONTINENTAL.

If you like superbly prepared continental fare but are put off by the stuffiness of high-brow Euro-wannabe restaurants, this is the place. Rustic elegance is the best description for the dining experience in this century-old dairy barn. The oddly slick exterior, which looks as if it could house a Ponderosa-style chain restaurant, doesn't offer a clue to just how pleasantly romantic the interior is. Heavy beams define the soaring space overhead, the walls are appropriately of barnboard, and the small bar is crafted of a slab of pine. A rooster motif predominates (predictably enough, since chantecleer is French for rooster), fresh flowers decorate the tables, and, when the weather's right, a fire blazes in the arched fieldstone fireplace. Swiss-born chef Michel Baumann, who's owned and operated the inn since 1981, changes his menu every three weeks, but his selections might feature entrees such as veal sweetbreads in a Madeira morel sauce, grilled prime veal chop, or frog legs Provençal. Arrive expecting an excellent meal; you won't go away disappointed.

3 Brattleboro & the Southern Green Mountains

It's a misty late summer morning when you rouse your adventurous self (the one who's not on speaking terms with your sleeping-in self) and set off to a nearby trailhead outside the village of Townshend. You make your way through this sleepy village of white clapboard, where only the pickup trucks are making their rounds, and park near the base of Bald Mountain. A mild tang is in the air even though it's August, and the ascent up the rocky trail feels good. After 45 minutes you come upon a ledge with a view to the east, where successive ridges fade from green to blue to gray then go. Directly below, clouds blanket the valley, as if it's packed with gauze. After a few minutes it's time to head back, knowing that a delicious breakfast awaits in town.

The southern Green Mountains are New England writ large. If you've developed a preconception of what New England is but haven't ever visited here, this is probably the place you're thinking of.

The hills and valleys around the bustling town of Brattleboro, in Vermont's southeast corner, contain some of the state's best-hidden natural treasures. Travel along the main valley floors—along the West or the Connecticut rivers, or on Route 100—tends to be fast and quick. To really soak up the region's flavor, turn off the main roads and wander up and over rolling ridges, and into narrow folds in the mountains that hide peaceful villages. If it suddenly seems to you that the landscape hasn't changed all that much in the past two centuries, well, you're right. It hasn't.

This region is well known for its pristine and historic villages. You'll stumble across them as you explore—you can't help but find them. And no matter how many other people have found them before you, there's almost always a sense that these are your own private discoveries.

A good strategy is to stop for a spell in Brattleboro to stock up on supplies or sample some local music. Then set off for the southern Green Mountains, settle into a remote inn, and continue your explorations by foot, bike, or canoe. In winter, you can plumb the snowy white hills by cross-country ski or snowshoe.

The single best source of regional travel information on the region is the state **visitors' center** (☎ **802/254-4593**) on I-91 in Guilford, south of Brattleboro.

BRATTLEBORO

Set in a scenic river valley, Brattleboro is not only a good spot for last-minute provisioning, but also has a funky, slightly dated charm that's part 1940's, part 1970's. The rough brick texture of this compact, hilly city has aged nicely, its flavor only enhanced with its adoption by "feral hippies" (as a friend of mine calls them), who live in and around town and operate many of the best local enterprises.

While Brattleboro is very much part of the 20th century, its heritage runs much deeper. In fact, Brattleboro was Vermont's first permanent settlement. (The first actual settlement, which was short-lived, was at Isle La Motte on Lake Champlain in 1666.) Soldiers protecting the Massachusetts town of Northfield built an outpost here in 1724 at Fort Dummer, about a mile and a half south of the current downtown. The site of the fort is now a small state park. In later years, Brattleboro became a center of trade and manufacturing, and was the home of the Estey Organ Co., which once supplied countless home organs carved in an ornate Victorian style to families across the nation.

Brattleboro remains the commercial hub of the southeast Vermont, located at the junction of I-89, Routes 5 and 9, and the Connecticut River. It's also the most convenient jumping off point for those arriving from the south via the interstate.

ESSENTIALS

GETTING THERE   From the north or south, Brattleboro is easily accessible via Exit 1 or 2 on I-91. From the east or west, Brattleboro is most easily reached via Route 9.

VISITOR INFORMATION   The **Brattleboro Chamber of Commerce,** 180 Main St., Brattleboro, VT 05301 (☎ 802/254-4565), next to the Dunkin Donuts, dispenses travel information year-round between 8am and 5pm weekdays.

EXPLORING THE TOWN

Here's an easy strategy for exploring Brattleboro: Park. Walk.

The commercially vibrant downtown is blessedly compact, and strolling around on foot is the best way to appreciate its very human scale and handsome commercial architecture. Even if you're en route to a destination to the north, it's well worth a stop for a bite to eat and some light shopping.

A number of unique enterprises fill downtown storefronts. Among those worth checking out are **Tom and Sally's Handmade Chocolates,** 55 Eliot St. (☎ 802/258-3065), where you can pick up freshly made hand-crafted chocolates (don't overlook the marked-down bags of broken pieces), and **Sam's Army & Navy Dept. Store,** at 74 Main St. (☎ 802/254-2933), a sprawling emporium that's filled to the rafters with durable clothing and camping and hunting supplies. Sam's offers free freshly popped popcorn while you browse.

Also enjoyable for kids and curious adults is the **Brattleboro Museum & Art Center** (☎ 802/257-0124) at the Union Railroad Station. Founded in 1972, the center offers wonderful exhibits highlighting the history of the town and the Connecticut River Valley, along with paintings and sculpture by artists of local and international repute. Call about lectures, which in the past have included discourses by renown local summer guy John Kenneth Galbraith. The museum is open daily except Mondays from 12 noon to 6 pm from mid-May through October. It's located downtown near the bridge to New Hampshire. Admission is $2 for adults, $1 for seniors and college students, free for children under 18.

North of town on Route 5, where the highway crosses the West River (a Connecticut River tributary), you can sign up for a guided river tour on the **Belle of**

Brattleboro (☎ 802/254-1263). This sturdy, wood-decked river boat, which may recall the African Queen among incurable romantics or those with poor vision, seats about 50 at picnic table–style seating under a yellow canopy. A variety of cruises is offered, but all offer a glimpse of Brattleboro's wildlife and small-town allure from the languid West and Connecticut Rivers. Tours run frequently in summer, and cost $7 for adults and $4 for children; there's an additional fee for cruises featuring meals or on-board entertainment.

OUTDOOR PURSUITS

A soaring aerial view of Brattleboro might be had by hiking Wantastiquet Mountain, which is just across the Connecticut River in New Hampshire. You can drive to the trailhead, but somehow it's more adventurous to walk from downtown (figure on a round trip of about three hours). To reach the base of the "mountain" (a term that's just slightly grandiose), cross the river on the two green steel bridges, then turn left on the first dirt road; go ²/₁₀ of a mile to a parking area on your right. The trail begins here; trekkers ascend via a carriage road (stick to the main trail and avoid the side trails) that winds about 2 miles through forest and past open ledges to the summit, which is marked by a monument dating from 1908. From here, you'll be rewarded with sweeping views of the river, the town, and the landscape beyond. Retrace your steps back to town or your car.

Canoeists stuck in Vermont without their canoe will find salvation at **Connecticut River Safari** (☎ 802/257-5008 or 802/254-3908) where Route 5 spans the West River north of town. Located in a shady riverside glen, this is a fine spot to rent a canoe or kayak to poke around for a couple of hours ($10 for two people), a half day ($15), or a full day ($20). Explore locally, or arrange for a shuttle upriver or down. The owners are exceedingly helpful about providing information and maps to keep you on track. Among the best areas for snooping, especially for bird-watchers, are the marshy areas along the lower West River and a detour off the Connecticut River locally called "The Everglades." Pack a lunch and make a day of it.

The Brattleboro area is equally well suited for exploring by bike. Rentals and good advice on day trip destinations are both available at the **Brattleboro Bicycle Shop,** at 178 Main St. (☎ 802/254-8644 or 800/272-8245). Rentals are $20 per day.

WHERE TO STAY

Naulakha. Landmark Trust, 28 Birge St., Brattleboro, VT 05301. ☎ **802/254-6868.** 1 4-bedroom house; accommodates up to 8 people. Apr–Oct $850–$1,850 per week; Nov–Mar $1,125–$1,150 per week. Rates are estimated; billing is in English pounds. MC, V.

This unique property, owned and managed by the British-based Landmark Trust, is available for rent only by the week during the peak season. (It can be obtained for shorter stays, with a minimum of three nights, in winter.) What makes this forthright, two-story shingled home in the hills outside of Brattleboro so extraordinary is its rich literary heritage. The home was built for British writer Rudyard Kipling, who lived here for several years in the mid-1890s while working on *The Jungle Book* and *Captains Courageous.* Kipling never quite fit in in rural Vermont. A local newspaper reported, "Neighbors say he is strange; never carries money, wears shabby clothes and often says Begad; drives shaggy horses and plays with the baby." He left somewhat abruptly, selling the home with much of its furniture in place.

It's a superb place to unwind in summer, strolling the 55-acre grounds, admiring the views from the porches, or just knocking a ball around on Kipling's tennis court. Even during the prime summer season, the rate works out to just $66 per night per room . . . providing you can find three compatible companions with whom to share your vacation.

Latchis Hotel. 50 Main St., Brattleboro, VT 05301. ☎ **802/254-6300.** Fax 802/254-6304. 30 rms. A/C TV TEL. $49–$98 double. AE, MC, V.

This wonderful downtown hotel fairly leaps out in Victorian-brick Brattleboro. Built in 1938 in an understated art deco style (it's one of only two genuinely art deco buildings in Vermont), the Latchis was once the cornerstone for a small chain of hotels and theaters. It no longer has its own orchestra or commanding dining room (although the theater remains), but it's still owned by the Latchis family and has an authentic if slightly dated flair.

Guests enter through a narrow lobby decorated with subtle art deco detailing, then walk or ride the elevator to guest rooms on the three upstairs floors. The colorful hallways are reminiscent of a film noir piece—you can't but wonder what's going on behind all the doors. For the most part, the guest rooms are comfortable, not luxurious, with simple maple furniture and old-time radiators that keep the place toasty in winter. From the hotel, it's easy to explore town on foot, or you can wander the first floor hallways to take in a first-run movie at the Latchis Theatre or quaff a pint at the Windham Brewery (see below).

40 Putney Rd. 40 Putney Rd., Brattleboro, VT 05301. ☎ **802/254-6268** or 800/941-2413. Fax 802/258-2673. 4 rms. A/C TEL. $80–$95 double. Rates include breakfast. AE, DISC, MC, V.

This stately home of white brick and gray slate sits off Route 5 at the northern edge of downtown Brattleboro. Built in the early 1930s as a home for the superintendent of the nearby Brattleboro Retreat, this small French chateau–style mansion was converted to a B&B in 1991 and now offers Brattleboro's most elegant accommodations. The common rooms have hardwood floors and dark wood detailing, which nicely offsets the pale muted colors of the walls. Wingback chairs and a bowback sofa face the fireplace; there's always a decanter of port set out for guests. Innkeepers Joan and Pete Broderick are gracious hosts, offering complimentary juices in an upstairs refrigerators, and the *New York Times* and *Boston Globe* on Sundays.

Guest rooms are well-appointed with country modern furnishings, including hooked and chenille rugs. The best of the four rooms is the two-room suite, which features built-in bureaus and a large tiled bathroom. Guests are welcome to enjoy the landscaped backyard along the West River, or stroll into town on a riverside path. Breakfasts are at the gourmet end of the scale, and are served on the pleasant backyard patio in summer. No smoking.

WHERE TO DINE

⑤ Common Ground. 25 Eliot St., Brattleboro. ☎ **802/257-0855.** Reservations not accepted. Lunch $2.25–$7.50; dinner $3–$7. No credit cards. Mon and Wed–Thurs 11:30am–8pm, Fri–Sat 11:30am–9pm, Sun 10:30am–2pm and 5:30–9pm. WHOLE FOODS.

The Common Ground, which opened two years after the Woodstock Music Festival, is now a well-established culinary landmark occupying a funky, hectic space on the second floor of a downtown building. The tone is set walking up the stairway, where business cards tout trauma touch therapy, astrological readings, and meditation and movement services. At the top of the stairs, diners choose from a well-worn interior space, or a pleasant greenhouse addition. The Common Ground is operated as a worker-owned cooperative, and service is cordial if not always brisk.

There's little variation be ween the lunch and dinner menu; both draw heavily from local and organic ingredients. A meal might include grilled tofu with tahini, brown rice with tamari ginger sauce, or a marinated sea vegetable salad. Or stick with the basics: a bowl of brown rice, beans, and a tortilla costs just $2.50. Sandwiches include tempeh reuben, Vermont cheddar, and the classic peanut butter and jelly (made with organic Valencia peanut butter and cider jelly and served on wholewheat bread). There's often live entertainment in the evenings.

Curtis Bar-B-Q. Route 5, Putney. ☎ **802/387-5474.** No credit cards. Wed–Sun 10am–dark. Closed Nov–spring. BARBEQUE.

Just uphill from Exit 4 off I-91 (about nine miles north of Brattleboro) you suddenly smell the delicious aroma of barbecue sizzling over open pits. Do not pass this place by, because you will change your mind later and waste a lot of time and gasoline back-tracking. After all, this is the best barbecue in Vermont, and possibly in New England.

This classic roadside food joint, situated on a scruffy lot next to a Mobil station, has a heap of charm despite itself. (The five signs commanding "All dogs must be leashed" set a strangely appropriate mood for dining here.) This self-serve restaurant consists of two blue school buses and a tin-roofed cooking shed; guests take their booty to a smattering of picnic tables scattered about the lot. Place your order, grab a seat, dig in, and enjoy.

La Sirena. 39 Main St., Brattleboro. ☎ **802/257-5234.** Reservations recommended on weekends. Main courses $5.95–$11.50. MC, V. Tues–Sat 5–8:30pm, Sun 3–8:30pm. Also open for lunch Tues and Fri starting at 11:30am. MEXICAN.

Good, simple, filling Mexican fare awaits at this understated downtown restaurant. Located in a storefront across from the Latchis Theatre, La Sirena is lightly decorated in a south-of-the-border motif (no piñatas) in soft pastel colors. It can be a bit noisy when it's crowded (especially on weekends), but you're likely to register few complaints about the food, which runs toward favorites like tacos, burritos, tostadas, and chimichangas. The menu isn't extensive, but the meals are always well prepared and come with unlimited tortilla chips and a zesty salsa.

Latchis Grille & Windham Brewery. 6 Flat St., Brattleboro. ☎ **802/254-4747.** Reservations for parties of 6 or more only. Café items $6–$10; main courses $12.95–$18.95. AE, MC, V. Tues–Sun 5–9pm; also open Sat–Sun and daily in summer 11:30am–3pm. INTERNATIONAL.

The Latchis Grille is situated beneath the Latchis Theatre and Latchis Hotel. And it's well worth venturing downstairs, both for the international flair of the food and to sample the excellent homemade ales, stouts, and lagers made on-site by the Windham Brewery. The Latchis Grille, while subterranean, is comfortably decorated with paintings and old lithographs. The rectangular dining room has soft lighting and upbeat jazz; enclosed at one end is an informal, tile-floored bar great for quaffing the local stuff—including a surprisingly delicate raspberry brown ale. There's also Guinness on tap (a reliable sign of a good bar), and homemade draft root beer.

Few will fail to find menu items that appeal. Appetizers range from crab and shrimp over polenta to roasted quail to Tibetan momos (steamed lamb and pork dumplings). Entrees include grilled pork chops served with an onion and cranberry confit, grilled filet mignon flamed in bourbon, and fresh fettucine with artichokes, proscuitto, mushrooms, spinach, and feta. The quality of the meals can be spotty at times, but when the chef hits it right, it's done very well indeed.

Peter Havens. 32 Elliot, Brattleboro. ☎ **802/257-3333.** Reservations strongly recommended. Main courses $15–$21. MC, V. Tues–Sat 6–9pm. REGIONAL/AMERICAN.

Peter Havens has been serving up the most consistently reliable fine dining in Brattleboro since it opened in 1989. Situated downtown in an upscale, contemporary building, Peter Havens doesn't offer a creative menu. You won't find towering appetizers that defy architectural principles, or wheelbarrow-loads of this year's trendy herb in your meal, but you will get choice ingredients served with panache and flair. The restaurant has but a handful of tables, so make a reservation if you have your heart set on dining here.

All appetizers are priced at $6.50 (except for soup at $4), and range from paté to gravlax to a smoked filet of lemon-peppered trout. Fewer than 10 entrees are on the menu, but among these you'll find a grilled filet mignon served with a green peppercorn bourbon sauce, and duck breast roasted with a black currant and port sauce. For seafood, there's scallops with roasted peppers and crabmeat in a light cream sauce, and salmon with a delicately sweet Zinfandel and shallot sauce. Wines are limited, but the selection is decent.

WILMINGTON REGION

Set high in the hills on the winding mountain highway midway between Bennington and Brattleboro, Wilmington has managed to retain its charm as an attractive crossroads village despite its location on two busy roads. The town draws its share of tourists (especially from New York and New Jersey) but still has the feel of a gracious mountain village.

From Wilmington, the ski resorts of Haystack and Mt. Snow are easily accessible to the north via Route 100, which is brisk, busy, and close to impassable on sunny weekends in early October. Heading north, you'll first pass through West Dover, a very attractive, classical New England town with a prominent steeple and acres of white clapboard.

Between West Dover and Mt. Snow, it becomes increasingly evident that developers and entrepreneurs discovered the area in the years following the founding of Mt. Snow in 1954. Some regard this stretch of highway as a monument to lack of planning. While the development isn't dense (this is no North Conway, N.H.), the buildings represent a not-entirely-savory melange of architectural styles, the most prominent of which is Tyrolean Chicken Coop Nightmare. Many of these buildings began their lives as ski lodges and have since been reincarnated as boutiques, inns, and restaurants. The silver lining is this: The unsightly development prompted Vermont to later pass a progressive and restrictive environmental law, which has saved many other areas from degradation.

Much of the development along Route 100 ceases just north of Mt. Snow. Also, remember that you're not restricted to Route 100, no matter what the locals tell you. The area is packed with smaller roads, both paved and dirt, that make for excellent exploring.

ESSENTIALS

GETTING THERE   Wilmington is located at the juncture of Routes 9 and 100. Route 9 offers the most direct access from both Bennington and Brattleboro. The Mt. Snow area is located north of Wilmington on Route 100.

VISITOR INFORMATION   The **Mt. Snow/Haystack Region Chamber of Commerce,** Main Street, P.O. Box 3, Wilmington, VT 05363 (☎ **802/464-8092**), maintains an information booth May through September at the intersection of Route 9 and Route 100. The **Mt. Snow Lodging Bureau and Vacation Service** (☎ **800/ 245-7669**) can assist with booking rooms in the area.

THE MARLBORO MUSIC FESTIVAL

The renowned Marlboro Music Festival offers classical concerts performed by highly talented student musicians on weekends from July through mid-August in the agreeable town of Marlboro, east of Wilmington on Route 9. Concerts take place in the

700-seat auditorium at Marlboro College, and advance ticket purchases are strongly recommended. Call or write for a schedule and ticket forms. Between September and June contact the festival's winter office at **Marlboro Music,** 135 S. 18th St., Philadelphia, PA 19103 (☎ **215/569-4690**). In summer, write **Marlboro Music,** Marlboro, VT 05344, or call the box office (☎ **802/254-2394**).

WHAT TO SEE & DO

After snooping around the village of Wilmington, strike south for the historic village of Whitingham, birthplace of Mormon prophet Brigham Young (1801–77). The son of an impoverished basket maker, Young continued the work of Mormon pioneer Joseph Smith after Smith was murdered by a mob in Illinois in 1844. Young brought his followers to Utah, where he founded Salt Lake City. Enjoy the village's historic character, then strike for the top of nearby Town Hill, which offers fine views and a marker commemorating Young.

To the west of Wilmington is the 5,060-acre George Aiken Wilderness Area, one of six such designated wildernesses in the Green Mountain National Forest. Named after a former Vermont senator, the Aiken Wilderness is unique in that no trails have been cut—it's a haven for hearty bushwhackers who don't mind slogging through wetlands in search of solitude or brook trout. A trail does run along the wilderness's eastern border; it's accessible via Forest Road 74, which leaves southward from Route 9 west of Wilmington 8.4 miles. More information can be obtained from the **Green Mountain National Forest's headquarters** in Rutland (☎ **802/773-0300**).

Less rugged adventures might be had at the **Mt. Snow Country Club** (☎ **802/ 464-3333**), which offers intensive golf classes each summer. The school has a national reputation for excellence, and weekend and mid-week classes are offered from late spring through fall on its 18-hole championship golf course set amid dramatic mountain scenery.

For winter travelers, the Mt. Snow area offers several excellent cross-country ski centers. **Timber Creek Cross Country Touring Center** (☎ **802/464-0999**) in West Dover near the Mt. Snow access road is a popular area with beginners and holds snow nicely thanks to its high elevation. The **Hermitage Ski Touring Center** (☎ **802/464-3511**) attracts more advanced skiers to its varied terrain and 30 miles of trails. The **White House Ski Touring Center** (☎ **802/464-0999**), at the inn by the same name on Route 100, offers the easiest access to the Vermont woods and a good range of terrain. And the **Sitzmark ski center** (☎ **802/464-3384**) maintains 24 miles of cross-county trail that covers terrain with 550 feet of elevation gain.

Mountain Biking

Mt. Snow was one of the first resorts to foresee the growing appeal of mountain biking, and the region remains one of the leading destinations for those whose vehicle of choice has knobby tires. Mt. Snow established the first mountain bike school in the country, and it remains one of the best places to be formally introduced to the sport.

The **Mountain Bike Center** (☎ **800/245-7669**) at the base of the mountain offers equipment rentals, maps, and advice.

Independent mountain bikers can also explore some 140 miles of trail and abandoned road that lace the region. For a small fee, you can take your bike to the mountaintop by chairlift and coast your way down along marked trails, or earn the ride by pumping out the vertical rise to the top. Fanning out from the mountain are numerous abandoned town roads that make for less challenging but no less pleasant excursions.

Skiing

Mt. Snow/Haystack. Mt. Snow, VT 05356. ☎ **802/464-3333,** or 800/245-7669 for lodging. Vertical drop: 1,700 feet. Lifts: 21 (1 high speed), 3 surface lifts. Skiable acreage: 650. Lift tickets: $47 weekends, $42 weekdays.

These two former ski resorts, once competitors, are now both owned by American Skiing Company, which owns numerous other New England resorts. Bear in mind that the figures above are for the combined ski areas—neither one is all that big. The main mountain is noted for its widely cut runs, and is an excellent destination for intermediates and advanced intermediates. Advanced skiers head to the North Face, which is its own little world. Because it's the most southerly of the Vermont ski areas and the closest to the Boston–New York megalopolis, it can become quite crowded at times. Haystack, which is 10 miles distant by car (it's much closer if you're a crow) is a classic older New England ski mountain, with challenging, narrow runs. Lift lines are typically much shorter at Haystack.

Mt. Snow's village is attractively arrayed along the base of the mountain. The most imposing structure is the balconied hotel overlooking a small pond, but the overall character is shaped more by the unobtrusive smaller lodges and homes. While once famed for its groovy singles scene, Mt. Snow's post-skiing activities today tend to center around families and downtime in the condo. With its conscientious landscaping and agreeable location, Mt. Snow is among the most aesthetically appealing New England ski areas in summer, a season when few resorts lavish much attention on their facilities.

WHERE TO STAY

Inn at Sawmill Farm. Route 100 (P.O. Box 367), West Dover, VT 05356. ☎ **802/464-8131.** Fax 802/464-1130. 21 rms. A/C. $340–$400 double. Rates include breakfast and dinner. AE, MC, V. Closed last week of Apr and first week of May.

"Interior designers say you can't mix plaid with floral," says innkeeper Rodney Williams as he walks through his barn-turned-common room at Sawmill Farm. "But this works," he says, indicating the bright floral upholstered couch on the bold tartan carpet. Well, whatever. But rest assured, the fashion police won't find anything else to fault at this very elegant, very cordial, and very expensive inn, which is part of the exclusive Relais & Chateaux chain. Many guests book rooms just to be close to the restaurant (see "Where to Dine," below), which serves memorable meals.

The rooms in this old farmhouse, parts of which date back to 1797, are each different, but all share a similar contemporary country styling and colonial reproduction furniture. The rooms are generally spacious; among the best are Cider House #2, with its rustic beams and oversized canopy bed, and the Woodshed, a quiet cottage with a beautiful brick fireplace and a cozy loft. After 6pm, men are requested to wear jackets in all public areas of the inn.

Facilities: Guests have the run of the 28-acre grounds, set near the quintessential New England village of West Dover, and can fish for rainbow trout in the two ponds or lounge by the swimming pool.

Trail's End. 5 Trail's End Lane ($^1/_2$ mile off Route 100 between Haystack and Mt. Snow), Wilmington, VT 05363. ☎ **802/464-2727.** 15 rms (2 with shower only). Summer $90–$140 double, fall $100–$160 double, winter $110–$170 double. Rates include full breakfast. AE, MC, V. Closed Easter to late May.

When the current innkeepers bought Trail's End in 1985, it was a rough ski lodge 30 years old, with bunk beds nailed into the walls. Since acquiring it, Bill and Mary Kilburn have carved out an inviting, friendly spot that attracts repeat visitors who come for the instant camaraderie with other guests and their gregarious hosts.

Trail's End's carpeted guest rooms are spotlessly clean, styled in a light country fashion with pine and wicker furniture. But few guests seem to spend much time in their rooms. They congregate around the 22-foot stone fireplace in the main common room, in the stone-floored library and game room, or in the informal second-floor loft—or they hang out in the kitchen with Bill as he obsessively polishes his gleaming stove. At breakfast, the congregating continues around three massive round tables. Introverts, it should go without saying, will not be happy here. Others will.

Facilities: In summer, guests enjoy the heated outdoor pool and a clay tennis court set amid 28 acres of forest owned by the inn.

White House of Wilmington. Route 9, Wilmington, VT 05363. ☎ **802/464-2135** or 800/541-2135. 23 rms. $108–$178 double. Rates include full breakfast. Fireplace rms are $30 less in summer. AE, MC, V.

The White House of Wilmington, a fanciful Greek Revival–style home with two prominent porticos (built in 1915 by a wealthy lumber baron), sits impressively on the crest of an open hill just east of Wilmington. The interior is spacious and open, with hardwood floors, arched doorways, and superb detailing throughout. Formal without being stuffy, the inn has an especially appealing bar on its enclosed porch, which can't be beat as a spot to sip something soothing while watching the sun sink over the Vermont hills.

Dining/Entertainment: The inn's restaurant is well regarded for its continental cuisine, served in an attractive dining room with hardwood floors, dark wood trim, pink tableclothes, and a intricate fireplace mantel. Entrees include duck stuffed with walnuts, apples, and grapes (the chef's specialty); veal piccatta; and filet mignon au poivre.

Facilities: The inn boasts an attractive swimming pool, tennis courts, and, for winter travelers, 27 miles of groomed cross-country ski trails. The inn also accommodates snowmobilers.

WHERE TO DINE

✪ **Inn at Sawmill Farm.** Route 100, West Dover. ☎ **802/464-8131.** Reservations strongly recommended. Men requested to wear jackets. Main courses $27–$32. AE, MC, V. Daily 6–9:30pm. Closed the last week of Apr–first week of May. CONTINENTAL.

Let's talk wine. About 36,000 bottles of wine. That's what's lurking in the inn's custom-made wine cellar, and what garnered it a coveted "Grand Award" from Wine Spectator magazine.

But that's the least of the reasons diners flock here. The food is deftly prepared by innkeeper/chef Brill Williams (son of innkeepers Ione and Rodney Williams), with entrees ranging from pan-seared salmon in saffron sauce to breast of pheasant with a forestiere sauce. For a little foreign intrigue, you might opt for the sautéed breast of chicken, served with a surprisingly delicate Indonesian curry sauce and caramelized banana.

The atmosphere is near perfect. While the garden dining room is less posh than the popular formal dining room (housed in a portion of an old barn), the soft tones, wide pine planks in the floors, and live piano music filling the air lend the whole dining room a soft and romantic feel. Beautiful silverware and glassware accent the mood. The service is superb, although the slavish attention and overall formality instantly makes informal folks somewhat edgy.

Le Petit Chef. Route 100, Wilmington. ☎ **802/464-8437.** Reservations recommended. Main courses $15–$25 (mostly $19–$22). AE, MC, V. Wed–Thurs and Sun–Mon 6–9pm, Fri–Sat 6–10pm. FRENCH.

Situated in an old Cape Cod–style house on Route 100, Le Petit Chef has attracted legions of satisfied customers who flock here to sample Betty Hillman's superb and creative cooking. The interior has been updated and modernized at the expense of some character, and the service can be spotty at times, but the quality of the food typically overcomes these shortcomings. By all means, start with the signature "Bird's Nest," an innovative mélange of shiitake mushrooms and onions cooked in a cream sauce and served in a basket of deep-fried potato. The main courses are equally succulent, with selections like a filet of salmon baked in a horseradish crust, loin of venison sautéed and served with sun-dried cherry sauce, and spicy shrimp sauteed with leeks and peppers and served on crispy noodles.

Skyline Restaurant. Route 9, Hogback Mt., Marlboro. ☎ **802/464-3536.** Reservations recommended for window seats. Lunch $4.95–$16.25 (most $5–$8); dinner $10.95–$16.95. Daily 7:30am–9pm (until 8pm in winter). AE, DC, DISC, MC, V.

The Skyline is a classic knotty-pine, stone-fireplace, tourist-stop restaurant atop a 2,350-foot ridge between Brattleboro and Wilmington. It's the sort of place that feels like it hasn't changed a whit since it opened in 1950—and it really hasn't, except that one young waitress was sporting a nose ring on my last visit. The restaurant claims a 100-mile southerly view through its massive plate-glass window; the maps on the paper placemats help you identify the mountains in sight, from Grand Monadnock in New Hampshire to the Berkshires in Massachusetts.

One problem: The restaurant is often in the clouds, which knocks the view down to 100 feet or so. ("Then I'm your view," the waitresses tell customers.) The menu offers basic New England fare (waffles for breakfast, club sandwiches for lunch, baked sugar-cured ham for dinner) at reasonable prices. Opt for the rich and tasty Indian pudding for dessert.

NEWFANE & TOWNSHEND

For many travelers, these two villages about five miles apart on Route 30 are the epitome of Vermont. Both are set deeply within the serpentine West River Valley, and both are built around open town greens. Both towns consist of impressive white clapboard homes and public buildings that share the grace and scale of the surrounding homes. Both towns boast striking examples of early American architecture, notably Greek Revival.

Don't bother looking for strip malls, McDonald's, or garish video outlets hereabouts. Newfane and Townshend feel as if they've been idled on a sidetrack for decades while the rest of American society steamed blithely ahead. That's not to say these villages have the somber feel of a mausoleum. On recent visits in autumn, a swarm of teenagers was skateboarding off the steps of the courthouse in Newfane, and a lively basketball game was underway at the edge of the green in Townshend. There's life here.

For visitors, inactivity is often the activity of choice. Guests find an inn or lodge that suits their temperament, then spend the days strolling the towns, undertaking aimless backroad driving tours, soaking in a mountain stream, or striking off on foot for one of the rounded, wooded peaks that overlook villages and valleys.

ESSENTIALS

GETTING THERE Newfane and Townshend are located on Route 30 northwest of Brattleboro. The nearest interstate access is off Exit 3 from I-91.

VISITOR INFORMATION There's no formal information center serving these towns. Brochures are available at the state **visitors' center** (☎ **802/254-4593**) on

I-91 in Guilford, south of Brattleboro. Visitors might also try the Townshend Country Store for local advice.

EXPLORING THE AREA

Newfane was originally founded on a hill a few miles away in 1774; in 1825 it was moved down to the valley floor. Some of the original buildings were dismantled and rebuilt, but most date from the early- to mid-19th century. The National Historic District is comprised of some 60 buildings around the green and scattered on nearby side streets. You'll find styles ranging from Federal through colonial revival, although Greek Revival appears to predominate. A strikingly handsome courthouse—where cases have been heard for 170 years—sets on the edge of the shady green. This structure was originally built in 1825; the imposing portico was added in 1853. For more detailed information on area buildings, obtain a copy of the free walking tour brochure at the Moore Free Library on West Street.

About a dozen antique shops line Route 30 through the West River Valley, as well as on Route 35 north of Townshend. They provide good grazing on lazy afternoons, and are a fine resource for serious collectors. The **Newfane Antiques Center** (☎ **802/365-4482**) houses 20 dealers on three floors and offers a broad selection ranging from bric-a-brac to quality furniture. Other dealers include the **A. Richter Gallery** (☎ **802/365-4549**) in Townshend, which specializes in early prints and posters, and **Schommer Antiques** (☎ **802/365-7777**) in Newfane Village, which carries a good selection of 19th-century furniture and accessories.

Hard-core treasure hunters should time their visit to hit the **Newfane Flea Market** (☎ **802/365-4000**), which features 100 plus tables of assorted stuff. The flea market is held Sundays May through October on Route 30 just north of Newfane village.

OUTDOOR PURSUITS

Three miles outside of Townshend is **Townshend State Park** (☎ **802/365-7500**) and Townshend State Forest. Located at the foot of Bald Mountain, the park consists mostly of a solidly built campground constructed by the Civilian Conservation Corps in the 1930s. But you can park here to hike Bald Mountain, one of the better short hikes in the region. A 3.1-mile loop trail begins behind the ranger station, following a bridle path along a brook. The ascent soon steepens, and at 1.7 miles you'll arrive at the 1,680-foot summit, which turns out not to be bald at all. But open ledges offer views toward Mt. Monadnock to the east, and Bromley and Stratton mountains to the west. The descent is via a steeper 1.4-mile trail that ends behind the campground. The park is open early May through Columbus Day; the day use fee is $1.50 for adults, $1 for children. Ask for trail maps at the park office. The park is reached by crossing the Townshend Dam (off Route 30), then turning left and continuing to the park sign.

More sedentary pleasures may be found at Townshend Dam, a recreation area managed by the Army Corps of Engineers. There's a small beach and picnic area on the upstream side of the dam. A modest day use fee is charged.

For more swimming, continue northwest on Route 30 to the photogenic town of Jamaica. **Jamaica State Park** (☎ **802/874-4600**) offers campsites and picnicking along the West River (there's good swimming and splashing in the river), and a trail to Ball Mountain Dam. Some of New England's premier white-water canoeing and kayak racing takes place on the river below the dam in the spring and fall; races are scheduled around controlled releases from the dam.

WHERE TO STAY

Four Columns Inn. West St. (P.O. Box 278), Newfane, VT 05345. ☎ **802/365-7713** or 800/ 787-6633. 15 rms. A/C TEL. $110–$175 double, including full breakfast; foliage season $200–$275 double, including breakfast and dinner. AE, MC, V.

You can't help but notice The Four Columns Inn in Newfane: It's the regal, white clapboard building with four Ionic columns, setting just off the green. The inn is decorated in a light country style throughout, and is located on lushly landscaped grounds. It's a great base for exploring the village. If you've stayed here in the past and found the management to be a little impersonal and haughty, give it another try; new innkeepers Pam and Gorton Baldwin acquired the inn in early 1996.

Dining/Entertainment: Perhaps the inn's greatest attraction is the well-respected dining room, which serves creatively prepared meals such as scallops and shrimp with vegetables in a green curry, and grilled duck with a sour cherry and rosemary sauce.

✪ **Windham Hill Inn.** Windham Hill Rd., West Townshend, VT 05359. ☎ **802/874-4080** or 800/944-4080. 18 rms, including 5 in nearby barn. A/C TEL. $195–$230 double, including breakfast and dinner. AE, DC, DISC, MC, V. Closed Apr and Thanksgiving weekend through Christmas. Turn uphill across from the country store in West Townshend and climb 1¹/₄ miles up a demanding hill to a marked dirt road; turn right and continue to end.

The Windham Hill Inn is one of the most elegant, quiet, and remote inns you'll find in Vermont. Situated at the end of a dirt road in a high upland valley, the inn was originally built in 1823 as a farmhouse, and remained in the same family until the 1950s, when it was converted to an inn. Under the new ownership of innkeepers Pat and Grigs Markham, the Windham Hill has ratcheted up several notches in quality as costly and extensive renovations have managed to meld the best of the old and the new. The guest rooms are wonderfully appointed in elegant country style. Ask to see the five rooms in the barn, which are a bit more rustic but marvelous examples of adaptive reuse.

Windham Hill is at the pricey end of the scale, but it's a guaranteed treat for those with limited leisure time who don't wish to take a chance on their vacation. This is a no-smoking inn.

Dining/Entertainment: The newly expanded dining room is still the picture of elegant simplicity, with light ash flooring and simple table settings. The views of the small pond are lovely, but not enough to distract from the delicious meals, which feature creative French cooking with a strong emphasis on local and seasonal ingredients.

Facilities: The inn is located on 160 acres, with 6 miles of cross-country ski trails groomed in the winter, and fine hiking through mixed forest and meadows in the summer.

West River Lodge. R.R. 1 (P.O. Box 693), Newfane, VT 05345. ☎ **802/365-7745.** 8 rms (2 with private bath; 6 others share 3 baths). $70–$80 double. Rates include full breakfast. DISC, MC, V. Closed during mud season.

This is as close as you'll come to a dude ranch vacation in the East—and you can enjoy it without the early morning wake-up call. Situated in a beautiful, broad valley with views of farmland and countryside, the West River Lodge caters to equestrians in the summer and cross-country skiers in the winter. This is not the place to be if you prefer to be left alone on your vacation. Guests become part of the family here, with everyone sitting down to eat at 7pm, and sharing stories in cluttered and cozy common rooms after the meal. Many guests couple their stay with horseback riding classes or tours at the adjacent West River Stables. The stables, which have been offering English riding instruction since 1948, are run by Roger Poitras and his staff, who well know the hidden bridle trails and are happy to share their knowledge with you. If you're not a horse person, you can just enjoy farm life (there are also dogs, cats, and cows), or walk down the dirt lane to a fine swimming hole.

WHERE TO DINE

Townshend Corner Store. Corner of Routes 30 and 35, Townshend. ☎ **802/365-4624.** Breakfast $1.55–$4.25; lunch and dinner items $1.60–$4.05. No credit cards. Daily 6:30am–7pm. LUNCHEONETTE.

"Sit long—talk much" reads the sign behind the counter. It's posted over the day's ice cream selections, which, quite frankly, don't vary much from yesterday's selections. Or tomorrow's. But the sign offers good advice for getting the most out of this classic country store, located on the green in Townshend. The dining area takes up about half the room, and in summer is likely to be occupied by a mix of locals and tourists, each eyeing the other warily. But don't fret it. Just sidle up to the worn, red laminate counter with the red toadstool-shaped stools, and enjoy the simple, filling luncheonette fare. Particularly good are the old-fashioned milkshakes and pies, and the thick slabs of bacon that come with breakfast.

Townshend Country Inn. Route 30, Townshend. ☎ **802/365-4141.** Reservations recommended during peak season. Main courses $12.75–$15.95. DISC, MC, V. Thurs–Tues 5–9pm; Sun 11am–2:30pm. Closed two weeks in Apr. AMERICAN/NEW ENGLAND.

This 1775 farmhouse is situated off Route 30 just south of Townshend, and is a good destination for reliable if not gourmet meals. Diners choose from two dining rooms (or a cozy tavern) decorated in traditional New England style. It's an inn that aspires toward elegance, but also serves saltines in cellophane with the soup. There's usually a good selection of nightly specials, and a variety of pasta dishes. The cuisine tends toward traditional New England, but often with a multicultural detour, like the maple-curry-dill salad dressing. Entrees include chicken breast stuffed with fontinella cheese, and veal scallopini with black olives, sun-dried tomatoes, and mushrooms in a brandy cream sauce.

GRAFTON & CHESTER

When I first visited Grafton, I was fully prepared to dislike it. I'd heard from others that it was pristine and quaint, the result of an ambitious preservation plan by wealthy benefactors. I figured it would be too precious, too fussy, too much an overwrought picture-book recreation of New England as envisioned by the D.A.R.

But it only took me about a half-hour of aimless wandering to come away a serious booster of the place.

Grafton was first founded in 1763, and soon grew into a thriving settlement. By 1850, the town was home to some 10,000 sheep, and boasted a handsome hotel that provided shelter for guests on the stage between Boston and Montréal. A cheese cooperative was organized in 1890. The soapstone industry flourished. But as agriculture and commerce shifted west and to the cities, Grafton became a mere shadow of a town—by the Depression, many of the buildings were derelict, for three decades afterwards, much of the town could be purchased for a song.

In 1963, Hall and Dean Mathey of New Jersey created the Windham Foundation. These two brothers had been entrusted by a wealthy relative, who had recently died, to come up with a worthy cause for her fortune. It took a few years, but they eventually hit on Grafton, where their family had summered, and began purchasing and restoring the dilapidated center of town, including the old hotel. The foundation eventually came to own some 55 buildings and 2,000 acres around the town—even the cheese cooperative was revived. Within time the village again came to life, although it's now teeming with history buffs and tourists rather than farmers and merchants.

The Windham Foundation has taken great care in preserving this gem of a village, even to the point of burying utility lines so as not to mar the landscape with wires. It's not a museum like Sturbridge Village or Colonial Williamsburg, but an active town with some 600 residents. It just happens to have dozens of museum-quality homes and buildings.

More commercial Chester, in contrast, is less pristine and feels more lived in. The downtown area has a pleasant neighborly feel to it, along with a handful of intriguing boutiques and shops set along the long, narrow green. Chester is a great destination for antiquing, with several good dealers in the area. When heading north of town on Route 103, be sure to slow enough to enjoy the Stone Village, where a neighborhood of well-spaced, austere stone homes line the roadway. Many of these homes were said to be major stopping points on the Underground Railroad.

ESSENTIALS

GETTING THERE   The most direct route to Bellows Falls is via I-91; get off at either Exit 5 or 6 and follow signs to town via Route 5. Grafton is 12 miles west of Bellows Falls on Route 121, at the intersection of Route 35. Tip: The trip north on Route 35 from Townshend to Grafton is exceedingly scenic and pastoral.

VISITOR INFORMATION   The **Grafton Information Center,** Grafton, VT 05146 (☎ **802/843-2255**), is located on Route 35 just south of the village. For information about Chester, contact the **Chester Chamber of Commerce,** P.O. Box 623, Chester, VT 05143 (☎ **802/875-2939**).

EXPLORING GRAFTON

Grafton is best seen at a languorous pace, on foot, when the weather is welcoming. Don't expect to be overwhelmed with grandeur. Instead, keep a keen eye out for telling historical details.

Start at the Grafton Information Center (see above), which offers parking and access to the rest of the village. Exhibits in the main center provide some background on the village's history. Barns nearby house other informative exhibits.

From here, follow a footpath past the barns and through a small covered bridge to the **Grafton Cheese Co.** (☎ **800/472-3866**), a small, modern building where you can buy a snack of award-winning cheese and peer through plate glass windows to observe the cheesemaking process. (*Note:* Outwardly, it's not very complicated or interesting.)

Cross back over the covered bridge and bear right on the footpath along the cow pasture to the Kidder Covered Bridge, then head into town via Water Street, continuing on to Main Street. Toward the village center, white clapboard homes and shade trees abound. Appreciate it. This is about as New England as New England gets.

On Main Street, stop by the **Grafton Historical Society** Museum (☎ **802/843-2344;** open weekends only) for photographs, artifacts, and memorabilia of Grafton. The nearby **Grafton Museum of Natural History** (☎ **802/843-2347;** open weekends only) offers intriguing displays on Vermont wildlife.

Afterward, stop by the **Old Tavern** at Grafton, the impressive building that anchors the town and has served as a social center since 1801, and enjoy a beverage at the rustic Phelps Barn Lounge, or a meal in one of the dining rooms. (See below.) From here, you can make your way back to the information center by wandering on pleasant side streets. If you'd like to expand your range and cruise the outlying areas by bike, ask about rentals at the tavern. Horse and buggy rides are also available here.

If you're visiting in winter, Grafton offers superb cross-country skiing at the **Grafton Ponds Cross-Country Ski Center** (☎ 802/843-2400), located just south of the cheese factory on Route 35. Managed by the Old Tavern, Grafton Ponds has 18 miles of groomed trails (with snowmaking on 3 miles) and a warming hut near the ponds where you can sit by a fire and enjoy a steaming bowl of soup. Ski and snowshoe rentals are available; a trail pass costs $12 for adults, $8 for seniors, and $6 for children 12 and under.

WHERE TO STAY

Inn at Long Last. Route 11 (P.O. Box 589), Chester, VT 05143. ☎ **802/875-2444.** 30 rms (some with shower only). $160 double, including breakfast and dinner; $110 double on Mon, including breakfast only. MC, V. Closed Apr and mid-Nov.

"This place succeeds where others are just cutesy," wrote one recent guest in the hotel's guest book. And that about sums it up. This three-story downtown hostelry, originally built in 1923, has a low-key charm and quirky ambience. Owned by Jack Coleman, formerly the president of Haverford College in Pennsylvania, the inn features eclectically furnished guest rooms, each decorated with a theme. The Frederick Law Olmsted Room, for instance, features prints of Olmsted-designed parks and two books about the landscape architect on the bedside table. The Charles Dickens Room has volumes by the author, and a regal Victorian veneer. Take a look around and find a room that suits you. Downstairs the lobby has the feel of a bustling stagecoach stop, with highly polished floors, braided and Oriental rugs, a stone fireplace, and a tidy collection of miniature soldiers in lighted cases. Guests are made to feel like family here, and it's a fun family to be part of.

✪ **The Old Tavern at Grafton.** Routes 35 and 121, Grafton, VT 05146. ☎ **802/843-2231** or 800/843-1801. 66 rms (2 with shower only). $115–$165 double. Rates include continental breakfast. Discounts available May–June and midweek in summer. MC, V. Closed Apr.

Countless New England inns seek to replicate the service and gracious style of a far larger resort, but fall short because of understaffing and a woeful lack of capital. But the Old Tavern at Grafton succeeds, and wildly so. It should be noted this is called Old Tavern, not "Ye Olde Taverne," a good reflection of the understated quality and professional service that has pervaded the establishment since a management change a few years ago. Note also that the Old Tavern advertises only lightly, yet still draws capacity crowds through word of mouth.

The inn seems more intimate than its 66 guest rooms would suggest, since the rooms are spread throughout the town. Fourteen are in the exceptionally handsome colonnaded main building, 22 are across the street in the Homestead Cottage, and the remaining rooms are scattered among seven historic guest houses in and around the village. All rooms are decorated with antiques and an upscale country elegance, but the rooms in the Homestead Cottage (which is actually two historic homes joined together) have a more modern, hotellike character.

The common areas in the inn are formal in a Federal-style sort of way, but those determined to relax can still do so. And, of course, there's the village of Grafton to reconnoiter, which requires but a few steps from the front door.

Dining/Entertainment: See "Where to Dine," below, for a review of the inn's dining room. The Phelps Barn Lounge, a modest, unassuming pub out back, features Vermont microbrews and evening entertainment from Brattleboro and beyond.

Facilities: As for recreation, the inn boasts swimming in an attractive sand-bottomed pool, hiking, bike rentals, two tennis courts, and, in winter, ice-skating, cross-country skiing, and platform tennis.

WHERE TO DINE

Inn at Long Last. Route 11, Chester. ☎ **802/875-2444.** Reservations recommended. Main courses $12–$19.50. MC, V. Sun and Tues–Thurs 6–8pm, Fri–Sat 6–9pm; Sun 11am–2pm. Closed Apr and mid-Nov. REGIONAL.

Located off the lobby of this handsome downtown hotel, the dining room at the Inn at Long Last has a formal setting with an informal character. Start with a cocktail at the ornate bar (imported from a hotel in Bangor, Maine), then take a seat in the tastefully decorated dining room. The meals are creative and professionally prepared by chef Russ Jones. You might start with slices of grilled smoked pork tenderloin with apple-pistachio butter, or a mushroom and gruyère tortellini. Then graduate to a grilled breast of chicken with a fennel-artichoke ratatouille, or a salmon served with a Thai-melon salsa. Leave time afterward to sit in the lobby and digest for a bit, enjoying the fire, the piped-in music, and the soothing ticking of the grandfather clock.

Old Tavern at Grafton. Routes 35 and 121, Grafton, VT 05146. ☎ **802/843-2231** or 800/843-1801. Reservations recommended. Lunch items $4.95–$8.25; main dinner courses $13.95–$20.95. MC, V. Daily 8am–10am, noon–2pm, and 6–9pm. Open for pub fare 2–5pm during foliage season. Closed Apr. REGIONAL.

The Old Tavern extends the elegance and grace of the inn to its dining rooms. Patrons choose from among three dining areas—two feature an Early American theme, and the third has an airy, open garden room feel. "Appropriate dinner attire" is requested, but there's still a fairly loose, relaxed air to the place in the evening. The menu features classic New England fare, updated for more adventurous palates and with healthier choices in mind. Lunch might feature a horseradish-garlic burger, or baked scrod with almond bread crumbs. Dinner is more ambitious, with entrees like roasted rack of lamb, panéed mignons of venison, and a house favorite, lobster pie. Lighter entrees included grilled chicken breast and vegetarian pizza.

LUDLOW & OKEMO

Ludlow is home to Okemo Mountain, a once-sleepy ski resort that's been nicely upgraded and updated in the past decade. Ludlow is also notable as one of the few Vermont ski towns that didn't go through one of those unfortunate Tyrolean identity crises. Centered around a former mill that produced fabrics and, later, aircraft parts, Ludlow has an unpretentious made-in-milltown-Vermont character that seems quite distant from the prim grace of white-clapboard Grafton. Low-key and unassuming, it draws skiers by the busload in winter (it's especially popular with travelers from the New York City metropolitan area); in summer, it's a good place to put your feet up on the rail and watch the clouds float over the mountaintops.

ESSENTIALS

GETTING THERE   Ludlow is situated at the intersection of Route 193 and Route 100. The most direct route from an interstate is Exist 6 of I-93; follow Route 103 westward to Ludlow.

VISITOR INFORMATION   The **Ludlow Area Chamber of Commerce,** P.O. Box 333, Ludlow, VT 05149 (☎ **802/228-5830**) staffs a helpful information booth at the Okemo Marketplace, at the foot of Mountain Road.

EXPLORING THE AREA

The intriguing history of Ludlow and the surrounding region is the subject of the **Black River Academy Museum** (☎ 802/228-5050), located on High Street near the village green. Open during summer and early fall, the museum includes an exhibit on Pres. Calvin Coolidge, who graduated from the Academy in 1892. Other exhibits explore the role of industry and farming in the Black River Valley.

In winter, cross-country skiing is offered at the **Fox Run Cross Country Ski Center** (☎ 802/228-8871), which has 12 miles of groomed trail over a golf course and up into the hillside forest. The trail mileage is relatively low, and the price is quite high at $12 for a one-day trail pass.

Ludlow's nightlife is easy to get a handle on. It consists of pub-style restaurant **Savannah's** (☎ 802/228-4279), which offers live music on Thursday, Friday, and Saturday. It's located in the Okemo Marketplace at the foot of Mountain Road. At Okemo's mountain village, you might also check out **Priority's** (☎ 802/228-2800) and **Dadd's** (☎ 802/228-9820) for electronic games and entertainment.

SKIING

Okemo. Ludlow, VT 05149. ☎ **802/228-4041,** or 800/786-5366 for lodging. Vertical drop: 2,150 feet. Lifts: 10 chairlifts (2 high-speed), 2 surface lifts. Skiable acreage: 470. Lift tickets: $47 weekend, $43 weekday.

Okemo fans like to point out a couple of things. First, this is one of the few family-owned mountains remaining in Vermont (it's been owned by Tim and Diane Mueller since 1982). Second, it now offers some good advanced trails on the newly cut south face, ridding it of the accusations that it's just an intermediate's mountain. Okemo still doesn't attract the yahoos, who gravitate to way-gnarlier Killington to the north. As such, it's still first and foremost a mountain for families, who not only like the varied terrain but the friendly base area that's of a scale not too intimidating for kids.

When Okemo opened in the 1956, it boasted "America's longest poma lift" at 6,250 feet long. Anyone who recalls poma lifts will regard this as a hollow boast—you'd be more tired when you got to the top than to the bottom. Today, Okemo is still equipped state-of-the-art equipment, but the equipment is thankfully much improved. Lifts include two high-speed chairs, including the 6,500-foot North Star Quad that whisks skiers to the summit with considerable ease.

A ROAD TRIP TO BELLOWS FALLS

A trip southeast through the canyon of Proctorsville Gulf to the riverside village of Bellows Falls is a recommended activity for an idle day, or to schedule into your travel in or out of the Ludlow area.

Bellows Falls has a rough-edged industrial charm. Set in a deep valley at the edge of the Connecticut River, Bellows Falls went through several booms, each time riding the wave of a new technology. America's first canal was first constructed here in 1802, offering a way for boats carrying freight to bypass the tumultuous falls, which are still dramatic during spring runoff. After the train eclipsed the canal, Bellows Falls was the junction of three train lines in the 19th century, which provided another infusion of cash. Advances in paper, farm machinery manufacturing, and hydroelectric power also led to a rise in the town's economic fortunes.

Today, Bellows Falls isn't riding much of any economic wave, but offers a glimpse of these earlier times through the varied architecture around town. A compact downtown of Victorian brick, the town is overlorded by town hall's crenelated clock tower, which, if you squint, looks as if it could rise above a square in Venice. Handsome commercial architecture of brick attests to an earlier affluence. Note especially the handsome Romanesque brick post office, which is near the site of the early canal.

An uncommonly well-written brochure guides visitors on a walking tour of Bellows Falls, offering a quick spanning of the centuries from the remains of the early canal to examples of Craftsman-style homes dating from the 1920s. The brochure is available at the **Great Falls Regional Chamber of Commerce,** 55 Village Square, Bellows Falls, VT 05101 (☎ **802/463-4280**). Be sure also to stop by the visitor's center at the hydroelectric dam for a tour of the clever fish ladder with its canallike locks. This allowed the reintroduction of salmon to the upper Connecticut River when it opened in 1982.

Before leaving town, swing by the classic Miss Bellows Falls Diner at the north edge of downtown. This 1920s diner has been a Bellows Falls fixture since the 1940s, when it was towed here from Massachusetts. Today it features the original marble countertop along with the good home cooking.

WHERE TO STAY

During ski season, contact the **Okemo Mountain Lodging Service** (☎ **800/786-5366** or 802/228-5571) for reservations at a variety of area accommodations, including slopeside condos. Those looking for a longer stay should check with **Strictly Rentals** (☎ **802/228-3000**), which can arrange for stays of a weekend or longer.

The Castle. Route 103 (at Route 131; P.O. Box 207), Proctorsville, VT 05153. ☎ **802/226-7222** or 800/697-7222. Fax 802/226-7853. 10 rms (2 with shower only). $135–$185 double, including breakfast; $190–$240 double, including breakfast and dinner. Off-season discounts available. AE, MC, V. Closed two weeks in Apr.

Sit in the lobby long enough and you'll hear someone walk in and exclaim, "Look at this place!" And the first floor of this stunning stone mansion on a rise overlooking Route 103 is exquisite. The original owner had an obvious thing for wood, and the house, built in 1901, is opulent with a dark, chocolatey woodworking throughout. Somewhat paradoxically, this makes the house a little gloomy during the day, but it glows with a golden luster at night, warmly lit by burning logs in the fireplaces.

The upstairs guest rooms, six of which feature wood-burning fireplaces, have come a long way since Boston corporate refugees Erica and Richard Hart bought the place in early 1995. Out went the 1950s-era furniture and design aesthetic; in came a truckload of antiques, handsome carpets, updated bathrooms, and CD players in all the rooms. There's still a ways to go—some of the old details are nice, like the spherical glass doorknobs; others aren't, like cracked and discolored tiles in some of the bathrooms, and outdated electrical fixtures. And be forewarned that some of those bathrooms are quite small. The innkeepers are amid a six-year plan to restore the place; look for improvements with each visit. In summer, guests can also avail themselves of the swimming pool and tennis court.

Black River Inn. 100 Main St. (Route 103), Ludlow, VT 05149. ☎ **802/228-5585.** 10 rms, 2 with shared bath (6 with shower only). Double with private bath, $105–$125 weekend, $85–$105 midweek; double with shared bath, from $95 weekend. All rates include breakfast. AE, DISC, MC, V.

The centerpiece of the Black River Inn is in the Lincoln Room, the only first-floor guest room. It contains a four-poster walnut bed made in 1794 and slept in by none other than Abraham Lincoln himself—there's even documentation (of sorts) framed on the wall. The rest of this brick Federal home is equally historic, including the vibrant, zebralike wood floors in the dining room and kitchen, and a countrified living room with working fireplace. The guest rooms are decorated in a Victorian country style, with a melange of antiques including oak, maple, walnut, and brass; many have handsome pine floors. Most of the rooms are very small, but seem large compared to their Lilliputian bathrooms. Two rooms share a bath, but several others have private "detached baths" requiring a walk down the hall. In those rooms, robes are provided.

WHERE TO DINE

Cappuccino's. 41 Depot St., Ludlow. ☎ **802/228-7566.** Reservations recommended on weekends. Main courses $8.95–$13.95. No credit cards. Wed–Sun 5–9pm, with later hours on weekends. PASTA.

Set in a former corner store just off Ludlow's main drag, Cappuccino's offers tasty, filling meals at a reasonable price. Inside the setting is bright and cheery, although it strays a bit into "Ye Olde Candy Shoppe" look, and the atmosphere is upbeat. The menu offers a decent range of hearty pasta dishes, including ravioli served with sautéed chicken, pasta with crabmeat and shrimp in a sherry tomato cream, and a filling, tasty $8.95 pasta with a simple red meat sauce. Nonpasta entrees include steak with shrimp, roasted duck, and chicken breast stuffed with crabmeat and shrimp.

The Castle. Route 131 (at Route 103, just south of Ludlow), Proctorsville. ☎ **802/226-7222.** Reservations recommended weekends and peak seasons. Main courses $14.25–$24. AE, MC, V. Wed–Sun 5:30–9pm. FRENCH.

The Castle's dining area occupies two rooms of exquisite woodworking on the first floor of this grand 1901 stone mansion. (Guest rooms are upstairs; see above.) The mood is set with candles on the tables, diffuse lighting, and jazz playing softly in the background. Chef Mark Dickerson, a New England Culinary Institute grad who's also worked in New Orleans and the Virgin Islands, prepares straightforward meals with a classical French touch. You might start with crab-stuffed prawns or a baked Roquefort and pear tart, then graduate to veal with artichoke and capers, or a delicious brook trout stuffed with prawns and served with a citrus buerre blanc sauce. When I last visited, the desserts gracefully ushered guests back from France to New England, with offerings such as lemon tartlet, apple-cranberry cobbler, and maple crème brûlée.

Harry's Cafe. Route 103 (four miles north of Ludlow), Mount Holly. ☎ **802/259-2996.** Reservations recommended on weekends. Main courses $10.95–$16.95. AE, MC, V. Wed–Sun 5–10pm. ECLECTIC.

Along a dark stretch of road north of Ludlow you'll pass a brightly lit roadside café with a red neon "Harry's" over the door. This isn't a hamburger joint, as you might assume, but a highly creative restaurant that serves up some of the tangiest sauces in Vermont. Inside, the atmosphere seems more fast-food restaurant than cozy bistro, and that's obviously not what draws the crowds here. It's the food, which seems to span the globe.

Entrees are a veritable culinary U.N., with New York sirloin, jerk pork, flautas, spicy Thai curry, fish and chips, Portuguese seafood stew, and chicken breast stuffed with riccotta cheese, basil, and sun-dried tomatoes. All dishes share the menu with apparent harmony. If you like the sauces you can take some home; owner Trip Pearce bottles and sells six different sauces, and does a brisk mail order business as well.

4 Central Vermont

The towns of Central Vermont each come from a distinctly different mold. There's Woodstock, a classic New England town set around a handsome green and nestled

Central Vermont & the Champlain Valley

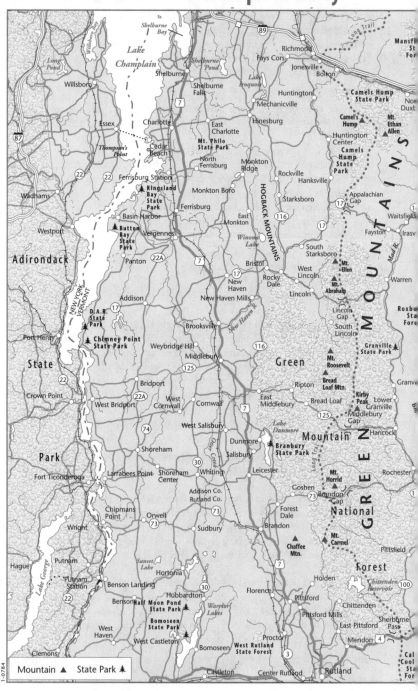

Mountain ▲ State Park ⚲

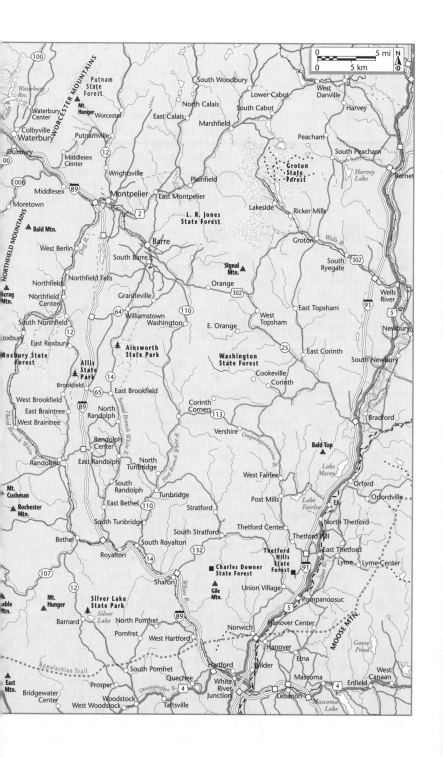

100

Putnam State Forest

South Woodbury

West Danville

Waterbury Res.

Lower Cabot

North Calais

South Cabot

Harvey

Mt. Hunger

Worcester

East Calais

Marshfield

Peacham

Waterbury Center

South Peacham

Colbyville

Waterbury

Putnamville

Harvey Lake

12

WORCESTER MOUNTAINS

Duxbury

Middlesex Center

Groton State Forest

Barnet

00

100B

Moretown

Wrightsville

Plainfield

Lakeside

Ricker Mills

Middlesex

89

Montpelier

East Montpelier

Groton

302

Bald Mtn.

2

L. R. Jones State Forest

South Ryegate

NORTHFIELD MOUNTAINS

West Berlin

Barre

Wells R.

Wells River

Dog R.

South Barre

Signal Mtn.

91

5

Northfield Falls

Orange

302

East Topsham

Newbury

Scrag Mtn.

Northfield

Northfield Center

Graniteville

110

West Topsham

64

Williamstown

Washington

E. Orange

25

East Corinth

South Newbury

South Northfield

12

Ainsworth State Park

Washington State Forest

Cookeville

Roxbury

East Roxbury

14

Corinth

Roxbury State Forest

Allis State Park

Brookfield

East Brookfield

Corinth Corners

113

Bradford

65

West Brookfield

North Randolph

89

Vershire

East Braintree

West Braintree

Ompompanoosuc R.

Third Branch White R.

Bald Top

Randolph Center

Lake Morey

Randolph

East Randolph

North Tunbridge

West Fairlee

Orford

Mt. Cushman

South Randolph

Tunbridge

Post Mills

Lake Fairlee

Orfordville

Rochester Mtn.

East Bethel

110

Stratford

Ely

North Thetford

Second Branch White R.

South Tunbridge

Thetford Center

Bethel

South Stratford

Thetford Hill

East Thetford

Royalton

14

South Royalton

132

Charles Downer State Forest

Thetford Hills State Forest

91

Lyme

Lyme Center

First Branch White R.

107

Sharon

Gile Mtn.

Union Village

MOOSE MTN.

able Mtn.

12

Mt. Hunger

Silver Lake State Park

Pompanoosuc

5

Goose Pond

Barnard

Silver Lake

North Pomfret

89

Norwich

Hanover Center

Pomfret

West Hartford

Hanover

Etna

East Mtn.

Appalachian Trail

South Pomfret

White R.

Hartford

Wilder

Mascoma

West Canaan

Bridgewater Center

Prosper

Quechee

White River Junction

Lebanon

Enfield

4

Woodstock

Ottauquechee R.

4

Mascoma Lake

West Woodstock

Taftsville

91

in a quiet valley. White River Junction and Rutland, on opposite ends of the region, both have blue-collar ancestry and handsome commercial architecture. And Killington is home to the Northeast's largest ski area, and bustles in winter with a vital, urban energy.

Between these major towns and resorts are pristine hills (including some of Vermont's most rugged peaks), tumbling rivers, and lush, verdant farmlands. You won't find quite as many perfect New England villages in this region. But off the main highways, you'll discover little traffic and good access to hiking—the Long and Appalachian trails share a trail corridor as they come in to this region, then split just above Route 2 as they head toward their separate destinations. If you need a small-town fix, head to Plymouth Notch, where you'll find the wonderfully preserved white-clapboard village where Calvin Coolidge was born, reared, and sworn in as president.

WHITE RIVER JUNCTION & NORWICH

White River Junction is a Vermont rarity: an industrial-era town that was built on the fruits of industry rather than wrenched from the earth on hardscrabble farmlands or in deep quarries. Industry, in this case, was the railroad. In 1847, White River Junction had only one farmhouse. Within 15 years, five different rail lines had established terminals here, and the town was bustling, noisy, and full of grit. Rail has suffered a well-documented decline since that golden era, and White River Junction has slipped from prominence along with the mighty steam trains and the lonesome whistle, but it retains a shopworn dignity and grace.

To the north, Norwich is a peaceful New England town slightly off the beaten track. The town has a fine selection of woodframe and brick homes, and boasts a pair of superb restaurants and an excellent science museum for kids. First settled in 1761, Norwich has long-established ties with Hanover across the river. Many Dartmouth faculty and staff commute from Norwich, and the two towns even share a school district.

ESSENTIALS

GETTING THERE   White River Junction is easily reached via either I-89 or I-91, which converge just south of town. Norwich may be reached from Exit 13 on I-91, or by driving north from White River Junction on Route 5. White River Junction is also served by daily **Amtrak** service (☎ **800/872-7245**), originating in Washington, D.C.

VISITOR INFORMATION   The **White River Chamber of Commerce,** P.O. Box 697, White River Junction, VT 05001 (☎ **802/295-6200**), staffs a seasonal information booth on the corner of Route 5 and Sykes Avenue (near the intersection of I-89 and I-91). It's open 9:30am to 4:30pm daily during the peak season (summer and foliage season). Between Memorial Day and July 4, and between Labor Day and foliage, it's open weekends only. The chamber's main office is open year-round Monday to Friday 9am to 5pm at 15 South Main Street in downtown White River Junction.

EXPLORING THE REGION

White River Junction's compact old downtown is clustered near the river and a confusion of old train tracks. Downtown was never particularly cheerful or quaint—the grit of the railyards always overpowered it—but today it maintains a quiet dignity in the face of strip-mall sprawl that keeps growing and growing on the ridge above town. With the exception of a couple of restaurants, downtown rolls up the sidewalk at dusk. It's easy to get a glimpse of the town's sooty history with a brief excursion by foot or car. A monument of sorts to its rail heritage may be found near the Amtrak station, where an old Boston & Maine locomotive and caboose are on display.

Also downtown, at 58 South Main St., is the **Catamount Brewing Company** (☎ 802/296-2248), one of the more prominent success stories in the New England microbrewery boom of the past decade. The brewers have attracted a broad regional audience for its amber ales, gold ales, porters, and specialty beers like bock, Octoberfest, and Christmas ale. A brewery tour provides a quick education in the making of a fine beer, and (more importantly) samples are offered at the conclusion. Tours are held daily July through October at 11am, 1pm, and 3pm (no 11am tour on Sundays). From November through June, tours are Saturdays only at 11am, 1pm, and 3pm.

A few miles south of White River Junction in the historic town of Windsor is the **American Precision Museum** (☎ 802/674-5781), a narrowly focused but broadly informative museum. The collections in part commemorates Windsor's role as the birthplace of the state's machine tool industry, and as home to countless inventors and inventions. More generally, it serves up an overview of the surprisingly intriguing history of machine tools and rifles. The museum is located in the 1846 Robbins, Lawrence and Kendall armory, itself an historic site.

What inventions, you ask? Ashael Hubbard put Windsor on the map in the early 19th century, when he moved here from Connecticut and invented the hydraulic pump. Other inventions followed, not only from Hubbard, but from his relatives and other inspired Windsor residents. These include the coffee percolator, the underhammer rifle, the lubricating bullet, and an early variant of the sewing machine. The museum covers this unique history with varied and engaging displays. It's open mid-May through October 9am to 5pm Monday to Friday, and 10am to 4pm weekends and holidays. After November 1, the museum is open by appointment only. Admission is $5 for adults, and $3 for seniors and children 6–17. Children under 6 are free.

Note also that just a short hop across the Connecticut River from Windsor is the lovely St. Gaudens Historical Site, along with North Star Canoes, which rents bikes and canoes. (see Chapter 6 on New Hampshire).

Fun for Kids

Montshire Museum of Science. Montshire Rd., Norwich. ☎ **802/649-2200.** $5 adults, $3 children 3–17, under 3 free. Daily 10am–5pm. Use Exit 13 off I-91 and head east; look for museum signs almost immediately.

This is not your average New England science museum of dusty stuffed animals in a creaky building in need of attention. Located on the border between New Hampshire and Vermont (hence the name), the Montshire is a new, architecturally engaging, hands-on museum that draws kids back time and again. The Montshire took root in 1976, when area residents gathered up the leavings of Dartmouth's defunct natural history museum and put them on display in a former bowling alley in Hanover. The museum grew and prospered, largely owing to the dedication of hundreds of volunteers. In 1989, the museum moved to this beautiful 100-acre property sandwiched between I-91 and the Connecticut River.

Exhibits are housed in a open, soaring structure inspired by the region's barns. The museum contains some live animals (don't miss the leaf cutter ant exhibit on the second floor), but it's mostly fun, interactive exhibits that involve kids deeply, teaching them the principles of math and science on the sly. Even preschoolers are entertained here at "Andy's Place," a play area with aquariums, bubble-making exhibits, and other magical things. Outside, there's a science park masquerading as a playground, and four nature trails that wend through this riverside property of tall trees and chirpy birds.

WHERE TO STAY

Thanks to its location at the crossroads of two interstates, White River Junction has several chain hotels near the highways. The **Holiday Inn** (☎ 802/295-3000 or 800/648-6754) has 140 rooms, an indoor pool and a restaurant. The **Howard Johnson Lodge** (☎ 802/295-3015 or 800/446-4656) features 112 rooms, an indoor pool, and a sauna. And the new **Comfort Inn** (☎ 802/295-3051 or 800/628-7727) offers 71 rooms, free continental breakfast, an outdoor pool, and a guest laundry room.

Hotel Coolidge. 17 North Main St., White River Junction, VT 05001. ☎ **802/295-3118** or 800/622-1124. 33 rms, some with shower only. A/C TV TEL. $45–$55 double. Rates $10 higher during foliage season. AE, DC, DISC, MC, V.

This 1925 downtown hotel (named after John Coolidge, the father of Calvin) is a stout, three-story brick structure that once bustled with jobbers, salesmen, and wholesalers during the heyday of rail travel. That era has passed, more or less leaving the hotel behind with it. The handsome lobby promises a low-key hospitality, with Doric columns, a brick fireplace, and reasonably modern furniture. The service is bright and helpful. Off the lobby is Cashie's, a comfortable restaurant that serves dependable if not exciting Yankee fare.

Like the town itself, the guest rooms are a bit threadbare and worn. The furnishings might have been au courant in the early 1970s, but now seem somewhat weary with age. With a thorough makeover (and, say, a million dollars or two), The Coolidge could stand proud as a first-class, luxury hotel. But as it stands now, it's a good find for travelers on a budget. Hostel-style rooms with shared bath are even cheaper, starting at $27.50.

Juniper Hill Inn. Juniper Hill Rd., Windsor, VT 05089. ☎ **802/674-5273** or 800/359-2541. 16 rms (5 with shower only). $85–$140 double, including breakfast; $135–$190 double, including breakfast and dinner. DISC, MC, V.

The Juniper Hill Inn isn't quite in White River Junction (it's about 12 miles south in Windsor), but it's worth mentioning as one of the more inviting retreats in the state. Set high atop a hill overlooking the Connecticut River Valley, this monumental 1902 manor home is a true period piece—guests half expect to run into Bertie Wooster by the pool or playing croquet on the grounds. It's more mannered and elegant than many Vermont inns, getting its inspiration from various colonial revivals. Palladian windows, a slate roof, and six chimneys grace the exterior; the richly appointed lobby features coffered paneling. The 16 guest rooms are each different, but all feature amenities like fresh flowers, hair dryers, and a decanter of sherry. Four-course candle-lit dinners are served to guests by request; one-day advance notice is requested.

Norwich Inn. Main St. Norwich, VT 05055. ☎ **802/649-1143.** 26 rms. A/C TV TEL. $55–$109 double. AE, MC, V.

Sally and Tim Wilson spruced up the dowdy Norwich Inn after they bought it in 1991, adding stenciling and richer colors and lending this 1797 inn a pleasant country flair. Many guest rooms feature brass and canopy beds; history buffs will prefer the 14 rooms in the main inn to those in the motel-style annex. The main building is alleged to also host one uninvited guest: the ghost of Mary Walker, who is evidently atoning for the sin of selling bootleg liquor at the inn during Prohibition.

Dining/Entertainment: The dining room has a sterling reputation, with guests seated in either a handsome formal room or on the porch in summer. Keeping in the tradition of Mary Walker, in 1993 the inn opened Jasper Murdock's Alehouse, which claims to be America's smallest brewery. Pub fare is available, along with a selection of hand-crafted ales, porters, and stouts.

WHERE TO DINE

✪ Itas'ca. 2 N. Main St., White River Junction. ☎ **802/295-1025.** Reservations recommended for dinner. Lunch $4.75–$9.25; dinner $16.25–$19.25. DISC, MC, V. Tues–Fri 11:30am–2pm; Wed–Sat 6–9pm. Schedule subject to occasional change; call ahead. WHOLE FOODS/GOURMET.

On a ground floor storefront of the 1890 Bates Block in downtown White River Junction, Itas'ca's interior comes as a bit of magic. It's bright, cheery, and modern, with clean pine trim and brick walls festooned with handsome quilts and other sizeable works of local art. But the real magic comes from the kitchen. Executive Chef Ravi Scher, who trained at the Culinary Institute of America, emphasizes organic, natural, and local foods, preparing them in a way that does not in the least resemble damp silage, an effect I've encountered at other whole food restaurants.

Delectable dinner appetizers include "guiltless Caesar salad" made with a yogurt Parmesan dressing, and Bahamian conch chowder. Entrees change frequently, but might include a fillet of natural beef stuffed with local Brie, black olives, and tomato risotto; or a grill-roasted leg of lamb with red kuri squash and bourbon barbecue sauce. The restaurant's name comes from the Latin "veritas caput," which translates as "true source."

✪ La Poule à Dents. Carpenter Street (off Main Street across from the Citgo station), Norwich. ☎ **802/649-2922.** Reservations recommended. Main courses $17.75–$25. AE, CB, DC, DISC, MC, V. Daily 6–10pm. FRENCH.

La Poule à Dents, in the sleepy town of Norwich, wakes up visitors with some of Vermont's most elegant and exquisite dining. Housed in an historic 1820 home with a canopied terrace off one side, this fine restaurant has the feel of an elegant French auberge—quiet, dark, and intimate. It's a perfect spot for a romantic meal, or to celebrate a major occasion.

The menu reads like the inventory of a Flemish still life capturing the bounty of the hunt. Begin your meal with an array of appealing appetizers, which range from Vermont quail to smoked breast of Pékin duck (served with an orzo, fig, and walnut salad) to hand-rolled pepper fettucini with goat cheese, shiitake mushrooms, and thyme. But save room for the main courses, with appealing choices like baby pheasant with wild rice and a pinot noir sauce, or loin of boar with braised red cabbage and a Reisling and stock reduction sauce flavored with juniper berries.

Polka Dot. North Main Street and Joe Reed Drive, White River Junction. ☎ **802/295-9722.** Breakfast $1.15–$4.10; lunch $1.25–$4.35; dinner $4.75–$7.50. Daily 5am–8pm. Closed Thanksgiving and Christmas. DINER.

Classic diner fare is served up daily in this local institution, a relic of the days when a slew of White River Junction diners catered to railwaymen working the frequent freight and passenger trains. (Amtrak still makes a stop across the way.) The interior is painted an eye-searing robin's egg blue, and the walls are hung with railroad photos and train models. You can sidle up to the counter and order a fried egg sandwich ($1.25), or grab one of the booths for a filling, decently prepared meal that's not likely to cost much more than $5. If you're here for breakfast, be sure to try the delicious homemade doughnuts.

WOODSTOCK

In 1847, Woodstock native and noted sculptor Hiram Powers unveiled his statue of a nude, entitled "Greek Slave." It caused a huge uproar nationwide, not only because of Powers's depiction of nudity, but because of his depiction of slavery at a time when slavery was emerging as the nation's most divisive issue.

Woodstock seems an odd spawning ground for someone who would foment a national scandal. Because today Woodstock is dedicated to preserving the mannered past, not to challenging the unsettled future. Travelers simply can't drive to Woodstock on a route that isn't pastoral and scenic, putting one in mind of an earlier, more peaceful era. The superb village green is surrounded by handsome homes, creating what amounts to a comprehensive review of architectural styles of the 19th and early 20th centuries.

Much of the town is on the National Register of Historic Places, and 500 acres surrounding Mt. Tom (see below) has been deeded to the National Park Service by the Rockefeller family and is in the process of becoming a National Historic Park (It's expected to open by the year 2000).

In fact, some joke that downtown Woodstock might as well be named Rockefeller National Park, given the attention and cash the Rockefeller family has lavished upon the town in the interest of preservation. (For starters, Rockefeller money built the faux-historic Woodstock Inn and paid to bury the unsightly utility lines around town.)

Woodstock, which sits on the banks of the gentle Ottauquechee River, was first settled in 1765, rose to some prominence as a publishing center in the mid-19th century (no fewer than five newspapers were published here in 1830), and began to attract wealthy families who summered here in the late 19th century. To this day, Woodstock just feels as if it should have a prestigious prep school just off the green, and it comes as some surprise that it doesn't.

Wealthy summer rusticators were instrumental in establishing and preserving the character of the village, and today the very wealthy have turned their attention to the handsome farms outside of town. Few of these former dairy farms still produce milk; barns that haven't been converted to architectural showcase homes more than likely house valuable collections of cars or other antiques.

Woodstock is also notable as a former center of winter outdoor recreation. The nation's first ski tow (a rope tow powered by an old Buick motor) was built in 1933 at the Woodstock Ski Hill near today's Suicide Six ski area. While no longer the skiing center of Vermont, Woodstock remains a worthy destination during the winter months for skating, cross-country skiing, and snowshoeing.

One caveat: Woodstock's excellent state of preservation hasn't gone unnoticed, and it draws hordes of travelers. During the peak of foliage season, it can even be hard to view the green for all the tour buses driving around it.

ESSENTIALS

GETTING THERE   Woodstock is 13 miles west of White River Junction on Route 4 (take Exit 1 off I-89). From the west, Woodstock is 20 miles east of Killington on Route 4.

VISITOR INFORMATION   The **Woodstock Area Chamber of Commerce,** 18 Central St., Woodstock, VT 05091 (☎ **802/457-3555**), staffs an information booth on the green between June and October. Ask about the guided village walking tours.

EXPLORING THE REGION

IN TOWN   I've got plenty of company when I say that Woodstock is one of my favorite New England villages. Few others can top it for sheer grace and elegance. The heart of the town is the shady, elliptical Woodstock Green. Admiral Dewey spent his later years in Woodstock, which may help explain the canard promulgated by some that the Green was laid out in the shape of Dewey's flagship. In fact, the town's basic design was more or less laid out by 1830, well before Dewey made his mark on history.

At the east end of the green is Woodstock's compact commercial area, with a small but good selection of boutiques and restaurants. To the south is the regal Woodstock Inn (see below). To the north is Middle Covered Bridge, one of three in town and I'd argue the most photographed covered bridges in existence; it was built in 1969 by one of the few master craftsmen still living. Around the rest of the green and along the shady side streets are architecturally outstanding buildings where you can neatly trace the evolution of American architecture.

For a simple, 20-minute walking tour of the village, leave from the green through the covered bridge over the Ottauquechee River and make a right on River Street. You'll follow along the river past trim homes, then past a shady forest before connecting within a few minutes to Elm Street. Turn right into town, taking the time to admire the remarkable homes along the route. You'll soon walk into Woodstock's downtown; veer right at the T-intersection and you're soon back at the green.

While en route, stop by the **Woodstock Historical Society,** 26 Elm St. (☎ **802/ 457-1822**). Housed in the 1807 Charles Dana House, this beautiful home has rooms furnished in Federal, Empire, and Victorian styles, and offers displays of dolls, costumes, and examples of early silver and glass. The Dana House is open from May through October. Hours are 10am to 5pm Monday through Saturday, and Sunday from noon to 5pm. Admission is free.

OUTSIDE WOODSTOCK   Less than a half-mile north of town on Route 12 (Elm Street) is the **Billings Farm and Museum** (☎ **802/457-2355**), a working farm well worth visiting for a glimpse of life in a grander era. The farm was built by Frederick Billings, the man who is credited with completing the Northern Pacific Railroad then saving the rail during the Panic of 1873. (The town of Billings, Mont., is named after him.) This dairy farm was renown late in the last century for its scientific breeding of Jersey cows and its fine architecture, especially the gabled 1890 Victorian farm house. Now owned by Billings' grandaughter and her husband, Laurence Rockefeller, the farm includes hands-on demonstrations of farm activities, exhibits of farm life, an heirloom kitchen garden, and active milking barns.

The museum is open daily May through October from 10am to 5pm, and on weekends in November and December. The farm is also open for special events in winter, including sleigh rides. Admission is $6.50 adults, $5.50 seniors, $5 children 13–17, $3 children 5–12, and $1 children 3–4.

Bird watchers will enjoy a trip to the **Vermont Institute of Natural Science** (☎ **802/457-2779**), which also houses the Vermont Raptor Center. The center is home to 25 species of birds of prey that have been injured and can no longer survive in the wild. The winged residents change from time to time, but typically range from majestic bald eagles to the diminutive saw-whet owl. Serious birders might also choose to spend some time in the institute's Pettingill Ornithological Library. Other attractions include an herbarium, nature trails, and exhibits of live animals, including snakes, bees, and tarantulas. The institute is located $2^1/2$ miles south of the village on Church Hill Road. It's open daily 10am to 4pm, but is closed Sundays from November through April. Admission is $5 adults, $2 for children.

About 5 miles east of Woodstock is the riverside village of Quechee. Formerly a town of prosperous woolen mills, Quechee is emerging as a huge, if low-key, resort community. Some 6,000 acres of the surrounding countryside is owned by the Quechee Lakes Corporation, which has developed second homes and other amenities, including a golf course and polo field.

The small village, with a handful of boutiques and restaurants, still revolves spiritually and economically around the restored brick mill building along the falls. **Simon Pearce Glass** (☎ **802/295-2711**), which makes exceptionally fine and exceptionally pricey glassware, occupies the former Downer's Mill, where it houses its glassmaking operation, a retail store, and a respected restaurant (see below). Visitors can watch glassblowing take place weekdays and on summer weekends from a catwalk viewing gallery. Open daily from 9am to 5pm.

To learn more about the area's history, you should pick up a copy of "By the Old Mill Stream," a brochure and map describing 39 historic sites in Quechee. It's available for $2 at the **Quechee Chamber of Commerce** (☎ **802/295-7900**) at 15 Main St.

OUTDOOR PURSUITS

Outdoor activities in the Woodstock area aren't as rugged as those you'll find in the Green Mountains to the west, but they'll easily occupy you for an afternoon or two.

Don't leave the village without climbing Mt. Tom, the prominent hill that overlooks Woodstock. Start your ascent from Faulkner Park, named after Mrs. Edward Faulkner, who created the park and had the mountain trail built to encourage healthful exercise. (To reach the trailhead from the Woodstock Green, cross Middle Covered Bridge and continue straight on Mountain Avenue. The road bends left and soon arrives at a grassy park at the base of Mt. Tom.)

The trail winds up the hill, employing one of the most lugubrious sets of switchbacks I've ever experienced. Designed after the once-popular "cardiac walks" in Europe, the trail sometimes seems to require hikers to walk for miles only to gain a few feet in elevation. But persevere. This gentle trail eventually arrives at a clearing overlooking the town. A steeper, rockier, and more demanding trail continues 100 yards or so from here to the summit. At the top, a carriage path encircles the summit like a friar's fringe of hair, offering fine views of the town and the Green Mountains to the west. You can follow the carriage path down to Billings Farm, or retrace your steps back to the park.

Experienced and aspiring equestrians should head to the **Kedron Valley Stables** (☎ **802/457-1480**), about 4¹/₂ miles south of Woodstock on Route 106. A full menu of riding options is available, ranging from a one-hour beginner ride ($30) to a five-night inn-to-inn excursion ($1,350 per person including all meals and lodging, double occupancy). The stables rents horses to experienced riders for local trail rides, offers sleigh and carriage rides, and has an indoor riding ring for inclement weather. It's open every day except Thanksgiving and Christmas.

Five miles east of town, Route 4 crosses Quechee Gorge, a popular if somewhat overrated tourist attraction. The sheer power of the glacial runoff that carved the gorge some 13,000 years ago must have dramatic, but the 165-foot gorge itself isn't all that impressive. More impressive is the engineering history. This chasm was first spanned in 1875 by a wooden rail trestle, when 3,000 people gathered along the gorge to celebrate the achievement. The current steel bridge was constructed in 1911 for the railroad, but the tracks were torn up in 1933 and replaced by Route 4.

The best view of the bridge is from the bottom of the gorge, which is accessible by a well-graded gravel path that descends south from the parking area. The round-trip requires no more than a half-hour. If the day is warm enough, you might also follow the path northward along the gorge's rim, then descend to the river to splash around in a fine, rocky swimming hole near the spillway.

Skiing

The area's best cross-country skiing is at the **Woodstock Ski Touring Center** (☎ 802/457-2114) at the Woodstock Country Club, just south of town on Route 106. The center maintains 36 miles of trails, including 12 miles of trail groomed for skate-skiing. And it's not all flat; the high and low points along the trail system vary by 750 feet in elevation. Lessons and picnic tours are available. The full-day trail fee is $11 for adults and $8 for children under 14.

Suicide Six ski area (☎ 802/457-6661) may have an intimidating name, but at just 650 vertical feet it doesn't pose much of a threat to either life or limb. Owned and operated by the Woodstock Inn, this venerable family ski resort (it first opened in 1934) has two double chairs, a complimentary J-bar for beginners, and a spiffy new base lodge. Beginners and intermediates will be content here. Lift tickets are $32 for adults, $21 for seniors and children under 14. The ski area is located two miles north of Woodstock on Pomfret Road.

WHERE TO STAY

Jackson House Inn. Route 4, Woodstock, VT 05091. ☎ **802/457-2065.** 12 rms, all with shower only. A/C. $135–$250 double. Rates include full breakfast. No credit cards.

The graceful aesthetic inside the Jackson House Inn, just outside of Woodstock on Route 4, is unrivaled anywhere in New England, if not the United States. Everything in this pale yellow 1890 Victorian is immaculate and perfectly chosen, from the Oriental rugs and 300-year-old tallcase clock in the first-floor common room, to cherry and maple floors so beautiful you'll feel guilty for not taking off your shoes. The guest rooms, which are each decorated in different period styles (Empire, Federal, etc.), are equally well appointed. The inn features the elegant touches you'd expect for the high price, like decanters of sherry and Bose speakers in the rooms. But there are others you wouldn't expect, like the small fitness room in the basement with steamroom, tanning bed, and juice bar; the video library; and the three-acre backyard with formal English gardens and a pond stocked with rainbow trout.

The sole disadvantage of the Jackson House is its location just off Route 4—not far from the sound of traffic—which somewhat detracts from rural tranquility the innkeepers have otherwise succeeded in achieving. No smoking.

✪ **Kedron Valley Inn.** Route 106, South Woodstock, VT 05071. ☎ **802/457-1473** or 800/836-1193. Fax 802/457-4469. E-mail kedroninn@aol.com. 27 rms, 2 with shower only. TV. $119–$191 double; foliage season and Christmas week $180–$275 double. Rates include full breakfast. Discounts available spring and midweek. DISC, MC, V. Closed Apr and briefly prior to Thanksgiving.

This is a stand-out inn. Located in a complex of Greek Revival buildings at a country crossroads about 5 miles south of Woodstock, the inn is run by Max and Merrily Comins, a cordial couple who offer guests a bit of history, a bit of country style, and a whole lot of good food and wine. The attractive guest rooms in all three buildings are furnished with a mix of antiques and reproductions, and all have heirloom quilts from Merrily's collection; 14 feature wood-burning fireplaces. Don't be alarmed if you're put in the newer, motel-like log building by the river. The rooms are equally well appointed, with canopy beds, custom oak woodwork, and fireplaces. Room 37 even has a private streamside terrace. All guests can share in the inn's pond located above and behind the main house. *Editor's note:* My dog Lucy loves this place!

Dining/Entertainment: The country-elegant dining room has two fireplaces and a nice view of the grounds, and features a menu of contemporary American cuisine built on a classical French foundation. You might start with fresh spinach agnolotti filled with pesto and served with a dressing of sun-dried tomato, then move on to salmon stuffed with a scallop, shrimp and salmon mousse and wrapped in a puff pastry.

Three Church St. 3 Church St., Woodstock VT 05091. ☎ **802/457-1925.** 11 rms, including 5 with shared bath (1 rm with tub only, 2 with shower only). $70–$95 double. Rates include full breakfast. Rates $10 higher during foliage season and Christmas week. MC, V. Closed Apr.

This sturdy brick Greek Revival B&B with a white clapboard ell is located just off the west end of the Woodstock Green, and is well situated for exploring the town. It's also an excellent value, especially if you don't mind sharing a bathroom with other guests and can overlook small imperfections like the occasional water stain on the ceiling. The inn's main foyer is stylish in a fusty, old-fashioned sort of way, featuring an antique highboy and writing desk, an Oriental carpet on the parquet floor, and an elegant staircase sweeping upward to the second floor. Guest rooms are furnished eclectically and comfortably with country antiques. Room 3 (shared bath) is the nicest of the bunch, very bright with painted floors, a fireplace (nonworking), and a nice bookshelf. The inn is situated on three acres that border on the river, complete with tennis court and swimming pool.

✪ **Twin Farms.** Barnard, VT 05031. ☎ **802/234-9999** or 800/894-6327. Fax 802/234-9990. 14 rms and cottages. A/C TEL TV. $700–$850 double; $850–$1,500 cottage. Rates include all meals, liquor, and many amenities. Children under 18 not accepted. AE, MC, V. Closed Apr.

Twin Farms offers uncommon luxury at an uncommon price. Housed on a 300-acre farm that was once home to Nobel Prize–winning novelist Sinclair Lewis and his wife, journalist Dorothy Thompson, Twin Farms has carved out an international reputation as low-key, exceptionally tasteful small resort. The clientele includes royalty and corporate chieftains looking for simplicity and willing to pay dearly for it. The inn consists of the main inn with 4 guest rooms, and 10 outlying cottages, including four that opened in 1995. The rooms are impeccable, designed by talented interior decorators who commissioned craftsmen and artisans to create much of the furniture and adornment. The inn is owned by the Twigg-Smith family, who are noted art collectors in Hawaii. Some of the work on display at the inn and in guest rooms includes originals by David Hockney, Roy Lichtenstein, Milton Avery, and William Wegman.

Dining/Entertainment: Meals are understatedly sumptuous affairs served at locations of your choosing—at your cottage, along a stream, or in one of the dining areas around the estate. Don't bother looking for a menu; the gourmet chefs serve what's fresh, and your meal is likely to include ingredients from the organic vegetable and herb gardens on the property.

Woodstock Inn & Resort. 14 The Green, Woodstock, VT 05091. ☎ **802/457-1100** or 800/ 448-7900. 143 rms, 2 townhouses. A/C TV TEL. $145–$279 double. AE, MC, V.

The Woodstock Inn, an imposing white brick structure behind a garden off the Woodstock Green, appears a venerable and long-established institution at first glance. But it's not—at least not this building. Constructed in 1968–69, the inn happily shunned the more unfortunate trends in '60s architecture for a dignified look suitable for Woodstock. Everyone's the better for it. Inside, guests are greeted by a broad stone fireplace, and sitting areas are tucked throughout the lobby in the manner of a 1940s-era resort. Guest rooms are tastefully decorated in either country pine or a Shaker-inspired style. The best rooms are in the new wing (built 1991), and feature rich carpeting, refrigerators, fireplaces, and built-in bookshelves.

Dining/Entertainment: The dining room is classy and semiformal, with continental and American dishes served on elegant green-bordered custom china. Entrees are in the $20 to $25 price range.

Facilities: There's a Robert Trent Jones golf course at the inn-owned Woodstock Country Club, two swimming pools (indoor and out), hiking trails, putting greens, and a fitness center with tennis, squash, racquetball, and steamrooms. In winter, the resort maintains 36 miles of groomed cross-country ski trails.

WHERE TO DINE

Bentley's. 3 Elm St. ☎ **802/457-3232.** Reservations recommended for parties of 4 or more. Lunch items $4.50–$8.25; main dinner courses $12.95–$18.50; brunch items $6.25–$7.75. AE, CB, DC, DISC, MC, V. Mon–Thurs 11am–9:30pm, Fri–Sat 11am–10pm, Sun 10:30am–9:30pm. Open later for drinks and dancing on weekends. AMERICAN.

There's a famous photo of Winston Churchill with his elbow on a bar, glowering at a photographer. That photo could have been shot at the bar at Bentley's, with its affluent, English gentleman's club feel. Beyond the bar, the dining room affects a Victorian elegance, but not ostentatiously so. The menu offers American standards with a twist (stuffed clams, steak flambéed with Jack Daniels, champagne trout), but also opens its doors to international fare, like focaccia, Mediterranean-style sauté of mixed vegetables, and chorizo quesadillas. There's a fine brunch on Sunday; spite your doctor and go for the New England corned beef hash with poached eggs and hollandaise sauce.

Stick around late enough on weekend evenings and witness a transformation: The tables get swept off a dance floor; the ceiling rolls back to reveal high-tech lighting; and Bentley's becomes Woodstock's hot place (did someone say only place?) to dance the night away.

۞ The Prince and the Pauper. 24 Elm St. ☎ **802/457-1818.** Reservations recommended. Dinner $32 fixed price. DISC, MC, V. Sun–Thurs 6–9pm, Fri–Sat 6–9:30pm. NEW AMERICAN/CONTINENTAL.

It takes a bit of sleuthing to find The Prince and the Pauper, located down Dana Alley (next to the Woodstock Historical Society's Dana House). But it's worth the effort. This is Woodstock's best restaurant, with an intimate but informal setting. Ease into the evening by starting off in the lounge with its tap-room atmosphere (it's open an hour before the restaurant), then move over to the rustic-but-edged-with-elegance dining room. Start with an appetizer of lobster ravioli or smoked Coho salmon, then enjoy the grilled boneless rack of lamb grilled baked in a puff pastry with spinach and mushroom Duxelles, or a grilled swordfish with spicy Thai ginger sauce. The $32 fixed-price dinner offers good value, but if that's out of your budget, head to the lounge and order off the bistro menu ($10.95 to $15.95), with a selections like barbeque pork, Maryland crab cakes, and Indonesian curried lamb. There's also a selection of pizzas at $9.95.

Simon Pearce Restaurant. The Mill, Quechee. ☎ **802/295-1470.** Reservations recommended for dinner. Lunch items $6.75–$11.50; dinner main courses $16–$24. AE, DC, DISC, MC, V. Daily 11:30am–2:45pm and 6–9pm. REGIONAL/AMERICAN.

The setting can't be beat. Housed in a restored 19th-century woolen mill with wonderful views of a waterfall (spotlit at night), the Simon Pearce is a collage of exposed brick, buttery yellow pine floorboards, and handsome wooden tables and chairs. Meals are served on Simon Pearce pottery and glassware (if you like your setting, you can buy it afterward at the sprawling retail shop). The restaurant atmosphere is a wonderful concoction of formal and informal, ensuring that everybody feels comfortable here whether in white shirt and tie or (neatly pressed) jeans.

You might start off your evening with Maine crab cakes with roille, or cheese croquettes with tomato chutney. Then move on to the chile-cured roast tenderloin of pork with grilled corn salsa, or perhaps the seared tuna with sesame, noodle cakes, wasabi and pickled ginger. Simon Pearce is also open for lunch, when the menu lightens to include delectable entrees like warm goat cheese salad, grilled chicken sandwich with roasted peppers and parmigian aioli, and tarragon chicken salad with scallions and toasted almonds.

KILLINGTON

In 1937 a travel writer described the town near Killington Peak as "a small village of a church and a few undistinguished houses built on a highway three corners." The area was rugged and remote, isolated from the commercial centers to the west by imposing mountains, and accessible only through the challenging Sherburne Pass.

That was before Vermont's second highest mountain was developed as the Northeast's largest ski area. And before a wide, five-mile-long access road was slashed through the forest to the mountain's base. And before Route 4 was widened and improved, easing access to Rutland. In fact, that early travel writer would be hard-pressed to recognize the region today.

Since the mountain was first developed for skiing in 1957, dozens of restaurants, hotels, and convenience stores have sprouted along Killington Road to accommodate the legions of skiers who descend on the area during the long skiing season, which typically runs October through May.

Killington Road is a brightly lit, highly developed modern ski resort access road. There's not much to remind visitors of classic Vermont between the highway and the base lodge. Suburban-style theme restaurants dot the route (The Grist Mill has a waterwheel; Casey's Caboose has a red caboose), along with dozens of hotels and condos ranging from high-end fancy to low-end dowdy.

It's also become a choice destination for those who ski for the nightlife as much for the moguls. With some 60 bars within striking distance, Killington cultivates a hard-partying personality. The area has a frenetic, where-it's-happening feel in winter. (That's not the case in summer, when the empty parking lots can trigger mild melancholia.) Those most content here are skiers who like their skiing BIG, and travelers who want a wide selection of amenities and are willing to sacrifice charm for choice.

ESSENTIALS

GETTING THERE   Killington Road extends southward from Routes 4 & 100, just east the intersection with Route 100 north. It's about 12 miles east of Rutland on Route 4. Many of the inns offer shuttles to the Rutland airport.

VISITOR INFORMATION   The **Killington & Pico Areas Association,** P.O. Box 114, Killington, VT 05751 (☎ **802/773-4181**), supplies seasonal travel information from the Killington Ltd. Ski Shop on Route 4 just west of Route 100. It's open May through Oct. from 10 am to 6 pm. For winter information, contact the **Killington Travel Service** (☎ **800/372-2007**) or the **Killington Lodging Bureau** (☎ **800/621-6867**). For the Pico Mountain area, try the **Pico Lodging Bureau** (☎ **802/775-9140**).

Hey, Colorado! Don't Look Back!

If you haven't already heard of Leslie B. Otten, ski mogul of New England, the chances are you soon will.

Otten started his career working for a company that owned several other area resorts. Early on, he was sent to western Maine to manage sleepy Sunday River, which then consisted of a handful of runs and some creaky T-bars. Sensing far greater potential, Otten bought the ski mountain from his bosses, along with thousands of acres of adjacent land, and began expanding aggressively, investing more than $100 million over the years in high-speed chairlifts, high-tech snowmaking, and accommodations. Before long, Sunday River had gained huge respect for its challenging runs and superb snow conditions, and was regularly beating out Maine favorite Sugarloaf/USA as the most popular ski area in the state.

As it turns out, Otten was just warming up. A few years ago he bought Sugarbush in Vermont, along with both Attitash and Cranmore in New Hampshire, upgrading the facilities to the tune of millions of dollars. And then in February 1996, his LBO Enterprises snapped up a brace of other prestigious New England ski areas when it bought SKI Ltd., its major competitor. Otten now also owns Killington (New England's biggest ski mountain), Mt. Snow, and Haystack in Vermont, plus Waterville Valley in New Hampshire and former rival Sugarloaf/USA in Maine.

Otten's aim: to boost the profile of skiing in New England, and in turn better compete with the Rockies and the West for the attentions of U.S. skiers. Ambitious? Of course. And Otten just might be the guy to do it.

ALPINE SKIING

Killington. Killington, VT 05751. ☎ **802/422-3261,** or 800/621-6867 for lodging. Vertical drop: 3,150 feet. Lifts: 2 gondolas, 16 chairlifts (2 high-speed), 2 surface lifts. Skiable acreage: 935. Lift tickets: $48.

Killington is the Northeast's largest ski area, and it's been likened to a huge mall that's run with brisk efficiency if not much of a personal touch. That's a bit unfair, because Killington's personality is not found in its service, but in its trails, which range from long, old-fashioned, narrow trails with almost no discernible downhill slope to killer bump runs high on its flanks.

Skiers new to Killington are in a bit of a quandary. The two-sided trail map is virtually worthless since it's impossible to follow. But make one wrong turn and you'll end up on a no-slope green trail practically walking back to the bottom.

My advice: At the outset, focus on one lift and follow the lift signs—don't even try to figure out the trail signs. After a couple of runs, the layout will start to make sense. Then move on to another lift. And if you're reasonably competent on skis, don't be intimidated by the black diamonds. Many of these expert slopes are intersected by beginner or intermediate escape trails, but this isn't always indicated at the major intersections. Take some chances.

Killington is a superb mountains for both experts and beginners. Intermediates might find the lack of blue trails a bit frustrating, and may be more content at Pico. Also bear in mind that Killington's trails are heavily congested on weekends; I'd advise moving over to Pico for at least Saturday and possibly Sunday.

Pico. Sherburne Pass, Rutland, VT 05701. ☎ **802/775-4345,** or 800/898-7426 for lodging. Vertical drop: 1,967 feet. Lifts: 7 chairlifts (2 high speed), 3 surface lifts. Skiable acreage: 200. Lift tickets: $41 weekends, $37 weekdays.

Pico claims to offer skiing on five peaks; the casual observer will discern three, maybe four. But they're fine peaks, with a good variety of terrain and with trails maintained in good condition. The lower mountain has fine, open intermediate cruising runs that are served by a detachable quad. The upper mountain offers some beautiful glade skiing; the Outpost double chair serves serious expert slopes. Among its greatest charms, Pico rarely inconveniences its guest with lift lines, even on weekends.

Pico's "village" at the base is modest, subdued, and quietly appealing. It's fairly sleepy at night (nightlife mavens head over to Killington Road), which makes it a good choice for families looking for a tranquil stay near the slopes.

CROSS-COUNTRY SKIING

The intricate network of trails at the **Mountain Top Inn** (☎ 802/483-2311 or 800/ 445-2100) has had a loyal local following for years, but it's now attracting considerable attention from far-flung skiers as well. The 66-mile trail network runs through mixed terrain with fabulous views, and is nicely groomed for both traditional and skate-skiing. The area is often deep with snow owing to its high ridgetop location in the hills east of Rutland, and snowmaking along key portions of the trail ensure that you won't have to walk across bare spots during snow droughts. The resort maintains three warming huts along the way, and lessons and ski rentals are available. The trails cover a wide variety of terrain, with a elevation gain of 670 feet. Trail passes are $13 adult, $10 child.

SUMMER ACTIVITIES

MOUNTAIN BIKING   Mountain bikers challenge themselves on Killington's five mountains as they explore 50 miles of trails. The main lift is equipped to haul bikes and riders to the summit, delivering spectacular views. Riders then give their forearms a workout applying breaks with some vigor and frequency while bumping down the slopes. Explore on your own, or sign up for a full- or half-day tour.

The **Mountain Bike Shop** (☎ 802/422-6232) is located at the Killington Base Lodge and is open from June through mid-October from 9am to 6pm daily. A trail pass is $5; trail pass with a one-time chairlift ride is $15; unlimited chairlift rides are $25 per day. Bike rentals are also available, starting at $20 for 2 hours, or $32 for a day. Helmets are required ($3 per day).

HIKING   Those who'd like to explore the rocky highlands but are a bit unsure of themselves in the wild should head for the **Merrell Hiking Center** (☎ 802/ 422-6708) at the Killington Base Lodge. The center's staff can offer helpful recommendations on area trails based on your experience and inclinations. Five dollars gets you a trail pass for hiking on Killington Peak, a map, and a pocket field guide. Another $5 will allow you to cut to the chase by taking the chairlift to the 4,195-foot summit to explore the ridgeline before hiking down. (This also offers a way for hikers with bad knees to stay active: Hike to the summit, then avoid the knee-jarring descent by riding the chairlift down.) Guided nature hikes and other specialized tours are available on request, as are rentals of boots and backpacks.

Hikers on their own might set their sights on Deer Leap Mountain and its popular three-hour loop to the summit and back. The trail departs from the Inn at Long Trail off Route 4 at Sherburne Pass. Park across from the inn, then head north through the inn's parking lot onto the Long Trail/Appalachian Trail and into the forest. Follow the white blazes (you'll return on the blue-blazed trail you'll see entering on the left). In ¹/₂ mile, you'll arrive at a juncture. The Appalachian Trail veers right to the New Hampshire's White Mountains and Mt. Katahdin in Maine; Vermont's Long

Trail runs to the left. Follow the Long Trail, and after some rugged climbing over the next 1.9 miles, turn left at the signs for Deer Leap Height. Great views of Pico and the Killington area await you in $^4/_{10}$ of a mile. After a break here, continue down the steep, blue-blazed descent back to Route 4 and your car. The entire loop is about 2.5 miles.

Hikers can also find a mix of enjoyable trails in rolling hills blanketed with mixed forest at the 16,165-acre Calvin Coolidge State Forest, about 10 miles south of the Killington area, including short nature trails at Calvin Coolidge Historic Site.

To the north along Route 100, the Green Mountain National Forest has linked a number of exhibits and outdoor activities along the White River Travelway. This area along the White River between Stockbridge and Granville was one of the original routes used by Native Americans, and later was taken over by European settlers for stagecoach travel. Recreational areas along the river provide for hiking, canoeing, and wildlife watching, and interpretive exhibits help visitors understand the subtle links between the cultural and natural history of the area. For a brochure describing the travelway, contact the **Rochester Ranger District** (☎ **802/767-4777**) on Route 100 in Rochester.

BIRDWATCHING   Vermont Ecology Tours (☎ **802/422-3500** or 800/ 368-6161) offers breakfast with the birds from its headquarters on Killington Road. Guests meet at the office (or are picked up at their hotel) at 7:30 am for a two-hour tour of local habitats, including lake, woodland, and marsh. The tour, on a 13-passenger minibus, includes coffee and use of binoculars; bring something to eat. The cost is $12.

AN ADVENTURE IN HISTORY

President Calvin Coolidge State Historic Site. Route 100A, Plymouth. ☎ **802/672-3773.** Admission $4.50 adults, children under 14 free. Late May to mid-Oct daily 9:30am–5:30pm.

When told that Calvin Coolidge had died, literary wit Dorothy Parker is said to have responded, "How can they tell?" Even in his death, the nation's most taciturn president rarely got the respect even Dan Quayle received. A trip to the Coolidge Historic District should at the least raise Silent Cal's reputation among visitors, who'll get a strong sense of the President raised in this mountain village, a man shaped by harsh weather, unrelieved isolation, and a strong sense of community and family.

Situated in a high upland valley, the historic district consists of a group of about a dozen unspoiled buildings open to the public, and a number of other private residences that may be observed from the outside only. It was at the Coolidge Homestead (open for tours) that in August 1923 Vice-President Coolidge, on a vacation from Washington, was awoken in the middle of the night and informed that President Warren Harding had died unexpectedly. His father, a notary public, administered the oath of office.

With sloping, open meadows surrounding the village, visitors can plainly see the distinct patterns of life in an early Vermont town, where commerce and residential life clustered tightly and barn animals roamed the rest. A new mile-long walking trail offers access to the area's meadows and woods.

Be sure to stop by the Plymouth Cheese Factory in a trim white shop just uphill from the Coolidge Homestead. Founded in the late 1800s as a farmer's cooperative by President Coolidge's father, the shop is now run by the President's son, who in his 90s still stops by daily in summer. Excellent cheeses are available here, including a spicy pepper cheddar. "It's got some authority," an elderly clerk warned me, and she was right.

WHERE TO STAY

Killington offers hundreds of guest rooms along the access road between Route 4 and the mountain. Prospective visitors can request lodging information from the **Killington and Pico Areas Association** (☎ 802/773-4181). Or they can line up a vacation with a single phone call to the **Killington Lodging Bureau** (☎ 800/621-6867). The accommodating staff will take care of all your travel needs, including air or train reservations.

Expensive

Cortina Inn. Route 4 (1.5 miles west of Pico), Killington, VT 05751. ☎ **802/773-3333** or 800/451-6108. Fax 802/775-6948. E-mail cortina1@aol.com. 97 rms. A/C TV TEL. Winter and foliage season $175–$275 double; summer $140–$240 double. Rates higher during holidays. Rates include breakfast. AE, DISC, MC, V.

Travelers seeking modern amenities within striking distance of Vermont's wilds and ski mountains will be content at Cortina Inn. The original lodge, situated on Route 4 between Pico and Rutland, was built in 1966, with additions in 1975 and 1987. The interior still feels a bit like a private ski chalet—albeit one with really long hallways. Why, there's even a sunken conversation pit with a two-sided fireplace, and a spiral staircase up to the second level.

Guest rooms vary slightly in their modern country style, but all are comfortably furnished. Especially nice is Room 201 (the priciest of the bunch) with a loft, fan window, refrigerator, and Adirondack-style log furniture. Innkeepers Bob and Breda Harnish do a good job making this inn, with nearly 100 rooms, feel like a smaller and more intimate place. Especially appealing is the attention paid to detail—the hotel staff even brushes off the car windows of guests each morning after a snowstorm.

Dining/Entertainment: Evening meals are available on premises at Zola's Grill (see below). There's also a tavern, and afternoon tea is served in winter.

Services: Free shuttles to both Killington and Pico during ski season.

Facilities: Extras include a brick-walled indoor pool, a fitness room, a mountain biking center, eight tennis courts, and a small pond along the highway that's just big enough to practice a few canoe strokes. There's also a game room for kids, and another game room for adults (with pool and darts) off the downstairs tavern.

Inn of the Six Mountains. Killington Rd. (P.O. Box 2900), Killington, VT 05751. ☎ **802/422-4302** or 800/228-4676. Fax 802/422-4321. 103 rms. TV TEL. Winter $139–$179 double midweek, $179–$219 double weekend, $229–$269 double holidays. Off-season discounts available. Rates include full breakfast. AE, DC, DISC, MC, V.

With its profusion of gables and dormers, the Inn of the Six Mountains stands as the most architecturally dramatic of the many hotels along Killington Road. The lobby is welcoming in a modern, Scandinavian sort of way, with lots of blonde wood and stone, and the location is convenient to Killington's base lodge, just a mile up the road. But for a luxury hotel that offers only "deluxe rooms" and suites, and charges accordingly, the attention to detail comes up short. While the guest rooms are tastefully decorated in a Shaker-inspired sort of way, many have scuffed walls, weary carpeting, and bruised and gouged furniture. This might be expected in a ski dorm, but not in a luxury inn.

Facilities: There's a handsome restaurant, a festive lounge, an attractive indoor pool, and a well-equipped fitness center.

Mountain Top Inn. Mountain Top Rd., Chittenden, VT 05737. ☎ **802/483-2311** or 800/445-2100. Fax 802/483-6373. 35 rms plus 20 units with 1–4 bedrooms. A/C TEL. Summer and fall $176–$216 double; winter $176–$206 double midweek, $196–$246 double weekends and holidays; off-season $98–$168 double. AE, MC, V.

The Mountain Top Inn was carved out of a former turnip farm in the 1940s, but has long since left its root-vegetable heritage behind. Situated on 1,300 ridgetop acres with expansive views of the Vermont countryside, the inn has the feel of a classic, small Pocono resort hotel, where the hosts make sure you've got something to do every waking minute. Overall, the Mountain Top doesn't offer good value to those only looking for simple room and board. But those who like to be active outdoors and who prefer to stay put during their vacation will be kept plenty busy for their money.

Dining/Entertainment: The pleasant dining room, with heavy beams and rustic, rawhide laced chairs, features regional American cuisine with a continental flair. Entrees, which range from $12.95 to $20.95, might include pork tenderloin served with apples and an applejack brandy sauce, or New England seafood pie.

Facilities: In winter, excellent cross-country skiing on 66 miles of trails is included in the room rates. Come summer, horseback riding reigns supreme as the activity of choice.

Moderate

Ⓢ **Butternut on the Mountain Motor Inn.** Killington Road, Killington VT 05751. ☎ **802/422-2000** or 800/524-7654. 18 rms, with showers only. A/C TV TEL. High season $70–$110 double. Off-season discounts. MC, V.

The Butternut Motor Inn is fewer than 100 yards off Killington Road—but that's distance enough to lend a quieter, more solitary air. The inn has the character of a no-frills ski lodge from the 1960s, but it's been updated with modern touches like air-conditioning and cable televisions. The owners have even managed to pack some small surprises into the little space, including a wee indoor pool, and a Jacuzzi that could accommodate three strangers or six very good friends. There's even a lounge area with a fireplace on the second floor, and a restaurant with a full bar and darts on the first floor. It's a reasonable value for the price, especially during midweek in ski season.

Inn at Long Trail. Route 4, Killington, VT 05751. ☎ **802/775-7181.** 22 rms, some with showers only. Midweek $78–$98 double, including full breakfast. Two-night minimum on weekends and during foliage season at $300–$398 double, including two nights, two dinners, and two breakfasts. AE, MC, V. Closed late Apr to late June.

The Inn at Long Trail, situated in an architecturally undistinguished building at the intersection of busy Route 4 and the Long and Appalachian trails, is not a drive-by. The interior of this rustic inn is far more charming than the exterior. "Rustic" can be a travel-guide code word for "shabby," but that's not the case here. Tree trunks support the beams in the lobby, which sports log furniture and bannisters of yellow birch along the stairway. The older rooms in this three-floor hotel (built in 1938 as an annex to a long-gone lodge), are furnished simply in ski-lodge style. Comfortable, more modern suites with fireplaces, telephones, and TVs are offered in a motellike addition.

Just off the lobby is a relaxing, woody pub—an ideal place to knock back a pint of Guinness after a day on the trails. The back dining room maintains the Keebler elf theme, with a stone ledge that juts through the wall from the mountain behind. Innkeepers Murray and Patty McGrath (along with their children Connor and Brogan) emphasize the Gaelic in both atmosphere and cuisine. The menu features a selection of hearty meals popular with hungry hikers and skiers, including the inn's famed Guiness stew, corned beef and cabbage, and Irish poached salmon. Delicious homemade bread accompanies the meals. And there's live Irish music in the pub on weekends during the busy seasons.

WHERE TO DINE

No one goes hungry in Killington. A vast smorgasbord of restaurants lines the access road, offering a wide variety of choices. Restaurant goers should exercise some discretion, since a number of establishments are designed for volume rather than quality.

Expensive

✪ **Hemingway's.** Routes 100 and 4. ☎ **802/422-3886.** Reservations recommended. Summer main courses $22–$28; winter fixed-price menu $42–$45; vegetarian menu $36.50; tasting menu $60–$65 (with wines). AE, MC, V. High season Tues–Sun 6–10pm, off-season Wed–Sun 6–9pm. Closed briefly in mid-Apr and early Nov. AMERICAN/ECLECTIC.

Hemingway's is an unusually elegant spot. Opened by Linda and Ted Fondulas in 1982, the restaurant has become recognized nationally, and was named one of the nation's 25 top restaurants by *Food & Wine* magazine in 1992, and one of the 50 most distinguished U.S. restaurants by *Conde Nast Traveler* in 1993. It's continued to improve since then.

Located in the 1860 Asa Briggs House, a former stagecoach stop now fronting a busy stretch of highway between Killington and Woodstock, Hemingway's offers dining in three formal areas. The wine cellar has an old-world intimacy and is suited for groups out for a celebration; the two upstairs rooms are elegant with damask linen, silver flatware, crystal goblets, fresh flowers, and white gloves on the waiters. Fellow diners tend to be dressed casually but neatly (no shorts or T-shirts). The food is superior, and dinner comes at a price that's actually quite reasonable given the quality of the cooking and the superb presentation. (And just compare the cost of dining here with the cost at any other of the *Food & Wine* 25.)

The menu changes frequently to reflect available stock. Guests might start with a salmon carpaccio with coconut, seaweed, and brioche toast, or a wild mushroom and truffle soup, then move on to risotto with lobster, shrimp and grilled asparagus, or a Napolean of beef tenderloin with Roquefort pastry. For dessert, guests might conclude their feast with a citrus tart with Grand Marinier, or cappuccino ice cream in a caramel cage.

Moderate

Charity's. Killington Road. ☎ **802/422-3800.** Reservations not accepted. Lunch items $5.95–$6.75; main dinner courses $12.95–$15.95. AE, DC, MC, V. Daily 11:30am–11pm. PUB FARE.

Rustic, crowded, bustling, and boisterous, Charity's is the place to head after a day on the slopes if you like your food big and your company to be young. (Lunch time in summers is a decidedly more mellow affair.) The centerpiece of this barnlike restaurant adorned with stained-glass lamps and turn of the century prints is a handsome old bar crafted in Italy, then shipped to West Virginia, where it completed a run of nearly a century before being dismantled and coming to Vermont in 1971. The menu offers a good selection of burgers, plus a half-dozen vegetarian entrees, like veggie stir-fry and red pepper ravioli.

Zola's Grille. At Cortina Inn, Route 4. ☎ **802/773-3333.** Reservations recommended during peak seasons. Main courses $8.95–$19.95. AE, DISC, MC, V. Winter daily 6–9pm; off-season daily 6:30–8:30pm. REGIONAL/AMERICAN.

Set inside the modern Cortina Inn, this comfortable, carpeted dining room is soothing in its rich forest-green hues. Many (but not all) of the diners sit with ease in floral wingback chairs; brass table lamps illuminate many of the tables. The background music is uptempo classical, and the waitstaff is genuinely concerned that you're enjoying your meal. Entrees range from Cajun shrimp to garlic and lime roasted chicken, and veal medallions to swordfish. Pasta Zola is the budget item ($8.95), and features pasta with grilled veggies, sun-dried tomatoes, and spinach. The dishes fall short of gourmet, but are conscientiously prepared and the selections nicely varied. On Sundays Zola's lays out an extravagant, all-you-can-eat brunch between 10:45am and 1:30pm. Fill yourself and then some for $13.95.

Inexpensive

Mother Shapiro's. Killington Road. ☎ **802/422-9933.** Reservations not accepted. Breakfast $2.99–$8.75; lunch/munchies $3.95–$7.25; main dinner courses $9.95–$13.95. AE, DISC, MC, V. Daily, breakfast 7am–1pm, lunch and munchies 11:30am–2am, dinner 4:30–10pm. PUB FARE/AMERICAN.

Mother Shapiro's motto is "Such a nice place." That understated approach sets the tone for this funky, locally popular establishment. "Mother" is actually Jay Shapiro, a mustachioed entrepreneur who founded the restaurant in 1980. He's made this a fun, relaxed place, done up in a sort of Victorian vaudeville/brothel look. The menu nags ("no whining," "don't make a mess," "no substitutions concerning this menu unless it's not too busy, then we'll talk") while offering a broad if not overly creative selection of dishes. Individual breakfasts are nearly large enough for two. Dinners include teriyaki steak and pot roast, and a more-than-filling all-you-can-eat ribs dinner for $13.95. This spot is often tremendously busy with locals (especially at breakfast), and offers a good bar menu after hours for those whose hunger catches up with them long after the sun has set.

PPeppers. Killington Road. ☎ **802/422-3177.** Reservations not accepted. Lunch items $3.50–$6.95; main dinner courses $7.95–$12.95. AE, DC, MC, V. Daily 7am–midnight. PASTA/ECLECTIC.

This 1950s-style retro restaurant is a festive and upbeat kind of place—and almost always crowded with visitors and locals alike after a long day on the slopes. Situated in a strip-mallish complex near the top of Killington Road, PPeppers sets the mood with a black-and-white tile floors, red lightshades, and red chili pepper accent lighting. Take a seat at a genuine naugahyde booth, or grab a stool at the wooden counter. Despite the name, the food isn't all spicy here—the menu is diner fare, expanded for a more sophisticated clientele. But the hamburgers are great, the pasta above average, and the service is far more friendly than you'll find in many ski mountain establishments.

RUTLAND

Rutland is a no-nonsense, blue-collar town that's never had much of a reputation for charm. Today, it's undergoing a low-grade renaissance, attracting new residents who like the small-city atmosphere and easy access to the mountains.

Located in the wide valley flanking Otter Creek, Rutland was built on the marble trade, which was mined out of bustling quarries in nearby Proctor and West Rutland. By 1880, Rutland boasted more residents than Burlington, and had the distinguished honorific of "Marble City." Many fine homes from this era still line the streets, and the intricate commercial architecture, which naturally incorporates a fair amount of marble, hints at a former prosperity.

Rutland remains the regional hub for central Vermont, with much of the economic energy along bustling Route 7 north and south of downtown. The downtown itself shares its turf with an oddly incongruous strip mall, which appeared during one of those ill-considered spasms of mid-century urban renewal. The discount retailer that occupied the plaza recently migrated to its natural range on the edge of town, leaving the plaza somewhat woebegone. (As of this writing, discussions were underway for another discounter to occupy the space.) At the same time, the more historic parts of downtown are holding their own, and even benefitting from a minor rebirth as boutiques and new restaurants carve out their territory.

Rutland is a good spot for errands and a meal or two, easily worth a stop if you're en route from north or south. More than that, Rutland has the feel of a real place with real people, a good antidote for those who've felt they've spent a bit too much time in tourist-oriented ski resorts.

ESSENTIALS

GETTING THERE   Rutland is at the intersection of Route 7 and Route 4. Burlington is 67 miles to the north; Bennington is 56 miles south. Rutland is also served by scheduled air charters to Farmingdale, NY, via **NY Air Charter** (☎ 800/ 692-4724).

VISITOR INFORMATION   The **Rutland Chamber of Commerce,** 256 N. Main St., Rutland, VT 05701 (☎ 802/773-2747) staffs an information booth at the corner of Route 7 and Route 4 West from Memorial Day through Columbus Day. It's open daily from 10am to 6pm. The chamber's main office is open year-round Monday to Friday 9am to 5pm.

FESTIVALS   The **Vermont State Fair** (☎ 802/775-5200) has attracted fairgoers from throughout Vermont for more than a 150 years. It's held the first week of September at the fairgrounds on Route 7 south of city. Gates open 8am daily.

EXPLORING THE TOWN

A stroll through Rutland's historic downtown will delight architecture buffs. Look for the detailed marble work on many of the buildings, such as the Opera House, the Gryphan's Building, and along Merchant's Row. Note especially the fine marble exterior of the Chittenden Savings Bank at the corner of Merchant's Row and Center Street. Nearby South Main Street (Route 7) also has a good selection of handsome homes built in elaborate Queen Anne style.

Shoppers can also look for small finds at a variety of unique downtown shops tucked under awnings here and there. Among those worth seeking out is **Michael's Toys,** 13 Center St. (☎ 802/773-1488), which will make young kids wide-eyed. It's located at the head of a creaky Dashiel Hammett–esque stairway in a second-floor workshop filled with rocking cows, wooden trucks, and handcarved wooden signs. You half expect to find a gnome hard at work; instead it's the pleasant Michael, who doesn't care much for last names.

In the vacant storefronts of downtown, look for the handiwork of "The Phantom Gallery," which gives the work of local artists good exposure in abandoned shops.

A stop worth making, especially as a rainy day diversion, is the **Chaffee Center for the Visual Arts,** 16 S. Main St. (☎ 802/775-0356). Housed in a Richardsonian structure dating from 1896, with a characteristically prominent turret and a mosaic floor in the archway vestibule, the Chaffee showcases the abundant artistic talent from Rutland and beyond. While it owns no permanent collections, it does feature a changing exhibits of local artists, and much of the work is for sale. The building is on the National Register of Historic Places, and the glorious parquet floors have been restored to their original luster. The Chaffee is open daily except Tuesdays from 10am to 5pm (noon to 4pm on Sundays), and admission is by donation.

WHERE TO STAY

Rutland has a selection of basic roadside motels and chain hotels, mostly clustered along Route 7 south of town. Room ratess at the **Comfort Inn at Trolley Square** (☎ 802/775-2200 or 800/432-6788) include a free continental breakfast. The

Holiday Inn (☎ 802/775-1911 or 800/462-4810) has an indoor pool, hot tub, and sauna. Likewise, the **Howard Johnson Rutland** (☎ 802/775-4303 or 800/446-4656) features an indoor pool and sauna, with the familiar orange-roofed restaurant next door. The **Best Western Hogge Penny Inn** (☎ 802/775-0356 or 800/828-3334), which is on Route 4, offers individual rooms and suites, along with a swimming pool and tennis court.

ⓢ **Inn at Rutland.** 70 N. Main St., Rutland, VT 05701. ☎ **802/773-0575** or 800/808-0575. 10 rms, some with showers only. TV TEL. Sept–Oct and mid-Dec to Mar $69–$140 double; Apr–Aug and Nov to mid-Dec $49–$99 double. Rates include breakfast. CB, DC, DISC, MC, V.

Built as a family home in the 1890s by the grain empire Burdett family, the Inn at Rutland is a pale grey Victorian with a slate roof overlooking busy Route 7 on the north side of town. It's elaborate on the outside, and even more so on the inside. Gracefully curving walls, stamped plaster wainscotting, oak trim, and leather wallpaper are among the detailing worthy of note. The downstairs parlors are a bit formal in a fusty, Edwardian sort of way, but no matter. Guests are likely to spend their time in their rooms, most of which are unusually spacious and all of which are tastefully done in high Victorian style. Rooms facing Route 7 are a bit noisier, but this solidly wrought house seems to absorb most of the sound. Note also that the third floor rooms are less opulent with detail, but the top floor also houses the Washington and Rutland rooms, two of the largest and most peaceful of the bunch.

Innkeepers Tanya and Bob Liberman have operated the inn with gracious hospitality since 1993. One incidental note: the couple moved to Vermont from Bob's native Atlanta because Tanya, who's from Russia, was nostalgic for the snow and the cold.

WHERE TO DINE

Rutland has experienced not quite an explosion but at least a resounding burst in dining choices in the past two years. Never known for creative restaurants, Rutland now has some fine establishments that will appeal to travelers with more adventurous palates. There's also a healthy number of places that fall under the category of old reliables.

The **Coffee Exchange** (☎ 802/775-3337) is a casually hip café housed in a former downtown bank at 101–103 Merchant's Row. You've got your choice here: Grab a seat at a sidewalk table, or move inside and pick a room. (The bank vault is tiny and painted enchantingly, and you can have a lively conversation with yourself by using the echo.) A good selection of coffees is available, along with delectable baked goods like banana-nut tarts, croissants, and superb cheese danishes.

ⓢ **Black Cactus Café.** 12 Wales St. ☎ **802/773-5944.** Reservations not accepted. Main courses $5.95–$14.95 (most $6–$8). AE, MC, V. Mon–Sat 11:30am–10pm, Sun 4–10pm. MEXICAN.

My rule of thumb: The more piñatas displayed in a Mexican restaurant, the worse the food. The Black Cactus, which opened in 1994, has no piñatas. A good omen, and one that proves prophetic. Located on a downtown side street, the Black Cactus has a modern, bright, and colorful dining room that seats only 40 customers at its handful of tables. (Many prefer to sit at the beautiful faux-woodgrain bar.) A draught microbrew or frozen margarita will get you started, and then it's on to the very reasonably priced and tasty main courses, which include chili rellenos, burritos, enchiladas (with both red and green sauce), and quesadillas. For desert, throw diet to the wind with the sweet chimichanga: apples, bananas, strawberries, and raisins fried in a tortilla and served with a dollop of vanilla ice cream.

Capers Bistro. 97 State St. ☎ **802/775-9700.** Reservations recommended. Lunch items $5.95–$8.75; main dinner courses $9.95–$12.95. MC, V. Mon–Fri 11:30am–2pm; Mon–Sat 5:30–10pm. FRENCH/CALIFORNIAN.

Caper's four owners opened this restaurant in late 1995 with the goal of recreating the feel of a small Parisian bistro. And for the most part they've succeeded, doing so in a somewhat dowdy part of town a short distance from the historic district. With black-and-white checkerboard floors and lush tomato-squash walls, the bistro is intimate without being oppressive. The meals also shine, prepared by chefs who've trained at the New England Culinary Institute and under Wolfgang Puck. Lunch ranges from a simple cheese and fruit plate to a sliced pork sandwich with assiago, fontina cheeses, and aioli. For dinner, you might start with clams, sausage, and Yukon Gold potatoes, then segue to lamb shank with corn risotto and a red wine sauce, or potato-wrapped salmon with artichoke and veal stock reduction. Capers is a rare surprise for pedestrian Rutland, and local gourmands are rooting for its survival over the long haul.

Royal's Hearthside. 37 North Main St. ☎ **802/775-0856.** Reservations recommended on weekends. Lunch items $4.95–$9.95; main dinner courses $10.95–$19.95. AE, MC, V. Mon–Sat 11am–3pm and 5–10pm, Sun noon–9pm. AMERICAN.

Royal's Hearthside falls under the category of "old reliable." Situated at the busy intersection of Route 4 and Route 7, this local institution is calming and quiet on the inside. It's done up in a sort of Ye Olde Colonial American style, although some rooms are more aggressively colonial than others. Expect spindle-backed chairs, faux pewter sugar bowls, and Brandenburg concertos playing loudly in the background.

Meals don't tax the staff in the creativity department, but entrees are solidly prepared. They run along the lines of baked stuffed shrimp, broiled rack of lamb, grilled swordfish, an assortment of grilled meats, and an array of specials. Luncheons include sandwiches, burgers, and omelettes. If you're looking for a dinner bargain, arrive early for one of the $9.95 specials. "We take care of people who come early," the waitress assured me.

Vacant Chair. 121 West St. ☎ **802/775-7708.** Reservations recommended on weekends. Lunch items $5.95–$7.95; main dinner courses $7.95–$15.95. DISC, MC, V. Mon–Sat 11am–10pm, Sun 11am–3pm. VICTORIAN/AMERICAN.

A Civil War theme restaurant? Well, why not? Fans of Shelby Foote and James MacPherson will have no shortage of diversions to educate and entertain themselves in this restaurant, which features regional American fare prepared with recipes dating from the mid- to late 19th century. The owners scoured the country for Civil War–era cookbooks (mostly southern), and strive for authenticity in preparing the meals. Special entrees include a custardy "plantation eggplant" made with three types of cheese, and a unique oyster loaf. Or choose from more familiar dishes like chicken pot pie, Brunswick stew, Mark Twain steak (pan-fried and served with a creamed mushroom sauce), or Jefferson baked noodles and cheese. The education of diners continues on the walls, which feature photos and documents relating to the Late Unpleasantness.

MIDDLEBURY

Middlebury is a gracious college town set amid bucolic countryside. The town center is idyllic in a peculiarly New-England-as-envisioned-by-Hollywood sort of way. It's centered around a slightly awkward, sloping green; above the green is the commanding Middlebury Inn; shops line the downhill sides. In the midst of the green is a handsome chapel, and the whole scene is lorded over by a fine, white-steepled

Congregational church built between 1806 and 1809. Otter Creek tumbles dramatically through Middlebury, flanked by a historic district where you can see the intriguing vestiges of former industry. In fact, Middlebury has 300 buildings listed on the National Register of Historic Places. About the only disruption is the constant growl of trucks downshifting as they drive along the main routes through town.

Historic Middlebury College, which is within walking distance of downtown, doesn't so much dominate the village as coexist nicely alongside it. The college has a sterling reputation for its liberal arts educations, but may be best known for its intensive summer language programs. Don't be surprised if you hear folks conversing in exotic tongues while walking through town. Students commit to total immersion, which means no lapsing by gossiping in English while they're enrolled in the program.

ESSENTIALS

GETTING THERE   Middlebury is located on Route 7 about midway between Rutland and Burlington.

VISITOR INFORMATION   The **Addison County Chamber of Commerce,** 2 Court St., Middlebury, VT 05753 (☎ **802/388-7951** or 800/733-8376), is located in a handsome, historic white building just off the green facing the Middlebury Inn. Brochures and assistance are available weekdays during business hours. Ask also for the map and guide to downtown Middlebury, published by the Downtown Middlebury Business Bureau, which lists shops and restaurants around town. Downstairs is the Vermont Folklife Center, offering exhibits on the crafts, arts, and culture of Vermont.

WHAT TO SEE & DO

The best place to begin a tour of Middlebury is the **Addison Country Chamber of Commerce** (see above), where you can request the chamber's self-guided walking tour brochure.

The historic **Otter Creek district,** set along a steep hillside by the rocky creek, is well worth exploring. While here, you can peruse top-flight Vermont crafts at the **Vermont State Crafts Center at Frog Hollow,** 1 Mill St.(☎ **802/388-3177**). The center, picturesquely situated overlooking tumbling Otter Creek, is open daily and features the work of some 300 Vermont craftspeople, with exhibits ranging from extraordinary carved wood desks to metalwork to glass and pottery. The **Middlebury Center** also features a pottery studio and a resident potter who's often busy at work. The **Crafts Center** also maintains shops in Manchester Village and at the Church Street Marketplace in Burlington.

Beer hounds should schedule a stop at the **Otter Creek Brewing Co.,** 85 Exchange St. (☎ **800/473-0727**), for a tour and free samples of their well-regarded beverages, including the Copper Ale and Stovepipe Porter. The brewery is open Monday through Saturday 10am to 6pm and Sunday 11am to 4pm.

Located atop flat ridge with beautiful views of both the Green Mountains and farmlands rolling toward Lake Champlain, prestigious Middlebury College has a handsome, well-spaced campus of gray limestone and white marble buildings that's best explored by foot. The architecture of the college, founded in 1800, is primarily colonial revival. Especially appealing is the prospect from the marble Mead Memorial Chapel, built in 1917 and overlooking the campus green.

At the edge of campus is the **Middlebury College Center for the Arts,** which opened in 1992. This architecturally engaging center houses the **Middlebury College Museum of Art** (☎ **802/388-3711,** ext. 5007), a small museum with a selective sampling of European and American art, both ancient and new. Classicists will savor the displays of Greek painted urns and vases; modern art aficionados should head for the powerful "Imagem da Minha Revolta," a 1988 installation by Brazilian artist Franz Krajcberg that deftly depicts the tragedy of the destruction of the rainforest. The museum is located on Route 30, and is open Tuesday to Friday 10am to 5pm, and weekends noon to 5pm. Admission is free.

Equestrians should head 2.5 miles outside of Middlebury to the **Morgan Horse Farm** (☎ **802/388-2011**), which is owned and administered by the University of Vermont. The farm has roots dating back to the late 1800s, and was for a time owned by the federal government, which in turn gave the farm to the university in 1951. The farm is credited with preserving the Morgan breed, a horse of considerable beauty and stamina that served admirably in war and exploration, and are now prized as show horses. The farm and its 70 registered stallions, mares, and foals is open for guided tours daily May through October from 9am to 4pm daily. There's also a picnic area. Admission is $3.50 for adults, $2 for teens, and free under 12. To reach the farm, head past the college on on Route 125 to Weybridge Street (Route 23); turn right and follow signs for approximately 2.5 miles.

Outdoor Pursuits

HIKING   The Green Mountains roll down to Middlebury's western borders, making for easy access to the mountains. Stop by the **U.S. Forest Service's Middlebury Ranger District office,** south of town on Route 7 (☎ **802/388-4362**), for guidance and information on area trails and destinations. Ask for the brochure "Day Hikes on the Middlebury & Rochester Ranger Districts," which lists 14 hikes.

One recommended stroll for people of all abilities—and especially those of poetic sensibilities—is the Robert Frost Interpretive Trail, dedicated to the memory of New England's poet laureate. Frost lived in a cabin on a farm across the road for 23 summers. (The cabin is now a National Historic Landmark.) Located on Route 125 about six miles east of Middlebury, this relaxing loop trail is just a mile long, and excerpts of Frost's are poems placed on signs along the trail. Also posted is information about the trail's natural history. The trail, which is managed by the Green Mountain National Forest, offers pleasant access to the gentle woods of these lovely intermountain lowlands.

SKIING   Downhill skiers looking for a low-key, low-pressure mountain invariably head to **Middlebury College Snow Bowl** (☎ **802/388-4356**), near Middlebury Gap on Route 125 east of town. This historic ski area, founded in 1939, has a vertical drop of just over 1,000 feet served by three chairlifts. The college ski team uses the ski area for practice, but it's also open to the public at rates of about half what you'd pay at Killington.

There's also cross-country skiing nearby at the **Rikert Ski Touring Center** (☎ **802/388-2759**) at Middlebury's Bread Loaf Campus on Route 125. The center offers 25 miles of machine-groomed trails through a lovely winter landscape.

WHERE TO STAY

Middlebury offers a handful of motels in addition to several inns. Two well-kept, inexpensive motels are located south of town on Route 7: **The Blue Spruce Motel** (☎ **802/388-4091**) and the **Greystone Motel** (☎ **802/388-4935**).

Middlebury Inn and Motel. 14 Courthouse Square, Middlebury, VT 05753. ☎ **802/388-4961** or 800/842-4666. 80 guest rms (3 with shower only). A/C TV TEL. Midweek $68–$134 double; weekends $75–$144 double, $122–$210 suite. MC, V.

The historic Middlebury Inn traces its roots back to 1827, when Nathan Wood built a brick public house he called the Vermont Hotel. It's come a long way since then, and now contains 80 modern guest rooms equipped with most conveniences. The rooms are good sized and most come furnished with a sofa or upholstered chairs in addition to the bed; rooms are decorated in rich, dark hues and colonial reproduction furniture. The eight guest rooms in the Porterhouse Mansion next door also have a pleasant, historic aspect. An adjacent motel is decorated in an early American motif, but it feels like veneer—underneath it's still a motel.

The inn's spacious lobby is decorated in an aggressive colonial American style, but has a nice feel with creaky floor, leather chairs, and bowback sofas. Late in the day, the lobby is filled with the rich golden glow of the setting sun, making the wonderful colors come even more alive. Two dining rooms offer breakfast, lunch, and dinner, and plan including breakfast and dinner is available at $34 per person additional.

Swift House Inn. 25 Stewart Lane, Middlebury, VT 05753. ☎ **802/388-9925.** Fax 802/388-9927. 21 rms (1 with shower only). A/C TEL. $75–$165 double. Rates include continental breakfast. AE, CB, DC, DISC, MC, V.

The Swift House Inn is a compound of three graceful old homes set in a residential area just a few minutes' walk from the town green. The main Federal-style inn dates back to 1814; inside, it's splendidly decorated in a simple, historical style that still bespeaks a modern crispness.

There's a dining room and tiny pub (see "Where to dine," below), and common rooms that are comfortable if not terribly cozy. Guests rooms are uncommonly well designed with antique and reproduction furnishings. Especially appealing is the Swift Room, with its oversized bathroom, whirlpool, and private terrace. About half of the 21 rooms have fireplaces or whirlpools or both; all but two rooms have televisions. Light sleepers may prefer the main inn or the Carriage House rather than the Gatehouse down the hill; the latter is on Route 7 and the truck noise can be an minor irritant at night. The Swift House offers lodging at reasonable prices for what guest receive, and the less expensive rooms are among the better deals in the state.

WHERE TO DINE

Swift House Inn. 25 Stewart Lane. ☎ **802/388-9925.** Reservations recommended during peak seasons, weekends, and college events. Main courses $10–$22 (most $15–$17). AE, CB, DC, DISC, MC, V. Thurs–Mon 5:30–9:30pm. REGIONAL.

Guests here are likely to feel as if they're having an exceedingly pleasant dinner in the house of an elderly, wealthy relative—one with the good taste to hire a creative cook who understood when and where to borrow from the Orient. The dining room on the first floor of this wonderful inn is divided among three rooms, some of which are detailed with lustrous cherry woodwork and 12-over-12 windows. In the cooler seasons, request a seat near the fireplace with its gorgeous mantle of polished cherry and marble. If time permits, arrive early for a single-malt scotch at the cozy pub. Then, to food.

For starters, you might opt for the grilled duck sausage with polenta and a tomato-caper chutney, or spicy pork wontons with a pickled-ginger and lime vinaigrette. Next, it's on to roasted venison with a fried fruit compote, or dill-crusted salmon with caviar and a ham and white-bean sauce. Deserts flirt with the sublime; the crème brûlée is among the best in the state.

Woody's. 5 Bakery Lane (on Otter Creek just upstream from the bridge in the middle of town). ☎ **802/388-4182.** Reservations recommended on weekends and during college events. Lunch items $3.95–$6.95; main dinner courses $9.95–$16.95. AE, MC, V. Mon–Sat 11:30am–3pm and 5–10pm; Sun 10:30am–3pm and 5–9pm. Closed Tues in winter. PUB FARE/PASTA.

Woody's is not Olde New Englande. Set down a small alley in the middle of town, Woody's features dining on three levels overlooking the creek in an exuberantly retro interior with a huge neon clock, lots of brushed steel, soaring windows, and red-and-black checkered linoleum floors. It's the kind of fun, hip place destined to put you in a good mood the moment you walk in. Lunches include burgers, sandwiches, and salads, along with burritos and pita melts. Dinner is heavy on the pasta selections (try the fettuccine with sea scallops sauteed and served with a sauce of sun-dried tomatoes, leeks, basil, and cream), but also features appetizing selections from the grill, like Cajun-grilled salmon and a char-roasted leg of lamb with a poached garlic flan.

5 Montpelier & Environs

The region surrounding Montpelier is wonderfully diverse, offering glimpses of various Vermonts within a short distance. There's old industry in Barre, new industry (if you count Ben & Jerry's Ice Cream as industry) in Waterbury, stalwart institutions of state government in Montpelier, and resort communities around Sugarbush and Stowe. Between and around these towns are classic New England villages. Think of the region as a Vermont sampler. You can see a lot of Vermont without spending a lot time in your car.

The terrain is mountainous and it contains the highest and fourth-highest peaks in the state, but traveling isn't slow or difficult thanks to broad valleys and fast roads that wind their way through.

MONTPELIER & BARRE

Montpelier is easily the most down-home, low-key state capitol in the United States. There's a hint of that in every photo of the glistening gold dome of the State Capitol. Rising behind it isn't a bank of mirror-sided skyscrapers, but a thickly forested hill. Montpelier, it turns out, isn't a self-important center of politics, but a small town that happens to house the state government.

The state capitol is worth a visit, as is the local art museum and historical society. But more than that, it's worth visiting just to experience a small, clean, New England town that's more than a little friendly. Barre is more commercial and industry-oriented, but shares an equally vibrant past. Between the two towns is six-mile stretch of road with motels, fast-food restaurants, and many of the other conveniences sought by travelers.

Montpelier centers around two main boulevards: State Street, which is lined with state government buildings, and Main Street, where many of the town's shops are located. It's all very compact, manageable, and cordial. If you so much as think about crossing the street, the drivers of the next car will probably stop and wave you across.

Lots of people I know have visited Montpelier and come away thinking, "Hey, I could live here!" The downtown has two hardware stores next door to one another (one had this sign posted on its front door recently: "We just oiled our floor and it may be slippery when wet until it gets wore in"), and two movie theaters, including the **Savoy** (☎ **802/229-0509**), arguably the best art house in northern New England. At the Savoy, a large cup of cider and a small popcorn slathered with real, unclarified butter cost me $2.20.

Nearby Barre (pronounced "Barry") has a more commercial, blue-collar demeanor than upscale Montpelier. The historic connection to the thriving granite industry is seen here and there, from the granite curbstones lining its long Main Street, to the signs for commercial establishments carved out of locally hewn rock. (The absence of any imposing granite buildings is a bit odd, however.) Barre attracted talented stone workers from Scotland and Italy (there's even a statue of Robert Burns), which gave turn-of-the-century Barre a lively, cosmopolitan flavor.

ESSENTIALS

GETTING THERE   Montpelier is accessible via Exit 7 off I-89. For Barre, take Exit 8. Amtrak's Vermonter stops at the Montpelier-Barre station just east of town. Call **800/872-7245.**

VISITOR INFORMATION   The **Central Vermont Chamber of Commerce,** P.O. Box 336, Barre, VT 05641 (☎ **802/229-5711**), is located on Airport Road (Exit 7 off I-89). From Montpelier, head toward Barre on Route 62 and look for signs.

EXPLORING THE TOWNS

Start your exploration of Montpelier with a visit to the gold-domed **State House** (☎ 802/828-2228). If you're in a hurry, you can take a self-guided tour, admiring the statue of Ethan Allen guarding the doors, and the long, stately halls with marble floors. If time allows and you're here in the right season, take one of the free guided tours, which are offered July through mid-October. The tours leave on the half-hour Monday to Friday 10am to 3:30pm, and on Saturdays from 11am to 2pm.

A short stroll from the State House, at 109 State St., is the **Vermont Historical Society** (☎ 802/828-2291). This is a great spot to admire some of the rich tapestry of Vermont's history. The museum is housed in a replica of the elegant old Pavilion House, a prominent Victorian hotel, and contains a number of intriguing artifacts, such as the gun once owned by Ethan Allen. The Governor's Corridor offers a rotating series of artwork from the collection. The museum is open Tuesday through Saturday from 9am to 4:30pm, and Sundays from noon to 4pm. Admission is $2 adults, $1 for students and seniors.

Also in Montpelier is the superb **T.W. Wood Art Gallery** (☎ 802/828-8743) a short drive away on College Street on the campus of Vermont College. (Drive east on State Street to East State Street; continue to College Street and turn right.) This handsome historical gallery contains oil paintings by noted 19th century portrait painter T.W. Wood, along with a broad assortment of paintings by other talented Vermonters. The gallery is open Tuesday through Sunday noon to 4pm. Admission is $2; children under 12 free.

For Rock Fans

Rock of Ages Quarry. Graniteville. ☎ **802/476-3119.** Tours, $4 adults, $3.50 seniors, $1.50 children 6–12. Mon–Fri 8am–3:30pm. Closed Nov–Apr. Drive south on Route 14 from Barre; watch for signs to quarry.

When in or around Barre, listen for the deep, throaty hum of industry. That's the Rock of Ages Quarry, set on a rocky hillside high above town near the aptly named hamlet of Graniteville. A free visitors' center presents informative exhibits, a video about quarrying, a glimpse at an old granite quarry (no longer active), and a selection of granite gifts.

For a look at the active quarry, sign up for a guided half-hour tour of the world's largest quarry. An old bus groans up to a viewer's platform high above the 500-foot, man-made canyon (it looks like something sculpted by Picasso in his cubist period), where workers cleave huge slabs of fine-grained granite and hoist them out using 150-foot derricks anchored with a spider's web of 15 miles of steel cable. It's an operation to behold. Afterward, visitors are invited to stop by the nearby manufacturing plant to see the granite carved into memorials, architectural adornments, and other pieces.

For a more poignant, less staged display of the local stonecutters craft, head to Hope Cemetery, located on a hillside in a wooded valley north of Barre on Route 14.

The cemetery is filled with columns, urns, and human figures carved of the fine-grained grey granite. It's more than a memorial park—it's a remarkable display of the talent of area stonecutters.

GETTING OUTSIDE

Hikers should set off for the rolling Worcester Range and its network of trails north of Montpelier. Trails tend to be slightly elusive and a matter of local knowledge hereabouts. Your best bet is to check with the **Green Mountain Club** (☎ 802/244-7037), north of Waterbury, for advice. The group offer guidebooks and can point you in the right direction.

For local advice on and equipment for canoeing, camping, or cross-country skiing, check with the helpful staff at **Onion River Sports,** which has two shops in the area. In Montpelier, stop by at 20 Langdon St. (☎ 802/229-9409). In Barre, they're on Main St. (☎ 802/476-9750).

WHERE TO STAY

Autumn Crest. RFD #1 (P.O. Box 1540), Williamstown, VT 05679. ☎ **802/433-6627** or 800/339-6627. 18 rms (5 with shower only). TV. $98–$148 double. Rates include full breakfast. AE, DISC, MC, V. Take Exit 5 from Route 89 and head east toward Williamstown; after the crest of hill, look for inn on left as you descend.

This two century-old farmstead set high in the rolling hills south of Montpelier will delight farm fans and landscape lovers, but may disappoint history buffs in search of creaky floors and architectural detailing. The five guest rooms in the handsome older farmhouse have been thoroughly modernized, so much so that they're just about indistinguishable from the rooms in the rear addition, which was built in the late 1980s. But the views can't be beat, especially in fall.

Outdoors, the inn features a barn and paddock with 10 horses, a farm pond for swimming (or skating in winter), and hills for strolling. There's also a in-house canine and cat, and guests are welcome to bring their own pets.

Dining/Entertainment: As an added bonus, the inn offers excellent dining (entrees are $16.50 to $23.50), with meals ranging from seafood Provençal to rack of lamb roasted with dijon and served with a hazelnut demi-glace.

Capitol Plaza Hotel. 100 State St., Montpelier, VT 05602. ☎ **802/223-5252** or 800/274-5252. Fax 802/229-5427. 42 rms. A/C TV TEL. Midweek $82 double; weekends (May–Sept) $92 double; foliage season $102 double. AE, DISC, MC, V.

The Capitol Plaza is Montpelier's business and conference hotel, but is well-located (across from the State Capitol) to serve travelers planning to explore the town. This solid brick building was originally constructed in the late 1950s, but underwent a makeover with a change of ownership to a family-run business in 1993. The carpeted lobby is small and has a colonial cast to it; the rooms on the three upper floors also adopt a light, faux-colonial tone, and feature the usual hotel amenities, including in-room coffee makers. The hotel is nothing fancy, but it is clean, comfortable, and very convenient. A simply decorated restaurant on the first floor is open for all three meals.

Inn at Montpelier. 147 Main St., Montpelier, VT 05602. ☎ **802/223-2727.** Fax 802/223-0722. 19 rms (4 with showers only). A/C TV TEL. $99–$153 double. Rates include continental breakfast. AE, DC, DISC, MC, V.

Two historic in-town homes house guests at the Inn at Montpelier, and both offer superb accommodations with most major amenities. The main cream–colored Federal-style inn, built in 1827, features a mix of historical and up-to-date furnishings, along with a sunny sitting room and deck off the rear of the second floor. The larger front rooms are nicely appointed, but so too are the much smaller rooms in the former servants' wing. If you'd prefer not to catch the wafting scents of dinner cooking, ask for a room at the adjacent house, built in 1807, and decorated with comparable flair. Room 27 is especially pleasant, and features a large private deck. The inn tends to be a shade more antiseptic and spartanly furnished than other historic inns, but it's more intriguing and comfortable than any chain hotel.

Dining/Entertainment: The inn's restaurant is very well regarded, with appealingly prepared entrees featuring pheasant breast, salmon filets, and hand-rolled fettuccine. Entrees are priced from $13 to $21.

WHERE TO DINE

A creation of the New England Culinary Institute, **La Brioche Bakery & Cafe** (☎ **802/229-0443**) occupies the corner of Montpelier's State and Main streets. It's a little bit of Europe in one of New England's more continental cities (Montpelier could slip into the Black Forest or the Vienna Woods without causing much of a stir). A deli counter offers baked goods like croissants and baguettes. Get them to go, or settle into a table in the afternoon sun outdoors.

Ⓢ Horn of the Moon. 8 Langdon St., Montpelier. ☎ **802/223-2895.** Reservations not accepted. Breakfast $2.50–$4.50; lunch/dinner items $3.95–$5.25. No credit cards. Tues–Sat 7am–9pm, Sun 9am–7pm. VEGETARIAN.

This relaxed, informal, and inexpensive restaurant overlooking a tributary of the Winooski was the first vegetarian restaurant in Vermont, and it remains one of the best. In fact, it's appealing enough to attract plenty of meat eaters, drawn by the Middle Eastern platter, the tasty sandwiches made on whole wheat flatbread, and the Mexican-style dishes like burritos and tostadas. If you're looking for a full three-course meal with dinner rolls and linens, you're better off around the corner at the Main Street Grill. But if you want wholesome, inexpensive food, get here early, and get here often.

Main Street Grill & Bar. 118 Main St., Montpelier. ☎ **802/223-3188.** Reservations usually not needed. Lunch items $3.75–$6.50; main dinner courses $5.95–$12.75. AE, DC, DISC, MC, V. Mon–Fri 7–10am, Sat 8–10am; Mon–Sat 11:30am–2pm, Sun 10am–2pm; daily 5:30–10pm. AMERICAN/ECLECTIC.

This airy, modern grill serves as a classroom and ongoing exam for students of the New England Culinary Institute, which is located just down the block. It's not unusual to see knots of students, toques at a rakish angle, walking between the restaurant and class. Diners can eat on the first level dining room, watching street life through the broad windows (in summer, there's seating on a narrow porch outside the windows), or burrow in the homey bar downstairs. Dishes change with the semester, but might include a vegetarian chili, vegetable stir-fry, portobello mushroom sandwich, or a robust penne with chicken, artichokes, and sun-dried tomatoes in a fennel cream sauce. The breakfast burrito is served with a tangy corn salsa, and is nearly large enough for two.

For fancier, more formal dining, head the second-floor Chef's Table, which is also part of the culinary institute. Entrees here range from $15.25 to $18.75.

MAD RIVER VALLEY

The Mad River Valley is one of Vermont's best-kept secrets, and has something of a Shangri-la quality to it. In places it appears to have changed little since it was first settled in 1789 by Gen. Benjamin Wait and a handful of early Revolutionary War veterans, including half a dozen said to have served as Minutemen at the battles of Concord Bridge and Lexington.

Since 1948, ski-related development has joined the early farms that were the backbone of the region for two centuries, but the newcomers haven't been too pushy or overly obnoxious. Save for a couple of telltale signs, you could drive Route 100 through the sleepy villages of Warren and Waitsfield (it's hard to tell where one stops and the other begins) and not realize that you've passed close to some of the choicest skiing in the state. The region happily hasn't fallen prey to condo or strip mall developers, as have some other ski areas in Vermont, and it still maintains an aggressively friendly and informal feel.

The region's character becomes less pastoral along the Sugarbush Access Road, but even then, development isn't heavily concentrated, not even at the base of Sugarbush, the valley's preeminent ski area. The better lodges and restaurants tend to be tucked back in the forest or set along streams, and it behooves travelers to make sure they have good directions before setting out in search of accommodations or food. Hidden up a winding valley road, Mad River Glen, the area's ski older and grumpier ski area, has a pleasantly dated quality that eschews glamor in favor of the rustic. Its slogan is: "Ski it if you can."

One warning: The valley may see accelerated changes in coming months. Ski mogul Les Otten, who owns Sunday River, Sugarloaf, and Killington, among other major New England ski areas, purchased Sugarbush in 1995 and is sinking $28 million in mountain machinery and lodging. The idea is to put Sugarbush on the map the same way he put tiny Newry, Maine, on the map in the course of making Sunday River one of New England's top ski destinations. Bathed in a brighter spotlight, the valley may be forced into the current century, but for now it remains one of Vermont's best destinations for those shunning nightime glitz in favor of good skiing and a down-home atmosphere.

ESSENTIALS

GETTING THERE   Warren and Waitsfield straddle Route 100 between Killington and Waterbury. The nearest interstate access is from Exit 10 (Waterbury) on I-89; drive south on Route 100 for 14 miles to Waitsfield.

VISITOR INFORMATION   The **Sugarbush Chamber of Commerce,** P.O. Box 173, Waitsfield, VT 05673 (☎ **802/469-3409** or 800/828-4748), on Route 100, is open Monday through Saturday 9am to 5pm.

EXPLORING THE VALLEY

Without a doubt the most unique way to explore the region is atop an Icelandic pony. The **Vermont Icelandic Horse Farm** (☎ **802/496-7141**) specializes in tours on these small, sturdy, strong horses. Day and half-day rides are available, but to really appreciate both the countryside and the horses, you should sign up for one of the multi-day treks. These range from one to five nights, and include lodging at area inns, all your meals (lunches are either picnics or enjoyed at a local restaurant), your mount, and a guide to lead through through the lush hills around Waitsfield and Warren. In winter, there's also skijoring, which can best be described as waterskiing behind a horse. The overnight trips range from $355 (based on double occupancy) for the two-day trip, to $1,095 for the six-day trip. Call for information and reservations for day and half-day trips.

The classic **Warren General Store** (☎ **802/496-3864**) anchors the former bustling timber town of Warren. Set along a tumbling stream, the store has uneven wooden floorboards, a potbellied stove, and a shelf stock fully updated for the 1990s with a good selection of gourmet foods and wines. Get a coffee or a sandwich at the back deli counter, and enjoy it on the deck overlooking the water. Afterward, browse the crafts gallery upstairs, which features local pottery, leather goods, and candles. The store is located in Warren Village just off Route 100 south of the Sugarbush Access Road.

Visitors can explore local rivers or lakes with the help of **Clearwater Canoe** (☎ 802/496-2708) on Route 100 in Waitsfield, just north of the covered bridge. These outgoing guides rent canoes and kayaks, and offer shuttle services for intrepid paddlers looking for adventures ranging from whitewater (best in the spring) to a placid summer afternoon paddle on the Waterbury Reservoir. Rates are $35 per day for canoe rental; guided tours run from 9am to 3pm and cost $45 per person, including transportation, equipment and instruction (bring your own picnic lunch). In a romantic mood? Ask about Clearwater's moonlight cruises.

Also in Waitsfield is the **Mad River Canoe Factory Showroom** (☎ 802/496-3127). Experienced canoeists will recognize the name of this respected canoe manufacturer, which makes fiberglass and other canoes of complex laminates suitable for running raging rivers and poking around placid ponds. The showroom, located on Mad River Green, is open weekdays from 10am to 4pm. Paddling accessories (and some good advice) are also available here.

South of Warren, Route 100 pinches through Granville Gulf, a wild and scenic area of tumultuous streams and sheer hillsides. The highway twists and winds through this troll-like defile, which stands in contrast to the more open vistas along most of Route 100. Look for the roadside pull-off at Moss Glen Falls, one of the state's loveliest cascades.

Hiking & Biking

A rewarding 14-mile bike trip along paved roads begins at the village of Waitsfield. Park your car near the covered bridge, and follow East Warren Road past the Inn at Round Barn Farm and into the farm-filled countryside. Near the village of Warren, turn right at Brook Road to connect back to Route 100. Return north on bustling but generally safe and often scenic Route 100 to Waitsfield.

Bike rentals, repairs and advice are available in Waitsfield at **Mad River Bike Shop** (☎ 802/496-9500). The shop is located on Route 100 just south of the junction with Route 17, and is open daily 9am to 6pm (until 5pm on Sunday).

Hikers in search of good exercise and a spectacular view should strike for Mt. Abraham, west of Warren. Drive west up Lincoln Gap Road (it leaves Route 100 just south of Warren Village), and continue until the crest, where you'll cross the intersection with the Long Trail. Park here and head north on the trail; about two miles along you'll hit the Battell Shelter, which can sleep eight hikers. (There's also a spring nearby.) Push on another $8/10$ of a mile up a steep ascent to reach the panoramic views atop 4,006-foot Mt. Abraham. Enjoy. Retrace your steps back to your car. Allow four or five hours for the round-trip hike.

For a less demanding adventure that still yields great views, head south from Lincoln Gap Road on the Long Trail. In about $6/10$ of a mile, look for a marked spur trail to Sunset Rock with open vistas of the Champlain Valley. A round-trip hike requires about one hour.

Skiing

Sugarbush. Warren, VT 05674. ☎ **802/583-2381,** or 800/537-8427 for lodging. Vertical drop: 2,600 feet. Lifts: 14 chairlifts (4 high-speed), 4 surface lifts. Skiable acreage: 412. Lift tickets: $45.

After absorbing nearby Glen Ellen Ski Area to create Sugarbush South and Sugarbush North in 1979, this sprawling but low-key resort struggled with solvency under several owners. Noted for its often icy and rocky runs, the mountain tended to attract young kids and older skiers who prized the classic New England ski trails. The neon-ski-suit and grunge-snowboard crowd stuck with Killington, one hour south.

With the purchase of Sugarbush by Les Otten in 1995—and a quick $28 million in improvements—Sugarbush aims to add some flash and zip to broaden its appeal. The "new" Sugarbush got underway by linking the two areas with a two-mile, 10-minute high-speed chairlift (no more irksome shuttle buses), and adding three other high-speed, detachable quad chairlifts. Snowmaking has been significantly upgraded (Otten is a master of snowmaking, if nothing else), and the improved slopes are generating a buzz among ski bums far and wide. Sugarbush is still a family-friendly area at heart with great intermediate cruising runs on the north slopes and some challenging expert slopes to the south, but expect a harder and glossier edge as the resort races to make up for lost time.

Mad River Glen. Waitsfield, VT 05763. ☎ **802/496-3551.** Vertical drop: 2,000 feet. Lifts: 4 chairlifts. Skiable acreage: 90. Lift tickets: $26 midweek, $30 weekends.

Mad River Glen is the George Burns of the Vermont ski world—it's been around forever, it's curmudgeonly, and it does what it does very well. High-speed detachable quads? Forget it. The main lift is a circa-1950 single-chair lift that creaks its way to the summit. Snowmaking? Don't count on it. Only 15 percent of the terrain benefits from the fake stuff; the rest is dependent on unreliable Mother Nature. Mad River's slopes are twisting and narrow, and hide some of the steepest drops you'll find in New England. Mad River Glen has long since attained the status of a cult mountain among serious skiers, and its fans seem determined to keep it that way.

But how long it stays that way remains to be seen. Longtime owner Betsy Pratt sold the ski area to a cooperative of about 1,000 Mad River skiers in late 1995. It's said that most of the new owners are adamant about retaining the rough-hewn character of the mountain, but another faction is pushing for changes and modernization.

WHERE TO STAY

✪ **Inn at Round Barn Farm.** East Warren Road, Waitsfield, VT 05673. ☎ **802/496-2276.** Fax 802/496-8832. 11 rms (some with shower only). $100–$185 double. Rates include full breakfast. $5 surcharge during holidays and foliage. AE, MC, V.

"We're basically for romantics," says Jennifer, the assistant manager of this extraordinary inn. And that's the all-encompassing definition of "romantic." Those seeking the romance of Vermont will find it here in spades. You arrive at the inn after passing through a covered bridge off Route 100; a mile later you come upon this spectacular structure, set along a sloping hill with views of fields all around. The centerpiece of the inn is the eponymous Round Barn, a strikingly beautiful 1910 structure that's used variously for weddings, arts exhibits, and Sunday church services. Owners Jack, Doreen and AnneMarie Simko have improved the grounds bit by bit since opening in 1987, and they're now beautifully landscaped with stone walls, gardens, and duck ponds—the next project is a sculpture garden.

Elegant, pine-floored guest rooms will appeal to couples looking to kindle their own romance. Each is furnished with an impeccable country elegance so deft that it doesn't overstay its welcome. Particularly wonderful is the Dana Room, a peaceful retreat set privately down a narrow corridor, with gas fireplace, cathedral ceilings, and a luxurious steam shower. It's $155 a night—and a good deal at that. Common rooms downstairs are furnished with comparable flair. Especially inviting is the library with its oriental carpet, grandfather clock, and always-full decanter of sherry. A breakfast solarium overlooks some of the inn's pastoral 85 acres. No smoking.

Facilities: In the winter you can explore the inn's 18 miles of groomed cross-country trails, and then work the knots out in what's perhaps the inn's best surprise: a modern 58-foot indoor lap pool hidden partially beneath the barn.

Ⓢ **Mad River Barn.** Route 17 (R.R. #1; P.O. Box 88), Waitsfield, VT 05673. ☎ **802/496-3310** or 800/631-0466. 15 rms. Summer $65 double; winter $95 double. Rates include breakfast. AE, DISC, MC, V.

The Mad River Barn, run by former Mad River Glen Ski area owner Betsy Pratt, is a classic, 1940s-style ski lodge that attracts a clientele nearly fanatical in its devotion to the place. While half of the rooms have TVs and steam showers, it's best not to come here expecting anything fancy. Do come expecting to have some fun once you're settled in. It's all knotty pine, with spartanly furnished guest rooms, and rustic common rooms where visitors feel at home putting their feet up. Most guests stay in a two-story barn behind the white clapboard main house; some stay at the annex up the lawn. In winter, guests can elect to get their dinners on the premises, served in boisterous family style. In summer, the mood is slightly more sedate (only breakfast is offered), but enhanced by a beautiful pool a short walk away in a grove of birches. The Mad River Barn isn't so much an institution or accommodation as a big family, and guests who approach it in that spirit won't go away disappointed.

Weathertop Lodge. Route 17 (about a mile west of Route 100), Waitsfield, VT 05673. ☎ **802/496-4909** or 800/800-3625. 9 rms. Summer $78–$93 double; winter $82–$107 double. Higher rates on weekends. Closed mid-Apr to May and mid-Oct to Thanksgiving. AE, DISC, MC, V.

The outside of the three-story Weathertop Lodge doesn't promise much—it's built in flagrant disregard to any architectural aesthetic—but inside it's a comfortable, homey place with some surprising amenities, like a sauna and hot tub. This converted 1970s ski lodge has nine rooms that are all a bit on the dark side, furnished in classic casual country style with stencilling on the walls, quilts on the beds, and ruffles on the pillows. The lodge is within easy striking distance of food, entertainment, and skiing, and is a good place for a soak and sleep after a day on the slopes. No smoking.

West Hill Inn. West Hill Road (R.R. #1, Box 292), Warren, VT 05674. ☎ **802/496-7162.** 7 rms (4 with shower only). Summer $85–$105 double; spring $80–$95 double; foliage and ski seasons $90–$115 double. AE, MC, V.

Nestled on a forested hillside along a lightly traveled country road, the West Hill Inn offers the quintessential New England experience with an easy commute to the slopes at Sugarbush. Built in the 1850s, this farmhouse was expanded in the summer of 1995 with a modern common room, which offers a handsome fireplace for warmth in winter and an outdoor patio for summer lounging. The guest rooms vary, but all are well-appointed in an updated country style. A room with a fireplace sits atop a spiral staircase; two Hobbit-like rooms are tucked under the eaves above a narrow staircase in the old part of the home.

Guests often linger amid the rich, colorful tones of the library, with its woodstove and walls of books, or borrow a VCR and one of the 80 movies before retreating to their rooms. Country breakfasts are served around a large dining room table, and the day's first meal tends to be an event as much as it is nourishment. It often takes some effort to pry yourself away from the good company to get outdoors before lunchtime rolls around.

WHERE TO DINE

Chez Henri. Sugarbush Village. ☎ **802/583-2600.** Reservations recommended. Bistro menu $3.50–$9.50; main dinner courses $13.50–$21.50. AE, MC, V. Ski season and summer daily noon–10:30pm. Open weekends only during shoulder seasons; call first to be sure. FRENCH.

The oldest restaurant in the valley, Chez Henri has lured customers back for years with its elegant French cuisine and its intimate, French-farmhouse atmosphere. The bistro is located, somewhat improbably, in a lower level of the ski complex at the base of Sugarbush Mountain. In the summer, diners can relax on a tent-covered terrace along a gentle brook. In winter, angle for one of the seats near the stone fireplace indoors.

Popular with couples, Chez Henri also offers a children's menu and does a good job of catering to the finicky set, who may not be entirely enamored of escargot or other things French. Entrees tend toward classical French, and include rabbit in red wine sauce, filet of beef peppercorn, and swordfish grilled with a coulis. Late in the evenings, tables move aside in the back room, the music cranks up, and Sugarbush shows up for dancing and mingling.

✪ The Common Man. German Flats Road, Warren. ☎ **802/583-2800.** Reservations highly recommended in season. Main courses $9.50–$19. AE, DISC, MC, V. Daily 6:30–9pm. Open at 6pm on Sat and till 10pm on busier nights. Closed Mon from mid-Apr to mid-Dec. CONTINENTAL.

Dapper proprietor Mike Ware personally greets guests arriving at The Common Man, and it's clear by the warm response from returning patrons that he and chef Patrick Matecat are doing something very right. It's spectacularly located in a century-old barn moved here in 1987 (the original barn was destroyed in a fire), and the interior is soaring and dramatic, but manages to be intimate as well. Chandeliers, floral carpeting on the walls (weird, but it works), and candles on the tables meld successfully and coax all but coal-hearted guests into a relaxed frame of mind.

The menu is as ambitious and appealing as the decor. Guests might start with an appetizer of salmon fillet dressed with green peppercorns and spices, or cheddar and walnut raviolis with basil-marinated sweet peppers. The feast continues with dishes ranging from braised rabbit served with a creamed Dijon sauce, to rainbow trout sautéed with pine nuts and sage.

The Den. Junction of Routes 100 and 17, Waitsfield. ☎ **802/496-8880.** Reservations not accepted. Lunch items $3.50–$6.95; main dinner courses $8.50–$13.95. AE, MC, V. Daily 11:30am–4pm and 5–10:30pm. AMERICAN.

Jonesing for a juicy burger without frills or fancy service? Look no further: The Den is your destination. A local favorite with a comfortable, neighborly feel, it's the kind of place where you can plop yourself down in a pine booth, help yourself to the salad bar while waiting for your main course, and cheer on the Red Sox on the tube over the bar. The menu offers pub fare, with all manner of burgers, plus reubens, roast beef sandwiches, chicken in the basket, and even pork chops with apple sauce and french fries.

⑤ John Eagan's Big World Pub. In Madbush Falls Country Motel, Route 100, Warren. ☎ **802/496-3033.** Reservations not accepted. Main courses $9.50–$16.25; burgers and sandwiches $6.25. AE, MC, V. Daily 5:30–9:30pm. GRILL/INTERNATIONAL.

Extreme skier John Eagan starred in 10 Warren Miller skiing films over the years, but really took a risk when he opened his own restaurant in December 1994. Located in a 1970s-style motel dining room that's sorely lacking in charm or élan (save for the bar made of ski sections signed by skiing luminaries like Tommy Moe), the Big World Pub compensates with a small but above-average pub menu that the chef pulls off with unexpected flair. Dishes include wood-grilled chicken breast glazed with Vermont cider, ginger, and lime; pan-roasted pork loin brushed with Dijon; and a delicious fresh tortellini with tossed shrimp and sausage. Try the unique "dog bones" appetizer—Polish sausage wrapped in puff pastry and served with sauerkraut and mustard. Wash your meal down with a pint of custom Eagan's Extreme Ale, brewed by Vermont's Catamount Brewery.

Sam Rupert's. Sugarbush Access Road, Warren. ☎ **802/583-2421.** Reservations recommended. Sandwiches $5.25–$6.50; main courses $10.95–$22.50. AE, MC, V. Ski season daily 11:30am–3pm and 6–9:30pm (till 10pm Fri–Sat). Off-season Wed–Mon 6–9:30pm. AMERICAN.

This longtime valley favorite took root as a pancake house in a rebuilt barn in 1958. It's evolved and improved steadily since then. During the winter, weary skiers take midday breaks from the slopes and head to this rustic, attractively decorated eatery to unwind over a chicken pot pie, a burger, or a hearty sandwich before limping back to the slopes. In the evening, the atmosphere takes on a soft and romantic glow ("There's probably not 100 watts in the whole place," says the manager), and the menu heads upscale, with entrees like sautéed shrimp served with bow tie pasta and a basil cream pesto sauce, Black Angus sirloin with a brown peppercorn sauce, or fish and veal prepared in a different way each day.

WATERBURY

Set along the Winooski River, Waterbury lies at the juncture of Route 100 and I-89, making it a commercial center by default if not by design. Waterbury tends to sprawl more than other Vermont towns, perhaps in part because of the flood of 1927, which came close to leveling the town, and in part because it's attracted an inexplicable number of food companies (including Ben & Jerry's Ice Cream and Green Mountain Coffee) that have built factories and outlets in outlying former pastures.

The downtown, with its brick commercial architecture and sampling of handsome early homes, is worth a quick tour, but most travelers are either passing through or looking for "that ice cream place." Despite its drive-thru quality, Waterbury makes a decent home base for further explorations in the Green Mountains, in Burlington 25 miles to the west, and in Montpelier 11 miles to the east.

ESSENTIALS

GETTING THERE   Waterbury is located at Exit 10 off I-89. Waterbury is also served by Amtrak's **Vermonter,** with daily departures from New York (☎ **800/ 872-7245**).

VISITOR INFORMATION   The **Waterbury Tourism Council,** P.O. Box 468, Waterbury, VT 05676 (☎ **802/244-7822**), operates a small, unstaffed booth stocked with helpful brochures on Route 100 just north of I-89. It's open daily from 7am to 10pm.

EATING YOUR WAY THROUGH WATERBURY

Waterbury is the home to a number of food emporia, and is developing a reputation as sort of a factory outlet center for deluxe comestibles. Most shops are located along Route 100 north of I-89.

Start a tour with the "anchor store"—Ben & Jerry's factory—that started it all. The saga of Ben & Jerry's has been repeated enough in the national press that its doesn't need much elaboration here. It all began when school buddies Ben Cohen and Jerry Greenfield went into the ice cream business in a garage in Burlington in 1978, using just $8,000 in capital and a culinary education acquired from a $5 correspondence course. Today, the pair sells millions of pints of their rich, creamy ice cream, has set up scoop shops all around the world, and their factory has become the top tourist attraction in Vermont.

The factory, about a mile north of I-89 on Route 100, has a festival marketplace feel to it, despite the fact that there's no festival, and no marketplace. During peak summer season vast crowds wait for the 30-minute, $1 tours (the afternoon tours fill up quickly, so get there early if you want to avoid a long wait). Once you've got your ticket, browse the small ice-cream museum (learn the long, strange history of Cherry Garcia), buy a cone of your favorite flavor at the scoop shop, or lounge on the promenade, which is scattered with Adirondack chairs and picnic tables. For kids, there's the "Stairway to Heaven," which leads to a playground, and a "Cow-Viewing Area," which needs no explanation. The tours are informative and fun, and conclude with samples of the day's featured product. For more information on the tours, call **802/244-8687.**

A short drive north of Ben & Jerry's on Route 100 is a modern outlet featuring the products of three other area food producers: **Green Mountain Chocolates** (☎ **802/244-1139**), **Cabot Cheese** (☎ **802/244-6334**), and **Green Mountain Coffee Roasters** (☎ **802/244-8430**). All three have set up under one roof, and it's a good spot for free-range grazing. Cabot is the most generous with its samples; Green Mountain Chocolates, alas, is quite stingy. But try the truffles and other handcrafted chocolates, and don't forget a steaming coffee for the road. The outlets are open daily 9am to 6pm (until 8pm on Fridays). Ask the Cabot clerks about tours of their cheese factory.

Yet further north on Route 100 is **Cold Hollow Cider Farm** (☎ **802/244-8771**), a tremendously popular attraction. Despite its claim to be "New England's Most Famous Cider Mill," it's really just a sprawling gift shop housed in a very un-Vermont red, mauve, and purple farm complex. Tempting samples of various foods are arrayed around the shop, but ubiquitous signs nag shoppers against taking too much, thereby inducing unwarranted guilt with every bite. The vaunted cider-making operation is in the back and observers are welcome, but it's not a very compelling display. My advice: Look for one of the dozens of less commercial, unheralded cider houses in the small towns around the state if you want to find the flavor of a real cider farm.

HIKING CAMEL'S HUMP

A short drive from Waterbury is Camel's Hump, the state's fourth highest peak at 4,083 feet. (It's also the highest Vermont mountain without a ski area.) Once the site of a popular Victorian-era summit resort, the mountain still attracts hundreds of hikers who ascend the demanding, highly popular trail to the barren, windswept peak. It's not the place to get away from crowds on sunny summer weekends, but it's well worth the effort for the spectacular vistas and to observe the unique alpine terrain along the high ridge.

The round-trip loop hike is about 7.5 miles (plan on six hours or more of hiking time), and departs from the Couching Lion Farm eight miles southwest of Waterbury on Camel's Hump Rd. (You're best off asking locally for exact directions.) At the summit, seasonal rangers are on hand to answer questions and to admonish hikers to stay on the rocks to avoid trampling the delicate alpine grasses, found in Vermont only here and on Mt. Mansfield to the north.

WHERE TO STAY

Thatcher Brook Inn. Route 100, Waterbury, VT 05676. ☎ **802/244-5911** or 800/292-5911. Fax 802/244-1294. 22 rms (some with showers only). TEL. Peak season (including holidays,

The Story of Ben & Jerry

The doleful cows standing amid a bright green meadow on Ben & Jerry's ice cream pints have become almost a symbol for Vermont. But Ben & Jerry's cows (actually, they're Vermont artist Woody Jackson's cows) have also become a symbol for friendly capitalism (or "hippie capitalism," as some refer to it).

The founding of the company has become a legend in business circles. Two friends from Long Island, N.Y., Ben Cohen and Jerry Greenfield, started up their company in Burlington in 1978 with $8,000 and a few mail order lessons in ice-cream making. The pair experimented with the flavor samples they obtained free from salesmen, and sold their products—not all of which were hugely popular—out of an old gas station in town. Embracing the philosophy that if it's no fun, why do it, they gave away free ice cream at community events, staged free outdoor films in summer, and plowed profits back into the community. This approach, along with the exceptional quality of their product, built a successful corporation with sales topping $150 million.

While competition from other gourmet ice cream makers and a widespread consumer desire to cut back fat consumption has made it tougher to have fun and turn a profit at the same time, Ben and Jerry are still at it, expanding their manufacturing plants outside New England, introducing ice cream to Russia, and concocting new products like fruit sorbet. While their products are sold almost worldwide, the company's heart is still in New England. Look for their shops in and around many towns and villages, and watch for their trucks with the doleful cows on the side.

Christmas week, President's Week, and foliage season) $90–$175 double; $75–$175 double off-season. Rates include full breakfast. AE, DC, DISC, MC, V.

Thatcher Brook Inn is located smack on busy Route 100 near the Ben & Jerry's factory, but creative innkeepers have pulled off the illusion that guests are miles away from this major artery. The circa-1899 white-clapboard building has a nice historical character, even though it's undergone significant renovations and expansions in recent years. The new additions have kept its Queen Anne–style architectural integrity in tact. The common areas downstairs are worn to a nice patina, whether it's the old sitting area in front of the fireplace, or the newer bar and grill with its Windsor chairs. The guest rooms are individually decorated with furniture varying from Ethan Allen new to flea-market oak, but the overall character takes its cue from the Laura Ashley country look. Guest rooms are no-smoking.

Dining/Entertainment: The inn's dining room is well respected (main courses are $12.95 to $23.95), with guests choosing from four dining areas decorated in soothing tones.

Stagecoach Inn. 18 N. Main St., Waterbury, VT 05676. ☎ **802/244-5056** or 800/262-2206. 10 rms, 7 with private baths (some with shower only). Foliage season, Christmas week, and President's Week $55–$110 double; other times $45–$90 double. Rates include full breakfast. AE, DISC, MC, V.

This handsome, gabled home, within walking distance of downtown, is full of wonderful details like painted wood floors, a pair of upstairs porches to observe the town's comings and going, an old library with a stamped tin ceiling, and a chessboard awaiting a game. There's even a full bar where guests can buy a drink after their day's explorations.

The home was originally built in 1826, but was gutted and revamped in 1890 in the ostentatious period style by an Ohio millionaire. In 1987, after some years of quiet disuse, it was converted to an inn by owners who took good care to preserve the historical detailing. Rooms are furnished in a not-too-heavy Victorian style, mostly with oak and pine furniture. The two third-floor rooms have the original exposed beams and skylights, and are pleasant and open. The three back rooms share a bath and are exceptionally comfortable and quiet, offering guests the feel of boarding at a friendly farmhouse.

WHERE TO DINE

Ⓢ **Marsala Salsa.** 13–15 Stowe St. ☎ **802/244-1150.** Reservations recommended on weekends. Main courses $6.95–$10.95. MC, V. Daily 3:30–10pm. INDIAN/MEXICAN.

Here's the story: The owner is from Trinidad and was raised on the cuisine of India, but spent time working at a Mexican restaurant in Nevada. The result? Marsala Salsa, a hybrid that offers two international cuisines, both surprisingly well prepared, at a more than reasonable price. The restaurant, located in a funky storefront in Waterbury's historic downtown, is decorated with a light and culturally ambiguous touch. Service is friendly and informal. Mexican entrees ranges from enchiladas with crabmeat, to delicious carne asada, to bistec picado—strips of sirloin charbroiled with a homemade avocado-lime butter. If your hunger tempts you to the Asian subcontinent, try the curries or tandoori chicken, or a wonderful shrimp shaag—a light curry with sauteed shrimp, spinach, and carrots. Desserts tend toward Mexican, with flan, deep-fried bananas and coconut cream caramel. Marsala Salsa is an unexpected oasis deep behind local culinary battle lines manned primarily by cheddar cheese and maple syrup.

STOWE

There's no getting around it: Stowe is a tourist destination. That's even evident in summer, when tell-tale ski racks don't grace every car. After all, how else to explain the shop called "Everything Cows" that sells bovine-themed giftware?

But Stowe, which bills itself as the "Ski Capital of New England," has managed the juggernaut of steady growth reasonably well and with good humor. There are condo developments and strip mall–style restaurants, to be sure. But there are still spectacular views of the mountains, and wonderful vistas across fertile farmlands of the valley bottom. And the village of Stowe has retained its charm and small-town feel.

Stowe is quaint, compact, and contains perhaps Vermont's most gracefully tapered church spire, located atop the Stowe Community Church. Most of the recent development has taken place along Mountain Road (Route 108), which runs northwest of the village to the base of Mt. Mansfield and the Stowe ski area. Here you'll find an array of motels, restaurants, shops, bars, and even a three-screen cinema. A free trolley connects the village with the mountain during ski season, so you can let your car get snowed in and still not miss out on anything.

ESSENTIALS

GETTING THERE   Stowe is located on Route 100 north of Waterbury and south of Morrisville. In summer, Stowe may also be reached via Smugglers Notch on Route 108. This pass, which squeezes narrowly between the rocks, is closed in winter.

VISITOR INFORMATION   The **Stowe Area Association,** P.O. Box 1320, Stowe, VT 05672 (☎ **802/253-7321**), maintains a handy office in the village center. Ask for advice, pick up brochures, or make lodging reservations at dozens of area inns and hotels. This is a good first stop if you show up in town without a place to stay.

Stowe's homepage on the Internet may be found at http://www.stowe.com/smr.

The **Green Mountain Club,** a venerable statewide association devoted to building and maintaining backcountry trails, has a **visitors' center** on Route 100 between Waterbury and Stowe. This is a good place to buy detailed hiking guides, and to ask the staff for hiking and camping suggestions and ideas.

FESTIVALS   The week-long **Stowe Winter Carnival** (☎ **802/253-7321**) takes places annually at the end of January, as it has since 1921. The fest features a number of wacky events involving skis, snowshoes, and skates, as well as nighttime entertainment in area venues. Don't miss the snow sculpture contest, or "turkey bowling," which involves sliding frozen birds across the ice.

Outdoor Pursuits

Stowe's forte is winter (see the sections on skiing, below), but it's also an outstanding fair-weather destination, surrounded by lush, rolling green hills and open farmlands, and towered over by craggy Mt. Mansfield, Vermont's highest peak at 4,393 feet.

Deciding how to get up Mt. Mansfield is half the fun. The toll road (☎ **802/253-7311**) traces its lineage back to the 19th century, when it served horses bringing passengers to the old hotel sited near the mountain's crown. (The hotel was demolished in the 1960s.) Drivers now twist their way up this road and park below the summit of Mansfield; a two-hour hike along well-marked trails will bring you to the summit and unforgettable views. The toll road is open from late-May through mid-October. The fare is $12 per car with up to 6 passengers, $2 per person additional; $7 per motorcycle (two people). Ascending by foot or bicycle is free.

Another option is the **Stowe gondola** (☎ **802/253-3000**), which whisks ski-less travelers to within striking distance of the summit at the Cliff House Restaurant—it's about a half-hour hike further beyond. Hikers can explore the rugged, open ridgeline, then descend just before twilight. The gondola runs mid-June through mid-October and costs $9 for adults, $4 for children 6–12.

The budget route up Mt. Mansfield, and to my mind the most rewarding, is by foot, and you have at least nine options for the ascent. The easiest but least pleasing route is up the toll road. Other options require local guidance and a durable map. Ask for information from knowledgeable locals (your inn might be of help), or stop by the **Green Mountain Club headquarters,** open weekdays, on Route 100 about 4 miles south of Stowe. GMC can also assist with advice on other area trails.

One of the most understated, most beloved local attractions is the Stowe Recreation Path, which winds 5.3 miles from behind the **Stowe Community Church** up the valley toward the mountain, ending behind the **Topnotch Tennis Center.** This exceptionally appealing pathway, completed in 1989, is heavily used by locals for transportation and exercise in the summers; in the winter, it serves as a cross-country ski trail. You can connect to the pathway at either end, or at points where it crosses side roads connecting to Mountain Road. No motorized vehicles or skateboards are allowed.

Bikes are available for rent ($10–$25 for four hours) at **The Mountain Bike Shop** (☎ **802/253-7919**), located in the Big Red Building along the Rec Path.

Fisherfolk should allow ample time to peruse **The Fly Rod Shop** (☎ **802/253-7346** or 800/535-9703), located on Route 100 two miles south of the village. This well-stocked shop offers fly and spin tackle, along with camping gear, antique fly rods, and rentals of canoes and fishing videos.

Maple Syrup & How It Gets that Way

Maple syrup is at once simple and extravagant: simple because it's made from the purest ingredients available, extravagant because it's an expensive luxury.

Two elemental ingredients combine to create maple syrup: sugar maple sap and fire. Sugaring season slips in between northern New England's long winter and short spring; it usually lasts around four or five weeks, typically beginning in early to mid-March. When warm and sunny days alternate with freezing nights, the sap in the maple trees begins to run from roots to the branches overhead. Sugarers drill shallow holes into the trees, and insert small taps. Buckets (or plastic tubing) are hung from the taps to collect the sap that drips out bit by bit.

The collected sap is then boiled off. The equipment for this ranges from a simple backyard fire pit cobbled together of concrete blocks, to elaborate sugar houses with oil or propane burners. It requires between 32 and 40 gallons of sap to make one gallon of syrup, and that means a fair amount of boiling. The real cost of syrup isn't the sap; it's in the fuel to boil it down.

Vermont is the nation's capital of maple syrup production, producing some 570,000 gallons a year. The fancier inns and restaurants all serve native maple syrup with breakfast. Other breakfast places will charge $1 or so for real syrup rather than the flavored corn syrup that's so prevalent elsewhere. (Sometimes you have to ask if the real stuff is available.)

You can pick up the real thing in almost any grocery store in the state, but it somehow tastes better if you buy it right from the farm. Look for handmade signs touting syrup posted at the end of farm driveways around the region throughout the year. Drive right on up and knock on the door.

A number of sugarers invite visitors to inspect the process and sample some of the fresh syrup in the early spring. Ask for the brochure "Maple Sugarhouses Open to Visitors," available at information centers, from the **Vermont Travel Division** (134 State St., Montpelier, VT 05602), or from the **agriculture department** at ☎ **802/828-2416.**

Alpine Skiing

Stowe Mountain Resort. Stowe, VT 05672. ☎ **802/253-3000** or 800/253-4754 for lodging. Vertical drop: 2,360 feet. Lifts: 1 gondola, 8 chairlifts (1 high-speed), 2 surface lifts. Skiable acreage: 487. Lift tickets: $45.

Stowe's been knocked from its perch as the ski capital of New England in recent years (Killington, Sunday River, and Sugarloaf all can make more substantial claims). But this historic resort, first developed in the 1930s, still has lots of funky charm and plenty of good runs. Especially notable are its legendary "Front Four" trails (National, Starr, Lift Line, and Goat), which have humbled more than a handful of skiers attempting to claw their way from intermediate to expert. The majority of the slopes are located on Mt. Mansfield; other trails are on adjacent Spruce Peak, which has a vertical drop of 1,550 feet. Other facilities include eight restaurants and limited night skiing.

Cross-Country Skiing

Stowe is an outstanding destination for cross-country skiers, offering no fewer than four groomed ski areas with a combined total of 93 miles of trails traversing everything from gentle valley floors to challenging mountain peaks.

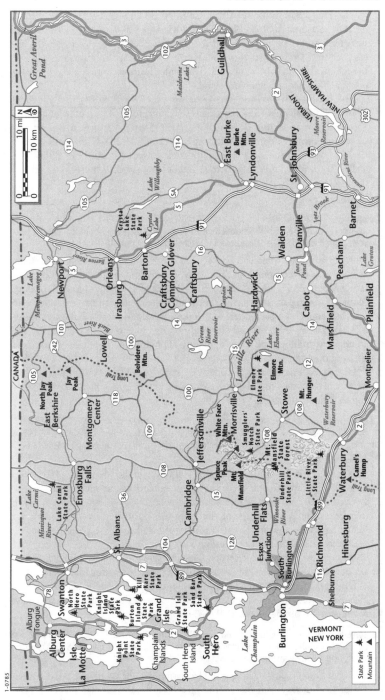

State Park ▲ Mountain

VERMONT
NEW YORK

The **Trapp Family Lodge Cross-Country Ski Center,** on Luce Hill Road, two miles from Mountain Road (☎ **802/253-8511** or 800/826-7000), was the nation's first cross-country ski center. It remains one of the most gloriously sited in the Northeast, set atop a ridge with views across the broad valley and into the folds of the mountains flanking Mt. Mansfield. The center features 36 miles of groomed trails on its 2,200 acres of rolling forestland.

The **Edson Hill Manor Ski Touring Center** (☎ **802/253-7371** or 800/621-0284) has 25 miles of wooded trails (15 miles groomed) just off Mountain Road. Also offering appealing ski touring are the **Stowe Mountain Resort Cross-Country Touring Center** (☎ **802/253-7311** or 800/253-4754), with 30 miles at the base of Mt. Mansfield, and **Topnotch Resort** ☎ **802/253-8585** or 800/451-8686), with 12 miles of groomed and ungroomed trails in the forest off Mountain Road.

WHERE TO STAY

Gable Inn. 1457 Mountain Rd., Stowe, VT 05672. ☎ **802/253-7730.** 19 rms (most with shower only). Summer $85–$155 double; foliage season $100–$175 double; winter $90–$175 double; off-season $65–$140 double. All rates include breakfast. AE, DISC, MC, V.

Don't be surprised when you first walk in to see other guests bubbling away in the hot tub next to the front door. This cozy, familial inn, housed in a gray farmhouse facing Mountain Road, is a relaxed kind of place. The main inn has 13 comfortable rooms of varying size and shape simply furnished with country antiques; a newer "carriage house" out back offers four rooms, mostly with cathedral ceilings, canopy beds, fireplaces, Jacuzzis, and air-conditioning. Two other "Riverview Suites" in an adjacent building are more opulently appointed, and include telephones and air-conditioning.

Dining/Entertainment: Breakfasts are served in a pleasant sun room with grand views across the road to distant Mt. Mansfield. The inn also offers tasty dinners with entrees ranging from $7.95 to $14.95.

✪ **Green Mountain Inn.** Main Street (P.O. Box 60), Stowe, VT 05672. ☎ **802/253-7301** or 800/253-7302. Fax 802/253-5096. 65 rms. A/C TV TEL. Winter and summer $109–$250 double. Higher rates on holidays, lower during off-season. Ask about packages. AE, DISC, MC, V.

This tasteful, historic structure is the only inn right in the village. It's a big place with 65 rooms spread through three buildings, but it feels far smaller, with personal service and cozy rooms. The rooms are all decorated with an early 19th-century motif that befits the 1833 vintage of the main inn. Primitive art, braided rugs, and stenciling on the wall in the guest rooms all blend nicely to create a mood that's pleasantly historic but not overzealously so. (About half the rooms are carpeted, so if you want the buttery golden wood floors, be sure to ask when you book.) Even the annex rooms, built some 25 years ago, have a pleasantly antiquarian flair.

Dining/Entertainment: The Green Mountain offers a raft of welcome amenities, including a beautiful outdoor pool set amid gardens, a fitness club, a library and game room, and two dining rooms. (See "Where to Dine," below).

Stowehof. 434 Edson Hill Rd. (P.O. Box 1139), Stowe, VT 05672. ☎ **802/253-9722** or 800/932-7136, Fax 802/253-7513. 50 rms plus two guest houses. A/C TV TEL. $70–$190 double. Rates include full breakfast. AE, DC, DISC, MC, V.

Stowehof's exterior architecture is mildly alarming in that aggressive neo-Tyrolean ski chalet kind of way. But inside, the place comes close to magic—it's pleasantly woodsy, folksy, and rustic in an Alpine way, with heavy beams and pine floors, ticking clocks, and massive maple tree trunks carved into architectural elements. Guests may feel a bit like characters in the Hobbit. The guest rooms are furnished simply, each decorated individually: some are bold and festive with sunflower patterns, others subdued and quiet.

Dining/Entertainment: Diners are are served in a cozy dining room, with entrees like Vermont venison stew, smoked pork chop, and the house specialty, wiener-schnitzel. Entrees range from $14.95 to $21.95.

Facilities: The inn has all-weather tennis courts and a beautiful pool outside the cantilevered sitting room. In the winter, sign up for a sleigh ride or a naturalist-led snowshoe hike.

✪ **Topnotch.** 4000 Mountain Rd. (P.O. Box 1458), Stowe, VT 05672. ☎ **802/253-8585** or 800/451-8686. Fax 802/253-9263. 90 rms. A/C TV TEL. Ski season $186–$570 double; off-season $130–$496 double; Christmas week $198–$685 double, with five-night minimum. Townhome accommodations $185–$695 depending on season and size. AE, DC, DISC, MC, V.

A boxy, uninteresting exterior hides a creatively designed interior at this upscale resort and spa. The main lobby is imaginatively conceived and furnished, with lots of stone and wood and an absolutely huge moosehead hanging on the wall. There's even a telescope to watch skiers schuss down the slopes across the valley. The guest rooms, linked by long, motel-like hallways, are nicely appointed if basic; ask for one of the top-floor rooms with cathedral ceilings.

Dining/Entertainment: Well-prepared, healthy dishes are offered in the inn's handsome stone-walled dining room (entrees $18 to $26).

Facilities: The spa facilities are the real draw here. Fitness classes are offered throughout the day, and guests spend much of their time around the exceptionally appealing 60-foot indoor pool with bubbling fountain and 12-foot whirlpool. There's an outdoor pool for summer use as well. Other activities include horseback riding, tennis (indoor courts provide for tennis all year), and cross-country skiing on the inn's property.

Trapp Family Lodge. Luce Hill Road, Stowe, VT 05672. ☎ **802/253-8511** or 800/826-7000. Fax 802/253-5740. 93 rms. TV TEL. Winter $138–$188 double (higher during school vacation); summer $118–$168 double. Breakfast $10 extra per person. Discounts available in spring and late fall. AE, DC, DISC, MC, V. Depart Stowe village westward on Route 108; in two miles bear left at fork near white church; continue up hill following signs for lodge.

The Trapp Family of Sound of Music fame bought this sprawling farm high above in Stowe in 1942, just four years after fleeing the Nazi takeover of Austria. Maria and Baron von Trapp's family continue to run this Tyrolean-flavored lodge. The original lodge burned in 1980, and guests still complain that its replacement lacks the character of the old place. But it's still a comfortable resort hotel, if designed more for efficiency than elegance. The guest rooms are a shade or two better than your standard hotel room, and most come with fine valley views and balconies.

Common areas with blonde wood and comfortably upholstered chairs abound, and make for comfortable idling. Especially nice is the second-floor library with fireplace.

Dining/Entertainment: The restaurant offers wonderful views for the lucky few with tables along the window, and well-prepared continental fare for all.

Facilities: Stowe's best cross-country skiing is just outside the door in winter.

WHERE TO DINE

The Harvest Market, 1031 Mountain Rd. (☎ **802/253-3800**), is the place for gourmet-to-go. The market offers basics like fruit and dairy products, but this isn't the place for the mundane. Browse the Vermont products and exotic imports (they've got eight different kinds of olives), then pick up some of the fresh-baked goods, like the pleasantly tart raspberry squares, to bring back to the ski lodge or take for a picnic along the bike path. There's also a great selection of wine and beer.

Cliff House. Atop Mt. Mansfield (gondola access). ☎ **802/253-3665.** Reservations required. Fixed-price dinner $39. AE, DC, DISC, MC, V. Open in winter on nights when night skiing is offered 5:30–9pm. Open irregularly in summer, but typically Thurs–Sun; call first. REGIONAL/ AMERICAN.

The setting is a somewhat stark, modern ski lodge. The food is well prepared if not quite worthy of a standing ovation. But talk about the views! Those are reason to hop the gondola to this high-altitude restaurant on the shoulders of Mt. Mansfield. Plan to arrive early enough to stroll the deck outside the restaurant; in summer, you can even come up in the late afternoon for the sunset atop Mansfield, then hike down to the Cliff House for diner. The restaurant offers a fixed-price dinner daily, with the charge including appetizer, salad, entree, dessert, and the gondola ride. Entrees draw on regional products, and might include spinach ravioli with Vermont chevre, native trout with forest mushrooms, or pan-seared tournedos of beef with roasted walnut spaetzle.

⑤ Miguel's Stowe-Away Lodge. Mountain Rd. ☎ **802/253-7574.** Reservations recommended weekends and peak ski season. Main courses $9.50–$12.50. AE, MC, V. Summer daily 5:30–10pm; other seasons daily 5–10pm. MEXICAN.

Located in an old, dark-red farmhouse midway between the village and the mountain, Miguel's packs in the locals who come for the most authentic Mexican food in the valley, if not in all of Vermont. Just like the big national chains, Miguel's has grown sufficiently popular to offer its own brand of chips, salsa, and other products in shops throughout New England. Start off with a killer margarita, then try out one of the appetizers like the queso fundido made with lamb sausage. Follow with dreamy crab enchiladas or the zesty zulu crisp—which includes just about everything they could scrounge up the kitchen. Miguel's offers superb quality for the money, and the kitchen pays attention to the little things, like using only Hass avocadoes for its guacamole rather than their watery Florida counterparts. Miguels also operates a branch on the Sugarbush Access Road in Warren.

The Shed. Mountain Rd. ☎ **802/253-4364.** Reservations recommended weekends and holidays. Lunch items $4.50–$7.95; main dinner courses $8.75–$15.95. AE, DC, DISC, MC, V. Daily noon–midnight (light fare only 10pm–midnight); Sun brunch 9am–11:30am. PUB FARE.

When The Shed burned down in early 1994, the gnashing of teeth and the tearing of sackcloth could be heard throughout the valley. Since opening three decades earlier, this friendly, informal place won converts by the sleighload with its solid pub food and feisty camaraderie. The good news is that the replacement structure has recaptured much of the original charm—especially the bar, with its barn-like interior that's already been worn to a nice patina. (The main dining room, alas, has the somewhat more sterile atmosphere of a chain restaurant.) The best news is that a new brewery was built along with the restaurant, and The Shed is cranking out some fine brews. Especially excellent is the dark Mountain Ale. The bar also serves up some fairly toxic West Indian rum drinks.

Whip Bar & Grill. Main St. ☎ **802/253-7301.** Reservations recommended. Sandwiches $4.95–$7.95; burgers and main dinner courses $5.50–$17.95. AE, DISC, MC, V. Mon–Thurs 11:30am–9:30pm, Fri–Sat 11:30am–10pm, Sun 11am–9:30pm (brunch served 11am–2pm). UPSCALE PUB FARE.

The Whip is located beneath the historic Green Mountain Inn in the village center, and management is quick to boast that it had the first liquor license in Stowe. This small, classy grill still has loads of pubby charm, and it's not hard to relax here after a day outside—even when facing the wall of antique whips (for horses, that is) that lends the bar its name. It's a good destination if you're hungry for something quick and fairly light. The menu offers a good selection of salads, sandwiches, and burgers. Slightly more ambitious meals include a lime and tequila marinated chicken quesadilla, and sesame-ginger stir fry.

6 Burlington

Burlington is a vibrant college town that's continually, valiantly resisting the onset of middle age. It's the birthplace of hippies turned mega-corporation Ben & Jerry's. It elected a socialist mayor in 1981, Bernie Sanders, who's now Vermont's representative to the U.S. Congress. Burlington is also home to the eclectic rock band Phish, which has been anointed by some as the heirs to the Grateful Dead tradition. And just look at the signs for offices as you wander downtown—an uncommonly high number seem to have the word "polarity" in them.

It's no wonder that Burlington has become a magnet for those seeking alternatives to big city life with its big city problems. The city has a superb location overlooking Lake Champlain and beyond to the Adirondacks of northern New York. To the east, visible on your way out of town, the Green Mountains rise dramatically, with two of the highest points (Mt. Mansfield and Camel's Hump) soaring above the undulating ridge.

In this century, Burlington turned its back for a time on its spectacular Lake Champlain waterfront (dubbed "New England's West Coast" by hyperactive marketers). Urban redevelopment focused on parking garages and high-rises; the waterfront lay fallow, open to development by light industry. In recent years the city has sought to regain a toehold on the waterfront, acquiring and redeveloping parts for commercial and recreational use. It's been successful in some sections, less so in others.

In contrast, the downtown is thriving. The pedestrian mall (Church Street) works here as it has failed in so many other towns. As a result, the scale is skewed to-wards pedestrians in the heart of downtown. It's best to get out of your car as soon as feasible.

ESSENTIALS

GETTING THERE   Burlington is at the junction of I-89, Route 7, and Route 2.

Burlington International Airport, about three miles east of downtown, is served by **Continental Express** (☎ 800/732-6887), **United Airlines** (☎ 800/241-6522), **USAir** (☎ 800/428-4322), and **Delta Connection** (☎ 800/345-3400).

Amtrak's Vermonter offers daily departures for Burlington from Washington, Baltimore, Philadelphia, New York, New Haven, and Springfield, Mass. Call **800/ 872-7245** for more information.

Vermont Transit Lines (☎ 802/864-6811), with a depot at 135 St. Paul St. facing City Hall Park, offers bus connections from Albany, Boston, Hartford, New York's JFK Airport, and other points in Vermont, Massachusetts, and New Hampshire.

VISITOR INFORMATION   The **Lake Champlain Regional Chamber of Commerce,** 60 Main St., Burlington, VT 05401 (☎ 802/863-3489), maintains an information center in a handsome brick building on Main Street just up from the waterfront and a short walk from Church Street Market. The center is open weekdays from 8:30am to 5:30pm.

A seasonal information booth is also staffed summers on the Church Street Marketplace at the corner of Church and Bank streets. There's no phone.

Burlington has three free weeklies that keep residents and visitors up to date on local events and happenings. (To confuse matters somewhat, the Free Press is the one paper that costs money.) Seven Days carries topical and lifestyle articles along with listings. The Vermont Times emphasizes local politics. And "Vox," a Vermont Times product, has an extensive cultural and nightlife calendar. All three are widely available at downtown stores and restaurants.

SPECIAL EVENTS First Night Burlington (☎ **802/863-6005**) turns the whole of downtown into a stage on New Year's Eve. Some 500 performers—from alternative rockers to vaudevillians—play at 34 venues (mostly indoors) for 10 hours beginning at 2pm. The evening finishes with a bang at the midnight fireworks. One nominal fee covers all performances.

The **Vermont Mozart Festival** (☎ **802/862-7352**) takes place in various locales in and around Burlington (and even further afield) from mid-July to August. Call for a schedule and information.

ORIENTATION

Burlington is comprised of three distinct areas: the UVM campus atop the hill, the waterfront along Lake Champlain, and the downtown area flanking the popular Church Street Marketplace.

University of Vermont The University of Vermont was founded in 1791, funded by a state donation of 29,000 acres of forestland spread across 120 townships. In the two centuries since, the university has grown to accommodate 7,700 undergraduates and 1,200 graduate students, plus 300 medical students. The school is set on 400 acres atop a hill overlooking downtown and Lake Champlain to the west, and offers a glorious prospect of the Green Mountains to the east. The campus has more than 400 buildings, many of which were designed by the most noted architects of the day, including H.H. Richardson and McKim, Mead and White. (By the way, UVM stands for "Universitas Virdis Montis," which translates as University of the Green Mountains.)

UVM doesn't have a college neighborhood with bars and bookstores immediately adjacent to the campus, as is common at many universities. Downtown serves that function. The downtown and the campus are five long blocks distant, connected via aptly named College Street. A shuttle, which looks like an old-fashioned trolley, runs daily on College Street between the Community Boathouse on the waterfront and the campus. It's in operation year round between 11am and 9pm, and it's free.

Church Street Marketplace The downtown centers around the Church Street Marketplace, which is alive with activity throughout the year. (See "Shopping," below.) Fanning from Church Street are a number of side streets, containing an appealing amalgam of restaurants, shops, offices, and malls. This is the place to wander without purpose and watch the crowds; you can always find a café or ice cream shop to rest your feet. While the shopping and grazing is good here, don't overlook the superb historic commercial architecture that graces much of downtown.

Waterfront The biggest project on the waterfront these days is the $6 million renovation centered around Union Station at the foot of Main Street. In 1995 two new buildings opened. The Wing Building, an appealingly quirky structure of brushed steel and other offbeat materials, blends in quite nicely with the more rustic parts of the waterfront. (A little too nicely, some of the tenants complain, noting the lack of

Burlington

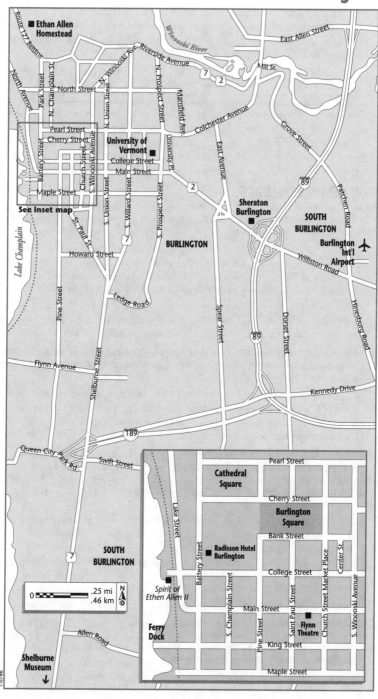

- Ethan Allen Homestead
- Route 127 Beltline
- Winooski River
- East Allen Street
- North Avenue
- Park Street
- N. Champlain St.
- North Street
- N. Winooski Ave.
- Riverside Avenue
- N. Prospect Street
- Mansfield Ave.
- Mill St.
- N. Union Street
- Colchester Avenue
- Grove Street
- Pearl Street
- Cherry Street
- University of Vermont
- University Pl.
- College Street
- Main Street
- East Avenue
- Battery Street
- Church Street
- S. Winooski Avenue
- Maple Street
- **See inset map**
- Lake Champlain
- S. Union Street
- S. Willard Street
- S. Prospect Street
- St. Paul St.
- Sheraton Burlington
- SOUTH BURLINGTON
- Patchen Road
- Howard Street
- BURLINGTON
- Burlington Int'l Airport
- Williston Road
- Ledge Road
- Spear Street
- Dorset Street
- Hinesburg Road
- Pine Street
- Flynn Avenue
- Shelburne Street
- Kennedy Drive
- 189
- Queen City Park Rd.
- Swift Street
- Pearl Street
- Cathedral Square
- Cherry Street
- Lake Street
- Burlington Square
- Bank Street
- Battery Street
- Radisson Hotel Burlington
- College Street
- Church Street Market Place
- Center St.
- SOUTH BURLINGTON
- Spirit of Ethan Allen II
- S. Champlain Street
- Pine Street
- Saint Paul Street
- Main Street
- S. Winooski Avenue
- Ferry Dock
- Flynn Theatre
- King Street
- Allen Road
- Maple Street
- Shelburne Museum
- 0   .25 mi   .46 km
- N

foot traffic to date.) Next door is the new Cornerstone Building, with a restaurant and offices, which offers better views of the lake from its higher vantage. Nearby is the city's Community Boathouse, which is an exceptionally pleasant destination on a summer's day (see below).

Bear in mind that Burlingtonians accept a fairly liberal definition of the adjective "lakeside." In some cases this might mean the shop or restaurant is 100 yards or so from the lake.

Elsewhere For upstairs/downstairs glimpse of Burlington, head to these two areas. Willard Street between Main and Cliff streets is lined with impressive mansions, some of which were built by the lumber barons when Burlington was a thriving port. North of town on North Street, a more rugged part of the city, you'll see how the other half lived in the remants of the city's proud working-class architecture.

EXPLORING BURLINGTON

Ethan Allen Homestead. Route 127. ☎ **802/865-4556.** Admission $3.50 adults, $3 seniors, $2 children 6–16. Mid-May to mid-June Tues–Sun 1–5pm; mid-June to mid-Oct daily 10am–5pm (Sun opens at 1pm). Take Route 127 northward from downtown; look for signs.

A quiet retreat on one of the most idyllic, least developed stretches of the Winooski River, the Ethan Allen Homestead is a shrine to Vermont's favorite son. While Allen wasn't born in Burlington, he settled here later in life on property confiscated from a British sympathizer during the Revolution. The reconstructed farmhouse is enduring tribute to this Vermont hero; an orientation center offers an intriguing multimedia accounting of Allen's life and other points of regional history. The Homestead is located in a sizeable park, which is open year-round. Admission to the park is free.

Robert Hull Fleming Museum. 61 Colchester Ave. (UVM campus). ☎ **802/656-2090.** $2 donation suggested. Year-round Sat–Sun 1–5pm; Labor Day to Apr Tues–Fri 9am–4pm; May to Labor Day Tues–Fri noon–4pm.

The University of Vermont facility houses a fine collection of art and anthropological displays, with especially strong collections from Europe and the United States. A selection of paintings by 20th-century Vermont artists are on permanent display. Call for a schedule of lectures and other events.

Lake Champlain ferries. King Street Dock, Burlington. ☎ **802/864-9804.** One-way fare for car and driver from Burlington to Port Kent $12; round-trip $5.50 for adult passengers; $1.50 children 6–12; children under 6 free. Burlington ferry operates mid-May to mid-Oct. Departures hourly in summer between 7:45am and 7pm. Schedule varies in spring, fall, and foliage season; call for current departures.

Car ferries chug across the often placid, sometimes turbulent waters of Lake Champlain from Burlington to New York State between late spring and foliage season. It's a good way to cut out miles of driving if you're heading west toward the Adirondacks. It's also a good way to see the lake and the mountains on a pleasant, inexpensive cruise. Take a round trip from Burlington with your binoculars; bring bite to eat.

Ferries also cross Lake Champlain between Grande Isle, Vt. and Plattsburgh, N.Y. (year-round), and Charlotte, Vt. and Essex, N.Y. (April through early January).

✪ Shelburne Museum. Route 7 (P.O. Box 10), Shelburne, VT 05482. ☎ **802/985-3346.** Summer admission (good for two consecutive days), $15 adults, $9 students, $6 children 6–14; winter tours, $7 adults, $3 children. Mid-May to late-Oct daily 10am–5pm. Nov to mid-May daily tours at 1pm (reservations recommended).

If you've allotted time to visit only one museum while in northern New England, this is the one. Established in 1947 by Americana collector Electra Havenmeyer Webb, the museum contains one of the most outstanding collections of American decorative, folk, and fine art. The museum is spread over 45 beautiful acres seven miles south of Burlington; the collections occupy some 37 buildings. The more mundane exhibits include quilts, early tools, decoys, and weathervanes. But the museum also collects and displays whole buildings from around New England and New York State. These include an 1890 railroad station, a lighthouse, a stagecoach inn, an Adirondack lodge, and a round barn from Vermont. There's even a 220-foot steamship, eerily landlocked on the museum's grounds. Spend a few hours here and you're bound to come away with a richer understanding of regional culture. The grounds also contain as museum shop, cafeteria, and picnic area.

In the winter, much of the museum is closed but tours of selected collections are offered daily at 1pm. Dress warmly.

The Spirit of Ethan Allen II. Burlington Boathouse, Burlington. ☎ **802/862-8300.** Narrated cruises (1¹/₂ hours) $7.95 adults, $3.95 children 3-11. Sunset cruises (2¹/₂ hours) $8.95 adults, $4.95 children. Specialty cruises (dinner, brunch, mystery theater) priced higher. Late May to mid-Oct.

The Spirit of Ethan Allen II is Burlington's premier tour boat. Accommodating 500 passengers on three decks, this sleek ship provides a good way of seeing Burlington, Lake Champlain, and the Adirondacks. The views haven't changed much since the area was explored by Samuel de Champlain, who first reached here in 1609. Food is available on all cruises, including all-you-can-eat buffets at dinner and on Sunday brunch. The scenic cruise departs daily every other hour beginning at 10am through 4pm. The sunset cruise departs at 6:30pm.

SHOPPING

The Church Street Marketplace is one of the more notable success stories of downtown development anywhere in the U.S. Situated along four blocks between Main Street and Pearl Street, and extending southward from the austerely elegant 1816 Congregational Church, the marketplace buzzes with the sort of downtown energy that urban planners everywhere are seeking. While decidedly trendy (there are Banana Republic and The Nature Company stores), the marketplace still makes room for a used book store and a $10 astrological reading joint. In summer, leave time to be entertained by buskers, sidewalk vendors, and knots of young folks just hanging out. In winter, there's the warm comfort of the Burlington Square Mall, an adjacent enclosed mall that's doing an admirable job of beating the suburbs at their own game.

Among the 100 or so shops hereabouts, a few are worth noting. **Pompanoosuc Mills,** 50 Church St. (☎ **802/862-8208**), sells an appealing line of simple, attractive wooden furniture. The **Vermont Trading Co.,** 66 Church St. (☎ **802/864-3633**), offers a colorful array of clothes in natural fabrics, along with a selection of imported goods. And avid readers can browse among the 80,000 titles at **Chassman & Bem,** 81 Church St. (☎ **802/862-4332**), usually open until 9 or 10 in the evening. Also worth seeking out is **Bennington Potters North,** 127 College St. (☎ **802/863-2221**), where shoppers can pick up fine pottery, kitchenware, and glass, including some items at discount prices.

North of Burlington in the riverside town of Winooski is the **Champlain Mill** (☎ **802/655-9477**), an attractive 1910 woolen mill that was converted to shops, restaurants, and offices in 1981. The mill hosts some 40 upscale retailers like Kenneth Cole and Patagonia, along with vendors of uniquely Vermont products, like Dakin Farms and its selection of locally smoked meats and cheeses.

OUTDOOR PURSUITS

Burlington is blessed with numerous attractive city parks. The most popular is **Leddy Park** (☎ 802/864-0123) on North Avenue, with an 1,800-foot beach, tennis courts, ball fields, trails, and a handsome indoor skating rink.

North Beach (☎ 802/862-0942) also features a long sandy beach, and camping for travelers with tents and RVs.

On the downtown waterfront look for the **Burlington Community Boathouse** (☎ 802/865-3377), a modern structure built with Victorian flair. A lot of summer action takes place at this city-owned structure and along the 900-foot boardwalk. You can rent a sailboat or rowboat, sign up for kayak or sculling lessons, or just wander around and enjoy the sunset.

Burlington's commitment to taking back its lake is best seen in the 9-mile Burlington Bike Path, which runs picturesquely along the shores of Lake Champlain to the mouth of the Winooski River. A superb way to spend a sunny afternoon, the paved bike route over a former rail bed passes through shady parklands and Burlington's backyards. Along the banks of the Winooski, you can admire the remains of an old bridge and scout around for marble chips.

Bike rentals are available downtown at the **Skirack,** 85 Main St. (☎ 802/658-3313), at $14 for four hours (enough time to do the whole trail), and up to $22 for a whole day. Skirack also rents in-line skates, which are also commonly used on the bike path. **Earl's Cyclery,** 135 Main St. (☎ 802/863-3832), and **North Star Cyclery,** 100 Main St. (☎ 802/863-3832), also rent bicycles.

A short drive east of the city is the **Catamount Family Center** (☎ 802/879-6001), a locally popular outdoor recreation center. It's open May to October and December to March. In summer there's mountain biking, orienteering, and cross-country running. Most of the 20 miles of trails pass through open fields and are suitable for novice mountain bikers. In winter, there's cross-country skiing and speed skating on the center's oval rink. Daily memberships are available. Drive east on Route 2 to the village of Williston; in the village, turn left (north) on North Williston Road; at Gov. Chittenden Road, turn right and continue to the center at 421 Gov. Chittenden Rd.

WHERE TO STAY

The good news is that Burlington has plenty of beds for visitors. The bad news? There's not much choice beyond oversized business-class hotels, cookie-cutter chain motels, and budget motels with rooms that smell vaguely funny. And other than the elephantine Radisson, there are few places to stay in Burlington's charming downtown. With its rich history and smattering of 19th-century mansions, it's something of a surprise that Burlington lacks a brick downtown hotel or a grand B&B.

The bulk of the motels are located along the two major access roads to the south and east. On Route 7 south of town, try the **Super 8 Motel** (☎ 802/862-6421 or 800/800-8000), the **Bel-Aire Motel** (☎ 802/863-3116), or the **Town & Country Motel** (☎ 802/862-5786). Clustered along Route 2 near I-89 and the airport are the **Holiday Inn** (☎ 802/863-6361), **EconoLodge** (☎ 802/863-1125 or 800/371-1125), and the clean, budget-priced **Swiss Host Motel and Village** (☎ 802/862-5734 or 800/326-5734).

In addition, a couple of no-frills bed and breakfasts are within walking distance of downtown. **Howden Cottage,** 32 North Champlain St. (☎ 802/864-7198), offers three small rooms in a cluttered 1825 house owned by local artist Bruce Howden. Breakfast is served in a new solarium. Double room rates are $45–$89. Also an easy stroll from downtown is the **Allyn House,** 16 Orchard Terrace (☎ **802/863-0379**). Located in an 1893 Victorian on a quiet residential block, the Allyn House also has three comfortable guest rooms. Rates are $55 per night.

✪ **The Inn at Shelburne Farms.** Harbor Road, Shelburne, VT 05482. ☎ **802/985-8498.** 24 rms (17 with private bath). TV. Spring $85–$210 double; summer $90–$220 double; fall $95–$250 double. AE, DC, MC, V. Closed mid-Oct to mid-May.

The numbers behind this exceptional turn-of-the-century mansion on the shores of Lake Champlain tell the story: 60 rooms, 10 chimneys, 1,000 acres of land. Built in 1899 by William Seward and Lila Vanderbilt Webb, this sprawling Edwardian "farmhouse" is the place to fantasize about the lifestyles of the truly rich and famous. From the first glimpse of the mansion as you come up the winding drive, you'll realize you've left the grim world behind. That's by design. Noted landscape architect Frederick Law Olmsted had a hand in the shaping the grounds, and noted forester Gifford Pinchot helped with the planting.

The 24 guest rooms are also splendidly appointed. Meals aren't included in the rates, but a restaurant on the property offers outstanding breakfasts and dinners. If you're traveling on a restricted budget, do this: Camp for a few nights, stay in a cheap motel, whatever it takes to free up a few dollars. Then pool your savings and book the least expensive room with the shared bath just to gain access to the mansion and the grounds. You'll feel like American royalty for a day.

Radisson Hotel Burlington. 60 Battery St., Burlington, VT 05401. ☎ **802/658-6500** or 800/333-3333. Fax 802/658-4659. 255 rms. A/C TV TEL. Winter $92–$102 double; summer $129–$139 double. AE, DISC, MC, V.

The nine-story Radisson offers the most extraordinary views and the best location in the city. As might be expected, it also offers all the amenities of an upscale national hotel chain, including an indoor pool, fitness room, covered parking, and two dining areas. Though built in 1976, renovations of the public areas in 1993 and the guest rooms in 1995 have kept the weariness at bay.

The hotel charges about $10 more for a lakeside room, and it's worth it. The views of the lake and the Adirondacks are spectacular; request a room ending with a "43"—these southwest corner rooms are bright and offer superb panoramas. Families with kids should angle for one of the five cabana rooms, which open up to the pool area.

Dining/Entertainment: If you end up with a city-view room, at least stop by the tiered bar and dining room, Seasons on the Lake, to savor the lake and mountain vistas.

Facilities: Indoor pool, fitness rooms.

Sheraton Burlington Hotel & Conference Center. 870 Williston Rd., Burlington, VT 05403. ☎ **802/865-6600** or 800/325-3535. Fax 802/865-6670. 308 rms. A/C TV TEL. May–Oct $85–$140 double; Nov–Apr $69–$125 double. AE, DISC, MC, V.

The largest conference facility in Vermont, the Sheraton also does a commendable job catering to individual travelers and families. This sprawling complex just off the interstate and a few minute's drive from downtown features a sizeable indoor garden area. The guest rooms all have two phones and in-room Nintendos (families take note); rooms in the newer addition (built in 1990) are a bit nicer, furnished in a simpler, lighter country style. Ask for a room facing the west (no extra charge) to enjoy the views of Mt. Mansfield and the Green Mountains.

Dining/Entertainment: The informal restaurant boasts its own gazebo.

Facilities: Indoor pool with retractable skylights for summer, two Jacuzzis, a fitness room, and an outdoor sundeck.

WHERE TO DINE

Burlington has as bounty of restaurants, easily enough to keep most diners content—especially if their tastes run toward spicy Asian food. As an added bonus, the best food isn't necessarily the most expensive in this city, which has a whole range of mid-priced restaurants that serve up tasty, filling meals without attaching a suction hose to your wallet.

Head to **Mirabelles** (☎ 802/658-3074) for coffee, pastries, and some of the other-worldliest desserts you'll find in the Northeast. Located at 198 Main St. just east of Church St., Mirabelles is small storefront with larger-than-life bakers. Try the triple-chocolate mocha mousse, the lemon-raspberry charlotte, or the delightful chocolate raspberry mousse cake. Have simpler tastes? Stick with the toothsome chocolate chip cookies, a bargain at 95¢. Mirabelles also has a shop in the Wing Building on the waterfront.

MODERATE

Daily Planet. 15 Center St. ☎ **802/862-9647.** Reservations recommended for parties of more than four. Lunch items $4.95–$6.50; main dinner courses $10.75–$18.25 (mostly $12–$14). AE, DC, DISC, MC, V. Mon–Fri 11:30am–3pm; Sun–Thurs 5–9:30pm, Fri–Sat 5–11pm. Sept–May Sat–Sun brunch 11am–3pm. ECLECTIC/GLOBAL.

This hugely popular, uncommonly creative spot is usually brimming with college students and downtown workers evenings and weekends. But it's worth putting up with the mild mayhem for some of the better food in town. The restaurant consists of several informal, comfortable dining rooms, including a solarium (pleasant during the winter brunch) and an adjacent bar, which has a loud, smoky saloon atmosphere with a stamped tin ceiling and a judicious use of neon.

The menu is wildly eclectic, and the dishes far better than the usual pub fare you might expect from a spot like this. For lighter appetites, the Planet enchilada, made with spiced beans, corn, and sweet potatoes is remarkably flavorful. Full entrees include grilled tuna on Tuscan white beans, Moroccan vegetable sauté, and filet of beef in a port sauce served with wild mushrooms and roast potatoes.

✪ **Five Spice.** 175 Church St. ☎ **802/864-4045.** Reservations recommended on weekends and in summer. Lunch items $5.25–$7.95; main dinner courses $9.95–$14.95. AE, CB, DC, MC, V. Sun–Thurs 11:30am–10pm, Fri–Sat 11:30am–11pm. PAN-ASIAN.

Five Spice is the best of Burlington's bumper crop of Asian restaurants. Located upstairs and down in an intimate setting with rough wood floors and aquamarine wainscoting, Five Spice is a popular draw among college students and professors. But customers pour in for the exquisite food, not for the scene. The cuisine is multi-Asian, drawing on the best of Thailand, Vietnam, China, and beyond. Try the excellent hot and sour soup. Then gear up for Indonesian beef or the superior kung pao chicken. The dish with the best name on the menu—Evil Jungle Prince with Chicken—is made with a light sauce featuring a winning combination of coconut milk, garlic, and lemongrass. If you're looking to save money, come for lunch rather than dinner. The menu's the same but the prices are about half the dinner menu.

Inn at Essex Junction. 70 Essex Way, Essex Junction. ☎ **802/878-1100.** Reservations recommended at Butler's; usually not needed at Birch Tree Cafe. At Birch Tree, lunch items $4.50–$10.95, main dinner courses $9.50–$12.95; at Butler's, main dinner courses $14–$22. AE, CB, DC, DISC, MC, V. Birch Tree daily 7am–10am, 11:30am–2pm (open at 11am on Sun), and 5:30–9:30pm. Butler's open for dinner only. REGIONAL/CONTINENTAL.

The Inn at Essex Junction, about a 15-minute drive from Burlington, is the auxiliary campus of the Montpelier-based New England Culinary Institute. It offers both formal and informal dining rooms with meals prepared and served by New England's prospective culinary stars. Both restaurants are housed in a large, gray faux-farmhouse complex located along the fringe of rare (for Vermont, at any rate) suburban sprawl. Inside, the setting is quiet and comfortable, inviting comparison with an upscale hotel restaurant. (In fact, there is a modern inn upstairs.)

Fortunately, the food far eclipses standard hotel fare at both the Birch Tree Cafe and Butler's Restaurant. In the light and airy café, you might be tempted by the Caribbean grilled chicken with a black bean salsa, or the honey-glazed pork chop. Amid the more intimate, country-inn elegance of Butler's, the fare is a bit more ambitious, with entrees like Dijon peppered rack of lamb, grilled salmon and shrimp with a horseradish cream, and oven-roasted veggies with goat cheese burritos.

Leunig's Bistro. 115 Church St. ☎ **802/863-3759.** Reservations recommended. Main courses $8.95–$18.95. AE, MC, V. Daily 7:30am–10pm, later on weekends. REGIONAL/ CONTINENTAL.

For years this local landmark, situated at the center-of-the-universe corner of College and Church streets, was called Leunig's Old World Café and Bar. In 1994, a pair of Boston transplants bought the place, changed the name to Leunig's Bistro, revamped the menu . . . and, voilà, a new Burlington culinary landmark was born. This boisterous, fun place has a hip, retro-old-world flair, with washed walls, a marble bar, and a Victorian back bar painted white and topped with cherubim. In summer, the inside spills onto the outside, with diners becoming part of the street scene on narrow patios. If you get the right table, this is Burlington's prime people-watching location.

The inventive seasonal menu features regional foods prepared with a continental touch. In winter, you might partake of the roasted pumpkin soup, followed by oyster stew or a delicious butternut squash ravioli with a light pesto sauce. In summer, there's poached asparagus with smoked salmon, or soft-shelled crabs with a lemongrass-coconut broth.

Mona's. 3 Main St. (in the Cornerstone Building). ☎ **802/658-6662.** Reservations recommended. Lunch items $5.25–$7.95; main dinner courses $8.95–$21.95 (mostly $10–$14). AE, CB, DC, MC, V. Mon–Fri 11:30am–11pm, Sat 11:30am–midnight, Sun 11:30am–10:30pm. NEW AMERICAN.

This restaurant overlooking the waterfront opened in late 1995 to great local acclaim, and quickly started attracting Burlington's business folk and grooverati. Located next to the train station, Mona's is an uptempo, contemporary kind of place rich with copper tones throughout. The first-floor ceiling is even made of copper, and seemingly emits an lurid, unearthly glow at sunset. Glimpses of Lake Champlain and the Adirondacks might be had out the first-floor windows; for better views, head upstairs and ask for a seat on the open deck.

The bustling open kitchen on the first floor produces some creative surprises. Appetizers include mushrooms baked with sun-dried tomato, artichoke, and cheddar; mussels steamed with lemon grass, ginger, and hot peppers; and a vegetable strudel with a port wine and fruit sauce. Entrees run the gamut, from a shellfish stew over linguini to polenta-crusted catfish to some mighty beefy steaks, including a 24-ounce porterhouse.

INEXPENSIVE

Al's. 1251 Williston Rd. (Route 2, just east of I-89), South Burlington. ☎ **802/862-9203.** Sandwiches 75¢–$3.55. No credit cards. Mon–Wed 10:30am–11pm, Thurs–Sat 10:30am–midnight, Sun 11am–10pm. BURGER JOINT.

Two words: French fries.

⑤ Bove's. 68 Pearl St. ☎ **802/864-6651.** Reservations not accepted. Sandwiches $1.30–$2.80; dinner items $3.85–$7.30. No credit cards. Tues–Sat 10am–10pm. ITALIAN.

A Burlington landmark since 1941, Bove's is a classic red-sauce-on-spaghetti joint (don't call it pasta) just a couple of blocks from chic Church Street Marketplace. The facade is stark black and white, its octagonal windows closed to prying eyes by Venetian blinds. Step through the doors and into a lost era; grab a seat at one of the vinyl-upholstered booths and browse the menu, which offers spaghetti with meat sauce, spaghetti with meatballs, spaghetti with sausage, and . . . . well, you get the idea. The red sauce is rich and tangy; the garlic sauce packs enough garlic to knock you clear out of your booth. If you resist the bar menu's Grasshoppers, Mai Tais, and other fondly remembered relics, you'll have plenty of money left to do up the town when you leave.

Nectar's Restaurant and Lounge. 188 Main St. ☎ **802/658-4771.** Reservations not accepted. Breakfast items $1.75–$6; lunch/dinner items $2.20–$6.75. No credit cards. Daily 5:45am until late. Breakfast served 5:45–11am. DINER.

Burlington in microcosm parades through Nectar's over the course of a long day. Early in the morning you'll find blue-collar workers and elderly gentlemen in ties enjoying heaping plates of eggs and hash browns. Midday finds downtown office workers in for lunch. And late in the evening it adopts a sort of retro chic as clubbers from Club Metronome and Nectar's lounge next door file through the cafeteria line for hamburgers, meat loaf, or just to get a local microbrew and hang with friends.

Vermont Pub & Brewery. 144 College St. ☎ **802/865-0500.** Reservations not accepted. Lunch items $3.25–$7.95; dinner items $8.50–$12.25. AE, DISC, MC, V. Sat–Thurs 11:30am–12:30am, Fri 11:30am–1:30am. Kitchen closes at 10pm; snacks available afterwards. PUB FARE.

Bustling and boisterous on weekends, this popular brewpub attracts college students and thirtysomethings alike—all drawn by the fresh beers brewed on premises. The proprietors are quick to note that their small-batch beer never travels more than a dozen feet from cellar to tap to you. Set in a slightly monstrous modern brick building facing City Hall Park, the interior is cookie-cutter quaint, a sort of TGIFriday's on hops. The bar area is set in a modern, bright solarium that's pleasant on a sunny day. Entrees run the pub fare gamut from meatloaf to Mulligatawny to Irish stew, and are invariably served with plenty of good cheer. Tours of the brewery are offered Wednesdays at 8pm and Saturdays at 4pm.

BURLINGTON AFTER DARK

There's always something going on in the evening in Burlington, although it might take a little snooping to find it in the slow season.

Flynn Theatre for the Performing Arts. 153 Main St. ☎ **802/863-5966.**

The Flynn is the anchor for the downtown fine arts scene. Run as a nonprofit and housed in a wonderful art deco theater dating to 1930, the Flynn stages events ranging from touring productions of Broadway shows to rock concerts to story-telling festivals. Call for the current schedule.

Royall Tyler Theatre. University of Vermont campus. ☎ **802/656-2094.**

Plays are performed by the University of Vermont theater department at this handsomely designed performance hall. Call for current schedule.

UVM Lane Series. Various venues. ☎ **802/656-4455.**

This university series brings renowned performers from around the country and the globe to Burlington for performances at the Flynn Theatre, Ira Allen Chapel, and the acoustically superb UVM Recital Hall. The series runs from September through April. Recent performers have included the San Francisco Opera performing The Marriage of Figaro, flutist Eugenia Zuckerman, and the Modern Mandolin Quartet.

Vermont Symphony Orchestra. 2 Church St. ☎ **802/864-5741.**

Outdoor pops performances punctuated by fireworks take place at various locations throughout Burlington and Vermont during the summer. In winter, the classical series moves indoors. Call for the current schedule.

NIGHTCLUBS

Burlington has thriving local music scene, one that's been infused with a bristling energy since Phish put the city on the map. The city government, recognizing a potential economic boon when it sees one, has worked to help incubate this scene. Check the local free weeklies for information on festivals and concerts during your visit, and to find out who's playing at the clubs.

The most popular clubs are located near the juncture of Main and College streets. At 188 Main St., **Nectar's** (☎ **802/658-4771**), half of which is a funky cafeteria-style restaurant (see "Where to Dine," below), features live bands seven days a week and no cover charge. On weekends it's packed with UVM students and abuzz with a fairly high level of hormonal energy. Look for the revolving neon sign.

One flight above Nectar's is **Club Metronome** (☎ **802/865-4563**), a loud and loose nightspot that features a wide array of acts with a heavy dose of world beat. This is a no frills place with tomato-red walls and disco mirror ball where you can dance or shoot a game of pool (or do both at once, as seems popular). The cover is generally less than $5, although national touring acts might run $12 or so.

Around the corner at 165 Church St. is **Club Toast** (☎ **802/660-2088**), which is a little rougher around the edges than the other two and often showcases local alternative rock bands. Cover charge is typically less than $5.

Other nightime options include the **Comedy Zone** (☎ **802/658-6500**) at the Radisson Hotel, and **CB's Dance Club** (☎ **802/878-5522**) in Essex, which features country dancing most nights. Call for the evening line-up and directions.

For gay nightlife, head to **135 Pearl** (☎ **802/863-2343**), Burlington's leading gay club, located at 135 Pearl St. Get a bite to eat, dance, or listen to live music Wednesday through Saturday. Open noon until 2am, it's a friendly place that attracts a diverse clientele.

7 Northern Vermont

Vermont's north country—that quarter of the state above Burlington and St. Johnsbury—has an edgy, wild, and remote character. Not that it's all wilderness—far from it. On the eastern side, near Lake Champlain, it's farmland, meadows, rolling hills and small villages. To the west, in Vermont's Northeast Kingdom, the villages are farther apart, and much of the forestland is owned by timber companies, which swoop in from time to time to remove broad swaths of forest for pulp and lumber.

What gives this region its character is its stubborn, old-fashioned insularity. Travelers get the feeling in much of southern Vermont that if tourists stopped coming, the economy would collapse, villages would decay, and the Volvo repair shops would close up. In northern Vermont, you get that feeling that if tourists stopped coming, not a single thing would change. Farmers would keep on baling their hay. Woodworkers in Newport would still get their paychecks. Timber cruisers would keep estimating the board feet in the woodlands, and loggers would take it out.

I've divided the region into two sections, the Lake Champlain Islands and the Northeast Kingdom, and suggested two tours of these appealing areas. There's a lot more to be seen, of course, both within these areas and in between. It's especially appealing to explore this region by bicycle. While some hills will command your undivided attention, the terrain tends to be a bit more open and forgiving than in the thickest part of the Green Mountains, and it seems you can always find a route along a river. The traffic is lighter, camping isn't all that hard to find, and you'll discover, perhaps inexplicably, that you've taken on a subtle sense of ownership of the region once you've passed through.

A DRIVING TOUR OF THE LAKE CHAMPLAIN ISLANDS

Few travelers studying a map of Vermont can stare at the archipelago of islands in northern Lake Champlain, hard against the Canadian border, and not wonder what's up there.

Well, here's what: not much. And therein lies much of the appeal.

These islands, connected by bridges, causeways, and roads, are linked primarily by a rich history, and a dependence on land and water. There are few amenities for tourists—just a handful of accommodations and only slightly more restaurants—but there's a stark, mercurial beauty in these low, largely open islands against the lake, which is sometimes placid and improbably blue, sometimes a hostile, dull gray, and flecked with frothy white.

The 30-mile main road is relatively straight and fast; the posted speed is typically 50 miles per hour. If you're going too slow, locals in pickup trucks will let you know by blowing by or hugging your tail. When the opportunity arises, veer off on one of the side roads and take it slow, or just pull over at one of the many parks to enjoy the scenery. If you've got a boat or kayak, you can explore several small island parks between the island and the mainland; some even offer camping. Camping is available at two parks (Grand Isle and North Hero state park) along the route described below.

While the area is open and appealing now, especially along the northern stretches, the handwriting is on the wall. Today, you'll pass many signs on former farms offering one-acre lots for sale. They're not moving especially fast these days, but that's not likely to be the case forever. Travel now to see this special area before it starts resembling former farmlands everywhere.

Further information is available from the **Lake Champlain Islands Chamber of Commerce,** P.O. Box 213, North Hero, VT 05474 (☎ **802/372-5683**).

Begin the tour at Exit 17 on I-89. Head northwest on Route 2, which you'll stay on much of this tour. Within a few minutes you'll arrive at:

1. **Sand Bar State Park.** This nicely maintained park (on the mainland side) has sweeping views to the north, a handful of picnic tables, and relatively protected swimming. There's a small fee in summer.

   Cross the water on the causeway (you can guess where the sandbar name comes from) to:

2. **Grande Isle.** This island, the largest of the bunch, is split into two villages, South Hero and Grand Isle. The area around South Hero doesn't quite qualify as rural. It's got a mix of architectural styles, from early stone farmhouse to modular home, and it's also blessed with a good number of convenience stores and small retail plazas. The landscape becomes less developed and more farmlike the farther north you travel.

At **Keeler Bay,** take a detour on Route 314 to the:

3. Lake Champlain Ferry to Plattsburgh, New York. The ferry runs year round (the only one of the three lake ferries to do so) and operates daily between 5am and 1am. This short detour is about 5 miles and offers wonderful views across the lake to the Adirondacks. Stop and watch the ferry operation for a bit; across the road is one of Vermont's several fish hatcheries, where you can learn about the state's stocking programs.

Continue on Route 314 back to Route 2, and head north again through the village of Grand Isle. Just north of the village, look for a rustic log cabin on the right side, next a historical marker reading:

4. "Pioneer Log Cabin." In fact, this is thought to be the oldest existing log cabin in the United States, dating back to 1783. Built by Jedediah Hyde, it's furnished with many of the Hyde family possessions. The cabin, which is managed by the Grand Isle Historical Society, is open in summer; there's a nominal admission fee.

Continue northward on Route 2 until you cross a bridge to North Hero Island. At this tip is:

5. Knight Point State Park. Situated on an old farm, this scenic property offers nice views, picnicking, and sheltered swimming that makes this park especially appealing for parents with young children. A small fee is charged in season.

Shortly beyond this park you'll come across the summer home of the:

6. Royal Lipizzan Stallions (☎ 802/372-5683). These stunning white horses, famed for their precise steps and leaping ability, take a holiday from their home in Florida by coming to a North Hero farm every summer for about six weeks. The breed dates back to 1580, and the name derives from Lipizza, which was once part of the Austro-Hungarian Empire. While relatively small, Lipizzans are very powerful and have remarkably expressive eyes. These stallions are trained by the Hermann family, which has been training Lipizzans for three centuries. Performances are offered Thursday through Sunday, but visitors are welcome to stop by anytime between mid-July and August.

Northward again, head through the picturesque village of North Hero, with its beautiful natural harbor, lapping waves, and westward views toward the Green Mountains. Continue on until you see signs for Route 129 and a small bridge to:

7. Isle La Motte. This is the most pastoral and remote of the Champlain Islands, although the western shore is thick with summer homes. The island was connected to Grand Isle in 1882, and for years there was a toll to cross the bridge (20¢ one way, 25¢ round trip). Today, the island's interior, for the most part, is farmland, although economics and the ever-assertive forest is making inroads against open fields.

Shortly after crossing to the island, turn right, following signs to:

8. St Anne's Shrine. This outdoor shrine with stations of the cross, grottoes, and a handsome outdoor chapel is run by the Edmundite Fathers and Brothers. It also happens to mark the first settlement in Vermont—in 1666 Captain Sieur de La Motte built Fort St. Anne on this very spot. It's also the site of the first mass said in Vermont. Daily masses are performed in summer; there's also a nice beach and a cafeteria. Nearby is a heroic statue of Samuel de Champlain originally sculpted for Expo '67 in Montréal.

Continue past the shrine for a slow circumnavigation of the island. The whole loop is about 12 miles, and it's especially appealing by bike. The terrain is flat, the traffic light, and the views are best seen from a bike saddle; a lot is lost through car windows. Bike rentals are available at **Champlain Islands Cycling** (☎ 802/928-3202), on Old Quarry Road near the village of Isle La Motte.

Upon leaving Isle La Motte, make a left just after the bridge. This road will take you through quiet farmland and past some stolid stone houses to the cheerless town of Alburg. If you're heading to New York State, turn left at the stop sign and continue through Alburg to cross at Rouse Point. If you're returning to the Burlington area, turn right on Route 2, then left on Route 78. After crossing the bridge, you'll pass through:

9. **Missisquoi National Wildlife Refuge** (☎ 802/868-4781), a 6,338-acre federal property with a 1.5-mile interpretive trail that runs through bosky northern forest, which is home to a broad range of birds and wildlife. The grounds are open daily from dawn to dark.

From here, it's a short hop to return to I-89 and southward to Burlington.

WHERE TO STAY

🄢 **Thomas Mott Homestead.** Blue Rock Road, Alburg, VT 05440. ☎ 802/796-3736 or 800/348-0843. 5 rms (3 with shower only). $65–$85 double. Rates include full breakfast. AE, CB, DC, DISC, MC, V. Blue Rock Road is about 1.5 miles east of Route 2 on Route 78; look for signs to inn.

Built in 1838, this small home has been been accommodating travelers since 1987 and is the islands' best destination for those seeking homey comfort and cordial hospitality. Ideally situated on a point overlooking the lake (although recently surrounded by a phalanx of expensive vacation homes), the Thomas Mott is exceptional for the attention to small things paid by innkeeper Patrick Schallert, a soft-spoken, retired wine dealer from California. Raspberries, blackberries, and blueberries from the yard are served with morning pancakes. Guests can select other options from the extensive breakfast menu, although why they would is unclear. Schallert also keeps a freezer stocked full of Ben & Jerry's ice cream for guests to help themselves when the mood strikes. Be sure to ask about the quails; Schallert raises them by the covey in the adjacent barn, releasing some 200 to 300 into the wild each year.

A DRIVING TOUR OF THE NORTHEAST KINGDOM

Vermont's Northeast Kingdom is one of northern New England's most spectacularly remote regions. Consisting of Orleans, Essex, and Caledonia counties, the region was given its memorable name in 1949 by Sen. George Aiken, who understood the area's allure at a time when few others paid it much heed.

Contrasts with southern Vermont aren't hard to find. Rather than pinched, narrow valleys, the Kingdom's landscape is far more open and spacious, with rolling meadows ending abruptly at the hard edge of dense boreal forest. The leafy woodlands of the south give way to spiky forests of spruce and fir. And rather than Saabs and Volvos, you'll see pickup trucks dominating the roads, and plenty of them.

Accommodations and services for tourists aren't as plentiful or easy to find here as in the southern reaches of the state, but some superb inns are tucked among the hills and in the forests.

This section includes a slightly convoluted driving tour of the Northeast Kingdom, along with some suggestions for outdoor recreation. If your time is limited, make sure you at least stop in St. Johnsbury, which has two of the most remarkable indoor attractions in the state (see the tour, below).

Visitor information is available from the **Northeast Kingdom Chamber of Commerce** in St. Johnsbury (☎ **802/748-3678** or 800/639-6379). Other helpful chambers of commerce in the region include **Barton** (☎ **802/525-1137**), **Lake Willoughby** (☎ **802/525-4496**), **Hardwick** (☎ **802/472-6894**), **Island Pond** (☎ **802/723-4326**), **Lyndon** (☎ **802/626-9696**), and **Newport** (☎ **802/334-7782**).

Begin at:

1. **Hardwick,** a small town with rough edges, set along the Lamoille River. It has an attractive, compact commercial main street, and some quirky shops.

   From here, head north on Route 14 a little over seven miles to the turn-off toward Craftsbury and:

2. **Craftsbury Common.** An uncommonly graceful village, Craftsbury Common is home to a small academy and large number of historic homes and buildings spread along a sizeable green and the village's broad main street. The town occupies a wide upland ridge, and offers sweeping views to the east and west. Be sure to stop by the old cemetery on the south end of town, where you can wander among historic tombstones of the pioneers, some of which date back to the 1700s. Craftsbury is an excellent destination for mountain biking and cross-country skiing, and is home to the region's finest inn (see below).

   From Craftsbury, continue north to reconnect to Route 14. You'll wind through the towns of Albany and Irasburg as you head north. At the village of Coventry, veer north on Route 5 to the lakeside town of

3. **Newport.** This crusty commercial center (pop. 4,400) is set on the southern shores of Lake Memphremagog, a spectacular 27-mile-long lake that's but 2 miles wide at it broadest point, and the bulk of which is located in Canada. Newport, improbably enough, has a small outlet zone on Main St. Look for discounted outdoor gear from **Bogner** (☎ **802/334-0135**), **Louis Garneau** (☎ **802/334-5885**), and **Great Outdoors** (☎ **802/334-2831**).

   ☕ **TAKE A BREAK** Newport's only lakeside restaurant is **The East Side,** located at 25 Lake Rd. (☎ **802/334-2340**). It's a good spot for lunch or a refreshing beverage while admiring shimmering, hill-encased Lake Memphremagog.

   From Newport, continue north on Route 5, crossing under I-91, for about seven miles to the town of Derby Line (pop. 2,000). This border outpost has a handful of restaurants and antique shops; you can park and walk across the bridge to poke around the Canadian town of Rock Island without much hassle. (The weaker Canadian dollar will likely yield a cheap lunch if you've held out this long.) Back in Derby Line, look for the:

4. **Haskell Free Library and Opera House,** at the corner of Caswell Avenue and Church Street (☎ **802/873-3022**). This handsome neo-classical building contains a public library on the first floor, and an elegant opera house on the second that's modeled after the old Boston Opera House. The theater opened in 1904 with the advertisements promoting a minstrel show featuring "new songs, new jokes, and beautiful electric effects." The theater is attractive in the extreme, with a scene of Venice painted on the drop curtain and carved cherubim adorning the balcony.

   What's most notable about the structure, however, is that it lies half in Canada and half in the United States. (The Haskell family donated the building jointly to the towns of Derby Line and Rock Island.) A thick black line runs through the seats of the opera house, indicating who's in the United States and who's in Canada. Because the stage is set entirely in Canada, stories abound from the early days of frustrated U.S. officers watching fugitives perform on stage. More recently, the theater has been used for the occasional extradition hearing.

From Derby Line, retrace your path south on Route 5 to Derby Center and the juncture of Route 5A. Continue south on Route 5A to the town of Westmore on the shores of:

5. Lake Willoughby. This glacier-carved lake is best viewed from the north, with the shimmering sheet of water pinching between the base of two low mountains at the southern end. There's a distinctive Alpine feel to the whole scene, and this underappreciated lake is certainly one of the most beautiful in the Northeast. Route 5A along the eastern shore is lightly traveled and well-suited to biking or walking. To ascend the two mountains by foot, see the "Outdoor Pursuits" section, below.

Head southwest on Route 16, which departs from Route 5A just north of the lake. Follow Route 16 through the peaceful villages of Barton and Glover. A little over a mile south of Glover, turn left on Route 122. Very soon on your left look for the farmstead that serves as home to the:

6. ✪ Bread and Puppet Theater. For the past three decades, Polish artist and performer Peter Schumann's Bread and Puppet Theater has staged elaborate summer pageants at this farm, attracting thousands of attendees who participate, watch, and lounge about the hillsides. The multiday fest takes place in a grown-over former quarry on the farm's property, and features huge, lugubrious, brightly painted puppets crafted of fabric and papier mâché. (For the exact dates, call **802/ 525-3031**.) The theme of the pageant is typically rebellion against tyranny of one form or another, and visitors get a distinct sense of reliving the 1960s. Think of it as Woodstock without the loud music.

Between June and October the venerable, slightly tottering barn on the property contains the Bread and Puppet Museum, housing many of the puppets used in past pageants. This is a remarkable display, and shouldn't be missed if you're anywhere near the area. Downstairs in the former cow-milking stalls are smaller displays, such as King Lear addressing his daughters, and a group of mournful washerwomen doing their laundry. Upstairs, the vast hayloft is filled to the eaves with soaring, haunting puppets, some up to 20 feet tall. The style is witty and eclectic; the barn seems a joint endeavor of David Lynch, Red Grooms, and Hieronymous Bosch. Admission is free, although donations are encouraged.

From Glover, continue south through serene farmlands to Lyndonville, where you pick up Route 5 south to:

7. St. Johnsbury. This town of 7,600 inhabitants is the largest in the Northeast Kingdom, and is the major center of commerce. First settled in 1786, the town enjoyed a buoyant prosperity in the 19th century, largely stemming from the success of platform scales, which were invented here in 1830 by Thaddeus Fairbanks and are still manufactured here. The town, which has not suffered from the depredations of tourist boutiques and brew pubs, has an abundance of fine commercial architecture in two distinct areas, which are joined by steep Eastern Ave. The more commercial part of town lies along Railroad Street (Route 5) at the base of the hill. The more ethereal part of town, with the library, St. Johnsbury Academy, and a grand museum, is along Main Street at the top of the hill. The north end of Main Street is also notable for its grand residential architecture.

☕ TAKE A BREAK Those with a literary-caffeine bent should strike for the **Northern Lights Café and Bookstore,** 79 Railroad St. (☎ **802/748-4463**). This shop has the best selection of reading matter in town (local works are especially well represented), and serves up delicious snacks and light meals, including sandwiches, homemade muffins, and a delectable blueberry coffee cake.

At the corner Main and Prospect streets in St. Johnsbury:

8. ✪ The Fairbanks Museum (☎ **802/748-2372**) is an imposing Romanesque red sandstone structure constructed in 1889 to hold the collections of obsessive amateur collector Franklin Fairbanks, the grandson of the inventor of the platform scale. Fairbanks was once described as "the kind of little boy who came home with his pockets full of worms." In adulthood, his propensity to gather and accumulate continued unabated. His artifacts include four stuffed bears, a huge moose with full antlers, art from Asia, and 4,500 stuffed native and exotic birds. And that's just the tip of it.

The soaring, barrel-vaulted main hall, reminiscent of an old-fashioned railway depot, embodies Victorian grandeur. Among the assorted clutter look for the unique mosaics by John Hampson. Hampson crafted scenes of American history—such as Washington bidding his troops farewell—entirely of mounted insects. In the Washington scene, for instance, iridescent green beetles form the epaulets, and the regal great coat is comprised of hundreds of purple moth wings. Words fail me here; you must see them.

There's also a planetarium and weather station. The museum is open Monday to Saturday from 10am to 4pm, and Sunday from 1 to 5pm, with longer hours in summer. Admission is $4 for adults, $3 for seniors, and $2.50 for children 5-17.

Also in town, at 30 Main St.:

9. ✪ The St. Johnsbury Athenaeum (☎ **802/748-8291**) is a quirky brick building with a truncated mansard tower and prominent keystones over the windows. This is the town's public library, but it also houses an extraordinary art gallery dating to 1873. It claims to be the oldest, unadulterated art gallery in the nation, and I see no reason to question the claim. Your first view of it is spectacular: After winding through the intimate library with its ticking regulator clock, you round a corner and find yourself gazing across Yosemite National Park. This luminous 10-by-15-foot oil was created by noted Hudson River School painter Albert Bierstadt, and the gallery was built specifically to accommodate this work. ("Now 'The Domes' is doomed to the seclusion of a Vermont town, where it will astonish the natives," groused the Boston Globe at the time.) The natural light flooding in from the skylight above nicely enhances the painting. Some 100 other works fill the walls. Most are painted reproductions of other paintings (a common teaching tool in the 19th century), but look for originals by other Hudson River School painters including Asher B. Durand, Thomas Moran, and Jasper Cropsey.

The Athenaeum is open Monday and Wednesday 10am to 8pm; Tuesday, Thursday, and Friday from 10am to 5:30pm; and Saturday 9:30am to 4pm. Admission is free, but donations are encouraged.

OUTDOOR PURSUITS IN THE NORTHEAST KINGDOM
HIKING

At the southern tip of Lake Willoughby, two rounded peaks rise above the lake's waters. These are the biblically named Mt. Hor and Mt. Pisgah, both of which lie within Willoughby State Forest. Both summits are accessible via footpaths that are somewhat strenuous but yield excellent views.

For Mt. Pisgah (elev. 2,751 feet), look for parking on the west side of Route 5A about 5.7 miles south of the junction with Route 16. The trail departs from across the road and runs 1.7 miles to the summit.

To hike Mt. Hor (elev. 2,648 feet), drive 1.8 miles down the gravel road on the right side of the above-mentioned parking lot, veering right at the fork. Park at the small parking lot, and continue on foot past the parking lot a short distance until you spot the start of the trail. Follow the trail signs to the summit, a round trip of about 3.5 miles.

Mountain Biking

The Craftsbury ridge offer several excellent variations for bikers in search of easy terrain. Most of the biking is on hard-packed dirt roads through sparsely populated countryside. The views are sensational, and the sense of being well out in the country very strong. The **Craftsbury Center at Craftsbury Common** (☎ 802/586-7767 or 800/729-7751) rents mountain bikes and is an excellent source for maps and local information about area roads. Bike rentals are $12 per day.

At **Jay Peak** (☎ 802/988-2611), mountain bikers can take their bikes via tram to the summit of the 3,968 mountain, then explore some 20 miles of trail while gravity does most of the work for them.

Cross-Country Skiing

The same folks who offer mountain biking at the Craftsbury Center also maintain 61 miles of groomed cross-country trails through the gentle hills surrounding Craftsbury. The trails maintained by **Craftsbury Nordic** (☎ 802/586-7767 or 800/729-7751) are pleasant, old-fashioned trails that emphasize pleasing landscapes rather than fast action. Trail passes are $11 for adults, $5 for juniors 6–12, and $7 for seniors (discounts available midweek.) **Highland Lodge** (☎ 802/533-2647) on Caspian Lake offers 36 miles of trails (about 10 miles groomed) through rolling woodlands and fields.

Alpine Skiing

Jay Peak. Route 242, Jay, VT 05859. ☎ **802/988-2611**, or 800/451-4449 for lodging. E-mail skijayvt@aol.com. Vertical drop: 2,153 feet. Lifts: 1 tram, 4 chairlifts, 2 surface lifts. Skiable acreage: 300+. Lift tickets: $38.

Located just south of the Canadian border, Jay is Vermont's best ski mountain for those who get away just to ski, and prefer to avoid all the modern-day glitter and trappings that seem to clutter ski resorts elsewhere. While some new condo development has been taking place at the base of the mountain, the mountain still has the feeling of a remote, isolated destination, accessible by a winding road through unbroken woodlands.

More than half of Jay's 62 trails are for intermediate skiers. But experts haven't been left behind. Jay has developed extensive glade skiing since 1994, taking excellent advantage of its sizeable natural snowfall, which averages more than 300 inches annually (more than any other New England ski area). Jay has also reopened its extreme chutes, which appeal to advanced skiers in search of a challenge. Jay Peak's ski school emphasizes glade skiing, making it a fitting place to learn how to navigate these exciting, challenging trails that have cropped up at most New England ski areas in recent years.

WHERE TO STAY

Highland Lodge. Caspian Lake, Greensboro, VT 05841. ☎ **802/533-2647**. 11 rms plus 11 cottages (2 rms with tub only). $200 double. Rates include breakfast and dinner. DISC,

MC, V. Closed mid-Mar to May and mid-Oct to Christmas. From Hardwick, drive on Route 15 east two miles to Route 16; drive north two more miles to East Hardwick. Head west and follow signs to inn.

The Highland Lodge was built in the mid-19th century, and has been accommodating guests since 1926. It's a great destination for a relaxing, old-fashioned holiday. Located just across the road from lovely Caspian Lake, this lodge has 11 rooms furnished in a comfortable country style. A wide porch runs the length of the inn, and white Adirondack chairs are well placed for shady reading or dozing.

Facilities: The main activities here tend to be relaxing rather than hectic: There's swimming and boating in the lake in summer, along with tennis on clay courts; in winter, the lodge maintains its own cross-country ski area with 30 miles of groomed trail. Behind the lodge is a nature preserve, which makes for quiet exploration. Bored? There's also badminton, croquet, and horseshoes.

✪ **Inn on the Common.** Craftsbury Common, VT 05827. ☎ **802/586-9619** or 800/ 521-2233. Fax 802/586-2249. 16 rms (3 with shower only). $200–$230 double; foliage season $250–$270 double. Rates include breakfast and dinner ($30 less for breakfast only). AE, MC, V.

This exceedingly handsome complex of three Federal-style buildings anchors the charming ridgetop village of Craftsbury Common. Innkeepers Penny and Michael Schmitt have been running this place with panache since 1973, and have created a beautiful, comfortable inn that offers just the right measures of history and luxury. Guests can unwind in the nicely appointed common rooms, or stroll the 15 acres of beautifully landscaped grounds.

Dining/Entertainment: Dinner starts with cocktails at 7pm, then guests are seated amid elegant Federal-era surroundings at 8pm. The menu changes nightly, but includes well-prepared dishes like venison ravioli and jumbo shrimp stuffed with scallops and served with a sherry sauce.

Facilities: There's a pool, clay tennis court, and croquet in the back gardens; in winter, cross-country skiing and snowshoeing are popular activities. If the weather turns sour, the inn has a collection of 250 videos to peruse.

6 | New Hampshire

There are two ways to get old-time New Hampshirites riled up and spitting vinegar. First, tell them you think that Vermont is a really great state. Then tell them you think it's weird that they still don't have a state income tax or sales tax.

At its most basic, New Hampshire defines itself by what it isn't, and that, more than not, is Vermont—a state regarded by local old-timers as one of the few communist republics still remaining. No, New Hampshire is not Vermont, and they'll thank you not to confuse the two.

Keep in mind that New Hampshire's state symbol is the Old Man of the Mountains, which is an actual site you can visit in the White Mountains. You'll see this icon just about everywhere you look—on state highway signs, on brochures, on state police cars. And it's an apt symbol for a state that relishes its cranky-old-man demeanor. New Hampshire has long been a magnet for folks who talk of government with tones normally reserved for scabies. That "Live-Free-or-Die" license plate? It's for real. New Hampshire stands behind its words. It hasn't quite accepted state planning as a legitimate task. Nor does New Hampshire have a bottle deposit law, or a law banning billboards. (Godless Vermont has both, as does its other heathen neighbor, Maine.)

New Hampshire savors its reputation as an embattled outpost of plucky, heroic conservatives fighting the good fight against intrusive laws and irksome bureaucrats. Without a state sales tax or state income tax, it's had to be creative. Many government services are funded through the "tourist tax" (an 8 percent levy on meals and rooms at restaurants and hotels) along with a hefty local property tax (the mere mention of which is another way to get local folks riled up). In fact, candidates for virtually every office with the possible exception of dogcatcher must take "The Pledge," which means they'll vow to fight any effort to impose sales or income tax. To shirk The Pledge is tantamount to political suicide.

The state's cranky spirit is perhaps best captured by its leading newspaper, the *Manchester Union Leader*. This conservative powerhouse has made and broken candidates in their quest for the White House during New Hampshire's influential first-in-the-nation primary. The paper's attitude has mellowed somewhat since the demise of cantankerous editor William Loeb, and it's dropped the vitriolic front-page editorials. But it still delivers plenty of fire and brimstone in its editorial section. (The newspaper also has the policy of printing all letters to the editor it receives. As such, it has become the outlet of choice for conspiracy theorists and people who believe the government is beaming radio waves at their brain.)

Get beyond New Hampshire's affable crankiness, and you'll find pure New England. Indeed, New Hampshire may represent the New England ethic distilled to its essence. At its core is a mistrust of those from outside the state, a premium placed on independence, a belief that government should be frugal above all else, and a laconic acceptance that, no matter what, you just can't change the weather. Travelers exploring the state with open eyes will find these attitudes in spades.

Travelers will also find wonderfully diverse terrain—from ocean beaches, to the broad lakes, to the region's most impressive mountains. Without ever leaving state's borders you can play Frisbee™ on a sandy beach, ride bikes along quiet country lanes dotted with covered bridges, hike rugged granite hills blasted by some of the most severe weather in the world, and canoe on a placid lake in the company of moose and loons. You'll also find good food and country inns you won't want to ever leave. But most of all, you'll find vestiges of that feisty independence that has defined New England since the first settlers ran up their flag three and a half centuries ago.

1 Enjoying the Great Outdoors

Visitors coming from the West scoff at the low elevations of New England's peaks. ("Four thousand feet? Four thousand feet? That's not even a foothill where we come from!")

Savvy eastern hikers indulge their guests with good humor. Then they take them to the White Mountains's brutally rugged, steep trails to snap their will and force them to beg for mercy—never mind the plentiful oxygen at these low elevations. After that, they tend to stay quiet.

The White Mountains's famed network of hiking trails will test anyone's mettle. The hard granite hills of the ancient mountains of New England resist the sort of gently graded trail through the crumbly earth found so often in the American West. And the White Mountains's early trail blazers were evidently a humorless lot, who found it amusing to build trails strait up sheer pitches and through tortuous boulderfields.

Despite (or perhaps because of) these trails, the White Mountains are the destination in New England for serious outdoorspeople heading north from Boston and New York. There's superb hiking in the summer, and fine skiing (both cross-country and alpine) in the winter. It's also a good place to test your meteorological acumen—the weather can change almost instantly on the high ridges, so backcountry explorers have to keep a keen eye out. A pleasant afternoon picnic can turn into a harrowing, cold experience for the unwary. Atop Mt. Washington, the region's highest peak, it's not unusual to see snow anytime of the year—mid-summer flurries aren't that uncommon.

More gentle outdoor recreation is found throughout much of the rest of New Hampshire, from canoeing on the meandering Connecticut River (which forms the border with Vermont), to sailing on vast Lake Winnipesaukee. If you're so inclined, come prepared for outdoor recreation, because it doesn't take much to find it.

An excellent general source of information is the **Appalachian Mountain Club,** 5 Joy St., Boston, MA 02108 (☎ **617/523-0636,** or 603/466-2727 in NH). The group sponsors outings and instructional workshops throughout the year across New England, but especially in the White Mountains. Signing up for a trip is an excellent way to get to know the area under the leadership of someone who knows the area well.

BACKPACKING   The White Mountains of northern New Hampshire offer the most extensive, most challenging, most beautiful backpacking in the Northeast. The bulk of the best trails are located within 773,000-acre White Mountain National Forest, which encompasses several 5,000-plus foot peaks and more than 100,000 acres of designated wilderness. Trails range from easy lowland walks along bubbling streams to demanding ridgeline paths buffeted by fierce winds. AMC huts offer shelter in eight dramatically situated cabins (called "huts") that boast a high degree of comfort. (Reservations are essential; call **603/466-2727**).

In addition, a number of three-sided Adirondack-style shelters are located throughout the backcountry on a first-come, first-served basis. Some are free; at others a small fee is collected. Pitching a tent in the backcountry is free subject to certain restrictions (e.g., no camping within a certain distance of a trail or river), and no permits are required. It's best to check with the forest headquarters (☎ **603/528-8721**) or a district ranger station for current rules and regulations.

The ridges around Mt. Washington attract the densest crowds. Backpackers in search of a more remote experience should head for trails in the Mt. Moosilauke/ Kinsman Notch area west of I-93, and the northern unit of the forest just west of Berlin.

The **Appalachian Trail** passes through New Hampshire, entering the state at Hanover, running along the highest peaks of the White Mountains, and exiting into Maine along the Mahoosuc Range northeast of Gorham. The trail is well maintained, although it tends to attract teeming crowds along the highest elevations in summer.

Rental equipment—including sleeping bags and pad, tents, and packs—is available at **Eastern Mountain Sports** (☎ **603/356-5433**) in North Conway at reasonable rates.

BIKING   There's superb road biking throughout the state. The best advice is to sacrifice the direct-line convenience of the major roads for the winding, twisting backroads. Southwest New Hampshire near Mount Monadnock offers a multitude of shady backroads for exploring, especially around Hancock and Greenfield.

In the White Mountains, my favorite one-day loop (bring lunch) is on the east side of the mountains outside of North Conway. Start in Conway and follow the Kancamagus Highway (Route 112) to Bear Notch Road. Turn right, then climb Bear Notch before descending to the town of Bartlett; turn right and follow busy Route 302 (the worst part of the trip) to River Road, which connects to West Side Road and continues back to Conway.

The White Mountains also offer plenty of opportunities for mountain bikers; trails are open to bikers unless otherwise noted. Bikes are not allowed in wilderness areas. The upland roads outside of Jackson offer some superb country biking. **Great Glen Trails** (☎ **603/466-2333**), near Mt. Washington, and **Waterville Valley Base Camp** (☎ **800/468-2553**), at the southwest edge of the park, both offer bike rentals and maintained mountain bike trails at a fee.

Mountain Road Tours (☎ **603/532-8708**) in southern New Hampshire can arrange inn-to-inn biking tours in the state.

CAMPING   Campers shouldn't have any problem finding a place to pitch a tent or park an RV in New Hampshire, especially in the northern half of the state.

The White Mountain National Forest maintains 20 campgrounds (no hook-ups), some very small and personal, others quite large and noisy. Sites tend to be fairly easy to come by midweek, but on summer and early fall weekends you're taking your chances if you arrive without reservations. Reservations are accepted by the **Forest Service** (☎ **800/280-2267**) at 11 of the campgrounds from 14 to 180 days before arrival.

New Hampshire

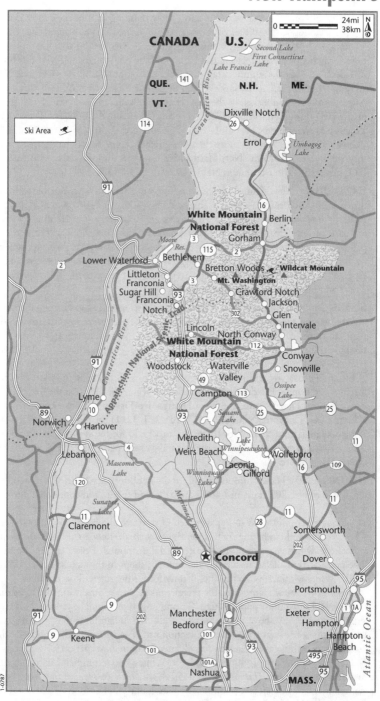

Fifteen of New Hampshire's state parks allow camping (two of these offer camping for RVs only). About half of these parks are located in and around the White Mountains. In 1995 the New Hampshire state park system began accepting reservations for many of the campgrounds it manages. Between January and May call **603/271-3627;** during the summer season, call the campground directly to reserve. Not all campgrounds participate; some remain first-come, first served. A list of parks and phone numbers is published in the *New Hampshire Visitor's Guide,* which is distributed widely through information centers, or by contacting the Office of **Travel and Tourism Development,** P.O. Box 1856, Concord, NH 03302 (☎ **603/271-2343**).

New Hampshire also has more than 150 private campgrounds. For a free directory, get in touch with the **New Hampshire Campground Owners' Association,** P.O. Box 320, Twin Mountain, NH 03595 (☎ **603/846-5511**).

CANOEING   New Hampshire has a profusion of river and lakes suitable for paddling, and canoe rentals are available widely around the state. Good flatwater paddling may be found along the Merrimack and Connecticut rivers in the southern parts of the state. Virtually any lake is good for dabbling about with canoe and paddle, although beware of stiff northerly winds when crossing vast Winnipesaukee. In the far north, 8,000-acre Lake Umbagog is home to bald eagles and loons, and is especially appealing to explore by canoe. In general the farther north you venture, the wilder and more remote your experience will be.

FISHING   New Hampshire ponds, streams, and rivers offer good fishing throughout the state. A vigorous stocking program keeps the waters active with fish. Brook trout account for about half of all trout stocked in the state's waters; lake and rainbow trout are also stocked. Other sportfish include small and largemouth bass, landlocked salmon, and walleye.

Fishing licenses are required for freshwater fishing throughout the state, but not for saltwater fishing. For detailed information on regulations, request the free "Freshwater Fishing Digest" from the **New Hampshire Fish and Game Department,** 2 Hazen Dr., Concord, NH 03301 (☎ **603/271-3211**). Fishing licenses for nonresidents range from $18.50 for three days to $35.50 for the season. Another helpful booklet, also available free from the fish and game department, is "Fishing Waters of New Hampshire."

HIKING   New Hampshire has hiking trails in abundance. The White Mountains alone offer 1,200 miles of trails; state parks and forests add considerably to the mileage.

Serious hikers will want to bypass much of the state and beeline for the Whites. The essential guide to hiking trails is the *Appalachian Mountain Club's White Mountain Guide,* which contains up-to-date detailed descriptions of every trail in the area. The guide is available at most book and outdoor shops in the state. See the section on the White Mountains later in this chapter for further suggestions on hikes.

In southwest New Hampshire, the premier hike is Mt. Monadnock, said to be one of the world's two most popular hikes (second only to Mt. Fuji in Japan). This lone massif, rising regally above the surrounding hills, is a straightforward day hike accessible via one of several trails. See the section on "The Monadnock Region & the Connecticut River Valley" later in this chapter for more information.

For other hiking opportunities outside the Whites, two recommended guidebooks are *50 Hikes in New Hampshire,* and *50 More Hikes in New Hampshire,* both written by Daniel Doan and published by Backcountry Publications, P.O. Box 175, Woodstock, VT 05091 (☎ **800/245-4151**).

If you like the heights but don't like the bother of schlepping gear, you might want to consider a llama-supported day hike. *Fairfield Llama Treks,* P.O. Box 96, Freedom, NH 03836 (☎ **603/539-2865**), offers a variety of hikes between 1.5 and 6 miles in the southern White Mountains. Guided trips include a hearty gourmet lunch atop picturesque mountaintops, and some time to bond with these doe-eyed relatives of the camel.

RAFTING   In the north, the Androscoggin River offers superb Class I-II whitewater and swift flatwater upstream of Berlin; below, the river is fetid with paper mill pollution and is best avoided.

Serious whitewater enthusiasts head to the upper reaches of the Saco River during spring run-off, where the Class III-IV rapids are intense if relatively short-lived along a 6.5-mile stretch paralleling Route 302.

ROCK CLIMBING   The White Mountains are renowned for their impressive, towering granite cliffs, especially Cathedral and White Horse ledges, which attract legions of rock climbers from throughout the United States and Europe. Ascents range from rather easy to extraordinarily difficult. The North Conway area hosts three climbing schools, and experienced and aspiring climbers alike have plenty of options for improving their skills. Classes range from one day to a week.

Contact **Eastern Mountain Sports Climbing School** (☎ 603/356-5433), the **International Mountain Climbing School** (☎ 603/356-7064), or the **Mountain Guides Alliance** (☎ 603/356-5310) for more information.

SAILING   New Hampshire's lakes region offers exceptional sailing with legendary northwest winds. But sailing is by and large the domain of those who own their own boats, since places willing to rent sailboats are few and far between. It's far easier to rent motorboats, which can be had at almost every marina along Winnipesaukee.

Sailboards may be rented at **Winni Sailboard School** in Laconia (☎ **603/ 528-4110**). On Lake Sunapee, you might try **Sargents Marine** (☎ **603/763-5032**) for sunfish rentals.

Coastal sailing is popular out of Portsmouth Harbor and Seabrook Harbor at Hampton Beach State Park. Sailors should be experienced with strong tides, and should be wary of the mud flats at low tide.

SKIING   While New Hampshire doesn't offer the sprawling, brawny mountains found in Vermont or Maine, it does offer everything from challenging slopes to gentle runs at 22 downhill ski areas.

New Hampshire's forte may be the small ski area that caters to families. These include Gunstock, Temple Mountain, Mt. Sunapee, King Pine, and Pats Peak, all with vertical drops of 1,500 feet or less. The more challenging skiing is in the White Mountains region; the best areas are Cannon Mountain, Loon, Waterville Valley, Wildcat, and Attitash. These all have vertical drops around 2,000 feet, and feature the services one would expect at a professional ski resort.

Ski NH (☎ **800/343-2250** or 603/745-9396 in NH) distributes a ski map and other information helpful in ski trip planning. To check on current downhill ski conditions, call **800/258-3608.**

The most impressive ski run in New Hampshire is one not served by a lift. Tuckerman Ravine drops 3,400 feet from a lip on the shoulder of Mt. Washington down to the valley floor. Skiers arrive from throughout the nation to venture here in the early spring (it's dangerously avalanche prone during the depths of winter), first hiking to the top then flying to the bottom of this dramatic glacial cirque. The slope is sheer and unforgiving; only very advanced skiers should attempt it. Careless or cocky skiers are hauled out every year on stretchers, and few years seem to go by without at least one skier's death. Contact the **AMC's Pinkham Notch camp** (☎ **603/ 466-2725**) for information on current conditions.

Ample cross-country skiing opportunities also exist. The state boasts some 26 cross-country ski centers, which groom a combined total of more than 500 miles of trails. The state's premier cross-country destination is the town of **Jackson** (☎ **603/ 383-9355**), with 55 miles of groomed trail in and around an exceptionally scenic village in a valley near the base of Mt. Washington. Other favorites include **Bretton Woods** (☎ **603/278-5181** or 800/232-2972) at the western entrance to Crawford Notch, also with more than 50 miles of groomed trail, and the spectacularly remote **Balsams/Wilderness cross-country ski center** (☎ **603/255-3951** or 800/ 255-0600) in the farthest reaches of the state.

My favorite inn with its own cross-country ski center is the **Franconia Inn** (☎ **603/823-5542** or 800/473-5299), which has nearly 40 miles of groomed trail on the scenic western edge of Franconia Notch.

SNOWMOBILING   Sledders will find nearly 6,000 miles of groomed, scenic snowmobile trails lacing the state, connected via an intricate trail network maintained by local snowmobile clubs. All sleds must be registered with the state; this costs $29 and can be done through any of the 200 off-highway recreational vehicle agents in the state. More information about snowmobiling in the state may be obtained from the **New Hampshire Snowmobile Association,** 722 Route 3A, Bow, NH 03304 (☎ **603/224-8906**).

The state's most remote and spectacular destination for snowmobilers is that nubby finger that thrusts up into Canada. It also happens to be the snowiest part of the state. The **Connecticut Lakes Tourist Association** (☎ **603/538-7405**) can provide information on services and lodging in the area. Your best bet for rentals or snowmobile tours of the area is **Pathfinder Sno-Tours,** based at Timberland Lodge in Pittsburg (☎ **603/538-6613**).

WINTER CAMPING/MOUNTAINEERING   The White Mountains attracts experienced recreationists who test their mettle against the blustery mountain peaks. The experience is unparalleled, if you're properly equipped—the Whites are never more untrammeled or peaceful than after a heavy winter's snowfall, and there are few other times you can enjoy the crystalline views from atop the region's highest peaks without sharing the experience with dozens of others.

Guided day hikes to the top of Mt. Washington are offered throughout the winter, and are suitable for people in reasonable shape with some hiking experience— no winter mountaineering experience is needed. **Eastern Mountain Sports Climbing School** (☎ **603/356-5433**) will outfit you with crampons and ice axe, and teach you their use on the lower slopes of the mountain. Many of the excursions fail to make the summit because of deteriorating weather conditions, but the experience of even being on the shoulders of wind-driven Mt. Washington is memorable nonetheless. Think of it as a low-rent trip to the Arctic.

Two of the AMC huts (Zealand Falls and Carter Notch) are kept open during the winter. Meals aren't served, but hikers need only bring food; the use of gas stoves and kitchenware are including in the rates ($15 per person; less for AMC members). Heat is provided by a woodstove at night in the common room (although not in the bunkrooms, so bring a heavy-duty sleeping bag); during the day you're free to explore these magnificent, snowy regions. Both huts require long ski or snowshoe hikes to reach them, although Zealand Falls is the less demanding of the two. Contact the AMC for more information at **603/466-2727.**

2 Seacoast

Every geography student at some point registers a small shock when they learn that New Hampshire isn't landlocked after all; it actually has a coast. Granted, it isn't much of a coast (just 18 miles of sand, rock, and surf), but travelers quickly learn that it manages to pack a lot of variety into a little space. The coast has honky-tonk beach towns, Newport-style mansions, vest-pocket state parks with swaths of warm sand, and a historic seaport city with a vibrant maritime history and culture. Ecologically, it's got low dunes, lush hardwood forests, and a complex system of salt marshes that has blocked development from overtaking the region entirely.

A short drive inland are more historic towns and a slower way of life that has, so far, managed to resist the inexorable creep of the Boston suburbs. While strip malls are belatedly establishing themselves throughout the region (particularly along Route 1), the quiet downtowns are holding their own and several have established themselves as fertile breeding grounds for small-scale entrepreneurs who've shunned the hectic life of far bigger cities.

A helpful, free guide to the region is available from the **Seacoast Council on Tourism,** 235 West Rd., Suite 10, Portsmouth, NH 03801 (☎ **800/221-5623** or 603/436-7678).

HAMPTON BEACH & HAMPTON

The **chamber of commerce**'s phone number in Hampton Beach is **1-800/ GET-A-TAN.** And that about says it all. During the peak of the summer season, as many as 200,000 people, many of them rather young, crowd the beaches on a sunny day, then spill over into the town and cruise the main drag by car, bike, and Rollerblade. The place bristles with a testosterone-fueled energy during the balmy months, then lapses into a deep, shuttered slumber the rest of the year.

This traveler's first impression of this beach town isn't one of sand and surf, however, but rather of asphalt—acres and acres of it—and strikingly undistinguished architecture. The town is separated from its sandy strand by a busy four-lane road and a series of parking strips. Along the northern part of the beach, which tends to be less commercial and more residential than the south, the view of the sea from the road is partially blocked by a stout white seawall, which also serves as a handy sunning perch. But stick around for a bit if you're initially less than enchanted; it takes more than a moment for the salty character of the town to reveal itself.

A short drive inland, the more relaxed town of Hampton draws its inspiration less from the sea and more from the classic New England village, although it has a besieged, somewhat bedraggled feel to it in summer. It remains a good destination for shopping, restaurants, and accommodations. Try here if seacoast lodging is booked up.

ESSENTIALS

GETTING THERE   Hampton Beach is reached from I-95 via Exit 2. Be forewarned that traffic to the beach can be taxing in the summer, particularly on weekends. Route 1A winds north through Rye Beach, ending eventually in Portsmouth. Hampton is on Route 1, a more commercial route that runs parallel to the coast. Traffic can also slow to a crawl here in midsummer.

VISITOR INFORMATION   The **Hampton Beach Chamber of Commerce,** P.O. Box 790, Hampton Beach, NH 03843 (☎ **603/926-8718** or 800/438-2826), maintains an information center summers at Hampton Beach State Park, which is located in the middle of Hampton Beach.

ON THE BEACH

What to do here? Head to the beach, of course. Never mind that the ocean water is frigid (60 degrees is warm here), or that you'll be comfortable splashing around only if the mercury soars sky-high. (And even then, the sweltering heat on shore looks pretty good after a few minutes underwater.) The sandy beach is a fine place to roll out a towel, to walk, or just to while away a day.

If you're staying at a Hampton Beach hotel, you're within walking distance of the surf. If not, metered parking is available in and around Hampton Beach, although spots are scarce during prime beachgoing hours. If town parking lots are full, head inland a block or so and search out commercial lots.

Six state parks and beaches, none of them very large, dot the seacoast between Hampton Beach and Portsmouth. All charge a nominal parking or entrance fee during the summer. **Hampton Beach State Park** (☎ 603/926-3784) is smack in the town of Hampton Beach, and is the place to be if you like boisterous crowds with your foamy surf. Farther up the coast, **Wallis Sands State Beach** (☎ 603/436-9404) offers an inviting, broad sweep of sand and ample parking. It's not quite as crowded or loud as the more southerly beaches. (Remember, this is all relative.) A mile and a half north of Wallis Sands is **Odiorne Point State Park** (☎ 603/926-3784), a 300-acre oceanside park for those popular among those looking for a more wooded seaside experience. The park marks the site of the first European settlement of New Hampshire (a Scotsman settled here in 1623), and boasts seven types of habitat, picnic areas, and a visitor's center.

NOT ON THE BEACH

Flower fans should detour briefly from the coastal route to visit **Fuller Gardens** (☎ 603/964-5414), located on Willow Avenue in North Hampton just north of the intersection of Routes 1-A and 101-D. The two-acre gardens adorn the grounds of the home of a former Massachusetts governor (the house is long gone), and feature extensive rose collections and a peaceful Japanese garden within the sound of the surf. After visiting the gardens, head to the shore and hike along the footpath. The gardens are open early May through mid-October from 10am to 4pm. Admission is $4.

A tour up Route 1-A is well worthwhile. This twisting oceanside road is dramatic in an understated sort of way (Big Sur it's not), with residential architecture becoming more elegant and immense as you make your way north to **Millionaire's Row.** Be forewarned that this won't be an activity you'll enjoy in isolation, particularly during the height of summer. The road is often congested and frustrating to navigate by car, with frequent, unexpected stops and limited visibility behind slow-moving motor homes.

A better option is to view the coast by bicycle, which affords a far more sane pace and opens up countless lounging options along the way. Route 1-A has a bike lane that periodically breaks away into a separate bike path with excellent views of the rocky coast.

WHERE TO STAY

Hampton Beach has dozens of motels scattered along its sandy shore, and they tend to clutter in greater density along the southern end near the center of town. Motels along Ocean Boulevard include the modern **Seaside Motel** (☎ 603/926-1655), **Springfield Motor Lodge** (☎ 603/926-5595 or 800/992-4297), **Oceancrest Inn & Motel** (☎ 603/926-6606) and **Jonathan's Motel** (☎ 603/926-6631 or 800/634-8243).

The New Hampshire Coast

York Harbor
Western Point
Godfreys Cove
Forty Acre Hill
Rachel Carson NWR
Brave Boat Harbor
Seapoint Beach
95
101
236
103
Newington Station
South Eliot
Kittery
Kittery Point
Newington
Pease AFB
Portsmouth
Little Harbor
Great Bay
Pierce Pt.
Pannaway Manor
Odiornes Pt.
1A
Elwyn Park
Lang's Corner
Fairhill Manor
Beays Brook
Wallis Sand
Rye N Beach
101
151
Rye
Fass Beach
Rye Harbor State Pk.
Straw Point
Duck Island
Appledore Island
Maine
New Hampshire
1
West Rye
Winnicut
Cable Road
Rye Beach
North Hampton
White Island
Star Island
95
101
1A
Little Boars Head
101
Hampton
Plaice Cove
North Beach
1
101
Great Boars Head
Hampton Beach
Hampton Harbor
Atlantic Ocean
Seabrook
Beckmans Point
Seabrook Beach
New Hamphire
Massachusetts
86
South Seabrook
Salisbury Beach
Salisbury
Salisbury Beach

Beach	☂
State Park	🌲
Major Railways	⊢⊢⊢⊢

0 — 5 mi

1-0789

Ashworth by the Sea. 295 Ocean Blvd., Hampton Beach, NH 03842. ☎ **603/926-6762** or 800/345-6736. 105 rms. A/C TV TEL. Peak season $95–$250 double; shoulder seasons $59–$225 double; off-season $55–$195 double. AE, DC, DISC, MC, V.

There are a few subtle architectural clues, but it's still hard to tell that this shorefront hotel was first built in 1912. After a number of renovations, it's all modern and polished to the hilt. The Ashworth is actually two buildings joined at the hip, with the 1912 south building linked to the less distinguished but comfortable north building, constructed in 1979. All rooms but six have private balconies. This friendly hotel does a lively business in conventions and meetings, but not such that it makes individuals or families feel like they've wandered somewhere they shouldn't.

Dining/Entertainment: The hotel has three dining areas. The main dining room was recently renovated to restore its Edwardian flavor (note the stamped tin ceilings), and serves traditional American fare including lobster Newburg, roast turkey, and filet mignon ($9.95 to $19.95). Sandwiches and other lighter fare is available at Breakers Cafe Lounge.

Facilities: Outdoor pool and deck on the second level overlooking the road and toward the beach.

Seaside Village. 1 Ocean Blvd. (Route 1A, 1,000 feet south of North Hampton Beach), North Hampton, NH 03862. ☎ **603/964-8204.** 19 rms. TV. $69–$99 daily (when available); $425–$750 by the week. AE, MC, V. Closed Oct 15–Apr 30.

Seaside Village is a classic, gray-shingled beach motel more reminiscent of sandy Cape Cod than of granite-and-spruce New Hampshire. If you're a beach fan, this is your place—it's the only motel in New Hampshire directly on the sand. During the day you can walk across low dunes to get to mile-long North Hampton Beach. In the evening, guests grill their dinner on the shared hibachis and prepare meals in the handy outdoor galley. All rooms have refrigerators and ceiling fans.

The trick here is to actually get a room. Most book up for the season the previous summer, although if you're in town it's worth calling to inquire if anything is available for the night. The older units (the Seaside has been operating for 60 years) are plain but neatly furnished, and the end units have nice views toward the sea. Expect some ambient noise (like your neighbor's plumbing) in these older rooms. Eight modern post-and-beam housekeeping cottages were built in the early 1990s and are a better, if more expensive, choice. The newer units are more solidly wrought, and have air-conditioning in the bedrooms.

WHERE TO DINE

J.B.'s Bagels/Java, 61 Lafayette Rd. (Route 1; ☎ **603/964-1877**), is easy to miss amid the haggard strip development of Route 1 between Hampton and North Hampton. But keep an eye out. Amid groovy surfer decor you can order coffee and bagels with tasty cream-cheese spreads (veggie, chives, or walnut-raisin). Eat inside or on the small deck with a Route 1 view. Better yet, stop by early in the morning (J.B.'s opens at 6am weekdays, 7am on weekends), add a bagel sandwich to the order, and head to one of the area beaches with your picnic. No credit cards.

Ron's Beach House. 965 Ocean Blvd., Hampton Beach. ☎ **603/926-7870.** Reservations recommended in summer. Lunch items $4.95–$9.95; main dinner courses $11.95–$19.95. AE, DC, DISC, MC, V. Mon–Sat 11am–10pm, Sun 10am–2pm and 4–10pm. SEAFOOD/AMERICAN.

No surprise: Seafood is the specialty at Ron's Beach House, a local institution owned by Ron Boucher, a graduate of the Culinary Institute of America. This white-shingled building just off Route 1A affords glimpses of Plaice Cove, and has become a local institution of sorts, providing an anchor for the often-transient Hampton Beach dining scene. Ron's attracts steady traffic in loyal repeat customers (during lunch, it's popular with ladies of a certain age), and many return time and again for the fresh seafood, which can be prepared baked, blackened, charbroiled, or steamed and served with an oriental dipping sauce. Entrees not from the sea include chicken, veal, and pasta dishes, but you're best off sticking with fish. Dining is on two floors and an outside deck, and there's a cozy bar on the second floor. The wine list, incidentally, is superb for any location, never mind a beach town.

Widow Fletcher Tavern. 401 Lafayette Rd., Hampton. ☎ **603/926-8800.** Reservations accepted for parties of 6 or more. Lunch items $4.95–$6.50; main dinner courses $4.95–$13.95. AE, MC, V. Daily 11am–11pm. BRITISH/AMERICAN.

Situated in what passes for downtown Hampton, a few miles from the sea, the Widow Fletcher has a distinctly British public house feel to it. The tavern sits on hectic Route 1, but once you cross the threshold, the crowds and congestion are left at the door. This early village home has a comfortable, well-worn patina, with heavy wooden beams and 14-inch pine plank floors. Dining is both upstairs and down in small rooms decorated with an eclectic selection of antiques, or at the sturdy bar. Guests can continue the Emerald Isles theme with an order of shepherd's pie, or bangers and mash (sausages and mashed potatoes). Or branch out and sample something more exotic. The house specialty isn't something Winston Churchill would likely recognize—it's a sirloin steak steak marinated in soy, ginger, and hoisin sauce. The portions are large and will satisfy those who've stoked up sizeable appetites after a day on the beach.

HAMPTON BEACH AFTER DARK

In the evening, the action's in Hampton Beach, which takes on a carnival atmosphere. Much of the town's organized nightlife is centered around **Hampton Beach Casino** (☎ **603/926-4541**), situated smack in the middle of town and fronting the ocean. The casino has shops, video arcades, waterslides, and parking for 700 cars (there's no gambling, despite the name). There's also a 2,000-seat performance hall where you can see yesterday's top performers.

EXETER

The inland town of Exeter is a piece of classic New England. It's got a bandshell around which the local traffic circles. It has varied commercial architecture in its small but vibrant downtown. It has wonderful residential architecture along its shady side streets. It's bisected by the historic Squamscott River, which once provided power to flanking mills. It has a fine selection of boutiques and shops worth browsing. It also has one of the nation's most prestigious prep schools, which is architecturally if not culturally integrated into the town itself. In short, it's a good stop if you want a quick view of what makes New England New England.

ESSENTIALS

GETTING THERE   Exeter is located on Route 108 south of Route 101. Take the Hampton exit on I-95 and head west to Route 108.

VISITOR INFORMATION   The **Exeter Chamber of Commerce,** 120 Water St., Exeter, NH 03833 (☎ **603/772-2411**), distributes travel information from its offices weekdays from 8:30am to 4:30pm.

EXPLORING THE TOWN

Exeter is best viewed on foot. Downtown boasts an eclectic mix of architecture, from clapboarded Georgian homes to intricate brick Victorians. The center of downtown is marked by the Swasey Pavilion, a trim 1916 bandstand with an intricate floral mosaic on the ceiling. Brass band concerts are still held here in the summer. Just up the hill from the pavilion is the imposing Congregational church, built in 1798, with its unusually handsome white spire. On Thursdays in summer and early fall, there's a farmer's market held from 2:30 to 5:30pm along Swasey Parkway near the river.

I'd strongly recommend picking up the booklet "Walking Tour of Exeter," published in 1994 by the Exeter Historical Society. It's available for $2 at the American Independence Museum, the Exeter Chamber of Commerce, or the historical society (47 Front St.). This guide and map offers a concise, well-written history of the town, along with historical and architectural facts about notable local buildings, such as 11 Pleasant St., where Abraham Lincoln's son lived while attending Exeter Academy.

With or without the guide, the grounds of the **Phillips Exeter Academy** (just southwest of the town center) are worth a stroll. The predominant style is Georgian-inspired brick buildings—it's hard to imagine misbehaving at a campus that seems this stern. (This hasn't deterred generations of troublesome prep school kids.) But look for the anomalies, like the 1971 prizewinning library by noted American architect Louis I. Kahn on Front St. near Abbot Place.

American Independence Museum. 1 Governor's Ln. (one block west of bandshell off Water St.). ☎ **603/772-2622.** Admission $4 adults, $2 children 6–12. May–Oct Wed–Sun noon–5pm.

This small, ambitious museum offers an insightful glimpse of colonial life during one-hour tours. Displays in the 1721 Ladd-Gilman House include Revolutionary War and Colonial Revival artifacts and furniture, although you won't see the museum's most prized possession: one of 25 Declarations of Independence known to exist. It turned up when someone finally got around to cleaning out the attic in the 1980s. Owing to its great delicacy, this revered document is brought out only for special occasions, although copies are always on display.

You'll learn all about the intriguing homestead, built by John Taylor Gilman, a 14-year governor of New Hampshire. Among the functions it served, the home was the state treasury during the American Revolution—look for displays of early currency in the treasury room. Descendents of Gilman occupied this home for decades, and in 1902 it was acquired by the state chapter of the Society of the Cincinnati, the oldest veterans group in the nation. In 1991 the group opened the house to the public (society members still meet here twice a year), and this engaging museum was born.

WHERE TO STAY

The Inn by the Bandstand. 4 Front St., Exeter, NH 03833. ☎ **603/772-6352.** 8 rms, all with fireplaces, some with showers only. A/C TV TEL. $89–$135 double. Rates include breakfast. AE, MC, V.

You can't help but notice this regal Federal-style house looming over the bandstand when wandering through downtown Exeter. Hosting guests only since 1992, the Inn by the Bandstand is handsomely decorated inside with a supple Victorian richness. The rooms are attractively furnished with a mix of antiques and reproductions. The first-floor suite is styled with deep maroons and forest greens, and furnished with leather wingback chairs. On the third floor are two rooms with the original hand-hewn beams (the home was built in 1809), and modern amenities include microwaves and refrigerators. Room rates include a fine continental breakfast, which typically features homemade muffins, coffee cake, fruit, and granola. While the downtown location is certainly handy, it can be a bit noisy as trucks gear down the hill next to the bandstand.

⑤ Inn of Exeter. 90 Front St., Exeter, NH 03833. ☎ **603/772-5901** or 800/782-8444. 50 rms. A/C TV TEL. $75–$100 double; $170 suite with fireplace. AE, DC, DISC, MC, V.

Located at the edge of the Exeter Academy campus and within easy walking distance of downtown, the Inn of Exeter has the dark, cool feel of a proper British drinking club. It's all dark wood and maroon carpets, with oil paintings on the walls, statuary in the alcoves, and a basket of apples on the front desk. The inn, which caters in large part to parents and staff associated with the academy next door, was built in 1932 and the solid brick building with its prominent chimneys could easily pass for a campus building. The rooms on three floors are tastefully furnished with reproduction American antiques, including some canopy beds. Room sizes vary, but all are welcoming and homey. While the inn isn't budget priced, it offers excellent value for the money.

Dining/Entertainment: The downstairs lounge and bar is clubby and dim, nicely capturing an era that elsewhere passed by long ago. The distinguished dining room serves three well-prepared meals a day. Dinner entrees might include chicken breast stuffed with lobster medallions and chives, salmon marinated in ginger and encrusted with sesame, or veal, a house specialty, which is served differently each night.

WHERE TO DINE

Loaf and Ladle. 9 Water St. ☎ **603/778-8955.** Reservations not required. Main courses $7–$11. AE, DC, DISC, MC, V. Mon–Sat 7:30am–9pm, Sun 9am–9pm. CAFE/BAKERY.

A handsome view of the river and colorful piscine art are the only distractions from the superb baked goods and other delicious fare served up with charm at the Loaf and Ladle. It's sometimes hard to get a grasp on the ever-evolving menu; it's constantly changing, updated on chalkboards as the day goes on. As one soup is drained by appreciative diners, another one goes up. Among the savory baked goods, the cinnamon buns are especially fine.

Starving Chef. 287 Water St. ☎ **603/772-5590.** Reservations recommended on weekends. Main courses at lunch $5.25–$8.95, at dinner $14.95–$17.95. AE, CB, DC, DISC, MC, V. Mon–Sat 11:30am–2:30pm, Sun 11am–2pm; Tues–Thurs 5–9pm, Fri–Sat 5–10pm. ECLECTIC.

This easy-to-miss 85-seat restaurant is tucked away on Water Street across from the American Independence Museum. Housed in a slightly shopworn clapboard home dating from 1834, the restaurant's interior shuns fancy in favor of simple and comfortable. Diners sit in an open room downstairs or in warrenlike smaller rooms upstairs (I'd go with the downstairs; it's more convivial). The menu offers a mix of American favorites like filet mignon and broiled swordfish, but steer yourself toward the chef's more creative entrees, which are influenced by the cooking of the Far East. Aunt Lydia's Chicken is a perennial favorite—it's a chicken breast sautéed with brussels sprouts, figs, dates, and cashews, served with a deliciously unique sauce of tamari, tamarind, and (oddly enough) French dressing. Other tempting entrees include shrimp in a Thai sauce, Szechuan beef and scallops, and quick-fried lamb marinated in garlic, ginger, onion, yogurt, and curry.

PORTSMOUTH

Portsmouth is a civilized seaside city of bridges and brick and seagulls, and is far and away one of the most attractive small cities on the whole of the eastern seaboard. Filled with elegant architecture that's more intimate than intimidating, this bonsai-sized city projects a strong and proud sense of its heritage without being overly precious about it.

Part of the city's appeal is its variety. Upscale coffee shops and fancy leather goods stores exist alongside old-fashioned barber shops and tattoo parlors. There's been a steady gentrification in recent years, which has brought a surfeit of twee shops, but the town still has a fundamental earthiness that serves as a tangy vinegar for the handful of overly saccharine spots. Portsmouth's humble waterfront must actually be sought out, and when found it's rather understated.

Portsmouth's history runs deep, which is instantly evident when walking through town. For the past three centuries, the city has served as a hub for the region's maritime trade. In the 1600s, Strawbery Banke (it wasn't renamed Portsmouth until 1653) was a center for the export of wood and dried fish to Europe. In the 19th century, it grew as a center of regional trade. Across the river in Maine, the Portsmouth Naval Shipyard was founded in 1800, and evolved into a prominent base for the building, outfitting, and repair of U.S. Navy submarines. Today, Portsmouth's maritime tradition continues with a lively trade in bulk goods (look for scrap metal and minerals stockpiled along the shores of the Piscataqua River on Market St.); the city's de facto symbol is the tugboat, one or two of which are almost always tied up near the waterfront's picturesque "tugboat alley."

Visitors to Portsmouth will find there's a whole lot to see in a little space. There's good shopping in the boutiques that now occupy much of the historic district, good eating at the many small restaurants, and plenty of history to explore among the historic homes and museums that crop up on almost every block.

ESSENTIALS

GETTING THERE   Portsmouth is served by Exits 3 through 7 on I-95. The most direct access to downtown is via Market St. (Exit 7), which is the last New Hampshire exit before crossing the river to Maine. By bus, Portsmouth is served by Concord Trailways and Vermont Transit.

VISITOR INFORMATION   The **Greater Portsmouth Chamber of Commerce,** 500 Market St., Portsmouth, NH 03802 (☎ **603/436-1118**), operates a very helpful tourist information center year-round between Exit 7 and downtown. The office is open daily in summer, weekdays only the remainder of the year. In summer the chamber staffs a second information booth at Market Square in the middle of the historic district.

ORIENTATION   Portsmouth consists of two main areas of interest to travelers. First, there's the historic commercial district, located around Market Square and extending to the shores of the Piscataqua River. Second, there's Strawbery Banke, the city's premier historic museum/neighborhood (admission charged), which is near the public gardens and a waterfront park.

PARKING   Most of Portsmouth can be easily reconnoitered on foot, so you need park only once. Parking can be tight in and around the historic district in summer. Happily, the municipal parking garage costs just 25¢ per hour; look for signs pointing you there just west of Market Square off Congress Street. Strawbery Banke also offers limited parking for visitors.

A "MUSEUM" NOT TO MISS

✪ **Strawbery Banke.** P.O. Box 300, Portsmouth, NH 03802. ☎ **603/433-1100.** $10 adults, $9 seniors, $7 children 7–17, $25 families. Early May to late Oct daily 10am–5pm. Special events held around Thanksgiving and the first two weekends of Dec. Look for directional signs posted around town.

If Portsmouth were a festival of historic homes and buildings, Strawbery Banke would be the main stage. In 1958 the city planned to raze this venerable neighborhood, first settled in 1653, to make way for urban renewal. A group of local citizens fought the tides of progress and won, establishing an outdoor history museum that's grown to be one of the largest in New England. The museum today consists of 10 downtown acres and 42 historic buildings, 10 of which have been restored to 10 different eras and are open to the public. (One admission fee buys access to all homes and exhibits.) While Strawbery Banke employs staffers to assume the character of historic residents (including Thomas Bailey Aldrich, a frequent early contributor to the *Atlantic Monthly*), the emphasis is more on the buildings, architecture, and historic accouterment, and less on "living history" as practiced as Sturbridge Village or Plimoth Plantation in Massachusetts.

The neighborhood surrounds an open lawn (formerly a tidal creek), and has a settled, picturesque quality to it. You'll find three working crafts shops on the grounds, where you can watch coopers, boatbuilders, and potters at work. The most

Portsmouth

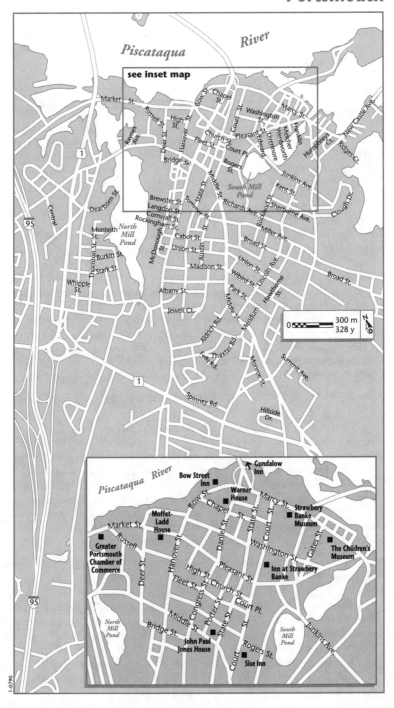

Main map labels:

Piscataqua River

see inset map

Market St.
Russell St.
Barnes Ave.
High St.
Deer St.
Hanover St.
Bridge St.
Fleet St.
Bow St.
Chapel St.
Washington
Court St.
Pleasant St.
Church St.
Court Pl.
Orchard
Livermore
Wentworth
Rogers St.
Marcy St.
Melcher
Franklin
Humphreys
Ct.
Ridges Ct.
New Castle Ave.

South Mill Pond

Dearborn St.
Central
Brewster St.
Langdon St.
Summer St.
State St.
Middle St.
Richards Ave.
Rockland St.
Sherburne Ave.
Kent St.
Junkins Ave.
Clough Dr.

Cornwall St.
Rockingham St.
North Mill Pond
Monteith St.
McDonough St.
Cabot St.
Union St.
Austin St.
Miller Ave.
Broad St.

Burkitt St.
Thornton St.
Stark St.
Madison St.
Union Ave.
Lincoln Ave.
Wibird St.
Broad St.

Whipple St.
Albany St.
Park St.
Hawthorne St.

Jewell Ct.
Middle St.
Meridium
Aldrich Rd.

0   300 m
    328 y

Thaxter Rd.
Fells Rd.
Monroe St.
Summit Ave.

Spinney Rd.

Hillside Dr.

Inset map labels:

Piscataqua River

Gundalow Inn

Bow Street Inn
Bow St.
Chapel St.
Warner House
Marcy St.
State St.
Strawbery Banke Museum

Moffet-Ladd House
Market St.
Russell St.
Daniel St.
Court St.
Washington St.
Cates St.
The Children's Museum

Greater Portsmouth Chamber of Commerce
Deer St.
Hanover St.
High St.
Pleasant St.
Inn at Strawbery Banke

Fleet St.
Church St.
Congress
Porter St.
Court Pl.
State St.
Court St.

North Mill Pond

Middle St.
Bridge St.
John Paul Jones House

Rogers St.
Sise Inn

South Mill Pond
Junkins Ave.

1-0790

169

intriguing home may be the split-personality Drisco House, half of which depicts life in the 1790s, and half of which shows life in the 1950s, nicely demonstrating how houses grow and adapt to each era. In 1997, the museum will open another home, which will depict the life of a Russian Jewish immigrant family in 1919.

A MAGICAL HISTORY TOUR

Portsmouth's 18th-century prosperity can be plainly seen in the regal Georgian-style homes that dot the city. A walking tour of the city will take in the most significant homes, many of which are maintained by various historical or colonial societies and are open to the public. A helpful map and brochure describing the key historic homes entitled "The Portsmouth Trail: An Historic Walking Tour" is available free at the city's information centers (see above). If you plan to tour more than one home, ask about the Portsmouth Passport, which offers a small discount.

John Paul Jones House. 43 Middle St. ☎ **603/436-8420.** $4 adults, $2 children 6–14. June to mid-Oct Mon–Sat 10am–4pm, Sun noon–4pm.

Revolutionary War hero John Paul Jones ("I have not yet begun to fight") was a boarder in this handsome 1758 home during the Revolutionary War, when he oversaw the construction of his sloop, *Ranger,* believed to be the first ship to sail under the United States flag (there's a model of it on display here). The home has been immaculately restored and maintained by the Portsmouth Historical Society; costumed tour guides offer tours of 45 minutes to an hour, providing a raft of information along the way about Jones and Sarah Wentworth, the widow who opened this large, Georgian-style home to boarders to support her sizable family. The house, which was built by six carpenters working six days a week for two years, contains a handsome collection of period furniture; there are also collections of china and period clothing, including elaborate wedding gowns.

Moffatt-Ladd House. 154 Market St. ☎ **603/436-8221.** $4 adults, $1 children under 12. June 15–Oct 15 Mon–Sat 10am–4pm, Sun 2–5pm.

The Moffatt-Ladd House, built for a family of prosperous merchants and traders, is as notable for its elegant garden as for the 1763 home, with its Great Hall and elaborate carvings throughout. Remarkably, the home remained in one family between 1763 and 1913, when it became a museum. Many of the furnishings have never left the house. The home will especially appeal to aficionados of early American furniture and painting; it's hung with portraits of some 15 family members. The terraced garden's design dates to the mid-19th century, but some of the roses can be traced back to plantings in 1768 and 1776. The home is owned by the National Society of The Colonial Dames of America in the State of New Hampshire.

Warner House. 150 Daniel St. Tel 603/436-5909. $4 adults, $2 children 7–12. Early June to Oct Tues–Sat 10am–4pm, Sun 1–4pm.

The Warner House, built in 1716, was the governor's mansion in the mid-18th century when Portsmouth served as state capital. This stately brick home with graceful Georgian architectural elements (note the alternating arched and triangular pediments above the dormer windows) is a favorite among architectural historians for its circa 1716 wall murals (said to be the oldest murals still in place in the U.S.), the early wall marbleizing, and the original white pine paneling. Benjamin Franklin visited the house in 1763 to personally supervise the installation of a lightning rod on the west wall.

Wentworth-Gardner House. 50 Mechanic St. ☎ **603/436-4406.** $4 adults, $2 children 6–14. Mid-June to mid-Oct Tues–Sun 1–4pm.

The Wentworth-Gardner is arguably the most handsome mansion in the entire Seacoast region, and is widely considered to be one of the best examples of Georgian architecture in the country. Built in 1760, the home features many of the classic period elements, including very pronounced quoins (the blocks on the building's corners), pedimented window caps, plank sheathing (this was meant to make it appear as if made of masonry), and an elaborate doorway featuring Corinthian pilasters, a broken scroll, and a paneled door topped with a pineapple, the symbol of hospitality. The inside is no less impressive, with hand-painted Chinese wallpaper and a vast fireplace in the kitchen featuring a windmill spit. This waterfront house was once owned by Wallace Nutting, the noted chronicler of old New England ways, and at one point was owned by the Metropolitan Museum of Art in New York, which had considered moving the house to Central Park.

BOAT TOURS

Portsmouth is especially attractive when seen from the water. A small fleet of tour boats ties up at Portsmouth, offering scenic tours of the Piscataqua River and the historic Isle of Shoals throughout the summer and fall.

The **Isle of Shoals Steamship Co.** (☎ **603/431-5500** or 800/441-4620) sails from Baker Wharf on Market Street and is the most established of the tour companies. The firm offers a variety of tours on the 90-foot, three-deck *Thomas Laighton* (it's a modern replica of a turn-of-the-century steamship) and the 70-foot *Oceanic,* which was especially designed for whale-watching. Among the most popular excursions are to the Isle of Shoals, allowing passengers to disembark and wander about Star Island, a dramatic, rocky island that's part of an island cluster far out in the offshore swells. Star Island has a rich history and today serves as the base for a summer religious institute. Reservations are strongly encouraged for this trip. Other popular trips include six-hour whale-watching voyages and a sunset lighthouse cruise. Fares range from $9 to $17 for adults, $5 to $15 for children.

Portsmouth Harbor Cruises (☎ **603/436-8084** or 800/776-0915) specializes in tours of the historic Piscataqua River aboard the *Heritage,* a 49-passenger cruise ship with lots of open deck space. Cruise by five old forts during the harbor cruise, or enjoy the picturesque tidal estuary of inland Great Bay, a scenic trip upriver from Portsmouth. Trips run daily, and reservations are suggested. Fares are $7.50 to $15 for adults, $5 to $8 for children.

KID STUFF

The **Children's Museum of Portsmouth,** located in an old meeting house at 280 Marcy St., two blocks south of Strawbery Banke (☎ **603/436-3853**), is a bright, lively arts and science museum that offers a morning's worth of hands-on exhibits of interest to younger artisans and scientists. Among the more popular displays are the miniature "submarine" and space shuttle cockpit, both of which invite clambering, and exhibits on earthquakes and lobstering. Admission is $3.50 for adults and children (free under 1 year old). It's open daily in summer 10am to 5pm (Sunday from 1 to 5pm.)

Another guaranteed kid-pleaser, especially on parched summer days, is **Water Country** (☎ **603/436-3556**), located on Route 1 three miles south of the Portsmouth Circle. This 18-acre water park includes New England's largest wave pool, and thrilling tubing rides called Raging Rapids and the Plunge. Gentler diversions, like sliding down the arms of Big Ollie the Octopus, will appeal to younger children. The park also has picnic areas and three snack bars. Admission is $21.95 for adults, $14.95 for children under four feet tall, and free for children under 2 years. Open 9:30am to 7:30pm daily during mid-summer; call for hours earlier and later in the season.

Shopping

Portsmouth's compact historic district has dozens of unique boutiques that sell items you won't find at the mall, including many hand-crafted products. The selection ranges from urban funky to country casual, so few are likely to leave disappointed. If you're serious about browsing, allow at least a couple of hours to wander through town. The following are just a sampling of the more intriguing places.

Choozy Shooz. 19 Market St. ☎ **603/433-4455.**

The most creative shoe store in the city, Choozy Shooz offers a wide selection of hip as well as eminently practical footwear.

City & Country. 50 Daniel St. ☎ **603/433-5353.**

This contemporary housewares store—a sort of Pottery Barn Lite—has a small but intriguing selection of glasses, table settings, flatware, and cooking implements, along with a mix of furniture and wrought iron accessories.

Harbor Treats. 4 Market Sq. ☎ **603/431-3228.**

This is a chocoholic's paradise, with a good selection of homemade fudges, chocolates, and truffles. Don't leave without trying the chocolate turtles.

Macro Polo. 89 Market St. ☎ **603/436-8338.**

Macro Polo takes retro and makes it retro chic. This pleasantly cluttered shop stocks pink flamingos, refrigerator magnets, movie kitsch, candies, coffee mugs, and T-shirts, most of which are embellished with off-beat humor. It's a popular spot with teens.

N.W. Barrett Gallery. 53 Market St. ☎ **603/431-4262.**

A contemporary gallery featuring the work of area craftspeople, this elegant shop offers up a classy selection of creative, exuberant crafts, including ceramic sculptures, glassware, lustrous woodworking, and a wide array of handmade jewelry.

Paradise Garage. 63 Penhallow St. ☎ **603/431-0180.**

Packed to the eaves with small stuff, this shop offers up an array of clever postcards, greeting cards, a good selection of car models (the kind you put together with glue), and vintage automobile bric-a-brac.

Slackers. 51 Ceres St. ☎ **603/427-1425.**

This appealing shop tucked away near Tugboat Alley features a selection of casual, contemporary clothing and footwear, including plenty from Patagonia. It's a draw for college students and young professionals.

Where to Stay

Portsmouth has a good selection of places to stay within walking distance of the downtown historic area. Less expensive, less stylish options include several chain hotels at the edge of town near I-95. Among them are the **Anchorage Inn,** 417 Woodbury Ave. (☎ **603/431-8111**); **Susse Chalet,** 650 Borthwick Ave. (☎ **603/436-6363**); and the **Holiday Inn of Portsmouth** (☎ **603/431-8000**), also on Woodbury Avenue.

Bow Street Inn. 121 Bow St., Portsmouth, NH 03801. ☎ **603/431-7760.** Fax 603/433-1680. 9 rms. A/C TV TEL. Aug to mid-Sept $105–$139 double; mid-May to July $99–$130 double; off-season $89–$119 double. Rates include continental breakfast. AE, DISC, MC, V.

This is a fine spot for travelers willing to give up charm to gain convenience. This former downtown brewery was made over in the 1980s in a bit of inspired adaptive reuse—condos occupy the top floor, and the respected **Seacoast Repertory Theatre** (☎ 603/433-4472) occupies the first.

The second floor is the Bow Street Inn, a modern nine-room hotel that offers superb access to historic Portsmouth. The guest rooms, set off a somewhat sterile hallway, are clean, comfortable, and for the most part unexceptional, although rooms 6 and 7 both feature fine views of the harbor. A couple of quibbles: The elevator may be the slowest in the Western world, and this is one of the very few lodgings in northern New England that doesn't offer free and easy parking. (Parking is on the street or at a nearby paid lot.) But the theater's right downstairs, and all of historic Portsmouth lies right outside your door. That's where the Bow Street's value lies.

Gundalow Inn. 6 Water St., Kittery, ME 03904. ☎ **207/439-4040.** 6 rms (2 with tubs and handheld showers.) July–Oct $105 double; May–June $95 double; Nov–Apr $80 double. Rates include full breakfast. MC, V. No children under 16.

The Gundalow Inn lies just across the river in Kittery, Maine, but it's very much linked in spirit to downtown Portsmouth. In fact, the inn allows travelers to combine the best of both worlds—guests can enjoy a relaxing, small-town inn, yet be just a half-mile walk across a bridge from New Hampshire's most historic and vibrant city. Innkeepers Cevia and George Rosol converted this 1889 home in 1990, and they've done a superb job of it. The rooms are tastefully restored and furnished with eclectic antiques, including vintage 1930s iron bedsteads. A first-floor common room and a small front porch allow guests to unwind with grace after a day's exertions. No smoking.

Breakfasts are notable for their delectability and generous portions, and typically include fruit soup, scones, and pancakes, along with something more exotic like smoked salmon or a dish with an East Indian tang.

Inn at Strawbery Banke. 314 Court St., Portsmouth, NH 03801. ☎ **603/436-7242** or 800/428-3933. 7 rms (5 with shower only). Peak season $90–$95 double; off-season $70–$75 double. Rates include full breakfast. AE, DISC, MC, V.

The Inn at Strawbery Banke, located in a home built in the early 1800s on historic Court Street, is ideally located for exploring Portsmouth. Strawbery Banke is but a block away, and Market Square is just two blocks. Innkeeper Sarah O'Donnell is a young and friendly host, and has done a nice job taking this antique home and making it comfortable for her guests. Rooms are small but bright, and feature stencilling, wooden interior shutters, and beautiful pine floors; one has a bathroom down the hall. There are two sitting rooms with televisions, and a dining room where a full breakfast is served between 8 and 9am.

✪ **Sise Inn.** 40 Court St., Portsmouth, NH 03801. ☎ **603/433-1200.** Fax 603/433-1200. 34 rms. A/C TV TEL. Late May–Oct $89–$175 double; Nov–early May $79–$150 double. Rates include continental breakfast. AE, DC, MC, V.

The Sise Inn is basically a modern, elegant, small hotel in the guise of a country inn. This solid gray Queen Anne–style home with jade and cream trim overlooks the busy intersection of Court and Middle streets, but inside it's peaceful and a world removed from the bustle of town. The original home was built for a prominent merchant in 1881; the hotel addition was constructed about a decade ago. The effect is surprisingly harmonious, with the antique stained glass and copious oak trim meshing well with the more contemporary elements. An elevator serves the three floors and there's modern carpeting throughout, but many of the rooms and suites feature antique armoires and updated Victorian styling. Among the most appealing rooms is #302, a two-level room with an upstairs bedroom and a private downstairs living room.

(The sofa folds out and there are two bathrooms, making this a good choice for families.)

An elaborate continental breakfast is served in the huge old kitchen and adjoining sunroom, and there's usually something to snack on in the afternoon. Be sure to admire the lustrous butternut trim surrounding the fireplace in the parlor.

WHERE TO DINE

The **Ceres Street Bakery,** 51 Penhallow St. (☎ 603/436-6518), is Portsmouth's original funky bakery, set off on a quiet sidestreet. It's less trendy than the more upscale Cafe Brioche smack downtown, and is a better place for local flavor and good home baking. It's a tiny space with just a handful of tables, so you're better off getting a cookie or slice of cake to go and then walking the couple of blocks to the waterfront rose gardens.

✪ **Blue Mermaid World Grille.** The Hill (between Hanover and Deer streets near the municipal parking garage). ☎ **603/427-2583.** Reservations recommended for parties of 6 or more. Lunch items $4.95–$8.75; main dinner courses $8.95–$16.95. AE, DC, DISC, MC, V. Sun–Thurs 11:30am–9pm, Fri–Sat 11:30am–10pm. Open one hour later in summer. ECLECTIC.

This place ranks among my favorites in Portsmouth for its good food, good value, and good attitude. Blue Mermaid is a short walk from Portsmouth's mainstream tourist destinations in a historic area called The Hill, whose main feature today is a large parking lot. Sited in an old house with lots of exterior charm, inside there's a certain Zen-like grace to the spare bar downstairs and dining room upstairs. It's not a pretentious place—bottles of hot sauce sit on the table, and Tom Waits drones on in the background. More locals than tourists congregate here.

The simple surroundings contrast nicely with the adventurous menu, which creatively builds on cuisines from around the world. You might try the spicy grilled Yucatán sausages served over pasta in a cilantro cream sauce; or pan-seared haddock in a coconut cream sauce served with plantain fritters; or skewered shrimp and scallops served with a watermelon salsa. More mainstream entrees include barbecue ribs, lamb with couscous, and salmon fillet, but why not be adventurous?

Portsmouth Brewery. 56 Market St. ☎ **603/431-1115.** Reservations accepted only for parties of 10 or more. Lunch items $4.50–$8.95; main dinner courses $8.95–$12.95. AE, CB, DC, DISC, MC, V. Mon–Sat 11:30am–12:30am, Sun 10am–12:30am (Sun brunch served until 2pm). PUB FARE.

Located in the heart of the historic district (look for the tipping tankard suspended over the sidewalk), the Portsmouth Brewery opened in 1991 and quickly attracted a young, hip clientele drawn by the superb beers. The high-ceilinged, brick-walled dining room is open, airy, echoey, and redolent of hops. Alberta Hunter is playing in the background. The brews are made in 200-gallon batches, and include specialties like Old Brown Ale, a hearty Murphy's Law Red Ale, and the delightfully creamy Black Cat Stout. The eclectic menu complements the robust beverages, with selections including burgers (try the "murder burger" with Cajun spices), stir-fry, burritos, white or red pizza, and beer-marinated beef kabobs. The food's OK; the beer is well above average.

⑤ **Press Room.** 77 Daniel St. ☎ **603/431-5186.** Reservations not accepted. Sandwiches $3.25–$5.25; main courses $5.25–$8.25. AE, DC, DISC, MC, V. Tues–Sat 11:30am–1am, Sun–Mon 5pm–1am. PUB FARE.

Diners flock here more for the convivial "Cheers"-like atmosphere and the easy-on-the-budget prices than for creative cuisine. Opened in 1976, the Press Room likes to boast that it was the first in the area to serve Guinness Stout, and so it's appropriate that the atmosphere reflects a certain Gaelic charm. It's the sort of place where locals like to gather to discuss the issues of the day ("BMWs? I hate BMWs!") and feel at home. As for character, it's got plenty. During winter and cool coastal days, a fire burns in the woodstove and quaffers flex their elbows at darts amid brick walls, pine floors, and heavy wooden beams overhead. Choose your meal from a basic bar menu, with inexpensive selections including a variety of burgers, nachos, fish and chips, stir-fries, and a selection of salads.

Dolphin Striker. 15 Bow St. ☎ **603/431-5222.** Reservations recommended. Main courses $13.95–$19.95. AE, DC, MC, V. Open Tues–Sun 11:30–2pm, daily 5pm–9:30pm (until 10:30pm Fri & Sat). SEAFOOD/NEW ENGLAND.

The Dolphin Striker is located in a historic brick warehouse in the middle of Portsmouth's most charming area and offers a good if not terribly exciting selection of traditional New England seafood dishes. There's grilled swordfish with sun-dried tomato butter, lobster and scallops with cheese tortellini, and a broiled scallops casserole. Seafood loathers can find refuge in one of several grilled dishes, including beef tenderloin, chicken, and duck breast. The main dining room features a rustic, public house atmosphere with wide pine-board floors and wooden furniture; you can also order meals downstairs in a comfortable pub decorated with a nautical theme. (Incidentally, the name of the restaurant isn't politically incorrect, as a note on the menu will inform you. Dolphin strikers were small spars used by schooners to prevent leaping dolphins from hitting and damaging the bowsprit.)

Muddy River Smokehouse. 21 Congress St. ☎ **603/430-9582.** Reservations not accepted Fri–Sat. Sandwiches $4.95–$6.95; main courses $7.95–$17.95 (mostly $9–$12). AE, MC, V. Sun–Wed 11am–9pm. Thurs 11am–10pm, Fri–Sat 11am–11pm. BARBECUE.

"So authentic you'll get a notion to marry your sister," claims the Muddy River T-shirt. And that's not far from the mark, if a bit cruel. This fun, lively restaurant, which opened in 1995, is a bit deceptive, like a speakeasy. The entrance is through an unremarkable, narrow storefront just down the block from historic Market Square. Guests pass through a long, open, brick-walled bar area decorated with neon and garbage-can lampshades, then suddenly arrive in a surprisingly cavernous, cacophonous dining room that has a cafeteria-like feel to it. Done up in a festive, faux-bayou atmosphere (there's an impressive wall mural), the dining room offers an appealingly wide-ranging menu. There's a superb assortment of mouth-watering barbecued beef ribs, pork ribs, chicken, and sausage (they're slow-smoked over hickory or applewood), and there's also sandwiches, burgers, and chili. This is definitely the place for the carnivore in your life. A limited menu is offered through midnight weekends downstairs in the lounge.

The Oar House. 55 Ceres St. ☎ **603/436-4025.** Reservations recommended. Lunch items $5.25–$9.95; main dinner courses $14.95–$19.95. AE, CB, DC, DISC, MC, V. Mon–Thurs 11:30am–9pm, Fri–Sat 11:30am–10pm, Sun 11:30am–8:30pm. SEAFOOD/NEW ENGLAND.

This intimate, dark, brick-walled spot place has the salty atmosphere of a seaside pub—it's not hard imagining having a final meal here before setting off on a whaling voyage. Situated across from the river on Ceres Street, The Oar House has been a Portsmouth fixture for nearly two decades, but happily hasn't set its menu in stone. The entrees have been revised and improved over the years, and it's still the preferred destination for those looking for traditional New England fare. The baked stuffed haddock served with a lobster sauce comes well recommended, as does the tangy bouillabaisse. There's a raw bar for snacking on shrimp, clams, and oysters; if you're not in the not in the mood for watery fare, there's also a choice of chicken, beef, lamb, and pork. The Oar House has gained a loyal following for its brunch (the menu changes each Sunday) and its award-winning Bloody Marys.

PORTSMOUTH AFTER DARK

Portsmouth's nightlife typically takes place in downtown bars over a pint or two of locally brewed beers. If you're geared up for something more active, check out the following options.

Dolphin Striker. 15 Bow St. ☎ **603/431-5222.**

Live jazz, classical guitar, and low-key folk rock is offered most Wednesday through Sunday evenings.

Elvis Room. 142 Congress St. ☎ **603/436-9189.**

The Elvis Room has fought battles against The King's lawyers (they didn't like the name) and unruly local teens who adopted the place as their own. They prevailed in both instances, and today this smoky, relaxed coffeehouse is a fine place to read a book, play some chess, or listen to eclectic live music. It's open later than anyplace else in the city.

Muddy River Smokehouse. 21 Congress St. ☎ **603/430-9582.**

Blues are the thing at Muddy River's downstairs lounge, which is open evenings Thursday through Saturday. Thursday nights draw the region's aspiring blues artists to open mike night; weekends offers wrenching blues with well-known performers from Boston, Maine, and beyond.

The Music Hall. 28 Chestnut St. ☎ **603/433-2400.**

This historic theater dates back to 1878, and was recently brought back to its former glory by a nonprofit arts group. A variety of shows are staged here, from magic festivals to comedy revues to concerts by the visiting symphonies and pop artists. Call for the current line-up.

The Press Room. 77 Daniel St. ☎ **603/431-5186.** Cover charge usually under $10.

A popular local bar and restaurant (see "Where to Dine," above), the Press Room offers casual entertainment most evenings, either upstairs or down. Tuesday nights are the popular Hoot nights, with an open mike hosted by local musicians. Friday nights are typically set aside for contemporary folk, starring name performers from around the region. But the Press Room might be best known for its live jazz on Sunday night, when the club brings in quality performers from Boston and beyond.

3 Manchester & Concord

These two Merrimack Valley cities tend to be overlooked by tourists making tracks for the lakes district or the White Mountains to the north. Quite frankly, neither town deserves billing as a top-of-the-ticket tourist destination. That's not likely to change in the near future, but to their credit both towns have made considerable strides to exert their magnetism on cars speeding by on the interstate. Manchester is making the most of its industrial heritage with conversions of its monolithic riverside mills. And since 1990 Concord has opened a slick new history museum and a fine new planetarium.

The two cities are vastly different. Manchester is a small city, Concord a big town. The main industry in Manchester was once the profusion of mills along the river— and it's an impressive sight to see these brick mastodons, since converted to more contemporary use, grazing at the river's edge. Smaller Concord is lorded over by the prominent dome of the state house, and has a more proper and genteel demeanor.

Both towns offer a mix of chain hotels and motels, but neither feature grand old hotels or alluring B&Bs within their borders. The best accommodations with easy access to downtown in both cities are the respective **Holiday Inns** (in Concord, ☎ **603/224-9534;** in Manchester, ☎ **603/625-1000**).

MANCHESTER

The history of Manchester is the history of its mills. Stoic, brick buildings today line both shores of the Merrimack River, reflecting a time when New England was the center of manufacturing for the nation. That era has passed, but visitors to Manchester can still be impressed by the old mills, some of which have been converted to restaurants and offices, others of which serve as university classrooms, and one of which has leapt eras by housing a technology center, complete with heliport on the roof. Some even remain active as working mills.

With 100,000 residents, Manchester is northern New England's largest city and it has a grittier, more urban feel than anywhere else in the three states. It's a good place for gathering supplies, for seeing a fine art museum, and most of all for getting a glimpse of the region's proud industrial heritage.

ESSENTIALS

GETTING THERE   Manchester is accessible from both I-93 and I-293. From the south, the easiest access is to get off at Exit 2 on I-293, then follow Elm Street into the town center.

The recently made-over **Manchester Airport** is served by Delta (☎ 800/221-1212), Continental (☎ 800/525-0280), United (☎ 800/241-6522), USAir (☎ 800/428-4322), and Comair.

Bus service is provided by **Vermont Transit** (☎ **802/864-6811**) and **Concord Trailways** (☎ **603/228-3300** or 800/639-3317), both of which make stops at the **Manchester Transportation Center,** 111 Canal St., at the intersection of Granite Street (☎ **603/668-6133**).

VISITOR INFORMATION   The **Manchester** Chamber of Commerce, 889 Elm St., Manchester, NH 03101 (☎ **603/666-6600**), provides brochures, maps, and a handy city guide from its second-floor office.

EXPLORING MANCHESTER

The best way to view the mill district is to get lost amid these canyons of brick. Don't worry; you'll eventually find your way out. Note also that you won't miss much if you're touring by car: These buildings are so massive you don't lose much detail driving by slowly.

The two main routes through the mill area are Commercial and Canal streets, which parallel the river. To explore by foot, leave your car at the small waterfront park beneath the bridge at Bridge Street. (Both restaurants mentioned below are near here.) For more adventurous exploring, walk around the hillside above the mill area, where you'll see a range of housing where millworkers lived in tenements and managers occupied more stately homes, all within easy walking distance of where they worked.

Amoskeag Fishways. Fletcher St. ☎ **603/626-3474.** Free admission. May to mid-June Mon–Fri noon–5pm, Sat–Sun 9am–5pm.

If you're here during the brief, six-week fish run in early summer, be sure to stop by this intriguing center with its underwater window that allows visitors to view salmon, shad, and two dozen other species of fish make their way up the Merrimack. Some 54 pools, each slightly higher than the next, skirt the hydroelectric dam, allowing the fish to leap from one to the other. You'll learn why Amoskeag (the Native American name for the falls and later for the mills) means "Great Fishing Place."

✪ **Currier Gallery of Art.** 192 Orange St. ☎ **603/669-6144.** $5 adults, $4 students and seniors, free for children under 18. Free Sat 10am–1pm. Sun–Mon and Wed–Thurs 11am–5pm, Fri 11am–9pm, Sat 10am–5pm. Cross the Queen City or Amoskeag Bridge to downtown, and follow Elm Street (Route 3) to Orange Street; go east on Orange six blocks and look for the museum on your left.

The Currier is northern New England's premier art museum—made all the more wondrous by its location in a weary industrial city. Housed in an elegant 1932 Beaux Arts building in a residential neighborhood a few blocks from downtown's main drag, the Currier recently underwent year-long renovations before reopening in March 1996.

The permanent collections include some 12,000 works of European and American art, with surprisingly fine pieces by Degas, Picasso, Monet, and John Singer Sargeant. Look for the especially haunting painting by Edward Hopper entitled "The Bootleggers." In addition to the extensive painting and sculpture on display, the museum has fine exhibits of silver, glass, furniture, and pewter. If you're planning to visit just one art museum in northern New England, this should be the one.

Robert Frost Farm. Route 28, Derry. ☎ **603/432-3091.** $2.50 adults, children under 18 free. Spring and fall Sat-Sun 10am–6pm; summer Thurs–Mon 10am–6pm. Closed late Oct to Memorial Day.

One of several New England spots to claim Robert Frost's affections, this graceful white clapboard farmhouse in Derry, about eight miles southeast of Manchester, was Frost's home between 1901 and 1909. Learn about the poet and his era while touring the house, and about the abundant wildlife on the property while exploring a network of trails through forest and field. The house and property is owned and managed by the New Hampshire Dept. of Parks and Recreation.

✪ **Zimmerman House.** c/o Currier Gallery of Art. ☎ **603/626-4158.** Standard tours $6 adults, $4 seniors and students; longer tours $10 and $7. Price includes admission to Currier Gallery. Tours Fri 2pm, Sat 1 and 2:30pm, Sun 1 and 2:30pm, and Mon 2pm. Tours depart from the Currier Gallery.

From the 1930s through the 1950s, famed architect Frank Lloyd Wright designed a number of "Usonian" homes—small-scaled, useful, elegant, and inexpensive to build. The Zimmerman House, built in a Manchester residential neighborhood in 1950, was one such home, but with a major exception: The owners didn't cut corners on costs here. The furniture and even the gardens were designed by Wright, and the home features luxe touches like Georgia cypress trim and red-glazed brick.

Only five Wright homes were built in the Northeast, and the Zimmerman home is the sole Wright home open to the public. Visitors are shuttled to the house from the Currier Gallery via van; choose from two tour lengths, 1 hour and 15 minutes, or 2 hours and 15 minutes.

WHERE TO DINE

Cafe Pavone. 75 Arms Park Dr. (at the foot of Salem Street, on the waterfront). ☎ **603/622-5488.** Reservations recommended. Lunch items $4.50–$8.95; main dinner courses $8.50–$17.95 (mostly $10–$12). AE, DC, DISC, MC, V. Mon–Thurs 11:30am–9:30pm, Fri 11:30am–10pm, Sat 4–10pm, Sun 4–9pm. PASTA.

Cafe Pavone combines the best of old and new in an elegant, upbeat trattoria housed in one of the few small brick buildings amid a complex of huge old mills. The old includes a staggeringly massive wall of granite along the back of the dining room, tile floors, and lively piped-in jazz in the background. The new is the cuisine, which includes some tasty pasta dishes including a spicy chicken and gorgonzola ravioli; fettucine with shrimp, scallops, and lobster; and individual pizza with deluxe toppings. Lunches tend to be along the same lines (although no pizza), but lighter on the wallet. Late in the day is the best time to be here, when the sun slants through the windows and bathes the place with a warm glow.

Stark Mill Brewery and Restaurant. 500 Commercial St. (just north of the Bridge Street bridge). ☎ **603/622-0000.** Reservations not accepted. Sandwiches $1.95–$5.95; main dinner courses $8.95–$14.95. AE, DC, DISC, MC, V. Daily 11am–1am. PUB FARE.

This warehouse-sized restaurant and lounge occupies the first floor of a huge former mill on the Manchester riverfront. Unlike other new brewpubs (this one opened in 1994), Stark Mill has plenty of native charm and is sparing on the cuteness. What the restaurant lacks in elegance it makes up for in edginess; it's one of Manchester's best spots for live and loud music on weekends.

The brewing operation is part and parcel with the bar: The stainless steel and copper vats rise up behind the liquor shelves, and there's no glass partition separating the producers from the consumers. The last time I visited an employee was even sitting in the restaurant slapping labels on 22-ounce bottles by hand. As for the food (a standard bar menu of pizzas, hamburgers, nachos, and burritos), well, let's just say the beer is excellent.

CONCORD

New Hampshire's capital is a graceful, compact city of 36,000 anchored by the distinguished gold dome of the State House. Visitors can wander a few blocks' radius from the dome and see a wide range of architectural styles, from the commercial brick architecture with elaborate cornices, to grand Richardsonian state office buildings, to low, solid buildings that draw heavily on classical tradition. For a state capital, everything is on a personal scale that's more comforting than overwhelming.

The one regret is that the city has turned its back on its Merrimack River, which flows picturesquely through the valley. Downtown is more or less blocked off from the riverside by I-93, parking lots, and uninspired commercial plazas. Adventurers must strike north or south to get access to the shores. One good spot for a riverside stroll is the 90-acre preserve and conservation center that's also headquarters of the **Society for the Protection of New Hampshire Forests** (☎ **603/224-9945**). The grounds are open daily from dawn to dusk at 54 Portsmouth Street, in East Concord just across the river.

ESSENTIALS

GETTING THERE   Concord is located near the junction of I-93 and I-89, and on the east-west state Route 9. The city is also served by **Concord Trailways** (☎ **603/228-3300** or 800/639-3317) and **Vermont Transit** (☎ **802/864-6811**). The **Concord Bus Terminal** is located on Depot Street (☎ **603/228-3300**).

VISITOR INFORMATION   Armfuls of brochures and other helpful information is available at the **Chamber of Commerce** of Greater Concord, 244 N. Main St., Concord, NH 03301 (☎ **603/224-2508**), during regular business hours.

EXPLORING CONCORD

Christa McAuliffe Planetarium. 3 Institute Dr. ☎ **603/271-7831.** $6 adults, $3 seniors & children 3-17. Schedule changes with the seasons, but shows are typically slated afternoons Thursday through Sunday; call for current schedule and reservations. Located at New Hampshire Technical Institute; take Exit 15E on I-93 and follow signs.

Housed beneath a glass pyramid on the technical institute campus, a five-minute drive from downtown Concord, the McAuliffe Planetarium is the state's memorial to Christa McAuliffe, the Concord schoolteacher who died in the 1986 Challenger explosion. The 92-seat theater presents five different hour-long astronomy shows throughout the week, showcasing its high-tech Digistar computerized projection system. Shows are tailored to different interests and age levels (some feature Sesame Street characters); be sure to ask before you enter. Visitors can peruse a handful of intriguing exhibits in the waiting area before the show.

Museum of New Hampshire History. Eagle Square (across from the State House, one-half block off Main Street). ☎ **603/226-3189.** Admission $3.50 adults; $1.75 children 6–18. Free Thurs evening. Tues–Wed and Fri–Sat 9:30am–5pm, Thurs 9:30am–8pm, Sun noon–5pm.

The New Hampshire Historical Society opened this handsome, modern museum in 1995 after years of displaying its collection in its more august and formal headquarters up the block. This compact, manageable museum is housed in a sturdy, stone-faced warehouse built in 1870; the exhibits focus primarily on New Hampshire's 19th century heritage, and include several interactive displays to keep kids amused. Permanent displays, including a handsome Concord Coach stage coach, occupy the first floor; upstairs you'll find exhibits that change throughout the year. Children especially enjoy the "fire tower," which pokes through the roof and allows glimpses of the Merrimack River and the state house dome.

Plan to stop by the original museum site at the historical society's headquarters at 30 Park St. A handful of paintings and furniture is still on display, but it's most impressive for the classical architecture wrought of New Hampshire granite. The rotunda inside is impressive; be sure also to note the portal sculpture above the front door by Daniel Chester French, who's best known for his sculpture of Lincoln in Washington's Lincoln Memorial.

State House. 107 N. Main St. ☎ **603/271-2154.** Free admission; self-guided tours Nov–July Mon–Fri 8am–4:30pm; Aug–Oct, Mon–Fri 8am–4:30pm and Sat–Sun 11am–4pm. Guided tours by reservation.

New Hampshire's state legislature consists of 412 representatives and senators, making it the third-largest legislative body in the English-speaking world (the U.S. Congress and the British Parliament are bigger). Despite its formidable size, the legislature still occupies the original chambers, which were built starting in 1816. Indeed, New Hampshire boasts the oldest state capitol in which the legislature still meets in its original chambers. New Hampshire's numerous citizen legislators are paid just $200 per year—an amount that hasn't changed since 1889.

Both chambers were restored in the mid-1970s, and visitors can catch a glimpse of both hallowed halls during a self-guided tour of the building. Stop by the visitors center in Room 119 and pick up a map and brochure, then wander the halls among the portraits of dour legislators. Especially impressive is the portrait of Benning Wentworth, New Hampshire's first governor, and the statue of revered native son Daniel Webster, who stands guard on the lawn in front.

A ROAD TRIP TO CANTERBURY SHAKER VILLAGE

A 20-minute drive north of Concord (take I-93 to Exit 18 and follow the signs) is one of the best-preserved Shaker communities of the 18 that once dotted the inland east from Kentucky to Maine. This village was founded in 1792; at its heyday in the late 19th century, some 300 Shakers communally owned 4,000 acres and more than 100 buildings, supporting themselves by selling herbs, making furniture, and growing most of the food they needed.

Today, this graceful outdoor museum features about two dozen buildings on 694 acres. Tours are offered on the hour and last about 90 minutes. You'll see the active herb gardens, the apiary, an impressive laundry facility, and an intriguing schoolhouse. Along the way, you'll learn a lot about this fascinating group of people who not only believed in equality of the sexes, but practiced it as well. They also practiced celibacy and pacifism, although they may be best remembered for the beguiling grace with which they crafted their signature furniture and storage boxes, and the distinguished style in which they built and maintained their buildings. After the tour, wander the trails that lace the property and enjoy the simple pleasures of the country air, or browse the extensive gift shop for Shaker reproduction furniture, books, and New Hampshire handicrafts.

Call **603/783-9511** for additional information. Admission is $8 adults, $4 children 6–16, $22 for a family. It's open daily May through October from 10am to 5pm; in April, November, and December, hours are Friday to Sunday 10am to 5pm.

A special treat is the dinner served at the Creamery on the grounds. There's a single seating at 7pm, with all guests gathered at long tables. The four-course meal is prepared from Shaker recipes; afterwards (in season), you'll be guided on a candlelight tour of the village. The price is $32 per person, and that includes tax and tip, as well as the village tour. The Creamery is also open for lunch and Sunday brunch.

WHERE TO DINE

Concord has a wonderful, old-fashioned candy shop in **Granite State Candies,** 13 Warren St., south of the State House (☎ **603/225-2591**). Hand-dipped milk and dark chocolates are the specialty in this palace of high-calorie delights, but you'll also find a wide selection of plain and fancy truffles, hard candies, marzipan, and just about anything else to tame a belligerent sweet tooth.

$ Capital City Diner. 25 Water St. ☎ **603/228-3463**. Breakfast items $2.25–$4.50; lunch items $2.95–$4.50; dinner items $4.25–$6.50. DISC, MC. V. Sun–Thurs 6am–9pm, Fri–Sat 6am–2am. Take Exit 13 off I-93. DINER.

This retro diner, housed in a former Howard Johnson's, is a relentlessly upbeat place with 50's music playing and 50's paraphernalia displayed throughout. There's even an alcove where you can buy period magazine covers, prints, and comic books. The meals are large and well-prepared, and include diner standards like burgers, club sandwiches, baked macaroni and cheese, and American chop suey. It's a great destination for families; a kid's menu and plenty of crayons are always on hand.

Thursday's. 6 Pleasant St. ☎ **603/224-2626**. Reservations accepted, but not usually needed. Breakfast items $2.75–$5.75; lunch items $4.25–$5.95; main dinner courses $7.95–$13.95. Mon–Thurs 7am–9pm, Fri–Sat 7am–10pm, Sun 9am–2:30pm. AMERICAN/WHOLE FOODS.

A favorite among Concord residents for its wholesome, well-prepared meals at reasonable prices, Thursday's offers creative selections like hot red pepper linguine, raspberry chicken, and crepe moussaka (made with eggplant, mushrooms, and zucchini). While the odds are you'll get a good meal whenever you arrive, the Sunday brunch is particularly appealing. The dim, woody interior of this friendly, busy spot just off Main Street is made less somber with creative use of latticework.

4 The Monadnock Region & the Connecticut River Valley

New Hampshire's southwestern corner is a pastoral region of rolling hills, small villages, rustic farmsteads, and twisting back roads. What the area lacks in major attractions, it makes up for in peaceableness and bucolic charm. The inns tend to be more basic and less elegant than those you'll find across the river in southern Vermont. But lodging prices will also appeal more to budget travelers looking to get a taste of history with their room and board. This is a popular area for Bostonians seeking a weekend respite from city life.

For most visitors, the chief activities include woodland walks, porch sitting, and idle drives to nowhere in particular. In fact, the best strategy for exploring the area may be to put away the map and turn randomly on a side road to see where you'll end up. Wherever it is, the odds are you'll find a quiet Currier & Ives quality.

PETERBOROUGH & ENVIRONS

Peterborough (pop. 5,000) was first settled in 1749, but it isn't a quaint colonial town gathered primly around a village green. It has more the feel of a once-prosperous commercial center, where the hum of industry provided harmony for a thriving economy. While the hum is a bit quieter these days, Peterborough is still a beautiful town with diverse architecture set picturesquely in a valley at the confluence of the Contoocook and Nubanusit rivers. Improbably enough, Peterborough has carved out a niche in the high-tech world as a publishing center for successful national computer magazines.

In the literary universe, Peterborough remains famous for inspiring Thornton Wilder to write *Our Town.* It's also home to the noted McDowell Colony, founded in 1907 to provide a retreat for artists, musicians, and writers to tap their creative talents without the distraction of preparing meals or attending to errands. It's hard to find a writer of note who didn't spend some time at McDowell.

The archipelago of three dozen or so villages that surrounds Peterborough and Keene has a strongly traditional New England demeanor; you half expect to hear town criers wandering through loudly offering the day's news. *Yankee* magazine and the *Old Farmer's Almanac,* which have done perhaps more than any other publications to shape the popular image of New England, are based in the unassuming town of Dublin to the west of Peterborough. Other quiet, picturesque villages abounding with the elements of classic New England include Hancock and Francestown. Both are well worth a detour.

ESSENTIALS

GETTING THERE   Peterborough is between Keene and Nashua on Route 101. A decent map is essential for exploring the outlying villages and towns on winding state and county roads. Unless, of course, you choose to get lost.

VISITOR INFORMATION   The **Peterborough Chamber of Commerce,** P.O. Box 401, Peterborough, NH 03458 (☎ **603/924-7234**), offers helpful advice either over the phone or at their information center located at the intersection of Routes 101 and 202.

OUTDOOR RECREATION

Mt. Monadnock stands impressively amid the gentler hills of southern New Hampshire. Although it's only 3,165 feet high (about half the height of Mt. Washington far to the north), its solitary grandeur has attracted hikers for more than two centuries. The knobby peak has been ascended by New England luminaries like Ralph Waldo Emerson and Henry David Thoreau. Today, more than 100,000 hikers strike for the summit each year to enjoy the views and follow in the footsteps of countless other pilgrims.

Some 40 miles of trails lace the patchwork of public and private lands on the slopes of the mountain. The most popular (and best marked) trails leave from near the **Mt. Monadnock State Park** (☎ 603/532-8862) entrance about four miles northwest of Jaffrey Center. (Head west on Route 124; after two miles follow the park signs to the north.) A round trip on the most direct routes will take someone in decent shape about three to four hours. Admission to the park is $2.50 for adults and children 12 and older; 11 and under is free.

An 18-mile drive north of Monadnock, not far from the towns of Hancock and Peterborough, is one of my favorite small parks in the region: **Greenfield State Park** (☎ 603/547-3497). This 400-acre park is a gem for car campers and geology buffs. The park was profoundly shaped by glaciers during the last Ice Age, and eskers, bogs, kames, and other intriguing geological formations may be spotted by knowing eyes (or ask a ranger). For more sedentary pleasures, the park boasts a small beach along scenic Otter Lake. There's also a 900-foot beach set aside for campers who avail themselves of the 252 wooded, well-spaced campsites. On weekends the campground bustles with activity, but it's a peaceable oasis midweek.

A REALLY BIG SMALL SHOW

New England Marionette Theatre. 24 Main St., Peterborough. ☎ **603/924-4333.** Ticket prices vary depending on the length of the show ($10–$22 adults; discounts for students and children). Performances are year-round at 8pm on Thurs, Fri, and Sat, and 2pm on Sun.

This is not your run-of-the-mill puppet theater with Flopsie and Mopsie nattering in whiny, high-pitched voices. This is puppetry practiced as fine art, and you're not likely to find it finer anywhere.

Located in an historic former Baptist church in downtown Peterborough, the New England Marionette Theatre specializes in opera, with the main performances typically lasting two-and-a-half hours. The theater, with its red velvet seats, is wonderfully designed to create the illusion that you're observing real people at a distance—and the artfulness of the puppeteers who control the marionettes only enhances the effect. Where else can you see *The Barber of Seville* acted in Italian (with projected English surtitles) by 32-inch "actors"? The cost is a bit pricey for an evening's entertainment in small-town New England, but it's an experience you're not likely to soon forget.

WHERE TO STAY

Benjamin Prescott Inn. Route 124, Jaffrey, NH 03452. ☎ **603/532-6637.** 9 rms (6 with shower only). $65–$85 double, $130 third-floor suite. Rates include full breakfast. AE, MC, V.

Col. Benjamin Prescott fought at the Battle of Bunker Hill, then came to Jaffrey in 1775. This three-story home, built by his sons, dates to 1853 and is a handsome yellow Greek Revival farmhouse along the highway in a pastoral area two miles outside of town. Throughout this pleasant inn you'll find a strong sense of history and connectedness to the past.

The interior appropriately matches the exterior, decorated in classical country farmhouse style with delicate stencilling on the walls and traditional pine farmhouse furniture. It's not overly austere—the innkeepers display folk art, ceramics, and other collectibles. The nine guest rooms, which are named after Prescott family members, are comfortably furnished; all have ceiling fans and phone jacks (phones provided on request), and two of the suites have air-conditioning. The best room in the house is the Col. Prescott, which is bright and airy and features two comfortable armchairs and a writing desk. Guests can wander the farmlands beyond the inn, or set off to hike Mt. Monadnock a short drive down the road.

⑤ **Birchwood Inn.** Route 45 (1¹/₂ miles south of Route 101), Temple, NH 03084. ☎ **603/ 878-3285.** 7 rms (1 with hall bath, some with showers only). June–Oct $60–$70 double; Nov–May $49–$59 double. Rates include breakfast. No credit cards.

This is a quiet village retreat, offering good rooms at good value. Thoreau visited this inn on his travels, and neither the town nor the inn feel as if they've changed all that much since. This handsome brick farmhouse with white clapboard ell is in the middle of the country crossroads town of Temple, near the Grange and a park with three war memorials (including one to the heroes of 1776). It's also an easy stroll to a historic cemetery with headstones dating back to the 1700s.

The inn is decorated throughout in a pleasantly informal country style. The seven rooms are each decorated with different themes (musical instruments, train memorabilia, historic newspapers, country store), which borders on kitschy but doesn't quite step over the line.

Dining/Entertainment: The common rooms are imbued with a rich sense of history. The dining room, where traditional New England meals are served, has wide pine floors and historic wall murals painted by the noted early 19th-century itinerant painter Rufus Porter. The BYOB tavern is also comfortable, and Judy and Bill Wolfe, who've been running this inn with considerable graciousness since 1980, make guests feel comfortable and at home.

⑤ **Fitzwilliam Inn.** Fitzwilliam, NH 03447. ☎ **603/585-9000.** 25 rms (plus three in annex; about ¹/₂ have private baths; the remainder share hallway baths). $45–$55 double with private bath; $40 double for shared bath. DISC, MC, V.

This handsome, three-story Greek Revival building towers over this quiet crossroads and its triangular green. Built in the early 1800s, the inn has a lot of history and a locally popular dining room, but elegance isn't its strong card. Some of the rooms have an old boarding house feel to them with beds crammed in every which way, and about half of the rooms share hallway baths. But if you're seeking a piece of New England heritage at a budget price, this is a worthy destination. The best bargain might be Room 31, a cozy, low-ceilinged room (shared bath) that's a quiet retreat under the inn's eaves.

Downstairs the sitting rooms have an eclectic mix of Victorian-era and contemporary country furniture, set on time-burnished pine floors. There's a piano, fireplace, ship's model, and a selection of books for browsing.

Dining/Entertainment: A quaint country dining room with baskets hung on heavy beams is in the back of the inn. The dining room serves three meals a day, mostly New England classics like lobster Newburg, stuffed chicken breast, or broiled steak. Complete dinners range from $12.95 to $21.95.

Monadnock Inn. 442 Main St. (P.O. Box B), Jaffrey Center, NH 03452. ☎ **603/532-7001.** Fax 603/532-7009. 15 rms (10 with private bath). $65 double with shared bath; $85 double with private bath. Rates include continental breakfast. AE, DISC, MC, V.

The Monadnock Inn is a handsome white clapboard building that sits behind a row of maples on Jaffrey Center's sleepy main street. The inn came under new ownership in early 1995, and the new owners have launched some long overdue renovations to bring this gracious inn back up to snuff.

Built in 1820, the Monadnock has long been a popular tourist destination, especially with travelers hell bent on climbing Mt. Monadnock, a short piece down the road. Today, the inn still has the peaceful air of the last century, with a welcoming line of rockers on the shady front porch. Guest rooms are decorated traditionally in New England country style. If you take a room with a shared bath, ask to see the bathroom first. Some are equipped with tubs not much bigger than sitzbaths, which may not prove entirely satisfactory.

Dining/Entertainment: Downstairs there's not much in the way of a common room for the guests, but there's a very cozy tavern with a woodstove and a rustic farmhouse atmosphere. The restaurant occupies several first-floor rooms. Lunch tends toward Monte Cristos and open-faced Reubens; dinner entrees include mixed grill, veal with hearts of palm, and tortellini with bay shrimp. Prices range from $14.75 to $19.95.

WHERE TO DINE

Latacarta. 6 School St., Peterborough. ☎ **603/924-6878.** Reservations recommended on weekends. Main courses $11.95–$18.95; café menu $8.95–$12. AE, MC, V. Tues–Sat noon–3pm; Tues–Thurs 5–8:30pm, Fri–Sat 5–9pm, Sun 4–8pm. INTERNATIONAL.

Built in the lobby of a converted theater one block off Peterborough's main drag, Latacarta offers few clues that it was once a theater—other than the aroma of popcorn wafting in from the back (the theater still shows films nightly, with the entrance on the side). Given the quirky heritage of the place, you would expect the owners to have some fun in designing it, but it's a relatively uninspired interior.

Likewise with the food, which is dependable if unexciting. Latacarta reaches for culinary heights and sometimes comes close to delivering. Entrees include delectable-sounding shrimp and wild mushroom ravioli, and grilled salmon, scallops and shrimp. But the presentation and service often fall short of the mark. If you're looking for fine dining in Peterborough this is the place, but it seems to be a hit-or-miss proposition.

Peterborough Diner. Depot Street, Peterborough. ☎ **603/924-6202.** Breakfast items $2.95–$6.60; lunch and dinner items $2.95–$9.95. AE, DISC, MC, V. Daily 6am–9pm. DINER.

This is a classic 1940s throwback on a Peterborough sidestreet. Behind the faded yellow and green exterior is a beautiful interior of wood, aluminum, tile, and ceiling fans, along with one of the best easy-listening jukeboxes in New England. The meals are just what you'd expect: filling, cheap, basic, and quick. Diner fans can buy Peterborough Diner refrigerator magnets and T-shirts when they settle their tab.

CORNISH REGION

Artists flocked to the quiet region in the late 19th century, and the subtle beauty of the area, still prevalent today, makes it abundantly clear why. The first artistic immigrants to arrive were the painters and sculptors, who showed up in the late 1880s and early 1890s, building modest homes in the hills. They were followed by politicians and the affluent, who eventually established a thriving summer colony. Among those who populated the rolling hills that looked across the river toward Ascutney were sculptor Daniel Chester French, painter Maxfield Parrish, and New Republic editor Herbert Crowley. Prominent visitors included Ethel Barrymore and presidents Woodrow Wilson and Theodore Roosevelt. A 1907 article in the New York Daily Tribune noted that artists made their homes in Cornish not "with the idea of converting it into a 'fashionable' summer resort, but rather to form there an aristocracy of brains and keep out that element which displays its lack of grey matter by an expenditure of money in undesirable ways."

The social allure eventually peaked and the area has lapsed into a peaceful slumber. Those who come here now do so for the beauty and seclusion, not for the gatherings and parties. Indeed, the country's most famous recluse (J.D. Salinger) lives in Cornish today.

The region lacks obvious tourist allure—there are no fancy hotels, no five-star restaurants—but it's well worth visiting and exploring. At twilight, you can see where Maxfield Parrish found his inspiration for the rich, pellucid azure skies for which his prints and paintings are so noted.

ESSENTIALS

GETTING THERE   Don't bother looking for Cornish proper; you won't find it. Cornish is really a few scattered villages with names like Cornish Flats and, somewhat grandiloquently, Cornish City. The best route for exploring the area is Route 12A along the Connecticut River north of Claremont.

VISITOR INFORMATION   Your best bet for local guidance is the **Greater Claremont Chamber of Commerce,** Tremont Square, Claremont NH 03743 (☎ **603/543-1296**), which dispenses travel information from the Moody Building in town.

EXPLORING THE CORNISH AREA

The region's premier monument to its former arts colony is the **St. Gaudens National Historic Site** (☎ **603/675-2175**), located off Route 12A. Noted sculptor Augustus St. Gaudens first arrived in this valley in 1885, shortly after receiving an important commission to create a statue of Abraham Lincoln. His friend Charles Beaman, a lawyer who owned several houses and much land in the Cornish area, assured him he would find a surfeit of "Lincoln-shaped men" in the area. St. Gaudens came, and pretty much stayed the rest of his life.

His home and studio, which he called "Aspet" after the village in Ireland where he was raised, is a superb place to learn more about this extraordinary artist. A brief tour of the house, which is kept pretty much as it was when St. Gaudens lived here, provides a brief introduction to the man. Visitors learn about St. Gaudens the artist at several outbuildings and on the grounds, where many replicas of his most famous statues are on display.

The 150-acre grounds also feature short nature trails, where visitors can explore the hilly woodlands, passing along streams and a millpond.

The historic site is open daily 9am to 4:30pm from late May through October. Admission is $2 for adults 17 and over; under 17 is free.

Covered bridge aficionados will want to seek out the **Cornish-Windsor Covered Bridge,** which is the nation's longest covered bridge. Spanning the Connecticut River between Vermont and New Hampshire, this bridge has an ancient and interesting lineage. A toll bridge was first built here in 1796 to replace a ferry; the current bridge was built in 1866, and extensively restored in 1989. When the late afternoon light hits it just right, this vies for the title of most handsome covered bridge in New England.

For a fisheye view of the bridge and the scenic, forested shores of the Connecticut River, rent a canoe a few miles downstream from the bridge at **Northstar Canoe Livery** (☎ **603/542-5802**). For $17 per person, Northstar will shuttle you 12 miles upstream, allowing a leisurely paddle back to your car over the next few hours. Or just rent by the hour and dabble in the currents.

WHERE TO STAY

Chase House. Route 12A, Cornish, NH 03745. ☎ **603/675-5391** or 800/401-9455. Fax 603/675-5010. 8 rms, 2 with shared bath (6 with shower only). A/C. $85–$105 double. Rates include full breakfast. MC, V. Closed Nov–Dec.

Every guest room in the Chase House has a biography of noted 19th-century politician Salmon P. Chase, who was born in the house in 1808. To refresh your memory: Chase was a founder of the Republican party, Lincoln's treasury secretary, chief justice of the Supreme Court, and namesake of Chase Manhattan Bank; his portrait appears on the $10,000 bill. His regal house, parts of which were built as early as 1766, is decorated appropriately in an early American style, with antiques and nice period touches. Serious history fans may find the house overly remodeled in a glossy, Yield-House sort of way, but others will find it comfortable and welcoming. Especially appealing is the new and spacious second floor common room, made from the timbers of an 1810 house moved from East Topsham, Vt. The best guest rooms are the queen suites in the new part of the house, which innkeeper Barbara Lewis has decorated with a deft country touch. The Chase House is especially popular with wedding parties, which rent the entire house and avail themselves of the whole 160-acre property.

HANOVER & ENVIRONS

If your notion of New England involves a sweeping green edged with stately brick buildings, be sure to head to Hanover, a thriving university town agreeably situated in the Connecticut River Valley. First settled in 1765, the town was home to the early pioneers who were granted a charter by King George III to establish a college. The school was named after the 2nd Earl of Dartmouth, the school's first trustee. Since its founding, Dartmouth College, the most northerly of the Ivy League schools, has had a large hand in shaping the community. One alumnus has aptly said of the school, "Dartmouth is the sort of place you're nostalgic for even if you've never been there."

Dartmouth has produced more than its share of illustrious alumni, including poet Robert Frost, Nelson Rockefeller, Supreme Court justice Salmon P. Chase, and children's book author Dr. Seuss. Perhaps the most famous son of Dartmouth was the renowned 19th-century politician and orator, Daniel Webster. In arguing for the survival of Dartmouth College in a landmark case before the U.S. Supreme Court in 1816 (when two factions vied for control of the school), Webster offered his famous closing line: "It is a small college, gentlemen, but there are those who love it." This has served as an informal motto for the school alumni ever since.

Today, a handsome, oversized village green marks the permeable border between college and town. In the summer, the green is an ideal destination for strolling and lounging. In the winter, look for the massive, intricate ice sculptures from the winter carnival. The best way to explore Hanover is by foot, so your first endeavor is to park your car, which can be trying during peak seasons. Try your hand at the municipal lots west of Main Street.

The town boasts a compact and prosperous commercial area, offering great browsing and shopping. While the area clearly caters to the affluent with its shops like Simon Pearce, The Gap, and several excellent bookshops, there's a good selection of small stores that are light on frills and fluff.

Just south of Hanover is the working-class town of Lebanon, another commercial center, which in many ways has a less artificial New England air to it. This colorful community has a village green to be proud of, a decent variety of shops, some surprising restaurants, and a quirky mall carved out of an old brick powerhouse. If you're looking for the *New York Times,* head to Hanover; if you need a wrench, head for Lebanon.

ESSENTIALS

GETTING THERE   Lebanon and its sibling West Lebanon are located on I-89 (Exits 17 to 20), and just across the river from I-91 (Exit 10). Hanover is north of Lebanon on Route 10 or Route 120.

Amtrak serves White River Junction, Vt., just across the river.

VISITOR INFORMATION   Dartmouth College alumni and other volunteers maintain an **information center** (☎ 603/643-3512) on the green in the summer and fall. Good sources of local information in the off-season are the **Hanover Chamber of Commerce,** P.O. Box 5105, Hanover, NH 03755 (☎ **603/643-3115**), located on Main Street across from the post office, and the **Lebanon Chamber of Commerce,** 2 Whipple Place, Lebanon, NH 03766 (☎ **603/448-1203**).

SPECIAL EVENTS   The **Dartmouth Winter Carnival,** held annually in mid-February, is the best way to make the most of the region's notorious cold weather. The festival features winter sporting competitions such as ski jumping, but it may be best known for the ice sculpture contest, in which elaborate if ephemeral artworks and cartoon characters grace the green. The festival is not necessarily family-oriented—it traditionally presents an opportune time for college kids to break the winter doldrums with the copious consumption of alcohol. Contact Dartmouth College (☎ **603/646-1110**) for more information.

EXPLORING HANOVER

Hanover is a superb town to explore by foot or on bike. Start by picking up a map of the campus, available at the Dartmouth information center on the green or at the Hanover Inn. (Free guided tours are also offered in the summer.) The expansive, leafy campus is a delight to walk through; be sure to stop by the **Baker Memorial Library** to view the murals by Latin American painter José Orozco. He painted "The Epic of American Civilization" while teaching here between 1932 and 1934. Given the school's current renown as a hotbed of conservativism, it's a bit surprising these paintings by the renown leftist have gone unscathed.

On the south of the green next to the Hanover Inn is the modern **Hopkins Center for the Arts** (☎ **603/646-2422**). The center attracts national acts to its 900-seat concert hall, and stages top-notch performances at the Moore Theater. Call for information on current shows. If the building looks vaguely familiar, there may be a reason for that. It was designed by Wallace Harrison, the architect who later went on to design New York's Lincoln Center, and it seems that this could have been a trial run for his later masterwork.

Adjacent to the Hopkins Center is the **Hood Museum of Art** (☎ **603/ 646-2426**). Although it houses one of the oldest college museums in the nation, it's in a decidedly contemporary, open building, constructed in 1986. The austere, three-story structure displays selections from the permanent collection, including a superb selection of 19th century American landscapes and a fine grouping of Assyrian reliefs dating from 883 to 859 B.C. The museum is open Tuesday through Saturday from 10am until 5pm (open until 9pm on Tuesday), and Sunday from noon to 5pm. Admission is free.

MT. KEARSARGE

Mt. Monadnock to the south is the most heavily visited peak in the area, but 2,931-foot Mt. Kearsarge ranks as among the most accessible. Located in the Sunapee Lake region southeast of Lebanon, Kearsarge can be ascended most of the way by car along a paved carriage road. The entrance is just outside the town of Warner (Exit 9 on I-89). State park rangers collect a toll at the base ($2.50 per person over 12 years old), then drivers snake their way 3.5 miles past dramatic vistas to a gravel parking lot high on the mountain's shoulder. From here, it's a simple half-mile hike to the summit along a well-marked, rocky trail with remarkable views to the south and southwest along the way.

The rocky, knobby summit offers superb panoramas of south-central New Hampshire's lakes and hills, although the views are cluttered slightly by an old

fire-tower and several small buildings bristling with antennae and other visual pollution of the information age. Another caveat: On crisp fall weekends, the summit
of Mt. Kearsarge has all the seclusion of Christmas Eve at the mall. You're better off
avoiding it then, and looking for your own peaks away from the crowds.

WHERE TO STAY

Several hotels and motels are located off the interstate in Lebanon and West
Lebanon, about five miles south of Hanover. Try the **Airport Economy Inn**
(☎ 603/298-8888 or 800/433-3466), **Days Inn** (☎ 603/448-5070), the **Radisson
Inn North Country** (☎ 603/298-5906), or **The Sunset** (☎ 603/298-8721).
Another area option is the Norwich Inn, a short hop across the river in Vermont (see
Chapter 5).

Hanover Inn. Wheelock Street (P.O. Box 151), Hanover, NH 03755. ☎ **603/643-4300** or
800/443-7024. Fax 603/646-3744. E-mail hanover.inn@dartmouth.edu. 92 rms. A/C TV TEL.
$197–$256 double. Parking $5 per day. AE, DC, DISC, MC, V.

The Hanover Inn has been owned and operated by Dartmouth College for more than
a century, which helps explain all the rich forest-green hues throughout (it's
Dartmouth's signature color). Housed in a handsome colonial revival building facing the Green, this exceptionally well-maintained inn is the destination of choice for
parents and dignitaries visiting the college. (It's also where performers appearing at
the adjacent Hopkins Center stay, so you might bump into musical celebrities in the
halls.) For such a large inn the common areas are quite limited (the ground floor is
mostly occupied by two restaurants) but the hotel connects via tunnels and enclosed
walkways to the student center and the Hood Museum, so it's easy to stretch your
legs, even in winter.

Rooms are priced according to size (there are three different sizes), and each is
nicely furnished in a contemporary country style. Most have canopy or four-poster
beds and down comforters. Ask for a view of the Green, if available, since there's no
extra charge. Also note that the fourth-floor rooms seem a bit smaller owing to lower
ceilings and dormer windows.

Mary Keane House. Lower Shaker Village, Enfield, NH 03748. ☎ **603/632-4241.** 7 rms. TV.
$59–$99 double; foliage season $89–$149 double. AE, DC, MC, V.

Situated at Lower Shaker Village about 25 minutes from Dartmouth, the Mary Keane
House is an ideal spot for quiet relaxation and gentle recuperation of a harried soul.
Built in 1929 (two years after the Shakers had abandoned the village), this two-story
yellow Georgian Revival doesn't share much with the Shaker village in architecture
or spirit—in fact, it's filled with lovely Victorian antiques, which seem anathema to
the Shaker sensibility. But it's kept immaculately clean (something the Shakers would
appreciate), and it's right in the Shaker village, so guests can explore the buildings
and museum by day (the grounds are especially peaceful at twilight), paddle one of
the inn's canoes on Lake Mascoma, or swim at the small private beach. Room 3 is a
particular gem, with Corinthian columns, a formal sitting room, plenty of space to
unwind, and a refined country-Victorian elegance.

WHERE TO DINE
In Hanover

Café Buon Gustaio. 72 South Main St. ☎ **603/643-5711.** Reservations recommended.
Main courses $8–$19. AE, CB, DC, DISC, MC, V. Tues–Thurs 5:30–9:30pm, Fri–Sat 5:30–10pm.
ITALIAN.

Four words sums up Café Buon Gustaio: simple setting, elegant fare. Tucked away
on the quiet end of Hanover's Main Street in a 19th-century home, the cafe is

Road Trips for Architecture Buffs

Two short trips from Hanover will amply reward those number Early American architecture among their passions.

One of the more remarkable if rarely visited architectural sites in New England is **"The Ridge"** in the town of Orford, north of Hanover. Atop a low ridge to the east of Route 10 in town you'll see seven similar, wonderfully austere white clapboard homes facing out toward the valley like the members of a formal wedding party portrait.

Built between 1773 and 1839, these structures not only attest to the affluence of the region two centuries ago, but many of the later homes show the authority of architect Asher Benjamin. His books, including the "American Builders Companion," strongly influenced home construction by local builders, and nowhere is this more evident than in Orford. The southernmost home was built in 1814–16, and is right from Benjamin's pages. In fact, it's known to have been built by a Boston architect—quite possibly Benjamin himself. The homes aren't open to the public, but the elegance and formality is writ large enough to be read from the roadside, and without glasses.

In the other direction, southeast of Hanover in the town of Enfield, is the **Lower Shaker Village,** a cluster of historic buildings on peaceful Lake Mascoma. "The Chosen Vale," as it was called by its first inhabitants, was founded in 1793; by the mid-1800s it had 350 members and 3,000 acres. From that peak, the community dwindled, and by 1927 the Shakers abandoned the Chosen Vale and sold the village lock, stock, and barrel to the Catholic church, which established a retreat here. In 1985, the village sold again, this time to private investors who developed some of the lakeshore with summer homes and created a restaurant and inn in the community's most impressive building. (As of this writing, the future of the inn and the restaurant was uncertain.)

Today, much of the property is either owned by the state of New Hampshire or the nonprofit **Museum of Lower Shaker Village,** founded in 1986. While not as extensively interpreted or as pristine as the Shaker Village at Canterbury (see "Concord and Manchester" section), this village is picturesque and contains some extraordinary specimens of architecture. It's worth stopping by for a self-guided walking tour and to view the small museum, which offers a heavier focus on Shaker industry than Shaker aesthetics.

After a few moments in the museum, ramble through the village and read about the buildings in the walking tour guide (free with your admission). Dominating the village is the imposing Great Stone Dwelling, an austere but gracious four-story building of granite erected between 1837 and 1841. When constructed, it was the tallest building north of Boston. The Enfield Shakers lived and dined here, with as many as 150 Shakers eating at long trestle tables. The first two floors of the building are open for viewing.

Lower Shaker Village (☎ **603/632-4346**) is on Route 4A, and is open Monday through Saturday from 10am to 5pm, and Sundays noon to 5pm. (The museum is open until 4pm November through May). Admission is $5 adults, $3 seniors, and $2.50 children 10 to 18.

a trattoria-style restaurant with a menu that changes frequently and a kitchen staff with the proven ability to pull off a good meal night after night. A handsome bar occupies part of one parlor; diners adjourn to the second, more intimate parlor.

Begin your meal with a grilled portobello mushroom with artichoke salad, or a lobster ravioli with roasted red pepper cream. Then feast on spaghettini served with tuna, capers, olives, and beans; or cannelloni of smoked chicken, peppers, scallions, and ricotta in a d'Abruzzi sauce. If you don't pine for pasta, there's usually a selection of pizzettas and grilled dishes, such as Black Angus steak with a five peppercorn butter, and swordfish with a spicy shrimp salsa.

✪ **Daniel Webster Room.** In the Hanover Inn, Wheelock Street. ☎ **603/643-4300.** Reservations recommended. Breakfast items $4.25–$9.50; lunch items $6.95–$13.50; main dinner courses $15–$23. AE, DC, DISC, MC, V. Daily 7:30–10:30am, 11:30am–1pm, and 6–9pm. CONTINENTAL.

The neoclassical Daniel Webster Room of the Hanover Inn will appeal to those looking for exceptionally fine dining amid a formal New England atmosphere. The inn's proper dining room is reminiscent of a 19th-century resort hotel, with fluted columns, floral carpeting, and regal upholstered chairs. The only concession to frivolity are the Tavern-on-the-Green–style white lights adorning the potted plants. The dinner menu isn't extensive, but that doesn't make it any less appealing. Entrees range from filet mignon with foie gras and truffled potatoes, to a more exotic Moroccan-spiced tuna with couscous. The restaurant has a commendable wine list, and is one of only two restaurants in New Hampshire to receive AAA's four-star rating.

Next door is the more informal Ivy Grill, set in retro, Miami Vice–like surroundings that come as a bit of a surprise at this staid inn. It's open daily from 11:30am to 10pm, and serves up lunches for under $10 and dinners like chicken with wild mushrooms and barbecue ribs with cornbread. Most entrees are $11 to $14.

🄢 **Lou's.** 30 S. Main St. ☎ **603/643-3321.** Breakfast items $2.10–$5.95; lunch items $3.85–$5.95. Mon–Fri 6am–3pm, Sat–Sun 7am–3pm. Bakery open for snacks until 5pm. BAKERY/DINER.

Lou's is a Hanover institution, attracting large crowds for breakfast on weekends and a steady clientele for lunch throughout the week. The mood is no-frills New Hampshire, with a black and white linoleum checkerboard floor and maple-and-vinyl booths updated with a modern country look. Breakfast is served all day here (real maple syrup on your pancakes is $1 extra), and the sandwiches are huge and delicious, served on fresh-baked bread. If you're inclined to blow your calorie budget, the baked goods are a fine temptation. The macaroons are especially good.

In Lebanon

Good Fortune. 45 Hanover St. (Courtyard Pavilion on the Mall). ☎ **603/448-3888.** Reservations recommended on weekends. Lunch dishes $4.75–$6.25; main dinner courses $10.95–$24.95 (mostly $11–$13). AE, DISC, MC, V. Sun–Thurs 11:30am–9:30pm, Fri–Sat 11:30am–10:30pm. CHINESE.

Situated in a miniature shopping mall at the west end of Lebanon's equally miniature pedestrian mall, Good Fortune serves up reliable Chinese food in unexceptional surroundings. While the place appears to borrow its decorating inspiration from chain-hotel restaurants, the food surpasses the decor. The meals are deftly prepared with a nice touch, light on the sauces, and are ample for big appetites. House specialties include a spicy dish of scallops served in a Szechuan mala sauce, and lamb served with a complementary pairing of spicy sauces. The other familiar Chinese classics are also on hand, from chicken cashew to pork lo mein. The truly famished should try the all-you-can-eat buffet, which costs $6.25 at lunch and $10.95 at dinner.

🄢 **Sweet Tomatoes Trattoria.** One Court St. ☎ **603/448-7711.** Reservations not accepted. Main courses $6.95–$10.95. MC, V. Mon–Fri 11:30am–2pm, Mon–Thurs 5–9pm, Fri–Sat 5–9:30pm. ITALIAN.

This is the original Sweet Tomatoes (there's another in Burlington, Vermont), located in an airy, contemporary ground floor space with huge windows facing Lebanon's attractive village green. The place is boldly decorated with floors and walls of polished tile; jars of seasoned vinegar line one wall and a muted fresco covers another. With all this echoing tile, the atmosphere tends to be boisterous and loud even with small evening crowds (if you're seeking quiet, head for the smaller, carpeted dining room off the back). The crowd is anything but homogeneous—it seems all ages and folks from every walk of life enjoy a good meal here. Expect a wait on weekends and anytime during midsummer or foliage, and be thankful the management keeps a magazine rack filled in the foyer.

The cuisine here is eclectic Italian, with dishes ranging from creative wood-fired pizzas (try the provolone, mushroom, artichoke heart, and roasted red pepper) to outstanding linguine, fusilli, and mostaccioli dishes employing mounds of fresh, local ingredients. Even with a good bottle of wine and desert, a full dinner here is relatively light on the wallet and guests invariably leave content.

5 The Lake Winnipesaukee Region

Unless you're bobbing in a canoe in the middle of New Hampshire's largest lake when a squall comes up, it rarely seems all that huge. That's because Lake Winnipesaukee's 180-mile shoreline is convoluted and twisting, warped around of dozens of inlets, coves, and bays, and further fragmented with some 274 islands. As a result, intermittent lake views from the shore give the illusion you're viewing a chain of smaller lakes and ponds rather than one massive body of water that measures 12 miles by 20 miles at its broadest points. (Incidentally, there's no agreement on the meaning of the lake's Indian name. Although "beautiful water in a high place" and "smile of the great spirit" are the most poetic interpretations, the more commonly accepted translation is "good outlet.")

How to best enjoy the lake? If you've got kids, settle in at Weirs Beach for a few days and take in the gaudy attractions. If you're looking for isolation, consider renting a lakeside cabin for a week or so on the eastern shore, find a canoe or sailboat, then explore much the same way travelers did a century ago. If your time is limited, a driving tour around the lake with a few well-chosen stops will give you a nice taste of the region's woodsy flavor.

WEST SHORE

Lake Winnipesaukee's West Shore has a more frenetic and congested atmosphere than its sibling shore across the lake. That's partly for historic reasons (the main stage and rail routes passed along the West Shore), and partly for modern reasons—I-93 runs west of the lake, serving as a sluice for hurried visitors streaming in from the megalopolis to the south. The West Shore offers the most diversions for short-attention spans. It also has more tourist amenities, including hotels, restaurants and shops, especially in Laconia and Meredith.

ESSENTIALS

GETTING THERE Interstate access to the West Shore is from I-93 at Exit 20 or Exit 23. From Exit 20, follow Route 3 north through Laconia to Weirs Beach. (It's less confusing and more scenic to stay on Business Route 3.) From Exit 23, drive nine miles east on Route 104 to Meredith, then head either south on Route 3 to Route 11, or strike northwest on Route 25.

VISITOR INFORMATION The **Greater Laconia/Weirs Beach Chamber of Commerce,** 11 Veterans Square, Laconia, NH 03246 (☎ **800/531-2347**), maintains a seasonal information booth on Business Route 3 about halfway between Laconia and Weirs Beach. It's open daily in summer from 10am to 6pm. Information is also available year-round at the chamber's office at the old railway station in Laconia. It's open Monday through Friday from 9am to 5pm and on Saturdays from 10am to 2pm.

The **Lakes Region Association,** P.O. Box 1545, Center Harbor, NH 03226 (☎ 603/253-8555 or 800/605-2537), doesn't maintain an information booth but is happy to send out a handy vacation kit with maps and extensive information about local attractions.

ENJOYING WEIRS BEACH

Weirs Beach is a compact resort town that reflects its Victorian heritage. Unlike beach towns that sprawl for miles, Weirs Beach clusters in that distinguished turn-of-the-century fashion along a boardwalk, just north of a sandy beach. At the heart of the town is a railroad that connects to the steamship line—a nice throwback to an era when summer vacationers weren't dependent on cars. The town attracts a mix of visitors, from history and transportation buffs, to beach nuts and young video game warriors.

But most of all, it attracts families. Lots of families.

In fact, Weirs Beach is an ideal destination for parents with kids possessed by an insatiable drive for novelty and flashing lights. Families might start the morning at **Endicott Beach** (named after the Royal Governor of Massachusetts Bay Colony, who sent surveyors here in 1652), swimming in the clear waters of Winnipesaukee. Arrive early if you want to find public parking, which costs 50¢ an hour with a five-hour maximum.

Afterward stroll along the boardwalk into town, which offers penny arcades, bumper cars, jewelry outlets, leather shops and delicious if unnutritious fare like crispy caramel corn.

Along the access roads to Weirs Beach are a number of activities that delight young kids and parents desperate to take some of the energy out of them. The **Surfcoaster** (☎ 603/366-4991) has a huge assortment of wave pools, water slides, and other moist diversions. It's on Route 11B just outside of Weirs Beach. Also on Route 11B is **Daytona Fun Park** (☎ 603/366-5461), which has go-karts, mini-golf, and batting cages. The **Weirs Beach Waterslide,** on Route 3 (☎ 603/366-5161), has four slides that produce varying levels of adrenaline. And the **Funspot** (☎ 603/366-4377) will keep kids (and uninhibited adults) occupied with video games, candlepin bowling, and a driving range.

Nearby Laconia is a good destination for drying out after the water rides or venturing on a rainy day. The town has a trim, miniature downtown that's been coming back bit by bit since the ill-fated pedestrian mall was torn up in 1994. Enjoy the eclectic architecture (there's a handsome white-spired church across from a Richardson-inspired train station), then quaff a home-brewed porter or ale at the **Winnipesaukee Pub and Brewery,** downtown at 546 Main St. (☎ 603/527-1300), which has an open, modern layout.

BY LAND & BY LAKE

Scenic train rides leave from town on the **Winnipesaukee Scenic Railroad** (☎ 603/279-5253), which offers one-and two-hour excursions from Weirs Beach throughout the day during the summer. It's a unique way to enjoy views of lake and forest; kids are provided a hobo lunch packed in a bundle on a stick. Fares for adults are $7.50 for the two-hour ride, and $6.50 for the one-hour ride. Children ages 4 to 11 are charged $5.50 and $4.50.

Hog Heaven

Laconia and Weirs Beach get VERY LOUD in mid-June, when some 150,000 motorcyclists descend on the towns to fraternize, party, and race during what's become the legendary Motorcycle Week.

This bawdy event dates back to 1939, when motorcycle races were first staged at the newly built Belknap Gunstock Recreation Area. The annual gathering gained some unwelcome notoriety in 1965, when riots broke out involving bikers and locals. The then-mayor of Laconia attributed problems to the Hell's Angels, claiming he had evidence that they had trained in Mexico before coming here to foment chaos. This odd episode was documented in Hunter S. Thompson's 1966 work, *The Hell's Angels.*

Laconia and Weirs Beach eventually recovered from that unwanted publicity, and today bike races take place at the Loudon Speedway just north of Concord, and at the Gunstock Recreation Area, which hosts the Hill Climb. But the whole of the Weirs Beach area takes on a leather-and-beer carnival atmosphere throughout the week, with bikers cruising the main drag and enjoying one another's company until late at night. Many travelers would pay good money to avoid Weirs Beach at this time, but they'd be missing out on one of New England's more enduring annual phenomena.

After riding the rails, head out onto the waters on the stately **M/S** *Mount Washington,* an exceptionally handsome 230-foot-long vessel with three levels and a capacity of 1,250 passengers (☎ **603/366-2628**). This ship, by far the largest of the lake tour boats, is the best way to get to know Winnipesaukee, with excellent views of the winding shoreline and the knobby peaks of the White Mountains rising over the lake's north end. As many as four cruises a day are offered in summer, ranging from a 2¹/₄-hour excursion ($12 adults, $5 children 4–12) to a 3¹/₂-hour dinner cruise ($32) that includes dinner and live music with two bands. The dinner cruises offer different themes, but don't look for alternative rock; most are along the lines of oldies nights and country-and-western. The ship operates from the end of May through mid-October, departing from the train station in Weirs Beach. (You can't miss it when it's at the dock.)

OUTDOOR PURSUITS

Few finer sights exist than watching the M/S *Mount Washington* steam cross the broad waters of the lake from atop Mt. Major, a popular and accessible peak near the lake's southern tip. The mountain isn't major by White Mountain standards (it's just 1,780 feet), but yields a great view of the waters and the more legitimate mountains to the north. The well-used ascent is 1.5 miles long; plan on somewhat more than an hour to get to the summit. The trail head is located four miles north of Alton Bay on Route 11.

Also near the lake is the **Gunstock Recreation Area** (☎ **603/293-4341**), a four-season area on Route 11A that's been attracting outdoorspeople since it was founded more than a half-century ago. This heavily forested, 2,000-acre park in the upland hills southeast of the lake features camping at 420 sites, fishing, swimming, and a plethora of hiking trails that wend through the scenic Belknap Mountains. (There's also skiing in winter; see below.)

A lower-elevation destination popular with swimmers is **Ellacoya State Beach** (☎ 603/293-7821), on Route 11 between Alton Bay and Weirs Beach. The 600-foot sandy beach has superb views across the waters to the rolling hills on the opposite shore, and offers basic amenities like changing areas and a snack bar. The beach also has RV camping with 38 sites featuring full hookups.

In Laconia, the **Winni Sailboarders School and Outlet,** 687 Union Ave. (☎ 603/528-4110), will put you on the water in either a kayak or on a sailboard on Opechee Bay, a long, fingerlike lake inlet. Lessons are also available.

Along the lake's northern shore, **Wild Meadow Canoes,** on Route 25 between Meredith and Center Harbor (☎ 603/253-7536 or 800/427-7536), rents canoes, kayaks, and small boats for exploring the big lake and some of the smaller waters nearby. A canoe rents for $25 per day.

SKIING   Gunstock, on Route 11A between West Alton and Gilford (☎ 800/486-7862), is a fine destination for families and intermediate skiers who like good views and great grooming as part of their ski experience. This venerable state-run ski area, with a vertical drop of 1,420 feet, has the comfortably burnished patina of a rustic resort dating from a much earlier era—no garish condos, no ski-theme lounges, no forced frivolity. But the mountain managers pride themselves on maintaining excellent ski conditions throughout the day on its 45 trails, and even closes several during lunch for mid-day grooming. Gunstock skiers have a choice of two double chair lifts, two triples, and a quad (plus two surface lifts); from the slopes, the views of iced-over Winnipesaukee and the White Mountains to the north are superb. Gunstock also offers night skiing on 12 trails served by three chairlifts. Adult lift tickets in 1995–96 were $28 midweek and $37 weekends and holidays. For juniors (ages 6–12) and seniors (65+), rates are $20 midweek and $22 weekends and holidays.

WHERE TO STAY

Creeping condomania has reduced the number of guest rooms in the lake area, but Business Route 3 (which runs picturesquely along Paugus Bay) still offers a good selection of motels, cottages, and motor courts, including many that will delight aficionados of 1950s-style architecture and neon. Try the **Naswa Lakeside Resort** (☎ 603/366-4341), which offers simple cottages and motel-style rooms on the water and features a popular restaurant and bar. The **Hi-Spot Motor Court** (☎ 603/524-3281) has its own beach and rowboats for guests, who choose from housekeeping cottages and motel rooms. If you'd prefer to be within walking distance of Weirs Beach attractions, the **Half Moon Motel and Cottages** (☎ 603/366-4494) is perfectly situated on a hillside overlooking the town and the lake beyond.

Inn at Mill Falls. Routes 3 and 25, Meredith, NH 03253. ☎ **603/279-7006** or 800/622-6455. Fax 603/279-6797. 78 rms in 2 buildings. A/C TV TEL. Summer and fall $79–$235 double; winter and spring $68–$195 double. AE, CB, DC, DISC, MC, V.

Located in the middle of Meredith, the Inn at Mill Falls is part of a complex of two dozen shops and restaurants in a renovated and expanded mill built around a small waterfall. The inn, which opened in 1985, has loads of architectural integrity, but it's best suited for those who prefer the amenities of modern hotel to the charm of a country inn. It's a thoroughly up-to-date hotel with nicely decorated guest rooms (the maple and pine furniture is by New Hampshire craftsmen), an indoor pool, and views across the highway to the Meredith Bay. Fifty-four of the guest rooms are at the old mill site; another 24 are across the way at Bay Point, a four-story building with superior lake views and turn-of-the-century boathouse styling.

Kona Mansion Inn. Kona Rd., Center Harbor, NH 03226. ☎ **603/253-4900.** 9 rms, plus 4 cottages and 2 chalets. A/C TV. $60–$140 double. MC, V. Closed late Oct–early May. Head south on Moultonboro Neck Rd. for 3.7 miles from Route 25; turn right on Kona Rd. and follow signs.

If you've always believed that somehow you've been gypped out of a huge inheritance, and were thereby deprived of your country estate with private golf course, then this might be the place for you. The exterior of this old mansion is extraordinary; the structure was built in 1895 by one of the partners of Jordan Marsh (a well-known New England department store chain). The low-roofed inn is all dark wood, terra-cotta tile, and Tudor accenting.

Unfortunately, the guest rooms are in dire need of updating. With cheap paneling, unfortunate carpeting, and nondescript furniture, the rooms seem like oddly out-of-place motel units dating from the early '70s. (Note that Room 5, which lacks TV and air-conditioning, is $60; the other rooms start at $85.) But if you don't expect luxury while you sleep, you can soak up all the luxury you need during the day.

Facilities: The inn sits amid a 9-hole, par-3 golf course, next to two asphalt tennis courts (both a bit weed-choked now), and up a short hill from the lakeshore, where guests can bathe at a small beach. The downstairs dining room is elegant, with a rich, vaguely medieval feel to it.

❸**Red Hill Inn.** Route 25B (P.O. Box 99), Center Harbor, NH 03226. ☎ **603/279-7001** or 800/573-3445. Fax 603/279-7003. 21 rms (some with shower or tub only). TEL. $85–$125 double at inn and farmhouse; $125–$150 cottage. Rates include breakfast. AE, CB, DC, DISC, MC, V. From Center Harbor, drive northwest 2.9 miles on Route 25B.

The Red Hill Inn is tucked in the rolling hills between Winnipesaukee and Squam Lake (where "On Golden Pond" was filmed), but borrows more of its flavor from the mountains than the lakeshore. Housed in an architecturally austere, three-story brick home dating from the turn of the century, the inn looks down a long meadow toward a small complex of elegant green-and-red shingled farm buildings at the foot of a hill. (Two of these have been converted to well-appointed guest quarters).

The rooms and common areas in the main inn are handsomely furnished in low Victorian style with floral wallpaper and maple floors. Room prices are based on views and size, but my favorite room (the Kearsarge) is one of the least expensive, with a very private brick and chocolatey-brown panelled sitting room, off which lies a small bathroom with clawfoot tub.

Despite a price that may seem average-to-high at first glance, the Red Hill delivers more for the dollar than most any other inn in New Hampshire. For an even better deal, ask about the inn's three-night midweek packages.

Dining/Entertainment: The inn's dining room serves lunch and dinner, with entrees such as medallions of venison au poive, or rack of lamb with a feta cheese and Dijon mustard topping.

WHERE TO DINE

Kellerhaus (☎ 603/366-4466) is the classic house of sweets. Located in a storybook-like stone and half-timber structure on Route 3 a third of a mile north of Endicott Beach, this old-fashioned place with bulls-eye windows on a hillside overlooking the lake features a diet-busting ice-cream buffet, where fanatics can select from a battery of toppings including macaroon crunch, butterscotch, chocolate, and whipped cream. The smorgasbord is $3.25 to $5.95, depending on the number of scoops you begin with. There's also a sizable gift shop with homemade candies providing snacks for the road.

Hart's Turkey Farm Restaurant. Route 3, Meredith. ☎ **603/279-6212.** Reservations recommended during peak season. Main courses $9.50–$17.75. AE, CB, DC, DISC, MC, V. Summer daily 11:15am–9pm; fall through spring daily 11:15am–8pm. POULTRY/AMERICAN.

Hart's Turkey Farm Restaurant is not good news if you're a turkey. On a typically busy day, this popular spot dishes up more than a ton of America's favorite bird, along with 4,000 dinner rolls and 1,000 pounds of potatoes. And let's not even talk about Thanksgiving.

Judging by name alone, Hart's Farm sounds more rural than it is. In fact, there are no turkeys to be seen nearby. It's in a nondescript roadside building on a busy, nondescript part of Route 3. Inside, it's comfortable in a faux Olde New Englande sort of way, and the service has that brisk efficiency found only in places where waitresses have been hoisting heavy trays for years. But diners don't flock to Hart's for the charm. They come here for filling meals that range from fried fish to filet mignon. And most of all, they come for turkey that's cooked right every time.

Hickory Stick Farm. 60 Bean Hill Rd., Belmont. ☎ **603/524-3333.** Reservations recommended. Main courses $10.95–$18.95. AE, DISC, MC, V. Memorial Day to Columbus Day Tues–Sun 5–8pm; limited schedule remainder of the year. Ask for directions when making reservations. AMERICAN.

The Hickory Stick Farm is well off the beaten path in the countryside outside of Laconia, but has managed to attract and keep happy diners since it first opened its doors in 1950. Ask for a seat on the screened in gazebo room during the balmy weather. When it turns chilly, angle for a table near the fireplace in the brick-floored dining room.

The restaurant is famous for its distinctive duck dishes, served with an orange-sherry sauce. The duck is slow-roasted for four to five hours, and the fatty layer is removed from beneath the skin. This method yields delicate and crispy skin, but moist meat. The duck attracts gourmands from Boston and beyond, but tasty country fare like vegetable lasagne, sirloin, and roast rack of lamb keeps the locals coming in night after night.

⑤ Las Piñatas. 9 Veteran's Square, Laconia. ☎ **603/528-1405.** Reservations suggested for parties of 5 or more. Lunch items $3.75–$7.99; main dinner courses $7.99–$9.99. MC, V. Daily 11am–2pm; Mon–Fri 5–8pm, Sat–Sun 5–9:30pm. MEXICAN.

Armando Lezama first came to Laconia from Mexico City in 1979 as a high school exchange student. He liked it. So he moved here with his family, opening what's most certainly the most authentic Mexican restaurant in New Hampshire. Housed in the stone railroad station on the edge of Laconia's downtown, Las Piñatas has a good menu of genuine Mexican dishes and frozen margaritas that seem especially tasty after a long day at the lake. While diners might gripe about the lackadaisical service or the overabundance of iceberg lettuce, the entrees boast authentic spicing—the beans are earthy and the salsa tangy. Everything is uniformly well-prepared, and offered at excellent prices. The menu includes Mexican regulars such as empanadas, tacos al carbón, and fajitas. Among the specialities are the delicious enchiladas de mole, made with the Lezama's homemade mole sauce. For dessert, try the coconut flan, or a bunuelo with maple syrup.

EAST SHORE

For some travelers, Winnipesaukee's eastern shore might recall Gertrude Stein's comment about Oakland: There's no there there. Other than the low-key town of Wolfeboro, the east shore is mostly islands and coves, mixed forests and rolling hills, rocky farms and the occasional apple orchard. While it's a large lake, its waters are also largely inaccessible from this side. Old summer homes and new gated condominium communities occupy some of the best coves and points. But narrow roads do touch on the lake here and there, and most roads are nicely engineered for leisurely cruising. The secret to getting the most out of the east shore is to take it slow and enjoy the small villages and quiet forests as if they were delicately crafted miniatures, not vast panoramas.

ESSENTIALS

GETTING THERE　Lake Winnipesaukee's east shore is best explored on Route 28 (from Alton Bay to Wolfeboro) and Route 109 (from Wolfeboro to Moulton-borough). From the south, Alton Bay can be reached via Route 11 from Rochester, or from Route 28, which intersects Routes 4 and 202 about 12 miles east of Concord.

VISITOR INFORMATION　The **Wolfeboro Chamber of Commerce,** P.O. Box 547, Wolfeboro, NH 03864 (☎ **603/569-2200**), offers regional travel information and advice from a converted railroad station at Depot Square, one block off Main Street in Wolfeboro (turn on Railroad Avenue).

EXPLORING WOLFEBORO

The town of Wolfeboro claims to be the first summer resort in the United States, and the documentation makes a pretty good case for it. In 1763, John Wentworth, the nephew of a former governor, built a summer estate on what's now called Lake Wentworth, along with a road to it from Portsmouth. Wentworth didn't get to enjoy his holdings for long—his Tory sympathies forced him to flee when the political situation heated up in 1775. The house burned in 1820, but the site now attracts archeologists. Tourists are lured to **Wentworth State Beach** (☎ **603/ 569-3699**) not so much because of history but because of the attractive beach, refreshing lake waters, and shady picnic area. The park is located five miles east of Wolfeboro on Route 109.

The town of Wolfeboro (pop. 2,800) has a vibrant, homey downtown that's easily explored on foot. Park near Depot Square and the gingerbread Victorian train station, and stock up on brochures and maps at the Chamber of Commerce office inside. Behind the train station, running along the former tracks of the rail line, is the **Russell C. Chase Bridge-Falls Path,** a rail-trail that (so far) runs pleasantly about ¹/₂ mile along Back Bay to a set of small waterfalls. (Plans call for extending the pathway much further in coming years.)

Near the falls, look for the **Wright Museum,** 77 Center St. (Route 77; ☎ **603/ 569-1212**), open 10am to 5pm daily in summer. This is an unusual museum, easily identified by the tank "crashing" out through the crumbling front wall. Founded in 1984, the Wright Museum celebrates life on "the home front" between 1939 and 1945, when America's boys were abroad fighting the good fight. If your notion of the good old days involves Frank Sinatra in saddle shoes and strawberry parfaits at a marble-topped fountain, you'll find a lot to bring back memories here. Admission is $5 adults, $4 seniors, and $3 students.

The ponderous **M/S *Mount Washington*** docks in Wolfeboro on its cruises from Weirs Beach (see the "Western Shore" section, above), but if you'd like a more intimate tour of the lake, sign up for a cruise on the Blue Ghost, an open, 19-foot U.S. mailboat that serves a handful of island communities around the lake. The three-hour tour departs from the Wolfeboro waterfront at 9:50am, and covers some 60 miles of the lake. Reservations are essential (call **603/569-1114**), and capacity is limited to eight passengers. The fare is $16 adults, $8 for children under 12.

For a superb view of the eastern shore, head seven miles north of Wolfeboro on Route 109 to the Abenaki Tower. Look for a parking lot and wooden sign on the right side of the road at the crest of a hill. From the lot, it's an easy, five-minute hike to the sturdy log tower, which rises about 60 feet and is ascended by a steep staircase. (This is not a good destination for acrophobes.) Those who soldier on to the top are rewarded with excellent views of nearby coves, inlets, and the Belknap Mountains southwest of the lake.

A QUIRKY CASTLE

Castle in the Clouds. Route 171 (four miles south of Route 25), Moultonborough. ☎ **603/476-2352** or 800/729-2468. $10 adults, $9 seniors, $7 students. (Grounds only, $4.) Mid-May to mid-June Sat–Sun 9am–5pm; mid-June to Labor Day daily 9am–5pm; Labor Day to third week of Oct daily 9am–4pm.

Cranky millionaire Thomas Gustav Plant built this eccentric stone edifice high atop a mountain overlooking Lake Winnipesaukee early in this century. Completed in 1913 at a cost of $7 million, the home is a sort of rustic San Simeon East, with orange roof tiles, cliff-hugging rooms, stained glass windows, and unrivaled views of the surrounding hills and lakes. Visitors drive as far as the carriage house (nicely converted to a snack bar and restaurant), where they park and are taken in groups through the house by knowledgeable guides.

Even if the castle holds no interest, the 5,200-acre grounds themselves are worth the admission price (there's a discount for those visiting the grounds only). The long access road is harrowingly narrow and winding (kids, don't try this in your mobile home), with wonderful vistas and turnouts for stopping and exploring along the way. I'd advise taking your time on the way up; the exit road is fast, straight, and uninteresting.

Equestrians can rent horses to explore the hills at $25 for a one-hour ride. (Reservations required.)

On your way out you're invited to visit the modern bottling plant, where Castle Springs Water is packaged for shipment to shops throughout the Northeast.

WHERE TO STAY & DINE

Wolfeboro Inn. 90 N. Main St., Wolfeboro, NH 03894. ☎ **603/569-3016** or 800/451-2389. Fax 603/569-5375. 44 rms. A/C TV TEL. $109–$219 double. Rates include breakfast. Add $20 on weekends. AE, DISC, MC, V.

This small, elegant hotel strives to mix modern and traditional, and succeeds admirably in doing so. Located a short stroll from downtown Wolfeboro, the inn dates back to 1812 but was extensively expanded and updated in 1985–86. The modern lobby features a small atrium with wood beams, slate floor, and a brick fireplace, and has managed to retain an Old World elegance and grace. Comfortable guest rooms vary in size, and most are furnished with early American reproductions. Some have fireplaces; others have views of Wolfeboro Bay. The inn also has some nice extras, including its own 75-passenger excursion boat (a free trip is included in room rates). On the downside, for an inn of this elegance and price it has only a disappointing sliver of lakeshore and a miniature beach for guests.

Dining/Entertainment: The main dining room has two areas to suit your mood: Sit near the fireplace in a low-ceilinged room decorated in a traditional early American style, or choose the upper, gazebo-like room, which is airy and summery. In the inn's early wing is the atmospheric Wolfe's Tavern, with pewter tankards hanging from the low beams, 60 brands of beer, and a selection of basic pub fare, including salads, burgers, and a variety of pasta dishes.

6 The White Mountains

The White Mountains are Northern New England's undisputed outdoor recreation capital. This cluster of ancient mountains is a sprawling, rugged playground that attracts kayakers, mountaineers, rock climbers, skiers, mountain bikers, bird watchers, and hikers.

Especially hikers. The White Mountain National Forest encompasses some 773,000 acres of rocky, forested terrain, more than 100 waterfalls, dozens of remote backcountry lakes, and miles of clear brooks and cascading streams. An elaborate network of 1,200 miles of hiking trails dates back to the 19th century, when the urban gentry took to the mountains in droves to build character, build trails, and experience the raw sublimity of nature. Trails ranging from easy and extraordinarily demanding lace the hillside forests, run along remote valley rivers, and traverse barren, windswept ridgelines where the weather can change dramatically in less time than it takes to eat lunch.

The spiritual center of the White Mountains is its highest point: 6,288-foot Mt. Washington, an ominous, brooding peak that's often cloud-capped, and often mantled with snow early and late in the season. This blustery peak is accessible by train, car, and foot, making it one of the most popular spots in the region. You won't find wilderness here, but you will find a surfeit of natural drama.

Flanking this colossal peak are the brawny Presidential Mountains, a series of fractured granite peaks named after U.S. presidents and offering spectacular views. Surrounding these are numerous other rocky ridges that lure hikers looking for challenges and a place to experience nature at its more elemental and raw.

As for camping, simple but comfortable "huts" (managed by the Appalachian Mountain Club) and three-sided lean-tos are scattered throughout the White Mountains, providing overnight shelter for campers. Meals are included at the huts, but it's surprisingly pricey. Shelters are sometimes free, sometimes a backcountry manager will collect a small fee. Backcountry tent camping is free throughout the White Mountains (no permit needed). Check with one of the ranger stations for restrictions.

Travelers whose idea of fun doesn't involve steep cliffs or icy dips in mountain streams still have plenty of opportunities for milder adventure. A handful of major arteries provide easy access to mountain scenery. Route 302 carries travelers through North Conway and Crawford Notch to the pleasant villages of Bethlehem and Littleton. Route 16 travels from southern New Hampshire through congested North Conway before twisting up dramatic Pinkham Notch at the base of Mt. Washington. Wide and fast Route 2 skirts the northern edge of the mountains, offering wonderful views en route to the town of Jefferson. I-93 gets my vote for the most scenic interstate in Northern New England, passing through spectacular Franconia Notch as it narrows to a two-lane road in deference to its natural surroundings (and local political will). And finally, there's the Kancamagus Highway, linking Conway with Lincoln, and providing some of the most spectacular White Mountain vistas in the region. Along the way, frequent roadside pull-offs and interpretive exhibits allow casual explorers to admire cascades, picnic along rivers, and enjoy sweeping mountain views. Several less demanding nature hikes are also easily accessible from various roadside turnouts.

Keep in mind that the White Mountains are a national forest, not a national park, a distinction that's sometimes lost on urbanites and foreign travelers. There's a big difference. National forests are managed for multiple uses, which includes timber harvesting, wildlife management, recreational development, and the like. This may disappoint those offended by clearcutting and logging roads. Fortunately, the level of cutting is not as excessive as in many Western forests, and the regrowth here also tends to be more rapid than in the arid West. Also bear in mind that about 15 percent of the White Mountains is designated as wilderness areas, from which mechanical devices (including mountain bikes) are prohibited. Strike for these areas if you're looking to step deep into the wilds.

As for accommodations, it's easy to find an area to suit your mood and inclinations. North Conway is the motel capital of the region, with hundreds of rooms, many quite charmless, but at very reasonable rates. The Loon Mountain and Waterville Valley area have a sort of planned condo village graciousness that delights some travelers and creeps out others. Jackson, Franconia Notch, Crawford Notch, and the Bethlehem-Littleton area are the best destinations for old-fashioned hotels and inns.

RANGER STATIONS & INFORMATION

Guidance for outdoor adventures can be obtained at the national forest visitor centers, which are located in various locations around the White Mountains. The **Saco Ranger Station** (☎ 603/447-5448) in Conway is on the Kancamagus Highway just 100 yards west of Route 16. The **Androscoggin Ranger Station** (☎ 603/466-2713) is at 80 Glen Rd. in Gorham. The **Evans Notch Ranger Station** (☎ 207/824-2134) covers the Maine portion of the White Mountains (about 50,000 acres) and located on Route 2 just north of Bethel. The **Ammonoosuc Ranger Station** (☎ 603/869-2626) is on Trudeau Rd. in Bethlehem. The **Forest Service's central White Mountains office** is in Laconia at 719 Main St. (☎ 603/528-8721).

General information and advice about recreation in the White Mountains is available at the **AMC's Pinkham Notch Camp** (☎ 603/466-2721) on Route 16 between Jackson and Gorham. The center is open daily from 6am to 10pm.

SPECIALIZED GUIDES

If you're serious about exploring the wind-scoured crags and mossy ravines of the White Mountains, you'll need supplemental guides and maps to keep you on track in great outdoors. Here's a short list of recommended guides, most of which are available at area bookstores:

- *AMC White Mountain Guide* (Appalachian Mountain Club, 1992, $16.95). This compact, 638-page book (no, that's not an oxymoron) is chock-full of detailed information on all the hiking trails in the White Mountains. It's printed in small type in a format suitable to throwing in your pack, and comes with a handy set of maps. This is the hiker's bible for the region.
- *Mount Washington: A Guide and Short History* (Countryman Press, 1992, $9.95). Peter Randall originally wrote this handy and informative guide in 1983, updating it in 1992. The guide will appeal to those interested in the history and hiking of the Northeast's tallest peak.
- *Fifty Hikes in the White Mountains* (Backcountry Publications, 1994, $14). The fourth edition of this popular guide, written by John Doan, offers a good selection of mountain rambles ranging from easy strolls to overnight backpack trips.
- *Ponds & Lakes of the White Mountains* (Backcountry Publications, 1993, $16). The White Mountain high country is studded with dramatic tarns (many left by retreating glaciers). This 350-page guide by Steven D. Smith offers 68 trips to help get you there.

The White Mountains & Lake Country

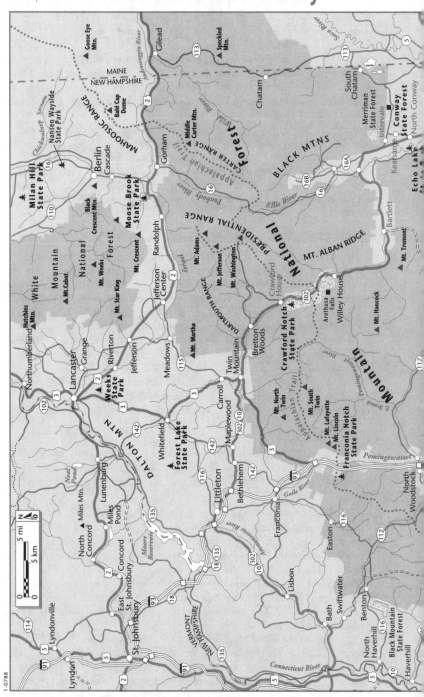

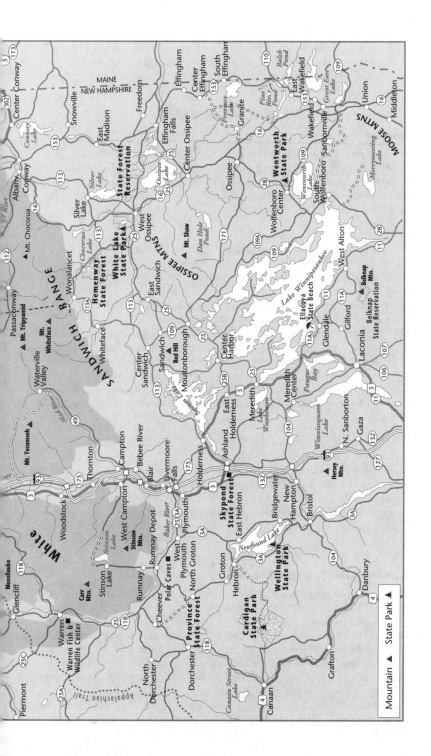

- *Waterfalls of the White Mountains* (Backcountry Publications, 1990, $17). Water lovers will get their money's worth from Bruce and Doreen Bolnick's guide to 100 mountain waterfalls, including roadside cascades and backcountry cataracts.

SUGGESTED ITINERARIES

If You Have 1 Day

Head to Franconia Notch State Park on the west side of the White Mountains. Visit the Flume, take a tram ride to the top of Cannon Mountain, enjoy roadside views of the Old Man of the Mountain, take a walk or bike ride along Echo Lake. You'll get a good introduction to the drama of the White Mountains without a lot of scurrying from place to place.

If You Have 2 Days

Day 1 Start at the town of Lincoln at Exit 32 of I-93, and drive to North Conway via the scenic Kancamagus Highway. Make a few brief shopping forays in town, and savor the views of the Mt. Washington Valley. Head to the village of Jackson for lunch and secure accommodations for the night. Spend the rest of the afternoon relaxing at Jackson Falls, and exploring by car or bike up Carter Notch Rd. and the other scenic backroads in the hills above the village.

Day 2 Retrace your path down Route 16 back to Route 302, turn right and drive through Crawford Notch. Go to the Mt. Washington Cog Railway on the far side of the Notch. Take the train ride to the summit of Mt. Washington (dress warmly). Upon your return, stop by the grand Mt. Washington Hotel for a celebratory snack. Continue west on Route 302 until reaching Route 3. Turn left (south) to I-93. Continue southward through scenic Franconia Notch, and tour the attractions as time allows.

If You Have 3 Days

Day 1 See Day 1 of two-day itinerary above.

Day 2 Spend the day exploring by foot around Pinkham Notch. Stop at Glen Ellis Falls en route to the base of Mt. Washington. Park at Pinkham Notch and hike to dramatic Tuckerman's Ravine for a picnic lunch. Return to your car and continue north to Wildcat Ski Area. Take the chairlift to summit for spectacular views of Mt. Washington, the Presidentials, and the Carter Range. Return to Jackson for the night.

Day 3 See Day 2 of two-day itinerary above.

If You Have a Week (and Like Things Rugged)

Day 1 Sign up for a one-day rock climbing course in North Conway, and spend the day muckled onto pencil-thin outcroppings at Cathedral Ledge. Learn the term "sewing machine leg."

Day 2 Drive on hairy Hurricane Road to Evans Notch in Maine and set up camp at one of the national forest campgrounds in the area. Limber up for forthcoming adventures with a hike up Baldface or Caribou mountains.

Day 3 More day hiking in Evans Notch, or head for Fryeburg and rent a canoe for a day trip on the gentle Saco River. See chapter 7.

Day 4 Head to Pinkham Notch Camp at the base of Mt. Washington and secure a bed for the night. Rent a mountain bike at Great Glen Trails (up the road toward Gorham) and spend the afternoon exploring the woods on wheels.

Day 5   With backpack in place, set off early to ascend the summit of Mt. Washington, then ramble 1.4 miles to AMC's dramatic Lake of the Clouds Hut for the night (advance reservations essential).

Day 6   Head south on the Appalachian Trail over Mt. Eisenhower for a dramatic, exposed traverse of about 6 miles to the AMC's Mitzpah Springs Hut (again, reservations essential). Bunk in for the night.

Day 7   Descend to Crawford Depot in the morning on Route 302 and catch the AMC shuttle (☎ **603/466-2727** for times and reservations) back to Pinkham Notch to retrieve your car. Head to North Conway for beer and pizza.

NORTH CONWAY & ENVIRONS

North Conway is the commercial heart of the White Mountains. Shoppers adore it because of the profusion of outlets, boutiques, and restaurants along Routes 302 & 16. (The two state highways overlap through town.) Outdoor purists abhor it, considering it a garish interloper to be avoided at all costs, except when looking for pizza.

No doubt, North Conway itself won't strike anyone as nature's wonderland. The shopping strip south of the village is basically one long turning lane flanked with outlet malls of every architectural stripe, motels, and chain restaurants. On rainy weekends and during the foliage season, the road can resemble a linear parking lot.

Regardless, North Conway is beautifully situated along the eastern edge of the broad and fertile Saco River Valley (often called the Mt. Washington Valley by local tourism boosters). Gentle, forest-covered mountains, some with sheer cliffs that suggest the distant, stunted cousins of Yosemite's rocky faces, border the bottomlands. Northward up the valley, the hills rise in a triumphant crescendo to the blustery, tempestuous heights of Mt. Washington.

The village itself is trim and attractive (if often congested), with an open green, quaint shops, Victorian frontier-town commercial architecture, and a distinctive train station. It's a good place to park, stretch your legs, and find a cup of coffee or a snack.

Visitors who'd prefer a more scenic, less commercial route bypassing North Conway's strip malls should detour to West Side Road. Arriving from the south, turn north at the light in Conway Village on to Washington St. One-half mile farther, bear left on West Side Road. The road passes near two covered bridges in the first halfmile, then dips and winds through the broad farmlands of the Saco River Valley. You'll pass working farms and farmstands, and some architecturally distinctive early homes.

You'll also come upon dramatic views of the granite cliffs that form the western wall of the valley. Stop for a swim at Echo Lake State Park (it's well-marked, on your left). At the first stop sign, turn right for North Conway Village, or turn left to connect to Route 302 in Bartlett, passing more ledges and cliffs.

ESSENTIALS

GETTING THERE   North Conway and the Mt. Washington Valley are on Route 16 and Route 302. Route 16 connects to the Spaulding Turnpike outside of Portsmouth, N.H. Route 302 begins in Portland, Maine.

VISITOR INFORMATION   The **Mt. Washington Valley Chamber of Commerce**, P.O. Box 2300, North Conway, NH 03860 (☎ **603/356-3171** or 800/367-3364), operates a seasonal information booth opposite the village green with brochures about attractions and inns. The staff can arrange for accommodations. It's open daily in summer (Monday to Friday 9am to 6pm, and weekends 9am to 8pm). In winter it's open weekends only.

The state of New Hampshire also operates an information booth with rest rooms and telephones at a vista with fine views of Mt. Washington on Routes 16 and 302 north of North Conway.

A TRAIN EXCURSION

A unique way to view the mountainous landscape around North Conway is via train. The **Conway Scenic Railroad** (☎ 603/356-5251 or 800/232-5251) offers regularly scheduled trips in comfortable cars pulled by either steam train or sleek early diesel engine. Trips depart from an 1874 train station just off the village green, which recalls an era when tourists arrived from Boston and New York to enjoy the country air for a month or two each summer. One-hour excursions head south to Conway; a slightly longer (and in my opinion, far more scenic) trip heads north to the village of Bartlett. In 1995 the rail line added a five-and-a-half hour excursion through dramatic Crawford Notch (I think of this as equivalent to the old "A" ticket at Disneyland), with stupendous views from high along this beautiful glacial valley. Ask also about the railway's dining excursions.

The train runs April through mid-December, with more frequent trips scheduled daily in mid-summer. Tickets are $8.50 to $16.50 for adults ($31.95 to $36.95 for Crawford Notch), $5 to $7 for children 4 to 12 ($16.95 to $21.95 Crawford Notch). Kids under 4 ride free on the Conway trip only. Reservations are advised.

SHOPPING

Consumers who get themselves into a lather about saving a few bucks on name-brand clothing and other merchandise should schedule a day or two for raking through the bargain racks of North Conway's outlets. You won't have to search hard to find these 200-plus shops. They're readily apparent along "the strip," which extends about three miles from the junction of Route 302 and Route 16 north of Conway into the village of North Conway itself. It's a town planner's nightmare, but a shopper's paradise.

Among the more notable outlet clusters are Outlet Village Plus at Settler's Green, with better than 30 name-brand shops; the Tanger Factory Outlet, which hosts the popular L.L. Bean shop; and Willow Place, with 11 shops like Dress Barn, Bed & Bath, and Lingerie Factory. Other outlets scattered along the strip include Anne Klein, American Tourister, Izod, Dansk, Donna Karan, Levi's, Polo/Ralph Lauren, Reebock/Rockport, J. Crew, and Eddie Bauer.

For those setting out on a White Mountain expedition, outdoor equipment suppliers in town include **International Mountain Equipment** (☎ 603/356-7013) and **Eastern Mountain Sports** (☎ 603/356-5433), both on Main Street just north of the green. There's also **Ragged Mountain Equipment** (☎ 603/356-3042), three miles north of town in Intervale on Routes 16 and 302. All three shops are excellent sources of advice on local destinations and weather conditions.

A final testimonial: A favorite shop of mine is **Chuck Roast Mountainwear** (☎ 603/356-5589), a North Conway–based manufacturer of outerwear, backpacks, and soft luggage. The daypack I purchased from them five years ago has held up superbly despite constant battering. All their goods come with a lifetime guarantee. Their outlet is at the Mt. Washington Outlet Center, not far from the L.L. Bean outlet.

Need a sugar buzz to keep browsing? Hidden amid the boutiques, galleries, and outlets of North Conway is the **Bavarian Chocolate Haus** (☎ 603/356-2663), a sweet-tooth's dream. Situated in a small faux-Tudor building in the shadow of the Hand Crafters Barn, this is the place to sate your chocolate cravings with a selection of hand-dipped chocolates and homemade fudge. Start with the truffles (there are 18 varieties) and—well, come to think of it, you just might want to stop with the truffles since they're that good. Sneak your bounty across the road to the small park and enjoy the great outdoors while dabbling in dietary crime.

ROCK CLIMBING

The impressive granite faces on the valley's west side are for more than admiring from afar. They're also for climbing. Cathedral Ledge and Whitehorse Ledge attract rock climbers from all over the Eastern seaboard, who consider these cliffs (along with the Shawangunks in New York State and Seneca Rocks in West Virginia) as sort of an eastern troika where they can put their grace and technical acumen to the test.

Experienced climbers will have their own sources of information on the best access and routes. (Guidebooks are also available at the outdoor outfitters mentioned above.) Inexperienced climbers should sign up for a class taught by one of the local outfitters, whose workshops run from one day to one week. Try the **Eastern Mountain Sports Climbing School** (☎ 603/356-5433), the **International Mountain Climbing School** (☎ 603/356-7064), or the **Mountain Guides Alliance** (☎ 603/356-5310).

To tone up or keep in shape on rainy days, the **Cranmore Sports Center** (☎ 603/356-6301) near the Mt. Cranmore base lodge has an indoor climbing wall open weekdays 5 to 9pm and weekends 2 to 8pm. The fee is $12, plus a one-time $5 belay test for newcomers. Private, semiprivate, and group lessons are also available.

SKIING

Mt. Cranmore. North Conway Village, NH 03860. ☎ **603/356-5544.** Vertical drop: 1,200 feet. Lifts: 6 chairlifts (1 high-speed quads), 4 surface lifts. Skiable acreage: 190. Ticket prices: Adult $39 weekend, $29 midweek; $20 and $15 for children under 12.

Mt. Cranmore is within walking distance of downtown North Conway, although I wouldn't dare try it in ski boots. The oldest operating ski area in New England, Mt. Cranmore is unrepentantly old-fashioned, and doesn't display an iota of pretense. It's not likely to challenge advanced skiers, but it will delight beginners and intermediates, as well as those who like the old-style New England cut of the ski trails.

WHERE TO STAY

Route 16 through North Conway is packed with basic motels that are reasonably priced in the off-season, but may be pricey during peak travel times such as fall foliage. Fronting the commercial strip, these motels don't offer much in the way of a pastoral environment, but most are comfortable and conveniently located. Try the **School House Motel** (☎ 603/356-6829), with a heated outdoor pool; The **Yankee Clipper Motor Lodge** (☎ 603/356-5736 or 800/343-5900), with a pool and mini-golf; or the slightly more pricey **Green Granite Motel** (☎ 603/356-6901 or 800/468-3666), with whirlpool suites, 88 rooms, and a free continental breakfast.

Expensive

Presidential Motel. 3440 North Main St./Route 16, North Conway, NH 03860. ☎ **603/356-9744.** 16 rms. A/C TV TEL. $92–$150 double. AE, DISC, MC, V.

The Presidential Motel celebrates its Pocono-retro chic. This is a standard issue roadside motel with one major exception: Every room has been fixed up with large Jacuzzis or hot tubs. There's a bed, and then there's a Jacuzzi (most of them are glossy lipstick red and heart shaped). Having them right next to the bed can be a bit disconcerting; picture sharing a room with a sporty red Ferrarri. The Presidential is a great place to unwind after a day of hiking or skiing, although it's way pricey for a motel.

The Golden Age of Resort Hotels

Lured by glowing written accounts and stunning landscape paintings, tourists poured into the White Mountains throughout the mid- and late 19th century. An excursion to see the noble peaks and the rushing torrents of the Whites quickly became the era's equivalent of a trip to Disney World. To cater to the boom, dozens of sprawling resorts cropped up throughout the mountains, appearing everywhere from the summits of windswept peaks to the open valleys with good views of the towering hills. In addition, farmhouses and boarding houses opened their doors to accommodate the less affluent summer visitors.

Fickle tourist tastes shifted away from the resorts and extended farm-stays in the early decades of this century, giving rise to motels and motor courts. Most of the grand resorts were shuttered, and eventually succumbed to time, termites, and fire.

Happily, some of the old hotels did survive—though just barely—and today have found new life as travelers have rediscovered the historic appeal of a grand resort vacation. The two most opulent surviving hotels are **The Balsams** at Dixville Notch, far north in the New Hampshire's most remote reaches, and the visually stunning **Mount Washington Hotel** at Bretton Woods, right at the base of the region's highest peak. Both recapture the grace and elegance of grand hotels, although at a price.

Some superb examples of the smaller-scale resorts are in Jackson, N.H. **The Eagle Mountain House** and the **Wentworth Resort Hotel** have both been nicely restored to reflect the flair of their era, and offer rooms at fair prices. To experience an upscale farm vacation resort, book a room at the lovely **Philbrook Farm Inn** in Shelburne, N.H., where the same family has been taking in guests seeking country air and mountain panoramas since 1853.

Red Jacket Inn. Route 16 (P.O. Box 2000), North Conway, NH 03860. ☎ **603/356-5411** or 800-752-2538. Fax 603/356-3842. 164 rms. A/C TV TEL. $89–$154 double, depending on season, time of week, and view. AE, DC, DISC, MC, V.

Set high on a grassy ridge overlooking the Saco Valley, the Red Jacket Inn is a 1970s-era resort that avoided that dated disco-era look through constant renovations. A modern, two-story building with two wings flanking a reception area, dining room, and indoor pool, the Red Jacket presents a quiet oasis on 30 acres above the hubbub of the highway. The spacious guest rooms are nicely furnished with colonial reproductions, and many offer private patios or balconies. If the weather's nice, splurge on a mountain-view room and enjoy the vistas of the Moat Mountains across the valley.

Dining/Entertainment: As for food, you're better off exploring locally. The resort's Champey's Restaurant is a rather dim and gloomy affair overdue for renovation. Not even wonderful views and a decent menu can enliven the atmosphere.

Facilities: The grounds are handsomely landscaped, and guests can entertain themselves at the swimming pool and tennis courts.

Four Points Hotel. Route 16 at Settler's Green (P.O. Box 3189), North Conway, NH 03860. ☎ **603/356-9300** or 800/648-4397. 200 rms. A/C TV TEL. Summer $89–$179 double; foliage season $105–$215 double; off-season $69–$149 double. AE, CB, DC, DISC, MC, V.

If you're looking for convenience, modern amenities, and easy access to outlet shopping, this Sheraton-run hotel is your best bet. Built in 1990 on the site of North Conway's old airfield, the Four Points is a four-story, gabled hotel adjacent (and architecturally similar) to Outlet Village Plus, one of the two or three million outlet centers based in North Conway. The Four Points offers impeccably clean, comfortable, basic hotel rooms.

Facilities: Guests have access to a pleasing brick-terraced indoor pool and Jacuzzi. Other extras include tennis courts, an outdoor pool, a fitness room, an above-average restaurant and tavern, and kids' karaoke nights.

Stonehurst Manor. Route 16 (1.2 miles north of North Conway village; P.O. Box 1937), North Conway, NH 03860. ☎ **603/356-3271** or 800/525-9100. 24 rms (2 with shared bath, some with showers only). A/C TV. $75–$125 double ($20–$30 surcharge during foliage season); $96–$156 double with breakfast and dinner included. MC, V.

The Stonehurst Manor seems determined to confound expectations. This imposing, eclectic Victorian stone-and-shingle mansion, set amid white pines on a rocky knoll above Route 16, wouldn't seem at all out of place in the south of France or on the moors of Scotland. The immediate assumption is that it caters to the stuffy and affluent. But don't assume. The main focus here is on outdoor adventure vacations, and it attracts a youngish crowd. The restaurant makes the best wood-fired pizza in the area (see "Where to Dine," below). And the rates aren't nearly as prohibitive as you might expect.

My advice is to request one of the 14 rooms in the regal 1876 mansion itself (another 10 are in a comfortable but less elegant wing built in 1952). These mansion rooms are all unique and furnished appropriately to the building's era. Room 21A, for instance, one of the nicest in the inn, has stained glass windows and a wicker-furnished private porch with sunset views toward Humphrey's Ledge. It's easy to slip into a fantasy that you're the guest of the Bigelow carpet tycoons—the wealthy Victorians who originally built this endearing edifice. Relax and enjoy it.

○ White Mountain Hotel and Resort. West Side Road (5.4 miles west of North Conway; P.O. Box 1828), North Conway, NH 03860. ☎ **603/356-7100** or 800/533-6301. 80 rms. A/C TV TEL. Summer $89–$179 double; foliage season $109–$189 double; winter $69–$139 double; off-season $59–$119 double. AE, DISC, MC, V.

This modern, upscale resort has the best location of any choice in the North Conway area. Sited at the base of dramatic White Horse Ledge near Echo Lake State Park and amid a new golf course community, the White Mountain Hotel was built in 1990 but borrows from the rich legacy of classic White Mountain resorts. Its designers have managed to take some of the more successful elements of a friendly country inn—a nice deck with a view, comfortable seating in the lobby, a clubby tavern area—and incorporate it into a thoroughly modern resort. The tones throughout are muted and rich, and overall sensibility seems more influenced by a European elegance than early American rusticity.

Guest rooms are comfortably appointed with dark wood and an earthy maroon carpeting, and are a solid notch or two above standard hotel furnishings. Minisuites offer a bit more elbow room and small refrigerators.

Facilities: Fitness center, heated outdoor pool, and Jacuzzi.

Moderate

Ө Cranmore Inn. 80 Kearsarge St., North Conway, NH 03860. ☎ **603/356-5502** or 800/ 526-5502. 18 rms, 14 with private bath (some hall baths, some with showers only). Summer $56–$74 double; foliage season and ski weekends $69–$84 double; off-season $44–$59 double. Rates include full breakfast. AE, MC, V.

The Cranmore Inn has the feel of a 19th-century boarding house—which is appropriate, since that's what it is. Open since 1863, this three-story Victorian home is hidden on a side street a short walk from North Conway's main attractions. Its distinguished heritage (it's the oldest continuously operating hotel in North Conway) adds considerable charm and quirkiness, but comes with some minor drawbacks, like uneven water pressure in the showers and some sinks with cracked or stained enamel. During my last visit, I had a window that wouldn't stay up and a window shade that wouldn't stay down. You should ask to see your room before you hand over your credit card.

That said, I'd return here in a second because of its charm, its graciousness, and the good humor of the innkeepers (all the more remarkable since they've been running the place for more than a dozen years, which is about 175 in innkeeper's years). The inn also has nice details like guests' names on placecards at breakfast in the dining room. The old-fashioned downstairs parlors are great for cribbage or mingling with other guests; the front porch allows you to monitor the rather sedate comings and goings of Kearsarge Street.

Inexpensive

Albert B. Lester Memorial Hostel. 36 Washington St., Conway, NH 03818. ☎ **603/ 447-1001.** 45 beds. $16 per person. Rates include continental breakfast. JCB, MC, V. Closed Apr 1–15; Nov 20–26; Dec 18–25. Turn north at the light in Conway on Washington Street; it's the third house on the left.

Conveniently situated near the center of Conway Village, the Lester Hostel is the best choice for those traveling on a shoestring but not enamored of camping. Rooms in this gracious black and white farmhouse are set up hostel-style and accommodate 45 people (some family rooms are available), but guests, many of whom are young Europeans, generally spend their time in the yard knocking around a volleyball or availing themselves of the barbecue. Not only will you save money here, but the congenial atmosphere is a great way to swap tips on area trails and attractions with newfound friends. The hostel is open daily 7:30am to 9:30am, and 5 to 10pm.

WHERE TO DINE

Bellini's. 33 Seavey St., North Conway. ☎ **603/356-7000.** Reservations not accepted. Main courses $9.95–$18.95. AE, DC, DISC, MC, V. Sun–Thurs 5–10pm, Fri–Sat 5–11pm. Closed 2 weeks in Nov and 2 weeks during mud season. ITALIAN.

Bellini's has a fun, quirky interior that's more informal than its Victorian exterior might suggest. Inside it features Cinzano umbrellas and striped awnings, black and white checkerboard floors, and huge potted plants—it's the kind of place to put you in a good mood right off. And the food, which runs the Italian gamut from fettuccini chicken pesto to braciola, can only but further improve your spirits. The pleasantly garlicky marinara sauce is only a notch above average, but much of the rest of the fare shines brighter. Particularly good are the toasted raviolis. This is a great place to sup with a gaggle of friends or your extended family, but a moon-eyed couple might also find a quiet niche to make a romantic evening of it.

Shalimar of India. 27 Seavey St., North Conway. ☎ **603/356-0123** or 800/561-0023. Reservations recommended in peak summer and winter seasons. Main courses $7.95– $15.95 (most $9–$10). AE, DISC, MC, V. Mon–Sat 11am–3pm and 5–10pm; Sun noon–9pm. NORTHERN INDIAN.

Shalimar is a pleasant surprise in a town where adventurous ethnic cuisine used to mean nachos fully loaded. Opened in 1994 by the folks who run a restaurant of the same name in Portland, Maine, Shalimar offers a wide variety of tasty, tangy dishes of Northern India. The meals are wonderfully prepared, and the chef is very accommodating to ensure just the right level of spice for your palate. The restaurant, located a short walk from the village green, offers several tandoori dishes, and a wonderfully spicy lamb vindaloo. If you're truly famished after a day on the slopes or the trails, try the royal dinner for one, two, or four guests—it's a rich banquet of Indian flavors from soup to dessert.

Stonehurst Manor. Route 16 (1.2 miles north of the village), North Conway. ☎ **603/356-3113** or 800/525-9100. Reservations recommended. Main courses $7.75–$21; pizza $8.95–$12.95. MC, V. Daily 6–10pm. AMERICAN/PIZZA.

It's likely these are the most elegant surroundings in which you'll ever consume a pizza. Wood-fired pizza was added to the menu about a decade ago, just ahead of the national trend, when the restaurant noticed inn guests arriving late from Boston didn't feel up to a full meal. So they added pizza in a number of elegant variations (chicken sausage and wild mushrooms; lobster, shrimp, and calamari), and the word spread. The pizza became a local institution, complementing the other superb dishes served here.

Diners have a choice of four dining areas in this first floor of this sumptuous 1876 mansion, and each area is decorated informally and comfortably. (In the summer, head for the screened patio overlooking the garden.) In addition to pizza, the chef serves up a raft of other creative dishes, including wood-fired roast duck with blackberry sauce, and baked haddock in parchment with vegetables. If you have a lighter appetite, try the slightly bizarre but tasty crab and artichoke sandwich served on a soft pretzel.

JACKSON & ENVIRONS

Situated in picturesque valley just off Route 16 about 15 minutes' drive north of North Conway, Jackson is an eddy swirling gently on its own, just out of the flow of the tourist mainstream. You enter Jackson, somewhat tentatively, on a single-lane covered bridge. The village center is tiny, but touches of old world elegance remain here and there—vestiges of a time when Jackson was a premier destination for the East Coast affluent, who fled the summer heat in the cities to board at rambling wooden hotels or retire to shingled country estates.

With the Depression and the subsequent rise of the motel trade in the 1940s and '50s, Jackson and its old-fashioned hostelries slipped into a decades-long quiet slumber. Then along came the 1980s, which brought developers winging in and out of the valley in private helicopters, condo projects sprouting in fields where cows once roamed, and the resuscitation of a few vintage wooden hotels that didn't burn or collapse during the dark ages.

Thanks to a new golf course and one of the most elaborate and well-maintained cross-country ski networks in the country, Jackson is today again a thriving resort in summer and winter. It's still out of the mainstream, and a peaceful spot quite distant in character from more commercial North Conway. Settle in to one of the old summer homes converted to an inn, park your feet parked on a porch rail, and you'll notice that not all that much has changed in the intervening century.

ESSENTIALS
GETTING THERE   Jackson is just off Route 16 about 11 miles north of North Conway. Look for the covered bridge on the right when heading north.

VISITOR INFORMATION   The **Jackson Chamber of Commerce,** P.O. Box 304, Jackson, NH 03846 (☎ **603/383-9356** or 800/866-3334), can answer your questions about lodging and attractions.

EXPLORING MT. WASHINGTON
Mt. Washington is home to a number of superlatives. At 6,288 feet it's the highest mountain in the Northeast. (Mt. Mitchell in North Carolina is slightly higher, robbing Mt. Washington of the "highest in the east" title.) It's said to have the worst

weather in the world outside of the polar regions. And it holds the world's record for the highest surface wind speed—231 miles per hour, set in 1934. Consider also that winds over 150 miles per hour are routinely recorded every month except June, July, and August, the result of the mountain's location at the confluence of three major storm tracks.

Mt. Washington may also be the mountain with the most routes to the summit. Visitors can ascend by railroad (see the "Crawford Notch" section, below), by car, by van, or by foot. There's an annual bike race and foot race to the summit, and each year winter mountaineers test their mettle by inching their way to the top equipped with crampons and ice axes.

The summit of Mt. Washington is a well-developed place, and not the best destination for those seeking brutish wilderness. There's a train platform, a parking lot, a snack bar, a gift shop, a museum, and a handful of outbuildings, some of which house the weather observatory, which is staffed year-round. And there are the crowds, which can be thick on a clear day. Then again, on a clear day the views can't be beat, with vistas extending into four states and to the Atlantic Ocean.

The best place to learn about Mt. Washington and its approaches is the **Pinkham Notch Camp** (☎ **603/466-2721**), operated by the Boston-based Appalachian Mountain Club. Located at the crest of Route 16 between Jackson and Gorham, Pinkham Notch offers overnight accommodations and meals (see below), maps, a limited selection of outdoor supplies, and plenty of advice from helpful staff. A number of hiking trails depart from Pinkham Notch, allowing for several loops and sidetrips.

About a dozen trails lead to the mountain's summit, ranging in length from 3.8 to 15 miles. (See Peter Randall's *Mount Washington: A Guide and Short History*, mentioned above, for details.) The most direct and, in many ways, most dramatic trail is the Tuckerman Ravine Trail, which departs from Pinkham Notch. Healthy hikers should allow four to five hours for the ascent, an hour or two less for the return trip. Be sure to schedule in time to enjoy the dramatic glacial cirque of Tuckerman Ravine, which attracts extreme skiers to its snowy chutes and sheer drops as late as June, and often holds patches of snow well into summer.

The **Mt. Washington Auto Road** (☎ **603/466-3988**) opened in 1861 as a carriage road, and since then has been one of the most popular White Mountain attractions. The steep, winding 8-mile road (it has an average grade of 12 percent) is partially paved and incredibly dramatic; your breath will be taken away at one turn after another. The ascent will test your iron will; the descent will test your car's brakes. If you're nervous at all, consider that there have been only two fatalities in more than a century, attesting to the road's sound engineering.

If you'd prefer to leave the driving to someone else, custom vans ascend regularly allowing you to relax, enjoy the views, learn about the mountain from informed guides, and leave the fretting about overheating brakes to someone else.

The Auto Road, which is on Route 16 north of Pinkham Notch, is open mid-May to late-October from 7:30am to 6pm (shorter hours early and late in the season). The cost for cars is $15 for vehicle and driver, and $6 for each additional passenger ($4 for children 5–12). The fee includes use of an audiocassette featuring a narrator pointing out sights along the way. Van rates are $20 for adults; $10 for children 5 to 12.

One additional note: The average temperature atop the mountain is 30 degrees fahrenheit. (The record low was -43 degrees fahrenheit, and the warmest temperature ever recorded atop the mountain, in August, was 72 degrees fahrenheit.). Even in summer visitors should come prepared for blustery, cold conditions.

If you'd prefer to observe Mt. Washington from a safe and respectful distance, head up **Wildcat Mountain** (☎ 603/466-3326 or 800/255-6439) on the enclosed gondola for a superb view of Tuckerman Ravine and Mt. Washington's summit. The lift operates weekends from Memorial Day to mid-June, then daily through October. The base lodge is located just north of Pinkham Notch on Route 16.

CROSS-COUNTRY SKIING

Jackson regularly makes rankings of the top five cross-country ski resorts in the nation, and there's one reason for that: the nonprofit **Jackson Ski Touring Foundation** (☎ 603/383-9355), which created and now maintains the extensive trail network. The terrain around Jackson is wonderfully varied, with 93 miles of trails maintained by the foundation (56 miles are regularly groomed).

Start at the foundation headquarters in the middle of Jackson, then head right out the back door and ski through the village. Gentle trails traverse the valley floor, with more advanced trails heading up the flanking mountains. Snowmaking blankets 2.6 acres in the valley, helping to extend the season and keep conditions up to par. One-way ski trips with shuttles back to Jackson are also available; ask if you're interested. Trail fees are $10 for adults, $5 for children 10 to 15, and free for children under 10. Ski rentals are available at the Jack Frost ski shop adjacent to the ski center.

For advanced backcountry skiers, an especially appealing trek is the Wildcat Valley Trail. Begin by buying a one-ride ticket at Wildcat Mountain ski area, then head off the back of the mountain and follow signs toward Jackson. The 10-mile trail boasts a vertical descent of 3,245 feet, and makes for an exciting, adventurous afternoon expedition. Ask at the ski center for details.

Beginning cross-country skiers may prefer the gentle terrain at **Great Glen Trails** (☎ 603/466-2333), about 15 minutes' drive north on Route 16. This area has a relatively easy selection of nicely groomed trails at the base of Mount Washington, offering exceptionally picturesque views of the White Mountains' most impressive peaks. There's also an open, sunny base lodge with a cafeteria and ski shop. The center claims to have 32 miles of trails, but they loop around in a fairly tight area and the distance seems far smaller. As of 1996 the trail network didn't seem extensive enough to make it worth buying a full-day pass ($11 weekends), but a half-day pass is available ($9) for mornings or afternoons. The ski center plans to expand its trail network in the coming years, which should add more and varied terrain.

ALPINE SKIING

Black Mountain. Jackson, NH 03846. ☎ **603/383-4490** or 800/475-4669. Vertical drop: 1,100 feet. Lifts: 4. Skiable acreage: 98. Lift ticket: Weekend $30 adult, $20 junior; weekdays $14 all.

Dating back to the 1930s, Black Mount is one of the White Mountains' pioneer ski areas. It remains the quintessential family mountain—modest in size, entirely nonthreatening, and perfect for beginners. It offers some great views from the top to boot. It feels a bit like you're skiing in a farmer's unused hayfield, which just adds to the charm. The original lift was a tow where skiers held on to shovel handles to get to the top.

Wildcat. Route 16, Pinkham Notch, NH 03846. ☎ **603/466-3326** or 800/255-6439. Internet http://www.skiwildcat.com. Vertical drop: 2,100 feet. Lifts: 1 gondola, 5 chairlifts. Skiable acreage: 120. Lift ticket: Adult $37 weekends & holidays, $25 midweek; junior (6–12) $22 weekends & holidays, $19 midweek.

Wildcat Mountain has a strong heritage as a venerable New England ski mountain. It also happens to offers the best mountain views of any ski area in the Whites.

Situated on national forest land just across the valley from Mt. Washington and Tuckerman Ravine, Wildcat has strong intermediate trails and some challenging expert slopes, including a newly cut double diamond with 60 percent drops. This is skiing as it used to be—there's no base area clutter, just a simple ski lodge. While there's no on-slope accommodations, you've got an abundance of choices within 15 minutes' drive. Spend the night bunkhouse-style just up the road at AMC's Pinkham Notch Camp, or enjoy the luxury comforts of Jackson's inns. A short trip to the north is the unassuming town of Gorham, which offers several good motels at accommodating rates and a handful of basic-fare restaurants.

OTHER OUTDOOR PURSUITS

The Jackson area offers an abundance of outdoor activities. In addition to exploring around Mt. Washington, hiking opportunities abound in the Carter Range to the north and on the various peaks surrounding Mt. Washington. Space here doesn't permit even a brief inventory of trails. Consult the *AMC White Mountain Guide,* or ask for advice from your innkeeper.

One suggested four-hour (round trip) hike offering a superb view is to the top of Doublehead. The hike departs from a trail head located 2.9 miles east of Jackson on Dundee Road. Views of the Presidential Range may be had from scattered ledges off the summits of both North and South Doublehead; it's a prime place to weigh more ambitious hiking options.

A new outdoor recreation facility north of the village is **Great Glen Trails** (☎ 603/466-2333), which opened in 1995 near the Mt. Washington Auto Road entrance. This network of trails offers hiking and mountain biking on scenic, gentle carriage path-like trails near the base of Mt. Washington. Walking is free (donations are encouraged); a full day bike pass is $9. Mountain bike rentals are $28 per day, and include a helmet and bike pass.

Golfers can tee up at the scenic **Wentworth Golf Resort** (☎ 603/383-9126), whose fairways and greens wend their way in and around the village of Jackson. The 17th hole even includes a covered bridge. Golf is also available in the pastoral upland valley spread out before the **Eagle Mountain House** (☎ 603/363-9111), a short drive from Jackson up beautiful Carter Notch Road.

A most agreeable way to spend the day is at Jackson Falls, along Carter Notch Road, just above the Wentworth Resort. A series of cataracts tumble down the rocky hillside, forming pools here and there that are custom-made for soaking on warm afternoon. Bring a book and while away a few peaceful hours.

KID STUFF

Parents with young children who find majestic mountains only slightly less interesting than veal aspic can buy brief peace of mind at two area attractions. **Story Land,** at the northern junction of Routes 16 and 302 (☎ 603/383-4293), is filled with improbably leaning buildings, magical rides, fairy-tale creatures, and other enchanted beings. Kids can take a ride in a Pumpkin Coach, float in a swan boat, ride the watery "Bamboo Chute," or spin on a lively carousel. A new "sprayground" opened in 1996, featuring a 40-foot happy octopus—if they're so inclined, kids can get a good summer soaking. Live shows and snacks easily fill out an afternoon. Story Land is open daily mid-June through Labor Day 9am to 6pm, and Labor Day to Columbus Day on weekends from 10am to 5pm. Admission, which includes all rides and entertainment, is $16 for visitors over 4 years old.

Next door is **Heritage New Hampshire** (☎ 603/383-9776), which endeavors to make state history easily digestible for both adults and kids. It's an indoor theme park in a Georgian-style building with a theme of old-time New Hampshire. Visitors learn about the famous Concord Coach and hear prominent politician Daniel Webster "speak" about his life and times. You'll come away with some context for the rest of your stay in the state. The museum is open daily mid-May to mid-October 9am until 5pm (until 6pm mid-June to Labor Day). Admission is $8 adults, $4.50 children 6 to 12, and free under 6.

WHERE TO STAY & DINE

Eagle Mountain House. Carter Notch Road, Jackson, NH 03846. ☎ **603/383-9111** or 800/ 966-5779. Fax 603/383-0854. 93 rms. TV TEL. $79–$149 double; $109–$169 suite. AE, DC, DISC, MC, V.

The Eagle Mountain House is a fine and handsome relic that happily survived the ravages of time, fire, and the capricious tastes of tourists. Built in 1916 and fully renovated in 1986, this five-story wooden classic is set in an idyllic valley above the village of Jackson. The lobby is rich with earth tones, polished brass, and oak accenting.

The guest rooms, set off wonderfully wide and creaky hallways, are furnished with a country pine look and feature stencilled blanket chests, pine armoires, and feather comforters. There's a premium for rooms with mountain views, but it's not really worth the extra cash. Just plan to spend your free time lounging on the wide porch with the views across the golf course toward the mountains beyond.

Dining/Entertainment: There's a handsome oak tavern off the lodge. The spacious, formal dining rooms seat about 150 guests, and provoke a distinct "well-here-we-are!" sense of glee when you first settle in for dinner under the high ceilings. The menu features creative New England classics, with offerings like Maine lobster pie and roasted cranberry duck.

Facilities: Other amenities include a nine-hole golf course, lighted tennis courts, a heated outdoor pool, and a small health club.

✪ **Inn at Thorn Hill.** Thorn Hill Road (P.O. Box A), Jackson, NH 03846. ☎ **603/383-4242.** 19 rms (some with showers only). $140–$200 double, including breakfast and dinner; peak season (foliage and Christmas) $176–$232; cottages $230–$275. AE, DC, DISC, MC, V.

This is a truly elegant inn. Housed in a classic shingle style home designed by Stanford White in 1895 (although now swathed in yellow siding), the Inn at Thorn Hill is just outside of town, surrounding by wooded hills that seem to greet it in a warm embrace. Inside, there's a comfortable Victorian feel, although mercifully sparing on the frilly stuff. The two sitting parlors are well-designed for lounging—one boasts a woodstove, piano, and views toward the mountains (cookies and tea are served here in the afternoon). There's also a TV room with jigsaw puzzles and a decent selection of books on the shelves. Classical music is piped throughout.

Dining/Entertainment: The dining room is decorated in what might be called Victorian great-aunt style, with rich green carpeting, press-backed oak chairs, and pink tablecloths. The inn serves some of the best meals in the valley.

The Lodge at Pinkham Notch. Route 16, Pinkham Notch, NH (Mailing address: AMC, 5 Joy St., Boston, MA 02108). ☎ **603/466-2727.** 108 beds in bunkrooms of 2, 3, and 4 beds. All have shared bath. Sun to Fri (except Aug) $45 per adult, $27 per child, including breakfast and dinner (discount for AMC members); Sat and Aug, $50 adult, $32 child. MC, V.

Guests flock to the Pinkham Notch Camp for the camaraderie as much as for the accommodations. Situated spectacularly at the base of Mt. Washington and with easy access to numerous hiking trails, the lodge is operated like a Scandinavian youth hostel, with guests sharing bunk rooms with new friends, and enjoying boisterous, filling meals at long family-style tables in the main lodge. A zealous warden even walks the hallways near dawn beating a pot with a wooden spoon to ensure no slackers try to shirk their obligation to GET UP AND HIKE!

The accommodations are spartan and basic, but that's overcome by the often festive atmosphere. Think of it as a field trip with a bunch of excitable teens—although the teens in this case often happen to be hardy mountain veterans in their 60s or 70s. In the winter I've been awoken in the pre-dawn darkness by eager mountaineers preparing their ascents in the parking lot to blaring Grateful Dead tapes. In the summer, I've spent hours swapping late-night tips on hiking destinations with grizzled hikers twice my age. It's not a place to be an introvert, but it is a place to feel part of the rich heritage of local mountain recreation.

Wentworth Resort Hotel. Jackson, NH 03846. ☎ **603/383-9700** or 800/637-0013. Fax 603/383-4265. 58 rms. A/C TV TEL. Weekdays $59–$119 double; weekends $89–$159 double. Higher rates during foliage season and Christmas week; discounts available Mar to mid-June. AE, MC, V.

The venerable Wentworth sits in the middle of Jackson Village, all turrets and eaves and awnings. Built in 1869, this Victorian shingled inn edged to the brink of deterioration in the mid-1980s, but was pulled back by a plucky entrepreneur, who added a number of condominium clusters around the golf course. The large guest rooms are good value for the money, decorated with a Victorian grace and elegance. Some rooms feature fireplaces, whirlpools, or clawfoot tubs.

Dining/Entertainment: The dining room is well-respected, serving up regional favorites like garlic and herb chicken and chargrilled salmon.

Facilities: It's no challenge to find something to do in the area. The inn has its own century-old, 18-hole PGA golf course, clay tennis courts, billiards (on an enclosed porch), and close proximity to hiking. For swimming, there's an outdoor heated pool, or you can stroll just up the road and plunge into the cold waters of Jackson Falls. In winter, you can cross-country ski out the door.

Wildcat Inn & Tavern. Route 16A, Jackson, NH 03846. ☎ **603/383-4245** or 800/228-4245. 15 rms, some with shower only, 2 with hall bathrooms. $84–$114 double. Rates include breakfast. AE, DC, MC, V.

The Wildcat Inn occupies a three-story farmhouse-style building in the middle of Jackson, directly across from the cross-country ski center. It's a comfortable, informal kind of place, better known for its restaurant and tavern than for its accommodations. Most guest rooms are cozy, two-rooms suites, carpeted and furnished eclectically. Sitting rooms typically contain contemporary sofas, chairs, and pine furniture, and offer cozy sanctuary after a day of hiking or skiing.

Dining/Entertainment: The downstairs dining room is in country farmhouse style, with old wood floors and pine furniture. Country-style meals are prepared with considerable flair, and include a tenderloin of beef topped with lobster, asparagus and Hollandaise sauce (main courses are $14.95 to $20.95). In the winter, the smart money stakes out a toasty spot in front of the tavern fireplace—one of the most popular gathering spots in the valley—to sip soothing libations and order from the bar menu, which has lighter fare like chicken quesadillas and spanakopita ($6.95 to $8.95).

CRAWFORD NOTCH

Crawford Notch is a wild, rugged mountain valley that runs through the heart of the White Mountains. Within the notch itself lies a lot of legend and history. For years after its discovery by Timothy Nash in 1771, it was an impenetrable wilderness, creating a barrier to commerce by blocking trade between the upper Connecticut River

Valley and commercial harbors in Portland and Portsmouth. That was eventually surmounted by a plucky crew who hauled the first freight through.

As the traffic picked up, the Crawford family offered lodging to the first teamsters, and later to the tourists who flocked here to experience the sublime feelings of raw nature. The Crawfords also led tours to the summit of Mt. Washington, and built the first horseback trail.

Nathaniel Hawthorne immortalized the notch with his short story about a real-life 1826 tragedy, in which the Willey family fled their home during a tempest when they heard an avalanche roaring toward the valley floor. The avalanche divided above the inn and spared the structure; the seven who fled were killed in tumbling debris. The only survivors were the family dog and two oxen. (You can still visit the site of the Willey home today.)

The notch is accessible along Route 302, which is wide and speedy on the lower sections, and becomes challenging only in its steepness as it approaches the narrow defile of the notch itself. (Modern engineering has taken most of the kinks out of the road.) The views up the cliffs from the road can be spectacular on a clear day; on an overcast or drizzly day, the effect is slightly foreboding and medieval.

ESSENTIALS

GETTING THERE   Route 302 runs through Crawford Notch about 25 miles from the towns of Bartlett and Twin Mountain.

VISITOR INFORMATION   **Twin Mountain Chamber of Commerce,** P.O. Box 194, Twin Mountain, NH 03595 (☎ **603/846-5407** or 800/245-8946), offers general information and lodging referrals at their information booth near the intersection of Routes 302 and 3. Open year round, but hours are shorter in the off-season.

WATERFALLS & SWIMMING HOLES

Much of the land flanking Route 302 falls under the auspices of Crawford Notch State Park, which was established in 1911 to preserve land that elsewhere had been decimated by aggressive logging. The headwaters of the Saco River form in the notch, and what's generally regarded as the first permanent trail up Mt. Washington also departs from here. Several turn-outs and trail heads invite a more leisurely exploration of the area. The trail network on both sides of Crawford Notch is extensive; consult the *AMC White Mountain Guide* for detailed information.

Engorged by snowmelt in the spring, the Saco River courses through the notch's granite ravines and winds past sizeable boulders that have been left by retreating glaciers and crashed down from the mountainsides above. It's a popular destination among serious whitewater boaters, and makes for a good spectator sport if you're here early in the season. During the lazy days of summer, the Saco offers several good swimming holes just off the highway. They're unmarked, but where you see cars parked off the side of the road for no apparent reason, you should be able to find your way to a good spot for soaking and splashing.

Up the mountain slopes that form the valley, hikers will spot a number of superb waterfalls, some more easily accessible than others. A day spent exploring the falls is a day well spent. A few to start with:

Arethusa Falls has the highest single drop of any waterfall in the state, and the trail to the falls passes several attractive smaller cascades en route. These are especially beautiful in the spring or after a heavy rain, when the falls are at their fullest. The trip can be done as a 2.6 mile round trip to the falls and back on Arethusa Falls Trail, or as a 4.5 mile loop hike that includes views from stunning Frankenstein Cliffs.

If you're arriving from the south, look for signs to the trail parking area shortly after passing the Crawford Notch State Park entrance sign. From the north, the trail head is $^1/_2$ mile south of the Dry River Campground. At the parking lot, look for the sign and map to get your bearings, then cross the railroad tracks to start up the falls trail.

Another hike begins a short drive north on Route 302. Reaching tumultuous **Ripley Falls** requires an easy hike of a little more than one mile round trip. Look for the sign to the falls on Route 302 just north of the trail head for Webster Cliff Trail. (If you pass the Willey House site, you've gone too far.) Drive in a bit and park at the site of the Willey Station. Follow trail signs for the Ripley Falls Trail, and allow about a half-hour to reach the cascades. The most appealing swimming holes are at the top of the falls.

Two attractive falls may be seen from the roadway at the head of the notch, just east of the crest. Flume Cascades and Silver Cascades tumble down the hills in white braids that are especially appealing during a misty summer rain. These falls were among the most popular sites in the region when tourists alighted at the train station about one mile away. They aren't nearly as spectacular as the two mentioned above, but they're accessible if you're in a hurry. Travelers can park in the lots along the road's edge for a better view.

A HISTORIC RAILWAY

Mt. Washington Cog Railway. Route 302, Bretton Woods. ☎ **603/846-5404** or 800/ 922-8825. Fare $35 adults, $24 children 6–12, under 5 free. Runs daily Memorial Day through late Oct, plus weekends in May. Frequent departures; call for schedule. Reservations recommended during peak season.

The cog railway was a marvel of engineering when it opened in 1869, and it remains so today. Part moving museum, part slow-motion roller coaster ride, the cog railway steams to the summit with a determined "I think I can" pace of about 4 miles per hour. But there's still a frisson of excitement on the way up and back, especially when the train crosses Jacob's Ladder, a rickety-seeming trestle 25 feet high that angles upward at a grade of more than 37 percent. Passengers enjoy the expanding view in relative comfort on this three-hour round trip (there are stops to add water to the steam engine, to check the track switches, and to allow other trains to ascend or descend). There's also a 20-minute stop at the summit to browse around.

It's hard to imagine anyone not enjoying this trip—from kids marveling at the ratchety-ratchety noises and the thick plume of black smoke, to curious adults trying to figure out how the cog system works, to naturalists who get superb views of the boney, brawny uplands leading to Mt. Washington's summit.

SKIING

Attitash Bear Peak. Route 302, Bartlett, NH 03812. ☎ **603/374-2368** or 800/223-7669. Vertical drop: 1,750 feet. Lifts: 10 chairlifts (including 1 high-speed quad), 1 surface lift. Skiable acreage: 214. Lift ticket: $43 weekends & holidays, $35 weekdays.

Attitash expanded in 1994 to include the adjacent 1,000-foot-high Bear Peak. The new area includes five trails and some new base facilities, which has taken some pressure off the main lift lines. Attitash is a good intermediate-to-advanced skier mountain with a selection of great cruising runs and a few that are somewhat more challenging. The base lodge is modern if unexciting. There's not much happening locally at night, so those still looking for action typically head to North Conway.

The ski area also offers a smart ticket program, which allows skiers to buy as many "points" as they'd like on a ticket. Points are deducted for each run (more points on weekends and on longer lifts). The advantage? If conditions deteriorate or if you're seized by the urge to shop in North Conway, you can do so then use up the rest of your points the next day. Points can also be transferred to others and are good for two years from date of purchase.

Bretton Woods. Route 302, Bretton Woods, NH 03575. ☎ **603/278-5000** or 800/232-2972. Vertical drop: 1,500'. Lifts: 4 chairlifts (including 1 high-speed quad), 1 surface lift. Skiable acreage: 150. Lift ticket: Adults $38 weekends & holidays, $31 weekdays; children 6–15 $25 weekends & holidays, $15 midweek.

Bretton Woods is a solid beginner-to-intermediate mountain with great views of Mt. Washington and a pleasant family atmosphere. The resort does a good job with kids, and offers some nice intermediate cruising runs and limited night skiing. There's even a speedy detachable quad chair, which skiers don't often find at resorts of this size. Accommodations are available on the mountain and nearby, but evening entertainment tends to revolve around hot tubs, TVs, and going to bed early. There's also an excellent cross-country ski center nearby.

WHERE TO STAY & DINE

The Bernerhof. Route 302, Glen, NH. ☎ **603/383-4414** or 800/548-8007. Fax 603/383-0809. 9 rms. A/C TV TEL. $69–$139 double including full breakfast; $119–$189 double including breakfast and dinner. Two-night minimum during peak season. AE, MC, V.

Situated off busy Route 302 en route to Crawford Notch, The Bernerhof occupies a century-old home that's all gables and turrets on the outside. Inside, the guest rooms are equally eclectic and fun, crafted with odd angles and corners. All are tastefully furnished in an elegant country style that's sparing with the frou-frou. Head for the roomy suites on the third floor—Room 8 is especially wonderful, with a Jacuzzi under a skylight, wood floors, a brass bed, and a handsome cherry armoire.

Dining/Entertainment: Downstairs, the rustic Black Bear Pub is all oakey and mellow—the type of place where you can relax with aplomb. There's a bear skin on the wall and 63 varieties of beers. The decor in the adjacent dining room is less inspired, but the food is superb and draws gourmands for miles. (The inn also hosts regular cooking schools.) Middle European fare, including several delicious veal dishes, is the specialty, but other creative entrees are available, like the chicken wallbanger, the inn's "moderately famous" dish of chicken breast layered with pesto, ham, and smoked gouda cheese. Dining is open to the public nightly, with entrees ranging from $15.95 to $21.95.

Mount Washington Hotel. Route 302, Bretton Woods, NH 03575. ☎ **603/278-1000** or 800/258-0330. 195 rms (6 with shower only). TEL. Midweek $185–$280 double, up to $585 suite, including breakfast and dinner; weekends and holidays $225–$315 double. AE, DISC, MC, V. Closed mid-Oct to mid-May.

Your first response to the Mount Washington Hotel will likely be one of disbelief. It seems as if some bizarre Edwardian glacier had flowed down from the mountains and settled resolutely in the valley. This five-story wooden resort, with its gleaming white clapboard and cherry-red roof, seems something out of a fable. Built in 1902 by railroad and coal magnate Joseph Stickney ("Look at me gentlemen . . . for I am the poor fool who built all this," he said at the grand opening), the resort attracted luminaries in its glory days like Babe Ruth, Thomas Edison, Woodrow Wilson, and silent-screen star Mary Pickford. In 1944 it hosted the famed Bretton Woods International Monetary Conference, which secured the dollar's role as the world's currency.

After large resorts fell out of fashion, the Mount Washington went through a succession of owners and fell on hard times. Threatened with demolition and put on the auction block in 1991, it was purchased for just over $3 million by a group of dedicated local business folks who launched the long process of bringing it back from the brink. Being frugal Yankees, they're renovating with operating profit, not with borrowed money, but the improvements are moving along nicely.

The guest rooms are furnished simply but comfortably (TVs are available only on request), but as at most other grand resorts, The Mount Washington was designed around public areas. Wide hallways and elegant common areas on the first floor invite strolling and indolence. A broad 900-foot wraparound veranda makes for relaxing afternoons.

The main hotel is open only seasonally, but three other properties—including a smaller 1896 inn, a motor inn, and contemporary townhomes—are open year-round. All in all, a trip to The Mount Washington is a fanciful trip back in time.

Dining/Entertainment: Meals are enjoyed in the impressive octagonal dining room, which was designed such that no guest would be slighted by being seated in a corner. (Jackets are requested for men at dinner.) In the evening, there's dancing to the house orchestra.

Facilities: 27-hole golf course, 12 red-clay tennis courts.

✪ **Notchland Inn.** Route 302, Hart's Location, NH 03812. ☎ **603/374-6131** or 800/866-6131. Fax 603/374-6168. 11 rms, 7 with shower only. Midweek $150–$170 double, including breakfast and dinner; weekends $170–$190; foliage season and holidays $180–$230. AE, DISC, MC, V.

The Notchland Inn appears just off the road in a wild, remote section of the valley, looking every bit like a redoubt in a Sir Walter Scott novel. Built of hand-cut granite between 1840 and 1862 by a prosperous Boston dentist, Notchland is today a superior inn perfectly situated for exploring the wilds of the White Mountains by day and basking in luxury at night. All 11 guest rooms are well-appointed with antiques and traditional furniture, and all feature fireplaces, high ceilings, and individual thermostats.

A stay here typically begins with a brief tour of the home, including the common rooms, one of which was remodeled at the turn of the century by Gustav Stickley himself, the father of the Mission Style. There are other treasures to be found, like an original oil painting by George L. Frankenstein, the prominent 19th-century artist whose name graces nearby cliffs, and a wood-fired hot tub in a gazebo overlooking a small pond. The Notchland is a no-smoking inn.

Dining/Entertainment: Dinners in the newly renovated dining room are as eclectic as they are well-prepared, and might feature Thai curries, gado-gado (a savory Malaysian salad), or three-pepper-crusted roast beef. Dinners are served at 7pm, and are available to the public (space permitting) at a prix fixe of $30.

WATERVILLE VALLEY & LINCOLN

On the southwestern edge of the White Mountains are two ski resorts tucked away in mountain valleys. Both have blossomed in recent years, not always with favorable results. Waterville Valley, which lies at the end of a 12-mile dead-end road, was the first to be developed. Incorporated as a town in 1829, Waterville Valley became a popular destination for summer travelers during the heyday of mountain travel late in the 19th century. Skiers first started descending the slopes in the 1930s after a few ski trails were hacked out of the forest by the Civilian Conservation Corps and local ski clubs. But it wasn't until 1965, when a skier named Tom Corcoran bought 425 acres in the valley, that Waterville began to assume its current modern air.

While the village has a decidedly manufactured character (it easily has as many parking lots as the average regional mall), Corcoran's vision has kept the growth within bounds. There's not much in the way of sprawl here; the village is reasonably compact, with modern lodges, condos, and restaurants clustered around the "Town Square," itself a sort of mall complex. The architecture is inspired by New England vernacular; there's not a Swiss chalet to be found. The village is also quite pleasant in summer, when the place abounds with outdoor activities like mountain biking, hiking, and swimming.

Some 25 miles to the north is Loon Mountain, which is located just outside the former paper mill town of Lincoln. (That's the distance by major roads in winter; it's shorter in summer by crossing Thornton Gap on Triploli Road.) The resort was first conceived in the early 1960s by Sherman Adams, a former New Hampshire governor and Eisenhower administration official. The mountain opened in 1966 and was quickly criticized for its mediocre skiing, but continual upgrading and expanding since then has brought the mountain greater respect.

Loon has since evolved from a friendly intermediate mountain served by a few motels to a friendly intermediate mountain served by dozens of condos and vast, modern hotels. Lincoln seems to embrace sprawl with the same zeal Waterville Valley shuns it. At times it seems that Lincoln underwent not so much a development boom in the 1980s as a violent development spasm. Clusters of chicken-coop style homes and condos now blanket the lower hillsides of this narrow valley, and fast-food restaurants and strip-mall-style shops line Route 112 from I-93 to the mountain.

The Loon area includes the adjacent towns of Lincoln and Woodstock on either side of I-93. Woodstock has more of the feel of a town that's lived in year-round. The Lincoln and Loon Mt. base village are both lively with skiers in the winter, but in the summer the area can have a post-nuclear fallout feel to it, with lots of homes but few people in evidence despite efforts to stage special events like lumberjack shows. The ambience is also compromised by that peculiar style of resort architecture that's simultaneously aggressive and bland.

ESSENTIALS

GETTING THERE   Waterville Valley is located 12 miles northwest of Exit 29 on I-93 via Route 49. Lincoln is accessible off I-93 on exits 32 and 33.

VISITOR INFORMATION   The **Waterville Valley Chamber of Commerce,** RFD #1, Box 1067, Campton, NH 03223 (☎ **603/726-3804** or 800/237-2307), staffs an information booth on Route 49 in Campton, just off I-93. The **Lincoln-Woodstock Chamber of Commerce,** P.O. Box 358, Lincoln, NH 03251 (☎ **603/745-6621** or 800/227-4191), has an information office open business hours at Depot Plaza on Route 112 in Lincoln.

The most comprehensive place for information about the region from Lincoln northward is the **White Mountains Visitor Center,** P.O. Box 10, North Woodstock, NH 03262 (☎ **603/745-8720** or 800/346-3687), located just east of Exit 32 on I-93. They'll send a visitor's kit, and they offer brochures and answer questions from their center, which is open 8:30am to 5pm daily.

HIKING & MOUNTAIN BIKING

Impressive mountain peaks tower over both Lincoln and Waterville Valley, making both areas great for hiking and mountain biking. As always, your single best source of information is the *AMC's White Mountain Guide,* which offers a comprehensive directory of area trails. Also check with Forest Service staff at the White Mountains Visitor Center for information on local outdoor destinations.

From Waterville Valley, a popular four-hour hike runs to the summit of Mt. Tecumseh, the shoulders of which host skiers in winter. The hiking trail starts about 100 yards north of the ski lodge, and offers wonderful views as you climb. From the 4,003-foot summit, you can return via the Sosman Trail, which winds its way down beneath the ski lifts and along ski runs closed for summer.

Outdoor novices who prefer their adventures neatly packaged will enjoy the **Waterville Valley Base Camp** (☎ 800/468-2553). The "camp," located at the Waterville Valley Town Square, offers mountain bike rentals, in-line skates, guided tours, lift access for bikers and hikers, and information on area trails. Rates start at $5 for a single ride on the lift, to $55 for a private four-hour guided hike.

In the Lincoln area, a level trail that's excellent for hikers in any physical shape is the Wilderness Trail along the East Branch of the Pemigewasset River. Head eastward on Route 112 (the Kancamagus Highway) from I-93 for 5 miles then watch for the parking lot on the left just past the bridge. Both sides of the river may be navigated; the Wilderness Trail on the west side runs just over three miles to beautiful, remote Black Pond; on the east side, an abandoned railroad bed makes for smooth mountain biking. The two trails may be linked by fording the river where the railbed is crossed by a gate.

The **Loon Mountain Bike Center** (☎ 603/745-8111, ext. 5566) offers more than 70 mountain bikes for rent at its facility at the mountain's base. There's also in-line skating at **Loon's skating center** (☎ 603/745-8111, ext. 5568), which features a skate arena and half-pipe.

Additionally, hikers will find easy access to various trail heads along the Kancamagus Highway (see below).

THE KANCAMAGUS HIGHWAY

The Kancamagus Highway—locally called "The Kanc"—is the White Mountain's most spectacular road. Officially designated a national scenic byway by the U.S. Forest Service, the 34-mile roadway joins Lincoln with Conway through 2,860-foot Kancamagus Pass. When the highway was built in 1960–61, it opened up 100 square miles of wilderness—a move that irked preservationists but has proven wildly popular with more casual tourists.

The route begins and ends along wide, tumbling rivers on relatively flat plateaus. The two-lane road, which is almost entirely within the boundaries of the national forest, rises steadily to the pass. Several rest areas with sweeping vistas allow visitors to pause and enjoy the mountain views. The highway also makes a good destination for hikers; any number of day and overnight trips may be launched from the roadside. One simple, short hike along a gravel pathway (it's less than $1/3$ mile each way) leads to Sabbaday Falls, a cascade that's especially impressive after a downpour. Six national forest campgrounds are also located along the highway.

Be sure to take your time and stop frequently. Think of it as a scavenger hunt as you look for a covered bridge, cascades with good swimming holes, a historic home with a fascinating story behind it, and spectacular mountain panoramas. All these things and more are along the route.

The highway is popular with serious bikers in training, but it's also a strong draw for casual peddlers in reasonable physical shape. The shoulders are wide enough to accommodate both bikes and RVs, and the grade is reasonably forgiving, especially on the eastern slope. Make sure your brakes are in good working order before setting off down the long descent.

SKIING

Loon Mountain. Lincoln, NH 03251. ☎ **603/745-8111,** or 800/227-4191 for lodging. Internet: http://www.mainstream.net/~loon/. Vertical drop: 2,100 feet. Lifts: 6 chairlifts

(1 high-speed), 1 high-speed gondola, 1 surface lift. Skiable acreage: 250. Lift tickets: $43 weekends, $36 weekdays.

Located on U.S. Forest Service land, Loon has been stymied in past expansion efforts by environmental concerns regarding land use and water withdrawals from the river. Loon finally got the go-ahead for limited expansion in 1994, and is now in the midst of a $12 million, six-year effort to expand and reshape the ski mountain, add uphill capacity, and improve snowmaking. That should reduce some of the congestion of this popular area and open up more room to roam. Today, most of the trails still cluster toward the bottom, and most are solid intermediate runs. Experts head to the north peak, which has a challenging selection of advanced trails served by a triple chairlift.

Waterville Valley. Waterville Valley, NH 03215. ☎ **603/236-8311** or 800/468-2553. Vertical drop: 2,020 feet. Lifts: 9 chairlifts (1 high speed), 4 surface lifts. Skiable acreage: 255. Lift tickets: $43 weekends, $37 weekdays.

While Waterville Valley has some good, steep drops, it's known mostly as a superb intermediate's mountain. There's been an effort to upgrade the mountain and offer more challenging trails, but recent turnovers put future improvements somewhat in limbo. (The ski area was purchased by New England ski-resort king Les Otten in 1996, but the U.S. Justice Department later ordered him to divest.) In 1995–96 the mountain opened a skiing glade (called Wide Weald), just off a double-diamond bump trail.

The ski resort has also taken strides to accommodate snowboarders—management built a snowboard playground called The Boneyard on Mt. Tecumseh (it features a bus buried up to its roof in snow and some hairy jumps), and it decreed that Snow Mountain (the beginners' mountain) is open only to snowboarders on weekends. (Snowboarders are welcome anywhere else on the mountain as well, of course.) There's also a good snowboard shop in the base complex.

WHERE TO STAY
In Waterville Valley
Golden Eagle Lodge. Snowsbrook Road, Waterville Valley, NH 03215. ☎ **603/236-4600** or 800/910-4499. Fax 603/236-4947. 118 rms. TV TEL. Winter $89–$239 per unit; summer $117–$177 per unit; spring $78–$138 per unit. Rates vary according to season and time of week. Premium charged on holidays. All rates subject to 7% "resort fee." Children stay free in parent's room. AE, DC, DISC, MC, V.

This sprawling, contemporary condominium project is centrally located in the village and is the most regal of the bunch. The lodge can accommodate two to six people in one and two-bedroom units, all of which have kitchens and basic cookware. The five-story resort strives for a modern-meets-rustic lodge appearance, generally to good effect. But guests don't travel great distances for the decor here; they come for the resort's amenities and location (an easy shuttle-bus ride to the slopes).

Facilities: There's an indoor pool and whirlpool on site. Room rates also include unlimited access to a nearby $2 million athletic facility, which features steam rooms, fitness room, indoor jogging track, and indoor racquet courts (an additional charge applies for the courts). In summer, guests also get 18 holes of free golf (midweek only) and the use of clay tennis courts.

Snowy Owl Inn. Village Rd., Waterville Valley, NH 03215. ☎ **603/236-8383** or 800/766-9969. Fax 603/236-4890. 80 rms. TV TEL. $89–$239 double. Discounts in off-season and summer. Rates include continental breakfast. AE, DISC, MC, V.

The Snowy Owl will appeal to those who like the amiable character of a country inn, but demand all the modern conveniences. Another modern resort project near Town

Square, it offers a number of pleasant extras like a towering fieldstone fireplace in the lobby and a rooftop observatory that offers a fine panorama of the surrounding hills. The rooms are basic motel-style rooms decently furnished and featuring pine accenting; about half have whirlpools and wet bars, and a few feature air-conditioning.

Facilities: There are indoor and outdoor pools and a game room, and rates include access to the valley athletic club and its numerous amenities.

In Lincoln & Woodstock

In addition to the places listed below, Lincoln offers a range of motels that will appeal to budget travelers. Among those worth seeking out are the **Kancamagus Motor Lodge** (☎ 603/745-3365 or 800/346-4205), the **Mountaineer Motel** (☎ 603/745-2235 or 800/356-0046), and **Woodward's Motor Inn** (☎ 603/745-8141 or 800/635-8968).

Mountain Club at Loon. Route 112 (R.R. 1; Box 40), Lincoln, NH 03251. ☎ **603/745-2244** or 800/229-7829. Fax 603/745-2317. 234 rms. A/C TV TEL. Winter midweek $109–$399 double, weekend $189–$499 double; summer and off-season starting at $79 double. AE, DC, DISC, MC, V.

Set at the edge of Loon Mountain's slopes, the Mountain Club is a huge, contemporary resort built during the real estate boom of the 1980s. It was managed for several years as a Marriott, and the decor tends to reflect its chain-hotel heritage. The lobby is done up in dark green tones with leather-like couches arrayed before a polished granite fireplace, and the rooms are adorned with copious oak veneer. Guest rooms are designed to be rented either individually or as a two-room suite; each pair features one traditional hotel-style bedroom with king-size bed, and one studio with a kitchen, sitting area, and a fold-down queen-size bed.

Facilities: The prime attraction of the resort (second to the ski-out-the-door access to the slopes) is the superb athletic facilities, which are connected via an enclosed walkway. There's an indoor and outdoor pool, small indoor basketball court, walleyball court, aerobics rooms, two outdoor tennis courts, a well-equipped fitness room, game room, and a heated outdoor whirlpool that's especially enjoyable during the deep freeze of winter. The free covered parking will be appreciated during heavy snowstorms, as will the resort's in-house restaurant and lounge.

The Mill House Inn. Route 112 (P.O. Box 696), Lincoln, NH 03251. ☎ **603/745-6261** or 800/654-6183. 95 rms. A/C TV TEL. Midweek $70–$125 double; weekend $95–$140 double. Discounts during summer and shoulder seasons. AE, DC, DISC, MC, V.

This middle-range, modern hotel is part of a larger complex called The Mill at Loon Mountain, which also includes condos and an all-suite hotel within a short drive. Conveniently located in the town of Lincoln with its restaurants and shopping (there's a free shuttle bus two miles to the slopes in winter), the Mill House is connected via an enclosed walkway to the Millfront Marketplace, a shopping center cobbled together from an old paper mill and some newly built structures. The lobby is tastefully done in a country-inn style; guest rooms are basic but decently decorated. The best rooms face the outdoor pool and the mountains; these also have private balconies.

Facilities: The inn boasts indoor and outdoor pools, a fitness room, and a game room.

Woodstock Inn. Main Street (P.O. Box 118), North Woodstock, NH 03262. ☎ **603/745-3951** or 800/321-3985. Fax 603/745-3701. 19 rms (11 with private bath). A/C TV TEL. Summer and winter $54–$135 double; foliage season $75–$140 double; off-season $39–$95 double. Rates include breakfast. AE, DC, DISC, MC, V.

Woodstock Station shares some qualities with Dr. Jekyll and Mr. Hyde. In the front, it's a fusty white Victorian with black shutters amid Woodstock's downtown commercial area. In the back, it's a modern, boisterous brew pub that serves up tasty fare along with its robust ales (see below). The inn features 19 guest rooms spread among three houses. If you're on a tight budget, go for the shared-bath rooms in the main house and the nearby Deachman house; the slightly less personable Riverside building across the street offers rooms with private baths, but at a premium. Rooms are individually decorated in a country Victorian style, furnished with both reproductions and antiques. There's a pervasive aroma of sachet and cedar in the main building that adds to the period mood. Woodstock Station is a fun place to hang your hat, and is the best local alternative to modern, oversized hotels.

WHERE TO DINE

Woodstock Station. Main Street. ☎ **603/745-3951.** Reservations accepted for Clement Room only. Breakfast items $3.95–$9.50; lunch and dinner items $5.49–$15.99 (dinner in Clement Room $11.95–$19.95). AE, DC, DISC, MC, V. Serving 7:30–11:30am, 11:30am–10pm (Woodstock Station), 5:30–9:30pm (Clement Room). PUB FARE/AMERICAN.

You've got a choice here: dine amid the Victorian frippery of the Clement Room on the enclosed porch of the Woodstock Inn. Or head to the relaxed brew-pub in the back, housed in a heavily doctored old train station. In the Clement Room, you can enjoy elegant American and continental fare like chicken breast with wild mushrooms, shrimp stuffed with clams, or beef Wellington.

The pub is far more informal, with high ceilings, knotty pine, and decorations consisting of vintage winter recreational gear. There's a large-screen TV, and live local music is featured some nights. The menu rounds up the usual pub suspects, like nachos, chicken wings, burgers, and pasta, all of which is prepared decently if without much creative flair. A new craft brewery opened on the premises in March 1995, and serves up tasty porters, stouts, and brown and red ales.

FRANCONIA NOTCH

Franconia Notch is rugged New Hampshire writ large. As travelers head north on I-93, the Kinsman Range to the west and the Franconia Range to the east begin to converge, and the road angles upward. Soon, the parallel mountain ranges press in on either side, forming tight and dramatic Franconia Notch, which offers little in the way of civilization but a whole lot in the way of natural grandeur. Most of the notch is included in a well-run state park that for practical purposes is indistinguishable from the national forest. Travelers seeking the sublime should plan on a leisurely trip through the Notch, allowing enough time to get out of the car and explore forests and craggy peaks.

ESSENTIALS

GETTING THERE   I-93 runs through Franconia Notch, gearing down from four lanes to two (where it becomes the Franconia Notch Parkway) in the most scenic and sensitive areas of the park. Several roadside pull-outs and scenic attractions dot the route.

VISITOR INFORMATION   Information on the park and surrounding area is available at the state-run **Flume Information Center** (☎ 603/823-5563) at Exit 1 off the Parkway. The center is open during the summer from Monday through Saturday 9am to 4:30pm. North of the Notch, head to the **Franconia/Eaton/Sugar Hill Chamber of Commerce,** P.O. Box 780, Franconia, NH 03580 (☎ **603/823-5661** or 800/866-3334) on Main Street next to the town hall. It's open Monday through Saturday 9am to 5pm.

EXPLORING FRANCONIA NOTCH STATE PARK

Franconia Notch State Park's 8,000 acres, nestled within the surrounding White Mountain National Forest, hosts an array of scenic attractions easily accessible from I-93 and the Franconia Notch Parkway. For information on any of the follow attractions, contact the **park offices** (☎ **603/823-5563**).

Without a doubt, the most famous park landmark is the Old Man of the Mountains, located near Cannon Mountain. From the right spot on the valley floor, this 48-foot-high rock formation bears an uncanny resemblance to the profile of a craggy old man—early settlers said it was Thomas Jefferson. If it looks familiar, it's because this is the logo you see on all the New Hampshire state highway signs. The profile, which often surprises visitors by just how tiny it is when viewed from far below, is best seen from the well-marked roadside viewing area at Profile Lake. In years past, harried tourists craning their necks to glimpse the Old Man while speeding onward resulted in some spectacular head-on collisions. Take your time and pull over. It's free.

The Flume is a rugged, 800-foot gorge through which the Flume Brook tumbles. The gorge, a hugely popular attraction in the mid-19th century, is 800 feet long, 90 feet deep, and as narrow as 20 feet at the bottom; visitors explore by means of a network of boardwalks and bridges. If you're looking for simple and quick access to natural grandeur, it's worth the money. Otherwise, set off into the mountains and seek your own drama with fewer crowds. Admission is $6 adults, and $3 for children 6 to 12.

Echo Lake is a picturesquely situated recreation area, with a 28-acre lake, a handsome swimming beach, and picnic tables scattered about all within view of Cannon Mountain on one side and Mt. Lafayette on the other. This is the best spot for a relaxing afternoon when the weather's in an agreeable mood. A bike path runs along the lake and continues onward both north and south.

Admission to the park is $2.50 for visitors over 12 years old.

For a high-altitude view of the region, set off for the alpine ridges on the Cannon Mountain Tramway. The old-fashioned cable car serves skiers in winter; in summer, it whisks up to 80 travelers at a time to the summit of the 4,180-foot mountain. Once at the top, you can strike out by foot along the Rim Trail for superb views. Be prepared for cool, gusty winds. The tramway costs $8 for adults, $4 for children 6 to 12. It's located at Exit 2 of the parkway.

HIKING

Hiking opportunities abound in the Franconia Notch area, ranging from demanding multi-day hikes high on exposed ridgelines to gentle valley walks. Consult AMC's White Mountain Guide for a comprehensive directory of area hiking trails.

A pleasant woodland detour of two hours or so can be found at the Basin-Cascades Trail (look for well-marked signs for The Basin off I-93 about 1 1/2 miles north of the Flume). A popular roadside waterfall and natural pothole, the Basin attracts teeming crowds, but few visitors slip away from the masses by continuing on the trail to a series of other cascades beyond. Look for signs for the trail, then head off into the woods. After about 1/2 mile of easy hiking you'll reach Kinsman Falls, a beautiful 20-foot cascade. Continue on about 6/10 of a mile beyond to Rocky Glen, where the stream plummets through a craggy gorge. Retrace your steps back to your car.

For a more demanding hike, set off for rugged Mt. Lafayette, with its spectacular views of the western White Mountains. Hikers should be well experienced, well equipped, and in good physical condition. Allow six to seven hours to complete the hike. A popular and fairly straightforward ascent begins up the Old Bridle Trail, which departs from the Lafayette Place parking area off the parkway. This trail climbs steadily with expanding views to the AMC's Greenleaf Hut (2.9 miles). From here, continue to the summit of Lafayette on the Greeleaf Trail. It's only 1.1 miles farther, but it covers rocky terrain and can be demanding and difficult, especially if the weather turns on you. If in doubt about conditions, ask advice of other hikers or the AMC staff at Greenleaf Hut.

A POETIC PLACE

The Frost Place. Ridge Road, Franconia. ☎ **603/823-5510.** Admission $3 adults, $1.50 children 6–15. Late May–June Sat–Sun 1–5pm; July to mid–Oct Weds–Mon 1–5pm. Head south on Route 116 from Franconia one mile to Ridge Road (gravel).; turn left and proceed a short way to the Frost House; park in lot below the house.

Although long associated with Vermont, Robert Frost wrote many of his most notable poems in New Hampshire, where he lived between ages 10 and 45. "Nearly half my poems must actually have been written in New Hampshire," Frost has said. "Every single person in my 'North of Boston' was a friend or acquaintance of mine in New Hampshire." The Frost Place is a humble farmhouse, where Frost lived simply with his family, and by wandering the grounds it's not hard to see how his granite-edged poetry evolved at the fringes of the White Mountains. First editions of Frost's works are on display, a slide show offers a glimpse into the poet's life, and a nature trail in the woods near the house is posted with excerpts from his noted poems.

SKIING

Cannon Mountain. Franconia Notch Parkway, Franconia. ☎ **603/823-5563.** Vertical drop: 2,146 feet. Lifts: 1 80-person tram, 6 chairlifts. Skiable acreage: about 200. Lift tickets: $37 weekend, $28 weekday.

Cannon Mountain, a state-run ski area, was once the place to ski in the East. One of New England's first ski resorts, Cannon remains famed for its challenging runs and exposed faces, and the mountain still attracts skiers serious about getting down the hill in style. Many of the old-fashioned New England–style trails are narrow and fun (if sometimes icy, scoured by the notch's winds), and the enclosed tramway is an elegant way to get to the summit. There's no base scene to speak of; skiers tend to retire to inns around Franconia or retreat southward to the condo villages around Lincoln.

WHERE TO STAY & DINE

Franconia Inn. 1300 Easton Rd., Franconia, NH 03580. ☎ **603/823-5542** or 800/473-5299. Fax 603/823-8078. 30 rms (2 with shower only), 2 suites. Midweek $75–$115 double; weekends $90–$130 double. Rates include breakfast. MAP rates also available. Closed Apr to mid-May. AE, MC, V.

This is a pleasant inn that's well-priced for what you get. Owned by Alec and Richard Morris, two brothers who bought the inn in 1981, the Franconia Inn is set along a quiet road in a bucolic valley two miles from the village of Franconia. A grass airstrip lies across the road, used by glider pilots (you can sign up for an hour-long soaring excursion over dramatic Franconia Notch).

The inn itself, built in 1934 after a fire destroyed the original 1886 inn, has an welcoming, informal feel to it, with wingback chairs around the fireplace in one common room, and jigsaw puzzles half completed in the paneled library. Families are always welcome; kids tend to gravitate to the basement game room for pinball, video games, and Ping-Pong. Guest rooms are nicely appointed in a relaxed country fashion.

Facilities: At the barn next door guests can rent horses to tour the network of scenic bridle trails. There's also an outdoor hot tub, clay tennis courts, bikes for guests to use free of charge, a heated pool, and golf courses nearby. In winter, guests ski on 38 miles of groomed ski trails that start right outside the front door.

BETHLEHEM & LITTLETON

A century ago, Bethlehem was about the same size as North Conway to the south, boasting an impressive number of sprawling resort hotels, summer homes, and even its own semiprofessional baseball team. (Joseph Kennedy, patriarch of the Kennedy clan, played for the team.) Bethlehem subsequently lost the race for the riches (or won, depending on your view of outlet shopping), and today is again a sleepy town high on a hillside.

Famous for its lack of ragweed and pollen, Bethlehem was once teeming with vacationers seeking respite from the ravages of hay fever. When antihistamines and air-conditioning appeared on the scene, the sufferers stayed home. Empty resorts burned down one by one. Around the 1920s, Bethlehem was discovered by Hasidic Jews from the New York City area, who soon arrived in number to spend the summers in the remaining boarding houses. In fact, that tradition has endured, and it's not uncommon to see bearded men wearing black walking the streets of Bethlehem, or rocking on the porches of Victorian-era homes.

Nearby Littleton, set in a broad valley along the Ammonoosuc River, is the area's commercial hub, but it boasts a surfeit of small-town charm. The town's long main street is still vibrant in an era when many main streets have been abandoned by retailers scrambling for the mall. (That hasn't been a problem here because there is no mall). The street has an eclectic selection of shops—you can buy a wrench, a foreign magazine or literary novel, locally brewed beer, pizza, whole foods, or camping supplies.

These two towns don't offer much in the way of must-see attractions, but offer good lodging, decent restaurants, and pleasant environs, and both are peaceful alternatives for travelers avoiding the tourist bustle to the south.

ESSENTIALS

GETTING THERE   Littleton is best reached via I-93; get off at either Exit 41 or 42. Bethlehem is about 3 miles east of Littleton on Route 302. Get off I-93 at Exit 40 and head east. From the east, follow Route 302 beyond Twin Mountain to Bethlehem.

VISITOR INFORMATION   The **Bethlehem Chamber of Commerce,** P.O. Box 748, Bethlehem, NH 03574 (☎ **603/869-2151**), maintains an information booth in summer on Bethlehem's Main Street near the golf course. The **Littleton Area Chamber of Commerce,** P.O. Box 105, Littleton, NH 03561 (☎ **603/444-6561**), offers information from its storefront office at 141 Main St.

EXPLORING BETHLEHEM

Bethlehem once had 38 resort hotels, but little evidence of that today. For a better understanding of the town's rich history, track down an "An Illustrated Tour of Bethlehem, Past and Present," available at many shops around town. This unusually informative guide offers a glimpse into the town's past, bringing to life many of the most graceful homes and buildings.

Bethlehem consists of a Main Street, and a handful of side streets. Several antique stores clustered in what passes for downtown are well worth browsing.

Harking back to its more genteel era, Bethlehem still offers two well-maintained 18-hole golf courses amid beautiful North Country scenery. Call for hours and greens fees. Both the municipal **Bethlehem Golf Course** (☎ **603/869-5754**) and private **Maplewood Casino and Country Club** (☎ **603/869-3335**) are on Route 302 (Main Street) in Bethlehem.

Just west of Bethlehem on Route 302 is **The Rocks** (☎ **603/444-6228**), a classic, Victorian gentleman's farm that today is the northern headquarters for the Society for the Protection of New Hampshire Forests. Set on 1,200 acres, this gracious estate was built in 1883 by John J. Glessner, an executive with the International Harvester Company. A well-preserved shingled house and an uncommonly handsome barn grace the grounds. Several hiking trails meander through meadows and woodlands on a gentle hillside, where visitors can enjoy open vistas of the wooded mountains across the rolling terrain. The Society operates a Christmas tree farm here, as well as regular nature programs. Admission is free.

WHERE TO STAY

Bethlehem, which has long been well-regarded for its selection of bed-and-breakfasts, has gone through considerable turmoil lately. Some notable establishments have closed, new ones have opened (if prematurely), and most have recently changed hands or are currently on the market. When the dust settles, I hope to include more reviews in the next edition. Meanwhile, persistent travelers should be able to find lodging in elegant, old homes with a little thoughtful snooping. Drop me a note if you turn up any real treasures.

✪ **Adair.** Old Littleton Road (just off Exit 40 on Route 93), Bethlehem, NH 03574. ☎ **603/ 444-2600** or 800/441-2606. Fax 603/444-4823. 8 rms. Summer, foliage season, and winter $125–$175 double; late fall and spring $105–$145 double. Rates include breakfast. AE, MC, V.

Adair opened in just 1992, but has rapidly become one of New England's most esteemed inns. Guests arrive up a long, winding drive flanked by birches and stone walls to arrive at a peaceful, Georgian Revival home that seems far older than its years. Built as a wedding gift for his daughter in 1927 by Washington attorney Frank Hogan (of Hogan & Hartson fame), the inn is set on beautifully landscaped grounds. Inside, the common rooms are open, elegant, and spacious. The guest rooms are impeccably well-furnished with a mix of antiques and reproductions. Innkeepers Patricia and Hardy Banfield have carved a wonderful retreat out of an extraordinary estate. It's the sort of place guests will return to time and again. This is a no-smoking inn.

Dining/Entertainment: If the first-floor sitting room with its fireplace and richly upholstered chairs seems too formal, head downstairs to the Granite Tap Room, a wonderfully informal, granite-lined rumpus room with a VCR and a bar with set-ups (bring your own spirits).

Facilities: A patio that overlooks an all-weather tennis court and swimming pool.

⑤ **Hearthside Village.** Route 302 (midway between Bethlehem Village and I-93), Bethlehem, NH 03574. ☎ **603/444-1000.** 16 cottages, all showers only. TV. $49.95–$59.95 ($10 less in off-season). MC, V. Closed mid-Oct to mid-May.

Hearthside Village is quirky motel court that seems partly conceived by Alfred Hitchcock, partly by Red Grooms. A little bit weird and a little bit charming at the same time, Hearthside claims to be the first motel court built in New Hampshire. The village—a colony of steeply gabled miniature homes—was built by a father and son in two constructive bursts, the first in the 1930s, the second in the late '40s. The six '40s-era cottages are of better quality, with warm knotty pine interiors. But all cottages are nicely if simply furnished, and most have a fireplaces (Duraflame-style logs only) and handy kitchenettes. Since acquiring the motel in 1990, Rhonda and Steve Huggins have done an outstanding job making it a friendly, fun place that appeals especially to families. There's a pool, an indoor playroom for tots filled with toys, and another recreation room with video games and ping-pong for older kids.

Rabbit Hill Inn. Route 18, Lower Waterford, VT 05848. ☎ **802/748-5168** or 800/762-8669. Fax 802/748-8342. 20 rms. $179–$269 double. Rates include breakfast and dinner. Discounts available midweek in winter. AE, MC, V. From I-93, take Route 18 northwest from Exit 44 for approximately two miles.

A short hop across the Connecticut River from Littleton is the lost-in-time Vermont village of Lower Waterford with its perfect 1859 church and small library. Amid this cluster of buildings is the stately Rabbit Hill Inn, constructed in 1795. With its prominent gabled roof and imposing columns, the inn easily ranks among the most refined in the Connecticut River Valley. From the porch and many of the guest rooms, the views of the northern White Mountains are unrivaled. The inn's interior is richly furnished with Federal-era antiques. More than half of the rooms have fireplaces, most have air conditioning, and innkeepers John and Maureen Magee go the extra mile to make this an appealing destination for couples in search of quiet romance. (Honeymoon packages are a specialty.)

Dining/Entertainment: Dinner is included in the rates, and features regional classics along with more creative fare like fresh tomato fettuccine tossed in a jalapeno sunflower seed pesto, and braised Vermont pheasant breast with bacon, grapes, and baby artichokes. There's also a pub with a Gaelic flair.

🖲 **Thayers Inn.** Main Street, Littleton, NH 03561. ☎ **603/444-6469** or 800/634-8179. 40 rms (3 with shared bath, some with shower only). TV TEL. $42.95–$59.95 double. AE, DC, DISC, MC, V.

Last century President Ulysses S. Grant addressed a streetside crowd from one of the balconies under the imposing eaves of Thayers Inn. You might try that, too, although you might not be as successful at scaring up a crowd. My advice: just grab a book, have a seat on the balcony, and watch life pass by on Littleton's Main Street. Thayers is a clean, well-run hostelry in an impressive historic building. That's an all-too-rare sight in small towns these days. This solid 1850 inn has a variety of rooms furnished comfortably and eclectically. Notable guests who have stayed here include Bette Davis, Horace Greeley, Nelson Rockefeller, and Richard Nixon. Each room on the four floors is different, and guests are encouraged to poke around and see what's available before deciding on their evening quarters.

WHERE TO DINE

Tim-Bir Alley. In Adair, Old Littleton Road, Bethlehem. ☎ **603/444-6142.** Reservations recommended. Main courses $13.95–$17.50. No credit cards. Wed–Sun 5:30–9pm. Closed Apr, Nov, and Sun in off-season. REGIONAL/CONTEMPORARY.

Hands down, the best dining in the northern White Mountains is at Tim-Bir Alley, housed in the area's most gracious country inn. Owned by Tim and Biruta Carr, Tim-Bir Alley began in a miniature storefront off a small alley in Littleton. Its reputation for gourmet cuisine outgrew its tiny size, and the pair eventually moved up the hill to Adair, occupying the spacious dining room. The setting is elegant and romantic, and the meals always memorable.

The ingredients are wholesome and basic, but the real art is in the preparation and presentation. Diners might start with a chicken and blue-cheese ravioli in roasted garlic broth, then follow with swordfish cooked with olives and sun-dried tomato, or tournedos of beef with mozzarella and roasted tomato and smoked bacon sauce.

Save room for the superb deserts, which range from a pear-walnut tart with maple-caramel sauce, to a chocolate-hazelnut paté.

7 The North Country

I've been traveling to New Hampshire's North Country for more than 25 years, and it's come to serve as a handy touchstone for me. Errol is a town that seems to never change, and that held true even during the boom times of the 1980s. The clean Errol Motel is always there. The Errol Restaurant still serves the best homemade donuts north of Boston. And the land surrounding the town is still possessed of a rugged, raw grandeur that hasn't been compromised like many of the former wildlands to the south.

Of course, there's a problem with these lost-in-time areas. It's the nothing-to-see-nothing-to-do syndrome that seems to especially afflict families with young children. You drive for miles and see lots of spruce and pine, an infrequent bog, a glimpse of a shimmering lake, and—if you're lucky—a roadside moose chomping on sedges.

But there is plenty to do. Whitewater kayaking on the Androscoggin River. Canoeing on Lake Umbagog. Bicycling along the wide valley floors. And visiting one of the Northeast's grandest, most improbable turn-of-the-century resorts, which happens to keep thriving despite considerable odds against it.

Some recent developments are encouraging for those of us who'd like to see the area remain unchanged. In what may be one of the last bursts of federal largess for a long time to come, the piney shoreline around spectacular Lake Umbagog was protected as a National Wildlife Refuge a few years ago. Part was acquired outright by the federal and state governments (Umbagog straddles the Maine–New Hampshire border), and part was protected through the purchase of development rights from timber companies. The upshot? Umbagog should remain in its more-or-less pristine state for all time.

As for Errol, some shops have closed, some have opened. But the Androscoggin River still flows through. And the police still set up a radar at the bend near the river to catch Canadian speeders heading south toward Old Orchard Beach on Friday, then turn around to catch them heading north on Sundays.

ESSENTIALS

GETTING THERE   Errol is at the junction of Route 26 (accessible from Bethel, Me.) and Route 16 (accessible from Gorham, N.H.)

VISITOR INFORMATION   The **Northern White Mountains Chamber of Commerce,** 164 Main St, Berlin, NH 03570 (☎ **603/752-6060** or 800/992-7480), offers travel information from its offices weekdays between 8:30am and 4:30pm.

A DRIVING TOUR

If you're not traveling with kids who constantly demand to know "when are we going to get there?" (*warning:* there's no there there in northern New Hampshire), a driving tour through the North Country can be the highlight of your trip to New Hampshire. The roads are in good shape and allow for easy traveling. The terrain, while not as dramatic as in the White Mountains to the south, features lush woods that are dense and moosey. And there's a sense of ruggedness in both the landscape and the people—a quality that's quickly being tamed elsewhere in the Northeast.

Weeks State Park (☎ **603/788-4004**), at the southwest corner of Coos County, is good place to begin. This park, located two miles south of Lancaster on Route 3, was the former summer home of U.S. Secretary of State John W. Weeks. Atop a low peak ascended via a twisty and narrow driveway, Weeks built an imposing manor house. The home isn't open to the public, but the adjacent stone firetower is and it offers some of the most sweeping views of the North Country anywhere. Visitors can climb the stairs to an open platform below the manned cabin; at the ranger's discretion, you can scramble up to the cozy aerie, where volunteers scout for forest fires during the dry season.

From here, follow Route 3 north through Lancaster and then continue 36 miles through the Connecticut River Valley to Colebrook. For a more scenic variation, cross the river at Northumberland to Vermont, and follow Route 102 north on the other bank, crossing over again at Colebrook. Colebrook is a logging town that often seems packed with pick-up trucks. A handful of small restaurants and motels cater to travelers and sportsmen.

Just north of Colebrook's town center, turn right on Route 145 north and drive 2.5 miles to Beaver Brook Falls. This 70-foot roadside waterfall combines a dramatic plunge at the top followed by a series of cascades. A grassy picnic area at the base is a good spot to enjoy a snack, and you can explore trails along the brook. In late summer the flow dries to an unimpressive trickle, but it's glorious during snowmelt in the spring, or following a summer thunderstorm.

Afterward, backtrack to Colebrook and head east on Route 26. Head eastward 10 miles until you reach The Balsams. You'll know when you've arrived. This extravagant resort rises from the woods, and seems about as probable as a 100-foot white pine in midtown Manhattan. Set along the edge of Lake Gloriette, the resort is worth a stop, if only for a refreshment and a chance to view the property. If you've got money to splurge, consider spending the night; see details below.

Dixville Notch, the town in which The Balsams lies, has a population of 30 or so, and gains national prominence every four years on the eve of Presidential elections. The residents stay up until midnight to vote, and when all have done so, the polls are closed and the votes tallied for the national press, which typically outnumbers the residents. The results are reported nationally on the morning of Election Day. (There's not much suspense. Dixville Notch always goes Republican.)

Adjacent to the resort, **Dixville Notch State Park** (☎ **603/788-2155**) offers limited hiking, including a delightful two-mile round trip hike to Table Rock. Look for the small parking area just east of the resort. The loop hike (it connects with a $^1/_2$ mile return along Route 25) ascends a scrabbly trail to an open rock with fine views of the resort and the flanking wild hills.

Continue eastward on Route 26 for 11 miles through a widening valley to Errol. This tiny North Country logging town has become a popular destination for outdoor enthusiasts.

The Errol Restaurant on Main Street specializes in what might be called "grub." But I use that term in an entirely complimentary way. The portions are generous, the food is well-prepared if basic, and many of the baked goods are homemade. Especially satisfying are the homemade donuts, which are crusty, tasty, and very filling. Pick some up for the road.

At the eastern edge of town, Route 26 crosses the Androscoggin River, which tumbles over a stretch of whitewater that's especially appealing to canoeists and kayakers. On a warm summer day, it's usually just a matter of minutes before you see colorful watercraft edge around the upper bend, then work their way to the calm water downstream of the bridge with various degrees of grace. It makes for good spectator sport.

From Errol, travelers choose from among three routes, each of which has its own allure. North of town Route 16 weaves through wild, marshy, and wooded terrain (you've got a reasonably good chance of spotting moose here) to cross the border into Maine. A short drive further will bring you to the scenic Rangeley Lakes area; see the Maine chapter that follows this one.

East of Errol Route 26 passes the tip of Lake Umbagog then crosses into Maine and snakes through dramatic Grafton Notch, which offers good hiking and exploring at Grafton Notch State Park. Again, see the Maine chapter for details.

South of Errol, Route 16 follows along the beautiful Androscoggin River, though scenic birch groves and woodlands. A few waysides and a riverside state campground offer distraction. In 33 miles, you'll come to the rough-hewn paper mill town of Berlin (pronounced BUR-lin), which you very well may smell before you arrive. South of Berlin you'll soon arrive at the crossroads town of Gorham, which offers a number of restaurants and motels, and easy access to the dramatic sights of the northern White Mountains.

OUTDOOR RECREATION

If you're heading to the North Country, be sure to bring your canoe or kayak, since this is a superb area for both whitewater and flatwater.

A great place to learn the fundamentals of whitewater is at **Saco Bound's Northern Waters whitewater school** (☎ 603/482-3848), located where the Errol bridge crosses the Androscoggin River. The school offers three- and five-day workshops in the art of getting downstream safely if not dryly. Many of the students camp along the river at the school's campground, although some reside a short walk away at the Errol Motel. Classes involve videos, dry-land training, and frequent forays onto the river—both at the Class I to III rapids at the bridge, and more forgiving rips downstream. The base camp is also a good place for last-minute boat supplies and advice for paddlers exploring the river on their own.

Excellent lake canoeing may be found at Lake Umbagog, which sits between Maine and New Hampshire. The lake, which is home to the **Lake Umbagog Wildlife Refuge** (☎ 603/482-3415), has some 40 miles of shoreline, most of which is wild and remote. Look for osprey and eagles, otter and mink. Some 30 primitive campsites are scattered around the shoreline and on the lake's islands. These are managed by **Umbagog Lake Campground** (☎ 603/482-7795), and are extremely pricey for backcountry sites ($18 for two). On the other hand, they're well maintained and you get a lot of wildlands for your money. The campground, which is located on Route 26 at the lake's southern tip, also rents canoes.

The area around Errol offers excellent roads for bicycling—virtually all routes out of town make for good exploring (although it's mighty hilly heading east). An especially nice trip is south on Route 16 from Errol. The occasional logging truck can be unnerving, but mostly it's an easy and peaceful riverside trip. Consider pedaling as far as what's locally called the Brown Co. Bridge—a simple, wooden logging road bridge that crosses the Androscoggin River. It's a good spot to leap in the river and float through a series of gentle rips before swimming to shore. Some small ledges on the far side of the bridge provide good location for sunning and relaxing.

Biking information and rentals are available in Gorham at **Moriah Sports,** 101 Main St. (☎ 603/466-5050).

WHERE TO STAY & DINE

✪ **Balsams Grand Resort Hotel.** Dixville Notch, NH 03576. ☎ **603/255-3400** or 800/255-0600 (800/255-0800 in NH). Fax 603/255-4221. 200 rms (1 with shower only). TEL. Winter $278–$298 double, including breakfast, dinner, and lift tickets; summer $298–$378 double, including all meals and entertainment; year-round $508–$575 suite. AE, DISC, MC, V. Closed early Apr to late May and mid-Oct to Christmas.

Located on 15,000 private acres in a notch surrounded by 800-foot cliffs, the Balsams is a rare surprise hidden deep in the northern forest. The inn is but one of a handful of great resorts dating back to the 19th century still in operation, and its survival is all the more extraordinary given its remote location. What makes this Victorian grande dame even more exceptional has been its refusal to compromise or bend to the trend of the moment. Bathing suits and jeans are prohibited from the public areas, you'll be ejected from the tennis courts or golf course if you're not neatly attired, and men are required (not requested) to wear jackets at dinner. The resort has also maintained strict adherence to the spirit of the "American plan"—everything but booze is included in the room rate, from green fees to tennis to boats on Lake Gloriette to entertainment in the three lounges in evening. Even the lift tickets at the resort's downhill ski area are covered.

The Balsam's rigorous old-world decorum only enriches the mood at this sprawling resort. The rooms are spacious and attractive; the public areas tastefully appointed with resort-style furnishings representing almost every decade between 1866, when the place first opened, and today. Navigating your way through the winding halls is not for the directionally challenged.

Dining/Entertainment: Meals are superb. Especially famous is the sumptuous luncheon buffet, served in summer, and featuring delightful salads, filling entrees like linguine with clam sauce and fried shrimp, and wonderful deserts (when did you last gorge yourself on chocolate eclairs?). There are also three lounges.

Facilities: Two golf courses (one 18 hole, one 9 hole), six tennis courts, a heated outdoor pool, and 45 miles of groomed cross-country ski trails.

⑤ Philbrook Farm Inn. North Road (off Route 2 between Gorham, N.H. and Bethel, Me.), Shelburne, NH 03581. ☎ **603/466-3831.** 18 rms plus 2 summer cottages (6 rooms have shared baths; of the private baths, 1 is tub only, 2 are shower only). $105–$130 double. Rates include breakfast and dinner. No credit cards. Closed Apr and Nov to Dec 26.

The Philbrook Farm Inn is a true New England classic. Set on 1,000 acres between the Mahoosuc Range and the Androscoggin River, this country inn has been owned and operated by the Philbrook family continuously since 1853. The inn has grown haphazardly since the Philbrooks acquired the early farmhouse, with additions in 1861, 1904, and 1934. As a result, the cozy guest rooms on three floors are eclectic—some have a country farmhouse feel, others a more Victorian flavor. Rooms are named after favored guests. I stayed in the room named after Albert Payson Briggs, who was a frequent visitor between 1872 and 1954.

The common areas are spacious and comfortable, with jigsaw puzzles and a century-and-a-half's worth of books lining the shelves. Guests spend their days swimming in the pool, playing croquet, or exploring trails in the nearby hills. Philbrook Farm is a wonderful retreat, well out of the tourist mainstream, and worthy of protection as a local cultural landmark.

Dining/Entertainment: The dining room has a farmhouse-formal feel to it; guests are assigned one table for their stay, and are served by waitresses in crisp, white uniforms. Meals tend toward basic New England fare, with specialities like cod cakes and baked beans with brown bread. Potatoes are served with almost every meal.

Maine 7

Humorist Dave Barry once wryly suggested that Maine's state motto should be "Cold, but damp."

Cute, but true. There's spring, which tends to last a few blustery, rain-soaked days. There's November, which alternates Arctic winds with gray sheets of rain. And then winter brings a character-building mix of blizzards and ice storms to the fabled coast. (The inland mountains are more or less blessed with uninterrupted snow.)

Ah, but then there's summer. Summer in Maine brings ospreys diving for fish off wooded points; gleaming cumulus clouds building over the steely-blue, rounded peaks of the western mountains; and the haunting whoop of loons echoing off the dense forest walls bordering the lakes. It brings languorous days when the sun rises before most visitors and it seems like noontime at 8am. (There's a tiny but vocal movement afoot to shift Maine to Canada's Atlantic Time Zone, which would move some of the precious daylight from 4 or 5am to the evening, where it might be put to better use.) Maine summers bring a measure of gracious tranquility, and a placid stay in the right spot can rejuvenate even the most jangled nerves.

The trick comes in finding that right spot. Those who arrive here without a clear plan may find themselves cursing their travel decision. Maine's Route 1 along the coast has its moments, but for the most part it's rather charmless—an amalgam of convenience stores, tourist boutiques, and restaurants catering to bus tours. Acadia National Park can be congested, Mount Katahdin's summit crowded, and some of the more popular lakes become obstacle courses of jet skis.

But Maine's size works to the traveler's advantage. Maine is nearly as large as the other five New England states combined. It has 3,500 miles of coastline, some 3,000 coastal islands, and millions of acres of undeveloped woodland. In fact, more than half of the state exists as the "unorganized territories," where no town government exists, and the few inhabitants look to the state for basic services. With all this space, and a little planning, you'll be able to find your piece of Maine.

Maine is typically characterized as being two states—Coastal Maine and the North Woods. Like most broad generalizations, it's not exactly true, but there's a kernel of truth in it. These two regions encompass the largest parts of the state, and have a major hand in shaping local character and history. But within them lie major differences. The coast south of Portland is sandy and flat; further to the east it's all rocky headlands and rolling hills. The choppy hills of western Maine around Rangeley Lake are far different than the open, flat timberlands north of Moosehead.

Wherever your travels take you, be sure to look for the varied layers of history, both natural and human. You'll find the mark of the great glaciers on the scoured mountaintops. You'll find the hand of man in two-century-old mansions on remote coves that bespeak a former affluence when Maine ruled the waves (or at least much of the early trade on those waves). Picking these layers apart is much of the fun in exploring Maine.

1 Enjoying the Great Outdoors

No other northern New England state offers as much diversity in its outdoor recreation as Maine. Bring your mountain bike, hiking boots, sea kayak, canoe, fishing rod, and snowmobile—there'll be plenty for you to do here.

But unlike New Hampshire and Vermont, Maine forces outdoor enthusiasts to be a little more creative and informed to get the most out of the state, since many of the best recreational destinations are a matter of local knowledge. There's Baxter State Park and Acadia National Park, but outside of these two well-known destinations much of the best recreation land remains hidden from plain view. Hikers often need to cruise confusing logging roads to reach some of the best trails. Canoeists need to spend hours with topographic maps to plot out the best routes. Sea kayakers need to research which of the myriad offshore islands are open to camping and which aren't.

A growing number of specialized guidebooks can help point visitors in the right direction; some of the best are mentioned below. And don't overlook another great resource: the dozens of outdoor shops around the state, where the staff tends to be friendly, and more than happy to send you in the right direction.

BEACHGOING   Swimming at Maine's ocean beaches is for the hearty. The Gulf Stream, which prods warm waters toward the Cape Cod shores to the south, veers toward Iceland south of Maine, and leave the state's 3,500-mile coastline to be washed by the brisk Nova Scotia current, an offshoot of the arctic Labrador Current. During the "warm" summer months, water temperatures along the south coast can top 60 degrees during an especially warm spell where the water is shallow, but it's usually cooler than that. The average ocean temperature at Bar Harbor in summer is 54 degrees.

Maine's beaches are found mostly between Portland and the New Hampshire border. Northeast of Portland there are a handful of fine beaches—including popular Reid State Park and Popham Beach State Park—but rocky coast defines this territory for the most part. The southern beaches are beautiful, but rarely isolated. Summer homes occupy the low dunes in most areas; mid-rise condos give Old Orchard Beach a "mini-Miami" air. For my money, the best beaches are at Ogunquit, which boasts a three-mile-long sandy strand, some of which has a mildly remote character, and Long Sands Beach at York, which has a festive, carnival atmosphere right along Route 1A.

Remember that in Maine, the term "sand beach" is not redundant. It simply distinguishes these from their more common cousins, the "pebble beach" and the "cobblestone beach." These probably don't require further definition, but you should be aware that some hyperbolic innkeepers might refer to a nearby "pebble beach" where closer examination shows the "pebbles" range in size from billiard-balls to bowling-balls.

Maine

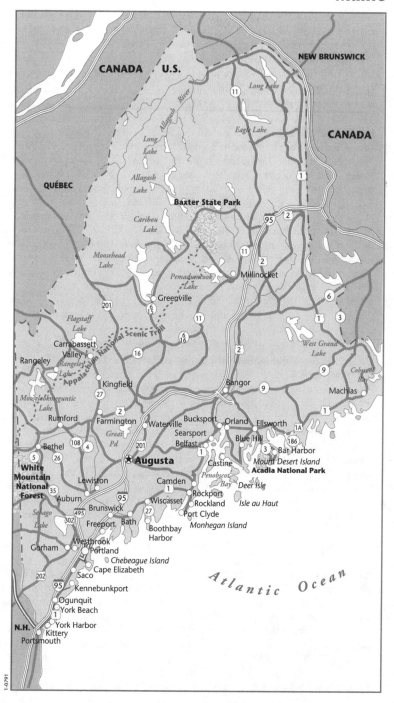

Don't overlook the sandy beaches at Maine's wonderful lakes, where the water is tepid by comparison to the frigid Atlantic. A number of state and municipal parks offer access. Especially popular are Sebago Lake State Park (☎ **207/693-6613**), about 20 miles northwest of Portland, and, for a more rustic experience, Lily Bay State Park (☎ **207/695-2700**), on Moosehead Lake, eight miles north of Greenville.

BACKPACKING   Compared to camping by canoe or sea kayak, backpacking opportunities are relatively limited in Maine. A couple of notable exceptions exist. The 2,000-mile Appalachian Trail, which ends (or begins, depending on your direction) at Maine's highest peak, is nothing short of spectacular as it passes through Maine. En route to Mt. Katahdin, it winds through what's known as the "100-Mile Wilderness," a remote, bosky, and boggy stretch where the trail crosses few roads and passes no settlements. It's the quiet habitat of loons and moose, and hikers are but brief transients. Trail guides are available from the **Appalachian Trail Conference,** P.O. Box 807, Harpers Ferry, WV, 25425 (☎ **304/535-6331**).

Another excellent destination for backcountry exploration is 200,000-acre **Baxter State Park,** 64 Balsam Dr., Millinocket, ME 04462 (☎ **207/723-5140**), in the north-central part of the state. The park maintains about 180 miles of backcountry hiking trails. The vast majority of travelers coming to the park are intent on ascending 5,267-foot Mt. Katahdin. But dozens of other peaks are well worth scaling, and just traveling through the deep woods hereabouts is a sublime experience. Reservations are required for backcountry camping, and many of the best spots fill up shortly after the first of the year. Reservations can be made by mail or in person, but not by phone.

Note that there is no backcountry camping at Acadia National Park.

BICYCLING   **Mount Desert Island** and **Acadia National Park** comprise the premier destination for bikers, especially mountain bikers who prefer easy-riding terrain. The 57 miles of well-maintained carriage roads in the national park offer superb cruising through thick forests and to the tops of rocky knolls with ocean views. No cars are permitted on these grass and gravel roads, so you've got them to yourself. Mountain bikes may be rented in Bar Harbor, which has at least three bike shops. The Park Loop Road (toll), while often crowded with slow-moving cars, offers one of the more memorable road biking experiences in the state. The rest of Mount Desert Island is also good for road biking, especially on the quieter western half of the island.

In southern Maine, Route 103 and Route 1A offer pleasant excursions for bikers along the coast. Offshore, bring your bike to the bigger islands for car-free cruising. Vinalhaven and North Haven in Penobscot Bay, and Swan's Island in Blue Hill Bay are all popular destinations for bikers.

CAMPING   Car campers in Maine have plenty of choices, from well-developed private campgrounds to primitive backcountry sites that are accessible by vehicle. **Baxter State Park** and **Acadia National Park** tend to fill up the fastest, but there's no shortage of other options. Maine has nearly 62,000 acres in state parks (not even including 202,000-acre Baxter), a dozen of which of which offer overnight camping. For more information about the state's parks, contact the **Department of Conservation,** State House Station #22, Augusta, ME 04333 (☎ **207/287-3821**). To make camping reservations at 11 of the state park campgrounds, call between January and August (☎ **207/287-3824** or 800/332-1501 in Maine). For reservations at Baxter State Park, see the "North Woods" section of this chapter.

On Maine's western border, the **White Mountain National Forest** offers superb camping at several campgrounds in the mountains of the Evans Notch Ranger District, RR #2, P.O. Box 2270, Bethel, ME 04217 (☎ **207/824-2134**).

Maine also has more than 200 private campgrounds spread throughout the state, many offering full hook-ups for RVs. For a guide to the private campgrounds, contact the **Maine Campground Owners Association,** 655 Main St., Lewiston, ME 04240 (☎ 207/782-5874).

CANOEING In the eyes of many, Maine means canoeing. From the thousands of lakes and ponds to the tumbling white water of mountain rivers, Maine offers a big allure for paddlers.

The state's most popular long-distance excursion is the **Allagash Wilderness Waterway** canoe trip, which can be done end-to-end in 7 to 10 days. Some 80 campsites are spaced along the nearly 100-mile route, which includes a 9-mile stretch of Class I-II white water. For a map and brochure, contact the **Bureau of Parks and Recreation,** Maine Department of Conservation, State House Station 22, Augusta, ME 04333. The Allagash is also served by a number of outfitters, who can provide everything from a complete guide service to a simple car shuttle. (See the "North Woods" section of this chapter.)

Other good canoe destinations include the **Saco River,** which ambles out of the White Mountains through western Maine and is noted for its popular sandbars and weekend crowds. There's the **upper West Branch of the Penobscot River,** which winds through through moose country and connects to one of Maine's most pristine lakes (a four-day paddle trip is outlined later in this chapter). And don't overlook the **lakes and rivers of Washington County** in far eastern Maine.

In fact, you can't travel very far in Maine without stumbling upon a great canoe trip. Two excellent sources of information are the *AMC River Guide: Maine* and *Quiet Water Canoe Guide: Maine,* both published by the Appalachian Mountain Club, 5 Joy St., Boston, MA 02108.

FISHING Maine draws anglers from throughout the Northeast who indulge their grand obsession on Maine's 6,000 lakes and ponds and its countless miles of rivers and streams. Want to find fishing? Just look at a map and head to those big blue areas.

Among the most appealing areas for serious freshwater anglers is the **Grand Lake Stream** region deep in the woods of Washington County, not far from the New Brunswick border and Canada. This area has a strong heritage as a fisherman's settlement, and a number of camps and outfitters cater to the serious angler.

Nearby **Dennys River** and the **St. Croix River** are good destinations for Atlantic salmon; troll the numerous lakes for trout and small-mouth bass. Among the classic fishing lodges in this area are **Weatherby's** (☎ 207/796-5558) and **Indian Rock Camps** (☎ 800/498-2821 or 207/796-2822).

Ice fishing is also enormously popular throughout the winter, and you'll see the huts of anglers clustered on lakes throughout the state from the time the ice freezes to the conclusion of the season at the end of March. If anyone tells you that Maine's waters are fished out, consider this: a Maine man landed a 23.5-pound brown trout while ice fishing in March 1996 at a pond in southwestern Maine.

Nonresident licenses are $48 for the season, or $20 for three days. Seven- and fifteen-day licenses are also available. You can purchase licenses at many outdoor shops or general stores. For a booklet of fishing regulations, contact the **Department of Inland Fisheries and Wildlife,** State House Station #41, Augusta, Maine 04333 (☎ 207/287-3371).

HIKING Maine isn't much of a hiker's state, even though it has 10 peaks over 4,000 feet. The reason is simple. Outside of Baxter State Park and Acadia National Park, Maine has surprisingly little public land. Recreation has historically occurred on the millions of acres of privately owned timber company land, and the emphasis there has been on canoeing, fishing, and hunting, not on recreational hiking.

That's not to say that Maine lacks great places to hike. There are trails, if you know where to look. **Acadia National Park** offers superb and surprisingly quiet hiking, given the huge popularity of the park. Happily for hikers, few visitors venture far from their cars, leaving the trail system relatively unpopulated. In western Maine, 50,000 acres of the White Mountains spill over the border from New Hampshire and boast an excellent network of trails. There are a number of pathways in and around Evans Notch that offer opportunities for hikers of all levels. Finally, there's the excellent and generally unheralded Bigelow Range near the Sugarloaf/USA ski resort, which offers challenging trails and stunning vistas from high, blustery ridges. The Appalachian Trail traverses the range; a good source of trail information is in the AT guide (see "Backpacking," above).

Two guides to the state's trails are highly recommended. *Fifty Hikes in Southern Maine* by John Gibson is a reliable directory to trails at Evans Notch, Acadia, and the Camden Hills area. *Fifty Hikes in Northern Maine* by Chloe Caputo, is the best guide for the Bigelow Range and Baxter State Park. Both are available from Backcountry Publications, P.O. Box 175, Woodstock, VT 05091 (☎ **800/ 245-4151**).

SEA KAYAKING   Sea kayakers nationwide migrate to Maine in the summer for world-class sea-kayaking. The 3,500 miles of rocky coastline and the thousands of offshore islands have created a wondrous sea kayaker's playground. Paddlers can explore protected estuaries far from the surf, or test their skills and determination with excursions across the choppy, open sea to islands far offshore. It's a sport that can be extremely dangerous (the seas can turn on you in a matter of minutes), but can yield plenty of returns for those with the proper equipment and skills.

The nation's first long-distance "water trail" was created here in 1987 when the Maine Island Trail was established. This 325-mile waterway winds along the coast from Portland to Machias, and incorporates some 70 state and privately owned islands along the route. Members of the Maine Island Trail Association, a private nonprofit organization, are granted permission to visit and camp on these islands, as long as they follow certain restrictions (e.g., don't visit designated islands during sea-bird nesting season). The association seeks to encourage low-impact, responsible use of these natural treasures. A guidebook, published annually, provides descriptions of all the islands in the network and is free with association membership (note that it's available only to members). Membership is $35 per year; contact the **Maine Island Trail Association,** P.O. Box C, Rockland, ME 04841 (☎ **207/596-6456** or 207/ 761-8225).

For novices, Maine has a number of kayak outfitters offering guided excursions ranging from an afternoon to a week. Recommended outfitters include the **Maine Island Kayak Co.,** 70 Luther St., Peaks Island, ME 04108 (☎ **207/766-2373**); **H2Outfitters,** P.O. Box 72, Orr's Island, ME 04066 (☎ **207/833-5257**); and **Maine Sports Outfitters,** P.O. Box 956, Rockport, ME 04856 (☎ **800/244-8799** or 207/236-8797).

SKIING   Maine has two major downhill ski resorts along with 10 smaller areas. The two big resorts, **Sugarloaf** and **Sunday River,** came under the same ownership in 1996, but both maintain distinct characters. Sugarloaf is compact and manageable, and offers the highest vertical drop in New England after Vermont's Killington. The resort's base area is self-contained like a campus and is a big hit with families. Sunday River is a younger resort and its base area is still a bit rough around edges—think of it more like a brash community college. But it offers diverse skiing terrain and state-of-the-art snowmaking and grooming. I'd go to Sugarloaf if I were expecting heavy natural snowfall; I'd choose Sunday River if the natural snow conditions were marginal or poor.

The medium and small mountains cater primarily to the local market but offer good alternatives for travelers who'd just as soon avoid the flash and crowds of a larger area. Of the mid-sized areas, Shawnee Peak and Saddleback have small resort complexes at or near their bases, and offer better bargains and fewer crowds; Shawnee Peak is open for night skiing until 10pm six nights each week. Mt. Abram, which is near Sunday River, has developed a solid reputation among telemark skiers. For a recorded announcement of current downhill ski conditions statewide, call **207/773-7669.**

Cross-country skiers have a glorious mix of terrain to choose from, although groomed cross-country ski areas aren't as extensive in Maine as in neighboring New Hampshire or Vermont. **Sunday River, Saddleback,** and **Sugarloaf** all feature cross-country ski areas at or near their downhill complexes. A more remote destination is **The Birches** (☎ 800/825-9453) on Moosehead Lake with 24 miles of groomed trails. The best place to combine remote backcountry lodging and skiing is **Little Lyford Pond Camps** (☎ via radio phone **207/695-2821**) outside of Greenville— it's accessible in winter only by skiplane or snowmobile.

For further information about cross-country ski areas in Maine, contact the **Maine Nordic Council** (☎ 800/754-9263).

SNOWMOBILING   Snowmobiling is in the midst of a boom in Maine as everyone from mechanics to doctors is discovering the appeal of this sport. Restaurants and lodges that were until recently shuttered through winter are now doing more business in the snowy months than the rest of the year. Communities throughout northern Maine, in particular, are spending tens of thousands of dollars grooming trails nightly for snowmobilers in a bid to attract their attention. Maine's **Interconnected Trail System** (ITS) serves as a superhighway for the North Woods; the woods are also laced with an elaborate network of local trails maintained by local snowmobile clubs. Overall, Maine has 11,000 miles of groomed trails maintained by 260 snowmobile clubs. If you plan your trip right, stops for gas, food, and warming up will be no more than 30 miles apart.

As in the other northern New England states, the further north you go the better the conditions are likely to be. Of particular note is the new sled trail that follows the perimeter of Moosehead Lake, with stops possible at Mt. Kineo and Pittston Farm, both of which offer food and lodging. For more information on the trail or rentals, contact the **Moosehead Region Chamber of Commerce,** P.O. Box 581, Greenville, ME 04441 (☎ **207/695-2702**).

Further to the north, just east of Baxter State Park's northern entrance, is **Shin Pond Village** (☎ **207/528-2900**), which offers basic lodging and snowmobile rentals through an affiliated business. Rates are reasonable (about $125 per day for a two-person sled) and the access to the trail system is superb. Sledders can ride on the perimeter road of Baxter State Park, or ride the beautiful 55-mile Bowlin-Mattagamon loop.

WHITE-WATER RAFTING   Maine has three northern rivers that get the adrenaline pumping: **the Dead, the Kennebec,** and **the Penobscot.** All three are dam-controlled, which means that good rafting is available throughout the season. The Dead River has a limited release schedule; during the average season, it's opened only a half-dozen times for rafting in early summer and fall; smaller releases allow paddling in inflatable kayaks during the summer. The Kennebec River offers monstrous waves just below the dam (some say they're comparable to the big water you'll find out West), then tapers off into a gentle afternoon paddle as you float out of a scenic gorge. The West Branch of the Penobscot River has a challenging, technical section called the Cribworks at the outset, several serious drops and falls after that, and dramatic views of Mount Katahdin along the route.

There are two main centers for rafting. West Forks is northwest of Skowhegan on Route 201 (the staging area for the Kennebec and Dead River trips). Outside of Millinocket on the way to Baxter State Park are staging areas for Penobscot River trips. Some outfitters are also based between the rivers in Greenville, at the tip of Moosehead Lake. Ask about lodging and rafting packages, which include overnight accommodations or camping (the quality varies widely), a meal or two, and other amenities like post-rafting hot tubs.

For a list of outfitters, contact **Raft Maine,** P.O. Box 3, Bethel, ME 04217 (☎ **800/723-8633** or 207/824-3694).

WINDJAMMING　An ideal way to combine time in the outdoors with relative luxury and an easy-to-digest education in maritime history is aboard a windjammer cruise on the coast. Maine boasts a sizeable fleet of vintage sailing ships that offer private cabins, meals, entertainment, and adventure. The ships range in size from 53 to 132 feet, and most are berthed in the region between Bath and Belfast. You choose your adventure: an array of excursions are available, from simple overnights to week-long expeditions gunkholing among Maine's thousands of scenic islands and coves.

Several windjammer festivals and races are held along the Maine coast through-out the summer; these are perfect events to shop for a ship to spend a few days on. Among the more notable events are the **Windjammer Days** in Boothbay Harbor (late June) and the **Camden Windjammer Weekend** in early September. Contact the appropriate chamber of commerce for more information. For more about windjamming, see the Rockland section of this chapter.

2　The South Coast

There are two good reasons to visit Maine's south coast: the beaches and the almost tactile sense of history you'll find in the coastal villages.

Thanks to the quirks of geography, almost all of Maine's sandy beaches are located in the 60-mile stretch of coastline between Portland and Kittery. And you're likely to find a sandy spot that appeals to you, whether you prefer dunes and the lulling sound of the surf or the carny atmosphere of a festive beach town. The waves are dependent on the weather—during a good Northeast blow they pound the shores and threaten beach houses built decades ago. During the balmy days of mid-summer the ocean can be as gentle as a farm pond, with barely audible waves lapping timidly at the shore.

One thing all beaches share in common: they're washed by the frigid waters of the Gulf of Maine. Bouts of swimming tend to be very brief and often accompanied by shrieks and whoops. The beach season is brief and intense, running from July 4th to Labor Day. Before and after, beach towns tend to be rather sleepy.

The South Coast wears its history on its sleeve. More than three centuries ago the early European settlers first settled here, only to be driven out by hostile Native Americans, who had been pushed to the brink by treaty-breaking British settlers and prodded by the mischievous French. Settlers later re-established themselves, and by the early 19th century the southern Maine Coast was one of the most prosperous regions in the nation. Shipbuilders constructed brigantines and sloops, and ship captains plied the Eastern seaboard, the Caribbean, and far beyond. Merchants and

Bethel
Bryant Pond
5
219 Livermore
17
26 Winthrop
North Waterford
5
117 Turner
4 202
11
South Paris
118 Norway
Mechanic Falls
495 201
117 Lewiston
Richmond
Lovell Auburn 196 Lisbon Falls 95
302 Bridgton
Long Lake 11
Bath
Casco 26 136 Brunswick
Naples 5 117
11 Gray Freeport
Hiram N. Windham Harpswell Peninsula 209
Cornish Sebago Lake Yarmouth Casco Bay
35 302
25 202 Portland
Limerick Westbrook South Portland
Hollis Center 4 95 Cape Elizabeth
11 Old Orchard Beach
Shapleigh 5 Saco Saco Bay
Alfred 111 Biddeford
109 Sanford 1
202 4 109 Kennebunk
Rochester North Berwick Kennebunkport
Berwick 95
Somersworth Wells Atlantic Ocean
Dover Ogunquit
New Hampshire Maine York
Durham Kittery
108 Portsmouth
1A
Exeter

0   16 km
0 10 mi.
N

1-0792

traders constructed vast warehouses along the rivers to store their goods. Many handsome and historic homes near the coast today attest to the region's former prosperity.

A second wave came in the mid- to late-19th century, when wealthy city dwellers from Boston and New York sought respite from the summer heat and congestion by fleeing to Maine's coast. They built shingled estates (called "cottages") with views of the Atlantic. After the turn of the century, aided by trolleys and buses, the wealthy rusticators were followed by the emerging middle class, who built bungalows near the shore and congregated at oceanside boarding houses to splash in the waves.

Today, the South Coast's primary business remains seasonal tourism, although more year-round residents have settled here in recent years. This includes a growing number of commuters who trek daily to Portsmouth and Boston. While tourist towns like York Beach shutter up around the time the first Canada geese are spotted heading south, businesses in the inland communities are up and running year round.

THE YORKS

"The Yorks" are comprised of three towns that share a name but little else. In fact, it's rare to find three such well-defined and diverse New England archetypes in such a compact area. York Village is rich with early American history and architecture. York Harbor is redolent of America's late Victorian era, when wealthy urbanites constructed rambling cottages at the ocean's edge. York Beach has a turn-of-the-century beach town feel, with loud amusements, taffy shops, a modest zoo, and small gabled summer homes set in crowded enclaves near the beach.

ESSENTIALS

GETTING THERE   The Yorks are accessible from Exit 1 of the Maine Turnpike. Route 1A, which departs from Route 1 just south of the turnpike exit, connects all three York towns and loops north back to Route 1.

VISITOR INFORMATION   Travelers entering the state on I-95 can stock up on travel information for the region and beyond at the **Kittery Information Center** (☎ **207/439-1319**), located at a well-marked rest area. Open until 9pm in summer, it's amply stocked with brochures, and the helpful staff can answer many questions.

The **York Chamber of Commerce,** P.O. Box 417, York, ME 03909 (☎ **207/363-4422**), operates an attractive, helpful information center at 599 Route 1, a short distance from the turnpike exit. A trackless trolly (a bus fitted out to look like an old-fashioned trolley) regularly links all three York towns and provides a convenient way to explore without having to scare up parking spots at every stop. Hop the trolley at one of the well-marked stops for a one-hour narrated tour ($3), or disembark along the way and explore by foot.

DISCOVERING LOCAL HISTORY

John Hancock is famed for his oversized signature on the Declaration of Independence. What's not so well known about him is his failure as a businessman. Hancock was the proprietor of Hancock Wharf, a failed enterprise that's only one of the intriguing sites open to the public in York Village, a fine destination for those curious about early American history.

First settled in 1624, York Village has several early homes open to the public from mid-June through September. The **Old York Historical Society** (☎ **207/363-4974**) operates a community museum comprised of seven buildings spanning three centuries in this quiet riverside town. One ticket ($6 adults, $2.50 children 6 to 16) provides admission to all buildings, or you can buy admission to individual buildings ($2). The museum is open Tuesday through Saturday 10am to 4pm and Sunday 1 to 5pm.

Tickets are available at Jefferds Tavern, across from the handsome old burying ground, where changing exhibits document facets of early life. Next door is the School House, furnished as it might have been in the last century. A 10-minute walk away on lightly traveled Lindsay Road you'll reach Hancock Wharf, which is next door to the George Marshall Store. Also nearby is the Elizabeth Perkins House with its well-preserved Colonial Revival interiors. The newest acquisition is an old bank building, which now houses the society's library and offices. The library is open to historical society members only.

The two don't-miss buildings in the society's collection are the intriguing Old Gaol, built in 1719 with its now-musty dungeons for criminals and debtors. The jail is the oldest surviving public building in the United States. Just down the knoll from the jail is the Emerson-Wilcox House, built in the mid-1700s. Added on to periodically over the years, it's a virtual catalog of architectural styles and early decorative arts. Docents make the building come alive during a tour.

Another extraordinary historic home is a short drive away in York Harbor. The **Sayward-Wheeler House,** owned by the Society for the Preservation of New England Antiquities, dates to 1718, and was built by Jonathan Sayward, a prominent merchant and politician. The home, which may be viewed by tour only, features wonderful collections of Queen Anne and Chippendale furniture. It's located at 79 Barrel Lane, and is open summer through fall. Tours are offered Wednesday through Sunday on the hour between noon and 4pm. Admission is $4.

Two Wonderful Walks

Two local strolls will allow visitors to stretch their legs and get the cobwebs out of their heads.

York Harbor and York Village are connected by a quiet pathway that follows a river and passes through shady woodlands. **Fisherman's Walk** departs from below Edward's Harborside Inn, near the Stage Neck Inn. (There's limited parking at tiny York Harbor Beach.) Follow the pathway along the river, past lobster shacks and along lawns leading up to grand shingled homes. Cross Route 103 and walk over the Wiggly Bridge (said to be, not implausibly, the smallest suspension bridge in the world), then head into the woods. You'll soon connect with a dirt lane; follow this and you'll emerge at Lindsay Road near Hancock Wharf (see above). Depending on your pace, the entire walk will take a half-hour to 45 minutes. For $1, you can catch the trolley back to your car.

Also departing from near York Harbor Beach is the **Cliff Walk,** a trail that follows rugged terrain along rocky bluffs and offers wonderful views of the open ocean and glimpses of life in some of the town's more grand cottages. The far end of this trail was destroyed by forceful ocean waves some years back; you'll have to retrace your steps back to the beach.

Shopping in Nearby Kittery

The consumer mecca of Kittery is four miles south of York on Route 1. Some 120 factory outlets flank the highway here, scattered among more than a dozen strip malls. Retailers include J. Crew, Polo Ralph Lauren, Bass Shoes, Nike, and Liz Clairborne. The area can be tough to navigate in peak season owing to the four lanes of heavy summer traffic and often capricious restrictions on turns. My advice: Wait until Freeport (60 miles to the north) to indulge your urge to acquire. In Freeport (as in Manchester, Vermont), you can park once and reconnoiter most of the outlet village on foot.

BEACHES

York Beach actually consists of two beaches—Long Sands Beach and Short Sands Beach—separated by a rocky headland and a small island capped with scenic Nubble Light. Both offer plenty of room for sunning and frisbees when the tide is out. When the tide is in, both are a bit cramped. Short Sands fronts the town of York Beach with its candlepin bowling and video arcades. It's the better bet for families who have kids with short attention spans. Long Sands runs along Route 1A, across from a profusion of motels, summer homes, and convenience stores. Parking at both beaches is metered (50¢ per hour).

WHERE TO STAY

For basic accommodations, try York Beach, which has a proliferation of motels and guest cottages facing Long Sands Beach. Even with this abundance, however, it's best to reserve ahead during prime season. And don't expect any real bargains during mid-summer, even among the most basic of motels.

If the following inns are booked, try these: **Anchorage Motor Inn** (☎ 207/363-5112), **Sea Latch Motor Inn** (☎ 800/441-2993 or 207/363-4400), or **Sunrise Motel** (☎ 800/242-0752 or 207/363-4542).

Dockside Guest Quarters. Harris Island (P.O. Box 205), York, ME 03909. ☎ **207/363-2868.** Fax 207/363-1977. 21 rms, 2 with shared bath. TV. Mid-June to early Sept, $60–$147 double. Rates up to 30% lower in off-season. MC, V. Closed weekdays Nov–May. Drive south on Route 103 from Route 1A; after bridge, turn left and follow signs.

David and Harriet Lusty established this quiet retreat in 1954, and recent additions (mostly new cottages) haven't taken away any of the friendly, maritime flavor of the place. Situated on an island connected to the mainland by a small bridge, the inn occupies nicely landscaped grounds shady with maples and white pines. Five of the rooms are in the main house, built in 1885, but the bulk of the accommodations are in small, townhouse-style cottages constructed between 1968 and 1974. These are simply furnished, bright, and airy, and all have private decks that overlook the entrance to York Harbor. (Several rooms also offer woodstoves.)

Dining/Entertainment: The inn runs a popular restaurant on the property, serving mounds of fresh seafood and New England classics.

Facilities: The innkeepers provide guests with the use of canoes, rowboats, and a 13-foot Boston Whaler at no additional charge. There's also badminton, croquet, and lounging in the gazebo overlooking the water.

Nevada Motel. Route 1A (P.O. Box 885), York Beach, 03910. ☎ **207/363-4504.** 21 rms. A/C TV TEL. Mid-June to Labor Day $78 double; off-season $56 double. AE, MC, V. Closed Oct 15–May 15.

This unassuming, classic 1953 beachfront motel is a low, white, two-story affair with turquoise trim offering simple, comfortable rooms, most of which are on the small side. But the sound of surf reaches the rooms through louvered windows (Long Sands Beach is just across Route 1A), and there's spacious deck on the second floor that affords wonderful views across the road to the ocean beyond. The Nevada is popular with a mix of guests, from families to couples, most of whom simply spend their day on the beach.

Stage Neck Inn. Stage Neck (P.O. Box 70), York Harbor, ME 03911. ☎ **207/363-3850** or 800/222-3238. 60 rms. A/C TV TEL. June through Labor Day $135–$205 double; early fall

$115–$185 double; winter $85–$130 double; spring $100–$150 double. AE, DISC, MC, V. Head north on 1A from Route 1; make second right after York Harbor post office.

A hotel in one form or another has been housing guests on this windswept bluff between the harbor and the open ocean since about 1870. The most current incarnation was constructed in 1972, and it defines modern elegance for the region. The hotel, while indisputably up to date, successfully creates a sense of old-fashioned intimacy and avoids the overbearing grandeur to which many modern resorts aspire, often with poor results. Almost every room has a waterview, and guests enjoy low-key recreational pursuits. It's but a few steps to York Harbor Beach. No smoking.

Dining/Entertainment: The dining room is outstanding, offering dinner entrees ranging from blackened Maine crab cakes to grilled pork medallions with apple-Dijon-garlic glaze.

Facilities: There are pools indoors and out, a Jacuzzi, and tennis courts overlooking the ocean.

Union Bluff Hotel. Beach St. (at the north end of Short Sands Beach), York Beach, ME 03910. ☎ **207/363-1333** or 800/833-0721 (out of state). 36 rooms, 4 suites. A/C TV TEL. Summer $95–$135 double; early fall $65–$85 double; spring and late fall $55–$75 double; winter $45–$65 double. $150–$200 suite, varying with seasons. AE, DISC, MC, V.

Viewed from Short Sands Beach, the Union Bluff Hotel, with its stumpy turrets, dormers, and prominent porches, has the look and feel of an old-fashioned beach hotel. So it's a bit of a surprise to learn it was built in 1989 (the fifth hotel to rise on this site since the late 1800s). Inside is a snug new facility with all the modern amenities. Rooms have oak furniture, wall-to-wall carpeting, and small refrigerators. There's a comfortable and quiet deck on the top floor for getting away from it all (alas, no ocean view). Step outside and you're at the beach and the Fun-O-Rama arcade with its candlepin bowling and banks of video games. (This can be a bit noisy in the evening if your room faces this direction.) Most rooms offer great views; the best rooms are the funky suites on the top floor, which offer beach vistas from sitting areas in the turrets.

On the ground floor there's a popular lounge and a restaurant; both are open only during the warmer months.

WHERE TO DINE

✪ **Cape Neddick Inn.** 1233 Rte. 1, Cape Neddick. ☎ **207/363-2899.** Reservations recommended. Full dinners $18–$27; light entrees served a la carte $10–$14. AE, MC, V. Summer daily 6–9pm; closed one or two days weekly during off season (call ahead). REGIONAL/CONTINENTAL.

This fine inn offers some of the consistently best dining in southern Maine. Located in an elegant structure (largely rebuilt after a recent fire) on a relatively undeveloped stretch of Route 1, the Cape Neddick Inn has a open, handsome dining area that mixes traditional and modern. The old comes in the cozy golden glow of the room. The modern is the artwork, which changes frequently and showcases some of the region's better painters and sculptors.

The highly creative menu also changes frequently to make the most of seasonal products. Depending on the season, the menu might include roasted chicken breast stuffed with shallots, basil, and boursin cheese and served with an artichoke wine sauce; or a horseradish and ginger-encrusted salmon with a soy and sake sauce. Save room for dessert, which tends to be extravagant.

⑤ Goldenrod Restaurant. Railroad Rd. and Ocean Ave. York Beach. ☎ **207/363-2621.** Breakfast $2.10–$5.25; lunch and dinner entrees $1.75–$7.50. MC, V. Memorial Day–Labor Day daily 8:30am–10:30pm; closed some weekdays during shoulder seasons. Closed Columbus Day to mid-May. AMERICAN.

This beachtown classic is the place for local color with breakfast or lunch. The Goldenrod has been a summer institution in York Beach since it first opened in 1896. It's easy to find: look for gawking visitors on the sidewalk at the plate glass windows, mesmerized by the ancient taffy machines hypnotically churning out taffy in volumes enough to make thousands of dentists very wealthy.

The restaurant, behind the taffy and fudge operation, is low on frills and long on atmosphere. Diners sit on stout oak furniture around a stone fireplace, or at the marble soda fountain. There are dark beams overhead and the sort of linoleum floor you don't see much anymore. Breakfast offerings are the standards: omelets, waffles, griddle cakes and bakery items. Lunch is fairly predictable, but equally well presented. As for dinner, you'd probably be better served heading to some place more creative.

Jama's Cafe. 433 Route 1, York. ☎ **207/363-7980.** Main courses $4.25–$11.95. AE, DC, DISC, MC, V. Mon–Fri 11:30am–9pm, Sat–Sun 11:30am–10pm. MEXICAN/AMERICAN.

Mexican food in northern New England all too often means soggy tortillas and vast amounts of preternaturally orange cheese. Jama's, situated away from the coast along a dowdy stretch of Route 1, is an exception. The Mexican food here is better than average for Maine, served up with an earthy, tangy salsa and an extravagant choice of margaritas (watermelon? blueberry? raspberry?). While the festive, south-of-the-border decor will put you in a frame of mind for Mexican entrees like fajitas or chimichangas, the menu also offers a selection of American classics, such as grilled sirloin and BBQ chicken.

OGUNQUIT

Ogunquit is said to come from a Wabanaki Indian word meaning "sandbar." And why not? It seems appropriate, given the grand sweep of picturesque Ogunquit Beach, which has attracted vacationers and artists for more than a century. Ogunquit's fame as an artist's colony dates to 1890, when Charles H. Woodbury arrived and pronounced the place an "artist's paradise." He was followed by artists such as Walt Kuhn, Elihu Vedder, Yasuo Kuniyoshi, and Rudoph Dirks, who was best known for creating the "Katzenjammer Kids" comic strip.

The town bristles with restaurants and inns and can feel overrun with tourists during the peak summer season, especially on weekends. The cure? Head for the expansive beach, which by and large has been protected from development, and is large enough to allow most of the teeming masses to disperse.

ESSENTIALS

GETTING THERE   Ogunquit is located on Route 1 between York and Wells. It's accessible from either Exit 1 or Exit 2 of the Maine Turnpike.

VISITOR INFORMATION   The **Ogunquit Welcome Center,** P.O. Box 2289, Ogunquit, ME 03907 (☎ **207/646-5533** or 207/646-2939), is located on Route 1 south of the village center. It's open daily Memorial Day through Columbus Day, and weekdays during the off-season.

GETTING AROUND   The village of Ogunquit is centered around an awkward four-way intersection that seems fiendishly designed to cause traffic foul-ups in summer. Parking in and around the village is also tight and relatively expensive (expect to pay $5 or $6 per day). As a result, Ogunquit is best reconnoitered on foot, by bike, or on the trackless trolley.

EXPLORING THE TOWN

The village center is good for an hour's browsing among the boutiques (check out the eclectic crafts at Maya's, 23 Shore Rd.) or sipping a cappucino at one of the several coffee emporia.

From the village you can walk the mile to scenic **Perkins Cove** along Marginal Way, a mile-long oceanside pathway once used for herding cattle to pasture. Earlier in this century, the land was bought by a local developer who deeded the right-of-way to the town. The pathway, which is wide and well-maintained, departs across from the Seacastles Resort on Shore Road. It passes tide pools, pocket beaches, and rocky, fissured bluffs, all of which are worth exploring. The scenery can be spectacular (especially after a storm), but Marginal Way can also be spectacularly crowded during fair weather weekends. To elude the crowds, try heading out in the early morning.

Perkins Cove, accessible either from Marginal Way or by driving south on Shore Road and veering left at the "Y" intersection, is a small, well-protected harbor that seems custom-designed for a photo opportunity. As such, it attracts visitors by the busload, carload, and boatload, and can often be congested. A handful of galleries, restaurants, and T-shirt shops catering to the tourist trade occupy a cluster of quaint buildings between the harbor and the sea. An intriguing pedestrian drawbridge is operated by whomever happens to be handy, allowing sailboats to come and go. Perkins Cove is also home to several tour boat operators, who offer trips of various durations throughout the day and at twilight. But if tourist traps give you hives, steer clear of Perkins Cove.

Not far from the cove is **The Ogunquit Museum of Art,** Shore Road (☎ 207/646-4909), one of the best small art museums in the country. Set back from the road in a grassy glen overlooking the rocky shore, the museum's spectacular view initially overwhelms the artwork as visitors walk through the door. But stick around a few minutes—the changing exhibits in this architecturally engaging museum of cement block, slate, and glass will get your attention soon enough, since the curators have a track record of staging superb shows and attracting national attention. (Be sure to note the bold, underappreciated work of Henry Strater, the Ogunquit artist who built the museum in 1953.) The museum is open July 1 to September 30 from 10:30am to 5pm Monday through Saturday, and 2 to 5pm on Sunday. Admission is $3 for adults, $2 for seniors.

For evening entertainment, head to the **Ogunquit Playhouse,** Route 1 (☎ 207/646-5511), a summer stock theater that has garnered a solid reputation for its careful, serious attention to stagecraft. The theater has entertained Ogunquit since the 1930s, attracting noted actors such as Bette Davis, Tallulah Bankhead, and Gary Merrill. Stars of recent seasons have included Gavin McLeod and Kitty Carlisle Hart.

BEACHES

Ogunquit's main beach is three miles long, and three paid parking lots are located along its length. The most popular access point (with the most expensive parking) is at the foot of Beach Street, which connects to Ogunquit Village. The beach ends at a sandy spit, where the Ogunquit River flows into the sea, and offers changing rooms and a handful of informal restaurants. It's also the most crowded part of the beach. Less crowded, less expensive options are at Footbridge Beach (turn on Ocean Avenue off Route 1 north of the village center) and Moody Beach (turn on Eldridge Avenue in Wells).

A ROAD TRIP TO LAUDHOLM FARM

A short drive north of Ogunquit, just above the beach town of Wells, is the **Laudholm Farm** (☎ **207/646-1555**), a historic saltwater farm owned by the nonprofit Laudholm Trust since 1986. The 1,600-acre property was originally the summer home of 19th-century railroad baron George Lord, but has been used for estaurine research since taken over by the trust. The farm has seven miles of trails through diverse ecosystems, which range from salt marsh to forest to dunes. A visitor center in the regal Victorian farmhouse will get you oriented. Tours are available, or you can explore the grounds on your own. Parking costs $5 in summer; it's free the rest of the year. There's no admission charge to the grounds or visitor center.

The farm is reached by turning east on Laudholm Farm Road at the blinking light just north of Harding's Books (which, incidentally, is located in Lord's former private railroad station). Bear left at the fork then turn right into the farm's entrance. The grounds are open 8am to 5pm daily.

WHERE TO STAY

The Aspinquid. Beach St. (P.O. Box 2408), Ogunquit, ME 03907. ☎ **207/646-7072.** Fax 207/646-1187. 62 rms. A/C MINIBAR TV TEL. June to Labor Day $95–$205 double; shoulder seasons $60–$115 double. AE, MC, V. Closed mid-Oct to mid-Mar.

Built on the site of the old Aspinquid Hotel in 1971, the new Aspinquid is a complex of modern, shingled buildings located an easy stroll across the bridge from Ogunquit's beach. Rooms range from basic motel units to two-room apartments, and all are equipped with most modern amenities. If the beach grows tiresome, on the grounds you'll find a spa, sauna, swimming pool, tennis courts, and a purebred Maine coon cat named Socrates. "If he is an unwanted visitor," notes a letter to the guests, "just shoo him out of your room."

Beauport Inn. 102 Shore Rd., Ogunquit, ME 03907. ☎ **207/646-8680** or 800/646-8681. 4 rms (2 with showers only). End of June to Labor Day $85; off-season $65. Rates include continental breakfast. Surcharge of $10 if staying just 1 night on weekends or holidays. AE, MC, V. Closed Dec 15–Mar 1.

Dan Pender opened this cozy bed-and-breakfast in 1988, where he offers four comfortable guest rooms furnished in a casual, summer-home style with eclectic antiques. The inn, which is on busy Shore Road between the village and Perkins Cove, makes a good base for exploring the area on foot, and guests can walk to most area restaurants. After a day wandering the town, unwind by lounging on the back deck or in the pine-panelled living room. The home is only about 60 years old, but has the feel of a place with a longer and more distinguished heritage.

Marginal Way House. Wharf Lane (P.O. Box 697), Ogunquit, ME 03907. ☎ **207/646-8801,** or 207/363-6566 in winter. 30 rms, some with showers only. TV. Peak season $75–$150 double; shoulder seasons $40–$130 double. No credit cards. Closed late Oct to mid-Apr.

If you travel for vistas, this is your place. Even if your room lacks a sweeping ocean view (and that's unlikely), you've got the run of the lawn and the guest house porch, both of which overlook Ogunquit River to the beach and sea beyond. This attractive compound centers around a four-story, mid–19th-century guest house, which is surrounded by four more-or-less modern outbuildings. The whole affair is situated on a large, grassy lot on a quiet cul-de-sac. Indeed, it's hard to believe that you're smack in the middle of Ogunquit, with both the beach and the village just a few minutes' walk away. All rooms have refrigerators ("for the caviar and champagne," the manager says), and all but two have air conditioning for those few days when the sea breeze fails. For longer stays, one and two bedroom efficiencies are available.

WHERE TO DINE

✪ **Arrows.** Berwick Rd. ☎ **207/361-1100.** Reservations strongly recommended. Main courses $25.95–$29.95. MC, V. May and Columbus Day–Thanksgiving Fri–Sat 6–9pm; June and Sept–Columbus Day Wed–Sun 6–9pm; July–Aug Tues–Sun 6–9pm. Closed Thanksgiving to Apr. Turn uphill at the Key Bank in the village; the restaurant is 1.9 miles on your right. REGIONAL/ NEW AMERICAN.

Ask well-heeled Mainers to name the five best restaurants in the state, and it's likely that Arrows will appear on most lists. Since owner/chefs Marc Gaier and Clark Frasier opened in 1988, they've managed to put Ogunquit on the national culinary map. And they've done so by not only creating a elegant and intimate atmosphere in a pleasant country setting, but by serving up some of the freshest, most innovative cooking in New England. The atmosphere is that of a classic European country inn, with oak chairs, white tablecloths, and a smartly uniformed waitstaff. The main dining room has heavy timbers overhead, and lighted views to the lush summer gardens.

The emphasis is on local products—very local products. The salad greens are grown in the gardens in back, and much of the rest is grown or raised locally. The food transcends traditional New England, and is concocted with some exotic twists and turns. Frasier lived and traveled widely in Asia, and his Far Eastern experiences often influence the menu, which changes nightly. Typically creative entrees might include grilled yellowfin tuna served with a melange of golden chanterelles, warm garden frisee, walnuts, and a wild mushroom broth; or smoked duck breast with baby bok choy, garlic, jasmine rice fritters, and Sichuan marinated eggplant. The wine list is superb. Arrows is not for the timid of wallet, but makes for a special evening.

Barnacle Billy's & Barnacle Billy's Etc. Perkins Cove. ☎ **207/646-5575.** Reservations not accepted. Lunch $3.65–$11.95; dinner $10.95–$18.95. AE, MC, V. Daily 11am–10pm. Closed Nov to mid-Apr. SEAFOOD.

This pair of side-by-side restaurants under the same ownership are a bit like brothers, one of whom became a fisherman, the other an executive. The original Barnacle Billy's, a local landmark since 1961, is a place-your-order-take-a-number-and-wait-on-the-deck-style restaurant with the usual nautical decor and pine furniture inside. Its fancier sibling next door has valet parking, sit-down service, and demonstrates better breeding.

In both places, you're largely paying for the same thing: the unobstructed view of Perkins Cove. At the original Barnacle Billy's, that means the food is at the high end of the price range for what you get (on my last visit the iced tea was $1.50 for a glass that was almost all ice). It's best to stick to simple fare, like chowder or boiled lobster. The prices are steeper but the value better next door, where the service seems less weary and more care is taken with the food. Entrees include a variety of broiled, fried, and grilled seafood, along with a selection of poultry and meat.

✪ **Hurricane.** Oarweed Dr., Perkins Cove. ☎ **207/646-6348.** Reservations recommended. Lunch items $6.95–$12.95; main dinner courses $13.95–$24.95. AE, DC, DISC, MC, V. Mon–Sat 11:30am–4pm, Sun 11:30am–4:30pm; Mon–Thurs 5:30–9:30pm, Fri–Sat 5:30–10:30pm. NEW AMERICAN.

Tucked away amid the T-shirt kitsch of Perkins Cove is one of the southern Maine's classiest dining experiences. The plain shingled exterior of the building, set along a curving, narrow lane, doesn't begin to hint at what you'll find on the inside. The narrow dining room is divided into two smallish halves, but soaring windows overlooking the Gulf of Maine make the rooms feel much larger than they actually are. During a storm, you're likely to feel as if you're on the prow of the ship.

Hurricane sneaks in surprises at almost every turn, from the waiters in white shirts and ties (you don't see that much in Maine beach towns), to the delicate Victorian-style back bar. The cuisine offers pleasant surprises as well, with creative concoctions like an appetizer of deviled Maine lobster cakes served with a tangy fresh salsa. Main courses include a lobster cannellonni with mascarpone cheese and shiitake mushrooms, and a baked salmon and brie baklava with a Key lime bearnaise. Added bonus: Hurricane makes the best martinis in town.

THE KENNEBUNKS

"The Kennebunks" consist of the villages of Kennebunk and Kennebunkport, both situated on the shores of tiny rivers. The region was first settled in the mid-1600s and flourished following the American Revolution when ship captains, ship builders, and successful merchants constructed the imposing, solid homes for which the region is noted. The two villages have decidedly different characters; a visit to these siblings provides contrasting looks at a coastal and an inland town.

While summer is the busy season, winter has its charm: the grand architecture is better seen through leafless trees. When the snow flies, guests find solace curling up in front of a fire at one of the inviting inns.

ESSENTIALS

GETTING THERE   Kennebunk is located off Exit 3 of the Maine Turnpike. Kennebunkport is 3.5 miles SE of Kennebunk on Port Road (Route 35).

VISITOR INFORMATION   The **Kennebunk-Kennebunkport Chamber of Commerce,** P.O. Box 740, Kennebunk, ME 04043 (☎ **207/967-0857**), can answer your questions year-round. It also maintains an information booth (open Memorial Day to Columbus Day) on Route 35 just west of the intersection with Route 9. The Kennebunkport Information Center (☎ 207/967-8600) is off Dock Square (next to Ben & Jerry's) and is open throughout the summer and fall.

EXPLORING KENNEBUNK

Kennebunk, an inland town just off the turnpike, is a dignified, small commercial center of white clapboard and brick. The **Brick Store Museum,** 117 Main St. (☎ **207/985-4802**), hosts shows of historical art and artifacts throughout the summer, switching to contemporary art in the off-season. The museum, which over-hauled its galleries in 1994, is housed (naturally enough) in a historic former brick store, as well as the three adjacent buildings. Admission is $3 (12 years and older). Open Tuesday through Saturday from 10am to 4:30pm.

Tom's of Maine, a natural toothpaste maker, is also headquartered here. Tom and Kate Chappell sell their all-natural toothpaste and other personal care products world-wide, but are almost as well know for espousing a green, socially-conscious business philosophy. (Tom wrote a 1993 book on the subject.) Tom's factory outlet sells firsts and seconds of its own products, as well as a selection of other natural products. The shop is at Lafayette Center, a sturdy brick industrial building converted to shops and offices at the corner of Main and Water streets.

When en route to or from the coast, be sure to note the extraordinary historic homes (including the renowned "Wedding Cake House") that line Port Road (Route 35).

EXPLORING KENNEBUNKPORT

Nearby Kennebunkport has better name recognition thanks to President George Bush, whose family has summered here for most of this century. It also has a tweedy, upper-crust feel that you might expect of a town where the former President feels comfortable. This historic village, whose streets were laid out during days of travel by foot and horse, is subject to epic traffic jams around the town center, called Dock Square. Your best strategy is to avoid driving near the square, park some distance away, then approach the square by foot.

Dock Square has a pleasantly wharflike feel to it, with low buildings of mixed vintages and styles (you'll find mansard, gabled, and hip roofs side by side), but the flavor is mostly clapboard and shingles. The boutiques and restaurants at the square are worth a quick browse, but Kennebunkport's real attractions are found on the surrounding blocks, where the side streets are lined with one of the richest assortments of early American homes in the country. The neighborhoods are particularly ripe with examples of Federal-style homes, in some of which you can spend the night (see "Where to Stay," below).

Aimless wandering is a good tactic for exploring Kennebunkport, but make an effort to swing by the **Richard A. Nott Memorial** in your travels. Situated on Maine Street at the head of Spring Street, this imposing Greek Revival house was built 1853 and is a Victorian-era aficionado's dream. It remained untouched by the Nott family through the years, and was donated to the local historical society with the stipulation that it remain forever unchanged. It still boasts the original wallpaper, carpeting, and furnishings. It's open afternoons mid-June through mid-October Wednesday through Saturday. Admission is $3 adults, $2 children 6 to 12.

Ocean Drive from Dock Square to Walkers Point and beyond is lined with opulent summer homes overlooking surf and rocky shore. This stretch is best appreciated by bike or on foot. You'll likely recognize the former president's home at Walkers Point when you arrive. If it's not familiar from the four years it spent in the spotlight, look for the swarming crowds with telephoto lenses.

A Museum on the Move

✪ **The Seashore Trolley Museum.** Log Cabin Rd., Kennebunkport. ☎ **207/967-2800.** http://www.biddeford.com:80/trolley/. $7 adults, $4 children 6–16, $5 seniors. Daily May through mid-Oct; weekends only through mid-Nov. Head north from Kennebunkport on North Street; look for signs.

A short drive north of Kennebunkport on Log Cabin Road is one of the quirkiest and most engaging museums in the state. The Seashore Trolley Museum, a place with an excess of character and an intriguing history, is well worth a visit. This scrapyard-masquerading-as-a-museum ("world's oldest and largest museum of its type") was founded in 1939 to preserve a disappearing way of life, and today the collection contains more than 200 trolleys from around the world, including Glasgow, Moscow, San Francisco, and Rome. Of course, there's also a streetcar named Desire from New Orleans. About 40 of the cars still operate, and the admission charge includes unlimited rides on a 2-mile track. The other cars, some of which still contain turn of the century advertising, are on display outdoors and in vast storage sheds.

A good museum inspires awe and educates its visitors on the sly. This one does so deftly, and not until visitors are driving away are they likely to realize how much they learned.

BEACHES

Several local beaches are suitable for an afternoon's relaxation. To the south of the Kennebunk River is **Kennebunk Beach** and **Gooch's Beach;** to the north is **Goose Rocks Beach.** These beaches tend to be less crowded and noisy than the beaches in York and Ogunquit to the south, or Old Orchard Beach to the north. Parking at the beaches requires a permit, which can usually be obtained at the town offices or from your hotel.

BIKING & KAYAKING

The Kennebunks are well-suited to both biking and sea kayaking. Bikes may be rented at **Cape Able Bike Shop** north of Kennebunkport (☎ **207/967-4382** or 800/220-0907). Some inns also will rent bikes to guests; ask when you reserve a room. **Kayak Adventures** (☎ **207/967-5243**) offers both kayak rentals and guided trips throughout the summer, weather permitting.

WHERE TO STAY

Expensive

Captain Lord. Pleasant St. and Green St. (P.O. Box 800), Kennebunkport, ME 04046. ☎ **207/967-3141.** Fax 207/967-3172. Internet www.biddeford.com:80/inntravel/inn0001.html. 16 rms. A/C TEL. $149–$199 double. $60 off during midweek in Jan–Apr. Two-night minimum on weekends. Rates include breakfast. DISC, MC, V.

It's simple: This is the best building in Kennebunkport, in the best location, and furnished with the best antiques. The Captain Lord is one of the most architecturally distinguished inns anywhere, housed in a pale-yellow Federal-style home that peers down a shady lawn toward the river. The adjective "stately" is laughably inadequate.

When you enter the downstairs reception area, you'll know immediately that you've transcended the realm of "wannaB&Bs." This is the genuine article, with grandfather clocks and Chippendale highboys—and that's just the front hallway. Off the hall is a comfortable common area with piped-in classical music and a broad brick fireplace. The rooms are furnished with splendid antiques. Some beds are high enough to require a running start to mount. The only complaint I've heard about this place is that it's too nice, too perfect, too friendly. That puts some people on edge. No smoking.

✪ **The Colony.** Ocean Ave. (about a mile from Dock Square; P.O. Box 511), Kennebunkport, ME 04046. ☎ **207/967-3331** or 800/552-2363. Fax 207/967-8738. Email colony@cybertours.com. Internet www.cybertours.com/colony/home.html. 135 rms in four buildings. TEL. $175–$265 double. Rates include breakfast and dinner. AE, MC, V. Closed mid-Oct to mid–May.

The Colony is one of the handful of oceanside resorts that has preserved intact the classic New England vacation experience. This gleaming white Georgian Revival (built in 1914) lords over the ocean and the mouth of the Kennebunk River. The three-story main inn has 105 rooms, most of which have recently been updated. The rooms are bright and cheery, simply furnished with summer cottage antiques. Rooms in two of the three outbuildings carry over the rustic elegance of the main hotel; the exception is the East House, a 1950s-era motor hotel at the back edge of the property with 20 charmless motel-style rooms.

Guest rooms lack TVs in the main inn, and that's by design. The Boughton family, which has owned the hotel since 1948, encourages guests to leave their rooms in the evening and socialize downstairs in the lobby, on the porch, or at the shuffleboard court, which is lighted for night-time play. During the day, activities include swimming in a heated saltwater pool (or at a small pebble beach across the street), golfing on the putting green overlooking the ocean, or renting bikes and exploring Ocean Avenue.

Dining/Entertainment: The massive, pine-panelled dining room seats up to 400, and guests are assigned one table for throughout their stay. Dinners begin with a relish tray, but quickly progress to a more contemporary era with regional entrees such as rainbow tortellini with lobster marinara sauce, or maple-cured ham with apricot-orange sauce. On Sundays, there's a jazz brunch.

Maine Stay Inn and Cottages. 34 Maine St. (P.O. Box 500), Kennebunkport, ME 04046. ☎ **207/967-2117** or 800/950-2117. Fax 207/967-8757. 17 rms (some with showers only), 11 cottages. A/C TV. Summer and foliage season $95–$185 double, $210 two-bedroom cottage; late fall to spring $85–$165 double. Rates include breakfast. AE, DISC, MC, V.

Built in 1860, this handsome white home with its prominent cupola is something of an architectural interloper in Kennebunkport, which had its biggest "development" phase a half-century earlier, when locals copied the austere Federal style of wealthy Boston merchants.

But never mind. Innkeepers Carol and Lindsay Copeland, who bought the inn in 1988, have instilled a strong sense of history as they've brought the inn into the modern era. Guest room decor might best be described as traditional-without-going-overboard-to-be-authentic. The common room is comfortably furnished. (I can't quite explain it, but I had the weird feeling that I had accidentally walked into Bararba Bush's house when I stepped through the front door.) Be sure to note the exceptionally fine staircase in the main hall. The cottages, arrayed along the property's perimeter, are equally appealing. While constructed in the 1950s, they've been updated with small kitchens, and many have gas fireplaces.

The inn is happy to accommodate children, and there's a small playground on the edge of the lawn. No smoking.

✪ **White Barn Inn.** Beach St. (¹/₄ mile east of junction of Routes 9 and 35; P.O. Box 560), Kennebunkport, ME 04046. ☎ **207/967-2321.** Fax 207/967-1100. 24 rms. A/C TEL. $140–$205 double; suites up to $375. Rates include breakfast. AE, MC, V.

The White Barn Inn pampers its guests like no other in Maine. Upon checking in, guests are shown to one of the inn's parlors and offered sherry or brandy while valets in dark uniforms gather luggage and park the cars. A tour of the inn follows, then guests are left to their own devices. They can avail themselves of the inn's free bikes (including a small fleet of tandems) to head to the beach, or walk cross the street and wander the quiet, shady pathways of Saint Anthony's Franciscan Monastery. The innkeepers plan to install a swimming pool behind the carriage house in 1996.

The inn has a heavily European atmosphere (no surprise: nearly half the staff is here on special visas from Europe), and the emphasis is on service. I'm not aware of any other inn of this size that offers as many unexpected niceties, like robes, fresh flowers in the rooms, bottled water, and turn-down service at night. The inn also serves some of the best fare in Maine (see "Where to Dine," below) in the adjoining barn. No smoking.

Moderate

Captain Jefferds Inn. Pearl St. (P.O. Box 691), Kennebunkport, ME 04046. ☎ **207/967-2311.** 12 rms plus 5 suites in adjacent carriage house. $85–$150 double; $145–$165 suite. Rates include breakfast. Two-night minimum July–Oct and holiday weekends. MC, V. Closed Dec 15–Apr 1.

Warren Fitzsimmons and Don Kelly are the owners of this handsome 1804 Federal home located in Kennebunkport's most historic neighborhood. They're also antique dealers, which will be obvious upon entering the inn. The common rooms are wonderfully and eccentrically furnished with collections of ceramic pitchers, miniature wicker chairs, turquoise-colored plates, and Majolica everywhere (they have 2,000 pieces in their collection). The remarkable thing is this: it doesn't feel cluttered.

On foggy days, guests can peruse the collections in the common room while warming themselves in front of the fire. When the weather's more cooperative, the cheerful sun room with its bamboo furniture makes a nice retreat. Breakfast is served indoors (and on the terrace in summer) in two sittings, at 8 or 9am. Most inn rooms have antique canopy beds, with the carriage house rooms somewhat more casually furnished. No smoking.

Kennebunkport Inn. Dock Square (P.O. Box 111), Kennebunkport, ME 04046. ☎ **207/ 967-2621** or 800/248-2621 (out of state). Fax 207/967-3705. 34 rms (some with shower only). A/C TV. Summer $84.50–$189 double; Sept–Oct $79.50–$189 double; off-season $69.50–$179 double. MAP rates available summer and fall. AE, MC, V.

Situated behind a scrim of maple trees a few steps from bustling Dock Square, the Kennebunkport Inn's exterior is busy with an amalgam of dormers, gables, porticos, awnings, and modern additions. Despite all this architectural frenzy, the stately 1899 inn manages the mean feat of both blending in with and standing out from its surroundings. Inside, it's impeccably maintained. The rooms are nicely furnished, many with turn-of-the-century antiques. (Some equally well-appointed rooms are located in the adjoining River House, built in the 1930s.)

Downstairs, there's a handsome, clubby lounge and a well-respected dining room, which is open summer and fall. For extended lounging, there's a pool and a relaxing front deck.

King's Port Inn. Junction of Routes 9 and 35 (P.O. Box 1172), Kennebunkport, ME 04046. ☎ **207/967-4340** or 800-286-5767. Fax 207/967-4810. 32 rms. A/C TV TEL. Summer $79– $115 double; spring and fall $59–$102 double; winter $39–$82 double. Rates include breakfast. AE, MC, V.

The King's Port Inn offers reasonably priced motel rooms within easy walking distance of Dock Square and area restaurants. That's the good news. The bad news: the structure is boxy and uninspired, the furnishings tend to be of a certain age, and the least expensive rooms are a bit gloomy. On the bright side, the current owners are remodeling bit by bit (ask about the remodeled rooms with two-person Jacuzzis), all rooms have small refrigerators, and room rates include the filling breakfast buffet.

WHERE TO DINE

Federal Jack's Restaurant and Brew Pub. Lower Village (south bank of Kennebunk River), Kennebunkport. ☎ **207/967-4322.** Reservations not accepted. Lunch items $5.25–$12.95; main dinner courses $6.25–$21.95. MC, V. Daily 11:30am–4pm; Sun–Thurs 5–9pm, Fri–Sat 5– 10pm. PUB FARE.

This light, airy, and modern restaurant is in a new retail complex that sits a bit uneasily amid the scrappy boatyards lining the south bank of the Kennebunk River. From the second floor perch (look for a seat on the spacious deck in warm weather) you can gaze across the river toward the shops of Dock Square, which is within easy walking distance across the nonworking draw bridge. The menu features basic entrees like hamburgers, BBQ pork ribs, and pizza, but everything is well prepared. Watch for specials like the tasty crab and artichoke bisque.

Don't leave without sampling the Shipyard ales, lagers, and porters brewed downstairs, which are among the best in New England. Shipyard brews a seasonal India Pale Ale in summer that's exceptional. Consider also the ale sampler, which provides tastes of various brews. Nontipplers can enjoy zesty homemade root beer.

✪ **White Barn Inn.** Beach St., Kennebunkport. ☎ **207/967-2321.** Reservations recommended. Fixed-price dinner $56. AE, MC, V. Daily 6–9pm (open later during peak season). Closed Jan. REGIONAL/NEW AMERICAN.

People don't come to the White Barn Inn just for special occasions, like anniversaries or birthdays. They come for really special occasions, like anniversaries or birthdays that end in "0" or "5." It's that kind of place (and one that charges that kind of price), but worth saving up for if you're bound and determined to make your stay in Maine unforgettable.

The setting is magical. The restaurant (attached to an equally magical inn, see above) is housed in an ancient, rustic barn with a soaring interior that might be compared without embarrassment to a cathedral's nave. (The furnace runs nearly full time in winter to keep the space comfortable.) There's a copper-topped bar off to one side, rich leather seating in the waiting area, a pianist setting the mood, and an eclectic collection of antiques displayed in the hay loft above. On the tables are floor-length tablecloths, and the chairs feature imported Italian upholstery that recalls early Flemish tapestries.

The menu changes frequently, but depending on the season you might start with a lobster spring roll with daikon, carrot, snowpeas and cilantro, then graduate to a grilled duckling breast with ginger and sundried cherry sauce, or a roast rack of lamb with pecans and homemade barbecue sauce. Anticipate a meal to remember. The White Barn won't disappoint.

Windows on the Water. 12 Chase Hill Rd. (above Lower Village), Kennebunkport. ☎ **207/ 967-3313** or 800/773-3313. Reservations recommended. Lunch items $6.95–$14.95; main dinner courses $13.95–$23.95. AE, DC, DISC, MC, V. Daily 11:45am–2:30pm; Sun–Thurs 5:30–9pm, Fri 5:30- 9:30pm, Sat 5:30–10pm. NEW ENGLAND/INTERNATIONAL.

First off, the name's a bit of a misnomer. It's more like Windows on the Kennebunkport Brewing Co., although some glimpses of the river might be had over the newer buildings, especially from the second floor dining room. But the compromised views aren't much of a loss, since the interiors of this modern restaurant are tastefully done, with pink tablecloths, oak chairs, and oak accenting. There's also a pleasant garden room with brick flooring and patio furniture, and dining upstairs in a room that's slightly more intimate if somewhat more antiseptic.

The food here is superb. The menu is based on classic New England cuisine, but with cooking techniques and spicing borrowed from around the world. There's seafood fettucine Milanese, lobster ravioli, and Thai lobster, the latter a delicious concoction served with soy, ginger, coconut milk, and curry. The full dinner menu is available at lunch, along with lighter entrees such as lobster croissants and chicken ceasar salad.

3 Portland

Portland is Maine's largest city, and easily one of the most attractive, liveable small cities on the East Coast. Actually, Portland has more the feel of a really large town than a small city. Strike up a conversation with a resident, and she's likely to give you an earful about how easy it is to live here. You can buy superb coffee, see great movies, and get delicious pad thai to go (Portland has five Thai restaurants). Yet it's still small enough to walk from one end of town to the other, and postal workers and bank clerks know your name soon after you move here. Despite its outward appearance of being an actual city, Portland has a population of just 65,000 (about half that of Peoria, Ill.).

In some ways, Portland is still figuring out what it wants to be when it grows up. It was a center for maritime trade in the 19th century, when a forest of masts obscured the view of the harbor. It's been a manufacturing hub, with locomotive factories, steel foundries, and fish packing facilities. It's been a mercantile center with impressive downtown department stores and a slew of wholesale dealers. Today, as the mall area of South Portland diverts much of the local economic energy, the city is bent on its downtown becoming a major tourist destination (plans for a $50 million aquarium are underway) and a regional center for the arts. These multiple layers of history, architecture, and commerce make Portland an especially rich destination.

ESSENTIALS

GETTING THERE   Portland is located off the Maine Turnpike (I-95). Coming from the south, downtown is most easily reached by taking Exit 6A off the turnpike, then following I-295 into town. Get off at the Franklin St. exit and follow this eastward until you arrive at the waterfront at the Casco Bay Lines terminal. Turn right on Commercial St. and you'll be at the lower edge of the Old Port. Continue on a few blocks to the visitor's center (see below).

    Concord Trailways (☎ **800/639-3317** or 207/828-1151) and **Vermont Transit** (☎ **800/537-3330** or 207/772-6587) offer bus service to Portland from Boston and Bangor. The Vermont Transit bus terminal is located at 950 Congress St. Concord Trailways, which is slightly more expensive, offers movies and headsets on its trips. The Concord terminal is at 161 Marginal Way.

    The **Portland International Jetport** is served by regularly scheduled flights on several airlines, including **Business Express** (☎ **800/345-3400**), **Continental** (☎ **800/525-0280**), **Delta** (☎ **800/221-1212**), **USAir** (☎ **800/428-4322**), **United** (☎ **800/241-6522**), **Pine State** (☎ **207/879-6111**), and **Down East** (☎ **800/983-3247**). The small and easily navigated airport is located just across the Fore River from downtown. Metro buses ($1) connect the airport to downtown; cab fare runs about $10.

    Amtrak (☎ **800/872-7245**) is planning to resume rail service to Portland in 1997 after a hiatus of several decades. Call for an update.

VISITOR INFORMATION   The **Convention and Visitor's Bureau of Greater Portland,** 305 Commercial St., Portland, ME 04101 (☎ **207/772-4994**), stocks a large supply of brochures and is happy to dispense information about local attractions, lodging, and dining. The center is open in summer weekdays 8am to 6pm and weekends 10am to 5pm; hours are shorter during the off-season. Ask for the free "Greater Portland Visitor Guide" with map.

    Casco Bay Weekly is a free alternative paper distributed Thursdays at many downtown stores and restaurants. The paper features extensive listings of performers at area clubs and other upcoming events.

SPECIAL EVENTS   **New Year's/Portland** (☎ **207/772-9012**) rings in January with a smorgasbord of events and entertainment throughout downtown Portland. Events for families are scheduled in the afternoon; adult entertainment including loads of live music kicks off later in the evening at numerous locales, including auditoriums, shops, and churches. One admission price buys entrance to all events.

    The **Old Port Festival** (☎ **207/772-6828**) takes place in early June when tens of thousands of revelers descend upon the historic Old Port section to herald the arrival of summer. Several blocks of the Old Port are blocked to traffic, and the throngs order food and buy unique goods from street vendors. Several stages provide entertainment, ranging from kids' sing-alongs to raucous blues. Admission is free.

ORIENTATION   The city of Portland is divided into two areas: **on-peninsula** and **off-peninsula.** (There are also the islands, but more on that below.) Most travelers

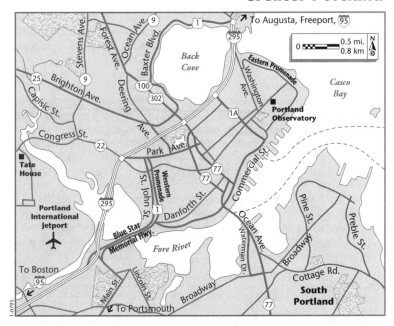

are destined for the compact peninsula, which is home to the downtown and where most of the city's cultural life and much of its commercial action takes place.

Viewed from the water, Portland's peninsula is shaped like a sway-backed horse, with the Old Port in the low spot near the waterfront, and the peninsula's two main residential neighborhoods (Munjoy Hill and the West End) on the gentle rises overlooking downtown. These two neighborhoods are connected by Congress Street, Portland's main artery of commerce. The western stretch of Congress Street (roughly between Monument Square and State Street) is Portland's emerging Arts District, home to a handsome art museum, three theaters, the campus of the Maine College of Art (located in an old department store), and a growing number of restaurants and boutiques.

PARKING   Parking is notoriously tight in the Old Port area, and the city's parking enforcement is notoriously efficient. Several parking garages are convenient to the Old Port, with parking fees less than $1 per hour.

EXPLORING THE CITY

Any visit to Portland should start with a stroll around the historic Old Port. Bounded by Commercial, Congress, Union, and Pearl streets, this several-square-block area near the waterfront contains some of the best commercial architecture in town, a plethora of fine restaurants, a mess of boutiques, and bars thicker than north woods black flies in June. The narrow streets and intricate brick facades reflect the mid-Victorian era; most of the area was rebuilt following a devastating fire in 1866. Leafy, quaint Exchange Street is the heart of the Old Port, with other attractive streets running off and around it.

Just outside the Old Port, don't miss the First Parish Church at 425 Congress St., an uncommonly beautiful granite church with an impressively austere interior that's changed little since it first opened its doors in 1826. Just down the block is Portland's elaborate granite City Hall, at the head of Exchange Street. Modeled after New York's City Hall, Portland's hall was built in 1909. In a similarly regal vein is the U.S. Custom House at 312 Fore St. During business hours wander inside to view the elegant woodwork and marble floors dating back to 1868.

Flanking the Old Port on the two hills are the downtown's two main residential areas. Drive eastward on Congress Street up and over Munjoy Hill and you'll come to the Eastern Promenade, a 68-acre hillside park with broad, grassy slopes extending down to the water and offering superb views of Casco Bay and its islands. Atop Munjoy Hill is the **Portland Observatory,** a quirky shingled tower dating from 1807 and once used to watch for ships coming into port. It was closed indefinitely for repairs and restorations in 1995; call for an update (☎ 207/774-5561).

On the other end of the peninsula is the Western Promenade. (Follow Spring Street westward to Vaughan; turn right then take your first left on Bowdoin Street.) This narrow strip of lawn atop a forested bluff has views across the Fore River, which is lined with less-than-scenic light industry, to the White Mountains in the distance. It's a great spot to watch the sun set. Around the Western Prom are some of the most grand and imposing houses in the city. A walk through the neighborhood reveals a wide array of architectural styles, from Italianate to Shingle to Stick style.

Children's Museum of Maine. 142 Free St. (next to the Portland Museum of Art). ☎ 207/ 828-1234. Admission $4 per person (child or adult). Summer Mon–Sat 10am–5pm, Sun noon–5pm. Fall–spring closed Mon–Tues.

The centerpiece exhibit of the Children's Museum is the camera obscura, a room-sized "camera" located on the top floor of this regal downtown building. Children gather around a white table in a dark room, where they see magically projected images of city streets and boats plying the harbor. The camera obscura rarely fails to enthrall, and it provides a memorable lesson in how a camera works.

There's plenty more to do here, from running a supermarket checkout counter to sliding down the firehouse pole to piloting the mock space shuttle from a high cockpit. Budget time also for lunch at the café, where you can order up a peanut butter and jelly sandwich, a tall glass of milk, and an oatmeal cookie. Make a deal with your kids: they behave during a trip to the art museum next door, and they'll be rewarded with a couple of hours in their own museum.

Maine Historical Society. 489 Congress St. ☎ 207/879-0427. Gallery and Longfellow house tour $4 adults, $1 children under 12. Gallery only $2 adults, $1 child. Longfellow House and gallery open June–Oct Tues–Sun 10am–4pm; gallery only June–Oct Wed–Sat noon–4pm.

Maine Historical Society's "history campus" includes three widely varied buildings in the middle of downtown Portland. The austere brick Wadsworth-Longfellow House dates to 1785 and was built by Gen. Peleg Wadsworth, father of noted poet Henry Wadsworth Longfellow. It's still furnished in an authentic early American style, with many samples from the Longfellow family furniture still on display. Adjacent to the home is the Maine History Gallery, located in a somewhat garish post-modern building that formerly housed a bank. Changing exhibits explore the rich texture of Maine history; a gift shop offers a selection of books and other items. Just behind the Longfellow house is the library of the Maine Historical Society, a popular destination among genealogists. Don't miss the small, peaceful garden hidden in the back next to the library.

✪ **Portland Head Light & Museum.** Fort Williams Park, 1000 Shore Rd., Cape Elizabeth. ☎ 207/799-2661. Grounds free; museum admission $2 adults, $1 children 6–18. Park grounds open daily year-round sunrise to sunset (until 8:30pm in summer); museum open daily June–Oct 10am–4pm; open weekends only in spring and late fall. From Portland, follow State

Downtown Portland

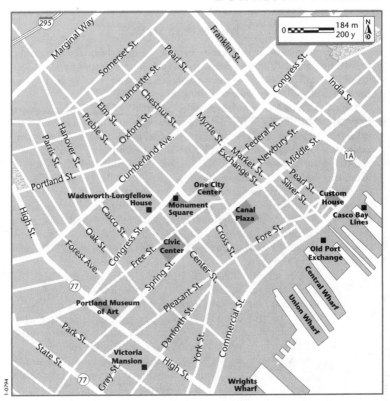

St. across the Fore River to the "T" ntersection at Broadway; turn left. At second light turn right on Cottage Rd., which soon becomes Shore Rd.; follow this about 2 miles until you arrive at the park, on your left.

Located a ten-minute drive from downtown Portland, this 1794 lighthouse is one of the most picturesque in the nation. The light marks the entrance to Portland Harbor, and was occupied continuously from its construction until 1989, when it was automated and the graceful keeper's house (1891) converted to a small, town-owned museum focusing on the history of navigation. The lighthouse is still active and thus closed to the public, but visitors can wander the park grounds, sit on the rocky headlands, and watch the sailboats and ships come and go. The park has a pebble beach, grassy lawns with ocean vistas, and picnic areas well-suited for informal barbecues.

Portland Museum of Art. 7 Congress Sq. (corner of Congress and High streets). ☎ **207/ 775-6148.** Admission $6 adults, $5 students and seniors, $1 children 6–12. Free Fri 5–9pm. Tues–Wed and Sat 10am–5pm, Thurs–Fri 10am–9pm, Sun noon–5pm.

This bold, modern museum was designed by I. M. Pei Associates in 1983, and displays selections from its own fine collections and a parade of touring exhibits. The museum is particularly strong in American artists who had a connection to Maine, including Winslow Homer, Andrew Wyeth, and Edward Hopper, and has fine displays of early American furniture and crafts. The museum shares the Joan Whitney Payson Collection with Colby College (the college gets it one semester every other

Ferries to Nova Scotia

A trip to northern New England can serve as an easy springboard for an excursion to Atlantic Canada. The most hassle-free way to link the two is by ferry. Two ferries connect Yarmouth, Nova Scotia with Maine, saving hours of driving time and providing a relaxing mini-cruise along the way.

The *Scotia Prince* departs each evening from Portland for an 11-hour crossing to Nova Scotia, arriving early in the morning. The ship is bustling with activity, from its café and restaurant to casino and glitzy floor show in the lounge. When the party winds down, you can retire to a cabin for a good night's sleep, awakening for breakfast before disembarking in Nova Scotia. Day cabins are available on the return trip, but you might be just as content sitting in the lounge or relaxing on a deck chair and watching for whales.

High season one-way adult fares are $78 (children 5 to 14 traveling with adults are half-price), with additional fares for a car ($98) or cabin ($32 to $95). Ask about package rates, which can dramatically bring the cost down for a family. For more information, contact **Prince of Fundy** (☎ **800/341-7540** or 207/775-5611 or 800/482-0955 in Maine).

Travelers at Acadia National Park can depart at 8am from Bar Harbor aboard the *Bluenose* for a six-hour cruise to Yarmouth, arriving early enough to explore the coves and woodlands of southern Nova Scotia before twilight. Enjoy the ship's buffet meal along the way, try your luck at slots or blackjack in the ship's Golden Anchor Casino, or just spend time on the deck watching for seabirds wheeling overhead. There's also a first-run film shown, and a kid's play room for the younger set.

One-way fares are $41.50 for adults (half price for children 5 to 12), plus $55 for cars and $36–$40 for a cabin (cabin rates are higher for the nighttime return trip). For more information, contact **Marine Atlantic** (☎ **800/341-7981** or 207/288-3395).

year). The collection features wonderful European works by Renoir, Degas, and Picasso.

Victoria Mansion. 109 Danforth St. ☎ **207/772-4841.** $4 adults, $2 children under 18. May–Oct Tues–Sat 10am–4pm, Sun 1–5pm. From the Old Port, head west on Fore St. to Danforth St. near Stonecoast Brewing; bear right and proceed three blocks to the mansion.

Widely regarded as one of the most elaborate Victorian brownstone homes in existence, this mansion (also known as the Morse-Libby House) is a remarkable display of high Victorian style. Built between 1859 and 1863 for a Maine businessman who made a fortune in New Orleans hotel trade, the towering, slightly foreboding home is a prime example of the Italiante style then in vogue. Inside, it appears that not a square inch of wall space was left unmolested by craftsmen or artists (11 artists were hired to paint the murals). The decor is ponderous and somber, but it offers an engaging look at a bygone era.

ON THE WATER

The 3¹/₂-mile **Back Cove Pathway** loops around Portland's Back Cove, offering nice views of the city skyline across the water, glimpses of Casco Bay, and a bit of exercise. The pathway is the city's most popular recreational facility; after work in summers, Portlanders flock here to walk, bike, jog, and windsurf (there's enough water two-and-a-half hours before and after high tide). Part of the pathway shares a noisy bridge with I-95, but the rest of it runs along quiet Baxter Boulevard. Look for shorebirds in the marshes.

The main parking lot is located across from Shop 'n Save Plaza at the water's edge. Take the Forest Avenue north Exit off I-95; turn right at the first light on Baxter Boulevard; at the next light turn right again and park in the lot ahead on the left.

Casco Bay Lines. Commercial and Franklin sts. ☎ **207/774-7871.** Fares vary depending on the run, but are generally $4.50–$13.75 round trip. Frequent departures 6am–midnight.

Six of the Casco Bay islands have year-round populations and are served by scheduled ferries from downtown Portland. (Most of these are part of the city of Portland; the exception is Long Island, which broke away in a secession bid a few years ago.) The ferries offer an inexpensive way to view the bustling harbor and get a taste of Maine's islands. Trips range from a 20-minute excursion to Peaks Island (the closest thing to an island suburb with 1,200 year-round residents), to the 5¹/₂-hour cruise to Bailey Island and back. All of the islands are well-suited to walking; Peaks Island has a rocky back shore that's easily accessible via the island's paved perimeter road (bring a picnic lunch). Cliff Island is the most remote of the bunch, and has a sedate turn-of-the-century island retreat character.

Eagle Island. Eagle Island Tours, Long Wharf (Commercial St.) ☎ **207/774-6498.** $15 adults, $9 children under 9 (plus state park fee of $1.50 adults, 50 cents children). One departure daily at 10am.

Eagle Island was the summer home of famed Arctic explorer and Portland native Robert E. Peary, who claimed in 1909 to be the first person to reach the North Pole. (His accomplishments have been the subject of exhaustive debates among Arctic scholars, some of whom insist he inflated his claims.) In 1904 Peary built this simple home on a remote, 17-acre island at the edge of Casco Bay; in 1912 he added flourishes in the form of two low stone towers. After his death in 1920 his family kept up the home, then later donated it to the state, which has since managed it as a state park. The home is open to the public, maintained much the way it was when Peary lived here. Island footpaths through the forest allow exploration to the open, seagull-clotted cliffs at the southern tip.

Eagle Tours offers one trip daily from Portland. The four-hour excursion includes a 1¹/₂ hour stopover on the island.

SHOPPING

Aficionados of antique and junk stores love Portland. Good browsing may be had on Congress Street. Check out the stretches between State and High streets in the arts district, and from India Street to Washington Avenue on Munjoy Hill. About a dozen shops of varying quality will be found in these two areas.

More serious antique hounds will want to take in an auction or two. Almost any day of the week you'll be able to find an auction within a hour's drive of Portland. The best source of information is the Maine Sunday Telegram. Look under the classifieds for listings of auctions scheduled for the following week.

For new items, the Old Port, with its dozens of boutiques and storefronts, is well worth browsing. I've listed the more notable shops below.

Abacus American Crafts. 44 Exchange St. ☎ **207/772-4880.**

A wide range of bold, inventive crafts of all variety—from furniture to jewelry—is displayed on two floors of this centrally located shop. Even if you're not in a buying frame of mind, this is a great place for browsing.

Amaryllis. 41 Exchange St. ☎ **207/772-4439.**

Portland's original funky clothing store, Amarylils offers unique clothing for women that's as comfortable as it is casually elegant. The colors are rich, the patterns unique, and much of the fabric is all-natural.

Fibula. 50 Exchange St. ☎**207/761-4432.**

Original, handcrafted jewelry is beautifully displayed at this tasteful shop in the heart of the Old Port.

Green Design Furniture. 267 Commercial St. ☎**207/775-4234.**

This inventive furniture shop sells a line of beautiful, Mission-inspired furniture that disassembles for easy storage and travel. These beautiful works, creatively crafted of cherry, must be seen to be appreciated.

Resourceful Home. 111 Commercial St. ☎**207/780-1314.**

Environmentally sound products for the home and garden are the specialty here, including linens and cleaning products.

SPECTATOR SPORTS

Portland Sea Dogs. Hadlock Field, P.O. Box 636, Portland, ME 04104. ☎**800/936-3647** or 207/874-9300. Tickets $4–$6. Season runs Apr–Labor Day.

The Portland Sea Dogs are the Double-A team affiliated with the Florida Marlins, and they play throughout the summer at Hadlock Field, a small stadium near downtown that still retains an old-time feel despite aluminum benches and other improvements. Games here are a great way to spend an afternoon or evening, and are geared towards families, with lots of entertainment between innings and a selection of food that's a couple of notches above basic hot dogs and hamburgers. (Try the tasty french fries and grilled sausages.)

The biggest problem is getting tickets—games tend to sell out a couple of weeks in advance. Pick a date, and call for reservations. If you have general admission seats, get there at least a half-hour early so you don't end up way down the left field line.

Portland Pirates. 85 Free St., Portland, ME 04101. ☎**207/828-4665,** or Civic Center box office 207/775-3458. Tickets $8–$13 adults, $5–$6.50 seniors and children (12 and under). Season runs Oct–Apr.

Portland's minor league hockey team plays a full roster at the Cumberland County Civic Center from fall into spring. Hockey is more a religion than a sport in the northern climates, and you're likely to see a good, fast game at this 6,000-seat center at a fraction of the cost of watching the Bruins play in Boston. Entertainment between periods will keep young kids amused.

ROAD TRIPS

OLD ORCHARD BEACH & OCEAN PARK   About 12 miles south of Portland is the unrepentantly honky-tonkish beach town of Old Orchard Beach, which offers treats for most of the senses (taste buds excluded). This venerable Victorian-era resort is famed for its amusement park, its pier, and its long, sandy beach, which attracts sun worshippers from all over, especially Quebec. (English-speaking folks quickly feel like a minority here.) Be sure to spend time and money riding some of the stomach-churning rides (if you'd prefer something more relaxing, head for the antique carousel), then walk on the seven-mile-long beach past the mid-rise condos that sprouted in the 1980s like an HO-scale Miami Beach.

The beach is broad and open at low tide; at high tide, space to put your towel down can be hard to come by. In the evenings, teens and young adults dominate the town. For dinner, do as the locals do and buy hot dogs and pizza and cotton candy; save your change for the video arcades.

A mile or so south of Old Orchard Beach on Route 9 is the quiet neighborhood of Ocean Park, which has a far more settled demeanor. And no wonder. It was founded in 1880 by Baptists who wanted to establish a summer retreat for their camp meetings. Set amid towering pines a few blocks for the ocean, the retreat still thrives, attracting congregants in summer. A tour through the area (especially on Temple Street) reveals a number of fine examples of late-Victorian summer cottages.

Old Orchard is just off Route 1 south of Portland. The quickest route to leave the turnpike at Exit 5, then follow I-195 and the signs to the beach. Be aware that parking is tight, and the traffic can be horrendous during the peak summer months.

SEBAGO LAKE & DOUGLAS HILL   Maine's second-largest lake is also its most popular. Ringed with summer homes of varying vintages, many dating from the early part of this century, Sebago Lake attracts thousands of vacationers to its cool, deep waters.

You can take a tour of the lake and the ancient canal system between Sebago and Long lakes on the *Songo Queen,* a faux-steamship berthed in the town of Naples (☎ 207/693-6861). Or just lie in the sun along the sandy beach at bustling **Sebago Lake State Park** (☎ 207/693-6613) on the lake's north shore (the park is off Route 302; look for signs between Raymond and South Casco). The park has shady picnic areas, a campground, a snack bar, and lifeguards on the beach (entrance fee charged). Even when it's crowded (which is to be expected on summer weekends), it's still always a relaxing place to go. Bring food for barbecuing.

To the west of the lake, the rolling wooded uplands hold some surprises. For a low-key excursion, head to the **Jones Museum of Glass and Ceramics** (☎ 207/787-3370), a place that captivates even visitors that have little interest in the history of glass or ceramics. Housed in beautiful old farm building near a compound of summer homes, the museum has hundreds of pieces of old and contemporary glass displayed in highly professional and engaging exhibits. You'll learn something, and come away intrigued.

The museum is located just off Route 107 south of Sebago (the town) on the lake's west side. The museum is conscientious about posting signs directing you there; look for them. It's open daily May through mid-November (afternoons only on Sunday). Admission is $5 for adults, $3 for students.

Just up the hill from the museum is Douglas Mountain, whose summit is capped with a 16-foot stone tower that's open to the public and affords fine views from Casco Bay to the White Mountains. The property is owned by The Nature Conservancy; the summit is reached via an easy one-quarter mile trail from the parking area. Look for wild berries during the late summer.

✪ SABBATHDAY LAKE SHAKER COMMUNITY   Route 26 from Portland to Norway is a fast, speedy road through hilly farmland and past new housing developments. At one point the road pinches through a cluster of stately historic buildings that stand proudly beneath towering elms. That's the **Sabbathday Lake Shaker Community** (☎ 207/926-4597), the last active Shaker community in the nation. The dozen or so Shakers living here today still embrace the ancient Shaker beliefs and maintain a communal, pastoral way of life. The bulk of the community's income comes from the sale of herbs, which have been grown here since 1799.

This community is open to the public daily in summer except on Sundays (when visitors are invited to attend Sunday services). Docents offer tours of the grounds and several of buildings, including the graceful 1794 meetinghouse. Exhibits in the buildings showcase the famed furniture lovingly crafted by the Shakers, and include antiques made by Shakers at other U.S. communes. You'll learn a lot about the Shaker ideology with its emphasis on simplicity, industry, and celibacy. After your tour, browse the gift shop for Shaker herbs and teas. Tours last either one hour ($5 adult, $2 children 6–12) or one hour and 45 minutes ($6.50 adult). Open daily except Sunday Memorial Day to Columbus Day from 10am to 4:30pm.

The **Shaker village** is located about 45 minutes from Portland. Head north on Route 26 (Washington Avenue in Portland). The village is 8 miles from Exit 11 (Gray) of the Maine Turnpike.

WHERE TO STAY

Two sizeable downtown hotels stand out against the skyline. The **Holiday Inn by the Bay,** 88 Spring St. (☎ **207/775-2311**), offers great views of the harbor from about half the rooms, along with the usual chain-hotel creature comforts. The **Radisson Eastland,** 157 High St. (☎ **207/775-5411**), is located in Portland's most venerable old hotel, and features two restaurants, a rooftop lounge, and a spacious lobby imbued with an old-world elegance.

Budget travelers should seek out less expensive accommodations by the Maine Mall in South Portland and off the Maine Turnpike near Westbrook—two areas that are patently charmless, but offer reasonable access to the attractions of downtown, about 10 minutes away. Try **Days Inn** (☎ **207/772-3450**) or **Coastline Inn** (☎ **207/ 772-3838**) near the mall, or the **Super 8 Motel** (☎ **207/854-1881**) or **Susse Chalet** (☎ **207/774-6101**) off turnpike Exit 8 near the Westbrook town line.

The Danforth. 163 Danforth St., Portland, ME 04102. ☎ **207/879-8755** or 800/991-6557. Fax 207/879-8754. 9 rms, some with shower only. A/C TV TEL. $95–$165 double. Rates include breakfast. Rates discounted in the off-season. AE, MC, V.

The Danforth is Portland's newest B&B (it opened in 1994), and brings with it a huge measure of class and elegance. Located in an imposing brick home constructed in 1821, The Danforth is something of a work in progress. It opened with just two guest rooms, but ongoing work has brought the total up to nine, where it will stop. Much of the effort has gone into renovating the building, and as such the guest rooms are still a bit spartanly furnished. The furnishings should catch up with the opulence of the architecture over time, but even so the inn's extras are exceptional throughout, from the working fireplaces in all rooms but one, to the richly panelled basement billiards room. Innkeeper Barbara Hathaway has done a superb job attending to details, from the direct-line phones in the rooms (equipped with data ports for cyber-travelers) to the smartly uniformed staff to the complimentary guest membership at the city's best health club. The inn is located at the edge of the Spring Street Historic District, and is within walking distance of many downtown attractions.

Inn at Park Spring. 135 Spring St., Portland, ME 04101. ☎ **207/774-1059** or 800/ 437-8511. 7 rms (2 with shared bath; some with shower only). $60–$115 double. Rates include continental breakfast. AE, DISC, MC, V.

This small in-town B&B is housed in a comfortable, historic brick home dating back to 1835, and is the best located inn for exploring the town on foot. The Portland Museum of Art is just two blocks away, the Old Port about 10 minutes, and great restaurants are all within easy walking distance. Guests can linger or watch television in the front parlor, or chat at the table in the kitchen. The rooms are all corner rooms, and most are bright and sunny. Especially nice is "Spring," with its great morning light and wonderful views of the historic rowhouses on Park Street, and "Gables," one of the shared-bath rooms on the third floor, which has a clean, contemporary design and abundant afternoon sun. Reservations are usually essential here, as the owner lives separately and comes to meet the guests.

✪ **Pomegranate Inn.** 49 Neal St., Portland, ME 04102. ☎ 207/772-**1006** or 800/356-0408. 8 rms. $95–$165 double. Rates include full breakfast. AE, DISC, MC, V. Free on-street parking. From the Old Port, take Middle Street (which turns into Spring Street) to Neal Street in the West End (about 1 mile); turn right and proceed to inn.

This is Portland's most gracious B&B, and one of the best in northern New England. Housed in a handsome, dove-gray Italianate home in the architecturally distinctive Western Prom neighborhood, the interiors are wondrously decorated with combination of whimsy and elegance—a combination that can be fatally cloying if attempted by someone without impeccably good taste. Look for the bold and exuberant wall paintings by a local artist Heidi Gerquest, and the wonderfully eclectic antique furniture collected and arranged by owner Isabel Smiles. If you have the chance, peek in some of the unoccupied rooms—they're all quite different with painted floors and faux-marble woodwork. The best room is in the carriage house, which has its own private terrace and fireplace. Breakfasts are invariably creative and tasty. The inn is well situated for exploring the West End, and downtown is about a 15-minute walk away. No smoking.

Portland Regency Hotel. 20 Milk St., Portland, ME 04101. ☎ 207/774-**4200** or 800/ 727-3436. Fax 207/775-2150. 95 rms. A/C MINIBAR TV TEL. Summer $149–$229 double; off-season $89–$175 double. AE, CB, DC, DISC, MC, V.

Centrally located on a cobblestone courtyard in the middle of the Old Port, the Regency has the city's premier hotel location. But it's got more than location going for it—it's also one of the most handsome and well-managed hotels in the state. Housed in a historic brick armory, the hotel offers a number of modern guest rooms nicely appointed and furnished with all the standard amenities. The hotel has a well-regarded dining room, an active tavern, and a well-equipped fitness room that doubles as a popular health club among Portlanders. The one complaint I've heard is about the noise: the walls are a bit thin, and on weekends the revelry on the Old Port streets can penetrate even the dense brick exterior walls. The Regency is planning a major expansion in a separate building that's to be finished in the spring of 1997. The addition will bring the number of rooms up to 156.

West End Inn. 146 Pine St., Portland, ME 04102. ☎ 207/772-**1377** or 800/338-1377. 5 rms (1 with detached bath, 1 with shower only). TV. $89–$169 double. Rates include breakfast. AE, MC, V. Parking on street.

This brick, mansard-roofed Victorian duplex sits in one of Portland's more distinguished residential neighborhoods. And John and Terri Leonard have done a superb job making this urban townhouse into a welcoming retreat. The downstairs parlor features gold-leaf detailing on the ceiling, leather furniture, and Oriental antiques. The five guest rooms on two upstairs floors have canopy beds and are nicely decorated with bold wallpaper and antiques. Look for nice touches like bottles of Poland Spring Water in the rooms, and towels that match the decor in the bathrooms. The inn is well situated for walks in the West End and the Western Prom, two lovely turn-of-the-century neighborhoods with some of Portland's best architecture.

WHERE TO DINE

Portland has an exceptionally vibrant dining scene, with dozens of restaurants offering up a smorgasbord of cuisines at a wide range of pricing. Residents will often tell you that their city has the most restaurants per capita after San Francisco. It's not true, but it might as well be. Restaurants seem to line every Old Port street and are tucked down every alley around town. For a city of this size, the selection is dazzling. Enjoy it.

EXPENSIVE

⑤ Street & Co. 33 Wharf St. ☎ **207/775-0887.** Reservations recommended. Main courses $11.95–$17.95. AE, MC, V. Sun–Thurs 5:30–9:30pm, Fri–Sat until 10pm. SEAFOOD/ CONTEMPORARY.

This is one of the best seafood restaurants in the state, if not all of New England. A pioneer establishment on now-trendy Wharf Street, Street & Co. specializes in seafood cooked just right. There's no smoke and mirrors—you pass the cramped kitchen on your way in, and some spectators watch the talented chefs practice their art through an alley window. The atmosphere of this intimate spot is a bit like something you might imagine stumbling onto while touring Provence: Low beams, dim lighting, and drying herbs hanging overhead nicely set the mood. Diners are seated at copper-topped tables, designed such that the waiters can deliver steaming skillets right from the stove. Try the lobster diavolo—a spicy melange of lobster, mussels, and clams in a delectable red sauce. If you're partial to calamari, be sure to order it here. They know how to cook it so it's perfectly tender, something that's becoming a lost art elsewhere. Street & Co. always fills up early, so reservations are strongly recommended. A few tables are reserved for walk-ins each night, though, so if you're in the neighborhood it can't hurt to ask.

⑤ West Side Restaurant. 58 Pine St. ☎ **207/773-8223.** Reservations recommended. Main courses $11.95–$18.95. MC, V. Tues–Thurs 11:30am–2pm and 5–9pm, Fri 11:30am–2pm and 5–10pm, Sat 9am–1pm and 5–10pm, Sun 9am–2pm and 5–9pm. NEW AMERICAN.

This intimate neighborhood bistro is quiet, elegant, and hugely popular with clued-in Portlanders. It's hard to even read all the way through the enticing menu without body-tackling a waiter and demanding to order immediately. The menu changes every two weeks but often features a good selection of game dishes: There's the Maine venison medallions with a wild mushroom, tarragon, and red wine sauce; duck breast with cranberries; and a tangy cassoulet with duck, lamb sausage, and pork. Other fine choices include delicate preparations of quail, sweetbreads, veal, salmon, and rabbit. The West Side is off the beaten path, but it's well worth hunting down. In the winter a woodstove makes the place toasty; in summer there's dining on a second-floor deck. Weekend breakfasts and weekday lunches are also first-rate.

MODERATE

⑤ Café Uffa!. 190 State St. ☎ **207/775-3380.** Reservations not accepted. Main courses $7.95–$10.95. MC, V. Wed–Sat 5:30–10pm, Sun 9am–2pm. MULTI-ETHNIC.

If you're looking to stretch your dollar without compromising on quality, this is your place. Launched a couple of years ago by three young friends, Uffa consistently manages to impress Portland's picky eaters with their creative international fare. The specialty is fish grilled to perfect tenderness over a wood-stoked fire, but there's plenty else to choose from. The chefs share a predilection for perfectionism, and even simple side dishes like black beans are cooked with unexpected flair. With its mismatched chairs, last-week's-flea-market decor, and high ceilings, Uffa attracts a young crowd with its aggressively informal styling. Sunday brunches are also superb, but be prepared to wait. There's often a line to get in.

Katahdin. 106 High St. ☎ **207/774-1740.** Reservations not accepted. Main courses $9.95–$14.95. DISC, MC, V. Mon–Thurs 5–10pm, Fri–Sat until 11pm. AMERICAN/REGIONAL.

Katahdin is a noisy, funky place that prides itself on its quirky salt shakers and its eclectic food. Local impoverished artists congregate here and order the nightly blue plate special, which typically features something basic like meatloaf. Wealthy business folks one table over dine on more delicate fare, like the restaurant's famed crab cakes. Other recommended specialties include the lobster spring roll appetizers, and the entree of grilled sea scallops with a spicy lime vinaigrette. Sometimes the kitchen nods, but for the most part it's good food at good prices. Reservations aren't accepted, but there's a big bar in the dining room where you can enjoy Portland's best martini while waiting for a table.

Tabitha Jean's. 94 Free St. ☎ **207/780-8966.** Reservations recommended. Lunch $4.95–$8.95; dinner $10.95–$15.95. AE, DC, DISC, MC, V. Mon–Fri 11:30am–3pm; Sun–Thurs 5pm–9pm, Fri–Sat 5–10pm. NEW AMERICAN.

Tabitha Jean's started out as a sort of casual neo-Cajun creole joint when it first opened a few years years ago. The concept didn't fly. So the owners (one of whom is novelist Stephen King's daughter) went back to the drawing board, upscaled the interior and the menu, and brought in a talented new kitchen staff. And the place is finally catching on among locals. Although situated on the ground floor of a less-than-scenic downtown parking garage, the interior is warm and welcoming with lots of soft wood tones, gentle lighting, and accenting in black—the chairs, the tiles, even the turtlenecks on the waiters are basic black. There's not much of a view, but creatively placed wood louvres take care of that. The meals are creative and considerable detail is paid to preparation. Entrees could include a roasted sweet-pepper florentine, a wild mushroom risotto, or a New York sirloin with garlic herb butter.

Uptown Billy's. 1 Forest Ave. ☎ **207/780-0141.** Reservations not accepted. Main courses $6.95–$20.95 (mostly $8–$10). AE, DC, MC, V. Mon–Sat 11:30am–2:30pm & 5–9pm (until 10pm Fri–Sat), Sun 3–8pm. BARBECUE.

Uptown Billy's is the place to go for a plate of pork ribs and a mess o' beans. Billy's started out in an authentic dive across the river in South Portland. Since moving uptown to a slightly larger venue, it's become "bistroized," adding somewhat more dainty dishes like salmon and grilled portobello mushrooms. But it's still best known for the slow-cooked pork spare ribs, which require at least a dozen napkins per rack. The meals come with cornbread, buttermilk biscuits, and a choice of side dishes like macaroni and cheese, potatoes, or a zippy coleslaw. Billy's hasn't lost any of its informal charm in the move, and you needn't be embarrassed by the BBQ sauce on your chin. On weekends there's live entertainment, which is typically jazz, blues, or rockabilly.

INEXPENSIVE

Fresh Market. 43 Exchange St. ☎ **207/773-7146.** Reservations not accepted. Main courses, $4.55–$5.60. AE, CB, DC, DISC, MC, V. Open Mon–Thurs 9am–8pm, Fri–Sat 9am–9pm, Sun noon–8pm. PASTA.

Located in the middle of the trendy Old Port is this low-key, low-budget pasta restaurant. Fresh Market offers cafeteria-style dining, but with selections far better than you'd usually find served on plastic trays and plates. Customers select a fresh pasta (enlivened with extras like black pepper or spinach), which is cooked on the spot and paired with a sauce of your choosing (like pesto or Alfredo). Meals come with bread and butter, and there's a decent selection of deserts. Elegant it's not, but it's invariably tasty and light on the wallet.

⑤ Seng's 2. 921 Congress St. ☎ **207/879-2577.** No reservations. Main courses $5–$9.95. No credit cards. Open daily 11am–10pm. THAI.

Portland's best Thai food is found in a small, somewhat dingy spot in a cheerless part of town near the bus station. Don't come here expecting atmosphere—unless you're a connoisseur of fluorescent lights. Come here expecting a big pile of delicious food at great prices. The spicy pad thai has developed a cult following among know-ledgeable Portlanders. Five dollars will buy you a plateful that's nearly big enough for two. The curries are delicious, as are the hot basil leaves with chicken, tofu, or beef. Everything is available to go.

WHERE TO GET A GOOD CUP OF COFFEE

Portland has been victim of an uncontrolled outbreak of coffee shops over the past few years, much to the delight of the city's caffeine addicts. The patriarch of the clan is **Green Mountain Coffee,** 15 Temple St. (☎ 207/773-4475), located in a large, modern shop in the middle of downtown. You can order a bagel sandwich with your latte next door at Bagelworks, then eat inside or out while watching slackers play hackey-sack out front.

At 13 Exchange St. is **Java Joe's** (☎ 207/761-5637), a loose sort of neo-beat coffee shop that's popular with goateed Scrabble players in the evening. Joe's serves great deserts, including a luscious tiramisu.

For my money, the best coffee in town is at **Portland Coffee Roasters** (☎ 207/761-9525), located at 111 Commercial St. at the corner of Pearl St. The beans are roasted on premises, and those who like coffee that packs a punch won't go away disappointed.

PORTLAND AFTER DARK

Portland is lively in the evenings, especially on summer weekends when the testosterone level in the Old Port seems to rocket into the stratosphere with young men and women prowling the dozens of bars and and spilling over onto the streets. Among the bars favored by locals are **Three-Dollar Dewey's** at the corner of Commercial and Union streets, **Gritty McDuff's Brew Pub** on Fore Street near the foot of Exchange Street, and **Brian Ború,** slightly out of the Old Port on Center Street. All three bars are informal and pubby, with guests sharing long tables with new companions.

Beyond the active Old Port bar scene, a number of clubs offer a good mix of live entertainment throughout the year. Check the free alternative paper, Casco Bay Weekly, for performers and showtimes.

NIGHTCLUBS

Granny Killam's. 55 Market St. ☎ 207/761-2787. Cover varies.

There's no telling what music you'll find at Granny's in the Old Port—they seem to book everything from metal to world beat to disco. This is a great venue for live music, but be prepared to stand in the back unless you get there early.

Morganfield's. 121 Center St. ☎ 207/774-5835. Ticket prices vary; generally $5–$15. Located near the Civic Center.

This intimate blues club resists the usual image of a smoky dive. Morganfield's has a high-tech filtering system that lets nonsmoking clubgoers go home at night with-out smelling of stale smoke (smokers can still light up under the vacuum at the far end of the club). It also has a superb sound system, Portland's best selection of microbrews on tap, and a bunch of pool tables. Acts range from local bands to national touring acts like Bo Diddley, Mose Allison, and Matt "Guitar" Murphy. There's also rockabilly, cajun, and zydeco nights.

Stone Coast. 14 York St. ☎ **207/773-2337.** Cover varies.

Portland's newest night club houses both a restaurant (with a Cajun menu) and brewpub in a painstakingly renovated 19th century cannery at the edge of the Old Port. Performers take the stage upstairs in the spacious Smoking Room, and range from local acoustic rock groups to touring acts like New Riders of the Purple Sage. This is the most upscale of the live music venues in Portland.

Zootz. 31 Forest Ave. ☎ **207/773-8187.** Cover varies for live shows; no cover on dance nights for early arrivals.

This is Portland's leading alternative music venue, with a good range of music both canned and live. This is also the best place in the city to dance. Zootz features popular all-ages shows and '70s nights. There's also a more informal club, called The Rec Room, downstairs.

THEATER

Portland has a small but lively theater community. Many of the companies take the summer off, but call or check the local papers for special performances.

Mad Horse Theatre Company. 955 Forest Ave. ☎ **207/797-3338.** Tickets $16–$25.

Located in an intimate theater situated incongruously along the commercial strip of outer Forest Ave., Mad Horse offers up a good mix of dramas and comedies ably performed by an ensemble of local actors. At press time, the theater was scouting for a new home downtown; call for more information.

Oak Street Theatre. 92 Oak St. ☎ **207/799-1421.**

This 90-seat black-box theater in the downtown arts district was carved out of an old, low-slung building on an easily overlooked side street. It's used by several theater groups and visiting performers throughout the year. Shows range from classical to avant garde. Call for the current lineup.

Portland Stage Company. Portland Performing Arts Center, 25A Forest Ave. ☎ **207/774-0465.** Tickets $18–$19.

The most professional of the Portland theater companies, Portland Stage offers slickly produced productions starring local and imported equity actors in a handsome second-story theater. About a half-dozen shows are staged throughout the season, which runs from October through May. Call to inquire about special summer shows.

4 The Western Mountains

Maine's Western Mountains are a treasury of sparkling destinations if your idea of getting away involves heading into the outdoors and away from the crowds. This rugged, brawny region, which stretches northeast from the White Mountains to the Carrabasset Valley, isn't as commercialized as the Maine Coast, and the villages aren't as quaint as you'll find in Vermont's Green Mountains. But it has azure lakes, ragged forests of spruce, fir, and lichens, and rolling hills and mountains that take on a distinct blue hue during the summer hiking season.

Cultural amenities are few here, but natural amenities are legion. Hikers have the famed Appalachian Trail, which crosses into Maine in the Mahoosuc Mountains (near where Route 26 enters into New Hampshire), and follows rivers and ridgelines northeast to Bigelow Mountain and beyond. Canoeists and fishermen head to the noted Rangeley Lakes area, a chain of deepwater ponds and lakes that has attracted sportsmen to rustic lodges along their shores for more than a century. And in the

Maine's Western Lakes & Mountains

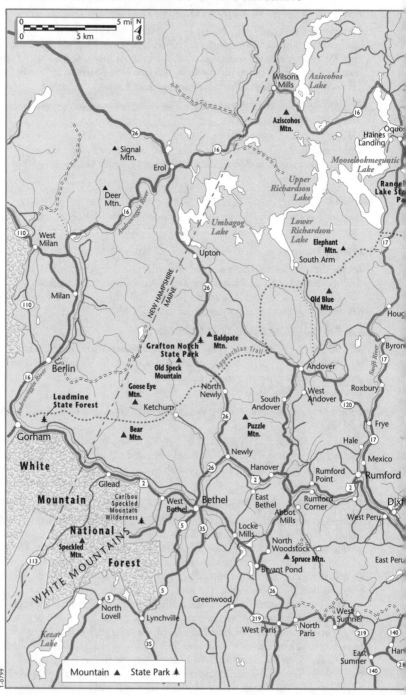

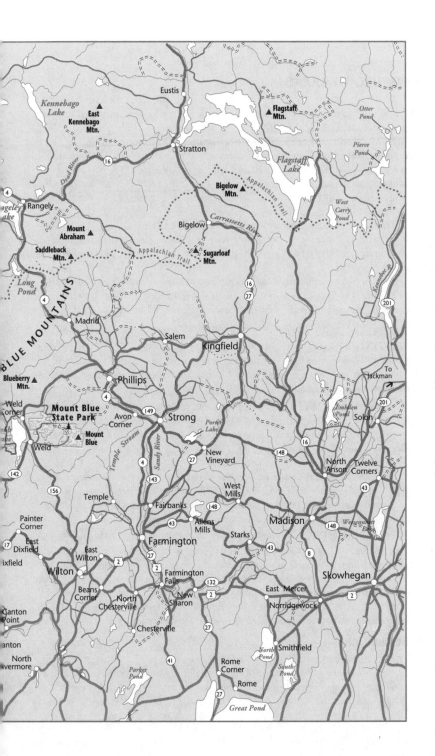

winter, skiers can choose among several downhill ski areas, including the two largest ski areas in the state, Sunday River and Sugarloaf.

FRYEBURG TO GILEAD

Travelers typically scurry through Fryeburg on their way from the Maine Coast to the White Mountains. They might buy a tank of gas or a sandwich here, but they don't give much thought to this town, set amid a region of rolling hills and placid lakes. Many don't realize that 50,000 acres of the White Mountain National Forest spill over from New Hampshire into Maine just above Fryeburg. And they simply don't know that the White Mountain foothills harbor some of the best hiking and canoeing in the region. Evans Notch has granite peaks and tumbling cascades. And the meandering Saco River is rife with sandbars that invite canoeists to pull over and laze away a sunny afternoon.

This region also contains what's arguably the best lake in Maine—scenic **Kezar Lake,** with its backdrop of the White Mountains. Kezar Lake is made all the more appealing because public access is more difficult than at most lakes, and very few roads touch its shores.

Day trippers from Portland and Boston have discovered the allure of this region (it's virtually in Portland's backyard), but it still lacks the crowds and commercialism of the more developed valleys of New Hampshire's White Mountains.

ESSENTIALS

GETTING THERE   Fryeburg is on Route 302 between Portland and North Conway, New Hampshire. It's about 1¼ hours northwest of Portland, and 15 minutes east of North Conway. Route 113 north to Gilead departs from Fryeburg on the west side of town.

VISITOR INFORMATION   The **Fryeburg Information Center** offers general information about lodging and attractions in the area. It's open in summer near the state line on Route 302. For information year-round, try the **Bridgton Lakes Region Chamber of Commerce,** P.O. Box 236, Bridgton, ME 04009 (☎ 207/647-3472).

Outdoor enthusiasts should head to the **Evans Notch Ranger District,** RR #2, P.O. Box 2270, Bethel, ME 04217 (☎ 207/824-2134). Rangers dispense information from their headquarters on Route 2 just north of Bethel. Or write in advance and request their helpful brochure describing a sampling of area hikes.

SPECIAL EVENTS   The **Fryeburg Fair** (☎ 207/935-3268) is Maine's largest agricultural fair, and is held during the 10 days prior to Columbus Day in early October. Staged at the peak of foliage season, this huge fair is even more colorful than its surroundings. It's a classic, old New England extravaganza, with snorting pigs, horse-pulling matches, serene llamas, pumpkins the size of Rhode Island, and contests for the best-looking and best-tasting pies. Tickets are $4 Monday to Thursday, $5 Friday to Sunday; seniors (over 65) and children under 12 get in free.

A SCENIC DRIVE

The 29-mile drive through Evans Notch from Fryeburg north on Route 113 to the crossroads of Gilead stands as one of the most alluring backroad drives in the state. You'll pass through open farmland hemmed in by rolling hills, and through tiny villages from which most commerce has long since fled. As you enter the national forest, you'll slowly gain elevation as the road narrows. Soon you're twisting up through craggy Evans Notch, before cresting the hill and coasting down through dense forest of birch and fir. The road, which is closed in winter, is narrow enough that the trees arch overhead, forming a shady tunnel in summer that turns a fiery gold in fall.

HIKING

Superb, hiking trails lace the rugged, low hills of Evans Notch on either side of Route 113, offering something for hikers of every stripe and inclination. There are far more trails than could possibly be covered in the limited space here. Hikers should request the national forest hiking brochure (see "Visitor Information," above), or consult one of the several trail guides covering the area. Among them are the *White Mountain Guide* and the *Maine Mountain Guide* (Appalachian Mountain Club), and *John Gibson's Fifty Hikes in Southern Maine* (Backcountry Publications).

An easy hike for which no trail guide is needed is to the summit of East Royce Mountain. The trail leaves from a small parking area on Route 113 just north of the road's high point. This well-marked 3-mile round trip follows a small stream before it begins a steeper ascent. The summit is bald and rocky, and affords fine views of Kezar Lake and the more imposing mountains to the west. Return via the same path.

Other recommended local hikes include the summit of Caribou Mountain in the heart of the Caribou Wilderness Area, and rugged Baldface Mountain, with its connecting ridgetop trail that follows the edge of a ragged glacial cirque carved out of the mountain eons ago.

CANOEING THE SACO RIVER

The Saco River is home to some of the most accessible and inviting canoeing in the state. The river rises in the White Mountains near Crawford Notch, then wends its way to the sea south of Portland, passing through the gentle farmlands around Fryeburg en route. The river is slow-moving but steady for much of its run through the region, with rapids enough to make it interesting but never threatening. The land flanking the river is mostly privately owned, but the owners graciously open their land to quiet recreation and camping. (They've also hired a seasonal ranger to make sure it stays clean and fire-free.) Thanks to glacial deposits, the river is notable for its numerous sandbars, which make for superb lounging. Bring your beach towel.

Trips ranging from a few hours to three days are easily arranged through commercial outfitters. The largest outfit is **Saco Bound** (☎ 603/447-2177), located on Route 302 in New Hampshire just over the state line. From their busy shop just across the highway from the river, the harried staff provides equipment, advice, shuttle service, and guided trips. For more personal, smaller-scale service, try **Saco River Canoe and Kayak** (☎ 207/935-2369) on Route 5, or **Canal Bridge Canoes** (☎ 207/935-2605) on Route 302.

A couple of caveats: In early summer, especially following a damp spring, mosquitos can be irksome along the river. Bring lots of repellent or opt for a trip later in the season. The bug population usually declines after July 4. By late August, they're all but gone.

Also, be aware that the Saco's popularity has soared in recent years. The upshot: You're not likely to find a true wilderness experience here, especially on weekends. Lunkheads fueled by beer and traveling in vast armadas descend in great number on many weekends to lend the river a frat-party atmosphere. In the late 1980s it became such a problem that the police set up "riverblocks" on busy weekends to check for sobriety and illegal substances. (The courts told them to cut it out.) It's mostly a weekend phenomenon; midweek, paddlers tend to be more sedate families and couples.

SKIING

Shawnee Peak. Route 302, Bridgton, ME 04009. ☎ **207/647-8444.** Vertical drop: 1,300 feet. Lifts: 4 chairlifts. Skiable acreage: 202. Lift tickets: $34 adult weekend & holiday, $26 midweek; $20 children 7-12 and seniors weekend, $17 midweek.

The friendly, family ski area of Shawnee Peak is a solid intermediate hill area located on Pleasant Mountain between Fryeburg and Portland. For skiers of moderate skills, it's a good alternative to the larger, more crowded resorts in the White Mountains and Maine. Shawnee Peak daily tickets are good until 5 pm (an hour later than most ski areas), and the mountain also also offers the area's best night skiing, with 17 of its 32 trails lit until 10 every night except Sunday. The ski lodge scene is low-key and family-oriented. Shawnee Peak is about an hour from Portland, and attracts a number of afterwork skiers.

WHERE TO STAY & DINE

✪ **Quisisana.** Route 5, Center Lovell ME 04016 (Winter address: P.O. Box 142, Larchmont, NY, 10538). ☎ **207/925-3500** or winter 914/833-0293. 16 rms in lodge; 38 cottages. Lodge $212–$224 double, including all meals; cottages $224–$304 double. One week stay required during peak season (Saturday arrival/departure); shorter stays available early in the season. Open mid-June to late-Aug. No credit cards.

This is not your average lakeside resort. The scenery across Kezar Lake to the White Mountains beyond is spectacular, but what makes this place stand alone is the music. It's everywhere. The 80-person staff consists of students recruited from the best conservatories in the nation, and you're never far from wafting notes, whether it's someone practicing an aria in a rehearsal hall near the lake, or a full-blown production number in a lakeside lodge. Guests typically stay for a week (it's required in mid-summer), and the musical menu changes day by day—Mondays feature musical theater, Tuesdays piano recitals, Wednesdays one-act operas, and so on. The recitals are always performed by exuberant students who rarely slip up—an astonishing feat given that practice time is sandwiched in between sweeping, cooking, laundering, and the other mundane tasks of resort management.

The setting is 47 lakeside acres studded with soaring white pines. The snug cabins set in the trees and along the lakeshore have the charm of an old summer camp, but include amenities like private baths and comfortable furniture. Days are spent canoeing, hiking, playing tennis, or simply sunning at the lake's edge. If it's rainy, the staff will often cobble together an extra recital to keep guests entertained. Dinner is served in a handsome dining hall in the main lodge, and entrees are creative and well-prepared. On Tuesdays nights cocktails are served at a grassy point along the lake, with chamber-music accompaniment—it's often a magical highlight to an always wondrous stay.

BETHEL

Until the mid-1980s, Bethel was a sleepy, 19th-century resort town with one of those friendly, family-oriented ski areas that seemed destined for certain extinction. Until a guy named Les Otten came along. This brash, young entrepreneur bought Sunday River Ski Area and proceeded to make it into one of New England's most vibrant and successful ski destinations. (Successful enough that he subsequently snapped up most of the major ski areas in New England, including Killington, Attitash, Sugarbush, Sugarloaf, Mt. Snow, and Waterville Valley.)

With the rise of the ski area, the white-clapboard town of Bethel (located about 7 miles from the ski area) has been dragged into the modern era, although it hasn't yet taken on artificial, packaged flavor of some other New England ski towns. The village (pop. 2,500) is still dominated by respected prep school Gould Academy, the village common, and the Bethel Inn, a turn-of-the-century resort that's managed to stay ahead of the tide by adding condos, but without losing its pleasant, timeworn character.

With the unparalleled success of the ski area, the handwriting is on the wall. In 1995 Bethel got its first multiscreen movie theater, and the next year construction started on a regional mall and hotel on the edge of town. Bethel will undergo certain change in the coming months, but with thoughtful planning by local officials most of the town is likely to retain its country-village character.

ESSENTIALS

GETTING THERE   Bethel is located at the intersection of Route 26 and Route 2. It's accessible from the Maine Turnpike by heading west on Route 26 from Exit 11. From New Hampshire, drive east on Route 2 from Gorham.

VISITOR INFORMATION   The **Bethel Area Chamber of Commerce,** 30 Cross St, Bethel, ME 04217 (☎ **207/824-2282**) has offices near the new movie theater and railroad depot. It's open year round Monday through Saturday from 9 am to 5 pm and on Sundays "by chance." (The Evans Notch Visitors' Center is also in Bethel; see "Visitor Information" in the "Fryeburg to Gilead" section, above.)

EXPLORING LOCAL HISTORY

Bethel's stately, historic homes ring the Bethel Common, a long, rectangular greensward created in 1807 atop a low, gentle ridge. (It was originally laid out as a street broad enough for the training of the local militia.) The town's historic district encompasses some 27 homes, which represent a wide range of architectural styles popular in the 19th century.

The oldest home in the district is the 1813 Moses Mason House, which is now a fine, small museum housing the collections and offices of the **Bethel Historical Society** (☎ 207/824-2908). Mason was doctor and local civic leader, and was willing to try anything once, including building his Federal-style house on a stone foundation. His compatriots assured him that the house would topple over in a gale. It didn't, and all local houses were soon built on stone foundations. Mason also commissioned an itinerant painter—possibly the renown landscape artists Rufus Porter—to paint his foyer and stairwell. The result is an engaging albeit primitive panorama (still in pristine condition) of boats at anchor at a calm harbor flanked by a still forest of white pine. View this and numerous other artifacts of the early 19th century while exploring the home. The museum, 14 Broad St., is open July and August 1 pm to 4 pm daily except Monday. Admission is $2 for adults and $1 for children.

Architecture buffs can sustain the Federal-home theme with a short road trip to **Waterford,** a wonderfully picturesque village first settled in 1793. About 20 minutes from Bethel along a fast-moving backroad route (head south on Route 5 from the Bethel Common to North Waterford, then continue on Route 35 to Waterford), this village has changed little since the late 19th century. Distinguished white clapboard homes surround a shady, small green, and the village touches on tranquil Keoka Lake, which has a small municipal beach. Stop for a swim, or head to the trail just off the Green leading summit of Mount Tir'em, a modest hike with a rewarding view.

GETTING OUTSIDE

Grafton Notch State Park

Grafton Notch straddles Route 26 as it angles northwest from Newry toward Errol, New Hampshire. The drive north from Bethel is remarkably scenic, passing initially through farmland in a fertile river valley before ascending through bristly forest beneath rough, grey cliffs on the hillsides above. The foreboding Old Speck Mountain towers to the south; views of Lake Umbagog open to the north as you continue on into New Hampshire. This route attracts few crowds, although it's often thickly populated with swift Canadian drivers in a hurry to get from Quebec to Old Orchard Beach.

Public access to the park is comprised of a handful of roadside parking lots near scenic areas. The best of the bunch is **Screw Auger Falls,** where the Bear River drops through several small and pleasant cascades before tumbling dramatically into a narrow and twisting gorge worn by glacial runoff through solid granite bedrock. Picnic tables dot the forested banks upriver of the falls, and kids seem inexorably drawn to splash and swim in the smaller pools on warm days. A short drive to the west, Mother Walker Falls is a miniature, bonsai-like waterfall, notable in that it's underground, hidden beneath a huge slab of granite that long ago tumbled down from the cliffs above. It takes a bit of sleuthing to find.

Road & Mountain Biking

One easy and scenic route perfect for a bike tour follows winding Sunday River Road for several miles into the foothills of the Mahoosuc mountains. Start near the Sunday River ski area, and head west along the river past a tranquil scene with covered bridge, and a few miles later past the Outward Bound school. Eventually, you'll head into the forested hills (the road eventually turns to dirt). This dead-end road is lightly traveled, and views from the broad valley floor are rewarding.

Hard-core mountain bikers should head to the **Sunday River Mountain Bike Park** (☎ 207/824-3000) at the ski area. Mountain bike trails of every caliber are open to bikers. Experienced trail riders will enjoy taking their bikes by chairlift to the summit, and caroming back down on the service roads and bike trails.

Hiking

The Appalachian Trail crosses the Mahoosuc Mountains northwest of Bethel. Many of those who've hiked the entire 2,000-mile trail say this stretch is the most demanding on knees and psyches. The trail doesn't forgive; it generally foregoes switchbacks in favor of sheer ascents and descents. It's also hard to find water along the trail during dry weather. Still, it's worth the knee-pounding effort for the views and the unrivaled sense of remoteness.

One stretch of the Appalachian Trail crosses Old Speck Mountain, Maine's third highest peak, in Grafton Notch State Park off Rt. 26. There are no views since the old fire tower closed a few years ago, but an easy-to-moderate hike from Rt. 26 to an 800-foot cliff called "The Eyebrow" provides a good vantage point of the Bear River Valley and the rugged terrain of Grafton Notch. Look for the well-signed parking lot where Route 26 intersects the Appalachian Trail in Grafton Notch State Park. Park your car, then head south on the AT; in 0.1 mi. you'll intersect the Eyebrow Trail and its moderate accent to the fine vistas.

The Appalachian Mountain Club's Maine Mountain Guide is highly reccommended for detailed information about other area hikes.

Alpine Skiing

The East's only **ski train** serves Sunday River from Portland, offering a relaxed way to get to the slopes and back. Launched in 1993 by Sunday River owner Les Otten, this train pulls out of an industrial lot on Portland's outskirts at 6:45 am, then follows rivers and historic train routes on its 2¼-hour run to Bethel Station. Skiers are then transferred to a fleet of buses for the final 7-mile shuttle to the slopes, and are usually on the slopes by 9:30 or 10 am.

The train cars are spacious if a bit cheerless, and allow sprawling and socializing for up to 283 passengers. Coffee and continental breakfast items are sold on the outbound leg; light meals and beer are available on the return trip. There's an adult-only bar car in the evening.

This isn't just basic transportation—although it's a delight when sloppy snows make driving hazardous. It's a whole experience, and one that's priced right. A weekend trip to sample Portland's restaurants and attractions could easily be packaged with a one- or two-day excursion to Sunday River, combining the best of urban Maine with some of the better skiing in New England.

The train runs on Fridays, Saturdays, and Sundays. When you buy a ski ticket, the train costs $15 round trip Friday; $20 on weekends. Contact **Sunday River** (☎ 207/824-3000) for more information.

Sunday River Ski Resort. P.O. Box 450, Bethel, ME 04217. ☎ **207/824-3000,** lodging 800/543-2754. Vertical drop: 2,340 feet. Lifts: 15 chairlifts (3 high-speed), one surface lift. Skiable acreage: 639. Lift tickets: $45 adults weekends, $41 weekdays.

Sunday River has grown by leaps and bounds in recent years, and today competes in the same league as other major New England winter resorts like Mt. Snow and Killington. Unlike ski areas that have developed around a single tall peak, Sunday River has expanded along an undulating ridge that encompasses some seven peaks. Just traversing from one side of the resort to the other, stitching runs together with chairlift rides, can take an hour. As a result, you rarely get bored making the same run time and again.

The descents offer something for virtually everyone, from steep bump runs to glade skiing to wide, wonderful intermediate trails. A few years ago, Sunday River was regarded as an intermediate's mountain. That changed dramatically with the expansion to the adjacent peaks and the addition of steep new runs. It's now got the reputation of a mountain with great bumps and sheer descents. Sunday River is also blessed with plenty of water for snowmaking, and makes tons of the stuff using a proprietary snowmaking system.

My chief complaint with Sunday River is that the superb skiing conditions are offset by an uninspiring base area. Everything seems a bit raw and unfinished at the bottom of the mountain. The lodges and condos are architecturally dull, dull, dull, and the less-than-delicate landscaping is the sort created by graceless bulldozers. And spread as widely as it is, there's no real sense of place, as is the case at more established resorts like Sugarloaf or Waterville Valley.

Ski Mt. Abram. P.O. Box 120, Locke Mills, ME 04255. ☎ **207/875-5003.** Vertical drop: 1,030 feet. Lifts: 2 chairlifts, 3 T-bars. Skiable acreage: 135. Lift tickets: $28 adult weekend, $18 midweek; children & teens $16–$22 weekends, $14–$18 midweek.

Mt. Abram is a welcoming intermediate mountain that's perfect for families on the uphill learning curve. It has a friendly, informal atmosphere that's in sharp contrast with nearby Sunday River. You don't have to expend much energy on logistics here planning when to meet up or at what base lodge. You don't have to expend as much cash, either.

Mt. Abram has carved out a niche as a telemark mountain. If you're interested in learning this newly rediscovered skiing technique, which employs the "free-heel" bindings used in cross-country skiing and a series of deep-knee bends in getting down the slopes, a number of clinics and packages are available throughout the week.

Golf

Duffers should make for the **Bethel Inn and Country Club** (☎ **207/824-2175**), which operates a scenic 18-hole golf course next to the inn. Equipment and golf carts are available for rent, and the club also features a driving range.

WHERE TO STAY

Bethel Inn. On the Common, Bethel, ME 04217. ☎ **207/824-2175** or 800/654-0125. 57 rms (some with showers only). TV TEL. Summer $190–$360 double including breakfast and dinner; winter $150–$260 double including breakfast and dinner. Lodging only in April and November. AE, DC, DISC, MC, V.

The Bethel Inn is a classic, old-fashioned resort built on the Common in 1913. You can tell which buildings are part of the inn by their distinctive color—Bethel Inn yellow. The main inn has a quiet, settled air throughout, which seems appropriate since it was built to house patients of Dr. John Gehring, who put Bethel on the map treating nervous disorders through a regimen of healthy country living. (Bethel was once known as "the resting place of Harvard" for all the faculty treated here.) The quaint, homey rooms aren't terribly spacious, but are welcoming and pleasingly furnished with country antiques. The deluxe rooms have separate sitting rooms; modern condominium lodging is also available, but these sorely lack the charm of the inn.

The resort, situated on 200 acres, has a number of welcome amenities, including a fitness center with an outdoor heated pool, a superb golf course, tennis, and the inn's Lake House, picturesquely located amid pines on a small lake a short drive away. In winter, there's cross-country skiing on the inn's 24 miles of trails, and a daily shuttle delivers guests to downhill skiing at Sunday River. The inn's fine-dining room serves notable meals in a classically elegant dining room, with specialties like a lobster-filled ravioli appetizer, and venison medallions and broiled duck breast for main courses. (Angle for a table on the enclosed porch.) While the cost is high, don't be scared off; the inn offers a number of packages that bring down the daily rate if you stay a few days. Call and inquire.

⑤ Holidae House. Main St., Bethel, ME 04217. ☎ **207/824-3400.** 7 rms (3 with shower only). TV TEL. Winter $75–$89 double weekends, $45–$58 midweek; summer $60–$70. Rates include breakfast. AE, MC, V.

Innkeeper Tom McGinniss has done an extraordinary job making over this century-old village home on Bethel's Main Street. The exterior is unusually handsome, painted in rich but muted colors, and the inside is superbly decorated in a style that nicely straddles high Victorian and low whimsical. Every room is furnished with antiques and Oriental carpets; some have delightful hand-painted ceiling murals and whirlpool tubs. (Number 5 was my favorite, decorated with a surfeit of classically inspired elegance.) The common room is fairly small for an inn of this size, but guests are likely to keep to their rooms most of the time—except perhaps when browsing the antiques shop in the barn out back. (Guests get wholesale prices.) The inn is a 5-minute walk from the Bethel Common, and a 10-minute drive to skiing at Sunday River.

L'Auberge Country Inn. Bethel Common (P.O. Box 21), Bethel, ME 04217. ☎ **207/824-2774** or 800/760-2774. 7 rms (1 with hall bath). $60–$100 double, including breakfast ($20 higher weekends and holidays). Two-night minimum on weekends. AE, DISC, MC, V. Closed mid-April to mid–May, and mid-Oct to Thanksgiving. Closed mid-April to mid–May, and mid-Oct to Thanksgiving.

L'Auberge was originally built as a barn in the 1890s, but other than a few exposed beams its lineage isn't immediately evident. Located on a spacious, shady lot down a small lane just off the Bethel Common, the inn has a settled, European air inside. You enter through a high-ceilinged living room with a Steinway, ticking antique hall clock, fireplace, and decanter of sherry. "Kit" the golden retriever may be present to give you a low-key greeting. The rooms are furnished in a comfortable country style, some with stencilling and brass beds. The inn is locally well known for its dining room, which serves delicately prepared continental fare. Guests choose from three small dining rooms; the best is an intimate space painted "gregarious red" that gives off a gentle, candle-lit glow in the evening. (The dining room is open to the public, reservations recommended. Entree prices range from $14 to $24.) In summer, Tuesday nights feature a traditional lobster bake.

Summit Hotel. P.O. Box 540, Bethel, ME 04217. ☎ **207/824-3000** or 800/543-2754. 230 rms. A/C TV TEL. $139–$400 double (from $89 in summer). AE, DISC, MC, V.

The Summit Hotel opened a few years ago to meet the huge demand for lodging on the mountain at Sunday River. Despite its name, the hotel is located at the base of the mountain just off the slopes, connected to the other base facilities via shuttle bus. And despite its pricey rates, it's more utilitarian than fancy, with long institutional hallways with drop ceilings and undistinguished mid-sized hotel rooms with basic furnishings. (The executive suites are far larger and a bit more lavishly appointed.) But the place can't be beat for convenience. Ski right out the front door to a nearby chairlift; when you return from skiing in the afternoon, you can jump right into the outdoor heated pool. There's also a café and restaurant in the building, and many of the rooms offer kitchenettes. Ask for a room with a private deck—there's no extra charge if they have one available.

Telemark Inn. RFD #2, Box 800, Bethel 04217. ☎ **207/836-2703.** 6 rms, all with shared bath. Summer, $90 double, including breakfast. Winter rate, $396 double includes two nights and all meals. MC, V. Closed April. Call for directions.

Built on a private inholding within the borders of the White Mountain National Forest, the Telemark Inn attracts wilderness adventurers and those whose vacation goal is to get away from the static of modern life. This small lodge was originally built in 1900 as a retreat for a successful businessman, and it retains a strong sense of turn-of-the century remoteness. Innkeeper Steve Crone, who opened the lodge in 1986, maintains a herd of a dozen or so llamas at the lodge; these gangly beasts see action in summer on guided hikes in the national forest. Independent-minded guests can explore the hills around the inn, soak in the nearby private swimming holes, or simply plop themselves in a chair and sip coffee until morning lapses into afternoon. In winter, guests cruise the 12 miles of private cross-country trails around the lodge, skate on the farm pond at the edge of the property, or strap on snowshoes to explore the deep, still woods.

WHERE TO DINE

Iron Horse Bar & Grill. Bethel Station (Cross St.), Bethel. ☎ **207/824-0961.** Reservations recommended. Main courses, $9.50–$20. AE, DISC, MC, V. Sun–Thurs 5–9pm (until 10pm Fri–Sat and ski season). AMERICAN.

Housed in two train cars sidetracked at Bethel Station (the new mall/hotel complex at the edge of town), the Iron Horse captures the atmosphere of a long-lost era. Guests enter through a coupling between the two cars. To the right is a lounge car where you might expect to run into John Cheever on his way back to the Westchester suburbs. To the left is the dining car, which has a romantic art deco-ish flair to it, with a striking wall mural in a Southwestern motif, white tableclothes, and etched glass partitions. Elegance notwithstanding, diners arrive in jeans in the summer and in ski togs in the winter. (This is Maine, after all.) The entrees are better than you'd find in most trains today, with dishes including Black Angus steak, chicken, seafood, and a selection of game, such as quail and wild boar. Be prepared for less-than-swift service (the waitress told us it's because the kitchen is so narrow), but count on a pleasant evening in unique surroundings.

Moose's Tale. Route 2 (at Sunday River Rd.), Bethel. ☎ **207/824-4253.** Reservations not accepted. Main courses, $3.95–$13.95 (most $6–$8). MC, V. Daily 11:30am–1am. PUB FARE.

Sunday River Brewing Co. opened this modern brew pub a few years ago on prime real estate at the corner of Route 2 and the Sunday River access road. This is a good choice if your primary objective is to consume superb ales and porters. The brews are excellent; the food (burgers, nachos, chicken wings) doesn't appear to strive for any culinary heights, and certainly doesn't achieve them. The design of the restaurant is a bit idiosyncratic; the best tables are by the stone fireplace in the main dining room, and in a side room near the pool tables. And, of course, there's the bar, which is the optimal place to be after a day skiing the slopes or hiking on the Appalachian Trail.

Mother's. Upper Main St., Bethel. ☎ **207/824-2589.** Reservations accepted for parties of 6 or more. Lunch $4.75–$8; dinner $6.50–$16.50. MC, V. Sun–Fri 11:30am–9:30pm (until 10pm Sat). May be closed briefly in late spring and late fall; call first. AMERICAN.

Appropriate to its name, Mother's is a homey, informal place housed in a pale green Victorian home adorned with gingerbread trim. Inside, diners are ushered to small, darkly panelled rooms, each of which has four or five tables and walls hung with portraits of dour Victorians. (In summer, there's also dining on the front deck.) The meals are basic and well-prepared, and the service is always friendly. For lunch there's hamburgers and crabcake sandwiches; for dinner, try the sea scallops with artichokes, or the pork ribs grilled with a lemon barbecue sauce.

RANGELEY LAKES

Mounted moose heads on the walls, log cabins tucked in the spruce forest, and cool August mornings that demand not one sweater but two come to mind when one speaks of the Rangeley Lakes region. Although Rangeley Lake and its eponymous town are at the heart of the region, it extends much further, consisting of a series of lakes that feed into and flow out of Rangeley. Upstream is Maine's fourth largest lake, Flagstaff, a beautiful, wind-raked body of water created in 1949 when Central Maine Power dammed the Dead River. (Below the dam it's no longer dead; in fact it's now noted for its white-water rafting—see "The North Woods" below). From Rangeley Lake, the waters flow into the Cupsuptic Pond, which in turn flow to Moose-lookmeguntic Lake, through the Upper and Lower Richardson Lakes, down the remote Swift River and to Lake Umbagog, which feeds the headwaters of the Androscoggin River.

The town of Rangeley (pop. 1,063) is the regional center for outdoor activities. It offers a handful of motels and restaurants, a few fishing guides, and a smattering of shops, but little else. Easy-to-visit attractions in the Rangeley area are few, and most regular visitors and residents seem determined to keep it that way. The wise visitor rents a cabin or takes a room at a lodge, then explores the area with the slow pace that seems custom-made for the area. Rangeley is Maine's highest town at 1,546 feet, and is usually cool throughout the summer.

Rangeley attracts a handful of low-key celebrities. It's been a longtime summer home to William Wegman, whose photographs of his Weimaraners in various outfits are often set in and around Rangeley. These photos have produced the fodder for a popular series of children's books, posters, and calendars.

ESSENTIALS

GETTING THERE   Rangeley is 122 miles north of Portland, and 39 miles north-west of Farmington on Route 4. The most scenic approach is on Route 17 from Rumford. Along the way, you'll pass one of the most scenic overlooks in New England, with a sweeping panorama of Mooselookmeguntic Lake and Bemis Mountain.

From New Hampshire, drive 111 miles north on Route 16 from North Conway through Gorham, Berlin, and Errol. Route 16 from Errol to Rangeley is especially remote and scenic.

VISITOR INFORMATION   The **Rangeley Lakes Region Chamber of Commerce,** P.O. Box 317, Rangeley, ME 04970 (**207/864-5571** or 800/685-2537) maintains an information booth in town at a small park near the lake that's open year-round Monday through Saturday from 9am to 5pm.

CANOEING

The Rangeley Lakes area is a canoeist's paradise. Azure waters, dense forests, and handsome hills are all part of the allure. Rangeley Lake has a mix of wild forest and old-time camps lining the lakeshore. The southeast coves of Mooselookmeguntic Lake suffered an unfortunate period of haphazard development during the 1980s, but much of the shore, especially along the Phillips Preserve (see above) and the west shore, are still very attractive. Upper Richardson Lake's shoreline is largely owned by the state, and is the most remote and wild of the chain. Primitive campsites along the shores of both Upper and Lower Richardson Lakes are managed by the **South Arm Campground** (☎ **207/364-5155**), located at the tip of Lower Richardson Lake and accessible via dirt road from the town of Andover.

Canoeists should exercise the usual cautions and keep a sharp eye on the weather. Stiff northerly winds can blow through with little warning, making it all but impossible to return to where you started. This is especially true on the Upper and Lower Richardson lakes, which angle northward—furious winds and frothy white-caps are not an uncommon summer phenomenon.

HIKING

The Appalachian Trail crosses Route 4 about 10 miles south of Rangeley. A strenuous but rewarding hike is along the AT northward to the summit of Saddleback Mountain, a 10-mile round trip that ascends though thick forest and past remote ponds to open, arctic-like terrain with fine views of the surrounding mountains and lakes. Saddleback actually consists of two peaks over 4,000 feet (hence the name). Be prepared for sudden shifts in weather, and for the high winds that often rake the open ridgeline.

An easier one-mile hike may be found at Bald Mountain near the village of Oquossuc, on the northeast shore of Mooselookmeguntic Lake. (Look for the trailhead one mile south of Haines Landing on Bald Mt. Rd.). The views have grown over in recent years (Minoxidil?), but you can still catch glimpses of the clear blue waters from above.

ALPINE SKIING

Saddleback Ski Area. P.O. Box 490, Rangeley, ME 04970. ☎ **207/864-5671.** Vertical drop: 1,830 feet. Lifts: 2 double chairs, 3 T-bars. Lift tickets: $32 adult weekend, $19–$27 juniors & students weekend; all tickets $17 midweek.

With only two chairlifts, Saddleback qualifies as a small mountain. But there's the surprise. Because Saddleback has an unexpectedly big-mountain feel. It offers a

Weird Science

One of the quirkiest destinations in Maine is Orgonon, former home of the controversial Viennese psychologist Wilhelm Reich (1897–1957). A tour of his hilltop estate includes a great story about a man with a mission, and an up-close look at an architecturally distinctive stone house. Even if the history of psychology or architecture don't hold any allure for you, take my advice and stop by anyway. It won't be a disappointment.

A brief overview: Wilhelm Reich was an associate of Sigmund Freud during the early days of psychoanalysis. But Reich took Freud's work one step further. He hypothesized that pent-up sexual energy resulted in many neuroses, and believed that a regimen of induced orgasms would result in a psychologically healthy being. This led to his involvement with the sexual politics movement in Europe in the 1930s. His theories forced a break with Freud, and the clouds of World War II forced his departure from Europe.

Once settled in Rangeley, Reich pursued his theories further and developed the science of "orgonomy," which held that units of "orgone" floated freely in the atmosphere, and if captured, could be used to cure patients not only of their neuroses but of illness such as cancer. Reich invented "orgone boxes," which were said to concentrate the orgone from the atmosphere, and patients sat inside to be cured. He also invented a rather large and fearsome looking orgone gun to capture orgone in the atmosphere, thereby producing rain by altering the atmospheric balance. Reich died in a federal prison in 1957, sentenced for contempt on matters related to the transport of his orgone boxes.

Orgonon, built in 1948 of native fieldstone, has a spectacular view of Dodge Pond and is built in a distinctive American Modern style, which doesn't exactly fit in with the local rustic-lodge motif. Visitors on the one-hour guided tour of the estate can see the orgone boxes and the orgone gun, along with the other intriguing inventions and stark, dramatic canvases created by Reich, who took up painting at age 55.

Orgonon (☎ 207/864-3443) is located 3.5 miles west of Rangeley on Route 4. Admission is $3 adults, free to children 12 and under; it's open July and August Tuesday through Sunday from 1 to 5pm, and in September on Sunday only.

vertical drop of 1,830 feet, but what makes Saddleback so appealing is its rugged alpine setting (the Appalachian Trail runs across the high, mile-long ridge above the resort) and the old-fashioned trails. Saddleback offered glade skiing and narrow, winding trails well before the bigger ski areas sought to re-create these old-fashioned slopes. The 2.5 mile Lazy River Trail is one of the more scenic beginner's descents in New England.

WHERE TO STAY & DINE

The Rangeley area has a scattering of bed-and-breakfasts, but many travelers destined here plan to spend a week or more either at a sporting camp or a rented waterfront cottage. Among the best-known of the sporting camps is **Grant's Kennebago Camps** (☎ 207/864-3608 or 800/633-4815), situated down a long and dusty logging road on Kennebago Lake—the biggest "fly-fishing only" lake east of the Mississippi. Rates are $100 per person per day, including all meals. **Mooselookmeguntic House** (☎ 207/864-2962) offers a cluster of cabins on or near the shores of Mooselookmeguntic, along with access to a handsome beach and marina.

For weekly rental of a private cabin, advance planning is essential. A good place to start is the local chamber of commerce's free "Accommodations and Services" pamphlet (☎ 207/864-5364 or 800/685-2537). The chamber can itself book cabins for the week for you.

Rangeley Inn. P.O. Box 398, Rangeley, ME 04907. ☎ **207/864-3341** or 800/666-3687. Fax 207/864-3634. 51 rms (several with shower only). TV (motel only). $69–$119 double. AE, DISC, MC, V.

The architecturally eclectic Rangeley Inn dominates Rangeley's miniature downtown. Parts of this old-fashioned, blue-shingled hotel date back to 1877, but the main wing was built in 1907, with additions in the 1920s and the 1940s. A 15-unit motel annex was built behind the inn on Haley Pond, but those looking for creaky floors and a richer sense of local heritage should request a room in the main, three-floor inn.

The rooms at the inn and motel are each unique—some in the motel have woodstoves, kitchenettes, or whirlpools; in the inn you'll find a handful of rooms with clawfoot tubs perfect for an evening's soaking. The gracious, old-worldish dining room serves hearty, filling meals with considerable flair. Ed and Fay Carpenter have run the place since the early 1970s, and have hospitality down to a science. During the heavy tour season (especially fall), bus groups tend to dominate, but the rest of the time it's perfect for couples or families looking for a place to slough off the stress of daily life.

Two Lakeside Campgrounds

While dozens of wilderness campsites, often accessible only by canoe, may be found throughout the region (check with the chamber of commerce for more information), two of the more accessible campgrounds bear mentioning. **Rangeley Lake State Park** (☎ 207/864-3858) occupies about a mile of shoreline on the south shore of Rangeley Lake. It has 50 attractive campsites with easy access to the waters of Rangeley Lake. Bring a canoe for exploring.

Along a narrow dirt road on the eastern shores of Mooselookmeguntic Lake is the **Stephen Phillips Wildlife Preserve** (☎ 207/864-2003), a private holding comprised of hundreds of lakeshore acres and several islands. The preserve offers camping on two islands (Toothaker and Students), both of which are accessible by canoe. Lakeside campsites are also available in the scrubby spruce forest that lines the lake; most sites are accessible by walking a few hundred feet from scattered parking areas, providing more of a backcountry experience than you'll find at most drive-in campgrounds. Canoes are available for rent at the office. The fee is $6 per night for two people, and campsite reservations are accepted.

CARRABASSETT VALLEY

The Carrabassett Valley can be summed up in six words: big peaks, wild woods, deep lakes.

The crowning jewel of the region is **Sugarloaf Mountain,** Maine's second highest peak at 4,237 feet. Distinct from other nearby peaks because of its pyramidal shape, the mountain has been developed for skiing, and offers the highest vertical drop in Maine, the best selection of activities daytime and nighttime, and a wide range of accommodations within easy commuting distance.

While Sugarloaf/USA draws the lion's share of visitors, it's not the only game in town. Nearby Kingfield is an attractive, historic town with a fine old hotel; to my mind, it has more the flavor of a town of the Old West than of classic New England. Other valley towns offering limited services for travelers include Eustis, Stratton, and Carrabassett Valley.

Outside of the villages, it's all rugged hills, tumbling streams, and spectacular natural surroundings. The muscular mountains of the Bigelow Range provide terrain for some of the state's best hiking. And Flagstaff Lake is the place for flatwater canoeing amid majestic surroundings.

ESSENTIALS

GETTING THERE   Kingfield and Sugarloaf are on Route 27. Skiers debate over the best route from the Turnpike. Some exit at Auburn and take Route 4 north to Route 27; others exit in Augusta and take Route 27 straight through. It's a toss-up time-wise, but exiting at Augusta is marginally more scenic.

VISITOR INFORMATION   The **Sugarloaf Area Chamber of Commerce** (☎ 207/235-2100) offers information year-round from its offices 9.5 miles north of Kingfield on Route 27. The office is open in summer 10am to 4pm Monday through Saturday. In winter, it's open weekdays 8am to 7pm, Saturday 10am to 6pm, and Sunday 11am to 3pm. The chamber will book lodgings in and around Sugarloaf; call **800/843-2732.** For accommodations on the mountain, contact **Sugarloaf** directly at ☎ **800/843-5623.**

ALPINE SKIING

Sugarloaf/USA. RR 1, Box 5000, Carrabassett Valley, ME 04947. ☎ **207/237-2000** or 800/843-5623. Internet http://www.sugarloaf.com. Vertical drop: 2,820 feet. Lifts: 13 chairlifts, including 1 gondola and 1 high-speed quad; 1 surface lift. Skiable acreage: 1,400 (snowmaking on 475 acres). Lift tickets: $45 adult weekend; $41 weekday.

Sugarloaf is Maine's big mountain, with the highest vertical drop in New England after Killington in Vermont. And thanks to quirks of geography, it actually feels bigger than it is. From the high snowfields (which accounts for much of Sugarloaf's huge skiable acreage) or the upper advanced runs like Bubblecuffer or White Nitro, skiers develop a bit of vertigo looking down at the valley floor. Sugarloaf attracts plenty of experts to its hard-core runs, but it's also a superb intermediate mountain, with great cruising runs. A gentle bunny slope extends down through the village; the "green" slopes on the mountain itself are a bit more challenging.

Sugarloaf has more of a destination feel to it than many resorts, since it's nearly three hours from Portland (five from Boston) and gets relatively little day-tripper traffic. Most people who ski Sugarloaf stay at the base complex, a well-run, convivial cluster hotel rooms, condos, mini-suites, and the like offering 7,500 beds. The accommodations, the mountain, the restaurants, and other area attractions are well-connected by chairlifts and shuttle buses, making for a relaxed visit here even during a fierce blizzard.

CROSS-COUNTRY SKIING

The **Sugarloaf Ski Touring Center** (☎ 207/237-6830) offers 57 miles of groomed trails that weave through the village at the base of the mountain and into the low hills covered with young, scrappy woodlands south of the Carrabassett River. The trails are impeccably groomed for striding and skating, and wonderful views open here and there to Sugarloaf Mountain and the Bigelow Range. The base lodge is simple and attractive, all knotty pine with a cathedral ceiling, and features a cafeteria, towering stone fireplace, and a well-equipped ski shop. Trail fees are $10 daily for adults; $7–$8 for juniors, seniors, and children. The center is located on Route 27 about one mile south of the Sugarloaf access road. A shuttle bus serves the area in winter.

HIKING

The 12-mile Bigelow Range has some of the most dramatic, high-ridge hiking in the state, a close second to Mt. Katahdin. The Bigelow Range consists of a handful of lofty peaks, with Avery Peak (the East Peak, renamed after Myron Avery, one of the Appalachian Trail's founders) offering perhaps the best views. On exceptionally clear days, hikers can see Mount Washington to the southwest and Mount Katahdin to the northeast.

A strenuous but rewarding hike for fit hikers is the 10.3 mile-loop that begins at the Fire Warden's Trail. (The trailhead is at the washed-out bridge on Stratton Brook Pond Rd., a rugged dirt road that leaves eastward from Rt. 27 about 2.3 miles north of the Sugarloaf access road.) Follow the Fire Warden's Trail up the extremely steep ridge to the junction with the Appalachian Trail. Head south on the AT, which tops the West Peak and South Horn, two open summits with stellar views. One-quarter mile past Horns Pond, turn south on Horns Pond Trail and descend back to the Fire Warden's Trail to return to your car. Hikers pass two lean-tos along this route (free, first-come, first-served), making this suitable for an overnight hike. Allow about eight hours for the loop; a map and hiking guide are strongly recommended.

A less rigorous hike with supremely rewarding views is to Cranberry Peak, the Bigelow peak furthest to the west. Plan on four to five hours to complete this hike along Bigelow Range Trail, which runs about 6.5 miles. The trail head is just south of the town of Stratton (from the south, turn right 0.2 miles after crossing Stratton Brook, then drive on a dirt road $1/2$ mile to a clearing). Follow the trail through woods and over a series of ledges to the 3,213-foot Cranberry Peak. Retrace your steps to your car.

Detailed directions for these hikes and many others in the area, may be found in the AMC's Maine Mountain Guide.

OTHER OUTDOOR PURSUITS

Skiers can take a break from the winter slopes and experience the northern forest from a vole's eye angle on the "The White Howling Express," a dog-sled ride that employs a team of robust, eager Samoyeds. Owner Tim Diehl offers $1 1/2$-mile trips on customized dogsleds from his headquarters on Route 27 just north of the Sugarloaf access road. Trips are run at regular intervals throughout the winter; in summer, the dogs pull wheeled carts along the course.

In summer, **Sugarloaf/USA's 18-hole golf course** (☎ 207/237-2000) attracts golfers by the cartload. It's invariably ranked the number one golf destination in the state by experienced golfers, who are lured here by the Robert Trent Jones, Jr. course design and dramatic mountain backdrop. Sugarloaf hosts a well-respected golf school during the season.

A MUSEUM FOR AUTO AND PHOTO BUFFS

Stanley Museum. School St., Kingfield. ☎207/265-2729. Suggested donation is $2 adults, $1 children, $3 family. Tues–Sun 1–4pm. Closed April and November, except by appointment.

The Stanley Steamer—an automobile powered with steam like a locomotive—is today an anachronistic footnote and prized collectible. But when manufactured between 1897 and 1925, it was state-of-the-art transportation, literally and figuratively smoking the competition. The Stanley Steamer was the first car to reach the summit of Mt. Washington, the first car to break the two-miles-in-one-minute barrier with a landspeed record of 127 mph in 1906, and the winner of numerous hill-climb competitions.

The Stanley Museum, housed in a handsome yellow Georgian former schoolhouse in Kingfield, chronicles the rise of the Steamer, and the backgrounds of the two Kingfield inventors, the twins F. O. and F. E. Stanley. Three working Steamers are on display. You'll learn that the Stanleys invented the car as a hobby—they established their first fortune inventing the dry-plate photographic process and building a company that was eventually purchased by George Eastman, the founder of Kodak.

Also on display are the extraordinary early photographs taken by their sister Chansonetta Stanley, who documented life in rural Maine and South Carolina at the turn of the century—a sort of self-appointed precursor to the WPA photographers. Her work has gained recent respect among serious collectors, and this exhibit will make it abundantly plain why that's so.

WHERE TO STAY

For convenience, nothing beats staying right on the mountain in winter. Skiers can pop right out the door and onto the lifts. Sugarloaf is nicely designed to allow skiers access to the village; a long, gentle slope extends from the base of the mountain through the clusters of condos and hotels, allowing skiers to glide home after a long day. A low chairlift takes you up to the base first thing in the morning.

Many of the condos are booked through **Sugarloaf/USA Inn** (☎ 207/237-2000 or 800/843-5623), which handles the reservations for far more than 300 condos and mini-suites. The units are spread throughout the base area, and are of varying vintage and opulence. All guests have access to the Sugarloaf Sports and Fitness Center. Another option at the base village is the **Sugarloaf Mountain Hotel** (☎ 800/527-9879), a towering structure right at the lifts with more than 100 guest rooms.

The Herbert. Main St. (P.O. Box 67), Kingfield, ME 04947. ☎ **207/265-2000** or 800/843-4372. 40 rms. $80–$140 double; discounts midweek. AE, DC, DISC, MC, V.

The Herbert has the feel of a classic North Woods hostelry—sort of Dodge City meets Northern Exposure. Built in downtown Kingfield in 1918, the three-story hotel featured all of the finest accoutrements when it was built—fumed oak paneling and incandescent lights in the lobby (look for the original brass fixtures), a classy dining room, and comfortable rooms. The Herbert's 1982 renovation cost $1 million, and was nicely done—right down to the two stuffed moose heads, the baby grand piano, and the fireplace in the lobby. The rooms are furnished in a fairly simple and basic style, although some feature whirlpool bathtubs (there's also a family whirlpool for rent at $10 per half-hour in the basement). Room furnishings tend toward flea-market antiques, with some newer additions. (This doesn't always translate into charming: I had a cheap imitation brass headboard missing rungs that rattled with every breath I took.) The Herbert is located about 15 miles from the slopes at Sugarloaf/USA.

Three Stanley Avenue. 3 Stanley Ave. (P.O. Box 169), Kingfield, ME 04947. ☎ **207/265-5541.** 6 rms (3 with private bath). Dec–March $50–$60 double; Apr–Nov $50–$55. All rates include breakfast. Two-night min on winter weekends. AE, MC, V.

Three Stanley Avenue is the bed-and-breakfast annex to the better-known restaurant next door, One Stanley Avenue. Set on a shady knoll in a quiet village setting just across the bridge from downtown Kingfield, Three Stanley Avenue has a old-fashioned Victorian boarding house feel to it, complete with a garish stained-glass window at the bottom of the stairs. The rooms are comfortably if not luxuriously appointed; three rooms share two baths, the other three have private baths. One of the greatest advantages of this spot is its location, just across a broad lawn from the restaurant, which consistently serves up some of the most creative (and expensive) regional cuisine in the state.

WHERE TO DINE

The Herbert. Main St., Kingfield. ☎ **207/265-2000** or 800/843-4372. Reservations recommended. Main courses, $12.95–$21.95. AE, DC, DISC, MC, V. Open daily 5pm–9pm (until 8pm on Sunday). REGIONAL.

This open but intimate dining room off the lobby of The Herbert hotel recalls the days when hotels served the best meals in town. The place has a nice Edwardian gloss to it—right down to the heavy sink for guests to wash their hands. The interior has been prettified somewhat, but not enough to lose its charm for the tourists and locals who flock here for tasty, creative meals. The chef offers some nice interpretations on regional classics, like shiitake mushrooms with venison medallions, and haddock baked with feta cheese and served with a lemon-garlic dressing. The meals are good, not excellent, but the service is friendly and the experience altogether enjoyable. Come early to enjoy a glass of wine in the lobby before you dine.

✪ **Hug's.** Route 27, Carrabassett Valley. ☎ **207/237-2392.** Reservations recommended, especially on weekends. Main courses, $10.95–$16.95. MC, V. Open Tues–Sun 5pm–9pm (until 9:30 on weekends). Closed May–Nov. Located $^7/_{10}$ mile south of the Sugarloaf access road. NORTHERN ITALIAN.

Hug's takes diners well beyond red sauce, offering a broad selection of delicately prepared pastas far finer than one should reasonably expect from a restaurant within the orbit of a ski area. This is a small place, set just off the highway in a fairy-tale like cottage. Inside are two intimate dining rooms; the dominant color is battleship gray, but it's enlivened with lipstick-red tablecloths and intriguing early ski pictures on the walls. Dinners are preceded with a tasty basket of pesto bread (very welcome after a day of hiking or skiing). The dinner selections are outstanding and uncommonly well prepared. The shiitake ravioli with walnut-pesto alfredo is superb, as is the chicken limon. The sole disappointment was the salad, which consisted largely of big, tasteless chunks of iceberg lettuce. (Although another disappointment is that it's closed in summer.) As for the name: No, you won't be greeted with a warm embrace. "Hug" was the original owner's nickname.

5 Freeport to Port Clyde

Veteran Maine travelers contend this part of the coast is fast losing its native charm—it's too commercial, too developed, too much like the rest of the United States. The grousers do have a point, especially regarding Route 1's roadside, but get off the main roads and you'll find pockets where you can catch glimpses of another Maine. Among the sights backroads travelers will stumble upon are quiet inland villages, dramatic coastal scenery, and a rich sense of history, especially maritime history.

The best source of information for the region in general is found at the **Maine State Information Center** (☎ **207/846-0833**) just off I-95 in Yarmouth. This state-run center is stocked with hundreds of brochures and free newspapers, and is staffed with a helpful crew that can provide information on the entire state, but is particularly well-informed about the mid-coast region.

FREEPORT

If Freeport were a mall (and that's not a far-fetched analogy), L.L. Bean would be the anchor store. It's the business that launched Freeport, elevating its status from just another town off the interstate to one of the two outlet capitals of Maine (the other is Kittery). Freeport still has the form of a classic coastal village (the main "Y" intersection in town was designed such that 100-foot masts could be hauled to the water's edge without making any sharp turns), but it's a village with a twist. Most of the old homes and stores have been converted to upscale shops, and now sell name-brand clothing and housewares. Banana Republic occupies an exceedingly handsome brick Federal-style home; even the McDonald's is in a tasteful, understated Victorian farmhouse—you really have to look for the golden arches.

While a number of more modern buildings have been built to accommodate the outlet boom (there are now more than 100 stores in town), strict planning guidelines have managed to preserve much of the local charm, at least in the village section. Huge parking lots off Main Street are hidden from view, making this one of the more aesthetically pleasant places to shop anywhere in the United States. But even with these vast lots, parking can be hard to find during the peak season, especially on rainy summer days when every cottage-bound tourist between York and Camden decides that a trip to Freeport is a winning idea. Bring a lot of patience, and expect teeming crowds if you come at a busy time.

ESSENTIALS

GETTING THERE   Freeport is on Route 1, but is most commonly reached via I-95 from either Exit 19 or 20.

VISITOR INFORMATION   The **Freeport Merchants Association,** P.O. Box 452, Freeport, ME 04032 (☎ **207/865-1212** or 800/865-1994) publishes a map and directory of retail businesses, restaurants, and overnight accommodations. The free map is available widely around town at stores and restaurants.

SHOPPING

At last count, Freeport had more than 100 retail shops between Exit 19 at the far lower end of Main St. and Mallett Rd., which connects to Exit 20. Shops have recently begun to spread south of Exit 19 toward Yarmouth. If you can't stand missing a single one, get off at Exit 17 and head north on Route 1. Among those with a presence in Freeport are The Gap, Anne Klein, Levi's, Boston Traders, Patagonia, Nike, J. Crew, Timberland, Maidenform, and many others.

L.L. Bean. Main & Bow sts. ☎ **800/341-4341.**

Monster outdoor retailer L.L. Bean traces its roots to the day Leon Leonwood Bean decided that what the world really needed was a good weatherproof hunting shoe. He married a watertight gumshoe bottom with a laced leather upper. Hunters liked it. The store grew. An empire was born.

Today L.L. Bean sells millions of dollars worth of clothing and outdoor goods to customers nationwide through its well-respected catalogs and it continues to draw hundreds of thousands through its door. This modern, multi-level store is the size of a regional mall, but tastefully done with its own indoor trout pond and lots of natural wood. L.L. Bean is open 365 days a year, 24 hours a day (note the lack of locks or latches on the front doors) and it's a popular spot even in the dead of night, especially around summer and holidays. (Stars from rock groups performing in Portland are frequently spotted shopping here after their shows.) Selections include Bean's own trademark clothing, along with home furnishings, books, shoes, and plenty of outdoor gear for camping, fishing, and hunting.

In addition to the main store, L.L. Bean stocks an outlet shop with a relatively small but rapidly changing inventory at discount prices. It's located in a back lot between Main Street and Depot Street—ask at the front desk of the main store for walking directions.

Cuddledown of Maine. 231 U.S. Route 1 (between exits 17 & 19). ☎ **207/865-1713.**

Down pillows are made right in this shop, which carries a variety of European goose-down comforters in all sizes and thicknesses.

DeLorme's Map Store. Route 1 (near Cricket's Restaurant). ☎ **207/865-4171.**

It all started a couple decades ago with the Maine Atlas and Gazetteer. Today, DeLorme produces and sells detailed atlases containing mini-topographic maps for numerous states, as well as award-winning computer CD-ROMs containing detailed road maps for the entire nation. The shop doesn't offer discounts, but the selection of DeLorme produces is comprehensive.

Harrington House Museum Store. 45 Main St. ☎ **207/865-0477.**

A shop to benefit the Freeport Historical Society, the Harrington museum store sells a broad array of unique Maine items including antique reproduction furniture, jewelry, and packaged gourmet foods.

J.L. Coombs Shoe Outlet. Route 1 (between exits 17 & 19). ☎ **207/865-4333.**

A Maine shoemaker since 1830, J.L. Coombs today carries a wide assortment of imported and domestic footwear, including a good selection of those favored by teens and college kids, including Dr. Marten, Ecco, and Mephisto. There's also outerwear by Pendleton and Jackaroos.

Maxwell's Pottery Outlet. 47 Main St. ☎ **207/865-1144.**

Maxwell's offers a good selection of practical and fancy pottery, candlestick holders, and other household accouterment. Prices are very reasonable.

Zandhoeven Chocolates. 21 Main St. ☎ **207/865-4405** or 800/897-0677.

When a pair of Maine friends brought chocolates back from a business trip to Belgium, friends and associates clamored for these rich, delectable sweets and started placing orders for their next trip. A business was born. Their second-floor shop is small but packs a powerful chocolate punch with its array of fresh imported sweets.

WHERE TO STAY

Harraseeket Inn. 162 Main St., Freeport, ME 05032. ☎ **207/865-9377** or 800/342-6423. 54 rms. A/C TV TEL. Summer & fall $155–$235 double; spring and early summer $140–$235; winter $105–$215. $10 discount midweek. All rates include breakfast buffet. AE, DC, DISC, MC, V. Take Exit 20 off I-95 to Main St.

The Harraseeket Inn is a large, thoroughly modern hotel two blocks north of L.L. Bean. It's to the inn's credit that one could drive down Main Street and not notice it. A late-19th century home is the soul of the hotel, but most of the rooms are in an architecturally similar 1989 addition that dwarfs the old house. (The new part is of steel and concrete, but not so as you could tell.) Guests can relax in the well-regarded dining room, in the common room with the baby grand player piano, or down in the faux-rustic Broad Arrow Pub with moose head, fireplace, and birchbark canoe. The guest rooms are on the large side and tastefully done, all with quarter-canopy beds and a nice mix of contemporary and antique furniture. About half have fireplaces, and a number have whirlpools. Plans call for construction of another addition with 26 rooms and an indoor pool beginning in December 1996.

Isaac Randall House. 5 Independence Dr., Freeport, ME 05032. ☎ **207/865-9295** or 800/ 865-9295. Fax 207/865-9003. 9 rms (some with showers only, some with hand-held showers in tub). A/C TEL. $70–$115 double, $125 in caboose. DISC, MC, V. Located one-half mile south of the L.L. Bean store on Route 1.

Freeport's first bed-and-breakfast, the Isaac Randall House is located in an 1823 farm-house that's been refurbished with nine handsome guest rooms, all with private bath. The most charming of the bunch is the "Pine" room, built in an adjoining shed with rustic barnboards and decorated in a Southwestern motif. (It also features a unique antique copper tub.) The least charming are the two smaller, modern rooms in an addition in back, and a dark "Loft" room upstairs. The caboose in the back yard sleeps up to four, and is as unique a place to lay your head as you'll find in Maine. Breakfast is served in a homey country kitchen with a Glenwood stove and ticking Regulator clock. The inn is well situated for exploring Freeport; its main disadvantage is its location sandwiched between busy Route 1 and I-95. The sound of traffic is never far away.

BRUNSWICK & BATH

Brunswick and Bath are two exceptionally handsome historic towns that have a strong commercial past, and today remain vibrant with commercial activity. Many travelers heading on Route 1 up the coast pass through both towns eager to reach the areas with higher billing on the marquee. That's a shame, for both these areas are well worth the detour.

Brunswick was once home to several mills along the Androscoggin River; these have since been converted to offices and the like, but Brunswick's broad Maine Street still bustles with activity. Brunswick is also home to Bowdoin College, one of the nation's most respected small colleges. The school was founded in 1794, offered its first classes eight years later, and has since amassed an illustrious roster of prominent alumni, including Nathaniel Hawthorne, Henry Wadsworth Longfellow, Franklin Pierce, and arctic explorer Robert E. Peary. Civil War hero Joshua Chamberlain served as president of the college after the war.

Eight miles to the east, Bath is nicely situated on the broad Kennebec River, and is a noted center of shipbuilding. The first U.S-built ship was constructed downstream at the Popham Bay colony in the early 17th century; in the years since, shipbuilders have constructed more than 5,000 ships. Bath shipbuilding reached its heyday in the late 19th century, but it continues to this day. Bath Iron Works is one of the nation's preeminent boatyards, constructing and repairing ships for the U.S. Navy. The scaled-down military has left Bath shipbuilders in a somewhat tenuous state, but it's still common to see the steely grey ships in the drydock (the best view is from the bridge over the Kennebec), and the towering red-and-white crane moving supplies and parts around the yard.

ESSENTIALS

GETTING THERE   Brunswick and Bath are both situated on Route 1. Brunswick is accessible via Exit 22 and 23 off I-95. Be prepared for traffic. Congestion along Route 1 in both towns may be heavy—especially when crossing the bridge over the Kennebec—during the peak summer season and when the shipyard lets its workers off around 3pm.

VISITOR INFORMATION   The **Bath-Brunswick Region Chamber of Commerce,** 59 Pleasant Street, Brunswick, ME 04011 (☎ **207/725-8797** or 207/443-9751) offers information and lodging assistance from its offices in downtown Brunswick. The chamber also staffs an information center on Route 1 just west of Bath.

FESTIVALS   In early August look for posters for the ever-popular **Maine Festival** (☎ **207/772-9012**), which takes place at Thomas Point Beach between Brunswick and Bath. What started as a sort of counter-culture celebration of Maine people and crafts has evolved and grown to a hugely popular mainstream event. Performers from throughout Maine gather at this pretty coveside park (it's a private campground the rest of the summer), and put on shows from noon past dark throughout the first weekend in August. Displays of crafts, artwork, and the products of small Maine businesses are also on display. An admission fee is charged.

WHAT TO SEE & DO

In Brunswick

Bowdoin Museum of Art. Walker Art Building, Bowdoin College. ☎ **207/725-3275.** Free admission. Tues–Sat 10am–5pm, Sun 2–5pm.

This stern, neo-classical building on the Bowdoin campus was designed by the prominent architectural firm of McKim, Mead, and White. While the collections are small, they include a number of exceptionally fine paintings from Europe and America, along with early furniture and artifacts from classical antiquity. The artists include Andrew and N.C. Wyeth, Marsden Hartley, Winslow Homer, and John Singer Sargent. The older upstairs galleries have soft, diffused lighting from skylights high above; it feels a bit as if you're underwater. The basement galleries, which feature rotating exhibits, are more modern and spacious.

Peary-MacMillan Arctic Museum. Hubbard Hall, Bowdoin College. ☎ **207/725-3416.** Free admission. Tues–Sat 10am–5pm, Sun 2–5pm.

While Admiral Robert E. Peary (class of 1887) is better known for his accomplishments (he "discovered" the North Pole at age 53 in 1909), Donald MacMillan (class of 1898) also racked up an impressive string of achievements in Arctic research and exploration. You can learn about both men and the wherefores of Arctic exploration in this manageable museum on the Bowdoin campus. The front room features stuffed animals from the Arctic, including some impressive polar bears. A second room outlines Peary's historic 1909 expedition, complete with extensive excerpts from Peary's journal. The last room includes varied displays of Inuit arts and crafts, some historic, some modern. This compact museum can be visited in about 20 minutes or so; the art museum (see above) is just next door.

In Bath

Maine Maritime Museum & Shipyard. 243 Washington St. ☎ **207/443-1316.** Admission $7.50 adult, $4.75 child 6–17, $21 family. Daily 9:30am–5pm.

You don't have to be a ship aficionado to enjoy the Maine Maritime Museum and Shipyard. But those who do love boats love it here and are hard to drag away. This up-to-date museum on the shores of the Kennebec River (it's just south of Bath Iron Works) features a wide array of displays and exhibits related to the boatbuilders art. The location is appropriate—it's sited at the former shipyard of Percy and Small, which built some 42 schooners in the late 19th and early 20th century. Indeed, the largest wooden ship ever built in America—the 329-foot Wyoming—was constructed on this lot in 1909. If you snoop around in the reeds, you can even find the ways used in launching the ship.

The centerpiece of the museum is the striking brick Maritime History Building. Here, you'll find changing exhibits of maritime art and artifacts. (There's also a gift shop with a good selection of books.) The 10-acre property houses plenty of additional displays, including an intriguing exhibit on lobstering and a complete shipbuilding shop, called the Apprenticeshop. Here, you can watch handsome wooden ships take shape in this year-long program, in which apprentices learn the craft of wooden shipbuilding from the keel up. Kids enjoy the play area (look for pirates from the crow's nest of the play boat). Be sure to wander down to the docks on the river to see what's tied up, or to inquire about cruises on the river (extra charge).

Exploring the Harpswell Peninsula

Extending southwest from Brunswick and Bath is the picturesque Harpswell peninsula. It's actually three peninsulas, like the tines of a pitchfork, if you include the islands of Orrs and Bailey, which are linked to the mainland by bridges. While close to some of Maine's larger towns (Portland is only 45 minutes away), the Harpswell peninsula has a remote, historic feel with sudden vistas across meadows to the blue waters of northern Casco Bay. Toward the southern tips of the peninsulas, the character changes as clusters of colorful Victorian-era summer cottages displace the farmhouses found further inland. Some of these cottages are for rent by the week, but many book up years in advance. Ask local real estate agents if you're interested.

There's no set itinerary for exploring the area. Just drive south until you can't go any farther, then backtrack and strike south again. Among the "attractions" worth looking for are the wonderful ocean and island views from South Harpswell at the tip of the westernmost peninsula (park and wander around for a bit), and the clever Cobwork Bridge connecting Bailey and Orrs islands. The hump-backed bridge was built in 1928 of granite blocked stacked in such a way that the strong tides could come and go and not drag the bridge out with it. No cement was used in its construction.

This is a good area for a bowl of chowder or a boiled lobster. One of the best off-the-beaten-track places for chowder is the down-home Dolphin Marina (☎ 207/ 833-6000) at Basin Point in South Harpswell. (Look for signs on Route 123 at Ash Point Rd. near the West Harpswell School.) Find the boatyard then wander inside, where you'll discover a tiny counter seating six and a handful of pine booths. The fish chowder and lobster stew are reasonably priced and tasty, and the blueberry muffins are delicious.

For lobster, several sprawling establishments specialize in delivering crustaceans fresh from the sea. On the Bailey Island side there's Cook's Lobster House (☎ 207/ 833-6641), which seats 280 diners and has been serving up a choice of shore dinners, most involving lobster, since 1955. Near Harpswell is the Estes Lobster House (☎ 207/833-6340), which serves lobster (including an artery-clogging triple lobster plate) amid relaxed, festive surroundings.

WHERE TO STAY

⑤ Driftwood Inn & Cottages. Washington Ave., Bailey Island, ME 04003. ☎ 207/ 833-5461, off-season 508/947-1066. 18 double rms, 9 single rms, 6 cottages (most rms share hallways baths). $65–$70 double, $45–$50 single; weekly $320 per person including breakfast and dinner; cottages $425–$525 per week. No credit cards. Open late May–mid-Oct; dining room open late June–Labor Day.

The oceanside Driftwood Inn dates back to 1910 and is a coastal New England classic. A rustic summer retreat on three acres at the end of a dead-end road, the inn is a compound of three weathered, shingled buildings and a handful of housekeeping cottages on a rocky, oceanside property. The spartan rooms of time-aged pine have a simple turn-of-the-century flavor that hasn't been gentrified in the least. Most rooms share baths down the hall, but some have private sinks and toilets. Your primary company will be the constant sound of surf surging in and ebbing out of the fissured rocks. The inn has a small pool and porches with wicker furniture to while away the afternoons, and roadway walks in the area are pleasant, but I'd advise bringing plenty of books and board games. The dining room serves basic fare in a wonderfully austere setting overlooking the sea; meals are extra, although a weekly American plan is available. The Driftwood isn't for those seeking luxury, but it's an ideal location to unwind at the ocean like they used to in the old days.

Harpswell Inn. 141 Lookout Point Rd., South Harpswell, ME 04079. ☎ **207/833-5509** or 800/843-5509. 13 rms plus 2 suites (6 rms share baths) . Summer & fall $58–$115 double; suites $150; off-season $48–$99. All rates include full breakfast. MC, V.

The Harpswell Inn is located idyllically on a pastoral backroad eight miles from Brunswick, and makes a good destination for those seeking quiet combined with modern comfort. This regal white-clapboard home can trace its roots back to 1761, although the main house was constructed in 1850. The home has been thoroughly made over in recent years—the common room is a bit too suburban for some tastes—and the guest rooms have been nicely modernized. The two 900-square-foot luxury suites in the rear carriage house offer a raft of amenities (although no phones), plenty of space, small kitchens, and glimpses through the trees to the water. The inn sits on three-and-a-half acres, and features a forested pathway along the cove's edge. No smoking.

BOOTHBAY PENINSULA

Although Boothbay Harbor is 11 miles from Route 1, this small but scenic harbor town exerts an outsized allure on passing tourists, and has become one of the prime destinations of travelers in search of classic coastal Maine. As a result, it's a popular stop for bus tours, and the village has been infiltrated by kitschy shops (T-shirts, stained glass unicorns) and mediocre restaurants that specialize in fried foods. The harbor is hemmed in somewhat by boxy, bland motels, but there's still an affable charm that manages to rise above the clutter, especially on foggy days when the horns bleat mournfully at the harbor's mouth. And visitors should also find some measure of satisfaction that a nickel will still buy 24 minutes at the town parking meters.

ESSENTIALS

GETTING THERE   Boothbay Harbor is 11 miles south of Route 1 on Route 27. Coming from the west, look for signs shortly after crossing the Sheepscot River at Wiscasset.

VISITOR INFORMATION   There are two visitor information centers in town. A mile before you reach the village is the seasonal **Boothbay Information Center** on your right (open June–October). If you zoom past it or it's closed, don't fret. The year-round **Boothbay Harbor Region Chamber of Commerce,** P.O. Box 356, Boothbay Harbor, ME 04538 (☎ **207/633-2353**) is at the intersection of Route 27 and Route 96.

WHAT TO SEE & DO

Boothbay Harbor is made for walkers. Pedestrians naturally gravitate to the long, narrow footbridge across the harbor, first built in 1901, but it's more of a destination than a link—other than a few restaurants and motels, there's really not much on the other side. The winding, small streets in town also offer plenty of boutiques and shops that cater to the tourist trade and offer decent browsing.

The most enjoyable way to see the Boothbay region is on a boat tour. Nearly two dozen tour boats berth at the harbor or nearby, offering a range of trips from an hour's tour to a full-day excursion to Monhegan Island. You can even observe puffins at their rocky colonies far offshore.

Two of Maine's larger, more modern boat tour firms are based in downtown Boothbay. **Balmy Day Cruises** (☎ **207/633-2284**) runs trips to Monhegan Island in the 65-foot *Balmy Days II,* allowing passengers about four hours to explore the island before returning (see "Monhegan Island" section below). The company also offers two-hour dinner cruises with onboard dinners of chicken, lobster roll, and lobster. **Cap'n Fish's Scenic Boat Trips** (☎ **207/633-3244** or 800/636-3244) offers sightseeing trips of one to four hours duration, including puffin and whale watches. The four boats in the fleet each carry between 130 and 150 passengers.

For a more personal excursion, two smaller touring boats come highly recommended, and both sail from Ocean Point, a few minutes east on Route 96. **Windborne Cruises** (☎ **207/882-1020**) can accommodate just six passengers on the 40-foot *Tribute,* a handsome Block Island sailboat. Capt. Roger Marin is a great storyteller and captivates his temporary crew with local tales. **Capt. Roger Duncan** (☎ **207/633-4780**) also can take six passengers on his 32-foot *Friendship* sloop, the *Eastward.* Duncan is the author of a superb maritime history of the Maine coast, and leaves his passengers well-informed about the coast and its quirks.

The most personal way to see the harbor is via sea kayak. **Tidal Transit Kayak Co.** (☎ **207/633-7140**), offers half and full-day tours of the harbor for $45 and $70; there's also a sunset tour (recommended) for $30. Tidal Transit is open daily in summer (except when it rains) on the waterfront at 47 Townshend Ave. (walk down the alley).

A short excursion to Ocean Point is well worthwhile. Follow Route 96 southward from west of Boothbay Harbor, and you'll pass through East Boothbay before striking toward the point. The narrow road runs through piney forests before arriving at the rocky finger; it's one of the few Maine points with a road around its perimeter, allowing wonderful ocean views. Bunches of colorful Victorian-era summer cottages bloom along the roadside like wildflowers.

Ocean Point makes for a good bike loop, as does a trip around Southport Island, which is connected to Boothbay Harbor via a bridge. Follow Route 238 around the island, stopping from time to time to enjoy the occasional sea views or to poke down gravel public roads. Mountain-bike rentals are available from $12 at Tidal Transit.

If dense fog or rain socks in the harbor, bide your time at the vintage **Romar Bowling Lanes** (☎ 207/633-5721). This log and shingle building near the footbridge has a superb harbor view and has been distracting travelers with the promise of candlepin bowling since 1946. On rainy summer days, the wait for one of the eight lanes can be up to an hour. While you're waiting you can play pool and video games, or order a $1.95 cheeseburger at the snack bar. It's not hard to find. You'll hear the pins crashing and the shrieks of victory from various points around the town.

WHERE TO STAY

Old Resorts

Newagen Seaside Inn. Route 27 (P.O. Box 68), Cape Newagen, ME 04552. ☎ **207/ 633-5242** or 800/654-5242. 26 rms (2 with shower only). $100–$175 double including breakfast. MC, V. Open mid-May–late Sept. Located on south tip of Southport Island; take Route 27 from Boothbay Harbor and continue on until the inn sign.

This 1940s-era resort has seen more glamorous days, but it's still a superb small, low-key resort offering stunning ocean views and walks in a fragrant spruce forest. The inn is housed in a low, wide, white-shingled building that's furnished simply with country pine furniture. There's a classically austere dining room with a well-regarded menu, narrow cruise-ship-like hallways with pine wainscotting, and a lobby with a fireplace. The rooms are plain and the inn is a bit threadbare in spots, but never mind that. Guests flock here for the 85-acre oceanside grounds filled with decks, gazebos, and walkways that border on the magical. For activities, there's badminton, shuffleboard, horseshoes, tennis, a new freshwater pool surrounded by a great deck for lounging, and an odd saltwater pool at oceanside with a small man-made beach. Rowboats are available free for guests to use. It's hard to overstate the magnificence of the ocean views, which may be the best of any inn in Maine. No smoking.

Spruce Point Inn. Atlantic Ave. (P.O. Box 237), Boothbay Harbor, ME 04538. ☎ **207/ 633-4152** or 800/553-0289. 65 rms. TV TEL. July–Aug $240–$330 double; June & Sept–Oct $178–$240. Rates include breakfast and dinner. AE, MC, V. Open Memorial Day to mid-Oct. Turn right on Union St. in Boothbay Harbor; proceed 2 miles to the inn.

The Spruce Point Inn was originally built as a hunting and fishing lodge in the 1890s, and evolved into summer resort in 1912. After years of quiet neglect, it benefitted in the late 1980s from a long-overdue makeover that thankfully retained much of the rustic charm. The eight guest rooms in the venerable, gabled main lodge are simply furnished and clean, but slightly austere and motel-like. Better are the rooms in the outbuildings flanking the lodge. These have a woodsy, country pine feel, and most have private porches with ocean views. The newer "Ocean Houses," built in 1988 at the back of the property, are contemporary, condominium-like townhouses with plenty of amenities but no character whatsoever.

Most guests occupy their time just puttering around the inn's 15-acre oceanfront grounds, or idling in the wicker chairs on the porch overlooking the rocky shore. Slightly more strenuous activities include croquet, shuffleboard, tennis on clay courts, putting on an Astroturf green, swimming at a newly rebuilt oceanside saltwater pool (there's also a heated freshwater pool at the forest's edge), and soaking in the whirlpool. Dinners are memorable events (see below). There's also a free shuttle bus to Boothbay, so guests can dabble in shopping or mild adventure without the hassle of downtown parking.

Inns & B&Bs

Five Gables Inn. Murray Hill Rd. (P.O. Box 335) East Boothbay, ME 04544. ☎ **207/633-4551** or 800/451-5048. 16 rms. $90–$135 double including breakfast buffet. MC, V. Open May–Oct. Drive through East Boothbay on Route 96; turn right after crest of hill on Murray Hill Rd.

The 125-year-old Five Gables Inn was painstakingly restored in 1988, and now sits proudly amid a small colony of summer homes on a quiet road above a peaceful cove. It's nicely isolated from the confusion and hubbub of Boothbay Harbor; the activity of choice here is to sit on the deck and enjoy the glimpses of the water through the trees. The rooms are pleasantly appointed, and the common room pleasantly furnished in an upscale country style. The new owners, De and Mike Kennedy from Atlanta, bought the inn in late 1995 and are proving to as helpful and congenial as their predecessors. This is a no-smoking inn.

Lawnmeer Inn & Restaurant. Route 27, Southport, ME 04576. ☎ **207/633-2544** or 800/ 633-7645. 32 rms. TV. $45–$120 double. MC, V. Closed mid-Oct to mid–May.

The Lawnmeer, situated just a short hop from Boothbay on the northern shore of Southport Island, offers easy access to town and a restful environment. This was originally built as a guest home at the turn of the century, and the main inn has been nicely updated with only slight loss of charm. More than half of the guest rooms are located in a motel-like annex, which makes up for its lack of character with private balconies offering views of the waterway that separates Southport Island from the mainland. American and continental fare is served in a comfortable, homey dining room with broad windows overlooking the water.

Sailmaker's Inn. Route 96 & Church St., East Boothbay, ME 04544. ☎ **207/633-7390.** 2 rms. TEL. $80–$95 double, including breakfast. CB, MC, V. Open May through Oct.

I normally wouldn't include a B&B with just two guest rooms, but I'm willing to make an exception in this case. Located in a striking Victorian home on a knoll in the sleepy town of East Boothbay, the Sailmaker's Inn is the pet project of Phil and Darla Parker, two Midwest expatriates who recently retired to Maine. The place will especially appeal to travelers who like a personal touch, and who have a fondness for high Victorian style (there's lots of walnut trim and an extravagant, steeply curving staircase to the second-floor rooms). A filling breakfast is served at a wonderful mahogany table, and Darla offers rich desserts in the evening. Guests can also use the inn's canoe to poke around the mill pond across the street.

Topside. McKown Hill, Boothbay Harbor, ME 04538. ☎ **207/633-5404.** 28 rms (1 with shower only). July 1–Labor Day $70–$95 double; June & Sept–Oct $50–$85. Closed mid-Oct to June. MC, V.

Okay, let's be up-front here. The looming old grey house on the hilltop above the motel-style building may bring to mind the Bates Motel, especially when a full moon is overhead. But get over that. Because Topside offers spectacular ocean views at a good price on its private hilltop compound located right in downtown Boothbay. The inn itself features six comfortable rooms, furnished with a mix of antiques and contemporary furniture. (Some may find the building a bit overly carpeted and wall-papered.) At the edge of the inn's cambered lawn are two outbuildings housing basic motel units, which have panelling and furniture that may recall the era when John Travolta was first popular. Just keep in mind that guests return here after year not for the dated styling, but for the spectacular ocean views.

WHERE TO DINE

When wandering through town, watch for **"King" Brud** and his famous hot-dog cart. The laconic Brud started selling hot dogs in town in 1943, and he's still at it. If he likes you, he'll give you a free postcard of him and his cart. Dogs are $1. He's usually at the corner of McKown and Commercial streets from 10 am till 4 pm from June through October.

Ⓢ **Boothbay Region Lobstermen's Co-op.** Atlantic Ave., Boothbay Harbor. ☎ **207/633-4900.** No reservations. Sandwiches $1.25–$8.75; dinners $6.50–$8.95. No credit cards. Open daily May to Oct 11:30am–8:30pm. By foot: cross footbridge and turn right; follow road for $^1/_3$ mile to co-op. SEAFOOD.

"We are not responsible if the seagulls steal your food" reads the sign at the order-ing window of this casual, harborside lobster joint. And that sets the tone pretty well. Situated across the harbor from downtown Boothbay, the lobstermen's co-op offers no-frills lobster and seafood. You order at a pair of windows, then pick up your meal and carry your tray to either the picnic tables on the dock or inside a garage-like two-story prefab building. Lobsters are priced to market (figure on $8 to $9), with extras like corn on the cob reasonably priced at 85¢. A bank of soda machines pro-vides liquid refreshment for 75¢ a can. This is a fine place for a lobster on sunny day, but it's uninteresting at best in rain or fog.

Lobsterman's Wharf. Route 96, East Boothbay. ☎ **207/633-3443.** Reservations for parties of 6 or more only. Lunch from $4.50; dinner $13.25–$22.95 (mostly $14–$16). AE, MC, V. Open April through Oct. SEAFOOD.

Slightly off the beaten path in East Boothbay, the Lobsterman's Wharf has the comfortable, pubby feel of a popular neighborhood bar, complete with pool table. And that's appropriate, since that's what it is. But it's that rarest of pubs—one that's popular with the locals, but also one that commands the respect of finicky diners and makes travelers feel at home. If the weather's agreeable, sit at picnic table on the dock, admiring views of a spruce-topped peninsula across the Damariscotta River; you can also grab a table inside amid the festive nautical decor. Entrees include a tasty mixed-seafood grill, a barbecue shrimp and ribs platter, grilled swordfish with bearnaise, and succulent fresh lobster offered four different ways.

✪ **Spruce Point Inn.** Atlantic Ave, Boothbay Harbor. ☎ **207/633-4152** or 800/553-0289. Reservations recommended. Main courses $14.75–$24.25. AE, MC ,V. Open daily 7:30am–9:30am and 6pm–9pm. Open Memorial Day to mid-Oct. Turn right on Union St. in Boothbay Harbor; proceed 2 miles to the inn. AMERICAN.

This classic resort dining room is certain to surprise you with its creativity. And what else would you expect from an inn that won a recent statewide cooking contest with a recipe for "lobster succotash"? Diners are seated in an elegant, formal dining room—the tables are lined up with an almost military precision, the maitre d' wears a tux, and men are requested to wear jackets at dinner. Guests enjoy wonderful sunset views across the mouth of Boothbay Harbor as they peruse the menu, which offers an inviting mix of seafood and meat dishes. The lobster spring rolls are terrific for starters. Next, you might opt for the two-texture duck (served with a shiitake and ginger gravy), or shrimp amaretto. If you're not feeling overly adventurous, you can take refuge in the more basic choices, like pork tenderloin, grilled chicken breast, or filet mignon.

PEMAQUID PENINSULA

The Pemaquid Peninsula is an irregular, rocky wedge driven deep into the Gulf of Maine. It's much less commercial than the Boothbay Peninsula just across the Damariscotta River, and more inviting for casual exploring. The inland areas are leafy with hardwood trees, and feature plenty of narrow, twisting backroads perfect for bicycling. Closer to the ocean point, the region takes on a more remote, maritime feel, and small harbors and coves predominate. Rugged and rocky Pemaquid Point, at the extreme southern tip of the peninsula, is one of the most dramatic destinations in Maine when the ocean surf is running.

ESSENTIALS

GETTING THERE The Pemaquid Peninsula is accessible from the west by turning southward on Route 129/130 in Damariscotta, just off Route 1. From the east, head south on Route 32 just west of Waldoboro.

VISITOR INFORMATION The **Damariscotta Region Chamber of Commerce,** P.O. Box 13, Main Street, Damariscotta, ME 04543 (☎ **207/563-8340**) is a good source of local information, and maintains a handy information booth on Route 1 during the summer months.

EXPLORING THE PEMAQUID PENINSULA

The Pemaquid Peninsula invites slow driving and frequent stops. Start out by heading south on Route 129 toward Walpole from the sleepy head-of-the-harbor village of Damariscotta. Keep an eye on your left for the austerely handsome Walpole Meeting House, one of three meeting houses built on the peninsula in 1772. (Only two remain.) It's usually not open to the public, but services are still held here during the summer and the public is welcome.

Just north of the unassuming fishing town of South Bristol, watch for the **Thompson Ice Harvesting Museum** (☎ **207/644-8551**). During winter's deep freeze, volunteers from around town carve out huge blocks of ice and relay them to the well-insulated ice house (a 1990 replica of the original icehouse) to be packed in sawdust. Summer visitors can peer into the cool, damp depths and see the glistening blocks (the harvest is sold to fishermen throughout the summer to ice down their catch), and learn about the once-common practice of ice harvesting through photos and other exhibits in a tiny museum.

Continue on Route 129 and you'll soon arrive at picturesque Christmas Cove, so named because John Smith anchored here on Christmas Day in 1614. While wandering about, look for the rustic, off-the-beaten-path **Coveside** (☎ 207/644-8282) a popular marina with a pennant-bedecked lounge and a basic dining room. The food is okay, nothing more, but the views are outstanding and you might even catch of glimpse of celebrity yachtsmen, like Walter Cronkite or William F. Buckley.

Backtrack about five miles north of South Bristol and turn right on Pemaquid Road, which will take you to Route 130. Along the way look for the Harrington Meeting House (the other 1772 structure), which is open to the public on occasional afternoons in July and August. It's an architectural gem inside, almost painfully austere, with a small museum of local artifacts on the second floor. Even if it's not open, stop to wander about the lovely cemetery out back, the final resting place of many sea captains.

Head south on Route 130 to the village of New Harbor, and look for signs to **Colonial Pemaquid** (☎ 207/677-2423). Open daily in summer from 9am to 5pm, this state historic site features exhibits on the original 1625 settlement here; archaeological digs are still taking place in the summer. The $2 admission charge (50¢ for children 6–12) includes a visit to stout Fort William Henry, a 1907 replica of a supposedly impregnable fortress that stood over the river's entrance. (It was not impregnable, as it turned out, with tragic results for the settlement.) There's a sand beach nearby for a bracing ocean dip.

Pemaquid Point, which is owned by the town, is the place to while away an afternoon (☎ 207/677-2494). Bring a picnic and a book, and find a spot on the dark, fractured rocks to settle in. The ocean views are superb, interrupted only by somewhat tenacious seagulls that may take a profound interest in your lunch. While here, be sure to visit the **Fishermen's Museum** (☎ 207/677-2726) in the handsome lighthouse. Informative exhibits depict the whys and wherefores of the local fishing trade, and should answer questions that may arise while watching lobstermen at work just offshore. There's a small fee to use the park in summer; admission to the museum is by donation.

Route 32 strikes northwest from New Harbor, and it's the most scenic way to leave the peninsula if you plan to continue to work your way eastward on Route 1. Along the way look for the sign pointing to the Rachel Carson Salt Pond Preserve, a Nature Conservancy property. The noted naturalist Rachel Carson studied these roadside tide pools extensively while researching her 1956 bestseller *The Edge of the Sea,* and today it's still an inviting spot for budding naturalists and experts alike. Pull off your shoes and socks, and wade through the cold waters at low tide looking for starfish, green crabs, periwinkles, and other creatures.

WHERE TO STAY

Bradley Inn. Route 130, 361 Pemaquid Point, New Harbor, ME 04554. ☎ **207/677-2105.** Fax 207/677-3367. 15 rms (including cottage & 2 suites). TV TEL. Summer & fall $95–$155 double; winter & spring $85–$120. Cottage $650 weekly in summer. Rates include continental breakfast. AE, MC, V.

The Bradley Inn is located within easy walking or biking distance to the point, but there's plenty of reason to lag behind at the inn. Start by wandering the nicely landscaped grounds, or enjoying a game of croquet in the gardens. If the fog's moved in for a spell, settle in for a game of Scrabble at pub, which is decorated with a lively nautical theme. This circa-1900 inn got a top-to-bottom makeover in 1991, when it was updated throughout. (This may be the only old inn in northern New England with fisheye-style peepholes in guest room doors.) The rooms are luxuriously appointed; the third floor rooms are the best, affording distant glimpses of John's Bay. The local seafood served in the Ships, the inn's restaurant, gets high marks.

WHERE TO DINE

Shaw's Lobster Pound. On the water, New Harbor. ☎ **207/677-2200.** Reservations not accepted. Lobster priced to market (usually $8–$11). No credit cards. Open noon until 8pm weekdays, 9 pm weekends. Closed mid-Oct until late May. LOBSTER POUND.

Shaws attracts hordes of tourists, but it's no puzzle to figure out why: It's one of the best-situated lobster pounds, with postcard-perfect views of the working harbor and the boats coming and going through the inlet that connects to the open sea. Customers stand in line to place their order, then wait for their name to be called. While waiting, you can stake out a seat on either the open deck or the indoor dining room (go for the deck), or order up some appetizers from the raw bar. This is one of the few lobster places with a full liquor license.

MONHEGAN ISLAND

Brawny and remote, Monhegan Island is Maine's premier island destination. Visited by Europeans as early as 1497 (although some insist earlier Norsemen carved primitive runes on neighboring Manana Island), the island was first settled by fishermen attracted to the sea's bounty in the offshore waters. Starting in the 1870s and continuing to the present day, noted artists discovered the island and came to stay for a spell. These included Rockwell Kent (the artist most closely associated with the island), George Bellows, Edward Hopper, and Robert Henri. The artists gathered in the kitchen of the lighthouse to chat and drink coffee; it's said that the wife of the lighthouse keeper accumulated a tremendously valuable collection of paintings. Today, Jamie Wyeth, scion of the Wyeth clan, claims the island as his part-time home.

It's not hard to figure why artists have long been attracted to the place: there's a mystical quality to it, from the thin light to the startling contrasts of the dark cliffs and the foamy white surf. There's also a remarkable sense of tranquility to this place, which can only help focus one's inner vision.

If you have the time, I'd strongly recommend an overnight on the island at one of the several hostelries. Day trips are popular and affordable, but the island's true character doesn't start to emerge until the last day boat sails away and the quiet, rustic appeal of the island starts to percolate back to the surface.

ESSENTIALS

GETTING THERE Access to Monhegan Island is via boat from either New Harbor, Boothbay Harbor, or Port Clyde. The hour and ten minute trip on the Laura B. from Port Clyde is the favored route among longtime island visitors. The trip from this rugged fishing village is very picturesque as it passes the Marshall Point Lighthouse and a series of spruce-clad islands before setting out on the open sea. The Laura B. is a doughty work boat (cargo including propane tanks and boxes of food is loaded on first; passengers fill in the available niches on the deck and in the small cabin). You can't bring your car, so pack light and wear sturdy shoes. Reservations are advised: **Monhegan Boat Line,** P.O. Box 238, Port Clyde, ME 04855 (☎ **207/372-8848**). Parking is available near the dock for a slight additional charge.

VISITOR INFORMATION Monhegan Island has no formal visitors' center, but it's small and friendly enough that you can make inquiries of just about anyone you meet on the island pathways. The clerks at the boat dock in Port Clyde are also quite helpful. Be sure to pick up the inexpensive map of the island's hiking trail at the boat ticket office or at the various shops around the island.

Because a forest fire could destroy this breezy island in short order, smoking is prohibited outside of the village.

WHAT TO SEE & DO

HIKE & WALK   Those are the chief activities on the island, and it's genuinely surprising how much distance you can cover on this 700-acre island (about 1¹/₂ miles long and ¹/₂ mile wide). The village clusters tightly around the harbor; the rest of the island is mostly wildland, laced with some 17 miles of trails. Much of the island is ringed along its shoreline with high, open bluffs atop fissured cliffs. Pack a picnic lunch and hike the trail around the perimeter, and plan to spend much of the day just sitting and reading, or enjoying the surf rolling in against the cliffs. During one afternoon sitting on a bluff near the island's southern tip, I spotted a half-dozen whale spouts over the course of a half hour, but never did agree with my friend whether it was one whale or several.

The inland trails are appealing in a far different way. The deep, dark Cathedral Woods is mossy and fragrant; sunlight only dimly filters through the evergreens to the forest floor. Look for the small "fairy houses" in the woods; these fanciful structures of twigs, bark, and other forest-floor detritus are crafted by island kids and visitors. You're welcome to build your own, provided you don't use live moss.

Birdwatching is an exceedingly popular activity in the spring and fall. Monhegan Island is on the Atlantic flyway, and a wide variety of birds stop at the island along their migration routes. Bring your binoculars.

The sole "attraction" on the island is the **Monhegan Museum,** located next to the 1824 lighthouse on a high point above the village. The museum, open from July through September, has an engaging collection of historic artifacts and will provide some context for this rugged island's history. But the real draw is the spectacular view from the grassy slope in front of the lighthouse. The vista sweeps across a marsh (which seems to attract a number of deer at twilight), past one of the island's most historic hotels, past melancholy Manana Island and across the sea beyond. Get here early if you want a good seat for the sunset; it seems most visitors to the island congregate here after dinner to watch the sinking of the sun. (Another popular place is the island's southern tip, where the wreckage of the *D.T. Sheridan,* a coal barge, washed up in 1948.)

One other popular activity is to visit the studios of Monhegan artists, who still gather here in great number. Artists often open their workspaces to visitors during limited hours, and are happy to have people stop by and look at their work, talk with them a bit, and perhaps buy something to bring home. Some of the art work is predictable seascapes and sunsets, but much of it rises above the banal. Look for the bulletin board along the main pathway in the village for walking directions to the studios and a listing of the days they're open.

WHERE TO STAY & DINE

Monhegan House. Monhegan Island, ME 04852. ☎ **207/594-7983** or 800/599-7983. 32 rms (all shared bath). $70 double. AE, DISC, MC, V. Open Memorial Day to Columbus Day.

The handsome Monhegan House has been accommodating guests since 1870, and it has the comfortable, worn patina of venerable lodging house. The accommodations are austere but comfortable; there are no closets, and everyone uses dormitory-style bathrooms down the hall. The downstairs lobby with fireplace is a welcome spot to sit and take the fog-induced chill out of your bones (even in August it can be cool here). The front deck is a nice place to lounge and keep a close eye on the comings and goings of the village.

Trailing Yew. Monhegan Island, ME 04852. ☎ **207/596-0440.** 37 rms in four buildings (1 rm with private bath). $108 double, including breakfast, dinner, taxes, and tips. No credit cards. Open mid–May to mid-Oct.

At the end of long summer afternoons, guests congregate near the flagpole in front of the main building at this rustic hillside compound. They sit in Adirondack chairs or chat with newfound friends. But mostly they're waiting for the ringing of the bell, which signals them in for dinner, as if at summer camp. Inside, guests sit around long tables, introduce themselves to their neighbors, then pour an iced tea and wait for the delicious, family-style dinner. (You're given a choice, but opt for the fresh fish.)

The Trailing Yew, which has been taking in guests since 1929, is a friendly, informal place, popular with hikers and birdwatchers (meals are a great time to swap tales of sightings) who tend to make fast friends here amid the welcome adversity of Monhegan Island. Guest rooms are eclectic and simply furnished in a pleasantly dated summer-home style; only one of the four guest buildings has electricity (although all bathrooms have electricity); guests in rooms without electricity are provided a kerosene lamp and instruction in its use (bring a flashlight just in case).

6 Penobscot Bay & Blue Hill

Traveling eastward along the Maine Coast, you'll notice around Rockland that you're heading nearly due north. The culprit is Penobscot Bay, a sizeable bite out of the Maine Coast that forces a northerly detour to cross the head of the bay where the Penobscot River flows in at Bucksport.

You'll find some Maine's best coastal scenery in this area—spectacular offshore islands, high hills along the water's edge, and heavily weathered rocks pounded by the surf. Although the mouth of Penobscot Bay is occupied by two large islands, its waters can still churn with vigor when the seas are running high.

The west shore of Penobscot Bay gets a heavy stream of tourist traffic, especially along Route 1 and the scenic villages of Rockport and Camden. These are good destinations to get a taste of the Maine Coast, especially for those in a hurry to get to Acadia National Park. Services for travelers are easy to find, although during the peak season a small miracle will be required to find a guest room without a reservation.

In contrast, the bay's eastern shore, formed by the Blue Hill Peninsula, Cape Rosier, and Deer Isle, is much more remote, laced with shady back roads and dotted with small inns. By and large it's overlooked by the majority of Maine's tourists, especially those who prefer to avoid narrow roads that suddenly dead-end or inexplicably start to loop back on themselves.

ROCKLAND & ENVIRONS

Few visitors refer to Rockland as "quaint." Located on the southwest edge of Penobscot Bay, Rockland has long been proud of brick-and-blue-collar waterfront-town reputation. Built around the fishing industry, Rockland historically dabbled in tourism on the side. But with the decline of the fisheries and the rise of the tourist economy in Maine, the balance is gradually shifting—Rockland is slowly being colonized by restaurateurs and other small-business folks who are painting it with an unaccustomed gloss.

There's a small park on the waterfront from which the fleet of windjammers comes and goes (see below), but more appealing than Rockland's waterfront is its commercial downtown—it's basically a long street lined with sophisticated historic brick

Penobscot Bay

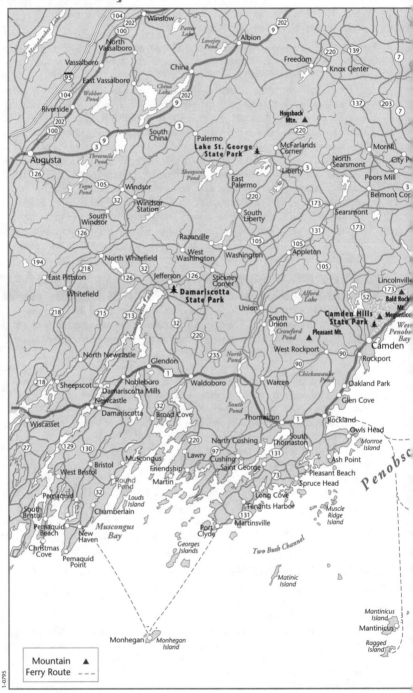

Mountain ▲
Ferry Route - - -

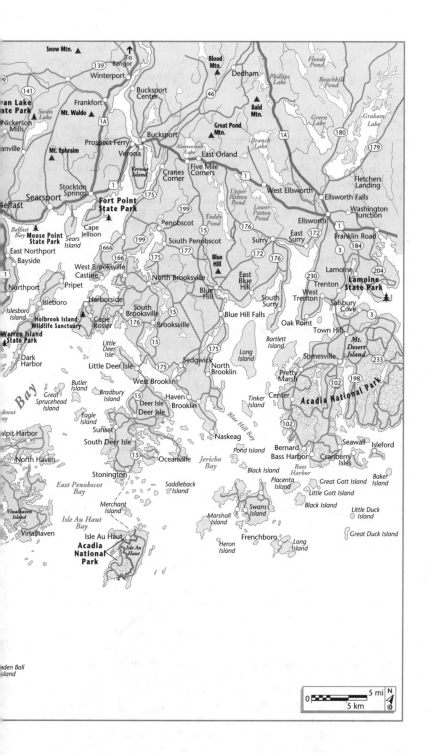

Snow Mtn. ▲

139
To
Bangor
Winterport

Blood
Mtn.
▲

Dedham

Floods
Pond

Beachhill
Pond

141

Bucksport
Center

46

Phillips
Lake

Frankfort

an Lake
ate Park

Swan
Lake

Mt. Waldo ▲

1A

Bald
Mtn.
▲

Green
Lake

Graham
Lake

Nickerson
Mills

Bucksport

Great Pond
Mtn.
▲

1A

180

anville

Mt. Ephraim ▲

Prospect Ferry

Verona

East Orland

Branch
Lake

179

Verona
Island

Cranes
Corner

Alamoosook
Lake

Five Mile
Corners

Stockton
Springs

1

West Ellsworth

Fletchers
Landing

Searsport

1

Fort Point
State Park

175

199

Upper
Patton
Pond

Ellsworth Falls

Washington
Junction

elfast

Penobscot

Toddy
Pond

Lower
Patton
Pond

Ellsworth

Belfast
Bay

Moose Point
State Park

Cape
Jellison

Sears
Island

166A

199

South Penobscot

15

176

Surry

172

East
Surry

Franklin Road

184

East Northport

166

175

177

172

176

3

Bayside

West Brooksville

Blue
Hill
▲

East
Blue
Hill

Lamoine

230

204

1

Northport

Castine

North Brooksville

Blue
Hill

West
Trenton

Trenton

Lamoine
State Park

Pripet

South
Surry

Salsbury
Cove

Isleboro

Harborside

Blue Hill Falls

Oak Point

3

Islesboro
Island

Holbrook Island
Wildlife Sanctuary

South
Brooksville

15

Town Hill

Mt.
Desert
Island

233

Cape
Rosier

176

Brooksville

Long
Island

Bartlett
Island

Somesville

Warren Island
State Park

15

Sedgwick

Pretty
Marsh

102

198

Dark
Harbor

Little
Deer
Isle

North
Brooklin

Acadia National Park

Bay

Butler
Island

Little Deer Isle

175

West Brooklin

Center

102

Great
Sprucehead
Island

Bradbury
Island

15

Haven

Tinker
Island

bscot
ay

Eagle
Island

Deer Isle

Brooklin

Blue Hill Bay

lpit Harbor

Sunset

Deer Isle

Naskeag

Bernard

Seawall

Isleford

North Haven

South Deer Isle

15

Oceanville

Pond Island

Bass
Harbor

Cranberry
Isles

Jericho
Bay

Black Island

Bass
Harbor

Stonington

Saddleback
Island

Placenta
Island

Great Gott Island

Baker
Island

East Penobscot
Bay

Merchant
Island

Little Gott Island

Black Island

Little Duck
Island

Vinalhaven
Island

Isle Au Haut
Bay

Marshall
Island

Swans
Island

Great Duck Island

Vinalhaven

Isle Au Haut

Acadia
National
Park

Isle Au
Haut

Frenchboro

Long
Island

Heron
Island

den Ball
sland

0   5 mi

5 km

N

architecture. If it's picturesque waterfronts you're seeking, head to Camden, Rockport, Port Clyde, or Stonington. But Rockland makes a great base for exploring this beautiful coastal region, especially if you have a low tolerance for primness and tourist hordes.

ESSENTIALS

GETTING THERE   Route 1 passes directly through Rockland. During the peak summer season, you can avoid the coastal congestion of Route 1 by taking the Maine Turnpike to Augusta, then heading to Rockland on Route 17. Rockland's tiny airport is served by **Colgan Air** (☎ **207/596-7604** or 800/272-5488) with daily flights from Boston and Bar Harbor.

VISITOR INFORMATION   The **Rockland/Thomaston Area Chamber of Commerce,** P.O. Box 508, Rockland, ME 04841 (☎ **207/596-0376** or 800/562-2529) staffs an information desk at Harbor Park. It's open daily 9am to 5pm in summer, open weekdays only the rest of the year.

EVENTS   The **Maine Lobster Festival** (☎ 207/596-0376 or 800/562-2529) takes place at Harbor Park the first weekend in August (plus the preceding Thursday and Friday). Entertainers and vendors of all sorts of Maine products—especially the local crustacean—fill the waterfront parking lot and attract thousands of festival-goers who enjoy this pleasant event with a sort of buttery bonhomie. The event includes the Maine Sea Goddess Coronation Pageant.

TWO FINE MUSEUMS

Farnsworth Museum. 352 Main St., Rockland. ☎ **207/596-6457.** $5 adults, $4 seniors, $3 children 8–18. Summer Mon–Sat 10am–5pm, Sun 1–5pm. Closed Mon Columbus Day– Memorial Day.

Rockland, for all its rough edges, has long and historic ties to the arts. Noted sculptor Louise Nevelson grew up in Rockland, and in 1935 cranky philanthropist Lucy Farnsworth bequeathed a fortune large enough to establish Rockland's Farnsworth Museum, which has since become one of the most respected small art museums in New England.

Located in the middle of downtown Rockland, the Farnsworth has a compact but superb collection of paintings and sculptures by renown American artists with some connection to Maine. This includes not only Louise Nevelson and three generations of Wyeths (N.C., Andrew, and Jamie), but Rockwell Kent, Childe Hassam, and Maurice Prendergast. The display space is modern and well designed, and the shows professionally prepared. This is a superb destination to while away a rainy afternoon. It's also a good place to reach a fuller understanding of the long, intimate relationship between artists and Maine.

The Farnsworth also owns two other buildings open to the public. The Farnsworth Homestead, located behind the museum, offers a glimpse into the life of prosperous coastal Victorians. And a 25-minute drive away in the village of Cushing is the Olson House, immortalized in the background of Andrew Wyeth's famous painting, *Christina's World.* Ask at the museum for directions and information.

Owls Head Transportation Museum. Route 73, Owls Head. ☎ **207/594-4418.** Internet: http://www.midcoast.com/~ohtm. $5 adults, $4.50 seniors, $3 children 5–12, families $15. April–Oct daily 10am–5pm; Nov–March Mon–Fri 10am–4pm, Sat–Sun 10am–3pm.

You don't have to be a car or plane nut to enjoy a day at the Owl's Head Transportation Museum, located three miles south of Rockland on Route 73. Founded in 1974, the museum has an extraordinary collection of cars, motorcycles, bicycles, and planes, nicely displayed in a tidy, hangar-like building at the edge of the Knox

County Airport. Look for the beautiful early Harley Davidson, and the sleek Rolls Royce Phantom dating from 1929. The museum is also a popular destination for hobbyists and tinkerers, who drive and fly their classic vehicles here for frequent weekend rallies in the summer. Call ahead to ask about special events.

WINDJAMMER TOURS

During the long transition from sail to steam, captains of the fancy new steamships belittled the old-fashioned sailing ships as "windjammers." The term stuck, and through a curious metamorphosis the name evolved into a term of adventure and romance.

Maine is the capital of windjammer cruising in the United States, and two of the most active Maine harbors are Rockland and Camden. Windjammer vacations combine adventure with limited creature comforts—sort of like lodging at a backcountry cabin on the water. Guests typically bunk in small two-person cabins, which usually offer cold running water and a porthole to let in fresh air, but not much else. Cruises last from three days to a week, during which these handsome, creaky vessels poke around the tidy inlets and small coves that ring beautiful Penobscot Bay. It's a superb way to explore Maine's coast the way it has historically been explored—from the outside looking in. The price runs around $100 per day per person, with modest discounts early and late in the season.

Cruises vary from ship to ship, and from week to week, depending on the inclinations of the captains and the vagaries of the mercurial Maine weather. The "standard" cruise often features a stop at one or more of the myriad spruce-studded Maine islands (perhaps with a clam bake on shore), hearty breakfasts enjoyed sitting at tables below deck (or perched cross-legged on the sunny deck), and a palpable sense of maritime history as these handsome ships scud through frothy waters. A windjammer vacation demands you apply all your senses, to smell the tang of the salt air, to hear the rhythmic creaking of the masts in the evening, and to feel the frigid ocean waters as you leap in for a bracing dip.

At least a dozen windjammers offer cruises in the Penobscot Bay region during the summer season (many migrate south to the Caribbean in the winter). The ships vary widely in size and vintage, and guest accommodations range from cramped and rustic to reasonably spacious and well-appointed. Ideally, you'll have a chance to look at at couple of ships to find one that suits you before signing up. If that's not practical, call ahead to the **Maine Windjammer Association** (☎ **800/807-9463**) and request a packet of brochures, which allow decent comparison shopping. If you're angling for a last-minute cruise, stop by the chamber of commerce office at the Rockland waterfront (see above) and ask if any berths are available.

While all the commercial windjammers are Coast Guard-inspected and each have unique charms, among the notable are the 44-passenger *Victory Chimes* (☎ **207/ 594-0755** or 800/745-5651), the largest schooner at 132 feet. The smallest in the fleet is the 7-passenger *Summertime* (☎ **800/562-8290**), a 53-foot schooner based in Rockland. The 26-passenger *J&E Riggin* is captained by a native Maine couple, who provide a lively running commentary on Maine history and lore. And the 31-passenger *Angelique* (☎ **207/236-8873** or 800/282-9989), based in Camden, may be the most handsome ship in the fleet, and features two below-deck hot-water showers.

WHERE TO STAY

East Wind Inn. P.O. Box 149, Tenant's Harbor, ME 04860. ☎ **207/372-6366** or 800/ 241-8439. Fax 207/372-6320. 26 rms, 14 with shared bath. Summer $78–$110 double, $125– $150 suites and apartments. Off-season $64–$82 double. Rates include continental breakfast.

AE, DISC, MC, V. Drive south on Route 131 from Thomaston to Tenant's Harbor; turn left at post office.

The East Wind Inn is a gracious anomaly—it manages to attract the corduroyed denizens of the old-money crowd, even though more than half the guest rooms share baths. How do you think old money got that way? Through frugality and thrift, that's how, and the East Wind's shared bath rates are among the better bargains in the region.

The inn itself, formerly a sail loft, is perfectly situated next to the harbor with water views from all rooms and the long porch. It's a classic seaside inn, with busy wallpaper, simple colonial reproduction furniture, and tidy rooms. (The 10 guest rooms across the way at a former sea captain's house have most of the private baths.) The atmosphere is relaxed almost to the point of ennui, the service very good, and the meals served in an Edwardian-era dining room. The menu includes hearty Yankee fare, usually with an ample selection of fresh-caught seafood.

LimeRock Inn. 96 Limerock St. Rockland, ME 04841. ☎ **207/594-2257** or 800/546-3762. 8 rms, (1 with shower only). $100–$160 double, including breakfast. MC, V.

This beautiful Queen Anne-style inn is located on a quiet side street just two blocks from Rockland's Main Street. Originally built for U.S. Rep. Charles Littlefield in 1890, it served as a doctor's residence from 1950 to 1994, after which it was renovated into a gracious inn. The innkeepers—two couples from New Hampshire—have done a stunning job of converting what could be a gloomy manse into one of the region's best choices for overnight accommodation. Excellent attention has been paid to detail throughout, from the choice of country Victorian furniture to the bottles of Poland Spring Water in the rooms. All the guest rooms are welcoming, but among the best is the Island Cottage Room, a bright and airy chamber wonderfully converted from an old shed and featuring a private deck and Jacuzzi. If it's big elegance you're looking for, choose the Grand Manan Room, which has a four-poster bed the size of the Astrodome, a fireplace, and a double Jacuzzi.

WHERE TO DINE

Next to the Farnsworth Art Museum you'll find **Second Read** (☎ 207/594-4123), a coffee shop masquerading as a used-book store. The selection of books is thin at best, but talk about your lattes! Enjoy a caffeine boost while sitting at the cluster of tables under high ceilings in front of the tall front windows. Light lunches are also available ($2.50 to $6.50). Open daily except Sunday 7:30am to 5:30pm.

☉ **Cafe Miranda.** 15 Oak St., Rockland. ☎ **207/594-2034.** Reservations strongly encouraged. Main courses $9.50–$14.50. DISC, MC, V. Open Tues–Sun. 5:30pm–9:30pm. ECLECTIC/ GLOBAL.

The pink flamingo stuck in the flowerbox outside this tiny restaurant and the offbeat notations scrawled on the menu ("Hungry? We have food! Coincidence?!") provide a clue that this isn't your small-town Maine chowderhouse. Further inspection of the menu confirms those suspicions. This tiny restaurant features a huge menu, and it's crammed with cuisines from around the world. Choose from the Szechuan dan dan noodles, poblano chiles stuffed with cheese and couscous, native mussels steamed in Thai curry, or flank steak wasabi. The one trait all entrees share is a sense of culinary adventure, and for a menu that grazes so far and wide, the chef pulls it off with considerable flair. While the prices aren't cheap compared to basic dinner fare available in town, Cafe Miranda offers excellent value for your buck.

CAMDEN

Camden is quintessential coastal Maine. Set at the foot of the wooded Camden Hills around a picturesque harbor that no Hollywood movie set could improve upon, the affluent village of Camden has attracted the gentry of the Eastern Seaboard for more than 100 years. The quirky mansions of the moneyed set still dominate the shady side streets (many have been converted into bed-and-breakfasts), and Camden is possessed of a grace and sophistication that eludes many other coastal towns.

Nor have Camden's charms gone unnoticed in recent years. The village and the surrounding communities have become a haven for retired U.S. Foreign Service and C.I.A. personnel, and has attracted its share of summering corporate bigwigs, including former Apple Computer C.E.O. John Sculley. (The area seems to be the destination of choice for retired computer executives: the family of Thomas Watson, the former C.E.O. of IBM, has a summer compound just offshore at North Haven.) More recently, the town received an economic injection from the phenomenal growth of MBNA, a national finance company, which has restored historic buildings and contributed significantly to Camden's current prosperity. It also explains the number of clean-cut young men in white shirts and ties you may see in and around town.

The best way to enjoy Camden is to park your car as soon as you can—which may mean driving a block or two off Route 1. The village is at a perfect scale to reconnoiter on foot, which allows a leisurely browse of the boutiques and galleries. Don't miss the hidden town park (look behind the library), which was designed by the landscape firm of Frederick Law Olmsted, the nation's most lauded landscape architect. I once stood in this small park at twilight and watched as a schooner maneuvered its way into the harbor, accompanied by the haunting sound of a bagpipe player standing at the bow. In the evening, make your way to The Waterfront Restaurant on Bayview Street (☎ 207/236-3747) to secure a seat on the deck overlooking the harbor. Enjoy a snack or cocktail as the evening calm settles over the town.

ESSENTIALS

GETTING THERE   Camden is located on Route 1. Coming from the south, travelers can shave a few minutes off their trip by turning left on Route 90 six miles past Waldoboro, bypassing Rockland. The most traffic-free route from southern Maine is to Augusta via the Maine Turnpike, then via Route 17 to Route 90 to Route 1.

VISITOR INFORMATION   The **Rockport-Camden-Lincolnville Chamber of Commerce,** P.O. Box 919, Camden, ME 04843 (☎ **207/236-4404** or 800/223-5459) dispenses helpful information from its center at the Public Landing in Camden. The chamber is open year round weekdays from 9am to 5pm and Saturdays 10am to 5pm. In summer, it's also open Sundays 12 noon to 4pm.

OUTDOOR PURSUITS

Camden Hills State Park (☎ **207/236-3109**) is nicely situated about a mile north of the village center on Route 1. This 6,500-acre park features an oceanside picnic area, camping at 112 sites, a winding toll road up 800-foot Mount Battie with spectacular views from the summit, and a variety of well-marked hiking trails.

One easy hike I'd recommend strongly is an ascent to the ledges of Mount Megunticook, preferably early in the morning before the crowds have amassed and when the mist still lingers in the valleys. Leave from near the campground and follow the well-maintained trail to these open ledges, which requires only about 30 to 45 minutes' exertion. Spectacular, improbable views of the harbor await, as well as glimpses inland to the gentle valleys. Depending on your stamina and desires, you can continue on the park's trail network to Mount Battie, or into the less-trammeled woodlands on the east side of the Camden Hills.

For a view from the water back to the hills, **Maine Sports Outfitters** (☎ 207/ 236-8797 or 800/722-0826) offers sea-kayaking tours of Camden's scenic harbor. The standard tour lasts four hours, and takes paddlers out to Curtis Island at the outer edge of the harbor. This is an easy, delightful way to get a taste of the area's maritime culture. Longer trips are also available. The outfitter's main shop, located on Route 1 in Rockport, has a good selection of outdoor gear and is worth a stop for outdoor enthusiasts gearing up for local adventures or heading on to Acadia.

The Camden area also lends itself well to exploring by bike. A pleasant loop of a couple of miles takes you from Camden into the village of Rockport, which has an equally scenic harbor and less tourist traffic. Head south on Union Street (look for the Belted Galloway cows) en route to the harbor, then return via Chestnut St. Take time to poke around the side streets with their stately homes and glimpses of the ocean.

Bike rentals, maps, and sound local riding advice is available at **Fred's Bikes** (☎ 207/236-6664) at 53 Chestnut St. in Camden.

Come winter, there's skiing at the **Camden Snow Bowl** (☎ 207/236-3438) just outside of town on Hosmer's Pond Rd. This small, family-oriented ski area has a handful of trails and a modest vertical drop of 950 feet, but good views of the open ocean and a superb toboggan run. Toboggans are available for rent, or you can bring your own.

WHERE TO STAY

Camden vies with Kennebunkport and Manchester, Vermont, for the title of bed-and-breakfast capital of New England. They're everywhere. Route 1 north of the village center—locally called High Street—is a virtual bed-and-breakfast alley, with many handsome homes converted to lodging. Others are tucked off on side streets. *One note:* Route 1 is thick with cars and RVs during the summer months, and you may find the steady hum of traffic diminishes the small-town charm of those establishments that flank this otherwise stately, shady road.

Despite the preponderance of B&Bs, the total number of rooms is fairly limited and lodging during peak season is tight. It's best to reserve far in advance. You might also try **Camden Accommodations and Reservations** (☎ 800/236-1920), which offers assistance with everything from booking rooms at resorts to finding cottages for seasonal rental.

Lastly, there's camping at Camden Hills State Park (see "Outdoor Pursuits," above).

Blackberry Inn. 82 Elm St., Camden, ME 04843. ☎ **207/236-6060** or 800/833-6674. 10 rms (six with shower only, one with detached bath). Peak season $85–$140 double; off season $55–$120. Rates include full breakfast. MC, V.

If your tastes run to Shaker austerity and simplicity, this is not your place. This 1850s inn, located on Route 1 along the commercial strip descending into Camden village, is cluttered in a high (some might say oppressive) Victorian style. The former home of the owner of the Knox Knitting Mill, its hallways are hung with portraits of stern Victorians, and some of the rooms feature stamped tin ceilings. The Rose Room is the best of the bunch, with a fireplace and claw-footed bathtub, offering a nice sanctuary at the back of the house. If you want more modern accommodations, ask for one of the two remodeled garden rooms. These bright, airy rooms are quiet and offer working fireplaces and Jacuzzis. A filling country breakfast is served family-style at a long table with press-backed chairs in the dining room, and typically includes fruit, baked goods, and a main course.

Lord Camden Inn. 24 Main St., Camden, ME 04843. ☎ **207/236-4325** or 800/336-4325. 31 rms. A/C TV TEL. Late June through August $128–$175 double; early summer and fall $118–$158; winter and spring $88–$138. All rates include continental breakfast. MC, V.

The downtown convenience can't be beat at this thoroughly modern hotel carved out of a Masonic Temple that dates to 1893. Converted to a hotel in 1983, the Lord Camden's guest rooms are each unique, and the hotel architects obviously had to be creative to adapt rooms of varying shapes and sizes. All are now carpeted and comfortably furnished with colonial reproductions, and the exposed brick walls add a nice touch of authenticity. The best and most expensive rooms are on the harbor side of the fourth floor. These offer balconies with unobstructed views of the harbor and the bay beyond. The service is a bit stiffer and more briskly efficient than you'll find at other Camden inns, but the whole town is at your doorstep and you can walk just about everywhere.

✪ **Maine Stay.** 22 High St., Camden, ME 04843. ☎ **207/236-9636.** 8 rms (6 with private bath; 4 with shower only). $80–$130 double including breakfast, discounts during the off-season. AE, MC, V.

The Maine Stay is Camden's premiere bed-and-breakfast. Located in a home dating to 1802 but expanded in Greek Revival style in 1840, the Maine Stay is a classic slate-roofed New England homestead set in a shady yard within walking distance of both downtown and Camden Hills State Park. The eight guest rooms on three floors all have ceiling fans and are distinctively furnished with antiques and special decorative touches. My favorite: the new downstairs Carriage House Room, which is away from the buzz of traffic on Route 1 and boasts its own stone patio.

The three downstairs country-style common rooms are perfect for unwinding, and the country kitchen is open to guests at all times—you might even help hand-grind the coffee. Breakfast is served in a country pine dining room, or, when the weather permits, on a deck overlooking the landscaped backyard. Hikers can set out on trails right from the yard into the Camden Hills.

Perhaps the most memorable part of a stay here, however, will be the hospitality of the three hosts—Peter Smith, his wife Donny, and her twin sister, Diana Robson. The trio is genuinely interested in their guests' well-being, and they offer dozens of day trip suggestions, which are conveniently printed out from the inn's computer for guests to take with them. It's a nice use of a modern technology at an inn that successfully strives to preserve the best of yesterday. No smoking.

✪ **Norumbega.** 61 High St., Camden, ME 04843. ☎ **207/236-4646.** Fax 207/236-0824. 12 rms (three with shower only). TV TEL. July through mid-Oct $195–$450 double; mid–May though June and late Oct $165–$375; November to mid-May $135–$295. All rates include full breakfast and evening refreshments. AE, MC, V.

You'll have no problem finding Norumbega. Just head north of the village and look for travelers pulled over taking photos of this Victorian-era stone castle overlooking the bay. One of the priciest hostelries in the state, Norumbega is the natural habitat of high-powered businessmen of a certain age. And it's no wonder they're attracted here. The 1886 structure is both wonderfully eccentric and finely built, full of wondrous curves and angles throughout. There's extravagant carved-oak woodwork in the lobby, and a stunning oak and mahogany inlaid floor. The downstairs billiards room is the place to pretend you're a 19th-century railroad baron. (Or an information-age baron—the home was owned for a time by Hodding Carter III.)

The guest rooms have been meticulously restored and furnished with antiques by current owner Murray Keatinge, who bought the place in 1987. Five of the rooms have fireplaces, and the three "garden level rooms" (they're off the downstairs billiards room) have private decks. Two rooms ranks among the finest of any inn in the United States—the Library Suite, housed in the original two-story library with interior balcony, and the sprawling Penthouse with its superlative views. The inn is big enough to ensure privacy, but also intimate enough to get to know the other guests—mingling often occurs at breakfast, at the optional evening social hour, and in the afternoon, when the inn puts out its famous fresh-baked cookies.

⑤ Sunrise Motor Court. Route 1 (HCR 60, Box 545), Lincolnville, ME 04849. ☎ **207/ 236-3191.** 13 rms (all shower only). TV. Peak season $49–$59 double; off season $45–$51. Open Memorial Day through Columbus Day. Located 4.5 miles north of Camden. DISC, MC, V.

Situated just far enough beyond of the congestion of Camden to provide a degree of remoteness, the Sunrise Motor Court is a classic 1950s-era establishment with excellent views of the bay—though these views are regrettably across Route 1 and through a latticework of utility lines. Yet, the place boasts a time-worn comfort, like a favorite old sweatshirt. The 13 cabins are arrayed along a grassy hillside at the edge of a wood, and are simply furnished with bed and maybe a few chairs. All boast small decks and outdoor chairs, allowing guests to relax and enjoy the serene view. (Note that two cabins behind the manager's house lack a view.) This is a good bet for budget-conscious travelers who want to experience the Camden area, yet not spend a small fortune doing so.

Whitehall Inn. 52 High St., Camden, ME 04843. ☎ **207/236-3391.** 50 rms, including 10 rms across the street in 2 cottages (5 rms with shared bath). TV TEL. July through late Oct $130–$165 double, including breakfast and dinner ($100–$135 with breakfast only). Discounts in late May and June. AE, MC, V. Open late May through late Oct.

The Whitehall is a venerable Camden establishment, the sort of place you half expect to find Cary Grant in a blue blazer tickling the ivories on the 1904 Steinway in the lobby. Set at the edge of town on Route 1 in a structure that dates to 1834, this three-story inn has a striking architectural integrity with its columns, gables and long roofline. This is the place you think of when you think of the time-worn New England summer inn.

Inside, the antique furnishings—including the handsome Seth Thomas clock, Oriental carpets, and cane-seated rockers on the front porch—are impeccably well cared for. Guest rooms are simple but appealing, and feature rotary dial phones that will provoke nostalgia in older visitors and mild befuddlement among youngest guests. The Whitehall also occupies a minor footnote in the annals of American literature—a young local poet recited her poems here for guests in 1912, stunning the audience with her eloquence. Her name? Edna St. Vincent Millay.

The Whitehall's dining room boasts a slightly faded glory and service that occasionally limps along, but remains a good destination for reliable American fare like veal with sweet vermouth, sage, and prosciutto; or baked haddock stuffed with Maine shrimp. (Entrees $14.75–$17.50.) And, of course, there's always boiled Maine lobster.

WHERE TO DINE

Mama and Leenie's Cafe. 27 Elm St., Camden. ☎ **207/236-6300.** Breakfast $3.95–$5.50; lunch & supper $4.50–$7.75. MC, V. Sun–Thurs 7am–7pm, Fri–Sat until 9pm. BAKERY.

This small, whimsically decorated downtown café is the place for a simple, wholesome meal. Or maybe not so wholesome. The breakfast menu, which is available all day long, includes delicious baked goods, blintzes served with sour cream and fruit, quiche, and Belgian waffles. (Don't be alarmed. There's also cholesterol-free French toast.) In the afternoon and evening, diners can satisfy their basic needs with salads and sandwiches, then indulge themselves with selections from the tempting baked goods counter. In summer, you can dine in the small adjacent courtyard that seats about a dozen. Or be more adventurous—everything on the menu is available to go. So grab a bite to eat and head to the summit of Mount Battie for a picnic.

Peter Ott's. 16 Bayview St., Camden. ☎ **207/236-4032.** Reservations not accepted. Main courses $13.95–$22.95 (most $14–$16). MC, V. Daily 5:30pm–9:30pm during season; closed for a couple of months in winter. AMERICAN.

Peter Ott's has attracted a steady stream of satisfied local customers and repeat-visitor yachtsmen since it opened smack in the middle of Camden in 1974. While it poses as a steak house with its simple wooden tables and chairs and its manly meat dishes (like char-broiled Black Angus with mushrooms and onions, and sirloin steak dijonaise), it's grown beyond that to satisfy more diverse tastes. In fact, the restaurant offers some of the better prepared seafood in town, including a fine pan-blackened seafood sampler and grilled salmon served with a lemon caper sauce. Be sure to leave room for the specialty coffees and its famous deserts, like the lemon-almond crumb tart.

Sea Dog Brewing Co. 43 Mechanic St. Camden. ☎ **207/236-6863.** Reservations not accepted. Main courses $2.95–$10.95. AE, DC, DISC, MC, V. Daily 11:30am–3pm and 5–9pm. Located at Knox Mill one block west of Elm St. PUB FARE.

The Sea Dog Brewing Co. is one of a handful of brew pubs that have found quick success in Maine, and it makes a decent destination for quick and reliable pub food like nachos or hamburgers. It won't set your taste buds to dancing, but it will satisfy basic cravings.

Located in the ground floor of an old woolen mill that's been renovated by MBNA, a national credit card company, the restaurant has a generic brew pub atmosphere that could be anywhere—maybe the Midwest, maybe a mall. While not original, the place is comfortable with its booths, wooden chairs and tables, a handsome bar, and views through tall windows of the old mill race. And the beers are uniformly excellent, although some suffer from a regrettable cuteness in naming (e.g., Old Gollywobbler Brown Ale).

BELFAST TO BUCKSPORT

Hasty travelers more than not whip around this northerly stretch of Penobscot Bay, scurrying from the tourist enclave of Camden to the tourist enclaves of Bar Harbor and Mount Desert Island. But it's a mistake to hurry through. Because there's some splendid history and architecture to be found here. Most of the businesses, especially off Route 1, cater to the local trade rather than tourists, so you'll find authentic coastal Maine if you but look for it.

This region was once famed for its fine shipbuilding. In the mid-19th century, Belfast and Searsport produced more than their share of ships and captains to pilot them on trading ventures around the globe. In the last century, the now-quiet village of Searsport had 17 active shipyards that turned out some 200 ships. In 1856 alone, 24 ships of more than 1,000 tons were launched from Belfast.

When shipbuilding died out at the turn of the century, the Belfast area was sustained by a thriving poultry industry. Alas, that too declined as the industry moved south. In recent decades, the area has attracted artisans of various stripes.

ESSENTIALS

GETTING THERE   Route 1 connects Belfast, Searsport, and Bucksport.

VISITOR INFORMATION   The **Belfast Area Chamber of Commerce,** P.O. Box 58, Belfast, ME 04915 (☎ 207/338-5900) staffs an information booth near the waterfront park that's open in summer. The **Searsport and Stockton Springs Chamber of Commerce,** P.O. Box 139, Searsport, ME 04974 (☎ 207/548-6510) maintains a seasonal information booth on Route 1. Further north, try the **Bucksport Bay Area Chamber of Commerce,** P.O. Box 1880, Bucksport, ME 04416 (☎ 207/ 469-6818).

EXPLORING THE REGION

Some splendid historic homes may be seen by veering off Route 1 and approaching downtown Belfast via High Street (look for the first "Downtown Belfast" signs). The Primrose Hill District along High Street was the most fashionable place for prosperous merchants to settle in the early and mid-19th century, and their stately homes reflect an era when stature was equal to both the size of one's home and the care one took in designing and embellishing it. Downtown Belfast also has some superb examples of historic brick commercial architecture, including the elaborate High Victorian Gothic building on Main Street that formerly housed the Belfast National Bank.

Near Belfast's small waterfront park you can take a fun excursion on the scenic **Belfast and Moosehead Lake Railroad** (☎ 207/948-5500 or 800/392-5500). The railroad was chartered in 1867 and financed primarily by the town; in fact, until 1991, the B&ML railroad remained the only railroad in the nation owned by a municipality. The rail line was purchased by entrepreneurs, who have spruced it up considerably. In 1995, the company acquired 11 vintage rail cars from Sweden, including a 1913 steam locomotive, and opened a new station in Unity, near the end of the 33-mile-long line. (The steam train departs from Unity; a diesel train runs from Belfast.)

The 1¹/₂-hour tours offers a wonderful glimpse of inland Maine and its thick forests and rich farmland. (The train also edges along Passagassawakeag River, a name which provokes considerable amusement among all but the most melancholy of children.) The train features a dining car, where beer and wine may be purchased, and entertainment in the form of a hold-up by some unsavory desperados known as the Waldo Station Gang. The train tends to be exceptionally popular with children and elderly visitors. An optional tour of northern Penobscot Bay on a handsome riverboat can also be packaged with the train excursions.

The train runs twice daily from mid–May to the end of October. The fare is $14 for adults, $7 for the first child (ages 3–16), and $3.50 for each additional child.

Just north of Belfast on Route 1 look for **Perry's Nut House** (☎ 207/338-1630), an enduring tourist trap of the highest order. Founded in the 1920s by Irving Perry, a Mainer who had invested a bit too aggressively in Southern pecan plantations, the Nut House was built along busy Route 1 with the idea of unloading Perry's nut surplus on unsuspecting tourists. Perry assembled and widely advertised his "world famous nut museum," stocking its exhibits with specimens from throughout Latin America and around the globe. Yellowing displays help provide context, with photographs and exhibits that chronicle the incredible story of the nut (e.g., "Shipping Filberts to Market"). Nuts, of course, are still available by the bag or the bushel, along with a lot of other tourist stuff.

At the northern tip of Penobscot Bay, the Penobscot River squeezes through a dramatic gorge near Verona Island, which Route 1 spans on an attractive suspension bridge. This easily defended pinch in the river was perceived to be of strategic importance in the 1840s, when the solid and imposing **Fort Knox** was constructed. While it was never attacked, the fort was manned during the Civil and Spanish-American wars, and today is run as a state park (☎ **207/469-7719**). It's an impressive edifice to explore, with subterranean chambers that produce wonderful echoes, and graceful granite staircases. Admission is $2 for adults, 50¢ for children under 12, and free for seniors and children under 5.

Across the river in the paper mill town of Bucksport is **Northeast Historic Film** (☎ **207/469-0924** or 800/639-1636), an organization founded in 1986 dedicated to preserving and showing early films related to New England. In 1992 the group bought Bucksport's Alamo Theatre, which was built in 1916 and closed (after a showing of "Godzilla") in 1956. Renovations are coming along slowly, but films are regularly shown at the bare-bones theater. Call to ask about ongoing film series. Visitors can also stop by the store at the front of the Alamo to browse through available videos and other items.

A SUPERB NAUTICAL MUSEUM

Penobscot Marine Museum. Church St. at Route 1, Searsport. ☎ **207/548-2529.** Adults $5, seniors $3.50, children 7–15 $1.50. Open daily Memorial Day through mid-October 10am–5pm (open 12 noon on Sundays).

The Penobscot Marine Museum is one of the best small museums in New England. Housed in a cluster of eight historic buildings atop a gentle rise in tiny downtown Searsport, the museum does a deft job in educating visitors about the vitality of the local shipbuilding industry, the essential role of international trade to daily life in the 19th century, and the hazards of life at sea. The exhibits are uniformly well organized, and wandering from building to building induces a keen sense of wonderment at the vast enterprise that was Maine's maritime trade.

Among the more intriguing exhibits are a wide selection of dramatic marine paintings (including one stunning rendition of whaling in the Arctic), black and white photographs of many of the 286 weathered sea captains who once called Searsport home, photographs of a 1902 voyage to Argentina, and an early home decorated in the style of a sea captain, complete with lacquered furniture and accessories hauled back from trade missions to the Orient. Throughout, the curators have done a fine job both educating and entertaining visitors. It's well worth the price if you're the least interested in Maine's rich culture of the sea.

WHERE TO STAY

Homeport Inn. Route 1 (P.O. Box 647) , Searsport, ME 04974. ☎ **207/548-2259** or 800/742-5814. 10 rms (six with private bath; 1 with shower only). $55–$75 double, including full breakfast. AE, DISC, MC, V.

Sitting in the front parlor of the Homeport Inn, guests would be excused for feeling a bit like they were sitting inside an Oriental carpet. The opulently furnished room is filled with tchothckes from Asia and elaborate decorative touches. In fact, this architecturally striking 1861 sea captain's house is imposing and elegant throughout, restored to a "T", and furnished appropriately to the period with Victorian furniture and heavy oil portraits. Guest who revel in authenticity will be delighted here.

Breakfast is served on an airy enclosed porch along the side (with glimpses of the bay beyond). After your meal, you can wander the grounds down to the water's edge, resting at benches placed for the guest's leisure. The main disadvantage is its location facing a fast-traveled stretch of Route 1 east of Searsport village. Guest rooms are a tough choice. Choose from either one of the four handsome period rooms in the old section of the house atop a grand staircase, or from six more modern rooms in the

Readers Recommend

Young's Lobster Pound. *"In the weeks before our trip along the Maine coast, visions of lobster danced in our heads. We expected the happy mollusk to be cheap 'n' plentiful throughout the region; we thought we'd find a down-home lobster pound on every corner. The reality, however, was very different: Lobster was everywhere, but mostly in dinner specials at restaurants that looked pretty much like the ones we had back home. We were surprised at how few and far between the "lobster in the rough" places that we'd envisioned were. But Young's, on Highway 1 just north of Belfast, was exactly the kind of place we were hoping to find: a no-frills joint serving up Maine lobster the way it was meant to be. You enter the hangar-like structure, choose your favorite from the tanks of live lobsters lining the walls (all pulled from the local waters by Young's boats that day), take a seat at one of the picnic tables overlooking the harbor (the view is terrific), and wait for your number to be called. In minutes, you're digging into a paper plate full of steaming lobster, accompanied by perfectly melted butter, vinegar 'n' salt potato chips, and all the handi-wipes you need—all for around $10. It's simply heavenly—and the ideal Maine coast experience."*

—Cheryl Farr, Brooklyn, NY

adjoining carriage house. The disadvantage of the old rooms is that they share a single bath; the disadvantage of the carriage house rooms is that they're somewhat lacking in historic charm. Also available are two-bedroom Victorian cottages, which rent by the week.

Rocky Ridge Motel. Route 1 (P.O. Box 1135), Stockton Springs, ME 04981. ☎ **207/ 567-3456** or 800/453-0754. 18 rms (16 with shower only). TV TEL. July & Aug $55–$60; off-season $29.95–$50. AE, DISC, MC, V.

The Rocky Ridge Motel, located between Searsport and Bucksport, is a standard issue Route 1 motel with dowdy 1970s-era furniture. But it has two things going for it. The rooms are impeccably clean. And it's within striking distance of a little known, thin strip of sandy beach called Sandy Point, which offers cool relief on sweltering days. With suit on and towel in hand, walk or drive across Route 1 and head down the country road to the park, which rarely attracts more than a handful of locals. You can take a dip in the upper reaches of calm Penobscot Bay, but be prepared to be cold. Very cold. Even this far inland the waters rarely warm to temperatures comfortable to nonaquatic species like humans.

WHERE TO DINE

Darby's. 105 High St., Belfast. ☎ **207/338-2339.** Reservations suggested for after 7pm on weekends. Main courses, lunch $3.95–$8.95, dinner $5.75–$13.95. DISC, MC. V. Daily 11am–9pm. AMERICAN/ECLECTIC.

This dark, sometimes smoky restaurant centers around a handsome bar and offers up filling fare that goes the extra culinary mile. Located in a Civil War-era pub with attractive stamped tin ceilings and a beautiful back bar with Corinthian columns, Darby's is a popular local hangout that boasts a comfortable, neighborhoody feel. Order up a Maine beer while you peruse the menu, which is surprisingly creative. Darby's offers most pub favorites, like burgers and Cajun chicken on a bulkie, but also features imports like pad Thai, enchilada verde, and Thai chicken salad. Try the Moroccan lamb or the smoked seafood pasta made with locally smoked fish. And if you like the artwork on the wall, ask about it. It's probably done by a local artist, and it's probably for sale.

⑤ Dockside Family Restaurant. 30 Main St., Belfast. ☎ **207/338-6889.** Reservations not accepted. Main courses, breakfast $2.50–$6.50, lunch $2.95–$7.95, dinner $7.50–$14.95. MC, V. Sun–Thurs 7am–8pm, Fri–Sat until 8:30pm. AMERICAN.

The uninspired grey shingled exterior of the Dockside, located on Main St. overlooking the harbor, hides an uninspired interior of red vinyl and pine banquettes. One suspects this is just to throw off the unknowing traveler and keep the snobs away. Beneath it all, it's a fun place, and hugely popular with the locals. The waitresses have been working here for years and have the patter down pat; the food is filling and often unexpectedly tasty. There's a whole range of fried fish (clams, shrimp, scallops, haddock), plus pizza, calzones, and a variety of sandwiches. But this is the place to splurge for one of the pricier things on the menu—the bowl of lobster stew ($10.95), which is made with succulent and plentiful chunks of lobster in a rich and creamy sauce. You won't go away disappointed.

MacLeod's. Main St., Bucksport. ☎ **207/469-3963.** Reservations recommended on weekends and in summer. Main courses, lunch $3.75–$9.95, dinner $8.95–$14.95. AE, DC, MC, V. Mon–Fri 11am–9pm, Sat–Sun 5–9pm. AMERICAN.

MacLeod's is a comfortable, pubby place in downtown Bucksport that often teems on weekends with Bucksport residents—from workers at the pulp mill to local businessmen. With its simple wood tables, Windsor chairs, and relentlessly upbeat background music, MacLeod's won't be confused with a place for fancy dining, but it does offer good meals, sizeable portions, and consistent quality. For lunch you might try the baked salmon loaf with fresh lemon dill sauce, teriyaki chicken on an onion roll, or a lobster melt on a croissant. For dinner, entrees include grilled lamb shishkabob, raspberry chicken, baked sea scallops, or a unique "lasagne al pescatore," made with shrimp, scallops, and crabmeat with a rich lobster sauce. Don't miss the locally famous chocolate silk pie for dessert.

Nickerson Tavern. Route 1, Searsport. ☎ **207/548-2220.** Reservations recommended, especially on weekends. Main courses $12.50–$18.50. MC, V. High season daily 5:30–9:30pm; off season closed Mon–Tues; closed mid-Jan–mid-Mar. REGIONAL/ECLECTIC.

It's easy to miss the Nickerson Tavern, located in a modest 1838 Cape-style home 2.8 miles east of Bucksport's downtown on Route 1. But do yourself a favor and turn around, joining the other gourmands who appreciate this gem set in a rustic part of coastal Maine. After you enter, you're ushered into a small parlor off the entrance. From here, you're seated in either the main dining room, which is decorated in an informal Colonial American motif with Indian Red paint, early china, and ancient bottles, or one of two smaller, slightly more formal side rooms.

The cuisine draws on regional delicacies, like lobster (of course), chicken, and duckling. The preparation is informed by French style, but dishes are made "without the heaviness and stuffiness of classic presentation," says the chef. You could begin with an appetizer of escargot, baked brie in puff pastry, or Maine mussels steamed in ale with garlic and dijon mustard. Then select from a delectable array of entrees, including lobster sauteed in butter with a cognac dill cream sauce, raspberry hazelnut chicken, or pork tenderloin served with a sauce of mushrooms, shallots, and capers.

CASTINE & ENVIRONS

If I had to choose the most elegant village in Maine, I would without hesitation choose Castine. It's not so much the stunningly handsome mid-19th-century homes that fill the side streets, virtually all of which are meticulously maintained. Nor is it the location on a quiet peninsula, 16 miles south of the hubub of tourist-jammed

Route 1. No, what lends Castine most of its charm are the splendid, towering elm trees, which still overarch many of the village streets. Before Dutch elm disease, much of America once looked like this, and it's easy to slip into a deep nostalgia for this most graceful of trees, even if you're too young to remember America of the elms. Through perseverance and a measure of luck, Castine has managed to keeps it elms alive, and it's worth the drive here for this alone.

For American history buffs, Castine offers more than trees. This outpost served as a strategic town in various battles between the British, Dutch, French, and feisty colonials in the centuries after it was settled in 1613. It's been occupied by all of them at some point, and historical personages like Miles Standish and Paul Revere passed through during one epoch or another. (Paul Revere, in one of his less heroic feats, was involved in the ignoble loss of 44 American ships during the Revolution after a failed colonial attack on British-held Castine.) The town has a dignified, aristocratic bearing, and it somehow seems appropriate that Tory-dominated Castine welcomed the British with open arms during the Revolution.

An excellent brief history of Castine by Elizabeth J. Duff is published in brochure form by the Castine Merchant's Association. The brochure, which also includes a walking tour of Castine, is entitled "Welcome to Castine" and is available widely at shops in town and at the state information centers.

Castine is also home to the **Maine Maritime Academy,** which trains sailors for the rigors of life at sea with the merchant marine. The campus is on the western edge of the village, and its hulking grey training ship is often docked in Castine, threatening to overwhelm the village with its sheer size. Tours of the ship are offered in summer.

One final note: Castine is mostly likely to appeal to those who can entertain themselves. It's a peaceful place to sit and read, or take an afternoon walk. If it's outlet shopping you're looking for, you're better off moving on. "This is not Bar Harbor," one local innkeeper puts it dryly.

ESSENTIALS

GETTING THERE   Castine is located 16 miles south of Route 1. Turn south on Route 175 in Orland (east of Bucksport) and follow this to Route 166, which winds its way to Castine. Route 166A offers an alternate route along Penobscot Bay.

VISITOR INFORMATION   Castine lacks a formal information center, but the clerk at the **Town Office** (☎ 207/326-4502) is often helpful with travel questions.

EXPLORING CASTINE

Don't leave the village without stretching your legs with a walking tour of Castine, using the walking tour brochure mentioned above.

One of the town's most intriguing attractions is the **Wilson Museum** (curator's ☎ 207/326-8545; call 5pm–9pm) on Perkins St., an attractive and quirky anthropological museum constructed in 1921. This small museum contains the collections of John Howard Wilson, a Castine resident and inveterate collector of rifles and other historic artifacts from around the globe. Don't miss the display of summer and winter hearses, or the early American kitchen. The museum is open May through September Tuesday through Sunday from 2 to 5pm and admission is free.

Next door is the **John Perkins House,** Castine's oldest home. It was occupied by the British during the Revolution and the War of 1812, and a tour features demonstrations of old-fashioned cooking techniques. The Perkins House is open July and August on Wednesday and Sunday from 2 pm to 5 pm. Admission is $4.

Also worth exploring is **Dyce's Head Light** at the extreme western end of Battle Avenue. While the 1828 light itself is not open to the public, it's well worth scrambling down the trail to the rocky shoreline along the Penobscot River just beneath the lighthouse. A small sign indicates the start of the public trail.

A TOUR OF CAPE ROSIER

Across the Bagaduce River from Castine is Cape Rosier, one of Maine's better held secrets. The bad news is, to reach the cape you need to backtrack to Route 175, head south toward Deer Isle, then follow Route 176 to the turnoff to Cape Rosier—about 18 miles of driving to cross one mile of water. Cape Rosier was home to the late Helen and Scott Nearing, who wrote the enduring back-to-the-land book *Living the Good Life*. It's no wonder they chose this bucolic place to settle. As a dead-end peninsula, there's no thru-traffic, and it still has a wild, unkempt flavor with salty views of Penobscot Bay.

A 10-mile loop around the cape starting on Goose Falls Road is suitable by bicycle or as a leisurely car trip. If the weather's agreeable, stop for a walk on the state-owned Holbrook Wildlife Sanctuary, a 1,200-acre preserve laced with trails and abandoned roads. The sanctuary is located at the northern end of the loop.

WHERE TO STAY

Castine Inn. Main St. (P.O. Box 41), Castine, ME 04421. ☎ **207/326-4365**. Fax 207/ 326/4570. 20 rms (some with shower only). $75–$125 double, including full breakfast. MC, V. Open mid–May through Oct.

The Castine Inn is a Maine Coast rarity—a hotel that was originally built as a hotel (not as a residence), in this case in 1898. This handsome cream-colored village inn, designed in an eclectic Georgian-Federal revival style, has a fine front porch and attractive gardens. Inside, the lobby takes its cue from the 1940s, with wingback chairs and loveseats, and a fireplace in the parlor. There's also an intimate, dark lounge decked out in rich green hues, reminiscent of an Irish pub. The elegant dining room has heavy wooden chairs and a wrap-around mural by Margaret Parker, one of the inn's owners. The meals served here, incidentally, are the best in town, featuring regional classics like crabmeat cakes, roast venison, fettucini with mussels, and lobster stew with corn and smoked bacon. Entrees are $12 to $18.

The guest rooms on the two upper floors are attractively, if unevenly, furnished in early American style—some aren't much of an improvement over standard motel rooms, but others are graciously appointed with antiques. Likewise, some rooms feature glimpses of the harbor, others don't. To avoid disappointment, ask to see your room before you hand over your credit card.

Pentagâet Inn. Main St. (P.O. Box 4), Castine, ME 04421. ☎ **207/326-8616** or 800/ 845-1701. 16 rms (7 with showers only). $95–$125 double, including full breakfast. MC, V. Open end-May through the third week of Oct.

Here's the big activity at the Pentagâet: Sit on the wrap-around front porch on cane-seated rockers. Watch Castine go by. That's not likely to be overly appealing to those looking for a fast-paced vacation, but it's the perfect salve for those seeking respite from urban life. This quirky yellow and green 1894 structure with its prominent turret is tastefully furnished downstairs with hardwood floors, oval braided rugs, and a woodstove—and somehow it's comforting to see an Encyclopedia Britannica lining the shelves of the sitting room. It's comfortable without being overly elegant, professional without being chilly, personal without being overly intimate.

The rooms on the upper two floors of the main house are furnished nicely and eclectically, with a mix of antiques and old collectibles. The five guest rooms in the adjacent Perkins Street building—a more austere Federal-era house—are furnished simply and feature painted floors. There's no air conditioning, but all rooms have ceiling fans. No smoking.

DEER ISLE

Deer Isle is well off the beaten path, but well worth the long detour off Route 1 if your tastes run to pastoral countryside with a nautical edge. Loopy, winding roads cross through forest and farmland, and travelers are rewarded with sudden glimpses of the azure ocean and mint-green coves. An occasional settlement crops up now and again.

Deer Isle doesn't cater exclusively to tourists, as many coastal regions do. It's still occupied by fifth-generation fishermen, farmers, long-time rusticators, and artists who prize their seclusion. The village of Deer Isle has a handful of inns and galleries, but its primary focus is to serve locals and summer residents, not transients. The village of Stonington, on the southern tip, is a rough-hewn sea town that's still dominated by fishermen and the occasional quarry worker.

ESSENTIALS

GETTING THERE   Deer Isle is accessible via several winding country roads from Route 1. Coming from the west, head south on Route 175 off Route 1 in Orland, then connect to Route 15 to Deer Isle. From the east, head south on Route 172 to Blue Hill, where you can pick up Route 15. Deer Isle is connected to the mainland via a high, narrow, and graceful suspension bridge, built in 1938, which can be somewhat harrowing to cross in high winds.

VISITOR INFORMATION   The **Deer Isle-Stonington Chamber of Commerce** staffs a seasonal information booth just beyond the bridge on Little Deer Isle. The booth is open daily in summer from 10 am to 4 pm, depending on volunteer availability.

EXPLORING DEER ISLE

Deer Isle, with its network of narrow roads to nowhere, is ideal for perfunctory rambling. It's a pleasure to explore by car, and is also inviting to travel by bike, although hasty and careening fishermen in pickups can sometimes be a bit unnerving. Especially tranquil is the road between Sunset and Stonington on the island's western side.

On the island's east side, a trip to the **Haystack Mountain School of Crafts** (☎ 207/348-2306) is a worthy excursion. Just south of the village of Deer Isle, turn east off Route 15 toward Stinson Neck and continue along this scenic road for seven miles. Look for the school's driveway, then head to the visitor's parking area.

The campus of this respected summer crafts school is visually stunning. Designed in the early 1960s by Edward Larrabee Barnes, the campus is set on a steep hillside overlooking the cerulean waters of Jericho Bay. Barnes cleverly managed to play up the views while respecting the delicate local landscape by building a series of small buildings on pilings that seem to float above the earth. These classrooms and studios are linked by boardwalks, many of which are connected to a wide central staircase, ending at the "Flag Deck," a sort of common area just above the shoreline. The buildings and classrooms are closed to the public, but visitors are welcome to walk to the Flag Deck and stop by the college store, which sells art supplies and craft books.

Stonington basically consists of one street that wraps along the harbor's edge. While a handful of bed-and-breakfasts and galleries have established themselves here, it's still a rough-and-tumble waterfront town with strong links to the sea, and you're likely to observe lots of activity in the harbor as lobstermen and urchin divers come and go. If you hear industrial sounds emanating from just offshore, that's likely to be the quarry on Crotch Island, which has been supplying architectural granite to builders nationwide for more than a century.

DAY TRIPS TO ISLE AU HAUT

Rocky and remote Isle au Haut offers the most unique hiking and camping experience in northern New England. This six-by-three mile island, located six miles south of Stonington, was originally named Ille Haut—or High Island—in 1604 by French explorer Samuel de Champlain. The name and its pronunciation evolved— today, it's generally pronounced "aisle-a-ho"—but the island itself has remained steadfastly unchanged over the centuries.

About half of the island is owned by the National Park Service and maintained as an outpost of Acadia National Park (see next chapter). A 60-passenger "mailboat" makes a stop in the morning and late afternoon at Duck Harbor, allowing for a solid day of hiking while still returning to Stonington by nightfall. At Duck Harbor the NPS also maintains a cluster of five Adirondack-style lean-tos, which are available for overnight camping. (Advance reservations are essential. **Contact Acadia National Park,** Bar Harbor, ME 04609, or call **207-288-3338.**)

A network of superb hiking trails radiates out from Duck Harbor. Be sure to ascend the island's highest point, 543-foot Duck Harbor Mountain, for exceptional views of the Camden Hills to the west and Mount Desert Island to the east. Nor should you miss the Cliff or Western Head trails, which track along high, rocky bluffs and coastal outcroppings capped with damp, tangled fog forests of spruce. The trails periodically descend down to cobblestone coves, which issue forth with a deep rumble with every incoming wave. A hand-pump near Duck Harbor provides drinking water, but be sure to bring food and refreshments for hiking.

The other half of the island is privately owned, some by fishermen who can trace their island ancestry back three centuries, and some by summer rusticators, whose forebears discovered the bucolic splendor of Isle au Haut in the 1880s. The summer population of the island is about 300, with about 50 die-hards remaining year-round. The mailboat also stops at the small harborside village, which has a few old homes, a handsome church, and tiny schoolhouse, post office, and store. Day trippers will be better served ferrying straight to Duck Harbor.

The **mailboat** (☎ **207/367-5193**) to Isle au Haut leaves from Stonington. In summer, the *Miss Lizzie* departs from behind the Atlantic Avenue Hardware Store for the village of Isle au Haut daily at 7 and 11am; the *Mink* departs for Duck Harbor daily at 10am. The round trip boat fare is $18 for adults to either the village or Duck Harbor. Children under 12 are half-price. Reservations are not accepted, but surprisingly few passengers are turned away, even in mid-summer. Parking is sometimes a problem, so plan to show up a half-hour before departure.

WHERE TO STAY

Pilgrim's Inn. Deer Isle, ME 04627. ☎ **207/348-6615.** 12 rms, 1 cottage (10 rms with private bath, 7 with shower only). $140–$165 double (cottage $90–$200), including breakfast and dinner. $5 additional in July and Aug. MC, V. Open mid-May through mid-Oct.

Set between an open bay and a millpond, the Pilgrim's Inn is a historic, handsomely renovated inn in a lovely setting. This four-story, gambrel-roofed structure will especially appeal to those intrigued by early American history. The inn was built in 1793 by Ignatius Haskell, a prosperous sawmill owner. His granddaughter opened the home to boarders, and it's been housing summer guests ever since. The interior is tastefully decorated in a style that's informed by early Americana, but not beholden to historic authenticity. The guest rooms are well-appointed with antiques and painted in muted colonial colors; especially intriguing are the rooms on the top floor with impressive diagonal beams.

While bikes are available for guest use and just strolling around the village is a pleasure, much inn life revolves around the wonderful dinners, which start with cocktails and hors d'ouevres in the common room at 6 pm, followed by one seating at 7 pm in the adjacent barn dining room. Only one entree is served at dinner, but it's not likely to disappoint. You might feast on tenderloin of beef with lobster risotto, or a bouillabaisse made of locally caught seafood. Dinner is open to the public by reservation at a fixed price of $29.50. This is a no-smoking inn.

BLUE HILL

Blue Hill, pop. 1,900, is fairly easy to find—just look for gently domed, eponymous Blue Hill Mountain, which lords over the northern end of Blue Hill Bay. Set between the mountain and the bay is the quiet historic town of Blue Hill, which clusters along the bay shore and a small stream. There's not much going on in town. This seems to be exactly what attracts summer visitors back time and again—and may explain why there are two excellent bookstores here. Many old-money families still maintain retreats set along the water or in the rolling inland hills. And Blue Hill offers several excellent choices for dining and lodging. It's a good destination for an escape, and will especially appeal to those deft at crafting their own entertainment.

When in the area, be sure to tune into the local community radio station, WERU at 89.9 FM. It started some years back in the chicken coop owned by Peter Yarrow (of Peter, Paul and Mary fame). The idea was to spread around good music and provocative ideas. It's become slicker and more professional in recent years, but still maintains a pleasantly homespun flavor.

ESSENTIALS

GETTING THERE   Blue Hill is located southeast of Ellsworth on Route 172. From the west, head south on Route 15 five miles east of Bucksport.

VISITOR INFORMATION   Blue Hill does not maintain a visitor information booth. Look for the "Blue Hill, Maine" brochure and map at state information centers, or write the **Blue Hill Chamber of Commerce,** P.O. Box 520, Blue Hill, ME 04614. The staff at area inns and restaurants are usually able to answer any questions you might have.

EVENTS   The Blue Hill Fair is a traditional country fair with livestock competitions, displays of vegetables, and carnival rides. The fair takes place at the fairgrounds northwest of the village on Route 172 on Labor Day weekend.

EXPLORING BLUE HILL

A good way to start your exploration is to ascend the open summit of Blue Hill Mountain, from which you'll have superb views of the azure bay and the rocky balds on nearby Mount Desert Island. To reach the trailhead, drive north on route 172, then turn west (left) on Mountain Road at the Blue Hill Fairgrounds. Drive 0.8 mile and look for the well-marked trail. An ascent of the "mountain" (elevation 940') is about a mile, and requires about 45 minutes. Bring a picnic lunch and enjoy the vistas.

Blue Hill has traditionally attracted more than its fair share of artists, especially, it seems, potters. On Union Street, stop by **Rowantrees Pottery** (☎ 207/374-5535),

Sea Kayaking & Camping Along "Merchant's Row"

Peer southward from Stonington and you'll see dozens of spruce-studded islands ringed with a salmon-pink granite between here and the dark, foreboding ridges of Isle au Haut. These islands are collectively called Merchant's Row, and they're invariably ranked by experienced boaters along the coast as the most beautiful in the state. Thanks to these exceptional islands, Stonington is among Maine's most popular destinations for sea kayaking. Many of the islands are open to day visitors and overnight camping, and one of the Nature Conservancy islands even hosts a flock of sheep. Experienced kayakers should contact the Maine Island Trail Association (☎ 207/761-8225) for more information about paddling here; several of the islands are open only to association members. Aspiring kayakers without experience should sign up for a guided trip. No outfitters are based in Stonington, but several Maine-based outfitters lead multi-day camping trips to Merchant's Row and Isle au Haut.

Contact **Maine Island Kayak Co.** (☎ **207/766-2373**) or **Maine Sports Outfitters** (☎ **207/236-8797**).

which has been a Blue Hill institution for more than half a century. The shop was founded by Adelaide Pearson, who said she was inspired to pursue pottery as a career after a conversation with Mahatma Gandhi in India. Rowantrees pottery is richly hued, and the potters who've succeeded Pearson continue to use glazes made from local resources. **Rackliffe Pottery** (☎ 207/374-2297) was founded by two former Rowantrees potters, and follows a similar local-source philosophy. Visitors are welcome to watch the potters at work. Both shops are open year-round.

Even if you're never been given to swooning over historic homes, you owe yourself a visit to the intriguing Parson Fisher House (contact **Blue Hill Tea & Tobacco,** ☎ **207/374-2161,** for information), located on Routes 176 & 15 a half-mile west of the village. Fisher, Blue Hill's first permanent minister, was something of a Renaissance man when he settled here in 1796. Educated at Harvard, Fisher not only delivered sermons in six different languages, including Aramaic, but was a writer, painter, and minor inventor whose energy was evidently boundless. On a tour of his home, which he built in 1814, you can see a clock with wooden works he made, and samples of the books he not only wrote but published and bound himself.

Parson Fisher House is open from July through mid-September daily except Sunday from 2 pm to 5 pm. Admission is $2 adults, children under 12 are free.

WHERE TO STAY

Blue Hill Farm Country Inn. Route 15 (P.O. Box 437), Blue Hill, ME 04614. ☎ **207/374-5126.** 14 rms (7 with private bath). Jun–Oct $70–$85 double; off season $58–$68. All rates include continental breakfast. MC, V.

Comfortably situated on 48 acres two miles north of the village of Blue Hill, the Blue Hill Country Farm Inn offers some of the most relaxing and comfortable common areas you'll find anywhere. The first floor of a vast barn has been converted to a spacious living room for guests, with a handful of sitting areas arrayed such that you can opt for privacy or the company of others. Or you can curl up in a cozy and intimate common room in the adjoining old farmhouse itself, amply stocked with a good selection of books. There's also the old kitchen, no longer used for cooking, but now a fine place to linger.

It's fortunate that the common areas are so exceptionally well done, because you're not likely to spend much time in the guest rooms, which tend to be small and spartanly furnished. The more modern rooms are upstairs in the barn loft and are nicely decorated in a country farmhouse style. But these are a bit motel-like with rooms set off a central hallway. The older rooms in the farmhouse have more character, but be forewarned that three share a single bathroom with a small tub and handheld shower. No smoking.

✪ **Blue Hill Inn.** Union St. (P.O. Box 403), Blue Hill, ME 04614. ☎ **207/374-2844**. Fax 207/374-2829. 11 rms (2 with shower only). $140–$190 double, including breakfast and dinner. MC, V. Closed the first two weeks of Dec, and from Jan through Mar.

The Blue Hill Inn has been hosting travelers since 1840, so it should come as no surprise that the place has got hospitality down pat. Situated on one of Blue Hill's busy streets and within walking distance of most everything, this Federal-style inn features an authentic colonial American motif throughout, with the authenticity enhanced by creaky floors, door jambs slightly out of true, and quirky touches, like a heavy iron safe employed as an end table. Innkeepers Mary and Don Hartley have furnished all the rooms pleasantly with antiques and down comforters.

The one part of the inn that doesn't feel old (and is the least interesting) is the dining room, which is built in a boxy, shed-like addition to the old house. But the superb French-style cooking of chef Andre Strong makes up for the slightly disappointing atmosphere. The limited menu, made chiefly with local, organic ingredients, might start with fiddlehead flan or penne with vodka tomato cream sauce, then follow with rabbit in a mustard wine sauce; lobster with carmelized ginger, shallots, and spinach; or guinea hen with grapes and wild mushrooms. The fixed price dinner ($30 for five course, $22 for three course) is open to the public, reservations required. This is a no-smoking inn.

✪ **John Peters Inn.** Route 176 East (P.O. Box 916), Blue Hill, ME 04614. ☎ **207/374-2116**. 14 rms. $95–$150 double, including full breakfast. MC, V. Open May–Oct.

Coming up the driveway of the John Peters Inn sends a signal that you're entering into another world, if not another dimension. The narrow dirt road ascends a gentle hill between a row of maples. To the right are glimpses of the bay; to the left is the 1810 home that, with the later architectural embellishments, could be a modest antebellum plantation home.

Inside, it's strictly New England and decorated in antiques with an uncommon elegance and an eye to detail by innkeepers Barbara and Rick Seeger. There's nothing grand here—it's all simple early American style done with exceptionally good taste. The guest rooms, nine of which boast fireplaces and four of which have private phones, all feature love seats or sofas, and are hard to tear oneself out of. But do try. The inn sits on 25 lovely shorefront acres, and has been lightly landscaped— to do more would be to gild the lily. There's also an unheated outdoor pool that will appeal mostly to those of stout constitution. Breakfast in the simply decorated dining room is a sublime treat, with offerings like freshly squeezed orange juice, poached eggs with asparagus, lobster omelettes, and a variety of waffles. This is a no-smoking inn.

WHERE TO DINE

The **Left Bank Bakery and Cafe** (☎ 207/374-2201) is Maine's preeminent counterculture outpost. Located on Route 172 north of town, the Left Bank serves up good food and good music, although not always accompanied by good service. (On my last visit four workers stood behind the counter chatting amiably while customers waited 15 minutes to place an order.) Tasty fresh-baked products are piled high at the counter in the older front section of the restaurant; a renovated side section down a few steps is open and airy, and hosts regular evening performances by notables like Maria Muldaur, Kenny Rankin, and Mose Alison. Call ahead to find out who's playing.

✪ **Firepond.** Main St., Blue Hill. ☎ **207/374-9970.** Reservations recommended. Main courses, $15.95–$21.95. AE, MC, V. Daily 5–9:30pm (closed Tues in fall). Closed Jan through mid-May. REGIONAL GOURMET.

Firepond, located right in the village of Blue Hill, is a drop-dead gorgeous restaurant that happens to serve exceptionally fine food. Ideally sited along a small stream in a former blacksmith's shop, Firepond has old-pine floors and is lavishly decorated with dry and live flowers. The decor flirts with a "Martha Stewart run amok" look, but it pulls back in the nick of time and carries its elegance unusually well. The best seats are downstairs in the covered porch overhanging the stream, but it's hard to go wrong anywhere here for setting a romantic mood. If you're not sure this is the place for you, try this: Stop by the handsome bar with its wrought-iron stools for a drink and an appetizer. The odds are you'll decide that staying for dinner is a good idea.

The meals are adventurous without being overly exotic. When I visited, the chef was in the process of opening a Russian restaurant in New York, and you could see the connection in dishes like "vegetarian caviar," a surprisingly delicate but earthy concoction of cabbage and mushrooms. More traditional regional fare dominates however, with grilled chicken served with a vegetable salsa and amarillo sauce, veal with sun-dried tomatoes, and lobster served on fresh pasta with a cream sauce of boursín and romano cheese. Whatever you choose, expect it to be prepared with an exceedingly deft touch.

⑤ **Jean-Paul's Bistro.** Main St., Blue Hill. ☎ **207/374-5852.** Lunch $4.95–$7.50. MC, V. Jul 1–Sept 15 daily 11am–5:30pm. Located at the intersection of routes 172 & 15. LIGHT FRENCH.

You get a lot of elegance for a little price at Jean-Paul's, which serves up lunch and tea throughout the summer. This is the place to head when the sun's shining overhead and summer blazes in its full glory. Behind this old farmhouse in the village center are stone terraces and a lawn that slopes down to the head of Blue Hill Bay. Choose either a table on the terraces, or plop yourself into one of the wide-armed Adirondack chairs on the lawn overlooking the water. (The lawn is a popular spot for solo diners who prefer to eat in the company of a good book.) Waiters in khakis and well-laundered T-shirts serve the lunches, which tend toward quiche, croissant sandwiches, and salads. The walnut tarragon chicken salad is tasty, as is the curried tuna. The delicious desserts make liberal use of local blueberries.

Jonathan's. Main St., Blue Hill. ☎207/374-5226. Reservations recommended in summer and on weekends year round. Main courses, $16.95–$19.95. MC, V. Daily 5–9:30pm; closed Mon–Tues in winter. NEW AMERICAN.

Here's some advice: Don't order the boiled lobster at Jonathan's. Not that there's anything wrong with it, but you're better off sampling the more innovative cuisine offered here, saving the boiled crustacean for a lobster-pound picnic table. The menu changes frequently, but among the fine dishes apt to be served here are grilled salmon wrapped in grape leaves and served with a feta salad; braised lamb shank simmered in ale and bourbon and served with a maple barbecue sauce; and venison medallions and wild boar sausage accompanied by portobello and shiitake mushrooms. Appetizers run along the lines of warm salad of smoked mussels and chevre, and grilled sopresatta and shrimp.

Located in the middle of Blue Hill, Jonathan's attracts the local hip crowd as well as the old-money summer denizens. The background music is jazz or light rock, the service brisk and professional, and the wine list is extensive and creative. Guests choose between the barn-like back room with a comfortable knotty-pine feel, or the less elegantly decorated front room facing Main Street, done up in green tablecloths, captain's chairs, and booths of white pine. My vote: Go for the back room—it's bigger, but paradoxically feels more intimate.

7 Mount Desert Island & Acadia National Park

Mount Desert Island is home to spectacular Acadia National Park, and for many visitors the two places are one and the same. It's true, Acadia dominates the economy and defines the spirit of Maine's largest island. And it does feature the most dramatic coastal real estate on the eastern seaboard.

Yet, the national park holdings are only part of the appeal of this popular island, which is connected to the mainland via a short, two-lane causeway. Beyond the parklands are scenic harborside villages and remote backcountry roads, quaint B&Bs and exceptionally fine restaurants, oversized 19th-century summer "cottages" and the unrepentantly ticky-tacky tourist trap of Bar Harbor. Those who arrive on the island expecting untamed wilderness invariably leave disappointed. Those who understand that Acadia National Park is but one chapter (albeit a very long one) in the intriguing story of Mount Desert Island will enjoy their visit more thoroughly.

Mount Desert (pronounced "dessert," like the after-dinner sweet) is divided into two lobes separated by Somes Sound, the only legitimate fjord in the continental U.S. (A fjord is a valley carved by a glacier that is subsequently filled with rising ocean water.) Those with a poetic imagination see Mount Desert shaped as a lobster, with one large claw and one small. Most of the parkland is on the meatier east claw, although large swaths of national park exist on the leaner west claw as well. The eastern side is more developed, with Bar Harbor the center of commerce and entertainment. The western side has a more quiet, settled air, and teems with more wildlife than tourists. The island isn't huge—it's only about 15 miles from the causeway to the island's southernmost tip at Bass Harbor Head—so visitors can take their time adventuring. The best plan is to explore mostly by foot, bicycle, or kayak.

ACADIA NATIONAL PARK

It's not hard to fathom why Acadia is consistently one of the biggest draws in the U.S. national park system. The park's landscape is a rich tapestry of rugged cliffs, restless ocean, and deep, silent woods. Acadia's landscape, like so much of the rest of northern New England, was carved by glaciers some 18,000 years ago. A mile-high ice-sheet shaped the land by scouring valleys into their distinctive U shapes, rounding many of the once-jagged peaks, and depositing huge boulders about the landscape, such as the famous 10-foot-high "Bubble Rock," which appears to be perched precariously on the side of South Bubble Mountain.

The park's more recent roots can be traced back to the 1840s, when noted Hudson River School painter Thomas Cole packed his sketchbooks and easels for a trip to this remote island, then home to a small number of fishermen and boat-builders. His stunning renditions of the surging surf pounding against coastal granite were later displayed in New York and helped trigger an early tourism boom as urbanites flocked to the island to escape the heat and to "rusticate." By 1872, national magazines were touting Eden (Bar Harbor's name until 1919) as a desirable summer resort. It attracted the attention of wealthy industrialists, and soon became summer home to

Mount Desert Island / Acadia National Park

Carnegies, Rockefellers, Astors, and Vanderbilts, who built massive summer cottages with literally dozens of rooms (one cottage even boasted 28 bathrooms).

By early in this century, the huge popularity and growing development of the island began to concern its most ardent supporters. Boston textile heir and conservationist George Dorr and Harvard president Charles Eliot, aided by the largesse of John D. Rockefeller, Jr., started acquiring large tracts for the public's enjoyment. These parcels were eventually donated to the federal government, and in 1919 the public land was designated Lafayette National Park, the first national park east of the Mississippi. Renamed Acadia in 1929, the park has grown to encompass nearly half the island.

Rockefeller purchased and donated about 11,000 acres—or one-third of the park. He's also responsible for one of the park's most extraordinary features. Around 1905 a row erupted over whether to allow noisy new motorcars on to the island. Resident islanders wanted these new conveniences to boost their mobility; John D. Rockefeller, Jr., whose fortune was ironically from the oil industry, strenuously objected, preferring the tranquility of the car-free island. Rockefeller went down to defeat on this issue, and the island was opened to cars in 1913. In response, the multimillionaire set about building an elaborate 57-mile system of carriage roads, featuring a dozen gracefully handcrafted stone bridges. These roads, which are today open only to equestrians, bicyclists, and pedestrians, concentrate most densely around Jordan Pond, but also ascend to some of the most scenic open peaks and wind through sylvan valleys.

Just the Facts

GETTING THERE   Acadia National Park is reached from the town of Ellsworth via Route 3. If you're coming from the south, you can avoid the coastal congestion along Route 1 by taking the turnpike to Bangor, picking up I-395 to Route 1A, then continuing south on Route 1A to Ellsworth. While this looks slightly longer on the map, it's by far the quickest route in summer.

Vermont Transit offers bus service to Bar Harbor between June and mid-September. Buses run every few hours from Boston and Portland to Bangor, where one bus daily connects to Bar Harbor. Contact Vermont Transit in Portland for details (☎ **207/772-6587** or 800/451-3292).

Daily flights from Boston to the airport in Trenton, just across the causeway from Mt. Desert Island, are offered by **Colgan Air** (☎ **207/667-7171** or 800/272-5488).

ENTRY POINTS   The main point of entry to Park Loop Road, the park's most scenic byway, is at the visitor center at Hulls Cove. Mount Desert Island consists of an interwoven network of park and town roads, allowing visitors to enter the park at numerous points. A glance at a park map (available at the visitor center) will make these access points self-evident. The entry fee is collected at a toll booth on Park Loop Road one-half mile north of Sand Beach.

VISITOR CENTERS   Acadia maintains two visitor centers. The **Thompson Island Information Center** (☎ **207/288-3411**) on Route 3 is the first you'll pass as you enter Mount Desert Island. This is open May through mid-October and is operated jointly by the park service and the island's chambers of commerce. It's a good stop for lodging and restaurant information; if you're primarily interested in information about the park itself, continue on Route 3 to the **National Park Service's Hulls Cove Visitor Center** (☎ **207/288-5262**), about 7.5 miles beyond Thompson Island. This attractive stone-walled center includes professionally prepared park service displays, such as a large relief map of the island, natural history exhibits, and a short introductory film. You can also request free brochures about hiking trails and the carriage roads, or purchase postcards and more detailed guidebooks. The center is open mid-April through October. In winter, information is available at the **park's headquarters** (☎ **207/288-3338**) on Route 233 between Bar Harbor and Somes Sound.

PARK ACCOMMODATIONS   Unlike many of the other "crown jewel" national parks, Acadia doesn't have its own rustic park lodge. In fact, the park itself offers no overnight accommodations at all, other than two campgrounds (see below). But visitors don't have to go far to find a room. Bar Harbor especially is teeming with motels and inns; the rest of the island has a smattering of hostelries. See "Where to Stay," below.

SEASONS   Visit Acadia in September if you can finagle it. Between Labor Day and the foliage season of early October, the days are often warm and clear, the nights have a crisp northerly tang, and you can avoid the hassles of congestion, crowds, and pesky insects. Not that the park is empty in September. Bus tours seem to proliferate this month, which results in crowds of tourists at the most popular sites. Not to worry: If you walk just a few feet away (literally, in some cases) you can find solitude and an agreeable peacefulness. Hikers and bikers have the trails and carriage roads to themselves.

Summer, of course, is peak season at Acadia. Some of the roads in and around the park can resemble New York's Central Park at rush hour if you arrive at the wrong time. That's no surprise. The weather is perfect for just about any outdoor activity in July and August. Most days are warm (in the 70s or 80s), with afternoons frequently cooler owing to ocean breezes. While sun seems to be the norm, come prepared for rain and fog, which are both frequent visitors to the Maine coast. And once or twice each summer a heat wave will settle into the area, producing temperatures in the 90s, dense haze, and stifling humidity, but this rarely lasts more than two or three days. Soon enough, a brisk north wind will blow in from the Arctic, churning up the waters and forcing visitors into sweaters at night. Sometime around the last two weeks of August, a cold wind will blow through at night and you'll smell the approach of autumn, with winter not far behind it.

The snowy season is growing in popularity, especially among resident Mainers who are notoriously stubborn in refusing to leave the state for vacations. After a coastal snowstorm, outdoor enthusiasts flock to the carriage roads to explore the snowy depths of the park with cross-country skis and snowshoes. Be aware that snow tends to be transitory along the coast, and it's not uncommon to have rain or a thaw follow close on the heels of a good blizzard.

AVOIDING THE CROWDS   Late summer and early fall are the best times to miss out on the mobs yet still enjoy the weather. If you do come during midsummer, try to venture out early morning and early evenings to see the most popular spots, like the Thunder Hole or the summit of Cadillac Mountain. Setting off into the woods is also a good strategy. About four out of five visitors restrict their tours to the loop road and a handful of other major attractions, leaving the Acadia backcountry open for more adventurous spirits. The carriage roads below Jordan Pond are closed to mountain bikes, and are a great place for an easy ramble without too much company.

The best guarantee of solitude is to head to the more remote outposts managed by Acadia, especially Isle au Haut and Schoodic Peninsula. These are covered in detail elsewhere in this guide.

REGULATIONS   Guns may not be used in the park; if you have a gun, it must be "cased, broken down, or otherwise packaged against use." Fires and camping are allowed only at designated areas. Pets must be on a leash at all times. Seat belts must be worn in the national park (this is a federal law). Don't remove anything from the park, either man-made or natural; this includes cobblestones from the shore.

FEES   A week-long park pass, which includes unlimited trips on Park Loop Road, costs $5 per car (no extra charge per passenger). Daily passes are not available.

RANGER PROGRAMS   Frequent ranger programs are offered throughout the year. These include talks at campground amphitheaters and tours at various locations around the island. Examples are the Otter Point nature hike, Mr. Rockefeller's bridges walk, Frenchman Bay cruise (rangers provide commentary on commercial trips; make reservations with boat owners), and a discussion of changes in Acadia's landscape. Ask for a schedule of events at the visitor center or either of the two campgrounds.

SEEING THE HIGHLIGHTS

Three or four days are a good minimum for exploring the park. If you're passing through just briefly, try to work in at least three of the four following activities.

DRIVE THE PARK LOOP ROAD   This almost goes without saying, since it's the park's premier attraction. This 20-mile road runs along the island's eastern shore, then loops inland along Jordan Pond and Eagle Lake. The road runs alternately high along the shoulders of brawny coastal mountains, then dips down along the boulder-strewn coastlines. The dark granite is broken by the spires of spruce and fir, and the earthy tones contrast sharply with the frothy white surf and the steely, azure sea. The two-lane road is one-way along the coastal stretches; the right-hand lane serves as a parking area, so it's easy to make frequent stops to admire the vistas.

Ideally, visitors will take at least two trips on the loop road. The first is for the sheer exhilaration and to get a feel for the lay of the land. On the second trip around, plan to stop more frequently, leaving your car behind while you explore the trails and coastline.

Attractions along the coastal loop include the **Robert Abbe Museum of Stone Age Antiquities** (☎ 207/288-3519), a small museum with anthropological artifacts that really isn't worth the $2 admission; scenic Sand Beach, which is the only sand beach on the island and offers good swimming during infrequent hot spells and brutally cold swimming the rest of the time; Thunder Hole is a shallow oceanside cavern into which the surf surges, compresses, and bursts out with explosive force and a concussive sound (young kids seem to be endlessly mesmerized by this); and Cadillac Mountain, at 1,530 feet the highest point on the island and the place first touched by the sun in the U.S. during certain times of year. The mountain top is accessible by car, but the lot at the summit is often overflowing. You're better off hiking to the top, or scaling a more remote peak.

HIKE A MOUNTAIN   This quintessential Acadia experience shouldn't be missed. The park is studded with low "mountains" (they'd be called hills elsewhere) that offer superb views over the island and the open ocean. The trails weren't simply hacked out of the hillside; they were crafted by experienced stonemasons and others with high aesthetic intent. The routes aren't the most direct, or the easiest to build. But they're often the most scenic, taking advantage of fractures in the rocks, picturesque ledges, and sudden vistas. See "Hiking" below for suggested climbs.

BIKE A CARRIAGE ROAD   The 57 miles of carriage road built by John D. Rockefeller, Jr. are among the park's most extraordinary hidden treasures. (See introduction above for a brief history.) While built for horse and carriage, these grass-and-gravel roads are ideal for cruising by mountain bike. Park near Jordan Pond and plumb the tree-shrouded roads that lace the area, taking time to admire the stonework on the uncommonly fine bridges. Afterwards, stop for tea and popovers at the Jordan Pond House, which has been an island tradition for over a century, although it's unlikely as much Lycra was in evidence 100 years ago. For bike rentals, see "Mountain Biking," below.

EAT A LOBSTER   While you can't feast on boiled lobster served oceanside within Acadia National Park, several lobster pounds offer the opportunity outside the park's borders. The best places are those right on the water, and where there's no pretension or fills. The ingredients for a proper feed at a local lobster pound are a pot of boiling water, a tank of lobsters, some well-worn picnic tables, a good view, and a six-pack of Maine beer. Among the best destinations for lobster are **Beal's Lobster Pier** (☎ 207/244-7178) in Southwest Harbor, which is one of the oldest pounds in the area. **Abel's Lobster Pound** (☎ 207/276-5827) on Route 198 five miles north of Northeast Harbor overlooks the deep blue waters of Somes Sound; eat at picnic tables under the pines or indoors at the restaurant. Abel's is more expensive than the others, but the setting—and the incredible lobster stew—make it worth the money. On the mainland just north of the causeway, turn on Route 230 and head four miles to **Oak Point Lobster Pound** (☎ 207/667-8548) for its lobster served up with a sensational view of the island's rocky hills.

OUTDOOR RECREATION

CANOEING   Mount Desert's several ponds offer scenic if limited canoeing, and most have public boat access. Canoe rentals are available at the north end of Long

Pond in Somesville from **National Park Canoe Rentals** (☎ 207/244-5854). Long Pond is the largest of the island ponds, and offers good exploring. Pack a picnic and spend a few hours reconnoitering the pond's three-mile length. Much of the west shore and the southern tip lies within Acadia National Park.

CARRIAGE RIDES   Carriage rides are offered by **Wildwood Stables** (☎ 207/ 276-3622), a national park concessioner located a half-mile south of Jordan Pond House. The one-hour Day Mountain trip departs three times daily, yields wonderful views, and costs $12 for adults, $7 for children 6–12, and $4 for children 2–5. Longer tours are also available; reservations are encouraged.

HIKING   **Acadia National Park** has 120 miles of hiking trails in addition to the 57 miles of carriage roads. The **Hulls Cove Visitors' Center** offers a one-page chart of area hikes; combined with the park map, this is all you'll need since the trails are well-maintained and well-marked. It's not hard to cobble together loop hikes to make your trips more varied. Coordinate your hiking with the weather; if it's damp or foggy, you'll stay drier and warmer strolling the carriage roads. If it's clear and dry, head for the highest peaks with the best views.

Among the most extraordinary trails is the **Dorr Ladder Trail,** which departs from Route 3 near The Tarn just south of the Sieur de Monts entrance to the Loop Road. This trail begins with a Homeric series of stone steps ascending along the base of a vast slab of granite, then passes through crevasses (not for the wide of girth) and up ladders affixed to the unyielding granite. The views east and south are superb.

An easy lowland hike is around **Jordan Pond,** with the northward leg along the pond's east shore on a hiking trail, and the return via carriage road. It's mostly level, with the total loop measuring 3.3 miles. At the north end of Jordan Pond, consider detouring up the prominent, oddly symmetrical mounds called The Bubbles. The ascents shouldn't take much more than 20 minutes each; look for signs off the Jordan Pond Shore Trail.

On the western side of the island, an ascent of Acadia Mountain and return takes about an hour and a half, but hikers should schedule in some time for lingering while they enjoy the views of Somes Sound and the smaller islands off Mount Desert's southern shores. This 2.5-mile loop hike begins off Route 102 at a trailhead three miles south of Somesville. Head eastward through rolling mixed forest, then begin an ascent over ledgy terrain. Be sure to visit both the east and west peaks (the east peak has the better views), and look for hidden balds in the summit forest that afford unexpected vistas.

MOUNTAIN BIKING   Acadia's carriage roads (see introduction, above) offer some of the most scenic, relaxing mountain biking anywhere in the United States. The 57 miles of grassy lanes and gravel road were maintained by John D. Rockefeller, Jr. until his death in 1960. Afterwards, they became somewhat shabby and overgrown until a major restoration effort brought them back beginning in 1990. The roads today are superbly restored and maintained. Where the carriage roads cross private land (generally between Seal Harbor and Northeast Harbor), they're closed to mountains bikes. Please respect these restrictions.

A map of the carriage roads is available at the park's visitor center. More detailed guidebooks are sold at area bookstores.

Mountain bike rentals are easily found along Cottage Street in Bar Harbor. Some bike shops include locks and helmets as basic equipment; ask what's included before you rent. Try **Bar Harbor Bicycle Shop** (☎ 207/288-3886) at 141 Cottage St.; **Acadia Outfitters** (☎ 207/288-8118) at 106 Cottage St.; or **Acadia Bike & Canoe** (☎ 207/288-9605) at 48 Cottage St.

SEA KAYAKING   Experienced sea kayakers flock to Acadia to test their paddling skills along the surf at the base of rocky cliffs, to venture out to the offshore islands, and to probe the still, silent waters of Somes Sound. Novice sea kayakers also come to Acadia to try their hand for the first time with guided tours, which are offered by several outfitters. While many new paddlers have found their inaugural experiences gratifying, others complain that the quantity of paddlers taken out on quick tours during peak season make the experience a little too much like a cattle call to truly enjoy. The following outfitters each offer half-and full-day tours: **Acadia Outfitters** (☎ 207/288-8118) at 106 Cottage St.; **Coastal Kayaking Tours** (☎ 207/288-9605) at 48 Cottage St., and **National Park Sea Kayak Tours** (☎ 207/288-0342) at 137 Cottage St.

CAMPING

The National Park Service maintains two campgrounds within Acadia National Park. Both are extremely popular; during July and August expect both to fill by early to mid-morning. The more popular of the two is **Blackwoods** (☎ 207/288-3274), located on the island's eastern side. Access is from Route 3 five miles south of Bar Harbor. Bikers and pedestrians have easy access to the loop road from the campground via a short trail. The campground has no public showers, but an enterprising business offers clean showers for a modest fee at an operation just outside the campground entrance. Camping fees are $15 and limited reservations are accepted through a commercial **reservation service** (☎ 800/365-2267).

Seawall (☎ 207/244-3600) is on the quieter, western half of the island near the fishing village of Bass Harbor. This is a good base for road biking, and several short coastal hikes are within easy striking distance. The campground is open late May through September on a first-come, first-served basis. No showers. The fee is $13 for those arriving by car, $8 for those coming by foot or bike.

Private campgrounds handle the overflow. The region from Ellsworth south boasts some 14 private campgrounds, which offer varying amenities. Contact the **Thompson Island Information Center** (☎ 207/288-3411) for details.

Another option is **Lamoine State Park** (☎ 207/667-4778), which faces Mount Desert across the cold waters of northernmost Frenchman Bay. This is an exceptionally pleasant, quiet park with private sites and a small beach about a half-hour's drive from the action at Bar Harbor. The campground rarely fills to capacity, even during the balmiest days of summer.

BAR HARBOR

Bar Harbor has its historical roots in the grand resort era of the late 19th century. Sprawling hotels and boarding houses once cluttered the shores and hillsides, as the newly affluent middle class flocked here in summer by steamboat and rail from Boston, New York, Philadelphia, and Washington, D.C. When the resort was at its peak near the turn of the last century, Bar Harbor had rooms enough to accommodate some 5,000 visitors. Along with the hotels and guest houses, hundreds of cottages were built by the most wealthy rusticators who came here season after season.

The tourist business continued to grow through the early part of the 1900s, then all but collapsed as the Great Depression and the growing popularity of automobile travel doomed the era of the extended vacation. Bar Harbor was dealt a further blow in 1947, when a fire fueled by an unusually dry summer and fierce northwest winds leveled many of the most opulent cottages and much of the rest of the town. (To this day, no one knows how the fire started.) The fire destroyed five hotels, 67 cottages, and 170 homes. In all, some 17,000 acres of the island were burned. Downtown Bar

Bar Harbor

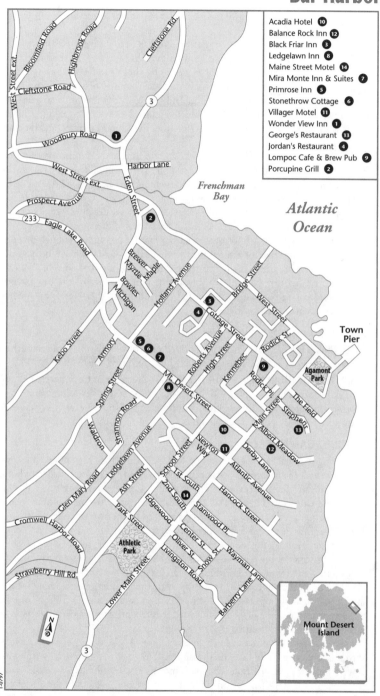

Acadia Hotel **10**
Balance Rock Inn **12**
Black Friar Inn **3**
Ledgelawn Inn **8**
Maine Street Motel **14**
Mira Monte Inn & Suites **7**
Primrose Inn **5**
Stonethrow Cottage **6**
Villager Motel **11**
Wonder View Inn **1**
George's Restaurant **13**
Jordan's Restaurant **4**
Lompoc Cafe & Brew Pub **9**
Porcupine Grill **2**

Frenchman
Bay

Atlantic
Ocean

Town
Pier

Agamont
Park

Athletic
Park

Mount Desert
Island

1-0797

Harbor was spared, and many of the grand homes in town along the oceanfront were missed by the conflagration.

After a period of quiet slumber, Bar Harbor has been rejuvenated and rediscovered in recent years as tourists have poured into this area and entrepreneurs have followed them, opening dozens of restaurants, shops, and boutiques. The less charitable regard Bar Harbor as just another tacky tourist mecca—Pigeon Forge, Tennessee, with moosehorns and spruce. And it does share some of those traits—the downtown hosts a proliferation of T-shirt vendors, ice-cream shops, and souvenir places. Crowds spill off the sidewalk and into the street in midsummer, and the traffic and congestion can be truly appalling.

But Bar Harbor's vibrant history, quirky architecture, and beautiful location along Frenchman Bay allow it to rise above its station in life as mild diversion for tourists. Most of the island's inns, motels, and B&Bs are located here, as are dozens of fine restaurants, making it a desirable base of operations. Bar Harbor is also the best destination for the usual supplies and services; there's a decent grocery story and laundromat, and you can stock up on other necessities of life.

As for the congestion, it's fortunate that Bar Harbor is compact enough that once you find a parking space or a room for the night, the whole town can be navigated conveniently on foot. Arriving here early in the morning also considerably improves your odds of securing parking within easy striking distance of the town center. *Suggestion:* Explore Bar Harbor before and after breakfast, then set off for the hills, woods, and coast the rest of the day.

Essentials

GETTING THERE   Bar Harbor is located on Route 3 about 10 miles southeast of the causeway. It's also accessible by daily bus from Bangor (see above).

VISITOR INFORMATION   The **Bar Harbor Chamber of Commerce,** P.O. Box 158, Bar Harbor, ME 04609 (☎ **207/288-5103**) stockpiles a huge amount of information about local attractions at its offices at 93 Cottage Street. Write or call in advance for a full guide to area lodging.

Exploring Bar Harbor

Wandering the small commercial area on foot is a good way to get a taste of the town. Don't overlook the residential side streets, which are leafy and quiet, lined with homes that range from Victorian quaint to unremarkable. One of downtown's special attractions is the **Criterion Theater** (☎ **207/288-3441**), a movie house built in 1932 in a classic art deco style and which has so far avoided the horrors of multiplexification. The 900-seat theater, located on Cottage Street, shows first-run movies in summer and is worth the price of admission for the beautiful interiors; the movie is secondary.

The best views in town are from the foot of Main Street at grassy Agamont Park, overlooking the town pier and Frenchman Bay. From here, set off past the Bar Harbor Inn on the Shore Path, a winding, wide trail that follows the shoreline for a short distance along a public right of way. The pathway passes in front of many of the elegant summer homes (some converted to inns), offering a superb vantage point to view the area's architecture.

From the path, you'll also have an open view of The Porcupines, a cluster of spruce-studded islands just off the shore. This is a good spot to witness the powerful force of glacial action. The south-moving glacier ground away at the islands, creating a gentle slope facing north. On the south shore, away from the glacial push (glaciers simply melted when they retreated north), is a more abrupt, cliff-like shore.

The resulting islands look like a small group of porcupines migrating southward—or so early visitors imagined.

One of the most elaborate of Bar Harbor's magnificent summer cottages—called The Turrets—is now the centerpiece of the **College of the Atlantic** (☎ 207/288-5015), a school founded in 1969 with a strong emphasis on environmental education. The Turrets is an impressively turreted stone castle built in 1895, featuring a broad porch and drop-dead spectacular views of the bay. Part of the ground floor has been converted to a natural history museum, which is open to the public. While the exhibits are well done and informative, the real value for visitors may be the home and its view. The museum is open daily 9am to 5pm June 15 to Columbus Day (10am to 4pm from Labor Day on); admission is $2.50 adults, $1.50 seniors and teens, and $1 children 12 and under.

Bar Harbor also makes a terrific base for offshore whale watching. Several tour operators offer excursions in search of humpbacks, finbacks, and others. The largest of the fleet is the *Friendship IV* (☎ **207/288-2386** or 800/942-5374), which operates out of the **Bluenose Ferry Terminal** one mile north of Bar Harbor. The tours are on a fast, twin-hulled excursion boat that can hold 140 passengers in a heated cabin. **Sea Bird Watcher Company** (☎ **207/288-2025** or 800/247-3794) runs whale tours on a 72-foot boat from the Golden Anchor Pier in Bar Harbor, and also offers birdwatching trips to offshore islands to view puffins and terns. **Frenchman Bay Boat Cruises** (☎ **207/288-3322** or 800/508-1499) takes passengers in search of whales aboard the 105-foot, two deck Whale Watcher, and offers a handy pick-up service at many hotels and inns.

WHERE TO STAY

Bar Harbor has hundreds of hotel, motel, and inn rooms, and they all share one thing in common: they are all filled during the busy days of midsummer. I've seen discouraged travelers sent packing for Bangor, some 50 miles north, when they discovered that not one empty bed existed on Mount Desert or in the Ellsworth area. It's essential to book your room as early as possible.

In addition to the inns listed below, there are dozens of motels, many of which line Route 3 north of Bar Harbor. Be aware that even the most basic of rooms can be quite expensive during the peak season, so you should be seated when calling to inquire about room rates. There's virtually no motel available for less than $50 during the summer; bed-and-breakfasts start at about $85.

Reputable motels and hotels offering rooms under $100 include the conveniently located **Villager Motel,** 207 Main St. (☎ 207/288-3211) a family-run motel with 63 rooms; the 79-room **Wonder View Inn,** 50 Eden St. (☎ 207/288-3358 or 800/341-1553) with its sweeping bay views; the downtown **Maine Street Motel,** 315 Main St. (☎ 207/288-3188 or 800/333-3188) and the budget **Acadia Hotel,** 20 Mount Desert St. (☎ 207/288-5721).

For a gourmet experience, don't overlook LeDomaine (see the "Down East" section), which has been catering graciously to guests for half-a-century on the mainland in Hancock.

A number of newer, full-service hotels cluster near the Bluenose Ferry Terminal; try this area first if you arrive late without a reservation.

✪ **Balance Rock Inn.** 21 Albert Meadow, Bar Harbor, ME 04609. ☎ **207/288-2610** or 800/753-0494. 21 rms. A/C MINIBAR TV TEL. Peak season $150–$350 double, including breakfast; off-season $95–$255. AE, DISC, MC, V. Open early May through Oct. Directions: Albert Meadow is off Main St. at Butterfield's grocery store.

Pillow Talk

Bar Harbor is the bedroom community for Mount Desert Island, with hundreds of hotel, motel, and inn rooms. Be forewarned that all share one thing in common: they're filled during the busy days of mid-summer. It's essential to book your room as early as possible.

A number of modern hotels and motels cluster along Route 3 just northeast of the village center; this is your best bet if you arrive without reservations. Be aware that even the most basic of rooms can be frightfully expensive in July and August. There's virtually no motel room available for less than $50 during the summer; bed-and-breakfasts start at about $85.

In the full listings on the adjacent pages there's space enough to review just a handful of the best choices. These represent only a fraction of the accommodations available. Don't despair if you can't book a room in any of these fine establishments. There are still dozens of other good options, including those listed below.

The Bar Harbor Inn (Newport Drive; ☎ 800/248-3351 or 207/288-3351) is a sprawling complex of 153 rooms in three buildings perfectly situated on the downtown waterfront. Great views abound from Oceanfront and Main Inn; the less expensive Newport building lacks the views but is comfortable and contemporary. Amenities include a pool and dining room overlooking the harbor. The inn is open year-round; rates are $115–$225 during the peak summer season, and include a continental breakfast.

The Acadia Inn (98 Eden St.; ☎ 800/638-3636 or 207/288-3500) opened in 1996. This modern, stylish three-story hotel features an outdoor pool and Jacuzzi. Peak season rates are $115–$225 including a continental breakfast.

The Golden Anchor (55 West St.; ☎ 800/328-5033 or 207/288-5033) is smack on the waterfront, with some rooms looking across the harbor toward the town pier and others out to Bar Island. (The less expensive rooms have no view at all.)

It's quite simple: If you can afford it, stay here. Everyone seems to speak in whispers, even the staff. It's not so much because it's a snooty place, but because one and all seem in awe of this oceanfront mansion, built in 1903. It's an architecturally elaborate affair of grey shingles with cream, maroon, and forest green trim. The common rooms are expansive yet comfortable, with pilasters and coffered ceilings, arched doorways and leaded windows. There's even a baby grand piano. The favored spot among serious loungers is the front covered patio with its green wicker furniture and a small bar off to the side. The sound of the sea drifts up here gently. And then there's the view, which I'd wager is the best in Maine: you look across a wonderful pool, and down a long lawn framed by hardwoods to the rich, blue waters of Frenchman Bay. The service is impeccable, and the rooms wonderfully appointed, many with whirlpool baths or fireplaces. The inn also features a fitness center in an air-conditioned carriage house on the property.

Black Friar Inn. 10 Summer St., Bar Harbor, ME 04609. ☎ **207/288-5091.** 7 rms (3 with private hall baths; 6 with shower only). A/C. $85–$135 double, including full breakfast. Discounts offered mid-Oct to mid-June. MC, V.

The Black Friar Inn, tucked on a sidestreet overlooking the municipal building parking lot, is easily overlooked. But this yellow-shingled structure with quirky pediments and a somewhat eccentric air offers surprises inside. A former owner "collected"

There's a pool and hot tub right at the harbor's edge, and an oceanfront dining room that serves basic fare. Peak season rates range from $110–$165.

The Park Entrance Oceanfront Motel (Route 3; ☎ **800/288-9703** or 207/288-9703) is nicely situated on 10 handsome waterfront acres close to the park visitor center. The inn has an attractive private pier and cobblestone beach, and an outdoor swimming pool and Jacuzzi. Summer rates are $129–$149.

Great views greet guests at the **Atlantic Eyrie Lodge** (Highbrook Rd., ☎ **800/422-2843** or 207/288-9786), perched on a hillside above Route 3. Peak rates are $125–$180. Some units have kitchenettes and balconies; all share access to the ocean-view pool.

The oceanside **Holiday Inn SunSpree Resort** (123 Eden St.; ☎ **800/234-6835** or 207/288-9723) has 217 rooms, a children's program, and numerous amenities, including a heated pool, putting green, marina, and restaurant and lounge. Rooms rates run $149–$189.

The Colony (Route 3, Hulls Cove; ☎ **800/524-1159** or 207/288-3383) consists of a handful of motel rooms and a battery of 55 cottages arrayed around a long green. The Colony is across Route 3 from a cobblestone beach, and a 10-minute drive into Bar Harbor. The rooms are furnished in a simple '70s style that won't win any awards, but all are comfortable; many have kitchenettes. Summer rates are $50–$90 for two.

Reputable motels and hotels offering rooms under $100 include the conveniently located **Villager Motel** (207 Main St.; ☎ **207/288-3211**), a family-run motel with 63 rooms; the 79-room **Wonder View Inn** (50 Eden St.; ☎ **800/341-1553** or 207/288-3358) with its sweeping bay views; the downtown **Maine Street Motel**, (315 Main St.; ☎ **800/333-3188** or 207/288-3188) and the B&B-style **Acadia Hotel**, (20 Mount Desert St.; ☎ **207/288-5721**).

interiors and installed them throughout the house. Among them is a replica of the namesake Black Friar Pub in London, complete with elaborate carved wood paneling (it's now a common room), stamped tin walls in the breakfast room, and a doctor's office (now a guest room). The Black Friar's rooms are carpeted and furnished with a mix of antiques, and most are quite small and cozy. The least expensive are the two garret rooms on their third floor, which have private bathrooms down a hall. The inn's friendly Brittany, named Falke, has the run of the place. No smoking.

Ledgelawn Inn. 66 Mt. Desert St., Bar Harbor, ME 04609. ☎ **207/288-4596** or 800/274-5334. Fax 207/288-9968. 33 rms (9 with shower only). A/C TV TEL. July and Aug 115–$225 double, including full breakfast; discounts in the off season. AE, DISC, MC, V. Open late May through late Oct.

The Ledgelawn features a handsome sun porch lounge with a full bar, and when you first set foot inside you half expect to find Bogart flirting with Bacall in a corner. This hulking cream and maroon 1904 "cottage" sits on a village lot amid towering oaks and maples, and has a mid-century elegance to it, although updated with modern amenities; on the property you'll find a pool and hot tub for soaking. Inside, the recently renovated common area around the fireplace has a plush, quiet, upholstered feel. The breakfast room is unexpectedly formal; it feels more like a place for fancy wedding reception. The guest rooms all vary somewhat as to size and mood, but all are comfortably if not stylishly furnished with antiques and reproductions. Some rooms feature fireplaces that burn Duraflame-style logs.

Mira Monte Inn. 69 Mount Desert St., Bar Harbor, ME 04609. ☎ **207/288-4263** or 800/553-5109. Fax 207/288-3115. 12 rms, 3 suites (some with shower only). A/C TV TEL. $115–$150 double, suites $180. Rates include breakfast. Open May through Oct. AE, DISC, MC, V.

This handsome greyish-green Italianate mansion, built in 1864, is blessed with a profusion of balconies and fireplaces—most guest rooms have one or the other; some have both. The common rooms are furnished in a pleasant country Victorian style, and there's a piano for evening entertainment. The two-acre grounds are handsomely landscaped, and include a cutting garden to keep the house in flowers. There's a nice brick terrace away from the street, which makes a fine place to enjoy breakfast on warm summer mornings. As for decor, the guest rooms tend to be a bit schizophrenic. Some are dim and almost sepulchral in that heavy Victorian style; others have the bright and airy feel of a country farmhouse. Ask to look first to find a room that fits your tastes. Unless you're traveling with a family, I'd avoid the suites in a separate outbuilding; they're not all that charming, and guests have the vague feel of staying in someone's borrowed apartment.

Mount Desert YWCA. 36 Mount Desert St., Bar Harbor ME 04609. ☎ **207/288-5008.** 35 rms (all shared bath). $25 single; $85 per week single; $140 per week double. No credit cards.

If you're a woman traveling alone, the undisputed best deal in Bar Harbor is the $25 bed at the YWCA, which is clean and centrally located. It's available only to women, and rooms can be rented by the night or week. If you choose to stay a week or more you'll be assessed a $10 membership fee and a $25 security deposit (refundable). The Y is open year round, but during summer it fills up rather fast; it's advisable to make reservations early.

Primrose Inn. 73 Mount Desert St., Bar Harbor, ME 04609. ☎ **207/288-4031** or 800/543-7842. 10 rms plus 5 efficiencies (1 with shower only). TV TEL. Peak season $90–$145 double, shoulder seasons $85–$140; suites $650–$850 per week. Daily rates include breakfast. Open May through late Oct. AE, DISC, MC, V.

This handsome pale-green and maroon Victorian stick-style inn, originally built in 1878, is one of the more noticeable properties on mansion row along Mount Desert St. It's distinctive architecture has been not only preserved, but improved upon with a major addition in 1987 that added 10 rooms with private baths, and resulted in a number of balconies being added. The inn is comfortable and tinged with elegance inside, although it has a distinctly informal air to it, which encourages guests to mingle and relax in the common room, decorated in a light country Victorian style and complete with piano. The guest rooms are all carpeted, and many feature whirlpools or fireplaces. The suites in the rear are spacious and comfortable, and the efficiencies make sense for families who could benefit from a kitchen (for rent by the week only). Light refreshments are served to all guests in the afternoon.

Stonethrow Cottage. 67 Mount Desert St., Bar Harbor, ME 04609. ☎ **207/288-3668** or 800/769-3668. 7 rms. TEL. $135–$175 double, including continental breakfast. MC, V.

The Stonethrow Cottage, which opened in 1995, feels very much like an English country cottage. Fans of Beatrix Potter will be at home here. Fans of a more rustic, early American style will not. Floral prints decorate the walls, and Kohler artist-edition sinks sport an aggressive floral motif. A music box signals guests to breakfast in the morning. The home dates to 1860, but three years of extensive renovating have given the interior a shiny, modern gloss, with whirlpools and bright gold fixtures in the bathrooms. The breakfast room is decorated in a faux-French empire style, which may strike some as a bit stiff and sterile. If you're looking for quiet, request one of the guest rooms facing the back lawn and away from the road. If you're looking for romance, ask for the honeymoon suite (naturally enough), with its whirlpool in a turret surrounded by three windows.

WHERE TO DINE
Expensive
George's. 7 Stephens Lane. ☎ **207/288-4505.** Reservations recommended. Entrees $20; appetizer, entree & dessert packages $29. AE, DISC, MC, V. Daily 5:30–10pm; shorter hours after Labor Day. Closed Nov–early May. MEDITERRANEAN-INSPIRED AMERICAN.

You may despair of ever finding George's. Don't. You must persevere. For George's is one of Bar Harbor classics, offering fine dining in informal surroundings for nearly two decades. (By the way, it's located in the small clapboard cottage behind Main St.'s First National Bank.) George's captures the joyous feel of summer nicely in its setting, with four smallish dining rooms (with plenty of open windows) and additional seating on the terrace outside, which is the best place to watch the gentle dusk settle over town. The service is upbeat, and the meals are wonderfully prepared. All entrees sell for one price ($20), and include salad, vegetable, and potato or rice. You won't go wrong with the basic choices, like steamed lobster or roast chicken, but you're better off opting for the more adventurous fare like tangerine scallops or the ever-changing preparations of game or lamb.

✪ **Porcupine Grill.** 123 Cottage St. ☎ **207/288-3884.** Reservations recommended. Main courses, $17.50–$21.95. AE, DC, MC, V. Summer and fall daily 5:30–9:30pm; off season Fri–Sun only. NEW AMERICAN.

The Porcupine Grill is a pleasant surprise. Housed in a nondescript home on the slightly frayed commercial end of Cottage St., the grill's interior is beautifully arrayed around a magnificent oak bar, which has the regal presence of a magnificent altar. Guest sit upstairs and down amid a smattering of antiques and enjoy the fresh flowers placed about as they peruse a wonderful menu, which is updated frequently to reflect the seasonal changes in the local bounty. You might begin with the delicate salmon cakes, served with a fresh ginger, chili, and coconut sauce, then move on to filet mignon served with portobello mushrooms and wild-boar bacon, or grilled sea scallops with a peppercorn and sun-dried tomato beurre blanc. The signature Porcupine stew is outstanding—a savory melange of lobster, scallops, fish, and mussels served in a tomato-caper broth. Desserts are equally superb.

Moderate
⑤ **Jordan's Restaurant.** 80 Cottage St. ☎ **207/288-3586.** Reservations not accepted. Breakfast $1.70–$6.25; lunch $1.95–$7.50. No credit cards. Daily 5am–2pm. Closed Jan through Mar. DINER.

This unpretentious breakfast and lunch joint has been dishing up filling fare since 1976, and offers a glimpse of Bar Harbor before the latest tourist invasion. It's a popular haunt of local working folks passing through town on one errand or another, but the staff is also genuinely friendly to tourists. Diners can settle into one of the pine booths or at laminated tables and order off the placemat menu, choosing among basic fare like grilled cheese with tomato or a serviceable hamburger that's just $2.75. The soups and chowders are all homemade. Breakfast is offered all day and it's the specialty here; the strawberry and blueberry pancakes are just about worth the drive from anywhere on the island.

Lompoc Cafe and Brewpub. 32 Rodick St. ☎ **207/288-9392.** Reservations not accepted. Sandwiches $3.75–$5.75; dinner $9.95–$13.95. DISC, MC, V. May–Nov daily 11:30am–1am. Closed Dec–April. AMERICAN/ECLECTIC.

The Lompoc Cafe has a well-worn, neighborhood bar feel to it, and it's little wonder that other waiters and waitresses from around Bar Harbor congregate here after hours. The café consists of three sections—there's the original bar in the pine-floored dining room, a small, tidy garden just outside (try your hand at bocce ball), and a small, barn-like structure at the garden's edge to handle the overflow. The on-site brewery produces five unique beers, including a locally popular blueberry ale (I don't much care for it), and the smooth Coal Porter, available in sizes up to the 20-ounce "fatty." Whisky drinkers will be busy here: the Lompoc also claims the largest selection of single-malts north of Boston. Bar menus are usually predictable but this one has some surprises, with an around-the-world-in-80-minutes style selection, with tasty entrees like Indonesian chicken, Mediterranean scallops, shrimp etouffe, and Vermont pork tenderloin. Live music is offered some evenings.

Miguel's Mexican Restaurant. 51 Rodick St. ☎ **207/288-5117.** Reservations not accepted. Main courses $6.95–$13.95. MC, V. Tues–Sun 5–9pm. Closed Nov–May. MEXICAN.

Miguel's serves what's possibly the best Mexican food in Maine amid a festive, boisterous atmosphere. It's slightly out of the limelight of downtown Bar Harbor (Rodick St. runs off Cottage St. just west of Main St.), but it's worth making the short trek if you've got a hankering for Mexican. It's not the best place for a quiet dinner—the terracotta tiles keep the sound bouncing around—but it is the place for delicious blue-corn crab cakes, shrimp fajitas, or the simple but tasty tacos al carbon. Try the rich, earthy homemade molé sauce, which is available with any dish for an extra 75 cents. If you're a drinker with a sweet tooth, the peach daquiris are dandy. During warm nights, there's dining on the patio in front, which is a bit quieter and more intimate.

ELSEWHERE ON THE ISLAND

Acadia National Park is the main island attraction, of course, and Bar Harbor has its charm and character. But there's plenty else to explore outside of these areas. Peaceful, charming villages, deep woodlands, and unexpected ocean views are among the jewels that turn up when one peers beyond the usual places.

ESSENTIALS

GETTING AROUND   The east half of the island is best navigated on Route 3, which forms the better part of a loop from Bar Harbor through Seal Harbor and past Northeast Harbor before returning up the eastern shore of Somes Sound. Route 102 and Route 102A provide access to the island's western half.

VISITOR INFORMATION   The best source of information on the island is at the **Thompson Island Information Center** (☎ 207/288-3411) on Route 3 just south of the causeway connecting Mount Desert Island with the mainland. Another reliable source of local information is **Mount Desert Chamber of Commerce,** P.O. Box 675, Northeast Harbor, ME 04662 (☎ 207/276-5040).

EXPLORING THE OTHER MOUNT DESERT ISLAND

On the tip of the eastern lobe of Mount Desert Island is the staid, prosperous community of Northeast Harbor, long one of the favored retreats among the Eastern Seaboard's upper crust. Those without personal invitations to come as house guests will need to be satisfied with glimpses of the shingled palaces set in the fragrant spruce forests and along the rocky shore. But the village itself is worth investigating.

Set around an attractive, narrow harbor, with the glorious Asticou Inn at its head, Northeast Harbor is possessed of a refined sense of elegance that's best appreciated by finding a vantage point, then sitting and admiring.

One of the best, least publicized places for enjoying views of the harbor is from the understatedly spectacular ✪ **Asticou Terraces** (☎ 207/276-5130). Finding the parking lot can be tricky: head one-half mile south on Route 3 from the junction with Route 198, and look for the small gravel lot on the water side of the road with a sign reading Asticou Terraces. Park here, cross the road on foot, and set off up a magnificent path made of local rock that scales the sheer hillside with expanding views of the harbor and the town. This pathway, with its precise stonework and the occasional bench and gazebo, is one of the Northeast's hidden marvels of landscape architecture. Created by Boston landscape architect Joseph Curtis, who summed here for many years prior to his death in 1928, the pathway seems to blend in almost preternaturally with its spruce-and-fir surroundings, as if it were created by an act of god rather than of man. Curtis donated the property to the public for quiet enjoyment.

Continue on the trail at the top of the hillside and you'll soon arrive at **Curtis's cabin** (open to the public daily in summer), behind which lies the formal Thuya Gardens, which are as manicured as the terraces are natural. These wonderfully maintained gardens, designed by Charles K. Savage, attract flower enthusiasts, students of landscape architecture, and local folks looking for a quiet place to rest. It's well worth the trip. A donation of $2 is requested of visitors to the garden; the terraces are free.

From the harbor visitors can depart on a seaward trip to the beguilingly remote **Cranberry Islands.** You have a couple of options: either travel with a national park guide to Baker Island, the most distant of this small cluster of low islands, and explore the natural terrain. Or hop one of the ferries to either Great or Little Cranberry Island and explore on your own. On Little Cranberry there's a small **historical museum** run by the National Park Service that's worth seeing. Both islands feature a sense of being well away from it all, but neither offers much in the way of tourist amenities so travelers should head out prepared for the possibility of shifting weather.

When leaving Northeast Harbor, plan to depart via Sargent Drive. This one-way route runs through Acadia National Park along the shore of Somes Sound, affording superb views of this glacially carved inlet.

On the far side of Somes Sound, there's good hiking (see above), and the towns of Southwest Harbor and Bass Harbor. These are both home to fishermen and boatbuilders, and are a far cry from the settlements of the landed gentry at Northeast and Seal harbors across the way. In Southwest Harbor, look for the intriguing **Wendell Gilley Museum of Bird Carving** (☎ 207/244-7555) on Route 102 just north of town. Housed in a new building constructed specifically to display fine woodcarving, the museum contains the masterwork of Wendell Gilley, a plumber who took up carving birds as a hobby in 1930. His creations, ranging from regal bald eagles to delicate chickadees, are startlingly lifelike and beautiful. The museum offers woodcarving classes for those inspired by the displays, and a gift shop offers fine woodcarving for sale. It's open daily except Monday June through October; open Friday through Sunday in May, November, and December. The museum is closed January through April. Admission is $3 adults, $1 children 5–12.

WHERE TO STAY

Asticou Inn. Route 3, Northeast Harbor, ME 04662. ☎**207/276-3344** or 800/258-3373. 44 rms. TEL. $224–$310 double, including breakfast and dinner. Main inn open early May to mid-Oct; 3-rm B&B cottage open year-round. DISC, MC, V.

The sprawling Asticou Inn, which dates back to 1883, occupies a prime location at the head of Northeast Harbor. Its weathered grey shingles and layered eaves gives it a slightly stern demeanor, but its yellow windowshades leaven its appearance with a mild eccentricity. The Asticou is, unfortunately, more elegant on the exterior than on the interior. The furnishings, including the plastic porch furniture, seems to have come from some best-forgotten interregnum between the dapper golden era and the present day. Nonetheless, a wonderful Old World gentility seems to seep from the creaking floorboards and through the thin walls. The rooms are simply furnished in a pleasing summer-home style, as if a more opulent decor was somehow too ostentatious. Jackets are requested on men in the evening; the dinner dance and elaborate buffet on Thursday nights in summer are hallowed island traditions and well worth checking out. Most rooms are located in the main inn, although others are across the road in the cheery Cranberry Lodge. The inn shares its grounds with some unfortunate UFO-like cottages.

Claremont. P.O. Box 137, Southwest Harbor, ME 04679. ☎ 207/244-5036 or 800/244-5036. Fax 207/244-3512. 30 rms (2 with tub only), 12 cottages. TEL. July–Labor Day $115–$145 double, including breakfast; $157–$187 including breakfast and dinner; off-season from $75 double. Open early June through mid-Oct.

The early prints of the Claremont, built in 1884, show an austere four-story wooden building with one severe gable overlooking Somes Sound from a low, grassy rise. And the place hasn't changed all that much since then. The Claremont offers nothing fancy or elaborate, just simple, clean, classic New England grace. It's wildly appropriate that the state's most high-profile and combative croquet tournament takes place here annually; all those folks in their whites seem right at home. Most of the guest rooms are bright and airy, furnished with antiques and some old furniture that doesn't quite qualify as "antique." The bathrooms are modern. Guests are assessed a premium for a "seaside" room overlooking the water; it's worth it. There's also a series of cottages, available for a three-day minimum. Some of these are set rustically in the piney woods; others offer pleasing views of the sound.

The common areas and dining rooms are pleasantly appointed in an affable country style. There's a library with rockers, a fireplace, and jigsaw puzzles waiting to be assembled. Two other fireplaces in the lobby take the chill out of the morning air. And Lucy and Buster, the inn's dogs—a golden retriever and a Siberian husky—make the place feel like home. Other amenities on the spacious, private grounds include a clay tennis court, rowboats, bicycles (free to guests), and, of course, the impeccably maintained croquet court. Meals are mainly reprises of American classics like grilled salmon, steamed lobster, and ribeye steak served with a mushroom demi-glaze.

Inn at Southwest. Main St. (P.O. Box 593), Southwest Harbor, ME 04679. ☎ 207/244-3835. 9 rms (3 with shower only; 2 with hall bath). Summer & early fall $105–$124 double; off-season $60–$90. All rates include full breakfast. Open Apr–Oct. MC, V.

Jill Lewis and her golden retriever, Bronco, acquired the architecturally quirky Inn at Southwest in early 1995, and both have done a fine job making this mansard-roofed Victorian a hospitable place. There's a decidedly turn-of-the-century air to this elegant home, but it's restrained on the frills. The guest rooms are named after Maine lighthouses, and are furnished with both contemporary and antique furniture. All rooms have ceiling fans and down comforters. Among the most pleasant rooms is Blue Hill Bay on the third floor, with its large bath, sturdy oak bed and bureau, and glimpses of the scenic harbor. Breakfasts are sit-down gourmet, and feature reason-to-get-up specialties like poached pears in wine sauce, eggs Florentine, and crab potato bake.

WHERE TO DINE

The Burning Tree. Route 3, Otter Creek. ☎ **207/288-9331.** Reservations recommended. Main courses $13.75–$19.50. Wed–Mon 5–9pm, daily in Aug. Closed Columbus Day–mid-June. REGIONAL/ORGANIC.

Located on busy Route 3 between Bar Harbor and Northeast Harbor, The Burning Tree is an easy restaurant to speed right by. But that would be a mistake. This low-key restaurant, with its bright, open and sometimes noisy dining room, serves up the freshest food in the area. Much of the produce and herbs come from its own gardens, with the rest of the ingredients supplied locally wherever possible. Seafood is the specialty here, and its consistently prepared with equal parts imagination and skill. The menu changes often to reflect local availability, with guests ordering from a selection scrawled on chalk boards. Typical appetizers include chili-orange noodle and scallop salad, and smoked salmon served with a corn and caper relish. Entrees might include Cajun crab and lobster au gratin, grilled swordfish with a watercress-lime sauce, or monkfish baked with clams, artichokes, and olives and served with a saffron orzo. Desserts are equally enticing, especially the ginger-orange cheesecake.

Jordan Pond House. Park Loop Rd., Acadia National Park (near Seal Harbor). ☎ **207/276-3316.** Reservations recommended for lunch, tea, and dinner. Lunch $5.50–$12, afternoon tea $5.50–$6.50; dinner $7.50–$14. AE, DISC, MC, V. Late May to late Oct daily 11:30am–8pm (until 9pm July–Aug). Afternoon tea served 2:30–5:30pm. AMERICAN.

The secret to the Jordan Pond House is location, location, location. The restaurant traces its roots back to 1847, when an early farm was established on this picturesque property at the southern tip of a pond looking toward The Bubbles, a pair of sizeable glacially sculpted mounds. Tragedy struck in 1979 when the original structure and its birch-bark dining room was leveled by fire. A more modern, two-level dining room was built in its place—it's got less charm, but it still has the location. If the weather's right, ask for a seat on the lawn with its unrivaled views. Afternoon tea is a hallowed Jordan Pond House tradition. Ladies Who Lunch sit next to Lycra-clad mountain bikers, and everyone feasts on the huge, tasty popovers and strawberry jam served with a choice of teas or fresh lemonade. Dinners are reasonably priced, and include classic resort entrees like prime rib, steamed lobster, and baked haddock.

☼ **Redfield's.** Main St., Northeast Harbor. ☎ **207/276-5283.** Reservations strongly recommended in summer. Main courses, $17.95–$19.95. AE, MC, V. June–Oct Mon–Sat 6–9pm; Nov–May Fri–Sat only. CONTEMPORARY.

One of the great surprises of Redfield's is that a restaurant with such a superb sense of service and such a fine mastery over the kitchen can thrive in such a small village. Then again, quietly wealthy Northeast Harbor isn't your typical small village. Located in a storefront in the tiny downtown, this restaurant is decorated with a subtle and restrained elegance. A couple of large sprays of flowers set the tone. Patrons can enjoy a libation at the wonderful marble bar (it was taken from an old soda fountain), then settle in and peruse the short but tempting menu, which draws its inspiration from cuisines around the world. Choices change with some frequency, but might include appetizers of smoked mussels with a sauce of corn, tomato, and serrano chili; or eggplant and roasted red peppers baked with cheddar on a corn tortilla. The delectable entrees are prepared with style and care, and include a salmon fillet with ginger-tamari sauce, and venison tenderloin with dried cranberries and blueberries.

8 Downeast Coast

The term "Downeast" comes from the old sailing ship days. Ships heading east had the prevailing winds at their backs, making it an easy "downhill" run to the eastern ports. Heading the other way took a bit more skill and determination.

Today, it's a rare traveler who gets far Downeast to explore the rugged coastline of Washington County. For reasons that have never been entirely clear to me, few tourists venture beyond Acadia National Park. But Downeast Maine has substantial appeal. There's an authenticity and remoteness that's been lost in much of coastal Maine. Those seeking a glimpse of a rugged, hardscrabble way of life where independence is revered above all else aren't likely to go away disappointed.

Many residents survive as their forebears did—by scratching a living from the land. Lobstering and fishing remain major sources of income, as do logging and other forest work. Picking wild blueberries in the barrens in late summer and tipping fir trees and making wreaths in late fall round out the income. In recent years, aquaculture has become an important part of the economy around Passamaquoddy Bay; travelers are likely to see vast floating pens where salmon are raised for markets worldwide. More than likely, locals you'll come across stitch together their livelihood with some of each, changing occupations as the seasons roll through.

I've cobbled together a driving tour that could be done in a leisurely two or three days, or in an abbreviated fashion in one hellishly long day from Mount Desert Island (not recommended).

ESSENTIALS

GETTING THERE   Downeast Maine is most commonly reached via Route 1 from Ellsworth. Those heading directly to Washington County in summer can take a more direct, less congested route via Route 9 from Bangor, connecting south to Route 1 via Route 193 or Route 192.

VISITOR INFORMATION   The **Machias Bay Area Chamber of Commerce,** P.O. Box 606, Machias, ME 04654 (☎ **207/255-4402**) provides tourist information from its offices at 23 E. Main St. (Route 1). The offices are open 9am to 5pm Tuesday through Saturday (also open Monday in summer).

A COASTAL DRIVING TOUR

To begin, head east from Ellsworth on Route 1 for 17 miles to West Gouldsboro, then turn south on Route 186 to Winter Harbor. Outside of Winter Harbor, look for the familiar brown-and-white National Park signs indicating:

1. **Schoodic Point.** A pleasing loop drive hooks around the tip of Schoodic Point, which is part of Acadia National Park. The one-way road (no charge) winds along the water and through forests of spruce and fir. Good views of the mountains of Acadia open up across Frenchman Bay; you'll also see buildings of an historic naval station housed on the point. Park near the tip of this isolated promontory and explore the salmon-colored rocks that plunge into the ocean. It's especially dramatic when the seas are running and the surf crashes loudly.

    From here, continue back to Route 186 then on through Prospect Harbor to rejoin Route 1 at Gouldsboro. Head eastward, detour off the highway at Columbia Falls, and look for signs to the historic:

2. **Ruggles House** (☎ **207/483-4637**). This fine Federal home dates from 1818, and was built for Thomas Ruggles, an early timber merchant and civic leader. The

Downeast Coast

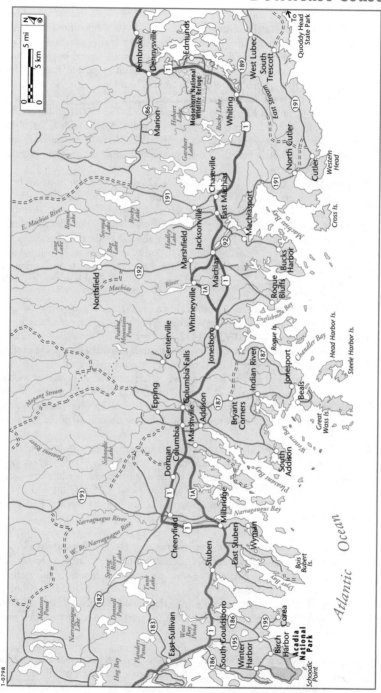

home is very grand and opulent, but in an oddly miniature sort of way. There's a flying staircase in the central hallway, pine doors handpainted to resemble mahogany, and extraordinary wood carvings in the main parlor, done over the course of three years by an English craftsman equipped, legend says, with only a penknife. Locals once said his hand was guided by an angel. The Ruggles House is open June through mid-October daily from 9:30 am to 4:30 pm (Sundays open at 11 am). Tours last 20 minutes to a half-hour, and a donation is requested.

East of Columbia Falls, head south on Route 187 to the rough-hewn fishing village of Jonesport. Look for signs to Beals Island. Cross the bridge; bear right at the fork after crossing the causeway to Great Wass Island. The pavement soon ends; continue slowly past the lobster pound to a small parking lot on the left, providing access to:

3. **Great Wass Preserve.** This exceptional 1,524-acre parcel was acquired by the Nature Conservancy in 1978, and contains an excellent five-mile loop hike covering a wide cross-section of native terrain, including bogs, heath, rocky coastline, and forests of twisted jack pines. Maps and a birding checklist are found in a stand at the parking lot. Follow one fork of the trail to the shoreline; work your way along the storm-tossed boulders to the other fork, then make you way back to your car. If a heavy fog has settled into the area, as often happens, don't let that deter your hike. The dense mist creates a medieval tableau that makes for magical hiking.

Continue along Route 187 back to Route 1, then head eastward to Machias. After crossing the bridge over the Machias River falls, take your second left to:

4. **Burnham Tavern** (☎ 207/255-4432). In June 1775, a month after the Battle of Lexington in Massachusetts, a group of patriots hatched a plan at the gambrel-roofed Burnham Tavern that led to the first naval battle of the Revolutionary War. The armed schooner Margeretta was in Machias harbor to obtain wood for British barracks. The patriots didn't think much of this idea, and attacked the ship using much smaller boats they had commandeered, along with muskets, swords, axes, and pitchforks. The patriots prevailed, killing the captain of the Margaretta in the process.

Visitors can learn all about this curious episode during a tour of the tavern, which was built on a rise overlooking the river in 1770. On display are booty taken from the British ship, along with the original tap table and other historic furniture and ephemera. The one-hour tours cost $2 for adults and 25¢ for children, and are held June through September on Monday through Friday from 9am to 5pm.

☕ **TAKE A BREAK**   The original owner of **Helen's Restaurant** (☎ 207/255-8423) retired in 1994, but this Machias institution still attracts crowds clamoring for good home cooking. The woodgrain-formica interior of this establishment on the eastern edge of town is nothing to write home about, but the homemade pies certainly are. Sidle up to the counter and try a slice of the famed strawberry pie, a perennial local favorite. Don't forget a scoop of vanilla ice cream on top.

From Machias, continue east on Route 1. At the riverside town of East Machias, turn south on Route 91. The road twists and winds past unremarkable homes and through an undistinguished landscape until it passes a huge defense radar installation. (You'll know it when you see it.) Afterwards, you'll come upon classic ocean views, framed with islands studded with spruce and fir, and an open boreal landscape of barrens and heaths. The Route 91 detour doesn't fit into any mold of classic New England beauty (you're never far from a mobile home), but there's a certain Spartan beauty to the entire area.

The town of Cutler has, to my mind, one of the most beautiful harbors in the state, flanked by a cluster of homes, some old, some new, on the hillside above. The town has a village store and not much else, other than a certain stalwart grace in the face of a poor economy and an unforgiving sea.

A couple of miles outside of Cutler keep an eye on the right for:

5. Cutler Coastal Trail. Marked by only a small sign at the edge of a wild meadow, this dramatic loop trail passes through diverse ecosystems, including bogs, barrens, and dark and tangled spruce forests. But the highlight of this trail, which traverses state-owned land, is the mile-long segment along the rocky headlands high above the noisy ocean. Some of the most dramatic coastal views in the state are along this isolated stretch, which overlooks dark-grey-to-black rocks and an often tumultuous sea. Visible on the horizon across the Bay of Fundy is the low, flat Canadian island of Grand Manan. Plan on at least two or three hours for the whole loop, although more time spent whiling away the afternoon hours on the rocks is well worthwhile. If it's damp or foggy, rainpants are advised to fend off the moisture from the low brush along the trail.

Back at your car, continue eastward, and after the harborside hamlet of South Trescott look for a right turn at a white farmhouse with green trim. This is a backroad shortcut to West Quoddy Head, over a narrow road that is partly paved, partly gravel, and which affords some glimpses of the ocean.

At the next stop sign, turn right and head to:

6. West Quoddy Head Light. This famed red-and-white light (it's been likened to a barbershop pole and a candy cane) marks the easternmost point of the United States, and ushers boats into the Lubec Channel between the U.S. and Canada. The light is operated by the Coast Guard and isn't open to the public, but visitors can walk along the high headlands at the adjacent state park. The park overlooks rocky shoals that are ceaselessly battered by high winds, pounding waves, and some of the most powerful tides in the world. Watch for fishing boats straining against the currents, or seals playing in the waves and sunning on the offshore rocks.

From the lighthouse, head to Route 1, backtracking part way on South Lubec Rd., then turn right into Lubec. Follow the signs to the international bridge leading to:

7. Campobello Island, and take a brief excursion out of the country and across the time zone. The U.S. and Canada maintain a joint national park here, called the **Roosevelt Campobello International Park** (☎ 506/752-2922). Head to the visitors center to collect information on hiking at the 2,721-acre park (some spectacular oceanside hikes await you along the 8 miles of trails), but at the very least take a self-guided tour through the wondrous Roosevelt "cottage," an 18-bedroom shingled summer home purchased by James Roosevelt in 1910. James was the father of President Franklin Delano Roosevelt, who summered here virtually every year between 1883 and 1921, when he was stricken with polio. A brief and informative film at the visitor's center helps set the stage; docents at the home can answer any questions you might have. The park is open daily Memorial Day weekend though mid-October from 10 am to 6 pm Eastern time. Admission is free.

CANOEING THE INLAND LAKES

Down East Maine isn't just bold coast and rocky headland. It also lays claim to some of the most scenic and remote lakes and rivers in the state. These tend to play second fiddle to the grand waterways of northern Maine (especially those north of Moosehead Lake), but for my money this area offers more wilderness with less cost and hassle than the more closely regulated and heavily traveled North Woods.

Canoeists could easily occupy themselves for a few days by paddling and portaging around the chain of lakes that feed into West Grand Lake. These bodies of water have wonderful names, like Pocumcus, Sysladobsis, and Scraggly Lakes. The surrounding forest, most of which is owned by timber companies, is less cut-over here than to the north, and a number of primitive campgrounds are managed by the state on islands and shorelines. They're rarely crowded, and often wonderful.

Also nearby are the headwaters of the Machias River. The upper river links the five Machias Lakes, and offers white water that edges into Class III, but is mostly solid Class I and II. A good three-day canoe trip in spring and early summer, when the water is sufficiently high, begins at Fifth Machias Lake and loops around to First Machias Lake. From here, the river takes a more serious turn and continues on through prized Class III white water and waterfalls (portaging needed) to Machias Bay and the coast. Consult the *Appalachian Mountain Club's Quiet Water Canoe Guide to Maine* and the *AMC River Guide/Maine* for more detailed instructions on river running and exploring the area lakes.

If you lack the experience or equipment to explore Washington County's backwaters, link up with **Sunrise County Canoe Expeditions** (☎ **207/454-7708**), which has been offering trips in Maine for 25 years. Adventures of between four and six days are offered throughout the summer on the Class II white water of the St. Croix River, which forms the border with Canada; early summer trips are offered on the more challenging Machias. The price is about $100 per day per person, which includes all equipment and food. Sunrise also offers outfitting and shuttle services for experienced paddlers who choose to travel on their own.

WHERE TO STAY & DINE

Le Domaine. Route 1 (P.O. Box 496), Hancock, ME 04640. ☎ **207/422-3395** or 800/554-8498. Fax 207/422-2316. 7 rms. $200 double ($125 single) including breakfast and dinner. AE, DISC, MC, V.

A gourmand's delight, Le Domaine has firmly established its reputation as one of the most elegant and delightful destinations in Maine. Set on Route 1 about 10 minutes east of Ellsworth, this inn has the continental flair of a impeccable auberge. While the highway in front can be a bit noisy, the garden and woodland walks out back offer plenty of serenity. The rooms are comfortable and tastefully appointed without being pretentious, but the real draw here is the exquisite dining room. Chef Nicole Purslow carries on the tradition begun by her mother in 1946 by offering superb French country cooking in the handsome candle-lit dining room with its pinewood floors and sizeable fireplace. The ever-changing sauces make the entrees sing here, and might feature the Atlantic salmon with a sorrel and shallot sauce, or rabbit served with a robust prune sauce. Plan to check in by 5:30 pm; dinner is served between 6 pm and 9 pm.

Lincoln House. Route 86, Dennysville, ME 04628. ☎ **207/726-3953.** 10rms (6 with shared bath). $116–$144 double, including breakfast and dinner. AE, MC, V.

Located far down east, the Lincoln House consists of a pair of regal, Federal-style mansions facing one another across the Denny's River and the head of tidal Denny's Bay. (The inn is visible from Route 1 as it winds along Cobscook Bay.) The main house, built in 1787, has six guest rooms that share four baths; the 1810 MacLauchlan House has four bedrooms, each with private bath. Both houses are tastefully furnished with antiques and will delight those who have an interest in American history. Ask about the homes' intriguing heritage—John James Audubon stayed in the main house during a birding trip down east in 1832. Rates include a tasty (but not gourmet) single-entree dinner, often featuring American classics like beef Wellington or lobster Newburgh. This is a good destination for those seeking a peaceful respite in a quiet village, and offers a good base for exploring Washington County.

9 The North Woods

Think of the much-mimicked perception/reality ads for Rolling Stone Magazine. Well, there's the perception of Maine's North Woods, and then there's the reality.

The perception is that this is the last outpost of big wilderness in the east, with thousands of acres of unbroken forest, miles of free-running streams, and more azure lakes and rocky mountains than you can shake a canoe paddle at. A look at a road map seems to confirm this, with only a few roads shown here and there amid terrain pocked with lakes. Indeed, Maine accounts for about half of New England, and northern forest with no formal governmental organization—called the "unorganized townships"—comprises about half of Maine. So about one-quarter of New England is undeveloped forest land in northern Maine.

But undeveloped does not mean untouched. The reality is that this forest land is a vast plantation, largely owned and managed by a handful of international paper and timber companies. An extensive network of small timber roads (about 25,000 miles at last count) feed off major arteries and open the region to extensive clear-cutting. This is most visible from the air. In the early 1980s, writer John McPhee noted that much of northern Maine "now looks like an old and badly tanned pelt. The hair is coming out in tufts." That's even more the case now with the acceleration of timber harvesting thanks to technological advances and demands for faster cutting to pay down debts incurred during the buy-and-sell real estate mania of the late 1980s.

While it's not a vast, howling wilderness, the region still has wonderful enclaves where moose and loons predominate, and where it hasn't changed all that much since Thoreau paddled through in the mid-19th century and found it all "moosey and mossy." If you don't arrive expecting utter wilderness, you're less likely to be disappointed.

BANGOR, ORONO & OLD TOWN

These three towns along the western banks of Penobscot River serve as gateways to the North Woods. Bangor, Maine's second largest city, is the last major urban outpost with a full-fledged mall. It's also a good destination for history buffs curious about the early North Woods economy. Bangor was once a thriving lumber port, shipping out millions of board feet cut from the woods to the north and floated down the Penobscot River. While much of the town burned in 1911 and later suffered from overzealous urban renewal, visitors can still discern a robust history just below the surface. Orono and Old Town, two smaller towns to the north, easily offer an afternoon's diversion on rainy days.

ESSENTIALS

GETTING THERE   Bangor is located just off the Maine Turnpike. Take I-395 east, exit at Main St. (Route 1A), and follow signs for downtown. The **Bangor**

Maine's Western Lakes & Mountains

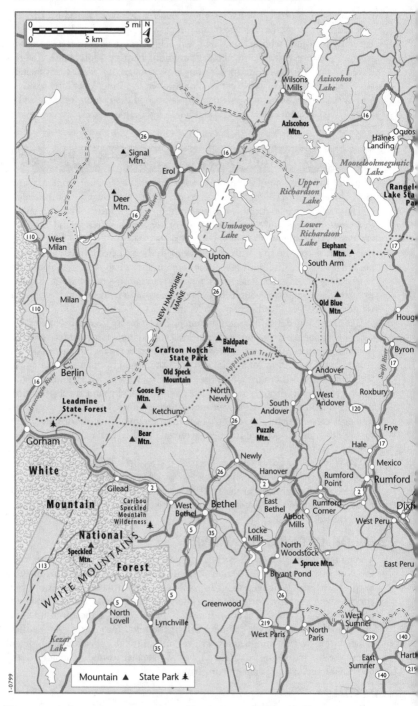

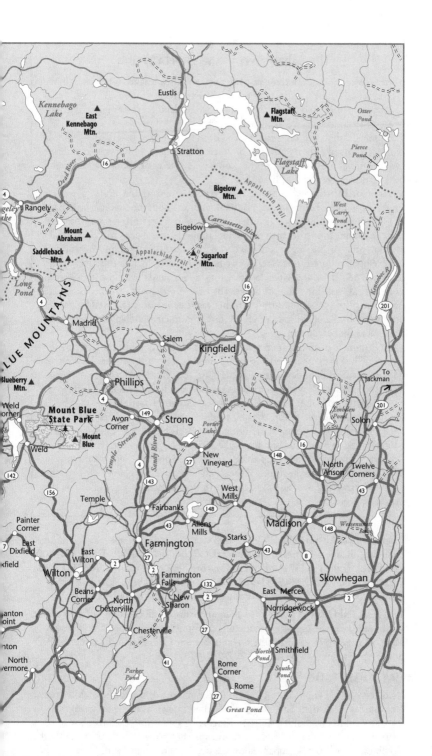

The Debate Over Maine's North Woods

Much of Maine's outdoor recreation takes place on private lands—especially in the North Woods, nine million acres of which are owned by fewer than two dozen timber companies. And this sprawling, uninhabited land is increasingly at the heart of a simmering debate over land-use policies.

Hunters, fishermen, canoeists, rafters, birdwatchers, and hikers have for years been accustomed to having the run of much of the forest. This has been with the tacit permission of the local timber companies, many of which had long and historic ties to woodland communities.

But a lot has changed in recent years, especially during the 1980s. The New England economic boom drove up land values throughout the region, which made lakefront and riverside property prized by outdoor recreationists far more valuable as second home properties than as standing timber. A number of parcels were sold off, and some formerly open land was closed to visitors. What's more, the wild and undeveloped nature of the forest was compromised in many areas (such along southern Moosehead and Mooselookmeguntic shores), and the handwriting seemed to be on the wall for much of the rest of Maine. At the same time, corporate turnovers in the paper industry led to increased debt loads, followed by greater pressure from shareholders to produce more from their woodlands, which led to accelerated timber harvesting.

Environmentalists maintain that the situation in Maine is a disaster in the making. They insist that the forest won't provide jobs in the timber industry or remain a recreational destination if the state continues on its present course. Timber companies deny this, and insist that they're practicing responsible forestry.

The Maine land-use debate has a long ways to go in sorting itself out, but a number of proposals to restore the forest are already circulating. These range from sweeping steps like banning clearcutting and establishing a new 2.6-million acre national park, to more modest notions like encouraging timber companies to practice sustainable forestry and keep access open for recreation through tax incentives. While the debate over the future of the forest isn't quite as volatile here as in the Pacific Northwest, few residents of the North Woods lack strong opinions on the matter.

International Airport (☎ 207/947-0384) is served by several national airlines, including Business Express, **Continental** (☎ 800/525-0280), **Delta** (☎ 800/221-1212), United and USAir Express. **Concord Trailways** (☎ 800/639-3317) and **Vermont Transit** (☎ 800/451-3292 or 800/642-3133) both offer bus service to Bangor from Portland; there's also connecting service to Bar Harbor.

VISITOR INFORMATION   The **Bangor Visitors' Information Office** is staffed in summer near the big, scary statue of Paul Bunyan at the convention center on Main St. near I-395. Contact the **Greater Bangor Chamber of Commerce,** P.O. Box 1443, Bangor, ME 04402 (☎ 207/947-0307).

WHAT TO SEE & DO

IN BANGOR   Despite the city's rich history and the distinguished architecture of the commercial district, Bangor is probably best known as home to horror novelist and one-man Maine industry Stephen King. King's sprawling Victorian home seems a fitting place for the Maine native author; it's got an Addams Family–like creepiness, which is only enhanced by the wrought-iron fence with bats on it. His home isn't open to the public, but it's worth a drive by. To find the house, take the Union St. exit off I-95, head toward town for six blocks, then turn right on West Broadway. I'll leave it to you to figure out which one it is.

The **Bangor Historical Society** (☎ 207/942-5766) offers a glimpse of life in Bangor during its golden days in the last century. The society is housed in a handsome brick home built in 1836 for a prominent businessman, and now features displays of furniture and historical artifacts. The society's collections are at 159 Union St. (just off High St.) and are open for one-hour guided tours Tuesday through Friday from 9 am to 4 pm.

IN ORONO & OLD TOWN   Orono is home to the University of Maine, which was founded in 1868. The campus is spread out on a plain and features a pleasing mix of old and contemporary buildings. On campus, the **Hudson Museum** (☎ 207/581-1901) features exhibits on anthropology and native culture. Housed in a modern, open building, the museum displays crafts and artwork from cultures around the world, including North America.

A few minutes north on Route 178 is the riverside town of Old Town, famous for its canoes, which have been made here since the turn of the century. The **Old Town Canoe Company** (☎ 207/827-5513) is still situated in its original brick factory in the middle of town, and sells new and factory-second canoes from its showroom at 58 Middle St. (Open in summer Monday through Saturday 9am to 6pm, Sunday 10am to 3pm.) Old Town no longer offers tours of the creaky old factory, but there's a continuously running video showing techniques used in contemporary canoe-making.

WHERE TO STAY

Bangor has plenty of guest rooms, but virtually all are located along an unattractive strip off the interstate and near the airport. If you're not choosey, or if you're arriving late at night, these are fine. Be aware that even these can fill up during the peak summer season, so reservations are advised. Try the **Comfort Inn** at 750 Hogan Rd., (☎ 207/942-7899 or 800/338-9966), **Howard Johnson's Motor Lodge** on Odlin Rd. (☎ 207/942-5251 or 800/654-2000), or the **Super 8 Motel** at 462 Odlin Rd (☎ 207/945-5681 or 800/800-8000).

Phenix Inn. 20 Broad St., Bangor, ME 04401. ☎ 207/947-0411. Fax 207/947-0255. 37 rms. A/C TV TEL. Summer/foliage $74.95 double; spring/winter $56.95. All rates include continental breakfast. AE, CB, DC, DISC, MC, V.

Bangor's only downtown hotel is in a striking brick building dating from 1873 and now on the National Register of Historic Places. The exterior shows a confident Victorian exuberance; the interior was modernized in 1983 when the electric and plumbing were replaced, and new walls installed. Trim, attractive guest rooms are comfortably furnished with mahogany reproduction furniture. Some rooms have four-poster beds, but all are carpeted and have wingback chairs for comfortable reading or watching television in the evening. Ask for one of the brighter, quieter corner rooms in the back. The hallway carpets are a bit worn and could use replacing, but overall the inn is a welcome downtown oasis. Plans call for adding a fitness room in 1996.

MOOSEHEAD LAKE REGION

Thirty-two miles long and five miles across at its widest point, Moosehead Lake is Maine's largest lake, and it's a great destination for hikers, boaters, and canoeists. The lake was historically the center of the region's logging activity; paradoxically, that preserved the lake and kept it largely unspoiled by development. Timber companies

Moosehead Lake Area

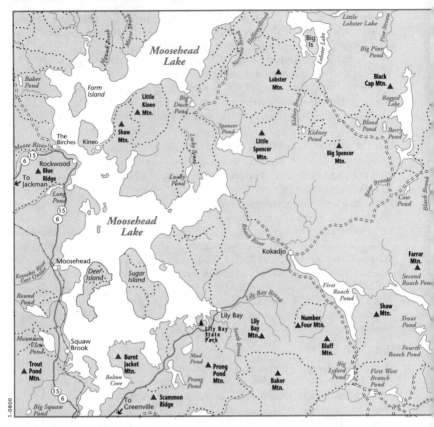

still own much of the twisting shoreline (although the state has acquired a large amount in recent years), and its 350-mile length is mostly unbroken second- or third-growth forest. The second-home building frenzy of the 1980s had some noticeable impact on the southern reaches of the lake, but the woody shoreline has absorbed most of the boom rather gracefully.

The first thing to know about the lake is that it's not meant to be seen by car. There are some great views from some roads—especially from Route 6/15 as you near Rockwood, and from the high elevations on the way to Lily Bay—but for the most part the roads are away from the shores, and rather uninteresting to drive. To see the lake at its best you should plan to get out on the water by steamship or canoe, or fly above it on a charter float-plane (see below).

Greenville is the "capital" of Moosehead Lake, scenically situated at the southern tip. Most lake services are located here, and you can stock up on groceries and camping supplies. The descent into Greenville on Route 6/15 is getting a bit cluttered with commercial strip development, but the town is still holding on to its remote, woodsy flavor.

ESSENTIALS

GETTING THERE   Greenville is 158 miles from Portland. Take the turnpike to the Newport exit (Exit 39) and head north on Routes 7/11 to Route 23 in Dexter, following that northward to Routes 6/15 near Sangerville. Follow this to Greenville.

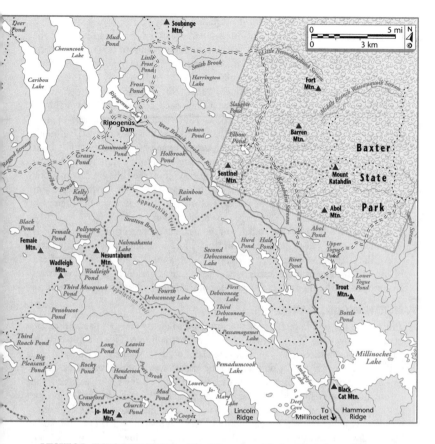

The famed map area shows locations including Deer Pond, Chesuncook Lake, Caribou Lake, Soubunge Mtn., Mud Pond, Little Frost Pond, Smith Brook, Harrington Lake, Fort Mtn., Frost Pond, Slaugter Pond, Barren Mtn., Ripogenus Dam, Jackson Pond, Elbow Pond, Baxter State Park, and more.

VISITOR INFORMATION   The **Moosehead Lake Chamber of Commerce,** P.O. Box 581, Greenville, ME 04441 (☎ **207/695-2702**) maintains an information booth open daily in summer just south of the village on Route 6/15.

HIKING

The famed **100-Mile Wilderness** of the Appalachian Trail begins at Monson, south of Greenville, and runs northeast to Abol Bridge near Baxter State Park. This is a spectacularly remote part of the state, and offers some of the best hiking in Maine. This trip is primarily for independent and experienced backpackers—there are no points along the route to resupply—although day trips in and out are a possibility.

One especially beautiful stretch of the trail passes by Gulf Hagas, sometimes called "Maine's Grand Canyon" (that's a bit grandiose, to my mind). The Pleasant River has carved a canyon as deep as 400 feet through slate in this area; the hiking trail runs along its lip, with side trails extending down to the river, where you can swim in the eddies and cascades. The gulf is accessible as a day hike if you enter the forest via logging roads. Drive north from Milo on Route 11 and follow signs to the Katahdin Iron Works (an intriguing historic site worth exploring), pay your fee at the timber company gate, and ask directions to the gulf. Also nearby is The Hermitage, a Nature Conservancy stand of 120-foot white pines that have been spared the woods-man's axe.

Nearer to Greenville, 3,196-foot Big Squaw Mountain (home to a ski area called, sensibly enough, Squaw Mountain) offers superb views of Moosehead Lake and the surrounding area from its summit. The hike requires about four hours, and departs about 5 miles northwest of Greenville on Routes 6/15 (turn west on the gravel paper company road and continue for one mile to the trailhead).

Another inviting hike is Mount Kineo, a sheer cliff that rises from the shores of Moosehead. This hike is accessible by water only; near the town of Rockwood look for signs advertising shuttles across the lake to Kineo (folks offering this service seem to change from year to year, so ask around). Once across, you can explore the grounds of the famed old Kineo Mountain House (alas, the grand, 500-guest-room hotel was demolished in 1938), then cut across the golf course and follow the shoreline to the trail that leads to the 1,800-foot summit. The views from the cliffs are dazzling; one hiker I know says he has no problems on any mountain except Kineo, which give him an inexplicable case of vertigo. Be sure to continue on the trail to the old firetower, which you can ascend for a hawks-eye view of the region.

A number of other hikes are available in the area, but get good guidance as the trails generally aren't as well-marked here as in the White Mountains or Baxter State Park. Ask at the chamber of commerce office, or pick up a copy of 50 Hikes in Northern Maine, which contains good descriptions of several area hikes. Also, several local hikes are outlined on the Internet at www.maineguide.com/mooshead/mooshike.html.

A NORTH WOODS CANOE TRIP

You can follow in Thoreau's footsteps into the Maine woods on a superb canoe excursion down the West Branch of the Penobscot River. This 44-mile trip is popularly done in three days. Put in at Roll Dam, north of Moosehead Lake and east of Pittston Farm, and paddle northerly on the smooth waters of the Penobscot. There are several campsites along the river; pick one and spend the night, watching for grazing moose as evening falls. The second day paddle to huge and wild Chesuncook Lake. Near where the river enters the lake is the Chesuncook Lake House, a wonderfully remote farmhouse dating from 1864 and open to guests (see "Where to Stay," below). Spend the night here. The final day paddle down Chesuncook Lake with its sweeping views of Mount Katahdin to the east and take out near Ripogenus Dam.

Allagash Canoe Trips, P.O. 713, Greenville 04441 (radio ☎ **207/695-3668**) has been offering guided canoe trips in the north woods since 1953. A five-day guided camping trip down the West Branch—including all equipment, meals, and transportation—costs $475 for adults, $350 for children.

If you'd prefer to go on your own, shuttling your car from Roll Dam to Ripogenus Dam is easily arranged. **Allagash Wilderness Outfitters** (radio ☎ **207/695-2821**) charges $43 to drive your vehicle from one end to the other so it will be awaiting you when you arrive.

If you're looking for less hassle and more drama, for about $250 two of you could depart from Greenville by seaplane (with your canoe lashed to the floats and your gear in the cargo bin) and be dropped off at Lobster Lake; four days later you'll be picked up at Chesuncook Dam and flown back to Greenville. Call Folsom's (see below) for details.

WHITE-WATER RAFTING

Big waves and steep drops await rafters on the popular run through Kennebec Gorge at the headwaters of the Kennebec River, located southwest of Greenville. Dozens of rafters line up along the boiling stream below the dam, then await the siren that signals the release. Hop in, and you're off, heading off through huge, roiling waves and down precipitous drops with names like Whitewasher and Magic Falls. Most of the excitement is over in the first hour; after that, it's a lazy trip the rest of the way down the river, interrupted only by lunch and the occasional water fight with other rafts. Also nearby is the challenging Dead River, which offers about a half-dozen release dates, mostly during the early summer.

A number of commercial white-water outfits offer trips throughout the summer at a cost of about $75 to $100 per person. Northern Outdoors, P.O. Box 100, **The Forks,** ME 04985 (☎ **800/765-7238**) is the oldest of the bunch, and offers rock-climbing, mountain-biking, and fishing expeditions as well. Rafting companies based in Moosehead Lake region include **Wilderness Expeditions,** P.O. Box 41, Rockwood, ME 04478, (☎ **800/825-9453**) and **Eastern River Expeditions,** Box 1173, Greenville, ME 04441 (☎ **800/634-7238**).

MOOSEHEAD BY STEAMSHIP & FLOAT PLANE

During the lake's golden days of tourism in the late 19th century, visitors could come to the lake by train from New York or Washington, then connect with steamship to the resorts and boarding houses around the lake. A vestige of that era is found at the **Moosehead Marine Museum** (☎ **207/695-2716**) in Greenville. A handful of displays in the small building suggest the grandeur of life at Kineo Mountain House, a sprawling Victorian lake resort that once defined elegance. But the real showpiece of the museum is the *S.S. Katahdin,* a 115-foot steamship that's been cruising Moosehead's waters since 1914. The two-deck ship (it's now run by diesel rather than steam) offers a variety of sightseeing tours, including a twice-a-week excursion up the lake to the site of the former Kineo Mountain House. Fares vary depending on the length of the trip.

Moosehead from the air is a memorable sight. Stop by Folsom's Air Service (☎ 207/695-2821) on the shores of the lake in Greenville just north of the village center on Lily Bay Rd. Folsom's has been serving the North Woods since 1946, and has a fleet of five float planes, including a vintage canary yellow DeHavilland Beaver. A 15-minute tour of the southern reaches of the lake costs $20 per person; longer flights over the region run up to $60. A nice adventure is the canoe-and-fly package. For $85 per person, Folsom's will drop you and a canoe off at Penobscot Farm; paddle up to Lobster Lake, where you'll get picked up and returned to Greenville later that day.

ALPINE & CROSS-COUNTRY SKIING

Big Squaw Mountain Resort (☎ **207/695-1000**), located just outside of Greenville, has been fighting an on-again-off-again battle with insolvency for years, but locals say it may have finally turned the corner. Founded by a paper company in 1963, the state took it over for a spell in the 1970s, and it's been owned by several private owners since then. Most recently, it was acquired in late 1995 by a husband and wife team intent on improving snowmaking and coaxing out the potential of this classic 1,750-foot ski mountain. The mountain features some good, winding old-fashioned runs (of the sort that the bigger mountains are now scrambling to re-create) and the views are terrific. The 18 slopes are served by two chairlifts and two surface lifts. Limited services, including ski rentals and a small cafeteria and restaurant, are located at the base. There's also 60 guest rooms on the mountain. Lift tickets are bargain-priced at $15 Monday through Thursday, and $20 Friday through Sunday.

Cross-country skiing is available at **The Birches** (☎ **800/825-9453**), a rustic resort on the shores of Moosehead north of Rockwood. The resort offers 15 log cabins and lodge accommodations. Some 24 miles of rolling backcountry trails are groomed daily.

SNOWMOBILING

You'll need more than just good luck finding a room in Greenville some weekends in winter. The town has become a snowmobilers' mecca of sorts, with hundreds of sledders descending on the town during good winter weather before striking out into the remote woods. The new Moosehead Trail, which runs around the perimeter of the lake, offers lodging and meals at various stops along the way. For snowmobile rentals, contact the **Kokadjo Trading Post and Camp** (☎ 207/695-3993), which is located about 15 miles north of Greenville, or the **Greenwood Motel** (☎ 207/695-3321).

WHERE TO STAY & DINE

Chesuncook Lake House. P.O. Box 656, Greenville, ME 04441. ☎ **207/745-5330.** 4 rms (all share 2 baths). $170 double, including all meals. Open May through Oct. (Two cottages available in winter.) No credit cards.

The Chesuncook Lake House is a perfect destination for those who like a bit of comfort with their adventure. This 1864 farmhouse, located on the shores of remote Chesuncook Lake, is accessible only via seaplane or 18-mile boat shuttle from Chesuncook Dam. (It can also be reached by canoe; see "North Woods Canoe Trip," above.) It's run with great rustic charm by Bert and Maggie McBurnie, who've been hosting guests here since 1957. (Bert grew up in Chesuncook Village when it was an active logging center; Maggie is from Paris, France.) The rooms are furnished simply and eclectically; there's running water in the shared bathrooms, and gas lamps provide the light in the evening. All meals are included, and Maggie's superb cooking makes good use of produce from her sizeable garden. During the day, guests can explore the remnants of Chesuncook Village (Thoreau passed through here in the mid-19th century), canoe over to 3,000-acre Gero Island, or just pass the time on the porch enjoying the views of Mt. Katahdin 35 miles to the east. If you stay three days or longer, the boat shuttle is free; otherwise there's a charge for it.

Greenville Inn. Norris St., Greenville, ME 04441. ☎ **888/695-6000** or 207/695-2206. 7 rms, 6 cottages (1 rm with hall bath). Summer $105–$165 double; off season $75–$135. All rates include continental breakfast buffet. DISC, MC, V.

This handsome 1895 lumber baron's home sits regally along a hilly side street a short walk from "downtown" Greenville. The interiors are sumptuous, with wonderful cherry and mahogany woodworking and a lovely stained-glass window of a pine tree over the stairwell. There's a handsome small bar, where you can order up a cocktail or Maine beer, then sit in front of the fire or retreat to the front porch to watch the late afternoon sun slip over Squaw Mt. and the lake. Four new cottages were built on the property in 1995, adding to the two others already there. The trim cottages are furnished in a light summer cottage style, and have views of the lake. The dinners served in the elegant dining room are delicious; the popovers are delectable and roughly the size of a football. The restaurant is open to the public, but is usually closed in winter; call first to confirm.

Inn at Moosehead. Lily Bay Rd. (P.O. Box 1167), Greenville, ME 04441. ☎ **207/695-4400.** Fax 207/695-2281. 5 rms. A/C TV. Summer & fall $145–$195 double; winter & spring $145–$175. Rates include full breakfast. Located 2.5 miles north of Greenville on Lily Bay Rd (head north through blinker). DISC, MC, V.

Guests face a dilemma at the Inn at Moosehead. Should you spend your time in the gracious common room, on the porch high above the lake, or in the spacious guest rooms, each of which have fireplace, whirlpool, and four-poster beds hand-carved by local artist Joe Bolf? Opened by Jennifer and Roger Cauchi in 1993, the inn has garnered plaudits from guests, who are impressed with the place's rustic elegance. Housed in a 1917 home built high on a hillside for a wealthy summer visitor, the Inn at Moosehead offers a nice mix of rustic and modern. The guest rooms are all carpeted, but there's Adirondack-style stick furnishings mixed in with wingback chairs and antique English end-tables. The dining room, where a full breakfast is served year round along with dinner in the winter, has a brisk, modern feel to it in contrast to much of the rest of the inn. The hosts are a good source of information for area activities. This is a nonsmoking inn.

✪ **Little Lyford Pond Camps.** P.O. Box 1269, Greenville, ME 04441. ☎ **207/695-2821** (radio phone via Folsom's). Fax 207/534-7428. E-mail 73002.2027@compuserve.com. $170 double, including breakfast, lunch, and dinner. Accessible by logging road in summer, by snow-mobile or ski-plane in winter. Closed in spring and late fall/early winter. No credit cards.

Kate and Bud Fackelman left Massachusetts for this remote lodge about a decade ago, and they've made this backwoods logging camp one of the most welcoming and comfortable spots in the North Woods. Bud is a renowned veterinary surgeon and maintains a limited practice by flying out from time to time and keeping up with communications through e-mail. Guests stay in small log cabins originally built to house loggers in the 1870s. Each has a small woodstove, propane lantern, cold running water, a private outhouse, and plenty of rustic charm. Guests gather in the more spacious main lodge for meals, to browse the inn's books, and to play board games in the evening. During the day, activities aren't hard to find, from fishing or canoeing at the two ponds down a short trail, or hiking the Appalachian Trail to Gulf Hagas, just two miles away. There's a wood-fired sauna and a solar shower for keeping clean. In winter, the cross-country skiing on the lodging's private network is superb.

BAXTER STATE PARK & ENVIRONS

Baxter State Park is Maine's crown jewel. This 201,000-acre state park in the remote north-central part of the state is unlike more elaborate state parks you might be accustomed to elsewhere—don't look for fancy bath houses or groomed picnic areas. When you enter Baxter State Park, you enter near-wilderness.

The park was singlehandedly created by former Maine governor and philanthropist Percival Baxter, who used his inheritance and investment profits to buy the property and donate it to the state starting in 1930. Baxter stipulated that it remain "forever wild," and caretakers have done a good job fulfilling his wishes.

You won't find paved roads, RVs, or hook-ups at the eight drive-in campgrounds. (Size restrictions keep the RVs out.) You will find rugged backcountry and beautiful lakes. You'll also find Mount Katahdin, that lone and melancholy granite giant rising above the sparkling lakes and severe boreal forest of northern Maine.

To the north and west of Baxter State Park are several million acres of forestland owned by timber companies and managed primarily for timber production. Twenty-one of the largest timber companies that collectively own much of the land manage recreational access through a consortium called North Maine Woods, Inc. If you drive on a logging road far enough, expect to run into a North Maine Woods checkpoint, where you'll be asked to pay a fee for day use or overnight camping on their lands.

One bit of advice: Don't attempt to tour the timberlands by car. Industrial forestland is boring when it's at its best, and downright depressing at it's cut-over worst. A better strategy is to select a pond or river for camping or fishing, and spend a couple of days getting to know a small area. Buffer strips have been left around all ponds, streams, and rivers, and it can often feel like you're getting away from it all as you paddle along, even if the forest sometimes has a Hollywood facade feel to it. Be aware that no matter how deep you get into these woods, you may well hear machinery and chainsaws in the distance.

ESSENTIALS

GETTING THERE   Baxter State Park is 86 miles north of Bangor. Take I-95 to Medway (Exit 56), and head west 11 miles on Route 11/157 to the mill town of Millinocket, the last major place for supplies. Head northwest through town and follow signs to Baxter State Park. The less-used entrance is near the park's northeast corner. Take I-95 to the exit for Route 11, drive north through Patten then head west on Route 159 to the park. The speed limit within the park is 20 miles per hour. Motorcycles and ATVs are not allowed within park boundaries.

VISITOR INFORMATION   Baxter State Park offers maps and information from its **headquarters** at 64 Balsam Dr., Millinocket, ME 04462 (☎ **207/723-5140**). For information on canoeing and camping outside of Baxter State Park, contact North Maine Woods Inc., P.O. Box 421, Ashland, ME 04732 (☎ **207/435-6213**). Help finding cottages and outfitters is available through the **Katahdin Area Chamber of Commerce,** 1029 Central Street, Millinocket, ME 04462 (☎ **207/723-4443**).

FEES   Baxter State Park visitors with out-of-state license plates are charged a day-use fee of $8 per car. (It's free to Maine residents). The day-use fee is charged only once per stay for those camping overnight. Camping reservations are by mail or in person only.

The private timberlands managed by North Maine Woods levy a day use fee of $3.50 per person for Maine residents, $7 per person for nonresidents. Camping fees are additional (see below.)

HIKING

With 180 miles of maintained backcountry trails and 46 peaks (including 18 over 3,000 feet), Baxter State Park is the destination of choice for serious hikers in Maine.

The most serious peak is 5,267-foot Mount Katahdin—the northern terminus of the Appalachian Trail. An ascent up this rugged, glacially scoured mountain is a trip you'll not soon forget. Never mind that it's not even a mile high (although a tall cairn on the summit claims to make it so). The raw drama and grandeur of the rocky, windswept summit is equal to anything you'll find in the White Mountains of New Hampshire.

Allow at least eight hours for the round trip, and be prepared to abandon your plans for another day if the weather takes a turn for the worse while you're en route. The most popular route leaves and returns from Roaring Brook Campground. In fact, it's popular enough that it's often closed to day hikers—when the parking lot fills, hikers are shunted to other trails. You ascend first to dramatic Chimney Pond, which is set like a jewel in a glacial cirque, then continue to Katahdin's summit via one of two trails. (The Saddle Trail is the most forgiving; the Cathedral Trail most dramatic.) From here, the descent begins along the aptly named "Knife's Edge," a narrow, rocky spine between Baxter Peak and Pamola Peak. This is not for acrophobes or the squeamish: in places, the trail narrows to two or three feet with a drop of hundreds of feet on either side. It's also not a place to be if high winds or thunderstorms threaten. From here, the trail follows a gentle ridge back down to Roaring Brook.

Katahdin draws the largest crowds, but the park maintains numerous other trails where you'll find more solitude and wildlife. A pleasant day hike is to the summit

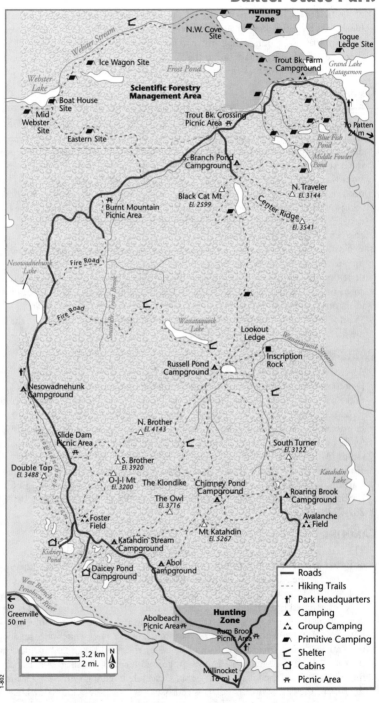

Webster Stream

N.W. Cove Site

Toque Ledge Site

Ice Wagon Site

Trout Bk. Farm Campground

Grand Lake Matagamon

Frost Pond

Scientific Forestry Management Area

Webster Lake

Boat House Site

Mid Webster Site

Trout Bk. Crossing Picnic Area

To Patten 24 m

Blue Fish Pond

Eastern Site

Middle Fowler Pond

S. Branch Pond Campground

N. Traveler △ *El. 3144*

Burnt Mountain Picnic Area

Black Cat Mt. *El. 2599*

Center Ridge

△ *El. 3541*

Nesowadnehunk Lake

Fire Road

South Br. Trout Brook

Fire Road

Wassataquoik Lake

Lookout Ledge

Wassataquoik Streams

Russell Pond Campground

Inscription Rock

Nesowadnehunk Campground

N. Brother △ *El. 4143*

South Turner *El. 3122*

Katahdin Lake

Slide Dam Picnic Area

S. Brother △ *El. 3920*

Double Top *El. 3488* △

O-J-I Mt *El. 3200*

The Klondike

Chimney Pond Campground

Roaring Brook Campground

Nesowadnehunk Stream

Foster Field

The Owl *El. 3716* △

Avalanche Field

Kidney Pond

Katahdin Stream Campground

Mt Katahdin *El. 5267*

Daicey Pond Campground

Abol Campground

West Branch Penobscot River

to Greenville 50 mi

Abolbeach Picnic Area

Hunting Zone

Rum Brook Picnic Area

Millinocket 16 mi ↓

Hunting Zone

0 ⌿⌿⌿⌿⌿ 3.2 km
2 mi.

N

	Roads
	Hiking Trails
⛨	Park Headquarters
▲	Camping
⁂	Group Camping
◼	Primitive Camping
Ⳇ	Shelter
⌂	Cabins
⚶	Picnic Area

1-802

361

of South Turner Mountain, which offers wonderful views of Mount Katahdin and blueberries for the picking in late summer. The trail also departs from Roaring Brook Campground and requires about three to four hours for a round trip. To the north, there are several decent hikes out of the South Branch Pond Campground. You can purchase a trail map at park headquarters, or consult *Fifty Hikes in Northern Maine.*

CAMPING

Baxter State Park has eight campgrounds accessible by car and two backcountry camping areas, but don't count on finding anything open if you show up without reservations. Park headquarters starts taking reservations in January, and dozens of die-hard campers spend a cold night outside headquarters on January 1st to secure the best spots. Many of the most desirable sites sell out well before the snow melts from Katahdin. The park is stubbornly old-fashioned about its reservations, which must be made either in person or by mail, with full payment in advance. No phone reservations are accepted. Don't even mention e-mail. Camping at Baxter State Park costs $6 per person ($12 minimum per tent site), with cabins and bunkhouses available for $17 per person per night.

North Maine Woods, Inc. (see above) maintains dozens of primitive campsites on private forestland throughout its 2 million-acre holdings. While you may have to drive through massive clearcuts to reach the campsites, many are located on secluded coves or picturesque points. A map showing logging road access and campsite locations is $3 plus $1 postage from North Maine Woods headquarters (see "Visitor Information," above). Camping fees are $4 per person in addition to the day use fee outlined above.

WHITE-WATER RAFTING

A unique way to view Mount Katahdin is by rafting the West Branch of the Penobscot River. Flowing along the park's southern border, this wild river offers some of the most technically challenging white water in the East. Along the upper stretches it passes through a harrowing gorge that appears to be designed by Cubists dabbling in massive blocks of granite. The river widens after this, interspersing sleepy flatwater (with views of Katahdin) with several challenging falls and runs through turbulent rapids. At least a dozen rafting companies offer trips on the Penobscot, with price around $75 to $100 per person, including a lunch along the way. Try **Unicorn Rafting,** P.O. Box T, Brunswick, ME 04011 (☎ **800/864-2676**), or **Magic Falls Rafting Co.,** P.O. Box 2820, Winslow, ME 04901 (☎ **207/663-2220** or 800/ 207-7238).

CANOEING

The state's premiere canoe trip is down the Allagash River, which starts just west of Baxter State Park and runs northward for nearly 100 miles to finish at the town of Allagash. The **Allagash Wilderness Waterway** was the first state-designated wild and scenic river in the country, and was protected in 1970. The river runs through heavily harvested timberlands, but a 500-foot buffer strip of trees protects the forest views along the entire route. The trip begins along a chain of lakes involving light portaging. At Churchill Dam, there's a nice stretch of Class I-II white water for about nine miles, then it's back to lakes and flatwater river paddling. Toward the end, there's a longish portage (about 150 yards) around picturesque Allagash Falls before finishing up above the village of Allagash. (Schedule in enough time for a swim at the base of the falls.) Most paddlers spend between seven and ten days making the trip from Telos Dam to Allagash. Eighty campsites are maintained along the route;

most have outhouses, fire rings, and picnic tables. The camping fee is $4 per night per person for Maine residents, $5 for nonresidents.

Several outfitters offer Allagash River packages, including canoes, camping equipment, and transportation. **Allagash Wilderness Outfitters,** Box 620, Star Route 76, Greenville, ME 04441 (radio ☎ **207/695-2821**) rents a complete outfit (including canoe, life-vests, sleeping bags, tent, saw, axe, shovel, cooking gear, first-aid kit, etc.) for $22 per person per day. Shuttling a car from Telos Dam to Allagash costs $145. **Allagash Canoe Trips** (☎ **207/695-3668**) in Greenville offers guided descents of the river, including all equipment and meals, for $625 adult, $475 children under 18.

SNOWMOBILING

Northern Maine is laced with a magnificent network of snowmobile trails. If the conditions are right, you can even cross over into Canada and take your sled to Quebec. Although a handful of maps and guides outline the network, the trails are still largely a matter of local knowledge. Don't be afraid to ask around. A good place to start is **Shin Pond Village,** RR#1, Box 280, Patten, ME 04765 (☎ **207/ 528-2900**). Six cottages and five guest rooms are available (starting at $40 double for guest rooms and $59 for the cottages), and snowmobile rentals are $100 to $125 per day. Shin Pond is located within one-quarter mile of two ITS trails (the chief snowmobile routes).

Index